Web Graphics
Bible

Web Graphics
Bible

Ron Wodaski

IDG
BOOKS
WORLDWIDE

IDG Books Worldwide, Inc.
An International Data Group Company

Foster City, CA ✦ Chicago, IL ✦ Indianapolis, IN ✦ Southlake, TX

Web Graphics Bible

Published by
IDG Books Worldwide, Inc.
An International Data Group Company
919 E. Hillsdale Blvd.
Suite 400
Foster City, CA 94404
http://www.idgbooks.com (IDG Books Worldwide Web site)

Library of Congress Catalog Card No.: 97-072193

ISBN 0-7645-3055-0

Printed in the United States of America

10 9 8 7 6 5 4 3 2 1

Distributed in the United States by IDG Books Worldwide, Inc.

1B/RV/QZ/ZX/FC

Distributed in the United States by IDG Books Worldwide, Inc.

Distributed by Macmillan Canada for Canada; by Transworld Publishers Limited in the United Kingdom and Europe; by WoodsLane Pty. Ltd. for Australia; by WoodsLane Enterprises Ltd. for New Zealand; by Longman Singapore Publishers Ltd. for Singapore, Malaysia, Thailand, and Indonesia; by Simron Pty. Ltd. for South Africa; by Toppan Company Ltd. for Japan; by Distribuidora Cuspide for Argentina; by Livraria Cultura for Brazil; by Ediciencia S.A. for Ecuador; by Addison-Wesley Publishing Company for Korea; by Ediciones ZETA S.C.R. Ltda. for Peru; by WS Computer Publishing Company, Inc., for the Philippines; by Unalis Corporation for Taiwan; by Contemporanea de Ediciones for Venezuela. Authorized Sales Agent: Anthony Rudkin Associates for the Middle East and North Africa.

For general information on IDG Books Worldwide's books in the U.S., please call our Consumer Customer Service department at 800-762-2974. For reseller information, including discounts and premium sales, please call our Reseller Customer Service department at 800-434-3422.

For information on where to purchase IDG Books Worldwide's books outside the U.S., please contact our International Sales department at 415-655-3023 or fax 415-655-3299.

For information on foreign language translations, please contact our Foreign & Subsidiary Rights department at 415-655-3021 or fax 415-655-3281.

For sales inquiries and special prices for bulk quantities, please contact our Sales department at 415-655-3200 or write to the address above.

For information on using IDG Books Worldwide's books in the classroom or for ordering examination copies, please contact our Educational Sales department at 800-434-2086 or fax 817-251-8174.

For press review copies, author interviews, or other publicity information, please contact our Public Relations department at 415-655-3000 or fax 415-655-3299.

For authorization to photocopy items for corporate, personal, or educational use, please contact Copyright Clearance Center, 222 Rosewood Drive, Danvers, MA 01923, or fax 508-750-4470.

ABOUT IDG BOOKS WORLDWIDE

Welcome to the world of IDG Books Worldwide.

IDG Books Worldwide, Inc., is a subsidiary of International Data Group, the world's largest publisher of computer-related information and the leading global provider of information services on information technology. IDG was founded more than 25 years ago and now employs more than 8,500 people worldwide. IDG publishes more than 275 computer publications in over 75 countries (see listing below). More than 60 million people read one or more IDG publications each month.

Launched in 1990, IDG Books Worldwide is today the #1 publisher of best-selling computer books in the United States. We are proud to have received eight awards from the Computer Press Association in recognition of editorial excellence and three from *Computer Currents'* First Annual Readers' Choice Awards. Our best-selling *...For Dummies*® series has more than 30 million copies in print with translations in 30 languages. IDG Books Worldwide, through a joint venture with IDG's Hi-Tech Beijing, became the first U.S. publisher to publish a computer book in the People's Republic of China. In record time, IDG Books Worldwide has become the first choice for millions of readers around the world who want to learn how to better manage their businesses.

Our mission is simple: Every one of our books is designed to bring extra value and skill-building instructions to the reader. Our books are written by experts who understand and care about our readers. The knowledge base of our editorial staff comes from years of experience in publishing, education, and journalism — experience we use to produce books for the '90s. In short, we care about books, so we attract the best people. We devote special attention to details such as audience, interior design, use of icons, and illustrations. And because we use an efficient process of authoring, editing, and desktop publishing our books electronically, we can spend more time ensuring superior content and spend less time on the technicalities of making books.

You can count on our commitment to deliver high-quality books at competitive prices on topics you want to read about. At IDG Books Worldwide, we continue in the IDG tradition of delivering quality for more than 25 years. You'll find no better book on a subject than one from IDG Books Worldwide.

John Kilcullen
CEO
IDG Books Worldwide, Inc.

Steven Berkowitz
President and Publisher
IDG Books Worldwide, Inc.

Eighth Annual Computer Press Awards 1992

Ninth Annual Computer Press Awards 1993

Tenth Annual Computer Press Awards 1994

Eleventh Annual Computer Press Awards 1995

Credits

Acquisitions Editor
Gregory Croy

Software Acquisitions Editor
Tracy Lehman Cramer

Developmental Editors
Nancy Stevenson
Susan Pines

Copy Editors
Deborah Kaufmann
Barry Childs-Helton

Editorial Assistant
Timothy Borek

Production Coordinator
Tom Debolski

Technical Reviewers
Coletta Witherspoon
Craig Witherspoon

Production Page Layout
Mario F. Amador
Vincent F. Burns
Laura Carpenter
Tom Debolski
Ritchie Durdin
Stephanie Hollier
Ed Penslien
Christopher Pimentel
Dina F Quan
Mark Schumann
Elsie Yim

Proofreader
Mary C. Oby

Indexer
Joan Griffits

Cover Illustration
Murder By Design

About the Author

Ron Wodaski lives on the shores of Puget Sound, far enough north of Seattle to have some peace and quiet, but close enough to cause trouble when he feels the need. He has had careers in both computing and journalism. His journalistic exploits include freelancing for National Public Radio, as well as writing for numerous newspapers and magazines. As for computers, he started as a programmer, rose to MIS Director, and decided that writing about computers was more fun than retiring into obscurity. He currently writes for various magazines, and you can visit him in virtual person at http://mmadweb.com.

This book is dedicated to every artist who ever shared a hard-earned secret with a struggling novice.

Preface

So you want to create your own web graphics. You want web pages that are as good as what you see out there on the wild Internet. You want home-grown graphics that you can be proud of.

Who Should Read This Book

If you know the basics of creating web pages but want to take your pages beyond the every day, this book is for you. If you want to know about the coolest techniques and software, and how to use them to create great graphics, this book will serve you well.

I have made heavy use of graphics in the book. You will always know how to carry out a step because you will see the step in graphic detail right in front of you. And I've covered every topic related to graphics on the Web.

How This Book Is Organized

Part I features a look at the best web graphics and how you can create graphics easily. You learn about adding graphics to web pages, using images as hyperlinks, finding free graphics, creating cool text effects, and understanding where hardware fits in.

Part II gets into details about publishing on the Web. You also get examples and explanations of file formats, image colors, interlacing, transparency, compression, and image maps.

Part III covers a myriad of design-related issues. Chapters in this part show you how to create buttons, doodads, and backgrounds, design and implement sophisticated sites, and use tables, frames, and animation.

The CD-ROM

Now take a look at the CD-ROM I've compiled, which is tucked neatly into the back cover of the book. I have included:

✦ A Web Tour for every chapter. These tours include sites that illustrate techniques from the chapters and places to download cool tools.

✦ A complete collection of custom graphics that you can use on your web pages.

✦ Shareware you can install right from the CD-ROM, without waiting for lengthy downloads.

✦ Tutorials with hundreds of sample files.

✦ Demo versions of key software tools.

A Site for Sore Eyes

And if you act now, I'll also include a complete web site where you can find links to all the cool tools out there, updated weekly. The web site, at `http://mmadweb.com/bible`, contains more free graphics, links, and downloads, as well as product reviews and other goodies that I will be adding from time to time.

The web site is also a gathering place where you can meet other readers of the book and discuss anything and everything about graphics on the Web. Or get help making your graphics better. Or just stop by to say "Hi!" to yours truly, Mr. Author.

How to Use This Book

There are some things you will want to know before you dive into the book. First, I want you to meet a friend of mine. He's a Web expert and a truly weird human being: Gustav Webb. We all know him as Uncle Webb. You'll have to excuse his manners; he's a bit crusty around the edges.

 Crusty! Well, Mr. Author, that's a darn site better than going along with the herd. When it comes to the truth, I don't pull my punches. I'm looking forward to watching over your shoulder and catching you in every addle-brained opinion you spout.

You see what I mean? Ornery little bugger, but we love him. After all, he knows more than anyone about graphics. If you don't believe me, just ask Uncle Webb. He will be your annoying but useful guide to the deep, dark mysteries of web graphics. I've also included the following icons:

Idea

Idea icons for additional things to try are located at the end of tutorials.

Caution!

Caution icons warn you about bugs and potential problems and missteps.

Tip

Tips further illuminate a point or offer information that makes your work easier.

CD

CD-ROM icons to identify something on the CD that comes with this book.

Tutorial

Tutorial icons identify the start of a step-by-step tutorial; most chapters contain detailed tutorials that you can work through.

Whenever possible, I point you to a place to download a free or trial version of the software used in a tutorial. Sadly, not every software package comes in a trial version, and you will need the commercial version of the software to operate those tutorials.

Should you come across anything that isn't clear, visit the web site for the book at `http://mmadweb.com/bible/index.htm`. You will find not only additional material, but lots of last-minute goodies that I think you'll enjoy.

Please note that the URLs listed in the book were correct at press time. Because the web changes constantly, you may find that some sites have moved or are defunct.

Have a blast! If you create some hot web graphics, and want me to include a link to your page on the Readers Pages list on my web site, send me the URL via e-mail at `bible@mmadweb.com`. You can also visit the page, at `http://mmadweb.com/bible/readers.htm`, and see what other readers have accomplished.

Acknowledgments

The writing of this book was a monumental effort, for the subject of graphics is a wide-ranging territory. I could not have written the book without the incredible, unimaginably deep support of my family: Donna, Justen, Chanel, and Chris. The book is over, and now you can have Daddy back.

I also owe a great deal of thanks to my assistant, Leslie Aickin, who found a way to get things done no matter what. Thank you also to Robin Comforto, who tracked down the software and hardware written about in the book. A special thank you to Amy Berger-McNitt, who helped bring Uncle Webb to life; you'll find her sketch on the CD-ROM.

Thanks to my development editor, Nancy Stevenson, who put up with the manic ravings of the author and still managed to wrap up this book. Thanks also to Greg Croy, whose support over the years has been a big factor in the success of my books.

Thanks also to the folks at Micron Computer, whose fine products I use day in and day out to test all this hardware and software. Nothing is tougher on a computer than bleeding-edge products, and I threw so many products at my computers that they should have fallen under the load. Instead, they thrived, and I am thrilled to give some credit for that.

I would also like to thank the various folks I run into via the Internet each day, who have either contributed ideas that eventually found expression here in this book, or who have asked questions whose answers evolved into sections of the book. And I would like to thank you, dear reader, for your trust in allowing me to show you the possibilities.

Contents at a Glance

Contents

Graphic Examples

The Best of the Web

To prepare for this chapter's tutorials, copy the following folder from the CD-ROM to the \My Web Stuff folder on your hard drive:

    \Tutorial\Chap01

This will copy files for all of the tutorials in this chapter to your hard disk. To create the \My Web Stuff folder, double-click the My Computer icon, and then double-click the hard drive where you want to create the new folder. Use the File | New | Folder menu selection to create the folder, and name it **My Web Stuff.** The easiest way to accomplish the copy is to open the Tutorial folder on the CD-ROM. Click on the Chap01 folder and drag it to the \My Web Stuff folder on your hard drive.

I have included a file in every chapter folder that serves as a gateway to all of the tutorial pages for each chapter. It is called viewme.htm, and you can double-click it at any time to look at the web pages I created for each chapter. For example, after you copy the tutorial files for this chapter, you can double-click the file \My Web Stuff\Chap01\viewme.htm to see what this chapter is all about.

There is an unmistakable trend unfolding on the World Wide Web. In case you missed it, I'm talking about the explosion of web pages filled with graphics. This is the latest step in an evolution that began with the first networked computers.

Let's get one thing straight *now.* That word — explosion — doesn't begin to convey what's going on around the Web. We're not headed toward virtual reality; we're headed for a virtual nightmare. There are too many web sites with too many graphics, and too many of those graphics are ugly, ugly, ugly. Not that I have much of an opinion on this subject.

Hey Unc: I'm writing this book at least in part to stem the tide of ugly pages. Cool your heels and let me explain.

That's the problem with old Uncle Webb — he has a bad habit of stating the obvious.

 Obvious, schmovious. You can't tiptoe around the problem. And ugly isn't the only problem. Ever try to figure out what you're supposed to do while waiting for someone's idea of the perfect web page to download? It's too short for coffee, and too long to bear.

We'll cover it all, Webbsy. Stay tuned.

The First Networks

In the beginning was the mainframe-based network — a bunch of little terminals hanging on to a great big computer for their very life. Of course "great big" is a relative term. At one time, a mainframe with 8K (that's kilobytes, at 1,024 bytes each) of memory was a Very Big Deal, and cost millions of dollars. Today, a PC with less than 16MB (that's megabytes, at 1,048,576 bytes each) is a baby. You can buy off-the-shelf computers with 64 or 128MB of memory for less than a very much-used car. And those terminals! They had no memory at all. Think of the horror of this situation: 8K of memory on a mainframe. No memory on the terminals. The terminals had to share that tiny little knot of memory between them — and there might be 100 terminals or more hanging from that mainframe. Figure 1-1 illustrates what I'm talking about. Yes, they really were called dumb terminals — dumb because they didn't have a brain (a.k.a. CPU, Central Processing Unit).

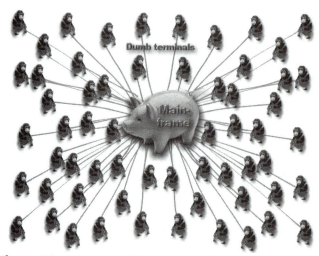

Figure 1-1: A typical mainframe network.

Then came the PC, and naturally a few folks got the idea of linking a few PCs together so you could move files around. There were even miniature versions of the old mainframe arrangement: one big powerful PC (a server), and lots of smaller PCs connected to it (and, because it made a lot of sense, to each other as well). There was a big difference, though: Even a small PC was a whole lot more powerful than a terminal. It had its own brain. The server just had to worry about moving data around the network, and to and from its hard disk. The PCs had their own brains (Pentiums these days) to work with. No more sharing the mental thing at all — every PC was free to be whatever it wanted to be. Figures 1-2 and 1-3 show two typical PC networking arrangements.

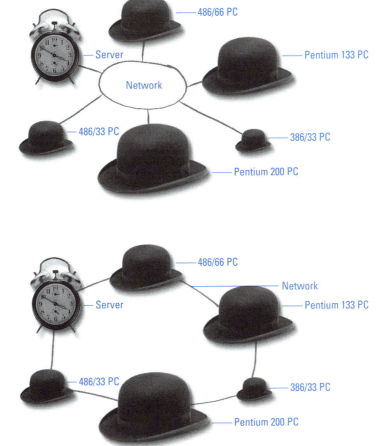

Figures 1-2 and 1-3: Two examples of PC network topography.

Out of this sea of big and small networks — PC-based, mainframe-based, whatever-based — came a Great Idea: Join all the little networks into one giant, if somewhat loose, network. An ÜberNetwork, if you will. This was the infant Internet, a network of networks (Figure 1-4). The actual Internet is vastly more complex than this — think of millions of computers linked together in thousands of different ways. It's a miracle that the Internet works at all.

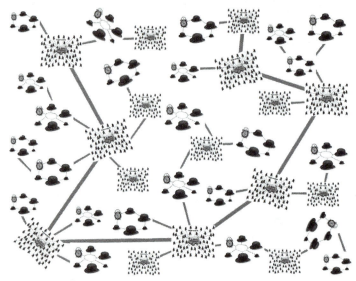

Figure 1-4: The Internet is a network of networks.

Initially, the Internet was largely text-based, as was most of computerdom at the time the Internet was conceived. I remember laughing at the early interest in the Internet. How could such a trivial thing — e-mail, Telnet, and other challenging sorts of "efficiencies" — ever amount to anything? The Internet was for scientists and nerds. And it was, for all its arcane tools, a Good Thing, mostly because it was better than the alternatives: The Post Office. Waiting until the next Big Meeting. And so on.

And then came the World Wide Web, adding (eventually) the missing ingredient that would take the Internet from *Cool Tool* to *Essential for Everyone*. Yes, I'm talking about graphics. I stopped laughing about the Internet when graphics showed up. It was immediately obvious that the old axiom — a picture is worth a thousand words — was as true as it had ever been.

The World Wide Web — most often referred to these days as the Web — added graphics and the explosion started, and it's still expanding. Today, you can navigate the Web, create great web pages, and you don't have to know very much about the underpinnings of the whole magic empire. You can learn these things, of course, and when you do you will be able to perform amazing tricks. That's for later chapters. For now, here's what you need to know to get started:

✦ A *URL (Uniform Resource Locator)* is just the address of a web page. You've seen URLs everywhere; they look like this: `http://www.mmadweb.com/index.htm`. If you've seen one URL, you've seen them all. From left to right, the URL consists of:

- The protocol (such as http, ftp, gopher)

- The domain name (like www.mmadweb.com, www.microsoft.com)

- The path and filename (for instance, /index.htm, or /products/images/myfile.gif,)

✦ A *web server* is the computer on which your web site's pages reside.

✦ *Publishing* is the act of moving your web pages, graphics, and other files from your local computer to a web server.

You'll learn more details about these concepts as you read through the book.

Graphic Pages

I suppose you've already noticed that there is a wide variation in the use of graphics on the Web. I break down all web pages into five categories:

✦ No graphics at all

✦ Heavy graphics

✦ Light graphics

✦ Good graphics

✦ Lousy graphics

Every page fits somewhere into one or more of these categories. Graphics-free pages are a cute idea, and they sure download in a hurry, but you've just heard my last comment about such pages. They have no place in this book.

Pages with heavy graphics might seem to be all the rage, but there are plenty of reasons for going light. If all that was needed was heavy graphics to make a great web page, you could hire (or become) a graphic artist and all would be well. But there are a thousand traps for the unwary web page creator, and most of them have something to do with graphics. Why do you think this book is so darn fat?

There are many different ways to define a good graphic, or a good web page. Beauty is only one criterion; the graphic (and the whole page) must also function effectively. It's more than possible to have a beautiful-looking web page that is a complete failure. It's also more than possible to have a pretty dumb-looking page that does its job effectively, and there's a certain beauty in that.

Ideally, a web page combines beauty and function. Such pages are immediately evident. They catch your eye *and* your imagination. Every web page ought to aspire to such greatness.

Having laid out five categories, I am going to cite some examples.

All-text pages

Oops, I lied. The example shown in Figure 1-5 isn't really all text. It looks like all text, but the buttons at the top of the page are little graphics. This makes a point I will remake a zillion times between now and the end of the book: Everything is graphical to some extent.

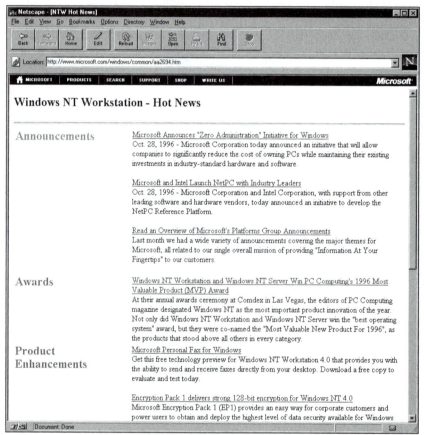

Figure 1-5: An all-text page that isn't all text.

Reprinted by permission from Mircosoft Corporation.

Look carefully at any page that appears to be all text. Chances are that something has been done to spice it up, graphics-wise. Is any of the text actually a graphic? Is there white space on the page to improve the appearance, readability, or layout of the page? When you start to pay attention to web pages, some of them are deceptively simple.

Pages with heavy use of graphics

Despite the fact that this book is titled *The Web Graphics Bible,* and despite the fact that graphics and multimedia are *the* buzzwords as we head into the twenty-first century, we are a long way from a time when just any page can make heavy use of graphics. The reason is a simple one: It takes much too long to download such a page. Graphics files are large and take a long time to download. The more graphics, the longer it takes. The kinds of pages where the visitor will be willing to wait for all of the graphics to download are few and far between.

By using few graphics efficiently, you increase the chances that visitors will linger to enjoy your page. There's no hard and fast line between fast and too long, but by the time you reach the end of the book you'll have a good sense of what works, and what doesn't.

To qualify as a "heavy user," a page has to have:

✦ Lots of images

✦ One or more large images, or a block of small images

✦ Sophisticated images

In short, graphics have to dominate the page. Much of the text on such a page will even be part of the graphics, not "real" text.

The site at `www.quantum.com` shows a heavy graphics page. This is a corporate page for Quantum, a company that makes hard drives. The preponderance of images is obvious. The background is a more dominant factor in this layout. If you look over the page carefully, the only true text on the page is a hyperlink at upper left that says "TEXT ONLY" — an ironic situation to say the least. This page easily meets the criteria for a heavy graphics page.

Quantum did a smart thing by putting the text-only hyperlink high on the page; it will usually display before the graphics finish downloading. If you are visiting the Quantum site and you just want to do some business (perhaps get technical information on a hard drive), the text-only pages give you a fast way to interact with the site.

The Internet is getting faster all the time. 28.8 Kbps was good, 33.6 is better, and 56K holds great promise (not to mention those fortunate to have ISDN connections, with a maximum of 128K/second transfer; or ADSL, Asymmetric Digital Subscriber Line connections). The more advanced technologies may or may not find their way to desktops, but as speed increases, the case for graphics-heavy pages increases. At some point, if very high transfer speeds become the norm, web pages might cease to exist on some sites — they will become more like television stations, broadcasting programs on multiple channels.

For now, very few sites are headed in this direction, but here's one example: Microsoft's MSN site (see Figure 1-6). Just when you think it's safe to invest in graphics, it'll be time to add video games to your web pages. Just about every link in Figure 1-6 either causes an animation to play, takes you to a page with one or more animations, or, at the very least, takes you to another graphics-heavy page. These pages are *slow* to download.

Figure 1-6: An extra-heavy graphics web site: Microsoft's MSN.
Reprinted by permission from Microsoft Corporation.

Pages with light use of graphics

If there is one thing I've learned while doing research for this book, it is that you can create great web pages with only minimal use of graphics. This sounds like heresy in a book on web graphics, but it's the truth. There are literally thousands of web pages out there to prove the point. I've included a few here, and the URLs of even more pages that make the point: Less is more.

Figure 1-7 is an example of a page with light use of graphics. There are just two graphics on the page: a graphic that repeats, tile-fashion, in the background, and a color version of the same image at top center.

Not only does the page go light on graphics, it's also very functional. The key information — a customer service phone number — is in large type near the top of the page, where visitors can find it quickly and easily. Links to more specific information are arranged in sequence on the page, with some support information in small type size to make it clear what each link is for.

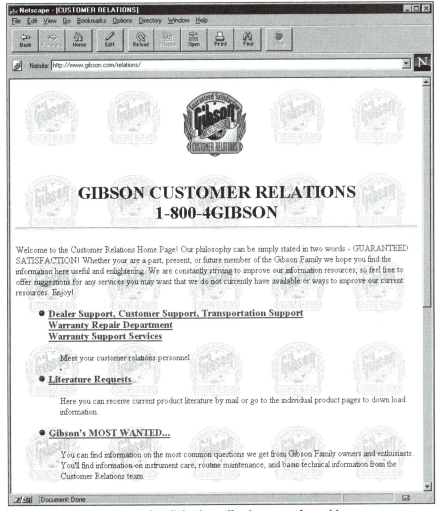

Figure 1-7: A page that makes light, but effective, use of graphics.
©1995 Gibson Guitar Corp.

Although graphics are the main subject of this book, it's not always clear what is graphical and what is not. The layout of text on the page, the font used for text, and other elements of the page all contribute to the overall design. In this sense, everything on the page has a graphical component. This is the sense I'm using throughout the book: If it's on the page, it contributes to the graphic appearance of the page.

And if you think the preceding tip grazes the edges of common sense, consider this: Even a page that's almost exclusively graphic can give the impression of light use of graphics.

Figure 1-8 shows a page that makes fairly light use of graphics. Most pages, as a matter of fact, fall into the middle ground — not light, not heavy. Most of the pages you'll see in this book certainly fall into that area. Light graphics and heavy graphics are both exceptions to the norm.

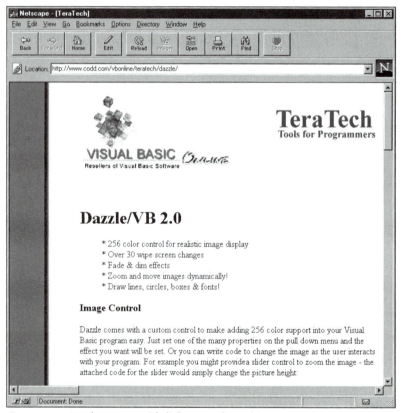

Figure 1-8: Another page with light use of graphics.

The page in Figure 1-8 uses an interesting technique for background images; see Chapter 17 for information about how to create similar left-edge backgrounds.

Pages with good or lousy graphics

The level of graphics sophistication on web pages has increased dramatically over the last few years. The trend toward fancy graphics doesn't always deliver something classy, however! It's easy to spend five hours to create a graphic that is a total bomb — it might not fit the needs of the page, it might be just plain ugly. Or you could create a very successful graphic in five minutes. It's the final web page that tells the tale of success or failure.

In fact, two pages on the same web site can illustrate the fine line between success and failure.

Don't just take his word for it! Beauty is always in the eye of the beholder. Every ugly web page has someone who loves it dearly. I may be an old curmudgeon , but I also know that taste is a relative concept. I should know; I've had my work criticized soundly by people who should know better! In the final analysis, it's your decision about what works, and what doesn't. There is no substitute for trusting your own creative judgment.

Anatomy of a Page

Figure 1-9 shows a matrix of sample web pages. You can't make out any of the details of these pages, but a certain pattern emerges. Certain parts of the web page tend to take on certain roles, or to contain certain kinds of information or designs.

As you look at the miniature web pages in Figure 1-9, several general themes are apparent:

✦ Most pages have a medium to large graphic at or near the top of the page.

✦ A separate row of links at the left edge of the page is common, but there are still plenty of pages that do not use this design feature.

✦ Very few pages use more than three columns.

✦ The trend is away from the traditional "center everything and pray for the best" and toward "carefully arrange the page elements into a coherent layout."

✦ Most pages have a white background. Light textured backgrounds are the next most common, and dark backgrounds are the least common.

✦ Many of the large commercial web sites have an ad at the very top of the page. The standard ad is narrow and about the width of a typical page.

Outside of these basic observations, the pages vary quite a bit. In this respect, web pages are a lot like magazine pages. From a design standpoint, there are many similarities between web pages and magazine pages. In fact, there are certainly more similarities between web pages and magazine pages than between web pages and the media that they are most often compared to: newspapers, television, and books.

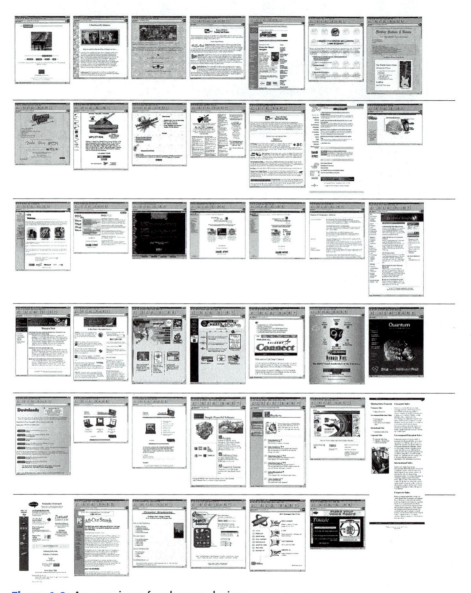

Figure 1-9: An overview of web page designs.

In addition to scanning web sites for cool pages, you can scan through magazines you like to find layout ideas for web pages. The fit will seldom be perfect, but good magazine layouts transfer reasonably well to the web page.

Aside from ads on the large commercial sites, these observations suggest a generic web page (see Figure 1-10).

Left hyperlinks   Heading

Figure 1-10: The components of a generic web page.

This is just one interpretation, of course, and you'll see quite a few "generic" web page layouts. Like great stories (think of Shakespeare, for example), great web pages use simple themes in elegant, original ways.

Best Page Designs

I'm sure that you are dying to create sizzling web pages, but let's look around for some inspiration first. In this section, I'll present what I feel are some of the best web *page* designs. In the next section, I'll present some individual *graphics* that I rate highly.

Given that there are millions of web pages out there, it's literally impossible to locate them all and make decisions about which is really the best. To simplify matters, and to illustrate just how arbitrary the concept of "best" is, I searched the Web using the string "graphic art" and simply divided the pages into best, good, average, and awful.

Let's look at a great web page that doesn't require a huge budget to create.

Figure 1-11 shows the World's Simplest Web Page. There's one graphic and a bit of text. As soon as I saw this web page — and, very importantly, the context in which it appears — I realized what a great web page it is. It breaks all the rules. There are no hotspots to jump to; there are no choices to make, no content to digest. Just a very simple message: *We're webtv, and we're simple and easy to use.* That's the right message for this web page, and thus it's a great web page. It also shows that going against convention can be the right solution to a problem.

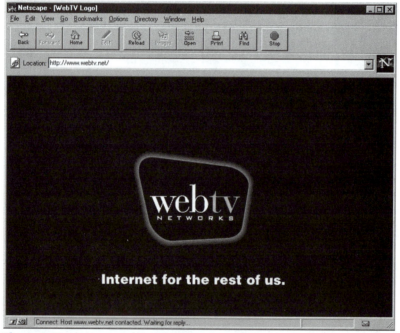

Figure 1-11: My unconventional choice for a "best page" award.
WebTV®, WebTV Network™, and the WebTV logo are trademarks of WebTV Networks, Inc.

Figure 1-12 shows another page from the webtv web site. It's also simple and direct, and these are admirable qualities that are ignored by too many web pages. The page has one purpose, and carries out that purpose in a direct, well-organized fashion. At the same time, the cute little TV controller at the left of the page provides access to any other part of the webtv site. You'll see this type of stacked graphic in Chapter 18, where you learn how a navigation bar is built up from smaller images.

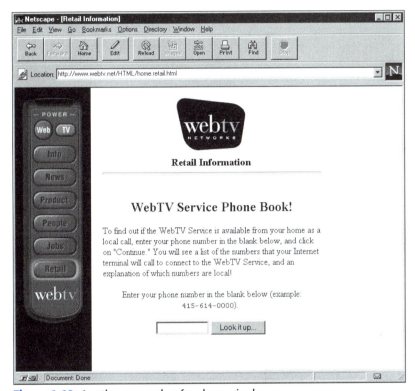

Figure 1-12: Another example of a clean, single-purpose page.
WebTV®, WebTV Network™, and the WebTV logo are trademarks of WebTV Networks, Inc.

Alas — and I say this in anticipation of Uncle Webb jumping in if I do not speak out — not every page has such a simple job to do, and we must give credit to other kinds of pages, too. After all, the criterion for success is not only how a page looks, but how well it does its job.

Figure 1-13 is an example of a page completely unlike the previous examples. This is the top-level page for the ESPN web site. This page has a gargantuan job to do. The amount of content on the ESPN web site is staggeringly large. This page has to provide interesting reading, supply links to the subsidiary parts of the web site, and still download quickly. To do this, it makes limited use of graphics. For a page that has to work, and work fast, that's a smart decision.

Figure 1-13: An example of a page that, while complex, gives you easy access to content.
Copyright ©1997. Starwave Corporation.

At what cost, though, does such a decision get made? The prior incarnation of ESPN's web site used a much more graphical approach (see Figure 1-14). I can argue (convincingly, I think) that the former design looks much better than the new design. But the new design functions much better, and is therefore, overall, a better page.

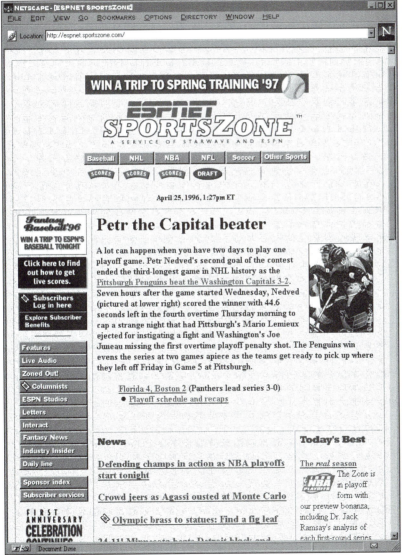

Figure 1-14: The old design for ESPN's web site.

This suggests a simple rule: Graphics must always serve the intended use of the page. It also suggests a second rule: Beautiful web pages ain't necessarily the best web pages.

This means that a large pretty graphic, if it interferes with the job the page is designed to do, reduces the value of the page. A small graphic, or even no graphic, is a better design choice in such a situation.

The bottom line is that a page has a job to do. Any graphic that gets in the way simply isn't a good graphic, no matter how clever, beautiful, or *avant garde* it happens to be.

Best Individual Graphics

In the previous section, the focus was on web pages that worked well with the graphics on the page. In this section, I take off the gloves of reason and present the most stunning examples of graphics I could find. Some of the newer 3-D graphics floating around the Web are simply astonishing.

At another extreme is the graphic shown in Figure 1-15. This is a "simple" line drawing with text, but it's got some character to it. Highly refined 3-D graphics are impressive, but sometimes a little vitality in a line drawing will have more impact.

The graphic in Figure 1-15 is more than a little retro, as is the graphic in Figure 1-16. If you can catch just the right angle on this sort of thing, it can make for an effective web page. The trick is to get the little things right.

Three of the (slightly) subtle ways in which Figure 1-16 works for me are:

✦ Notice the play on 3-D glasses at the left.

✦ The dots suggest the crude screened artwork of Andy Warhol (hmm…getting a bit out of period here! 3-D was hot in the '50s, while Andy was a creature of the '70s).

✦ The rocket is right out of Flash Gordon serials.

Your take on this graphic might be completely different. Know what you like, and learn from it. There are no experts when it comes to taste. You get to make up your own mind. Of course, it never hurts to know what your audience likes, so you can decide whether to flaunt or favor their expectations.

Figure 1-17 shows a highly creative graphic; it's from the Claris home page. This graphic has a strong style, and isn't very different from the kinds of graphics you will see in high-style magazines. If you are migrating content from other media, you can often migrate a lot of the graphics, too.

Figure 1-15: A completely different example of a great individual graphic.

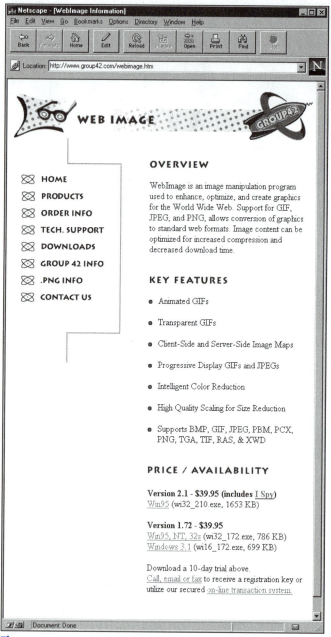

Figure 1-16: Another retro graphic with some intricacy and class.

WebImage, Group42 are trademarks of Group42, Inc.

Figure 1-17: A highly stylized graphic.

Handling Graphics with Your Browser

You can learn a lot from the graphics you encounter on the Web. If you see a graphic you like, and want to study it, you can use the more popular browsers to save a copy of the file on your hard disk.

Caution!

Just about all of the material you see on the Web is owned by someone. This ownership is called copyright. That means the owner has the right to copy it, and you don't. There are minor exceptions to this rule, but they are open to interpretation, so there are no clear-cut guidelines to safely follow. If you keep in mind that someone else created and owns these examples, and simply use them to further your own graphics education, you'll find that you'll get along with the rest of the folks on the Web much better.

Occasionally, you will find a web site that allows you to use its graphics for free, but don't ever make this assumption — look for something that explicitly spells out your rights to reuse graphics. Figure 1-18 shows an example of such a site. See Chapter 6, "Free Graphics and Clip Art," for important information about using graphics from this kind of source.

Figure 1-19 shows a page from the Woodshed site that displays tiles that you can use on your web page. You can click the name of the file to download it, but both the Internet Explorer and Navigator browsers come with tools to enable you to download any image you can see.

Downloading Graphics with Netscape Navigator 3

Tutorial

Download: From the Netscape web pages at `http://www.netscape.com`. Look for the *Download Now* icon near the top of the web page.

Level: Easy

Task: Download a graphic image to your hard disk

Before you start:

✦ Connect to the Web with Netscape Navigator 3.

✦ Go to the WoodShed site at `http://deckernet.com/ shed/graphics.html`.

Brick-wall backgrounds have a certain appeal, and there are several for you to download on this web page (refer to Figure 1-19). You can right-click an image to see a list of options. This is true whether or not the image is a hyperlink. The images on the WoodShed page are links. You can tell because the cursor changes to a pointing hand when it is over a hyperlink (text or image) (see Figure 1-20).

1. Right-click the image titled TILBRIX3.JPG to display the list of options (see Figure 1-21). There are a number of interesting options here.

2. Click Save Image As....

3. Save the image file to the `\My Web Stuff` folder. If this folder does not already exist, create it by clicking the Create Folder button.

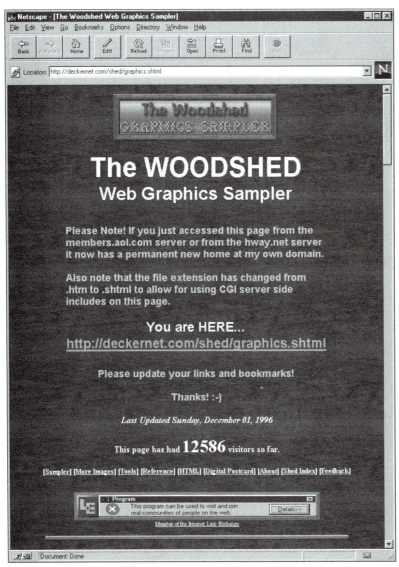

Figure 1-18: A web site that allows you to download free graphics.

You'll be clicking this image

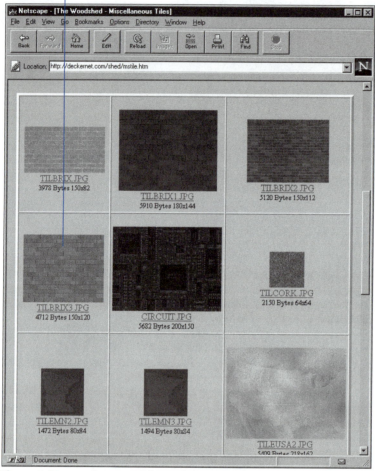

Figure 1-19: A web page with graphics you can download and use on your web pages.

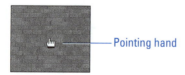
Pointing hand

Figure 1-20: The pointing-hand cursor in action.

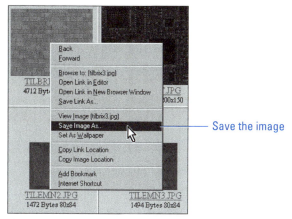

— Save the image

Figure 1-21: The right-click Netscape Navigator options for an image.

4. Open the file \My Web Stuff\Chap01\chap01A.htm on the CD-ROM to see this image used as a background (see Figure 1-22). To open this file in your default browser, double-click the file's icon.

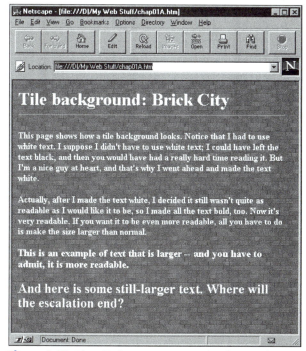

Figure 1-22: The tile image as a page background.

Some of the other options that become visible when you right-click are used for non-graphics tasks, such as downloading a page for editing, or copying URLs to the Clipboard.

Idea

Where to go from here:

✦ You can use the right-click download method at web sites that allow you to download free graphics. This allows you to download just what you need, and to see exactly what you are downloading.

✦ You can also use some of the other right-click options shown in Figure 1-21:

- *Browse to* (`tilbrix3.jpg`) will display the image in the browser.

- *View Image* (`tilbrix3.jpg`) will do the same thing.

- *Set as Wallpaper* will download the image, convert it to a bitmap (a .BMP file) and copy it to your Windows directory. It will then install the image as your wallpaper. Figure 1-23 shows the brick image as my desktop wallpaper.

Tile image as wallpaper

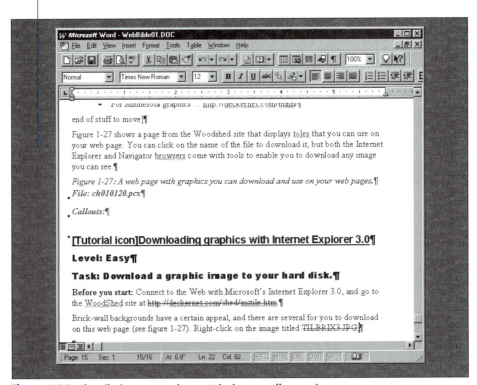

Figure 1-23: The tile image used as a Windows wallpaper image.

Downloading Graphics with Internet Explorer 3

Download: From Microsoft's web site at `http://www.microsoft.com/ie`

Level: Easy

Tutorial

Task: Download a graphic image to your hard disk

Before you start:

✦ Connect to the Web with Microsoft's Internet Explorer 3.

✦ Go to the WoodShed site at `http://deckernet.com/shed/mytiles.htm`.

You can also right-click an image in Internet Explorer 3.0 to see a list of options. As with Navigator, this is true whether or not the image is a hyperlink. The Internet Explorer pointing hand is also different.

1. Right-click the image titled TILBRIX3.JPG to display the list of options (see Figure 1-24). There are fewer options here (compare to Figure 1-21).

2. Click Save Picture As….

3. Save the image file to the `\My Web Stuff` folder. If this folder does not already exist, create it by clicking the Create Folder button.

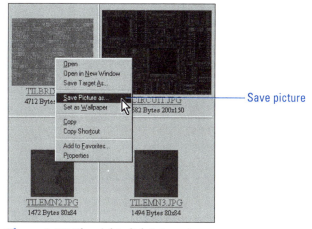

Figure 1-24: The right-click Internet Explorer options for an image.

If you simply accept the default filename (TILBRIX3.JPG), Internet Explorer will attempt to overwrite the existing copy you downloaded with Navigator. If you wish to save a separate copy, use a different filename. Click the Save button to save the image file.

I'm sure you've seen all the torrid press reports about browser wars. When it comes to right-click pop-up menus, Netscape's Navigator wins hands down. It puts more at your fingertips, and it does it without creating chaos. Take that, Microsoft (oh ye who created this Windows 95 right-click thorn-thicket in the first place!).

Idea

Where to go from here:

✦ See the tutorial for Netscape Navigator; some of the same options are available in Internet Explorer.

Web Tour #1: Visit Hot Web Sites

CD

The Web is full of pages. Some are good, some are awful, and some are great. If you want to visit a wide selection of pages that make interesting use of graphics, double-click the CD-ROM file:

```
\WebTour\Chapter1\index.htm
```

You'll see the web page for this chapter. Click the Web Tour icon and you will see a list of sites that we (that is, Uncle Webb and I) feel represent some darn good examples of web page design.

A Graphic View of the Web

To prepare for this chapter's tutorials, copy the following
folder from the CD-ROM to the \My Web Stuff folder on
your hard drive:

    \tutorial\chap02

This will copy files for all of the tutorials in this chapter to
your hard disk. See Chapter 1 for complete details on setting
up for tutorials.

As the Web becomes more and more graphically
oriented, knowing the ways in which graphics are used
on the Web becomes more important. In this chapter, you'll
learn why the World Wide Web is much like a bunch of Really
Big Pig Farms, and how graphics fit into the larger picture.
You'll also learn how to manage large collections of graphics,
and how to use graphics to make it easier for visitors to find
their way around a web site.

Web Overview

There are two kinds of readers reading this book: folks who
know what the Web is, and folks who don't. If you fit into the
latter category, I'm going to provide the pig's-eye-view of the
whole shootin' match.

Think of the Web as a giant pig farm. There are pigs
everywhere you look. Pigs to the left of you, pigs to the right
of you, and if you aren't careful, pigs on top of you. Figure 2-1
lays out the reality of the Web in graphic detail.

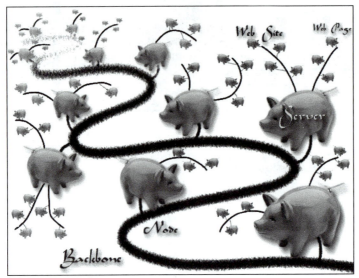

Figure 2-1: This is what the World Wide Web really looks like.

The primary organizational principle of the World Wide Pig Farm is the backbone. It's a snaky thing that connects all the really big pig farms to all the other really big pig farms. The really big pig farms are connected to the backbone at nodes. These really big pig farms can move pig slop at amazingly fast speeds because the nodes are connected to the backbone by a Really Big Pipe.

Tip

A Really Big Pipe is just a telephone connection, but it has lots and lots of capacity. Think of it as a Really Big Bundle of Wires that can carry either thousands of phone connections at normal speed, or a few connections at completely ridiculous speeds.

You find one or more Pig Servers sitting at each node. For the really big pig farms, there can be dozens of servers on a node. A server is a pig with one or more hard drives, and a really fast connection to its node.

The Pig Server has lots of little piglets (these are web sites, in case you are still trying to follow this insane ramble) that hang off of it. Think of little suckling pigs and you pretty much have the concept nailed down. In addition to the piglets, there are things like CGI scripts, data servers, and other deeply mysterious things on some web servers. There. Now you have a complete understanding of how the Web works. To put it more succinctly: There's this great big interconnected network out there, and anyone who connects to the network can look at your stuff, and you can look at theirs.

For reasons known only to the media elite, this is incredibly cool.

For once in his life, Mr. Author got something right. I hope he doesn't let it go to his head. There's plenty of pig slop to go around if he gets careless. Let's see how long he can dance to this tune.

How Graphics Fit In

Given this great big network that highly paid professionals manage to keep from collapsing in on itself, the idea is to make your little wayside pig farm cooler than the other pig farms. This is done with graphics.

Graphics come at a cost, however. If you were to create a complete web page with nothing but text (yes, I know this is a bizarre idea, but this is just a hypothetical discussion), the visitor could download it very quickly and start reading it. The visitor would also stop reading it fairly quickly because it has no graphics.

If you were to create a complete web page with *just* graphics, the visitor would wait and wait and wait while the graphics downloaded to his machine, and then he would get tired of waiting and go visit a different pig farm.

The trick — you are probably ahead of me on this one — is to use just enough graphics to make your web page Really Cool, without using so many graphics that visitors cough politely and then move on without ever really hearing what you have to say.

Organizing Your Graphics

The discussion of Really Big Pig Farms begs an important question: What about my pig farm? How do I organize it?

In a word: folders. Folders, which used to be called *directories* before Windows 95, are really just little pigpens. By organizing your web pages, images, and multimedia into pigpens, you can keep track of the various parts of your web site.

There are three fundamental kinds of pig farms (web sites):

◆ Family farms

◆ Big family farms

◆ Corporate farms

Each type of web site has its own organizational requirements, and those are explained shortly.

The basic unit of a web site is the web page. The web page doesn't actually contain graphics or multimedia elements. Graphics and multimedia are stored in separate files. Let's look at an example.

Web pages are built using a coding system called HTML (HyperText Markup Language). It's a way of specifying text attributes (such as bold and italic) and layout information (such as "put a graphic here" or "make this paragraph a heading"). You'll learn more about HTML in Chapter 4, "Images and Hyperlinks." Listing 2-1 shows the HTML code for a fairly simple web page created with Netscape Navigator Gold.

Listing 2-1: A sample of HTML

```
<!DOCTYPE HTML PUBLIC "-//W3C//DTD HTML 3.2//EN">
<HTML>
<HEAD>
   <TITLE></TITLE>
   <META NAME="Author" CONTENT="Ron Wodaski, Multimedia
      Madness, Inc.">
   <META NAME="GENERATOR" CONTENT="Mozilla/3.01Gold (WinNT; I)
      [Netscape]">
</HEAD>
<BODY>

<H2 ALIGN=CENTER>Pig Farm as Metaphor for the World Wide Web
<HR WIDTH="100%"></H2>

<P><IMG SRC="pignet.gif" HSPACE=5 HEIGHT=240 WIDTH=320
      ALIGN=RIGHT>
Think of the Web as a giant pig farm. There are pigs
      everywhere you look.
Pigs to the left of you, pigs to the right of you, and, if you
      aren't careful,
pigs on top of you. The figure at right lays out the reality of
      the web
in graphic detail. </P>

<P>The primary organizational principle of the World Wide Pig
      Farm is the
backbone. It's a snaky thing that connects all the really big
      pig farms
to all the other really big pig farms. The really big pig
      farms are connected
to the backbone at nodes. These really big pig farms can move
      pig slop
at amazingly fast speeds because the nodes are connected to the
      backbone
by a Really Big Pipe. </P>
</BODY>
</HTML>
```

The web page itself is shown in Figure 2-2. There is a headline at the top of the page, or horizontal rule, an image aligned at the right of the page, and some text.

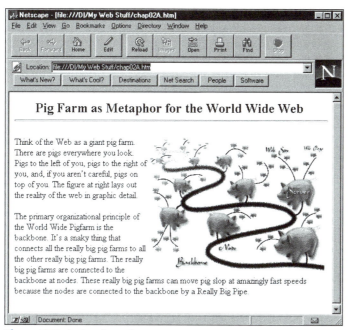

Figure 2-2: A simple web page.

In the preceding HTML, the reference to the image is highlighted in bold. It looks like this:

```
<IMG SRC="pignet.gif" HSPACE=5 HEIGHT=240 WIDTH=320
     ALIGN=RIGHT>
```

From left to right, this line of HTML does the following:

<	This is a special character that starts all HTML commands. Anything outside of these brackets is treated as text that should be displayed on the web page.
IMG	This is the first bit of actual HTML code, and it's called a *tag*. In this case, the tag tells the browser that an image reference is coming right up.
SRC="pignet.gif"	All of the remaining HTML codes are called *parameters*. The SRC parameter tells the browser where to find the image file pignet.gif.

HSPACE=5	This parameter tells the browser to put five pixels of horizontal space to the left and right of the image. Yes, there is a corresponding parameter for vertical space.
HEIGHT=240	This parameter defines the display height of the image. In this case, it is the same as the actual height of the image. You could also specify a larger or smaller display height.
WIDTH=320	This parameter defines the display width of the image.
ALIGN=RIGHT	This parameter defines how the image is aligned. In this example, the image is aligned at the right edge of the page.
>	The special character that ends all HTML commands. Look for other "<" and ">" characters to see other HTML commands in the example in Listing 2-1.

The important point here is not that you memorize the <IMG> tag. It is that images and other files are not actually stored "inside" the web page. They stay as separate files. When you organize the various files for your web site, it's important to know what you are organizing!

Family farms (small web sites)

A small web site usually consists of one or two web pages plus whatever graphics files are referenced on those pages. Figure 2-3 shows the files for a hypothetical web site. There is one web page (index.htm) with three images (image1.gif, image2.gif, and image3.gif).

```
\MYPAGE\INDEX.HTM
\MYPAGE\IMAGE1.GIF
\MYPAGE\IMAGE2.GIF
\MYPAGE\IMAGE3.GIF
```

Figure 2-3: Files for a small web site.

All four files are stored in a single folder (mypages). Figure 2-4 shows a highly sophisticated representation of this method of organization. This is the way of small web sites: Put it all in one folder, and hope for the best. If you do not have a large number of files, this works. If you get into double-digit file numbers (ten or more), the one-folder-holds-everything web layout becomes a pain in the neck. Here's the typical scenario:

 \mypages

Figure 2-4: How to organize a small web site.

✦ You build the web site with, let us say, eight files — two pages, six images.

✦ A week later, you realize you need another page and four more images. Now you are up to 13 files.

✦ Two weeks later, you go back because you want to change one of the graphics on one of the pages. You wind up having to open all of the image files in your image editor, one at a time, because you've forgotten which image is the one you want to change.

✦ A month later, you go back again, and you forget which image you changed, what images are on what pages, and what it was you wanted to do in the first place. You now own a mess. It's time to reorganize this mess as a medium-sized pig farm.

To avoid these kinds of hassles, you can organize your web site. The degree of organization required is directly tied to the number and variety of files used on the site.

Big family farms (medium-sized web sites)

When your file count starts to go up, it's time to move to a higher level of organization. Figure 2-5 shows a list of files for a medium-sized web site. There are three web pages, five images (three in GIF format, two in JPEG format) and two audio files. This is fewer than ten files, but there is significant variety in file type. This arrangement of files into folders (one folder for each type of file, with web pages all in the top-level folder) works for many web sites. It makes it easy to find the file you want.

```
\MYPAGES\PAGE1.HTM
\MYPAGES\PAGE2.HTM
\MYPAGES\PAGE3.HTM
\MYPAGES\IMAGES\IMAGE1.GIF
\MYPAGES\IMAGES\IMAGE2.GIF
\MYPAGES\IMAGES\IMAGE3.GIF
\MYPAGES\IMAGES\PHOTO1.JPG
\MYPAGES\IMAGES\PHOTO2.JPG
\MYPAGES\SOUNDS\AUDIO1.WAV
\MYPAGES\SOUNDS\AUDIO2.WAV
```

Figure 2-5: A medium-sized web site.

Figure 2-6 shows the folder layout for such a web site. If you add additional file types, such as video clips or animations, you simply create a new folder for the file type.

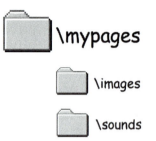

Figure 2-6: The folder organization for a medium-sized web site.

Corporate farms (really big web sites)

For larger web sites, the need for organization becomes acute. Simply dumping every image into a single folder won't work. To organize a large site, create folders that correspond to the overall structure of the web site. Figure 2-7 shows a list of files for a moderately large web site. In this list of files, there are (and excuse me if this comes off like a computerized version of "The Twelve Days of Christmas"):

✦ Five top-level web pages

✦ Three topic folders

✦ Two web pages and two folders in the first topic folder

✦ Three web pages and one folder in the second topic folder

✦ Two web pages and three folders in the third topic folder

Figure 2-8 shows the actual folder layout for this web site. This example uses three levels of folders. A very large web site might use four or even five levels of folders. Note that the subfolders for each topic look amazingly like the folder arrangement shown in Figure 2-6. This brings a brutal truth about large web sites to light. Tack the following to the side of your monitor:

The very best way to organize a large web site is to break it down into smaller, simpler web sites.

```
\OURSITE\INDEX.HTM
\OURSITE\TOPIC1.HTM
\OURSITE\TOPIC2.HTM
\OURSITE\TOPIC3.HTM
\OURSITE\TOPIC1\PAGE1.HTM
\OUTSITE\TOPIC1\PAGE2.HTM
\OURSITE\TOPIC1\GIF\IMAGE1.GIF
\OURSITE\TOPIC1\GIF\IMAGE2.GIF
\OURSITE\TOPIC1\GIF\IMAGE3.GIF
\OURSITE\TOPIC1\JPG\PHOTO1.JPG
\OURSITE\TOPIC1\JPG\PHOTO2.JPG
\OURSITE\TOPIC2\PAGE1.HTM
\OURSITE\TOPIC2\PAGE2.HTM
\OURSITE\TOPIC2\PAGE3.HTM
\OURSITE\TOPIC2\GIF\IMAGE1.GIF
\OURSITE\TOPIC2\GIF\IMAGE2.GIF
\OURSITE\TOPIC3\PAGE1.HTM
\OURSITE\TOPIC3\PAGE2.HTM
\OURSITE\TOPIC3\GIF\IMAGE1.GIF
\OURSITE\TOPIC3\JPG\PHOTO1.JPG
\OURSITE\TOPIC3\JPG\PHOTO2.JPG
\OURSITE\TOPIC3\VIDEO\VIDEO1.AVI
```

Figure 2-7: Files for a large web site.

Figure 2-8: The folder arrangement for a large web site.

You will never hear a better piece of advice on organizing your web site. Violate this rule at your peril. Am I making myself clear? This little rule is the Great Organizing Principle for web publishers. It can make the difference between the Web Site from Hell and a web site that practically manages itself.

If more than one person is making changes to a web site, the rule becomes even more important. Divide and conquer worked for Caesar, Charlemagne, my Aunt Ruth — and it works for web sites, too. To state the obvious: if there are five people (or five departments, or five monkeys) responsible for web site content, reality is just about begging you to create a web site with five smaller web sites within it.

 Even if one of those mini-web sites has just a single page, you still will never regret setting it up as a separate web site within a larger web site. Time and human nature have a tendency to complicate things — so don't just sit there, subdivide!

Thanks, Unc, for those words of wisdom. But let's not forget the Most Important Organizational Rule:

Use the exact same organization on your local hard disk and on the web server.

If you follow this rule, you will be much less likely to get lost when moving from one to the other.

If the idea of having two complete copies of your web site seems confusing, allow me to explain. The web site itself lives on a web server. Visitors can access the pages that sit on the web server. If your site is good, they are going to do that quite often. You do not want to do anything that will interfere with that process.

If you were to open files on the web site and make changes to them at the same time that people were reading them, chaos would result. For example, suppose you've made a few changes, and you save the file to the server. What if you've made a mistake? What if you aren't done yet, and the visitor sees a page that doesn't work right?

To avoid these problems, make all changes to the *copy* of your web site that sits on a local hard disk. Test it, refine it, and when it's perfect you can upload it to the web server. This is called publishing. Don't publish until you know that everything works. That way, visitors to your web site will be able to cruise around your site, using its various links, viewing its various images, and generally having a good time.

Now that you know how to organize your web site, it's time to do something really exciting, like learn what's available for creating really cool graphics that are worth organizing.

Web Signposts

Finding your way around the average web site is an exercise in dealing with chaos. If you can organize your web site, and make it easy for folks to navigate, your web site will definitely stand out. So far in this chapter, I've talked about the physical organization of the web site on your local hard disk and the server. Now let's take a look at the need to navigate around that web site.

When you are organizing your site for navigation, you may take a very different view of it than you do for maintenance purposes. For example, maintenance needs may suggest putting all images together — but that's hardly the way someone will navigate around your site!

Ideally, the overall scheme of your web site will be evident on not only your home page, but on every page on the site. This is usually accomplished with a navigation bar. Common locations for navigation bars are at the top of the page, at the left of the page, and at the bottom of the page (see Figure 2-9).

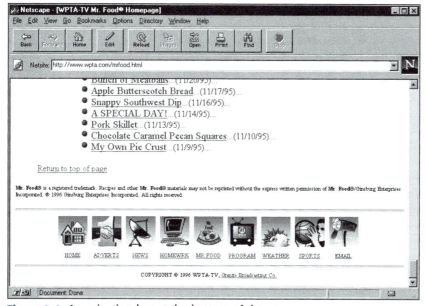

Figure 2-9: A navigation bar at the bottom of the page.
Copyright © WPTA-TV.

There are as many types, positions, and combinations as you care to invent. If you want to be original, consider putting your navigation bar at the right-hand side of the page. Or try both left and right (see Figure 2-10). Or top and left (Figure 2-11). Wherever you put your navigation bar, and however you construct it, there is just one important concept involved: Be sure to use one on every page. Multipage web sites without navigation bars are almost always awkward to navigate. It's too easy to get lost.

Figure 2-10: Navigation guides at left and right. And lots of them, too.

Reprinted with permission from The Detroit News.

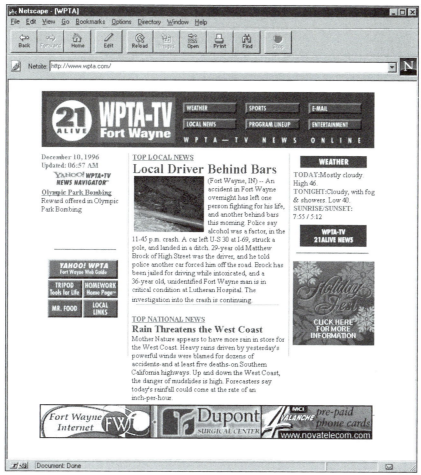

Figure 2-11: Navigation bars at the top and left.
Copyright © WPTA-TV.

Creating a good navigation bar requires an ability to see your web site the way visitors see it, and that's not easy to do when you are creating it yourself. There is a distinct tendency to feel that something is obvious. It's often not obvious to your visitors.

To see how a navigation bar works in principle, the following tutorial shows you how to create the images that make up the bar, and how to incorporate them into the pages on a web site.

Adding navigation bars with Navigator Gold 3.0

Download: From the Netscape web pages at `http://www.netscape.com`. Look for the *Download Now* icon near the top of the web page.

Level: Easy

Tutorial

Task: Add navigation aids to four pages

Before you start:

   ✦ Download and install Netscape Navigator Gold 3.0 or later.

The templates for the buttons used in the following demonstration were created with PhotoImpact, using the Web | Button Designer menu selection. I manually chose the colors and gradient for the buttons and then saved the result using the built-in GIF SmartSaver. You can learn how to build the button templates and add the text to them with Adobe Photoshop in Chapter 16.

Tip

CD

1. Double-click the file `\My Web Stuff\Chap02\chap02b.htm` to open it in Navigator Gold.

   If Navigator Gold is not your default browser, run Navigator Gold and use the File | Open File in Browser menu selection to open the file. You'll see a text-only (Gasp! Horrors!) web page (see Figure 2-12).

2. Click the Edit button to switch to Navigator Gold's Edit mode (see Figure 2-13). Once you are in Edit mode, you can use the tools above the web page to make changes to the page.

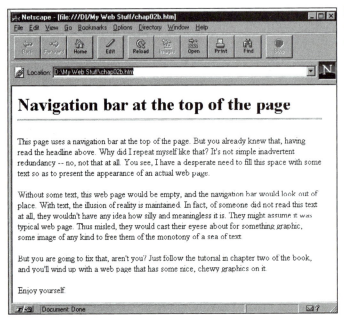

Figure 2-12: You will add a navigation bar to this page in the tutorial.

Figure 2-13: Navigator Gold's Edit mode.

Adding buttons

In this part of the tutorial, you will add four buttons to the page to create a toolbar. The buttons come in two varieties. One, shown in Figure 2-14, has the appearance of a button waiting to be pushed. The other, shown in Figure 2-15, looks like a button that has already been pushed. Each button will correspond to a web page — click the button, jump to the web page. The button for the currently displayed web page will appear already pushed, so the visitor will know not to click it.

Figure 2-14: A button yet to be pushed.

Figure 2-15: A button that has been pushed.

My book, *Creating Cool Navigator Gold Web Pages* (IDG Books Worldwide, ISBN 0-7645-3021-6) is a great place to learn how to use Navigator Gold effectively. Visit the book's web site at `http://www.olympus.net/biz/mmad/index.htm` for information about what the book covers.

Tip

1. Switch to Edit mode; the cursor is positioned at the upper left side of the page.

2. Click to the left of the top line to reposition the cursor.

3. Press the Enter key to add a blank line at the top of the page (see Figure 2-16).

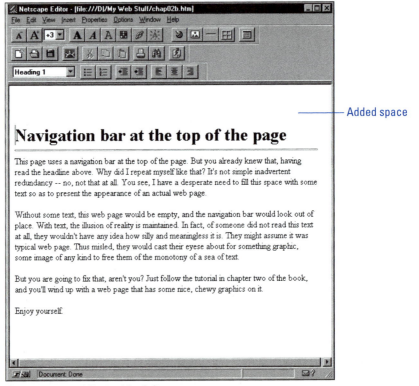

Figure 2-16: Adding a blank line.

  4. Click the Insert Image (or as I like to call it, Picture) icon on the toolbar to open the dialog box shown in Figure 2-17.

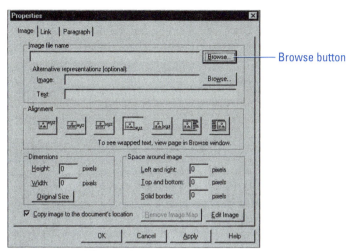

Figure 2-17: Adding a picture.

5. Click the Browse button to open the dialog box shown in Figure 2-18, and locate the file \My Web Stuff\Chap02\blueHom2.gif.

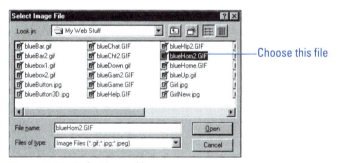

Figure 2-18: Selecting a file.

6. Click Open, then click OK to add the image to the page (see Figure 2-19).

This image is one of the already-pushed buttons. This page is the home page, so the pushed effect tells the reader not to click the button. The other buttons you add will be of the please-push-me variety.

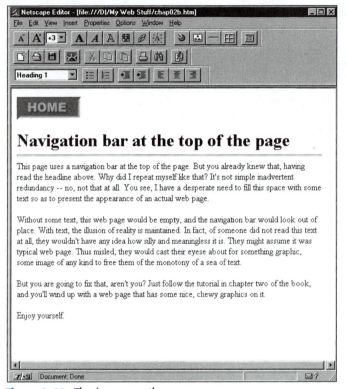

Figure 2-19: The image on the page.

When you are done adding the HOME button, the cursor is positioned to the right of the new button — the perfect place to add the next button.

7. Repeat the steps you used to add the first button, but adding the following image files, in the following order:

✦ BLUECHAT.GIF

✦ BLUEGAME.GIF

✦ BLUEHELP.GIF

When you have added all four buttons, the page should look like Figure 2-20. If there is space between the buttons, you probably pressed the spacebar at some point. You can delete the extra space with the Backspace or Delete keys, as appropriate.

Figure 2-20: All four buttons added to the page.

It's something of a tradition to center a top-of-page navigation bar.

8. Position the cursor anywhere in the line of buttons, and click the Center Text button in the toolbar. The result is shown in Figure 2-21.

For this example, all of the buttons look like buttons. You can also create variations that don't exactly look like buttons, but still use a row of separate images. If you design the images just right, they won't look like separate images at all.

Figure 2-21: Centering the navigation bar.

Adding hyperlinks

So far, the navigation bar has only earned the "bar" part of its name. To make it a navigation tool, you have to add hyperlinks to the images on the bar. Except, of course, the already-pushed button, which isn't designed to take the user anywhere.

1. To add a link with Navigator Gold, right-click the CHAT button. This displays a pop-up menu (see Figure 2-22).

2. Click Create Link Using Selected to display the dialog box shown in Figure 2-23.

Figure 2-22: Adding a hyperlink.

You can also add a hyperlink by clicking the image to select it, and then clicking the Link button. Another method: use the Insert | Link menu selection. Both of these options display the same dialog box shown in Figure 2-23.

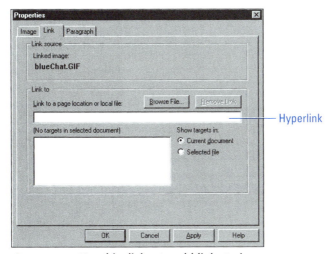

Figure 2-23: Use this dialog to add links to images.

3. Click the Browse button, and locate the file \My Web Stuff\Chap02\ chap02e.htm.

4. Click Open, and you are returned to the dialog box shown in Figure 2-23. The filename you selected appears on the Link to line (see Figure 2-24).

5. Click OK to add the link.

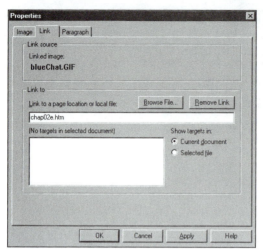

Figure 2-24: Adding the correct link.

 What happens next depends on what mood your Navigator Gold editor is in. If it's in a good mood, nothing will change — the CHAT button will look exactly the same. If it's in a bad mood, it will add a border around the CHAT button. No self-respecting navigation bar wants to have borders around the individual images that make up the bar; it spoils the whole effect. If Navigator Gold turns out to be in a bad mood, you can fix this problem. Refer to the last sections in Chapter 4 of this book for details of the solution (open the file in Notepad and add BORDER=0 to the IMG tag, if you know your HTML).

6. Add hyperlinks to the two remaining buttons:

✦ GAMES   `\My Web Stuff\Chap02\chap02c.htm`

✦ HELP   `\My Web Stuff\Chap02\chap02d.htm`

7. Save your work.

 8. To test a link, click the View in Browser button and click one of the buttons.

For example, if you click the GAMES, button, you should see the GAMES page (see Figure 2-25). If the Browse view is open in a separate window, close that window and return to the Edit mode window. Otherwise, click the Edit button to resume editing the file.

Figure 2-25: A hyperlink page.

Adding more navigation bars

Notice that there is no navigation bar on this page — let's add one. The process is similar. This time, however, you'll use the image \My Web Stuff\Chap02\ blueHome.GIF for the HOME button, and the image \My Web Stuff\Chap02\ blueGam2.GIF for the GAMES button.

1. Add all four buttons (see Figure 2-26).

2. Now add links to the buttons:

   ✦ HOME   \My Web Stuff\Chap02\chap02b.htm

   ✦ CHAT   \My Web Stuff\Chap02\chap02e.htm

   ✦ GAMES   none

   ✦ HELP   \My Web Stuff\Chap02\chap02d.htm

Figure 2-26: Adding buttons to the GAMES page.

3. Save your work.

4. To test a link, click the View in Browser button and click the HELP button. This displays the HELP page.

5. Add the buttons for the navigation bar, this time using the `blueHlp2.GIF` image instead of the `blueHelp.GIF` file. Figure 2-27 shows the result you want to achieve.

6. Add hyperlinks:

✦ HOME   `\My Web Stuff\Chap02\chap02b.htm`

✦ CHAT   `\My Web Stuff\Chap02\chap02e.htm`

✦ GAMES   none

✦ HELP   `\My Web Stuff\Chap02\chap02d.htm`

Figure 2-27: Adding the navigation bar to the HELP page.

7. Save your work.

8. To test a link, click the View in Browser button and click the CHAT button. This displays the CHAT page.

9. Add the buttons for the navigation bar, this time using the `blueCht2.GIF` image instead of the `blueChat.GIF` file. Figure 2-28 shows the result you want to achieve.

10. Add hyperlinks:

    ✦ HOME   `\My Web Stuff\Chap02\chap02b.htm`

    ✦ CHAT   `\My Web Stuff\Chap02\chap02e.htm`

    ✦ GAMES   none

    ✦ HELP   `\My Web Stuff\Chap02\chap02d.htm`

Figure 2-28: Adding the navigation bar to the CHAT page.

You have now added navigation bars to all four pages, with the appropriate button for each page showing as already pressed.

11. To test the complete web site, click buttons to go from page to page to page to . . . you get the idea.

12. If you find a problem, click the Edit button to return to Edit mode, make a change, then continue testing until all the links are correct.

Caution!

You may be wondering if it's okay to copy the navigation bar from one window to another. Unfortunately, there is a bug in Navigator Gold that creates trouble if you try this. The links to the image files on disk get messed up, so it's safer to follow the procedure outlined here. If the bug gets fixed, you will be able to simply drag the buttons from one window to another window, which makes the whole process much easier. To see if the bug is fixed in the version of Navigator Gold you are using, give it a try.

Idea

Where to go from here:

✦ If you have a lot of navigation buttons, arrange then in two rows or columns.

✦ Create a navigation bar that looks like a real-world object. Anything from a bar of soap to a TV remote control will work.

✦ If you expect that some visitors to your web site will still be using text-based browsers, provide an alternative navigation method using text. Use vertical bars between the choices.

Site Maps

A site map is a graphic or text representation of all the web pages on a given web site. Not all web sites have site maps — in fact, even though site maps are a growing trend, surprisingly few web sites make use of them. With a site map, one click should take you to a specific web page.

One of the problems with a site map is the effort required to maintain it. It's one thing to take a snapshot of your web site and commit it to a map; it's another to revise it as pages come and go.

The graphic quality of site maps is all over the map. There are all-text site maps.

Figure 2-29 shows one that is a combination of graphics and text. It's dense, and only the dedicated visitor will be able to find what he or she wants.

Figure 2-30 shows a more graphically oriented site map. It includes a flow chart that shows the relationship among the various pages on the site. A map like this is an excellent tool for budding web builders. It allows you to study the organization of a web site.

It is also possible to generate a site map using programs that run on the web server. These programs make it easier to maintain the site map, but the cost in readability can be high.

For information about site mapping as a science, visit `http://lislin.gws.uky.edu/Sitemap/Sitemap.html`.

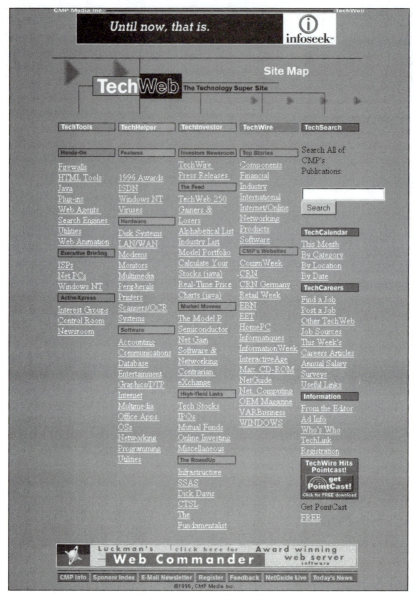

Figure 2-29: A site map that might as well be all text.

Copyright © CMP Media Inc.

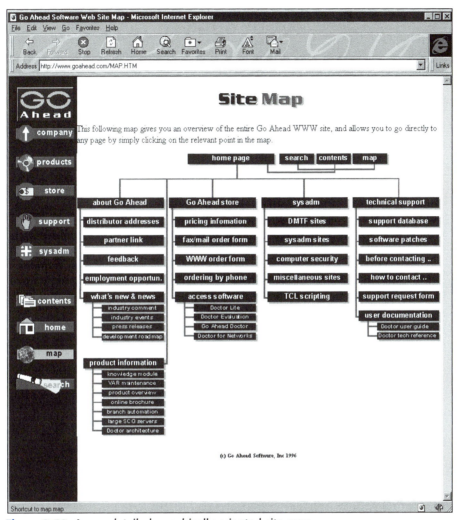

Figure 2-30: A very detailed, graphically oriented site map.

Web Tour #2: Visit Organized Web Sites

The best way to learn how to organize a web site is to look at how other web sites are organized. In most cases, you'll have to visit various pages on a web site and build your own map of how the site is organized by observing the URLs for the various pages and images. In a few cases, you can look at a web site at a directory level using an ftp (File Transfer Protocol) connection instead of an http (HyperText

Transfer Protocol) connection. The Web Tour for this chapter includes some of each, as well as links to some of the best and worst site maps.

To get started on the Web Tour of sites that are well organized, double-click the CD-ROM file:

`\WebTour\Chapter2\index.htm`

You'll see the web page for this chapter. Click the Web Tour icon to get started.

Easy Web Graphics You Can Create

To prepare for this chapter's tutorials, copy the following folder from the CD-ROM to the \My Web Stuff folder on your hard drive:

    \tutorial\chap03

This will copy files and folders for all of the tutorials in this chapter to your hard disk. See Chapter 1 for complete details on setting up for tutorials.

This is a big, thick book, but you don't need to know everything between the covers in order to create good-looking web graphics. This chapter is dedicated to the proposition that a little time and a little effort can generate big results. Sure, you could sweat over a hot computer all day to create the perfect graphic, but there's room for fast 'n' easy, too.

Before you create your first image, there are some general topics that are worth a look. I'll explain what an image editor is and how to use one, and then we'll play around with several different image editors so you can get a feel for what it's like to be in the driver's seat.

This chapter covers the mechanics of image creation. If you want more information about how to design killer graphics, see Chapters 8, 17, and 22.

Principles of Graphic Creation

There are many, many image editors floating around in the Windows 95 universe. Some of them are intended for creating images, and some are intended for editing images. A few are good at both tasks. To acquaint you with the possibilities of a good image editor, I've selected Adobe's Photoshop. Although it's often the image tool of choice for professionals, it's so well designed that just about anyone can work with it.

Photoshop packs a lot of power, but in this chapter my main intention is to use Photoshop to illustrate the kinds of things you can do with an image editor. Over the course of the book, you will see Photoshop over and over, and you'll learn much more than can be fit into a single chapter.

Other image editors provide many of the same features you'll see in Photoshop, though not necessarily as elegantly or powerfully. Some image tools, like Fractal Design Painter, go beyond Photoshop in surprising ways. The bottom line is that the features you are about to see are usually available in some form in any decent image editor.

Figure 3-1 playfully illustrates the kinds of things you can do with an image editor. The real power of image editing comes when you combine these various effects — you can make an image look very different by using the tools in an image editor.

Figure 3-1: The possibilities for image editing seem endless.

For example, Figure 3-2 shows a sample image open in Photoshop. The Photoshop tools palette is at the left of the Photoshop window. The palette at the bottom right of the Photoshop window is one of many that are available. Palettes allow you to change the way a tool works, or to access image properties easily.

Figure 3-2: An image open in Photoshop for editing.

Figure 3-3 shows the same image after several Photoshop tools have been used to make changes to the image. These changes included smearing the flower images, lightening the apple, using an airbrush to write "Hi!" on the apple, darkening the peaches, and applying a colored pencil filter to the pear.

Figure 3-3: The same image as in Figure 3-2, but with some changes.

Figures 3-4 and 3-5 show two more extreme changes to the image. These are just a few of the millions of ways you can change an image with Photoshop and other image editors. A good image editor is limited only by your imagination.

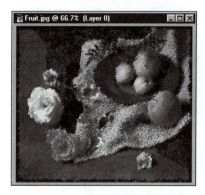

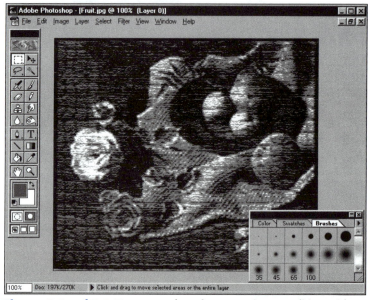

Figures 3-4 and 3-5: Two examples of extreme image editing with Photoshop.

Photoshop is a professional tool, and it is capable of effects and tricks that are beyond many other image editors. This chapter will show you the kinds of basic effects you can expect to use in various image editors.

Using Color, 3-D, and Borders Effectively

Unlike most of this book's pages, your web pages will use color images. However, this creates a dilemma that I call the More Colors Problem:

✦ The more colors you use in the image, the better it looks.

✦ The more colors you use in the image, the longer it takes to display on the web page.

There are tips and tricks you can use to reduce the impact of the More Colors Problem, but it is something that you will always have to be aware of. For an in-depth, more-than-you-ever-wanted-to-know approach to this issue, see Chapter 11. For a quick and dirty overview, read on.

There are two basic kinds of images you are likely to use on a web page: true-color images, and images that use a palette of colors. So-called true-color images can include up to 16.7 million different colors — that's more than your eye can distinguish, and such images are very lifelike. Color palettes are often limited to 256 or fewer colors. There's a big difference between 16,700,000 and 256, but if you are careful your images will not suffer greatly because of the difference.

Photoshop 4.0 (and most image editors) offers a simple way to convert images for use on the Web. In Photoshop, use the Image | Mode | Fixed Palette menu selection. This displays a dialog box of different palette options (see Figure 3-6). Choose Web as your palette setting, and note that the color depth is 216. That means that Photoshop will use 216 colors in the palette. This is less than 256, and there's a reason behind the difference. Those missing 40 colors are used by Windows and by other programs such as your browser, leaving just 216 for your images.

— Palette type set to Web

Figure 3-6: Selecting the palette type in Photoshop.

Converting a true-color image to a fixed-palette image isn't without penalty. Figure 3-7 shows a side-by-side comparison of a true-color image (left) and a fixed-palette image using 216 colors. In both cases, the images are magnified more than 3 times (332% larger than normal, to be exact). Note that the transitions between colors in the true-color image (shades of gray here, but you can check the color section of the book to see the actual colors) are relatively smooth. In the 216-color image, the boundaries between colors are much harsher, and the fine detail in the image gets lost.

Smooth pixelation   Rough pixelation

Figure 3-7: Compare a true-color image (left) to an image with only 216 colors (right).

Figure 3-8 shows a more extreme example. The 216-color image is still on the right, but the image on the left uses just 16 colors. The pear, in particular, is a complete mess using so few colors.

Fortunately, special software is now available that helps you reduce colors without sacrificing too much image fidelity. Figure 3-9 shows the color reduction possible using a product called HVS Color from Frontier Technology. This product uses information about the way that the eye sees color to perform color reductions. The result is an image that looks as close as possible to the original while using a much smaller selection of colors. The image on the left is true-color, while the image on the right uses just 64 colors. Note that the 64-color image uses a completely different method to control color changes.

Turn to the color section to see normal-size versions of these images.

Really rough pixelation   Rough pixelation

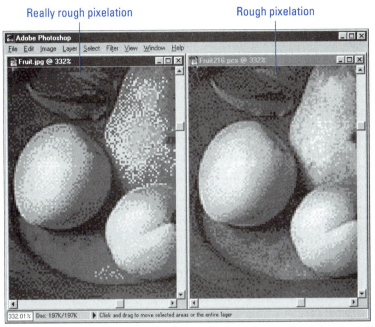

Figure 3-8: Compare a 16-color image (left) with a 216-color image (right).

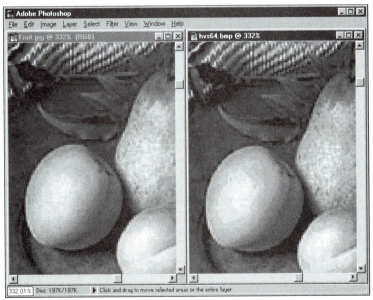

Figure 3-9: Compare a true-color image (left) with a 64-color image created with HVS Color.

Creating Color Buttons with Paint Shop Pro

Tutorial

Download: From Jasc's web site at `ftp://ftp.jasc.com`

Level: Easy

Task: Create a round, blue button using Paint Shop Pro

Before you start:

✦ Download Paint Shop Pro from Jasc's web site, and install it.

✦ Run Jasc's Paint Shop Pro: Click the Start button, and then click Programs │ Paint Shop Pro │ Paint Shop Pro 4. This displays an empty window as shown in Figure 3-10.

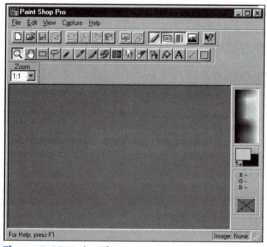

Figure 3-10: Paint Shop Pro 4.

1. To create a new image file, use the File │ New menu selection. This displays the New Image dialog box, shown in Figure 3-11.

2. Set the image width and height to 30 pixels, the background color to White, and select an image type of 16.7 million colors.

3. Click OK to create the new image. Figure 3-12 shows the appearance of the new image in Paint Shop Pro.

Width   Height

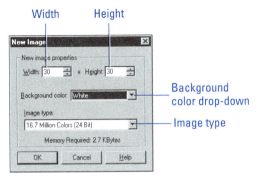

Background
color drop-down

Image type

Figure 3-11: Creating a new
image in Paint Shop Pro.

Do you see that crosshatching at the right of the image? That's what
Paint Shop Pro uses for a background. Come on — any sensible
image editor uses a solid gray background! That @#*&$#@
background is an annoying touch on an otherwise useful program.
Sometimes, it's hard to tell what pixels are in your image, and what
pixels are in the background. Get with it, Jasc, and fix this!

Ugly cross-hatching

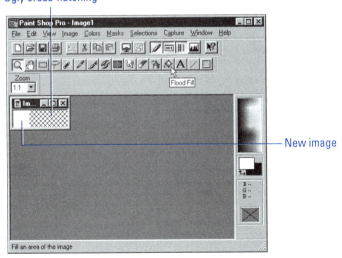

New image

Figure 3-12: A new image.

To create the round button, you will create a round selection, and fill it with color.

4. Click the selection tool (see Figure 3-13). Note that the list of options below the tools changes to reflect the options available for the selection tool.

5. Click the selection type (the default is Rectangle) to expose a drop-down list of types.

6. Click Circle to select it.

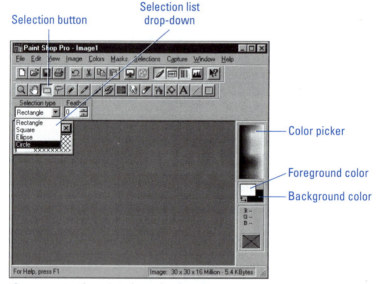

Figure 3-13: Choosing the Selection type.

The cursor changes to a large cross-hair, with a small circle icon at the lower right.

7. Click at the top left of the image, and drag to the lower right to select a circle (refer to Figures 3-14 and 3-15 to see the appropriate size of the selection).

Bucket icon cursor

Cross-hair

Figures 3-14 and 3-15: Filling an area with color.

Paint Shop Pro, like most image editors, has two colors available for immediate use: a foreground color (used for filling, painting, and drawing) and a background color (fills in spaces you leave behind when you move a selection).

8. To change the foreground color to blue, click in the color picker on a medium shade of blue (see Figure 3-13). The foreground color area changes to show the new foreground color.

Tip

To change the background color, right-click the color picker. To switch foreground and background colors, click the little two-headed arrow at the lower left of the foreground/background color areas.

9. Click the Flood Fill button (see Figure 3-12) to activate it. Note that the area just below the toolbar changes to reflect the settings for the flood fill tool. Note also that the cursor changes to a small bucket (the traditional symbol for a flood fill).

10. Place the small cross-hair over the circle selection (see the image in Figure 3-14), and click to fill the circle with blue (see the image in Figure 3-15).

11. To save the button, use the File | Save As menu selection. This opens the Save As dialog box.

I recommend that you save all of your tutorial files in one place. In all of the examples for this book, we'll reference a folder called My Web Stuff. To create this folder:

New Folder   12. Click the Create New Folder icon in the Save As dialog box. A new folder icon appears, with the name New Folder. The text is selected, and anything you type will replace this default name.

13. Type the folder name **My Web Stuff**.

14. Press Enter (or click outside the folder) to add the new name.

My Web Stuff   15. Double-click the new My Web Stuff folder to open it.

16. Click the Save as Type drop-down box and select the file type JPG - JPEG - JIFF Compliant. (You'll learn about file types in Chapter 11).

17. Enter the filename **blueButton**.

18. Click the Save as Type drop-down box and select the file type JPG-JPEG-JIFF Compliant.

19. Click the Save button to save your new button.

If you are curious about the Options button, visit Chapter 11, which reveals the inner secrets of JPEG and other image types.

CD

Open the file \My Web Stuff\Chap03\chap03A.htm on the CD-ROM to see this button in use on a web page. To open this file in your default browser, double-click the file's icon. Figure 3-16 shows the appearance of the page in Netscape Navigator.

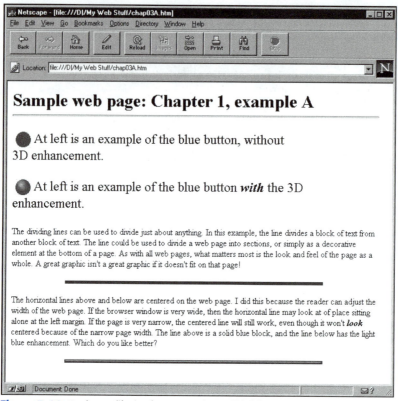

Figure 3-16: Saving a file in the My Web Stuff folder.

Adding 3-D Effects

Level: Easy

Task: Make a button 3-D

Tutorial

This is not the place to stop! To make the button useful, you gotta make it 3-D. Will one of you guys please explain how?

Sorry, Uncle Webb; you are right as usual. All this button needs to add some life to it is a highlight to make it look 3-D. Here's how to do it.

1. Click on the eyedropper tool (see Figure 3-16).

2. Move the tip of the tool into the color picker (see Figure 3-17).

3. Move the tip around until it is over a light blue color. You can tell what color you are over by looking at the color box at bottom right (see Figure 3-17).

4. When you have the light blue color you want (I used color values of red=177, green=235, and blue=243; you can find these values just above the color box), left-click to make that color the current foreground color.

5. Click the airbrush tool (see Figure 3-17) to activate it. The options for the tool appear below the toolbars. The default value shown in Figure 3-17 is suitable for creating a light blue highlight on the button.

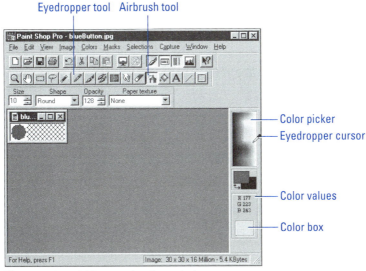

Figure 3-17: Picking a color for painting.

6. To paint with the airbrush, click and wiggle it around near the upper left of the blue button image you created earlier.

Figure 3-18 shows the effect created by the airbrush. Note that the airbrush tool gives a soft edge to the painting color.

Airbrush icon cursor

Figure 3-18: Painting with the airbrush.

Tip

If you make a mistake, stop painting immediately and press Ctrl+Z. This will remove the last brush stroke, and you can try again.

7. If you feel adventurous, you can set the opacity of the airbrush tool to a value of 15 (see Figure 3-19) and paint a much lighter highlight around the intense highlight you just created.

Figure 3-19 shows the result. The combination of a small, intense highlight and a broader, less intense highlight creates a 3-D effect.

8. Save your work in the file \My Web Stuff\blueButton3D.jpg.

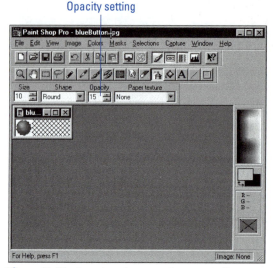

Figure 3-19: Creating the complete 3-D effect.

Idea

Where to go from here:

✦ Try creating a square button. Add the highlight to the left and top edges. Always try to simulate natural light reflections when you create a 3-D object.

 ✦ Use a darker shade of a color to create a shadow area on the round and square buttons.

✦ See Chapter 13, "Interlacing and Transparency," which tells you how to make the button backgrounds transparent on the web page.

Creating Lines and Dividers with PhotoImpact

Tutorial

Download: A trial version of PhotoImpact is not available from Ulead. Check the web site at http://www.ulead.com to see if this changes.

Level: Easy to Intermediate

Task: Create a dividing line using PhotoImpact

Before you start:

✦ Download and install the demo version of PhotoImpact.

In this tutorial, you are going to take a step up in sophistication. Paint Shop Pro is a useful image tool, but Ulead's PhotoImpact offers a slew of features that help you create files that work well on the Web.

Figure 3-20 shows the PhotoImpact window. The various tools and buttons are arranged around the PhotoImpact window — file, clipboard, and miscellaneous buttons at the top edge, tools on the left, tool settings at the bottom, and color controls on the right.

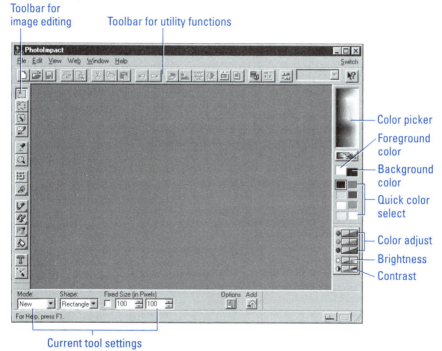

Figure 3-20: The PhotoImpact window.

1. Use the File | New menu selection to create a new file. This displays the New dialog box shown in Figure 3-21.

2. Click the radio button for User defined size, and set the width to 480 pixels, and the height to 8.

3. Make sure that the Data type button selected at the top of the dialog box is the one on the far right — True Color.

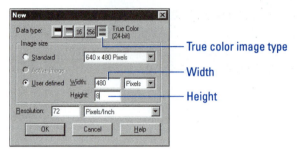

Figure 3-21: Creating a new file.

This creates a wide image, as shown in Figure 3-22. The image proportions are just right for creating a dividing line. You create the line by first selecting an area, and then filling it with color.

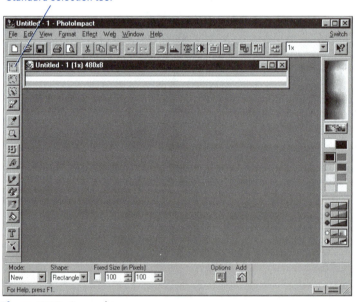

Figure 3-22: A new image.

4. Click the standard selection tool (see Figure 3-22) to activate it.

5. Click near the upper left corner of the new image, and drag to a point near the lower right corner.

6. Release the mouse button. You will see a rectangle formed by a dashed line, as shown in Figure 3-23. Note that the selection does not include the entire image area.

Figure 3-23: Creating a rectangular selection.

I deliberately left space around the selection. This space will help to separate the colored area of the image from surrounding text or images on the web page. To add more space above and below the image, use a larger image height when you create the image. To eliminate the space, make the image height and width exactly the size of the divider you plan to create.

PhotoImpact uses a different method for filling an area with color.

7. Use the Edit | Fill menu selection to open the Fill dialog box shown in Figure 3-24.

   The dialog box contains a row of basic colors at the top, as well as other ways to fill an image. This is a more sophisticated way of filling an image, and is typical of higher-end image editors.

8. Make sure the Selected color radio button is highlighted, as shown in Figure 3-24, and click the blue block of color.

9. Click OK to fill the selected area with color. Figure 3-25 shows the result.

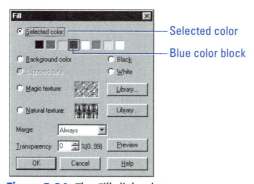

Figure 3-24: The Fill dialog box.

Figure 3-25: The area is filled with color.

Tip

The area within the selection boundary is usually referred to simply as "the selection." The dashed outline of the selection is sometimes affectionately referred to as *crawling ants* because, well, that's sort of what it looks like.

You probably expect to save this image using the old, familiar File | Save menu selection. Not if you plan to use the image on a web page! Instead:

10. Click that handy-dandy Web menu to drop down an intriguing list of possibilities (see Figure 3-26). You are going to save this image using the GIF file type.

11. Click the GIF SmartSaver selection to open the dialog box shown in Figure 3-27.

Figure 3-26: PhotoImpact's Web menu contains some juicy surprises.

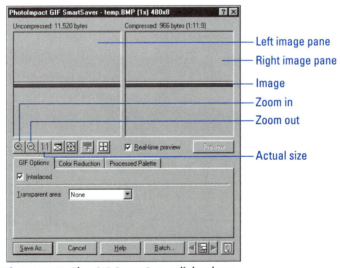

Figure 3-27: The GIF SmartSaver dialog box.

You can use this dialog box to gain control over your GIF images. There are two image panes in the window. The left pane shows the uncompressed image, including size and appearance. The right pane shows the compressed image. Note that the uncompressed size of the blue line is over 11,000 bytes, while the compressed version will be just 966 bytes. That's a substantial saving.

GIF images are compressed, but there is no loss in image quality. The JPEG file format uses even more compression, but at a slight cost in image quality. For detailed information about image compression, see Chapter 11.

The background of this image is white. If you were to add this image to a web page with a gray background, the white border would look pretty odd. You can specify one color in a GIF image to be transparent.

12. Click the drop-down list near the bottom of the SmartSaver dialog box labeled Transparent area.

13. Click Pick colors (see Figure 3-28).

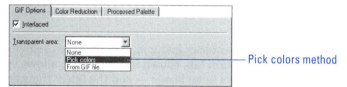

Figure 3-28: Setting the method for choosing the transparent color.

The appearance of the dialog box changes, as shown in Figure 3-29. You see instructions that tell you how to select what part of the image will be transparent.

14. To make the white area transparent, press the Ctrl key and click the white area in the left pane.

The white area changes to gray in both panes. The color change indicates white has been made the transparent color.

You can also create so-called "3-D" buttons with Paint Shop Pro, but for my money they aren't very good looking — much too crude. Take a gander at Figure 3-35, which shows the damage done. If you like it (someone must; they put it in the software, didn't they?), you can work your own black magic with the Image | Special Effects | Buttonize menu selection.

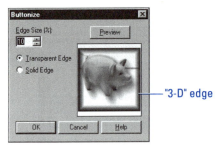

"3-D" edge

Figure 3-35: Creating a crude 3-D effect with Paint Shop Pro.

1. Begin by opening the file `\Our Web Stuff\Ron\pig.jpg` in PhotoImpact. Use the Web | Button Designer menu selection to display the dialog box shown in Figure 3-36.

   This dialog box allows you to create various kinds of borders for images. In addition to following along with this tutorial, I encourage you to experiment with the wide variety of tools included in the dialog box.

   The key features of this dialog box include:

   Button styles   Shows the four most commonly used button styles. You can switch to one of these styles by clicking it.

   Direction   Specifies whether the button 3-D effect is added to the button (outward), or uses a part of the existing button (inward).

   Options   Allows you to change the width of the button 3-D effect, select new colors, and so on. The exact options vary with the different styles.

   Preview   Shows the appearance of your button with the current style and options.

   More styles   Displays additional styles to choose from.

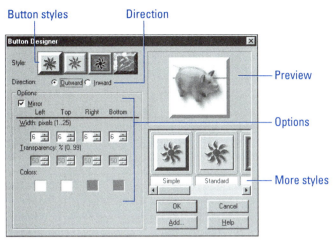

Figure 3-36: Using the PhotoImpact Button Designer.

2. As you can see in Figure 3-36, if you like the default button effect, you can click OK and you are done! How's that for a quick and easy tutorial?

 Harumph! Think you can get away that easy, do you? I'll show 'em something they won't soon forget! Did you notice how some of those buttons have colored edges? You can set the color of the edges yourself. For example, click the second style from the left at the upper left of the Button Designer dialog box. Look at Figure 3-37. See those colors at the bottom left? They're not colors at all — they're gray. Click each color, and the Windows Color dialog box pops up (Figure 3-38). Pick appropriate colors — say a very light blue for group one in Figure 3-37, and a medium blue for group two.

You might mention, Uncle, that the colors are grouped because the Mirror check box is checked.

 Twaddle! Even an idiot could see that. The borders of the image in the preview area change to reflect the new colors. You can also change the width and transparency for some button styles. Experiment! Take control of your buttons! Save your work on the hard disk in the \My Web Stuff folder you created earlier!

Group one

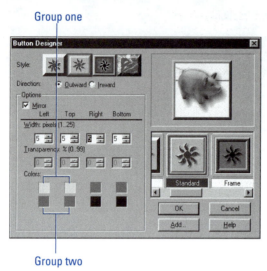

Group two

Figure 3-37: Changing the button style.

Figure 3-38: Changing colors.

Just a minute, Uncle. This is a JPEG (an acronym for Joint Photographic Experts Group, the folks who defined this file format) file, not a GIF file, and I'd like to point out some neat features in PhotoImpact for working with JPEG images.

3. Use the Web | JPEG SmartSaver menu selection to open the JPEG SmartSaver (see Figure 3-39).

   The appearance is similar to the GIF SmartSaver. Note that there is only one tab, and it is labeled Compression.

4. For this example, use the default settings of Smooth, Subsampling, and Mode.

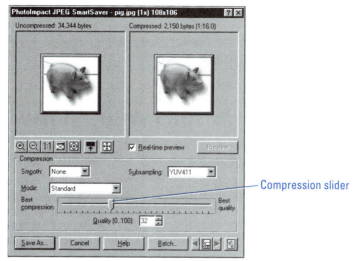

Compression slider

Figure 3-39: Using the JPEG SmartSaver.

5. For fun, move the compression slider to various settings and see what effect it has on the size and quality of the right-hand image.

At the setting shown in Figure 3-39 (a quality level of 32), the image compresses from 34,344 bytes down to 2,150 bytes — a 16:1 compression ratio. That's very good. There is a very slight degradation in the right-hand image, but not enough to be a problem. If you use a very low quality setting (less than 10), you get the result shown in Figure 3-40. The JPEG SmartSaver allows you to test such things interactively, which makes it easy to get the smallest possible file.

Figure 3-40: Using too much compression.

6. When you have the quality slider set to your satisfaction, click the Save As button and save this image to the folder \My Web Stuff, using the filename **pigButton.jpg.**

Tip

For more information about compression using GIF and JPEG file formats, see Chapter 11.

Idea

Where to go from here:

✦ PhotoImpact contains a wide variety of button types. Experiment with each type to see what it does to your images.

✦ Try using a patch of color for the button, instead of an image. Experiment with variations.

✦ Experiment with changing the border colors of images, as well as transparency and other options.

Creating Freeform Buttons with Photoshop

CD: A trial version of Photoshop is on the CD-ROM. To find out how to install it, view the web page at \demo\viewme.htm in your browser and click the \demo\adobe hyperlink.

Tutorial   **Level:** Easy to Intermediate

Task: Create a button using selections and fills

Before you start:

✦ Run Photoshop 4.0.

This tutorial introduces a little creativity into the button-making process. I wasn't sure whether to label this tutorial as Easy or Intermediate. If you have any design skill, it's Easy. If you are terrified at the prospect of putting pencil to paper, it's no worse than Intermediate.

1. Use the File | New menu selection to open the New dialog box in Photoshop.

2. Enter the name **MyButton** into the Name text box.

3. Set the image width and height to 30 pixels (see Figure 3-41). Verify that the mode is RGB Color, and that the Contents radio button is set to White. You can safely ignore the resolution setting; it's there for images used in print publication.

4. Click OK to create the new file. You'll see a new image window, as shown in Figure 3-42.

Tip

If the image is too small for you, use the Ctrl + Plus sign keys to enlarge it, and the Ctrl + Minus keys to shrink it. You are not changing the image size, just the size at which you are viewing it. You must use the Plus and Minus keys on the numeric keypad — not the keys in the row of number keys on the keyboard.

5. Click the selection tool (refer to Figure 3-41) and hold down the mouse button until a fly-out row of buttons appears (see Figure 3-43). The flyout contains alternative tools for creating different kinds of selections. From left to right, they are Rectangle, Ellipse, Row, Column, and Crop.

6. Without releasing the mouse button, drag to the ellipse tool and *then* release the mouse button. After you click, the ellipse replaces the rectangle as the symbol for the selection tool.

Selection tool   Name   Width   Height   Mode (type)

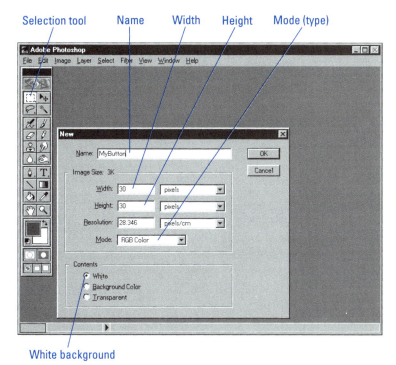

White background

Figure 3-41: Creating a new file.

Sensible background
Image

Figure 3-42: The new image.

7. Click at the upper left corner of the image, and drag to the lower right, to create a circle (see Figure 3-44).

Note that I dragged the lower right corner of the image window to expand it. I find it more comfortable to work with extra area around the image; it's less distracting. It's also a pain in the you-know-what when you try to click near the edge of the image, and click the window border instead!

8. Click the foreground color (refer to Figure 3-43) to open the Photoshop Color Picker dialog box (see Figure 3-45).

9. Use the color slider and the color panel to pick a medium-dark color. I used a maroon, with values of 128 for Red, 38 for Green, and 38 for Blue. You can type these numbers into the appropriate boxes (see Figure 3-45) to get exactly the same color.

10. Click OK when you have the color you want.

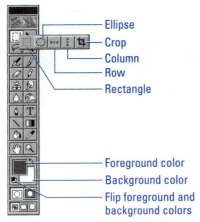

Ellipse
Crop
Column
Row
Rectangle

Foreground color
Background color
Flip foreground and
background colors

Figure 3-43: A fly-out menu appears when you hold down the mouse button on a tool.

Selection border

Figure 3-44: Selecting a circle.

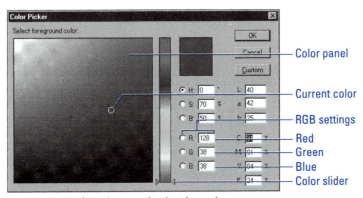

Color panel

Current color

RGB settings
Red
Green
Blue
Color slider

Figure 3-45: Choosing a color in Photoshop.

To make sure you create an exact circle, hold down the Shift key while you drag out the ellipse. This forces Photoshop to create only a circle. This tip also works when you want to create a square using the rectangle version of the selection tool.

Tip

11. To fill the selection with the new color, use the Edit ⏐ Fill menu selection. This opens the dialog box shown in Figure 3-46.

12. Select Foreground Color in the Use drop-down list. Verify that Opacity is set at 100%, and that the Mode is normal. If not, change these settings.

13. Click OK to fill the selection.

What to use for fill color

Figure 3-46: Filling a selection with the foreground color.

14. Click and hold the selection tool, and drag to select the rectangle in the flyout.

15. Use the Ctrl + D keys to deselect the circle. Then click and drag out a small rectangular selection as shown in Figure 3-47.

16. Use the Edit ⏐ Fill menu selection to fill the selection with white. Hint: In the Contents section of the Fill dialog box, set the Use drop-down to White.

Selection border

Figure 3-47: Creating a rectangular selection.

Now for the fun part. (Are you listening, Uncle Webb? Suddenly, you are strangely silent.)

17. Click on the lasso selection (see Figure 3-48) and hold.

18. Drag the cursor to the straight-line lasso tool and release to activate it.

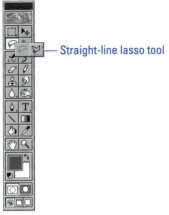 — Straight-line lasso tool

Figure 3-48: Selecting the straight-line lasso tool.

For the next few steps, it will help to enlarge your view of the image window.

19. Press Ctrl + Plus (that's the Plus key on the numeric keypad) three times to enlarge the view to 400%, as shown in Figure 3-49.

Figure 3-49: Enlarging the view.

20. Click at the points of the triangle shown in Figure 3-50 to select a triangular region. This requires a total of four clicks: once at one apex, then at the second, then at the third, then back at the first place you clicked to complete the triangle.

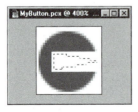

Figure 3-50: Selecting a triangular region.

21. Click the foreground color, and pick a nice blue. I used settings of red=6, green=69, and blue=195.

22. Then use Edit | Fill to fill the region with the foreground color. *Hint:* In the Contents section of the Fill dialog box, set the Use drop-down to Foreground.

You now have yourself a cute little doodad (see Figure 3-51). (See Figure 3-56 to see what this button looks like on a web page, or double-click now on the file \My Web Stuff\Chap03\chap03B.htm.)

Figure 3-51: Doodad extraordinaire.

Idea

Where to go from here:

✦ Photoshop has some very interesting built-in effects. Try adding effects to one or more portions of the button. Textures are often especially interesting.

✦ You can use the smudge tool to vary the edges of your doodads.

Creating Borders and Edges

Tutorial

CD: Install the trial versions of the plug-ins from the CD-ROM. To find out how to install, view the web page at \demo\viewme.htm in your browser and click the \demo\auto_fx hyperlink.

Level: Easy to Intermediate

Task: Apply edge effects

Before you start:

✦ Run Photoshop, then the plug-in program Photo/Graphic Edges.

Photo/Graphic Edges is a plug-in program for Photoshop. There are quite a few different plug-ins for Photoshop, and for good reason: Photoshop is the tool of choice for a vast number of professional artists. This large audience is a natural market for cool image tools, and Adobe, the folks who make Photoshop, has developed a sophisticated and standardized interface for Photoshop plug-ins and add-ons.

If you buy Photo/Graphic Edges, the CD starts up its installation routine automatically when you insert the CD into the drive. You do need to tell Photo/Graphic Edges where the Photoshop plug-in directory is (see Figure 3-52). This is true for any Photoshop plug-in that you install.

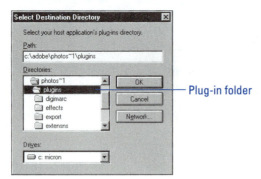

Plug-in folder

Figure 3-52: Selecting the
Photoshop plug-in directory.

Because Photo/Graphic Edges is a plug-in, you must run Photoshop first. First,
open the image file \My Web Stuff\Chap03\mygirl.pcx (see Figure 3-53) using
the File | Open menu selection. To apply the edge effect, you use the menu
selection Filter | Auto F/X | Photo/Graphic Edges to open the Photo/Graphic
Edges dialog box (see Figure 3-54). It's a fancy dialog box that allows you to build
the edge effect interactively. There are a number of controls at the bottom left,
and a preview of the current image at the upper right.

Figure 3-53: Opening a file in Photoshop.

Alter effect settings   Click here to select first effect

Figure 3-54: The Photo/Graphic Edges dialog box is photogenic.

To select an effect, you click the button labeled *Select Outset Effect.* This opens a list of effects. You can click one to highlight it, and click the Open button to apply the effect. Figure 3-55 shows several typical effects. You can specify effect properties, such as the blurring of the edge — if you want to add transparency to an image, you want a completely unblurred edge, for example. (See Chapter 13 for a discussion of image transparency.) You can also combine edge effects, as shown at bottom right of Figure 3-55.

Second effect

First effect

Figure 3-55: You can create a variety of interesting effects.

Figure 3-56 shows the results of the various tutorials in the second half of this chapter. The top row of pig buttons shows the crude 3-D effect available in Paint Shop Pro, while the lower row shows the results you get with PhotoImpact. You can look at the file itself: `\My Web Stuff\Chap03\chap03B.htm`.

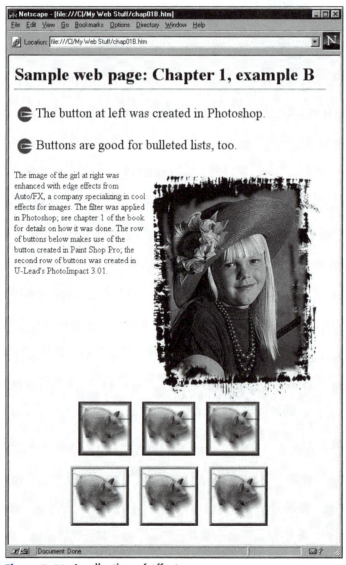

Figure 3-56: A collection of effects.

Creating 3-D Buttons in Fractal Design Painter

CD: To install the trial version of Painter from the CD, double-click the file `\demo\fractal\painter4\setup.exe`.

Level: Intermediate

Tutorial

Task: Create spectacular 3-D effects

Before you start:

✦ Download and install the demo version of Painter 4.

Adobe Photoshop sets the standard for image editing software. Fractal Design's Painter sets the standard for image creation software. Photoshop is well-designed and offers powerful tools, but Painter takes off in a different direction. It includes a wide range of tools that mimic natural drawing and painting tools — brushes, pencils, crayons, oils, and so on.

Yeah, yeah — quit throwing such high-sounding words at this software, and say it like it is: there isn't anything else out there that comes close to Painter. If you want the best, like me, you'll get your hands on this sucker, and soon!

Painter also includes some nifty tools for enhancing the appearance of images and buttons. Excellent color control, textures, papers, and drop shadows are just a few of the goodies available.

In this tutorial, you will use Painter to create a 3-D button. Figure 3-57 shows the Painter window. It looks kind of scary, with all those tools and little windows. Painter is a vast piece of software, with more nooks and crannies than an old Victorian house.

1. Use the File | New menu selection to create a new image. Set the width and height to 40 pixels (see Figure 3-58).

   Note that you can set the paper color (all Painter images have a background paper texture), and that Painter also supports creating movies. (The trial version does not support making movies.) You'll learn how to create an animation with Painter in Chapter 22, "Dynamic Graphics."

2. To create a circular selection, first click the selection tool (see Figure 3-59). Note that the control panel changes to reflect the options for the selection tool (see Figure 3-60).

3. Click the button with the dotted circle to change the selection shape from the default (rectangle) to a circle.

4. Click at the upper left of the image, and drag not quite all the way to the lower right corner (see Figure 3-61). Use the Shift key while dragging to create a perfect circle.

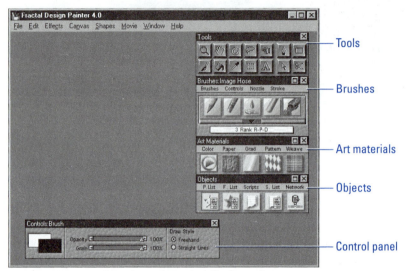

Figure 3-57: Fractal Design Painter is full of goodies.

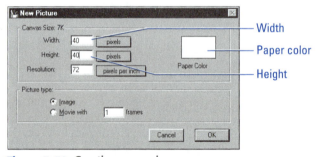

Figure 3-58: Creating a new image.

Figure 3-59: Choosing a tool.

Figure 3-60: Setting options for the selection tool in the control panel.

5. Release the Shift key and mouse button together to complete the selection.

 ——— Circular selection boundary

Figure 3-61: Selecting a circular area.

6. Use the Effects | Fill menu selection to open the Fill dialog box (see Figure 3-62). Note that you have quite a few options for the fill — patterns, gradations, and weaving, as well as color.

7. Make sure the Current Color radio button is selected.

   Speaking of color, you may have noticed that I didn't give any direction to pick a color before opening the Fill dialog box. That's because Painter lets you work with many of the other features even while a dialog box is open.

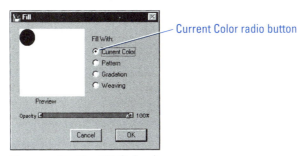 ——— Current Color radio button

Figure 3-62: The Fill dialog box.

8. To change the current foreground color while the Fill dialog box is open, click the Color icon in the Art Materials panel (see Figure 3-63).

9. Click the outer wheel to select a color, and in the inner triangle to choose saturation (amount of color) and value (lightness or darkness).

   I selected a red, with the saturation/value near the top right of the triangle, but any color will work. For best results, don't choose black, white, or a completely saturated color (the three points of the triangle).

   A glance at the Fill dialog box will show that the color you selected now appears (see Figure 3-64).

10. Click OK to fill the selection with the color (see Figure 3-65).

What's Modal?

Do you ever stop to think about all those dialog boxes you deal with in Windows? Probably not. But they come in two distinct flavors: modal, and nonmodal.

You are most familiar with the modal dialog box — even if you've never heard that word used to describe a dialog box. Modal dialog boxes demand your focused attention. Until you click OK or Cancel, that dialog box not only won't go away, it won't let you access the program that called it. That's the essence of a modal dialog box: It wants your answer now, before you can continue with anything else.

Fractal Design Painter makes frequent use of nonmodal dialogs. That means that you can leave the dialog box open, and work in the program. The Fill dialog box mentioned in the text is a good example of a nonmodal dialog box — you can change colors, create a pattern, or do a lot of other things while the dialog box is open.

However, there are some things you still can't do. You can't, for example, draw while the dialog box is open, or change the shape of the current selection. It might be better to call Painter's dialogs semi-modal — there are things you can do while they are open, and there are things you can't do.

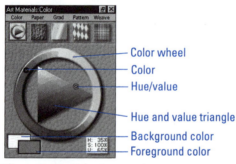

Color wheel
Color
Hue/value
Hue and value triangle
Background color
Foreground color

Figure 3-63: Selecting a color.

Figure 3-64: The new color appears in the Fill dialog box.

Figure 3-65:
The selection is filled with color.

11. To make the selection 3-D, first use the Edit | Float menu selection to float the selection, turning it into an object.

You will see a heavier, square border around the object that defines its logical boundary, not the literal selection boundary. Peek ahead to Figure 3-69 to see what it looks like.

To see the list of current objects, click the Object panel to activate it (refer back to Figure 3-57 for the location of this panel). You can rearrange the order of objects in the Object panel. You can also use the Object panel to access objects that are part of a group, enabling you to make changes to objects even after they are grouped. Painter's object orientation adds to its power.

Tip

12. Next, use the Effects | Surface Control | Apply Surface Texture menu selection. This opens the dialog box shown in Figure 3-67.

Fer cryin' out loud, Sonny, tell them to notice just how many Effects menu selections there are — and most of those selections open up a hornet's nest of additional possibilities. This is pure, raw power. If it ain't too much trouble, have a gander at Figure 3-66, which shows the Effects menu selections just for Surface Control. There's plenty more available for Tonal Control, Focus, Esoterica, and so on. It's enough to make you dizzy, just thinking about the possibilities!

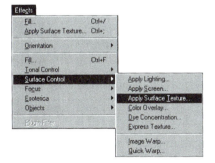

Figure 3-66: The Painter menus are deep, deep, deep.

There are a lot of options here, and you can create a wide range of interesting 3-D effects using texture. The default effect, paper grain, is interesting in its own right, but that's not why we are here!

13. Click the Paper Grain button at top right, which displays a variety of options.

Using Images as Links

In case you missed it in Chapter 1, I'll say it again: Any decent graphic image really *is* worth at least a thousand words. Adding hyperlinks to your images can make them worth millions — of *words*, of course — though it could be *dollars* for a commercial web site. If you were selling a product on the Web, a good picture could make the difference between "Just looking" and "I'll take one of those, please." Ah, but you *are* selling a product on the Web — at the very least, your web page itself! Millions of web pages are added to the Web every month; why should anyone visit yours? Because you are going to give them a web page worth visiting, that's why. And you can do that best with graphic links.

Most of this chapter shows how to add links to a web page using various web page editors. You may think that's a waste of time, but it's not. There are important differences in how web page editors handle graphic links; often the shortcomings of these editors are worth knowing about. Most of what I have to say about actual page design and image links will be said (appropriately) with pictures. All the usual rules for good graphics still apply: Small is better, fewer colors are better, and good design and tight integration into the overall page are still strict requirements. The sample graphics used in the tutorials are not just window-dressing; they are part of the lesson.

Adding Hyperlinks with Navigator Gold

Download: From the Netscape web pages at `http://www.netscape.com`. Look for the *Download Now* icon near the top of the web page.

Level: Easy

Tutorial

Task: Add different kinds of hyperlinks to images

Before you start:

✦ Download and install Netscape Navigator Gold from Netscape's web site.

✦ Open the folder `\My Web Stuff\Chap04\4A` on your desktop (see Figure 4-1).

Figure 4-1: The folder containing the starting files for this tutorial.

Although Netscape Navigator Gold won't let you create complex web pages (frames and forms aren't supported), it's a handy little editor for quickly laying out the text and graphics for a web page. It's also convenient — built right into the most popular Web browser, Netscape Navigator. (This may change when Netscape introduces its newest browser, Netscape Communicator, but the basic concepts will remain the same.) Navigator Gold also has some important limitations, as the tutorial points out.

To begin the tutorial, locate the following file:

```
\My Web Stuff\Chap04\4A\chap04a.htm
```

1. If Netscape Navigator Gold is your default web browser, locate the file and double-click its icon. Otherwise, run Navigator Gold from the Start ꟾ Programs ꟾ Netscape Navigator Gold ꟾ Netscape Navigator Gold menu selection, then choose the File ꟾ Open File in Editor menu selection.

2. Locate the file in the Open dialog box, and then click the Open button to open it in Navigator Gold. Figure 4-2 shows the file in Browse mode.

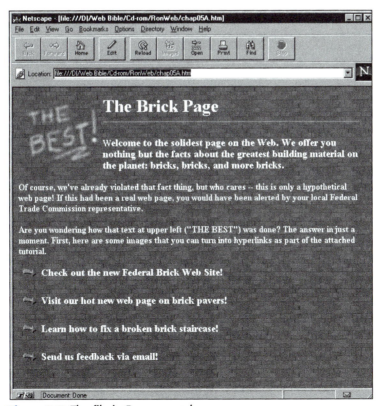

Figure 4-2: The file in Browse mode.

3. Click the Edit button to switch to Edit mode (see Figure 4-3).

Tip

Note that the file in Edit mode looks different from the way it looks in Browse mode. Navigator Gold is not a true what-you-see-is-what-you-get (WYSIWYG, pronounced *wizz-ee-wig*) editor. Always check the layout of your page by viewing it in Browse mode.

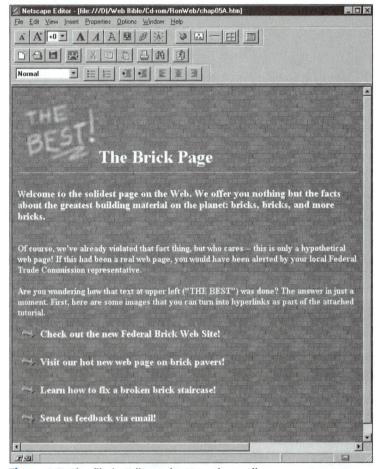

Figure 4-3: The file in Edit mode. Note the toolbar.

To add images or edit their properties, you use the Picture dialog box (see Figure 4-4). You can get to this dialog box in different ways. Some of the most common are as follows:

✦ Click the Insert Images button (which I like to call the Picture button) on the toolbar to add a new picture

✦ Click to highlight a picture, and then click the Picture button

✦ Right-click a picture, and then choose the Image Properties menu selection

✦ Use the Insert | Image menu selection to add a picture

✦ Click to highlight a picture, and then use the Insert | Picture menu selection

Tip

This is typical of Navigator Gold — there are usually several ways to accomplish any task. In most cases, you can choose between toolbar buttons, right-click pop-up menus, and the menu bar — or combinations of these. It's enough to make you dizzy until you figure out which way you like best.

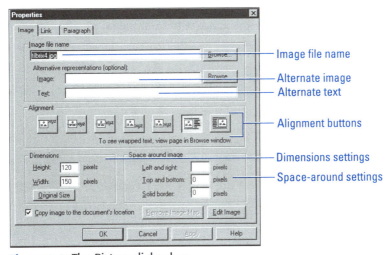

Figure 4-4: The Picture dialog box.

To see how this dialog box works in action, you will work with the file you already have open in Navigator Gold.

4. Switch to Edit mode if you haven't done so already.

In Figure 4-2 you can see that the text to the right of the image at the upper left is crowding too close to the image.

5. To add more space between the image and the text, right-click the image to open the Picture dialog box shown in Figure 4-4.

Tip

Perhaps you are wondering just exactly what is image here, and what is background. Click on the image while you are in Edit mode to select it. The image becomes outlined, and you can see what I've done: I used a simple trick, adding the spray text to a copy of the background image. When the image is inserted into the document, it merges with the background. This is more effective than trying to create transparency around a spray-painted bit of text. Figures 4-5 and 4-6 show the background image and the spray paint image side-by-side for comparison.

6. To add space, enter the number **24** into the text box for Left and Right pixels at the lower right of the dialog box (see Figure 4-7).

This specifies the number of pixels used for spacing. As a general rule, use small numbers for small images, and large numbers for large images. This image is a medium-to-large image.

Figure 4-5 (left): The background image.
Figure 4-6 (right): The same image with spray paint.

 Left and right
space settings

Figure 4-7: Setting space around an image.

You can also use this section of the dialog box to add space above and below the image, or to add a border with the width you specify. Left/right space is needed most frequently, and picture borders are used the least.

7. Click OK to view the result in Edit mode (see Figure 4-8).

Most editors support setting space around images. This is a fundamental feature of HTML, the language that is used to specify the arrangement of text and images on a web page.

Working with Hyperlinks

A web page isn't really a web page unless it contains hyperlinks. You are probably familiar with the most common type of link, which jumps to another web page. There are actually three general classes of links:

✦ Links that jump to files on the same web server, which I am calling links to files. They come in two varieties: links to files in the same directory as the current page (direct links), and links to files in other directories on the server (relative links).

✦ Links that jump to web pages on other web servers, which I am calling links to web sites.

✦ Links that aren't exactly links, such as those that pop up your e-mail program with the address already filled in. I am calling these MAILTO links.

The following sections describe each kind of link in detail.

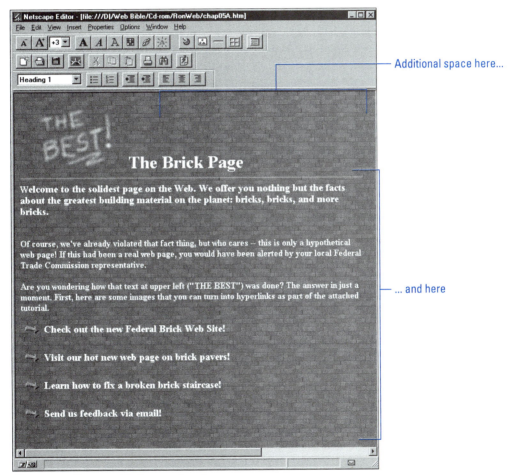

Figure 4-8: Space added around an image.

Adding direct links to files

The spray-paint image will draw the visitor's attention. The image makes the statement that this company is the best in their business. Visitors might want to see some proof, so the image should have a hyperlink to an appropriate page. To add a hyperlink that will jump to a specific page on this web site, right-click the image to display the pop-up menu shown in Figure 4-9, and choose Create Link Using Selected. This displays the same Picture dialog box, but with the Link tab selected (see Figure 4-10).

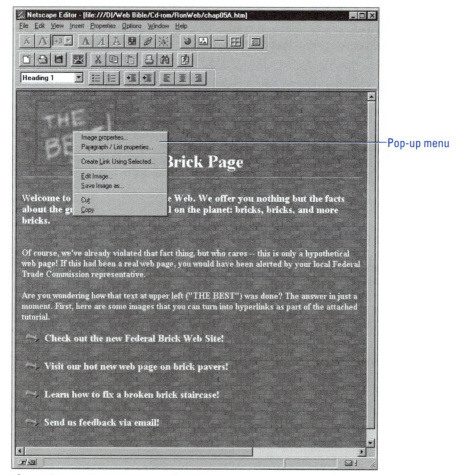

Figure 4-9: Right-clicking to add a link.

Tip

If you don't look closely, you might not realize that this is the same dialog box that you saw earlier. It looks very different. This dialog box uses tabs, and the appearance of the dialog box changes dramatically depending on which tab is active. Keep an eye on the top of dialog boxes with tabs because you never know when you'll need to click a tab to get to the version of the dialog box you really want.

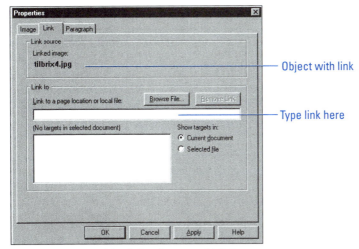

Figure 4-10: Use this dialog box to add links.

You can specify the file to link to in one of two ways:

✦ You can type the filename `chap04A2.htm` into the Link to a page location or local file text box.

✦ You can click the Browse button and locate the file `chap04A2.htm` in the Link to File dialog box. Click the Open button in that dialog box, and the filename appears in the Link to a page location or local file text box.

Whichever method you use, when you've specified the file, click OK to complete the link.

Here are some important things to note about this dialog box:

✦ The object that anchors the link is indicated at the top of the dialog box. In this case, that is the image file `tilbrix4.jpg`.

✦ You have the option of clicking the Browse button to scan your disk for the link file.

✦ You can click the Remove Link button to remove a link you no longer want to use.

✦ If the selected file has targets in it, you can choose to display them in the little window at the bottom left of the dialog box (more about this later).

Adding relative links to files

This is just one type of link you can add: a link to another file on the web site. You can use relative pathnames to specify other files on a web site. For example, if the file were in the parent directory, you would use this to specify the file:

```
..\Chap04A2.htm
```

If the other file were in a directory at the same level as the current file, but in a different folder, you might specify the path to the other file like this:

```
..\somefolder\Chap04A2.htm
```

If you use the Browse button to locate files for links, the correct relative pathname will be used automatically. If you aren't familiar with relative pathnames, always use the Browse button to add links to files to avoid errors.

Tip

The files for these links must always be in the same location on your computer's hard disk as they are on the web server. Otherwise the link will not be found when the user clicks the image.

Adding links to other web sites

You can also add links to other web sites. These are called URLs (Uniform Resource Locators). Most of the time, they start with `http://`. There are little arrows at the left of each item in the list at the bottom of the page you have open in Navigator Gold. Right-click the arrow next to the first item in the list (see Figure 4-11).

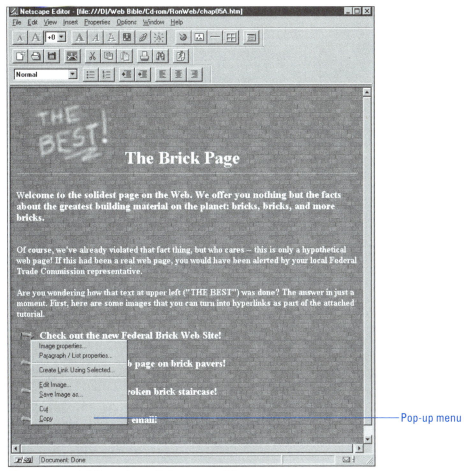

Pop-up menu

Figure 4-11: Adding a hyperlink to a small image.

Click the Create Link Using Selected menu choice to display the dialog box shown
in Figure 4-12.

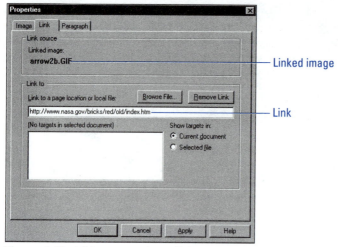

Figure 4-12: Adding a URL hyperlink.

You cannot browse for URL hyperlinks. You can type in the URL, but URLs are often so long and complicated it is usually safer to copy the URL to the Clipboard, and then paste it into the dialog box. To do so follow these steps:

1. Go to the web page in Netscape (or your favorite browser). Even if you must type the URL to get to it, doing it this way guarantees that you type the URL correctly; if you don't, you won't get where you want to go!

2. Copy the URL to the Clipboard. Either select the entire URL in the location where you typed it in, or right-click a link to the URL, and select the Copy Link to Clipboard or Copy Link Location menu selection (not available in all browsers).

3. Paste the URL into the dialog box shown in Figure 4-9. Click OK to add the hyperlink.

This is the safest way to guarantee that you've entered the URL correctly. For this example, either get your own sample hyperlink following the above procedure, or type in a sample hyperlink as shown in Figure 4-12:

```
http://www.nasa.gov/bricks/red/old/index.htm
```

Once you add the hyperlink to the arrow image, passing the pointer over it changes the cursor to a pointing hand (see Figure 4-13). Passing the pointer over an image that has no hyperlink doesn't affect the cursor (see Figure 4-14).

Cursor changes to
pointing hand on link

Figure 4-13: The cursor becomes a pointing
hand over an image that has a hyperlink.

Cursor stays
on arrow: no link

Figure 4-14: If the image is not a hyperlink,
the cursor does not change.

Adding a MAILTO link

You can also add links that aren't really links. The most common such beast is the
MAILTO, which is a link to an e-mail address. A MAILTO starts with (drum roll
please!) MAILTO. It can also be in lower case: mailto. A complete MAILTO looks
like this:

    MAILTO:name@domain.com

You should substitute a valid e-mail address for name@domain.com.

A link using a MAILTO, when clicked, will usually cause the user's mail program to
start with the To: field of the message already filled in. I say usually because some
browsers — most notoriously some versions of Microsoft's Internet Explorer —
will fail to start the mail program, or will start it and fail to put the To: information
in the message. The idea behind the MAILTO is to make it easy for someone to
send mail to a given e-mail address. If someone visits your site using Internet
Explorer, the MAILTO links won't work right. You should provide the e-mail
address in the text of the link so Internet Explorer users can send you e-mail the
old-fashioned way, by typing in the To: address themselves.

To add an e-mail address as a link to an image, you'll use the list at the bottom of
the page you have open in Navigator. Right-click on the little arrow to the left of
the second item in the list. In the pop-up menu, click the Create Link Using
Selected menu choice to display the dialog box shown in Figure 4-15. Fill in either
a valid e-mail address (such as your own; that's always a good way to test a
MAILTO without annoying other folks) or a made-up one as shown in Figure 4-15.

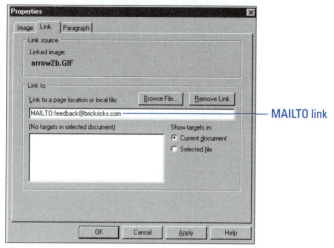

Figure 4-15: Adding a link to an e-mail address using a MAILTO.

Adding links to targets

At the start of this tutorial you added a link to a web page that was a file. Not all web pages are equal, however. Some web pages contain targets, and you can link not only to the web page, but also to the target on the page.

Some web page editors refer to targets as bookmarks. The concept is the same: You can jump to a specific destination on a web page. The target/bookmark must be added to the page by the person who creates it; you cannot aim at a target that doesn't already exist on the page.

I have included a web page that has targets in it in the tutorial files for this chapter. You copied it to your hard disk when you set up the tutorials at the beginning of the chapter. Each target has a name. To add a link that will jump to a target when clicked, follow these steps:

1. Begin by right-clicking the third little arrow on the web page.

2. In the pop-up menu, click the Create Link Using Selected menu choice to display the Properties dialog box with the Link tab active.

3. Click the Browse File button to display the Link to File dialog box.

4. Locate the file `\My Web Stuff\Chap04\4B\chap04b.htm` and click the Open button to select the file.

This returns you to the Properties dialog box, with the filename displayed in the "Link to a page location or local file" text box. The targets that I placed in the file are also displayed, in the "Select a named target in the specified file" list box. Figure 4-16 shows the file (with a relative pathname) and the list of targets already in the file.

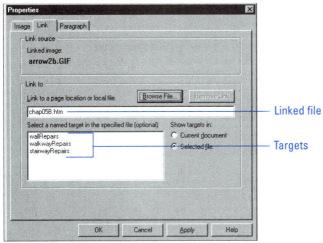

Linked file

Targets

Figure 4-16: Adding a link to a web page with targets/bookmarks.

Caution!

There is a bug in version 3 of Netscape Gold that causes trouble when you try to establish a link to a target on a web page. If you select one of the targets shown in Figure 4-16 just after using the Browse File button, the target will not be added to the link. The link will be to the file only. To add a link to a target, continue by following the steps below.

1. Click the Browse File button to locate the web page file.

2. Click OK to establish the link to the file.

3. Highlight the image again, and click the Hyperlink button on the toolbar.

4. The dialog box shown in Figure 4-16 appears again. Now you can click the target, then click OK to add the hyperlink.

Now the hyperlink includes both the filename and the target name. To verify this, highlight the image and click the Hyperlink button. Observe that the target name appears in the same text box as the filename (see Figure 4-17).

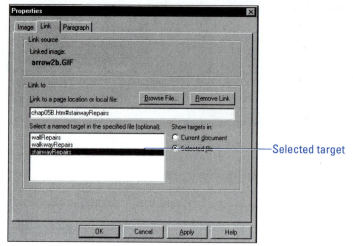

Figure 4-17: The target name has been added.

Inserting Low-Resolution Substitutes

Large graphic images take a long time to download. Interlacing (see Chapter 13) can make the downloading time pass more pleasantly, but there are other tricks you can use to placate your visitors while they wait for a large image to download. You can display some text in place of the image, and you can also use a low-resolution version of the image. The low-resolution image downloads quickly and, if the visitor lingers, is gradually replaced by the high-resolution version.

The low-resolution version can be either a small version of the image, or a black-and-white version of the image. If you use a small version of the image, the effect is similar to interlacing: The visitor sees the low-res image, and then sees a high-res image. Generally, it's better to simply use interlacing.

To add alternate text or a low-res image in Navigator Gold, click the image to highlight it, right-click to display the pop-up menu, and click Image Properties. This displays the Properties dialog box, shown in Figure 4-18. To add alternate text, type it into the space for alternate text. To specify an alternate image, use the second Browse button to locate the alternate image.

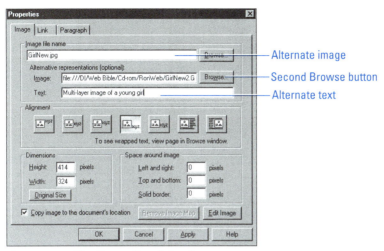

Alternate image

Second Browse button

Alternate text

Figure 4-18: The Properties dialog box.

Tip

If you are creating a black-and-white image for the low-res image, be sure to avoid using dithering when converting from color to black and white. Dithering results in surprisingly large file sizes. Instead, open the file in your image editor and use the Posterization feature to reduce the number of colors to a very small number, such as 4, 6 or 8. Experiment to get the best result. Then convert to black and white (2-bit color). The file size should be very small.

Figure 4-19 shows the appearance of a web page before the graphic starts to display. Navigator Gold automatically uses the WIDTH and HEIGHT parameters, reserving a space for the image on the page.

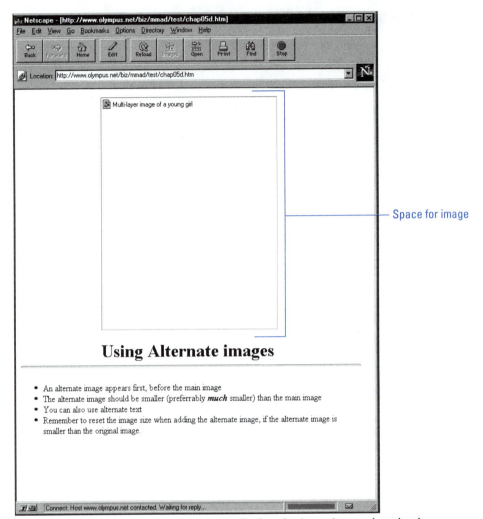

Figure 4-19: Alternate text for an image is displayed prior to image download.

Figure 4-20 shows the low-resolution image downloaded. In this example, the low-resolution image is 8,291 bytes, and the high-resolution image is 96,993 bytes. The low-res image downloads very quickly.

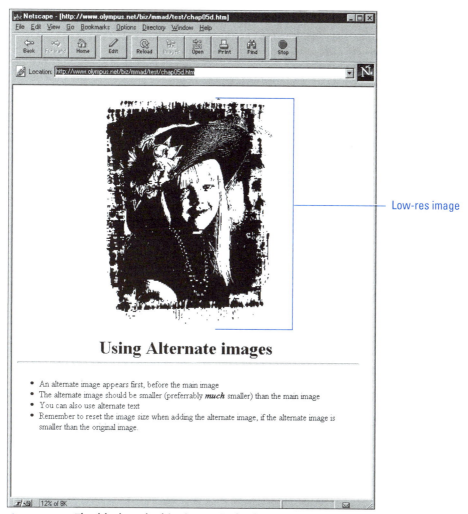

Low-res image

Figure 4-20: The black-and-white image is displayed.

To see the web page shown in Figure 4-20, double-click the file \My Web Stuff\Chap04\4D\chap04D.htm. To see the settings shown in Figure 4-18, click the Edit button to view the page in Edit mode, right-click the image, then select Image Properties on the pop-up menu.

Figures 4-21 and 4-22 show two stages during the download of the high-resolution image. If your hard disk is a fast one, you might find it hard to see the low-resolution image. If this is the case, double-click the original file on the CD-ROM.

The files will load more slowly from the CD, and you'll have more time to see the low-res image. The original file is located at \tutorial\chap04\4D\chap04D.htm.

Here it comes

Figure 4-21: The high-res image is beginning to display.

More of the high-res image

Figure 4-22: The high-res image is two-thirds displayed.

Many images will not require an alternate, low-res image. The most common use for such images is for a top-of-the-page graphic that is large and uses many colors.

Changing Link Appearance

The Picture dialog box shown originally in Figure 4-4 has seven buttons across the center of the dialog box. Table 4-1 lists these buttons and their alignments.

Table 4-1 Picture Dialog Box Buttons		
Button		**Alignment**
	TEXTTOP	Image aligns with top of text.
	ABSCENTER	Image aligns with center of text between ascenders (letters such as "b") and descenders (letter such as "y").
	CENTER	Image aligns with center of text x-height (between baseline and top of such letters as "a").
	DEFAULT	Aligns with baseline of text.
	ABSBOTTOM	Aligns with bottom of descenders (bottom of letters such as "y").
	LEFT	Aligns text at left edge of window, and text wraps around image.
	RIGHT	Aligns text at right edge of window, and text wraps around image.

To choose the alignment for an image, simply click the appropriate button while the Picture dialog box is open.

Tip

These buttons really belong in two distinct groups. The first five buttons have to do with the vertical alignment of an image. The last two buttons deal with the horizontal alignment of an image. You cannot control vertical and horizontal alignment at the same time. The LEFT and RIGHT buttons are the only alignment options that allow text to wrap around an image.

Figure 4-23 shows what happens to image alignment when the text in the same paragraph as the image has more than one line. Note that the second line of text wraps below the image for all alignments except LEFT and RIGHT. The original file shown in Figure 4-23 is one of the tutorial files for this chapter. Open it by double-clicking the file `\My Web Stuff\Chap04\4C\Chap04C.htm`.

Text breaks below image

Text wraps around image

Figure 4-23: Image alignment with more than one line of text.

Caution!

The exact result of alignment settings varies from one browser to another. Figure 4-24 shows image alignment displayed in Netscape Navigator 3, and Figure 4-25 shows image alignment displayed in Microsoft Internet Explorer 3. Internet Explorer does a better job of providing the alignment you would expect. In both figures, the order of alignment for each image is the same as shown in Table 4-1.

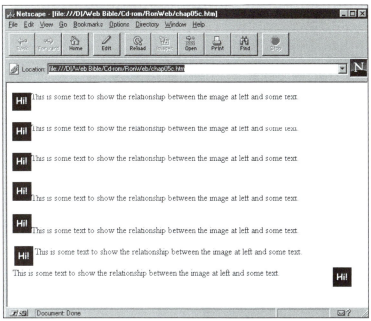

Figure 4-24: Image alignment in Navigator isn't exactly what you would expect.

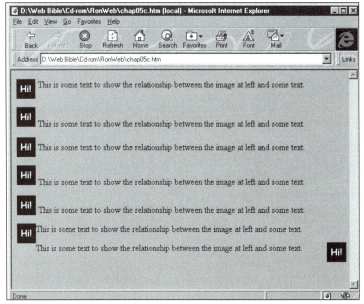

Figure 4-25: Internet Explorer provides the correct alignment for each alignment type.

Adding Borders

The Picture dialog box also allows you to add borders to images. By default, images have no border (the value for Border is zero). You can specify the pixel width of a border, and the browser will supply a border of that width when the image is displayed. Figure 4-26 shows an image without a border, and Figure 4-27 shows the same image with a four-pixel border.

To view these web pages, double-click the file `\My Web Stuff\Chap04\4E\chap04E.htm` (no border) and `\My Web Stuff\Chap04\4F\chap04F.htm` (with border).

Image borders are not often used on web pages, but if you like the look, there is no harm at all in using a border. There is one situation, however, where borders are automatically used with images. Images with a hyperlink have a two-pixel border attached unless you specifically specify a zero-width border.

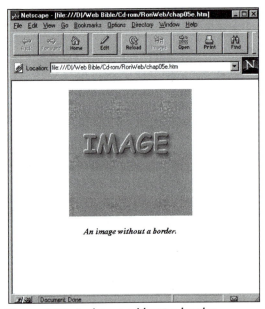

Figure 4-26: An image without a border.

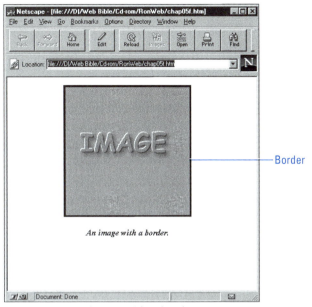

Border

Figure 4-27: An image with a border.

And this brings up a rather nasty bug in Navigator Gold 3. When you add a hyperlink to an image, it automatically gets a border. So far, so good. Now suppose you don't want a border. You do the right thing: You highlight the image, you set the border to zero width using the Image dialog box, and you save the file. Now for the bad news: The next time you save that file, Navigator Gold will assume you really want a border around that image, and will remove the BORDER=0 specification for the image. This is frustrating for anyone who doesn't want borders around their hyperlinked images. A casual glance at web pages shows that very few images with hyperlinks use borders. Hey, is anyone at Netscape listening? Fix this bug!

The images in Figures 4-26 and 4-27 do not use transparency. Transparent images look kind of silly with a border, and you will almost always want to protect such images from borders if a hyperlink is involved. That's a very annoying requirement in Netscape Gold because you have to open the file in Notepad and make the change manually. Most other editors present no problems in this situation.

Here's what a hyperlink created by Navigator Gold looks like in Notepad:

```
<A HREF="http://www.mmadweb/bible/index.htm"><IMG
     SRC="getmmad.gif"></A>
```

To remove the border, add `BORDER=0` to the HTML code:

```
<A HREF="http://www.mmadweb/bible/index.htm"><IMG
     SRC="getmmad.gif" BORDER=0></A>
```

See Chapter 5, "Adding Graphics to Web Pages," for detailed information about working with HTML, links, and images.

Web Tour #4: Images of the World Wide Web

Images with hyperlinks are a staple of the Web. You'll find them on almost every web page. However, in the interest of broadening your experience with images and links, you can visit some of my favorites by opening the file:

```
\WebTour\Chap4\index.htm
```

You'll see the web page for this chapter. Click the Web Tour icon and you will see a list of sites that offer free and/or fee graphics.

Adding Graphics to Web Pages

To prepare for this chapter's tutorials, copy the following folder from the CD-ROM to the \My Web Stuff folder on your hard drive:

    \tutorial\chap05

This will copy subfolders for all of the tutorials in this chapter to your hard disk. See Chapter 1 for complete details on setting up for tutorials.

I n Chapter 4, you learned how easy it is to add images to a page, and to add hyperlinks to images. In this chapter, you'll learn how to take the next steps toward power graphics. You'll find out about image maps, which allow you to have more than one link in an image. You'll also learn about the behind-the-scenes HTML codes that control graphics and links.

Adding Hyperlinks with FrontPage 97

Tutorial

Download: A trial version of FrontPage 97 is not available. Check the web site at http://www.microsoft.com to see if this changes.

Level: Intermediate

Task: Replace text hyperlinks with image map links

Before you start: Install FrontPage 97.

1. Run FrontPage 97 using the Start | Programs | Microsoft FrontPage menu selection. The dialog box shown in Figure 5-1 appears. When you copied tutorial files for this chapter, you copied a complete FrontPage 97 web site.

2. Click the radio button Open Existing FrontPage Web, as shown in Figure 5-1.

3. Click OK to continue.

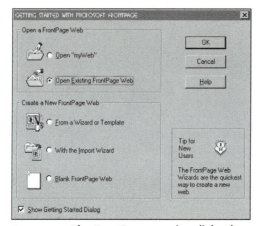

Figure 5-1: The FrontPage opening dialog box.

4. Type the path to the web site for this tutorial in the Web Server or File Location text box, as shown in Figure 5-2. The path is `\My Web Stuff\Chap05\myWeb`.

5. Click the List Webs button. The dialog box changes as shown in Figure 5-3.

6. Highlight the web `myWeb`, and click the OK button.

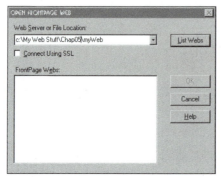

Figure 5-2: Locating the web site.

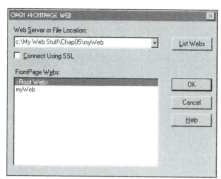

Figure 5-3: The list of available webs.

The FrontPage Explorer starts up, showing the various components of the web site (see Figure 5-4).

7. Double-click the file `folder1_nav.htm` (shown in Figure 5-4) to open the FrontPage 97 Editor.

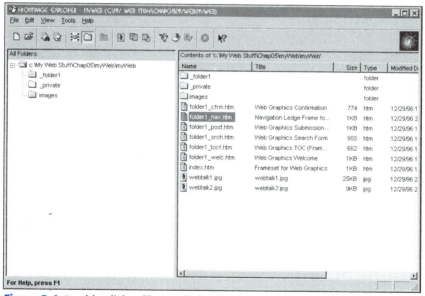

Figure 5-4: Double-click a file to edit it.

Figure 5-5 shows the web page open for editing in FrontPage 97. This is one of the default pages created by a FrontPage wizard. This particular page is the navigation bar for a threaded discussion web site on the topic of — what else! — web graphics. There are two hyperlinks at top right of the page that you will replace with hyperlinked images. While you have the page open, you will also add an image for the page title.

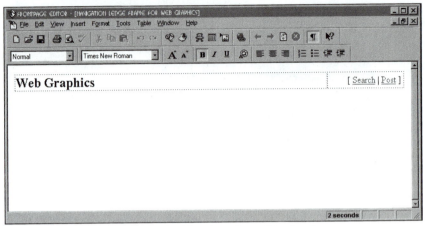

Figure 5-5: A web page created with a FrontPage 97 wizard.

Adding images in FrontPage is a little different from adding images in Navigator Gold. FrontPage is a more complex editor that offers more features. The basic unit of Navigator Gold is the web page — you edit specific web pages, one page at a time. FrontPage is really a site editor; you don't even have to know the filenames of your web pages. Figure 5-6 shows the FrontPage view of things: a web site at left, with the connections between site elements shown at right.

For this tutorial, you'll be replacing two text hyperlinks with image hyperlinks. Because FrontPage 97 makes it so easy to create image maps, you'll learn how to use a single image for both links. The first step is to identify the links.

8. Right-click the first link (see Figure 5-7) to display a pop-up menu.

9. Choose the Hyperlink Properties menu item to display the Edit Hyperlink dialog box shown in Figure 5-8.

There are several tabs at the top of the dialog box. These represent different kinds of links. In Navigator Gold, it was up to you to add different kinds of links. In FrontPage, you use a different tab in the Edit Hyperlink dialog box for different kinds of links.

Web colors page   Page for navigation   Page for navigation   Web colors page

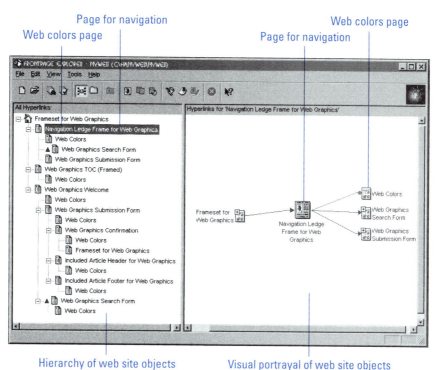

Hierarchy of web site objects   Visual portrayal of web site objects

Figure 5-6: FrontPage is web-site oriented.

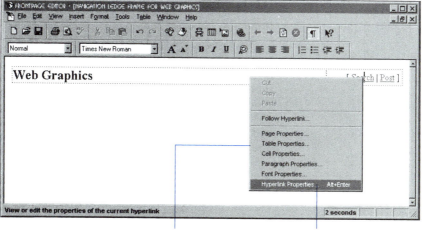

Pop-up menu   Hyperlink Properties menu selection

Figure 5-7: Right-clicking displays a FrontPage pop-up menu.

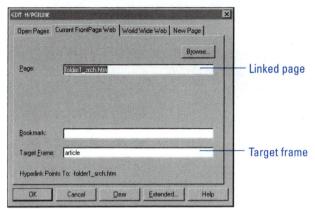

Figure 5-8: The Edit Hyperlink dialog box.

The linked page is `folder1_srch.htm`, and the target frame for the link is the frame called `article`. *Frames* are areas of the browser window. The latest versions of most browsers support frames. For now, it's enough to know that frames have names, and that you can define the frame in which a given web page displays.

10. Right-click the second text hyperlink to reveal that it is a link to the page `folder1_post.htm`, and it also displays in the frame `article`.

11. Delete the text links by selecting the text and pressing the Del key, leaving a blank table cell (see Figure 5-9).

 12. Click in the cell to locate the cursor in the cell, and then place an image by clicking the Image button on the toolbar.

13. To place the image, click the second tab in the Image dialog box (Other Location), and click the Browse button to display the dialog box shown in Figure 5-10.

14. Click the Open button to insert the image into the table cell (see Figure 5-11).

15. To set image properties, highlight the image and press Alt + Enter to display the Image Properties dialog box (see Figure 5-12).

You can use this dialog box to change the image source file, to specify transparency, interlacing, and compression options, add a hyperlink, and more. The Appearance tab (see Figure 5-13) of the dialog box allows you to set image alignment, spacing, and other image options.

Text links removed

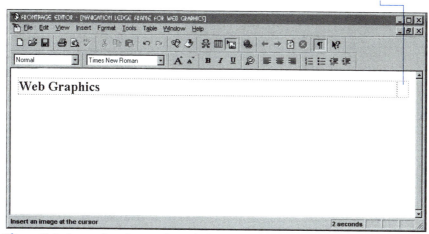

Figure 5-9: Removing the text hyperlinks.

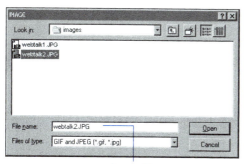

Image file

Figure 5-10: Choosing the image file to insert.

Image added

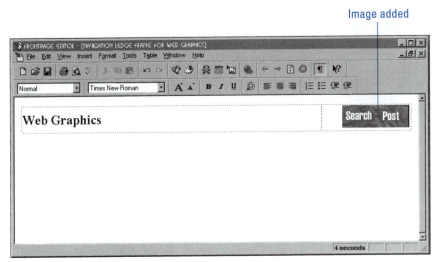

Figure 5-11: The image is inserted into the table.

Image filename   Browse button

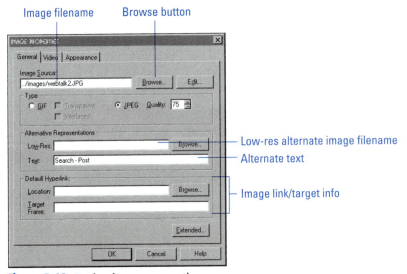

Low-res alternate image filename

Alternate text

Image link/target info

Figure 5-12: Setting image properties.

Alignment   Border   Left/right space

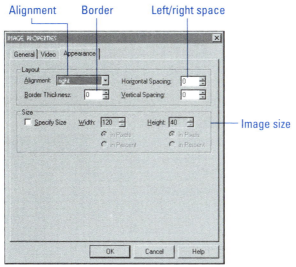

Figure 5-13: Setting image appearance.

16. Delete the text in the left table cell, and replace it with an image.

Figure 5-14 shows the result. I created both images in Fractal Design Painter; see Chapter 18 for more examples of negative text (also called cutout) graphics.

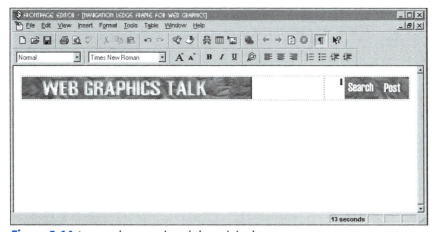

Figure 5-14: Images have replaced the original text.

The graphic on the right in Figure 5-14 still needs two hyperlinks to replace the original text hyperlinks. This requires a *client-side image map*. An image map is an image that contains multiple hyperlinks, and client-side refers to putting the map into the web page itself, instead of somewhere on the web server. Putting the map on the server results in a server-side image map. See Chapter 15 for detailed information about image maps.

17. Click the right-hand image, and then click the Rectangle tool in the Image toolbar (see Figure 5-15).

If a toolbar is not already displayed, use the View | Toolbars menu selection to choose which toolbars to display.

Tip

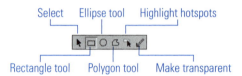

Figure 5-15: The Image toolbar.

18. Click and drag on the image to roughly outline a section of the Search portion of the image (see Figure 5-16). You do not need to outline the exact edges of the image. This is the hyperlink area — clicking in the area will jump to the hyperlink.

19. Release the mouse button once you have a small rectangle, and the Create Hyperlink dialog box appears (see Figure 5-16).

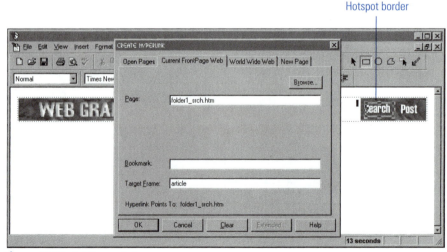

Figure 5-16: Adding a link.

20. For the Page, enter the original link (`folder1_srch.htm`). For the Target Frame, enter `article`.

21. Click OK.

22. Click the selection arrow in the Image toolbar, and then click and drag the handles on the hyperlink area to the edges of the image (see Figure 5-17).

23. Repeat this process for the Post side of the image, this time making the link to the page `folder1_post.htm`.

24. Adjust the hyperlink areas so they cover the whole image (see Figure 5-18).

Hotspot
selection handles

Hotspot border

Figure 5-17: Adjusting size of the hyperlink area.

Figure 5-18: Adjusting hyperlink areas.

25. Save your work (File | Save menu selection).

26. Open the web site's main page, `index.htm`, to display the page you've been working on in the top frame of a three-frame page (see Figure 5-19).

27. Click the Search hyperlink to jump to the Search page, where visitors can search for discussion topics.

   Clicking the Post hyperlink jumps to the Post page, where visitors can post their own messages.

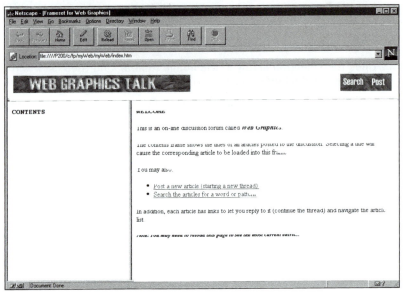

Figure 5-19: The completed web page.

Idea

Where to go from here:

✦ Create graphics for the web pages in the other two frames using the same techniques used to create the graphics in the top frame.

✦ Create a single graphic as a navigation bar across the entire top frame. One disadvantage to this approach is that the bar will not adjust its width to fit the width of the browser.

✦ Use FrontPage to add a table of contents page to the left frame.

Adding Images and Hyperlinks with HTML

Netscape Navigator Gold and FrontPage 97 both use dialog boxes where you can set the various properties of an image. There are differences between the dialog boxes, but the features of both web page editors are similar. You can set image alignment, you can add borders to an image, add space around an image, and so on.

All of these properties and features have their roots in the HTML codes used to add images to web pages. For example, here's some HTML code created in Navigator Gold that adds a graphic with alternate low-resolution image:

```
<IMG SRC="girlnew.jpg" LOWSRC="girlnew2.gif" HEIGHT=414
    WIDTH=324>
```

Everything between the angle brackets is HTML code. IMG is the *tag,* and in this case is referred to as the image tag. SRC, LOWSRC, HEIGHT, and WIDTH are *parameters* for the tag. In most cases, the tag is the first item between the angle brackets.

The following HTML code for an image comes from a file created with FrontPage, and is for the Search/Post image added in the previous tutorial. It includes additional parameters for the IMG tag.

```
<img align="right" src="webtalk2.jpg" width="120" ismap
       usemap="#FrontPageMap" hspace="0" height="40" border="0">
```

What does this mean for you? It means that you have a choice. You can use a web page editor and forget about ever knowing what an IMG tag is, or how it works. Or you can tweak your web pages to add features that aren't covered by your favorite web page editor, or, sometimes, correct problems caused by bugs or omissions in your web page editor.

Table 5-1 lists the most commonly used parameters for the IMG tag.

Table 5-1 **IMG Tag Parameters**	
Parameter	*Values*
ALIGN	TOP|MIDDLE|CENTER|BOTTOM|LEFT|RIGHT
ALT=text	The text you enter here will be displayed in place of the picture. It is also displayed before the picture is loaded.
BORDER=n	The size in pixels of a border around the image. If the image is a hyperlink, the border is in the hyperlink color.
HEIGHT=n	Specifies the height of the picture on the page. If necessary, the picture is stretched or shrunk to match. Most browsers use this parameter to set the height of the picture before it is loaded.
HSPACE=n	Specifies horizontal space to the left and right of the image.
ISMAP=image	Identifies the picture as an image map. Only required for server-side image maps.
SRC=url	Specifies the address of the picture to insert. This can be a filename, or a complete URL.
STYLE=css1 properties	Specifies style information.
USEMAP=url	Identifies the picture as a client-side image map. Specifies a map definition to use in response to clicks on the image.

(continued)

Table 5-1 *(continued)*	
Parameter	**Values**
VSPACE=n	Specifies vertical space above and below the image.
WIDTH=n	Specifies the width of the picture on the page. If necessary, the picture is stretched or shrunk to match. Most browsers use this parameter to set the width of the picture before it is loaded.

For example, to add the image myfile.gif to a page, with horizontal space of 8 pixels and vertical space of 4 pixels, you could use this tag:

```
<IMG SRC="myfile.gif" HSPACE=8 VSPACE=4>
```

To make an image into a hyperlink, all you need to do is add the appropriate hyperlink tags. The tag for establishing a link looks like this:

```
<A HREF=link>
```

Everything that follows this tag is linked. To indicate the end of the link text or image(s), use this tag:

```
</A>
```

For example, the following HTML creates a link to the page mypage.htm for the image file myfile.gif:

```
<A HREF="mypage.htm"><IMG SRC="myfile.gif"></A>
```

Text hyperlinks work in a similar fashion. The following HTML

```
Visit my <A HREF="mypage.htm">home page</A> now!
```

establishes a link for the text *home page.*

Here is another example of a hyperlinked image. The image is linked to a site that provides detailed information about using HTML:

```
<A HREF="http://www.microsoft.com/workshop/author/newhtml/
        default.htm"><IMG SRC="myfile.gif"></A>
```

To remove the border from an image that is used as a hyperlink, use the BORDER parameter with a value of zero:

```
<A HREF="mypage.htm"><IMG SRC="myfile.gif" BORDER=0></A>
```

Knowing how to work with the hyperlink and IMG tags gives you additional control over the images used on your page. The best way to learn is also the easiest. When you see an image on a page, use your browser to view the HTML source for the page, and identify the HTML codes used to place the image on the page, and to create any links that use images. You can also find online references to the current parameters for the <A> and <IMG> tags at various sites, including an excellent collection of pages about HTML on Microsoft's web site at
`http://www.microsoft.com/workshop/author/newhtml/default.htm`.

Web Tour #5: Images of the World Wide Web

Images with hyperlinks are a staple of the Web. You'll find them on almost every web page. However, in the interest of broadening your experience with images and links, you can visit some of my favorites by opening the file:

```
\WebTour\Chapter5\index.htm
```

You'll see the web page for this chapter. Click the Web Tour icon and you will see a list of sites that offer free and/or fee graphics.

Free Graphics and Clip Art

Everyone wants to have great graphics for their web site. There are many, many graphics already in use on the Web. It might seem natural to "borrow" graphics that you find on the Web for your own use. But there are laws against using someone else's intellectual property, and it's important to know how to buy, get, use, or create graphics for your web pages. This chapter focuses on the "buy" and "get" methods. You can buy graphics from clip art companies, and you can get graphics (often for free) from some web sites.

Understanding Copyright Issues

There is an extensive and very active debate going on about the role of copyright as it applies to the Internet. There are numerous court rulings about how copyright law applies to traditional media, from books to movies, from sculpture to photography. But there is a general sense that the rules should somehow be different for digital media.

For example, if someone takes a photograph of a sculpture or a painting, the copy is nothing like the original. You can't touch the object in a photograph.

With digital media, the copy is exactly like the original. I'm not talking about a digital copy of a real-world original; I'm talking about digital copies of digital originals. For all intents and purposes, the copy is indistinguishable from the original. How should copyright law apply to this situation? There are as many answers as there are people with an interest in the problem.

The safest course appears to be to assume that anything you find on the Web is off limits for copying unless there is a clear, unambiguous statement present on the web page giving you the right to use that material. In the simplest terms: If you didn't create it, don't use it unless you have permission.

However you obtain your images, be sure to pay close attention to the exact rights that you receive for each image. In some cases, you may be able to use the image for free, but only if you give credit to the source of the image. In other cases, you will have free rights to use the image however you wish.

If you are like most of us, you don't read those small-print licensing agreements that come with just about all software. When it comes to images, it's a good idea to break with tradition and read the fine print. By working within the exact rights granted to you, you can rest assured that you won't have trouble later when your web site is up and running.

Working with Clip Art Collections

There are many clip art collections available, most on CD-ROM. Common sources for these collections are your friendly neighborhood computer store (Computer City, Egghead Software, and so on), mail-order offers at the back of the popular magazines, and catalogs. In my never-ending search for cost-effective graphics, I have found that the stores carry lots of products that aren't well suited for Web use. Mail-order offers are whatever they are, and mostly they are sight unseen. This leaves catalog shopping as my preferred method of acquiring clip art.

The trick to effective catalog shopping is to use the right catalogs. I have found several that offer a combination of variety and quality. They are listed in the section "Where is the good stuff?" later in this chapter.

What is the good stuff?

The universe of clip art is far larger than you might imagine if you are not a graphics professional. There is an unending need for new and original art and photos for brochures, pamphlets, magazines, flyers, ads, and other printed publications. Most of this artwork doesn't translate well to the Web. Standard clip art, intended for use on the printed page, is often unsuitable for use on web pages. Common reasons include incompatible file formats and print-oriented colors. A few companies are starting to recognize the Web as a genuine marketing opportunity. Such companies are supplying art and photos intended specifically for use on web pages.

Ideally, clip art images are supplied in a noncompressed, true-color format so that you can make the decisions about how much and what kind of compression to use, what size the image should be, and so on. Some file formats are great for print work, but not terribly useful on the Web. For example, avoid so-called vector formats like EPS. These files contain outlines that use the PostScript language — ideal for printers that understand the language, and useless if you really wanted a bitmap. Most image editors can work with the common bitmap formats — BMP, PCX, and TIF. Look for clip art supplied in these file formats.

Figure 6-1 shows the kinds of clip art that don't usually work well for web pages. Such images are usually gorgeous and big — they would be great for an ad layout, but are useless for a web page. Figure 6-2 shows a collection of clips containing objects. Such images can be used as-is to illustrate an idea, or very small as a button or doodad on a page, or as the basis for your own Great Art.

Figure 6-1: These kinds of clip art aren't often useful for web pages.

Figure 6-2: Object art is often useful for web pages.

Both sets of images are from the same vendor: PhotoDisc (see the next section for contact information), which has made a strong effort to offer web-specific images. To get useful images for the Web, you have to sort through the clip art collections offered by various vendors.

Where is the good stuff?

The growth of the Web, and the growth of web-oriented graphics, are creating a demand for more graphics that work well on web pages. The best way to keep up with what's happening is to order catalogs from some of the better mail-order companies. These include:

Publishing Perfection, 800-852-2348. Focus is on hardware and software for graphics professionals. While you will find less web-specific stuff here, you will see what the professionals are using for all media.

Image Club, 800-661-9410. This is the one catalog that focuses most tightly on images, as the name implies. You'll find products direct from Image Club as well as many products from other vendors. In particular, you'll find photo and image collections that are ideally suited to web page design.

PhotoDisc, 800-528-3472 or `http://www.photodisc.com`. All of the images in this catalog are from a single company, but there are thousands and thousands to choose from. PhotoDisc offers web-specific images. Visit their web site to see how you can download sample images.

Almost all of the catalogs offer starter collections that include a variety of images. In most cases, you pay a nominal fee ($10 to $50) and you get one to five CD-ROM discs with thousands of sample images. This allows you to browse through a collection and decide if you want to purchase the complete CD for that collection.

There are also some magazines that are worth a look to see if they offer useful information for your needs:

Adobe magazine, 206-628-2321. Covers Adobe products and how to use them. Often contains useful, practical advice on how to work with images using various Adobe products. It costs $35 per year, but look for free initial subscription offers inside Adobe product packages.

New Media, `http://www.newmedia.com`. Covers multimedia, graphics, video and other "new media" technologies. Focus is on products, not on how-to; the product reviews are detailed and useful. Free to qualified subscribers; see web site for information on subscriptions.

Computer Artist, 918-831-9405. Covers all aspects of digital art, from fine arts to production issues. Focus has mostly been on using computers to create art for traditional media, but more and more of the articles are becoming useful to web artists.

These and other magazines can open your eyes to new possibilities. If you have a background in graphics, and want to start using your computer to create/edit graphics for use on the Web, magazines can offer you new ideas and techniques.

Can I edit clip art?

When you purchase a clip art collection, it usually arrives on a CD-ROM with from perhaps a hundred to thousands of images. The artwork and photos are usually yours to use as you like. This means you can edit an image in any way you see fit — darken it a bit to change the mood, or paint a cartoon face on it. Your sense of taste is the only limitation on what you can do to the image.

However, there are exceptions. Always read the rights statement that comes with a clip art collection carefully (before you buy it, if possible). A few of the more expensive clip art collections place restrictions on the art. The two most common restrictions are on how and where you can use the images.

For example, high-quality photographs intended for use in advertisements may come with restrictions that allow you to only use the images in ads, and without any modifications. The only way to know these things is to read the fine print that comes with the collections.

Working with Online Graphics Resources

Tutorial

Download: All you need to work through this chapter is a browser and an Internet connection.

Level: Intermediate

Task: Finding graphics online

Idea

Before you start: Open your web browser.

All of the sites mentioned in this section are available at the click of a button from the web page for this book: `http://www.mmadweb.com/bible/graphics.htm`.

There are many, many sources for graphics on the Web. They come in two flavors: free and not free. There are probably enough free graphics floating around on the Web to meet the average person's needs until the end of the next century, but if you have a specific need for a high-quality image that you cannot create yourself, paying for the graphic may be the right solution.

Caution!

Free may not mean free to use in any way you like. As with CD-ROM clip art collections, free art that you download over the Web often comes with restrictions. Check the rights given to you on the web site before you use the clip art, to make sure you can use it for the purpose you intend. When in doubt, ask by sending e-mail to the owner of the art. Be specific about how you intend to use the images if you want a meaningful reply.

You can use search tools to find graphics resources, or you can use some of the links in the Web Tour at the end of this chapter. You will find everything from horrible to elegant graphics available for the taking.

Finding free graphics

To search for graphics on your own, you can use one of two approaches: shotgun or fine-tuned. Figure 6-3 shows an example of the shotgun approach. In the figure, Infoseek is set up to search for web pages that contain the phrase "free graphics." That's as broad a search category as you can start with, but it's also exactly to the point: I want to see everything that's free and graphic.

Figure 6-3: Searching using the Infoseek search engine.

 And I could drive a truck through that setup, straight man! I don't suppose, Mr. Author, that you ever looked up "graphic" in the dictionary? If you did, you'd realize that you've just put your foot firmly in your mouth — which, come to think of it, is pretty graphic, too.

As if you've never tasted shoe leather, Webbsie. Look at Figure 6-4, which shows the results of the search: 4,157,227 web sites related to free graphics. I suppose it's no coincidence that the ad at the top of the page says "Unbelievable?"

The first few sites in the search result look promising: Jelane's Free Web Graphics, Free Graphics, Horizontal Rules & Objects, Backgrounds and Textures, and so on. That's how easy it is to locate web sites that offer graphics for the downloading.

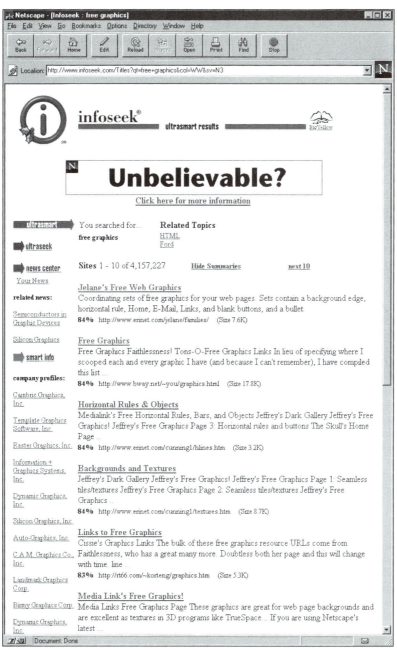

Figure 6-4: The results of the search: Too many web pages to visit in one lifetime.

Of course, you won't know whether the graphics are any good until you actually start visiting those web sites. I did a little visiting on my own, and found free graphics of every description and kind. Linnaeus himself couldn't have made order out of such vast chaos.

Figure 6-5 shows a web page on a site, located at `http://beta.pixelsight.com`, that had some of the most sophisticated free graphics that I found. In fact, not only were the graphics sophisticated, the site itself was very fancy. Figure 6-6 shows a page that allows you to choose from among quite a few tools for editing a graphic while online. The tools include a text editor, text effects, icon colors, button toolbar, icon editor, text colors, icon effects, button colors, and more.

Figure 6-5: A sophisticated web site for free graphics.

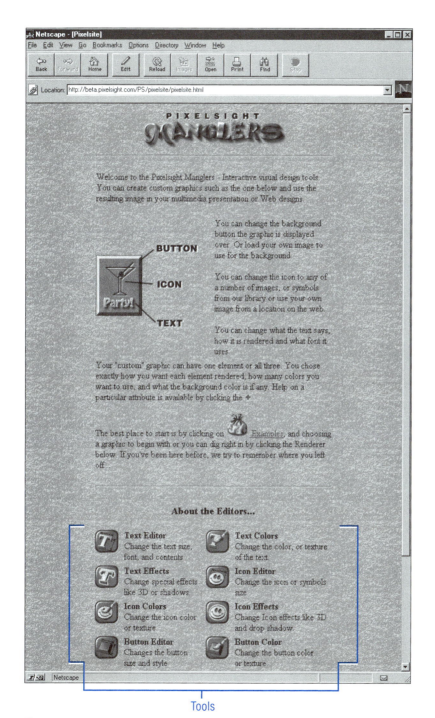

Tools

Figure 6-6: Tools for modifying your free graphics.

Figure 6-7 shows one of the tools, the Button Mangler, in action. You can click the little plus signs for more information on any aspect of the tool.

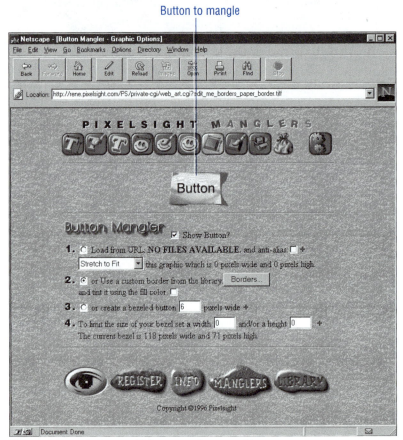

Figure 6-7: Tools for modifying your free graphics.

As we went to press, the Pixelsight site was so successful that it was being transformed into a commercial site. It's still well worth a visit because of the high quality of images and tools.

I found other interesting pages, too. The site at `http://gifwiz2.gifwizard.com` will perform color reduction on your graphic. Color reduction is important because it results in smaller image file sizes and faster downloads.

Another interactive site, at `http://coder.com/creations/banner`, allows you to design banners. Banners consist of text against a graphic background, such as a raised panel. It takes a bit of effort to create the banner, but it works. See Figure 6-8.

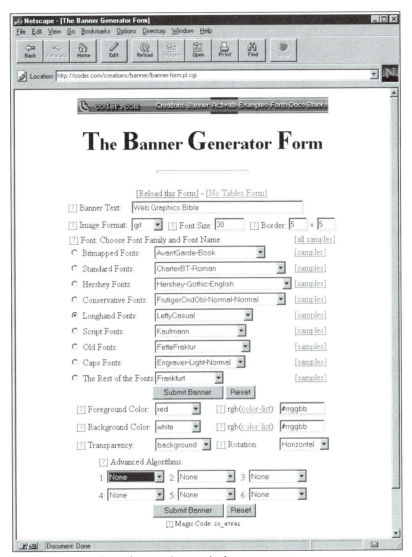

Figure 6-8: Creating a banner interactively.
Copyright © 1997 Prescient Code Solutions.

A site that features only graphics, and no interactivity is Free Web Graphics
(http://www.beeseen.com/beeseen/free; see Figure 6-9).

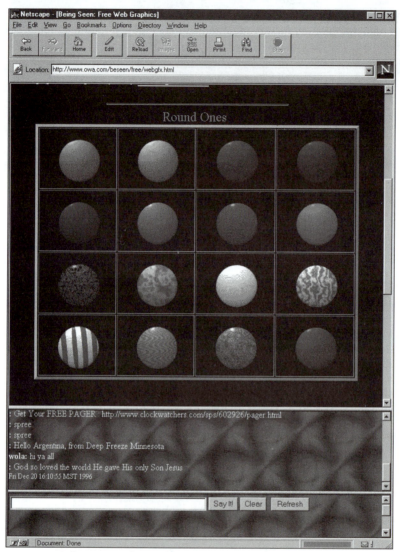

Figure 6-9: The Free Web Graphics site.
Courtesy of Being Seen.

Also worth a visit: Jelane's Families of Graphics at `http://www.erinet.com/jelane/families/families.html` (see Figure 6-10). These are groups of graphics that you can download and use on a web page. They include banners, buttons, horizontal lines, and so on. The Primordial Soup family is shown in Figure 6-11, and the Wood 1 family in Figure 6-12.

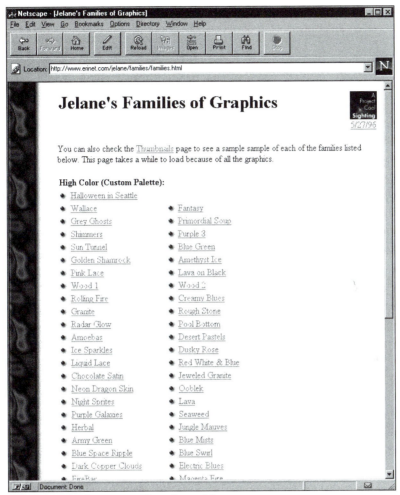

Figure 6-10: Jelane's Families of Graphics page.
Copyright © Jelane Ko Johnson 1996, 1997.

Figure 6-13: Searching for bananas on the Web.

I tried other search strings:

✦ free banana pictures

✦ free banana graphic

✦ free graphics banana (yes, changing word order resulted in different links!)

Searches based on variations on this theme were — dare I say it? — fruitless. But that silly pun gave me an idea. I searched on fruit images, and lo and behold, at last there was a link that offered some promise (see Figure 6-14). I pursued the links, and about eight links deeper I finally found what I was looking for. My search path (eight different web pages!) led to the final result at `www.csdl.tamu.edu/FLORA/mi 06/mi06064.jpg`.

Botanical image links
Botanical Image Collections On-line Return to the main botany index Agricultural Images from University of Maryland at College Park Algal Microscopy & Image Digitization Home Page, **96%** http://www.interaktv.com/BOTANY/BotImg.html   (Size 8.0K)

Figure 6-14: A link that offers some promise of bananas.

It was hardly worth the hour of searching. If nothing else, this search for a banana picture makes a great introduction to the next section in this chapter. It documents, better than any 1,000 words I might string together, the need for custom graphics for which you pay a fee. If I really needed a banana image, I could have searched instead for companies that create custom graphics for the Web. I could also create the image myself, but that's a subject for another chapter!

 I can't resist the temptation to rail a bit here about the horrible state of the Web search engines. The Web is much too large for these kinds of search engines. Think of the yellow pages: If you live in a major city, the yellow pages always turns up too many choices. Now imagine searching through the yellow pages for the world! But that's still not the equivalent of the Web. Searching the Web is like having yellow pages where anyone and everyone can put in a full-page ad. Scary, isn't it? It's a miracle that Mr. Author found any banana pictures at all.

 See the "Rights of Use" section later in this chapter for information about using free graphics that you find.

Graphics for a fee

Finding companies that provide web graphics for a fee was relatively simple. I searched using the string "web graphics." I found a combination of free and fee sites. Some of the fee sites are ones I mentioned already — they offer free graphics as a way to show what kind of work they can do. One example is Pixelsight (refer to Figure 6-5). Such companies offer the free graphics as samples, and will charge you for custom work.

Probably the most important consideration is the past performance of the company; always get references. Most graphics-for-a-fee sites will include links to pages that the company has provided graphics for, or pages that the company designed. Don't just look at these pages; talk to the customers! Most sites include an e-mail address — send an e-mail like the following:

```
I like the work that Company X did on your web site, and I'm
considering using them for my own project. Would you be kind
enough to take a moment and tell me how you liked their work? I
am most interested in:
```

- Did they complete the work on time?

- Was the price reasonable for the graphics and service you received?

- Was the company responsive to your requests and feedback?

- Would you use this company again?

The answers to these questions will go a long way toward helping you decide whether to use the company to create your web graphics.

Rights of Use

Many of the web sites that offer free graphics for downloading include a link to a page that sets out the rights you have for using those graphics. The exact rights vary from site to site. For example, the web site for the Woodshed (`http://deckernet.com/shed/graphics.html`) requires that you follow these rules for using their graphics:

✦ Send an e-mail to the company to get permission to use the graphic.

✦ Download the images and then upload them to your server. Given the way that the Web works, you could put a full URL to these graphics in your web page, but this puts an unfair load on the other person's server. It's very bad form to point to graphics on other web pages; always use your own graphics.

✦ Provide a link back to the source of the graphics. If the free graphics are downloaded from a personal or company web site that sells graphics or graphic services, they want you to provide some publicity for them in return for use of the images.

These are typical — and very reasonable — requests. You will see minor variations from one graphics site to the next. Some sites, such as PhotoDisc at `http://www.photodisc.com`, have more extensive requirements and restrictions. Always check out the rules before you download and use the graphics!

Web Tour #6: Sources for Web Graphics

There are uncountable sites for downloading free graphics on the Web, and more show up every day. You can visit some of my favorites (and a few dogs, just for the laughter you'll enjoy) by double-clicking on the file:

```
\WebTour\Chapter6\index.htm
```

You'll see the web page for this chapter. Click the Web Tour icon and you will see a list of sites that offer free and/or fee graphics.

Working with Text

To prepare for this chapter's tutorials, copy the following folder from the CD-ROM to the \My Web Stuff folder on your hard drive:

    \tutorial\chap07

This will copy files for all of the tutorials in this chapter to your hard disk. See Chapter 1 for complete details on setting up for tutorials.

Text, and the fonts you use to present that text, have a huge impact on the visual appearance of your web page. I could write an entire book about how to be creative with text (and I probably will, now that I'm thinking about it), but I have just one chapter in this book to address the huge number of ways you can spice up the headings, titles, bullets, hotspots and other text on your web pages.

Before we start, I think it's only fair for me to tell you One Great Secret of creating cool text effects. I've seen many suggestions for quick and easy text effects over the years, and the promise of instant results is always appealing. But the One Great Secret for text is identical to the One Great Secret of winemaking: Time is everything. If you take the time to deal with details when working with text, you will usually be much more satisfied with your results.

 If I had a nickel (or maybe a quarter these days, what with inflation and all) for every graphic designer who figured he'd add the text at the last minute, I'd be rich enough to put a Pentium Pro chip in my alarm clocks. For a properly balanced web graphic, plan on spending at least as much time on font selection and text manipulation as you spend on the rest of the graphics.

We're in total agreement for once, Uncle Webb. There's something about the way the human mind perceives text that is fundamentally different from how it perceives other graphics. Well-dressed text will turn heads, just like a debutante at a party or a muscle man at the beach. I submit Figure 7-1 in evidence. (If I'm wrong, I'll eat a whole page of Garamond 10-point type for breakfast for a week.)

Figure 7-1: A compelling web graphic that uses text and a strong image to hit you right between the eyes. Pow!

Text and Page Design

I'm going to start out slowly and build to the big, impressive text stuff later. The starting point is the text-handling built into the HTML language itself. The Netscape Navigator Gold Editor offers the basic HTML text possibilities: font, color, size, weight, and style.

Font   The design of the text. There are three types of fonts to be concerned about: serif, sans serif, and fixed-width (monospace). Within each type, there are many different designs to choose from. All are explained shortly.

Color   The color of the text. You can apply color to letters, words, phrases, sentences, paragraphs, or the whole web page.

Size	Unlike print publication, font sizes on an HTML page are limited to certain preset sizes. More about this later.
Weight	On the web page, you have two choices: normal and **bold.**
Style	On the web page, you have several choices: normal, *italic,* <u>underlined,</u> ~~strikethrough~~, and `preformatted` (monospaced font).

Font

Most web pages make extremely limited use of fonts. Early web browsers used a set of default fonts, and that was that: You had no choice. Today's browsers support font changes, but there are still obstacles to be wary of.

If you are not already familiar with fonts, see the sidebar, "Fonts Versus Text," for the juicy details. If you are familiar with fonts from desktop publishing or word processing, then you need to know that some of the problems that bedeviled you in those realms will haunt you on the web page, too. If a font is not installed on the machine displaying the web page, then the browser will simply use the default font.

Fonts Versus Text

Text is just what it seems: the letters, words, phrases, sentences, and paragraphs that you find on a page. It is a generic term that refers to anything you read, in any medium. Text is text is text.

Fonts are what you use to display text on the page, television screen, billboard, dollar bill or whatever medium you use for your text. Fonts come in a huge variety, from classics like Garamond and Goudy Old Style to modern inventions like Avant Garde and Kabel. There are also plenty of playful fonts, such as **Cooper** and **Ad Lib**.

Deciding which font to use can be a big decision. Figure 7-2 shows a hypothetical company name in three different fonts. The name itself, Madcap Enterprises, suggests that a playful or odd font might best represent the company's intended image. My pick from Figure 7-2 would be the font on top. You might pick a different font — there is often not one single, perfect choice for a font. It's a personal decision.

Figure 7-3 shows three more font examples, this time for the hypothetical investment company Meridian Funds Match, Inc. Prestige is the name of the game here, and either of the top two fonts could be a good choice. The third font, an informal one, gives the wrong impression. The first font is the most formal, while the second one a more "after-dinner" kind of formal.

If you drew the conclusion that font selection is an emotional, intuitive process, you understand how the game is played. Matching a font to its text is a subjective affair, and is always subject to personal preference. However, whatever your font choice, keep in mind how it fits with your web page's purpose and your visitors' needs.

Madcap Enterprises

Madcap Enterprises

MADCAP ENTERPRISES

Figure7-2: Three fonts for a hypothetical company name.

Meridian Funds Match, Inc.

Meridian Funds Match, Inc.

MERIDIAN FUNDS MATCH, INC.

Figure 7-3: A more refined company name requires a different font choice.

As web browsers gain the capability to display a variety of fonts, they also bring the familiar problems with fonts from the desktop publishing world to the Web. The most important problem is this: If you do not have a font, you cannot display it. Just because you have a font on your computer doesn't mean someone else has it, too. A page that you create on a Windows 95 computer might look good on another Windows 95 machine — if the fonts you used are installed on that machine. There is never a guarantee that any particular font will be available on a particular machine. Worse, if the visitor is using a different operating system, the font problem becomes much larger. Someone sitting at a UNIX terminal will have much less chance of seeing the right font.

It is one thing to add fonts to text as part of a graphic image — the font is reduced to the pixels in the image, and can be displayed without any trouble at all on any computer. It is quite another to apply a font to some ordinary text on a web page. If the displaying computer does not have that font installed, then the page will display in the default font instead of in the font you desired.

For the best results, only apply fonts that you know will be available on the visitor's machine. Most of the time, that means relying on the browser to display the default font.

If you are willing to accept that some people (perhaps even most people) will not be able to see the fonts you used, go ahead and use them as you will. If you want to gain some measure of control over what your web pages look like, you will follow a simple rule:

If you want to use a specific font, use it as a graphic on the page.

There is some room for bending this rule. There are certain fonts that Microsoft includes with Windows 95, for example. If you want to use some of those fonts on your page, almost everyone with Windows will see the fonts you intended, while those without Windows (or who did not install, or removed, those default fonts) will not.

These Windows fonts are Arial, Comic Sans, Courier New, MS Sans Serif, and Times New Roman. Figure 7-4 shows a web page that uses these fonts to create a distinctive appearance. The page is displayed in Internet Explorer 3.01. You can view it yourself at `\My Web Stuff\chap07\chap07e.htm`. Note that some fonts, such as Symbol and Wingdings, are not properly displayed.

Viewing this same page on a different computer, using a different browser (Netscape Navigator 3.0), results in a slightly different appearance (see Figure 7-5). However, the basic elements of the page design, including fonts, remain the same.

These basic fonts represent the three basic font families I mentioned earlier in this section. Refer to Figures 7-4 and 7-5 for examples of the fonts mentioned below.

Serif   Fonts with little doohickeys on the ends of the strokes that create each letter, such as **Times New Roman**. Serif is derived from the Dutch word *schreef*, which means simply line.

Sans serif   Fonts that have clean edges, such as MS Sans Serif and Arial.

Fixed-width Fonts in which every character has the same width, such as `Courier New`. (**Times New Roman** and Arial are proportional fonts because letters of the font take up different amounts of horizontal space.)

By using an image editor to create small graphic images that you can add to the page, you can use any font that appeals to you, and visitors to your site will see them accurately. Figure 7-6 shows a web page that uses graphics for fancy fonts. I used a yellow background on the page to make the white background of the images visible. The file is `\My Web Stuff\chap07\chap07f2.htm`. You could just as easily use a white background, as in Figure 7-7, so that it is not readily apparent that the headlines are actually images. The file is `\My Web Stuff\chap07\chap07f.htm`.

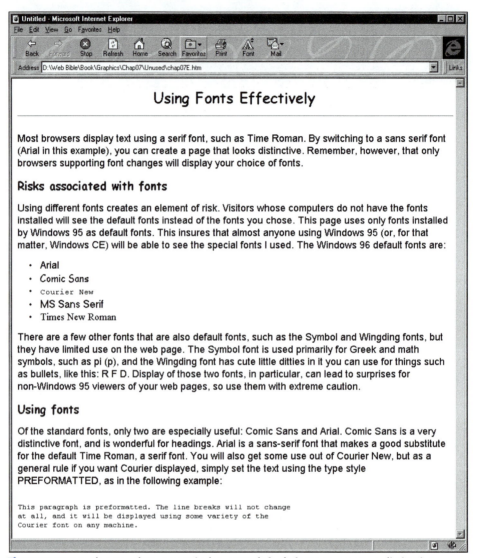

Figure 7-4: A web page that uses Windows 95 default fonts to create a distinctive appearance.

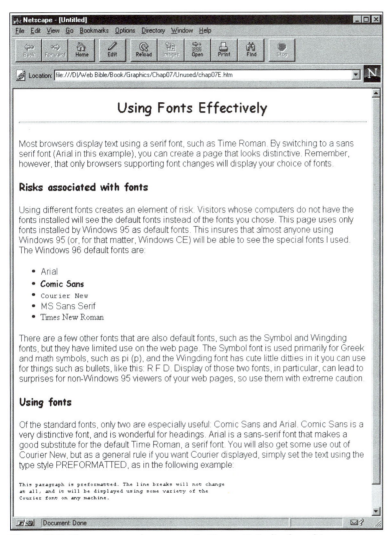

Figure 7-5: The same web page as in Figure 7-4, displayed in a different browser.

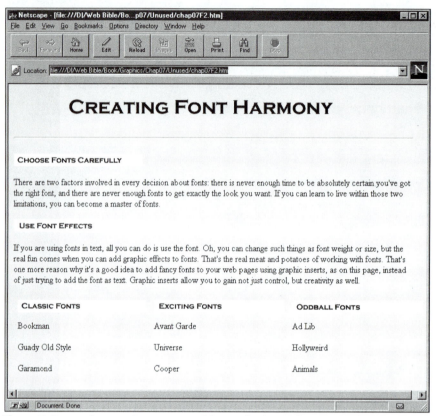

Figure 7-6: A web page that uses graphics to display an interesting font in headlines.

Substituting graphic images for text headlines gives you tremendous flexibility when working with fonts. You never need to worry whether the font is installed on users' machines, and you can create exactly the font size you want every time.

Color

When you are designing your web page, you have two basic choices for text color. You can apply color to a portion of the text on the page, or you can change the default color of all of the text on the page.

To change the color of letters, words, phrases, sentences, or paragraphs in a web page editor, just select the text you want to change, and specify the color. The exact method for specifying a custom color varies from one editor to the next. Netscape Navigator Gold's dialog box for setting a custom text color appears in Figure 7-8; simply select text, and apply a custom color to it.

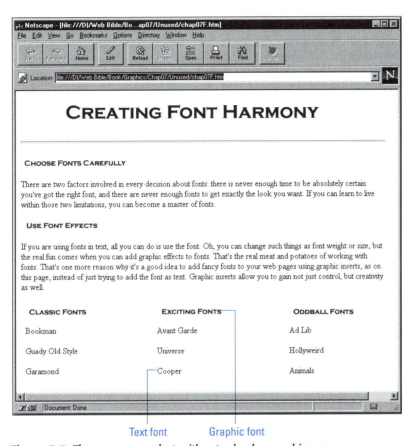

Text font   Graphic font

Figure 7-7: The same page, but without a background image.

Pick new color here   Select value here

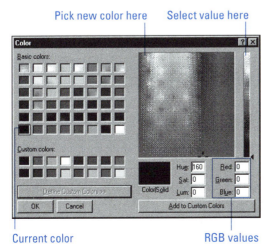

Figure 7-8: Choosing a font color in Netscape.

Current color   RGB values

Caution!

If you are working with Microsoft's Internet Assistant for Word for Windows 6.0 or 7.0, you cannot apply custom colors to hyperlinked text. If you do apply a custom color, it will not be saved. You can only apply custom colors to non-hyperlinked text.

When you are specifying default text color for an entire page, *omnis textus in quattuor genus divisa est* ("all text is divided into four kinds," with apologies to Mr. J. Caesar, Esq.):

Normal text   Most of the text on a page falls into this category. If you use a light background, black text is best — large areas of colored text can be tough to decipher. If you use a dark background, be sure to set the default text color to white or a very light color.

Link text   This is text that serves as a hyperlink to another web page. Specifically, it represents a link you have not visited, or have not visited recently.

Active link text   During the fraction of a second when you click linked text, the text changes to this color.

Followed link text   Once you have visited a link, the link text changes to yet another color.

You can set all of these colors in most web page editors. Figure 7-9 shows the dialog box in Navigator Gold for setting default font colors; most web editors have a similar dialog box. The default colors apply to all text that does not have a custom color; custom colors override the default colors.

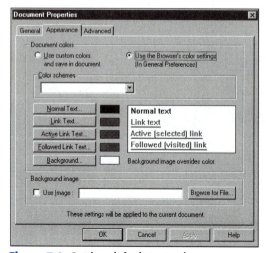

Figure 7-9: Setting default text colors.

Tip

Font colors should be selected as carefully as the colors you use to design your page. If you use a large number of different colors, you will get a web page that looks like spilled paint. The default colors — black text, bright blue hyperlinks, subdued blue followed hyperlinks — are actually a bit hard to take. Hyperlinks stand out dramatically on the typical web page, and can interfere with the readability of the page. Take a moment to step back and consider how all the colors involved work together — default text, the various links, graphics and images on the page, and so on. Unless you are purposely trying to create an agitated-looking web page, harmony of color is the best route.

Size

If you are familiar with desktop publishing, you know that there is a nearly infinite number of font sizes. Figure 7-10 shows a font in various sizes. They range from tiny (8 points) to huge (128 points). The unit of measurement for fonts, the point, is a very small distance, equal to 0.013835 inches (one seventy-second of an inch). Thus, 8-point type is still very small: 8/72 (1/9) of an inch high. Even fractional font sizes, such as 12.2, are legitimate.

Figure 7-10: Various font sizes from the print publishing world.

On the web page, a very finite universe of font sizes is available. There is a standard or reference font size, and all other font sizes are "measured" with respect to the reference. The seven available font sizes are -2, -1, 0, +1, +2, +3, and +4.

Zero is the standard font size, used for all normal text. There is no standard *point* size for this "standard" font size. It is up to the browser to determine the display size for normal text. It is also up to the browser to determine just what a -1 or a +3 change in font size means. Figure 7-11 shows a web page that includes multiple font sizes, displayed in both Netscape Navigator and Microsoft Internet Explorer. Notice that the font sizes are slightly different, and that the spaces between the lines are very different. Netscape Navigator (large outer window) uses much larger spacing between lines than Internet Explorer (smaller window).

Figure 7-12 shows the exact same pages as in Figure 7-11, but with Internet Explorer set to maximum font size (View | Fonts | Largest). Figure 7-13 shows Internet Explorer's minimum font size (View | Fonts | Smallest).

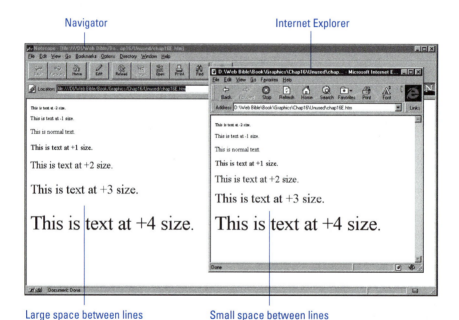

Figure 7-11: Comparing text sizes using two different browsers: Navigator (large window) and Internet Explorer (small window).

The bottom line is that you do not have exact control over either the size of a given piece of text, or the relative sizes of different font sizes. The user's browser settings, or the browser itself, will determine these things.

If you use cascading style sheets, you can specify an exact font size as well as many other aspects of your fonts. See the section "HTML 3.2 and Beyond," later in this chapter, for details.

Unlike the font sizes in print publishing, web font sizes are not absolute. It is up to the browser viewing the page to determine what font sizes to use as the standard size, and how much larger or smaller to make nonstandard sizes.

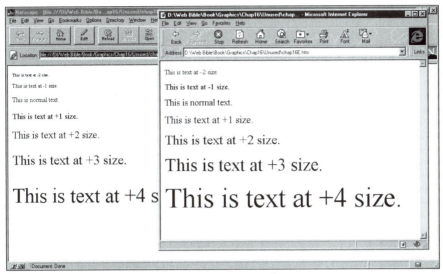

Figure 7-12: The largest font setting in Internet Explorer.

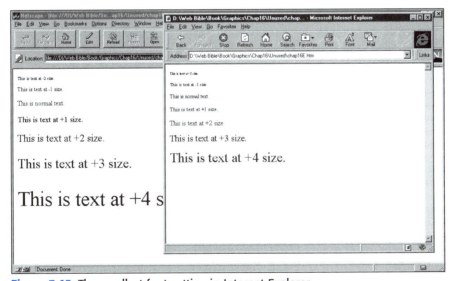

Figure 7-13: The smallest font setting in Internet Explorer.

You can change font sizes using the built-in HTML styles, such as the heading styles (Heading 1, Heading 2, and so on), or by applying plus and minus settings to text that you select. Figure 7-14 shows a page without text sizing, and Figure 7-15 shows the page with sizing applied. You can find these pages on the CD-ROM: \My Web Stuff\chap07\chap07c.htm and \My Web Stuff\chap07\chap07c2.htm.

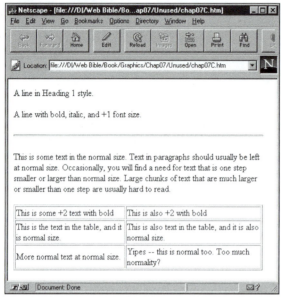

Figure 7-14: A page with all of the text the same size. Yuck!

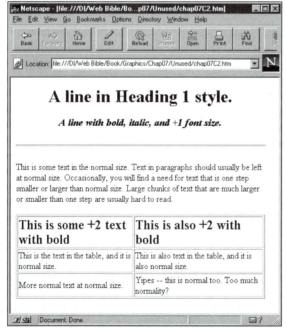

Figure 7-15: The same text as in Figure 7-14, but with different font sizes.

Font size changes the page. You can use large font sizes to break up the page into digestible portions. You can use small font sizes to cluster text together, and visually unite portions of the page. By using both together, you can control overall page organization.

Weight

There are many different weights available for fonts used in desktop publishing. Figure 7-16 shows a variety of weights available for just one font. When you create web pages, you are reduced to two weights: normal and bold. Bold is usually used for emphasis, but if you use too much of it the page starts to look out of control, as if the various emphasized words are competing with each other for your attention (see Figure 7-17). To look at this overly bold page yourself, double-click `\My Web Stuff\chap07\chap07d.htm`.

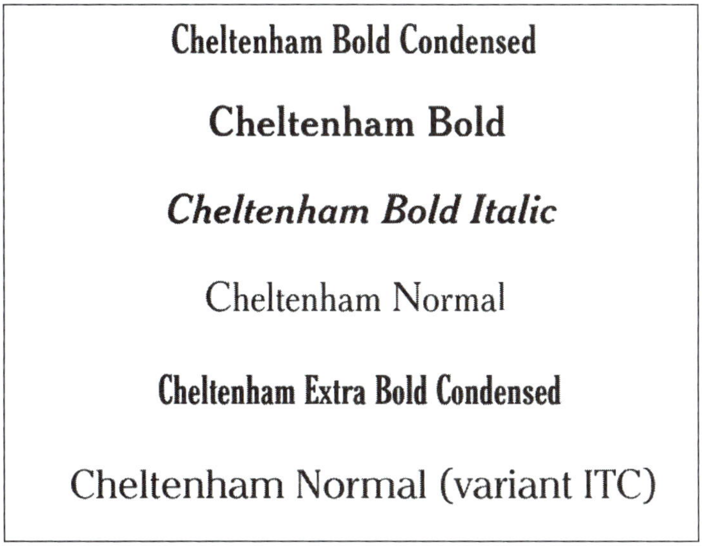

Cheltenham Bold Condensed

Cheltenham Bold

Cheltenham Bold Italic

Cheltenham Normal

Cheltenham Extra Bold Condensed

Cheltenham Normal (variant ITC)

Figure 7-16: Various weights and styles of the font Cheltenham.

Ninety-nine percent of the material on a typical page should be normal weight. Bold is fine for some, perhaps even most, hyperlinks, although you'll find different opinions on that subject. Some folks think that hyperlinks are distracting enough and should seldom be bold, while others feel hyperlinks are important and *should* stand out against the rest of the text. Follow your own taste on this one.

There is an exception to the rule about 99 percent normal text. If you use a dark background, you may need to make *all* of the text bold to make it readable. Look at your page using a variety of browsers to verify that the text stands out adequately from the dark background. This is usually an issue even if you have a black background and white text because white text just isn't as legible as black text.

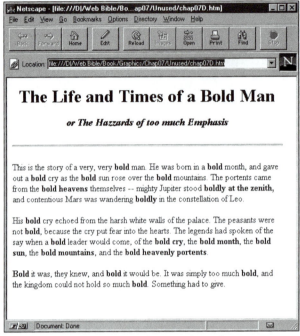

Figure 7-17: Too much bold makes for ugly pages.

Style

Text styles come in six varieties on the web page, plus two special-purpose styles:

Normal   This is the normal appearance of text for a given font.

Italic   Usually a slanted version of the text. Some fonts, especially very exotic ones, may not have an italic style available.

Underlined   Underlining is automatically applied to text hyperlinks, so you should have little use for it on your web pages. Underlining text sends a confusing message: is it a hyperlink, or not? If you get the urge and simply must underline text, you can.

Strikethrough   Strikethrough text is used mostly on legal documents, to indicate deleted text.

Preformatted   This is a special-purpose style. You can apply it to a block of text, in which case that text will appear in a monospaced font (typically some form of Courier, the standard typewriter-like font). Or you can apply it to an entire paragraph, in which case two things will happen: the font will be Courier, and the layout of the text on the web page will be identical to the layout in your web editor. Normally, for example, line breaks vary according to the width of the browser window. Figure 7-18 shows a web page with both normal and preformatted paragraphs. The file is \My Web Stuff\chap07\chap07g.htm. Figure 7-19 shows the same page with a greater window width — note that the preformatted paragraphs do not change width.

Tip

An important use of preformatted paragraphs is to create tables on web pages where you cannot use true HTML tables. Because the preformatted paragraph will not change width, you can add spaces to align text into vertical columns that will retain their shape no matter how the browser window is adjusted.

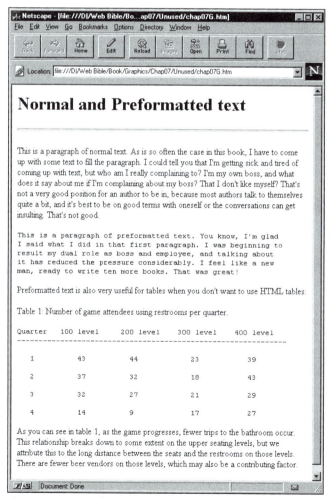

Figure 7-18: A web page with preformatted paragraphs.

Normal text   Preformatted text

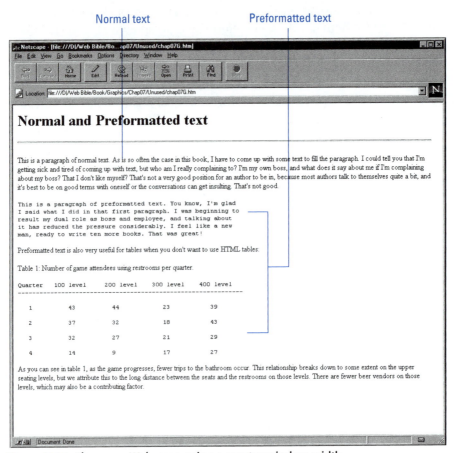

Figure 7-19: The same Web page using a greater window width.

Blinking	This is the forbidden text style. Once upon a time, back in the days of monochrome monitors, blinking text was a legitimate text style because many of those old monitors could not display styles like bold or italic. Today, with our sophisticated monitors, blinking text is usually considered annoying and is frowned upon. You can use it if you must, but keep in mind that many visitors will find it bothersome.
Subscript	This is a special-purpose style used with mathematical and chemical formulas. For example, the chemical formula for water is H_2O.
Superscript	This is a special-purpose style used with ordinal numbers (1st, 2nd, and so on), and footnotes, among other uses.

Some word processors call bold weight a text style, but that's technically incorrect. Weight is a separate characteristic of text. For example, it's quite possible to have text that is has a bold weight and an italic style.

HTML 3.2 and Beyond

As I am writing this chapter, an upheaval is in progress. HTML is the language of the web page, and it is evolving rapidly. The stuff I said about fonts will likely remain true for a long time, but there are rapid (and sometimes inconsistent) changes afoot in the world of web page text.

Web pages are built out of HTML code. I have included an example of some HTML code in Figure 7-20. Very basically, HTML consists of *tags* and text. The tags specify images, hyperlinks, text attributes, and other design- and layout-related aspects of the page. The text is, well, text.

Figure 7-20: The HTML code behind the web page at
`http://www.olympus.net/biz/mmad/index.htm`.

For example, the IMG tag allows you to add images to a web page. Like many tags, the IMG tag has *parameters*. These are individual subtags that specify exactly how the tag operates. The IMG tag has parameters like SRC (the file that is the source for the image) and WIDTH (how wide the image should be when displayed on the web page).

For better or for worse, HTML is not a static language. It keeps changing, and every change brings two things with it: fancier web pages, and confusion. The ability to create fancier web pages is nice, but the confusion that comes with the changes can create problems if you aren't prepared for them. Most of the confusion results when a given feature gets implemented in two or more ways. Typically, either Microsoft or Netscape will introduce a cool web page feature, and the other company will respond with its own version of that feature. The web world proceeds to duke it out over the competing methods until one or the other wins. Naturally, all the web pages built with the losing method have to be edited to support the winning method.

With that in mind, here is a quick survey of the font-related features on the HTML event horizon.

Desperately seeking fonts

As I pointed out earlier in this chapter, one of the distasteful aspects of font support in HTML is that you can specify any font you like, but you can never assume that the user's machine will have that font available. The FACE parameter of the FONT tag allows you to specify a list of fonts. The browser will search the user's hard disk for each font, and use the first font that it finds. For example, the HTML code

```
<FONT FACE="Garamond, Bookman, Times, Arial">
```

searches the user's machine for the fonts listed. If it does not find Garamond, it looks for Bookman, then Times, then Arial. The first font it finds is used to display the text.

To use this new parameter effectively (look for your favorite web page editor to support it in the near future), the list should begin with your ideal font, and end with one or more fonts that are typically default fonts found on most computers. Times and Arial are two good choices for default fonts, as they are available on most computers. Times is a serif font, and Arial is a sans serif font. Serif fonts are usually considered traditional, conservative fonts, while sans serif (literally, without serif) fonts are often considered modern.

In addition to the FACE parameter, you can also specify the COLOR and SIZE parameters. Colors are designated in hexadecimal notation, ranging from #000000 (white) to #FFFFFF (black).

Tip

To easily obtain the hex equivalent of a color, use a color utility program that displays a color and shows you the hex numbers that specify that color. You'll find a collection of links to such utilities on the web site for this book at `http://www.mmadweb.com/bible/utils`. There are even a number of online color pickers, such as the one at `http://thccy14.oz.nthu.edu.tw:6083/simon/java/Picker.html` (see Figure 7-21). This picker is a Java applet, and the source code is available on the web site if you want to use it to learn how it works. Among downloadable color pickers, try the RGB Color Box at `http://home1.inet.tele.dk/theill/rcb.htm` (see Figure 7-22).

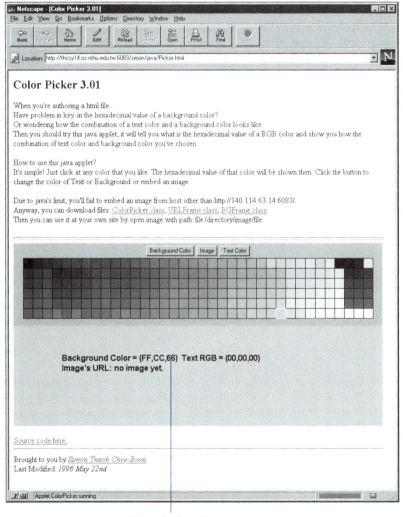

Hex codes for color

Figure 7-21: A web page that allows you to pick colors.

Pick color for . . .

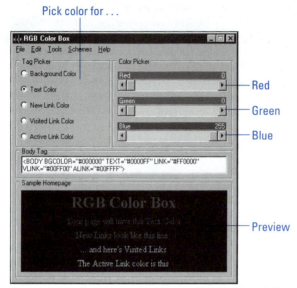

Red

Green

Blue

Preview

Figure 7-22: The RGB Color Box application for picking colors.

Layers upon layers

There's a new sheriff in town, and he's a lot more flexible than his predecessors. His name? Layer. Sheriff Layer Tag, to you. He's flexible, but he's tough: He's moving all the old HTML crooks out of town, and the nice respectable desktop publishing folks are moving in with their fancy hotels and mansions. Web pages will never be the same.

Web page layers are similar to the layers you encounter in Photoshop (see the tutorials later in this chapter). Layers sit on top of other layers, and they can be transparent, or even made temporarily invisible using JavaScript commands. Best of all, you can define the exact position of a layer on the page. This includes X,Y coordinates as well as Z-order (the order of the layer among the other layers). You can even nest layers inside of layers, either for convenience or to create maintenance headaches for the next time you try to edit the page!

Figure 7-23 shows an example of a page with layers. The fish image is actually an animation, and it sits in its own layer. The three vertical columns are also in layers. The middle column is in a layer above the fish image, and the two outside columns are in layers below the fish. The order of layers, from top to bottom is

✦ Middle column

✦ Fish

✦ Right outside column

✦ Left outside column

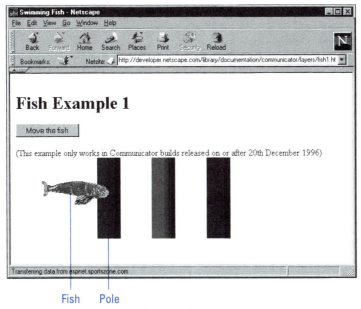

Fish   Pole

Figure 7-23: A web page that uses layers.

The fish moves when the button on the page is clicked, using a simple JavaScript script shown in Listing 7-1. The script uses a JavaScript reference to the fish layer using the layers array (document.layers["fish"]). It moves the entire layer in order to move the fish. Since the fish image is the only thing on the layer, this works well.

Listing 7-1: Using JavaScript to move an image.

```
<SCRIPT>
function movefish()
{
  var fish = document.layers["fish"];
  if (fish.left < 400) {
      fish.offset(5, 0);}
  else {fish.left = 10;}
  setTimeout("movefish()", 10);
  return;
}
</SCRIPT>
```

The HTML code for the page itself starts by defining the four layers and their contents. Note in Listing 7-2 that each LAYER tag includes LEFT and TOP parameters for providing a specific location for each layer.

Listing 7-2: Using HTML code for layers.

```
<LAYER NAME="bluepole" LEFT=160 TOP=150>
<IMG SRC=images/fish/bluepole.gif>
</LAYER>

<LAYER NAME="greenpole" LEFT=360 TOP=150>
<IMG SRC=images/fish/greenpol.gif>
</LAYER>

<LAYER NAME="redpole" LEFT=260 TOP=150>
<IMG SRC=images/fish/redpole.gif>
</LAYER>

<LAYER NAME="fish" LEFT=40 TOP=170  ABOVE="redpole">
<IMG SRC=images/fish/fish1.gif >
</LAYER>
```

Each new layer is placed above the previous layer. The fish layer is created last, and it would be the top layer, if not for the use of the ABOVE parameter. The relationship of the fish layer to the other layers is established by putting the REDPOLE layer above the fish layer using the ABOVE parameter. Figure 7-24 shows the fish moving across the page. It is behind the red pole (center) and above the green pole (right).

Layers are powerful tools for layout because they allow you to put one layer on top of another layer, and to position each layer exactly on the page. This is nothing short of a revolution in web page layout.

Caution!

The fish sample page will only work with Netscape Communicator, which is version 4.0 of Netscape Navigator. Because Communicator was in development at the time I was writing the book, and changes were likely, I elected not to include a sample layer page on the CD-ROM. There was no guarantee the page would work! Instead, when the final version of Communicator is available, I will have examples of pages using layers and graphics on the book's web site at http://www.mmadweb.com/bible/layers.htm.

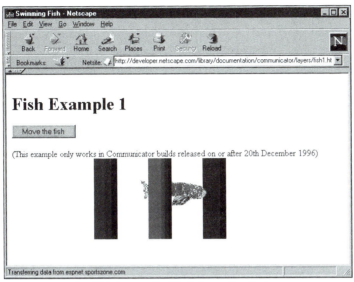

Figure 7-24: The fish layer is behind the red pole layer.

Between the style sheets

Style sheets allow you to define the way a web page should look, and to then import the style definitions quickly into your web pages. This means that all of your web pages can have a customized look that is consistent from one page to the next.

The official name for this is *cascading style sheets.* The styles from the master style sheet are inherited by the individual web pages that reference it. There are three different ways to make use of cascading styles: style sheets, style blocks, and in-line styles.

Tip

The term "style sheet" comes from print publishing, where the styles to be used in a publication were dummied up (that is, used in an example with nonsense text) and printed on sheets of paper that could be passed around to everyone working on the publication.

Style sheets

Style sheets represent the highest level of cascading style sheets. The style sheet is nothing more complicated than a web page that contains all of the style definitions. You can import these definitions into other web pages quickly and easily.

The top level of the cascade is a web page containing the styles. It isn't a real web page; it can contain dummy text that allows you to view the various styles. Instead of an .HTM or .HTML extension, the file has a .CSS extension. A typical style sheet file might look like the example in Listing 7-3.

Listing 7-3: A typical style sheet.

```
<STYLE TYPE="text/css">
BODY {font: 10pt "Arial"}
H1 {font: 19pt/21pt "Comic Sans MS";
        font-weight: bold;
        color: maroon}
H2 {font: 15pt/17pt "Comic Sans MS";
        font-weight: bold;
        color: blue}
P   {font: 10pt/12pt "Arial";
        color: black}
</STYLE>
```

To import a style sheet into a web page, add a LINK tag to the page's HTML code in the page header, like this:

```
<LINK REL=STYLESHEET
        HREF="http://www.myserver.com/styles/mainstyle.htm"
        TYPE="text/css">
```

Caution!

Cascading style sheets started with Microsoft and Internet Explorer 3.0; Netscape Navigator 3.0 does not display style sheet pages properly. The whole subject of style sheets will likely change with the advent of version 4.0 of both products, so I am only providing an overview here. For detailed information about style sheets, visit Microsoft's web page at `http://www.microsoft.com/workshop/author/newhtml/default.htm`.

Figure 7-25 shows a web page that uses the style sheet in Listing 7-3. If you have Internet Explorer 3.0 or later, you can view the web page by double-clicking the file `\My Web Stuff\chap07\chap07h.htm`. Figure 7-26 shows the same page viewed in Netscape Navigator 3.0, which does not support cascading style sheets. The page appears in default styles, and looks very different compared to the page in Figure 7-25.

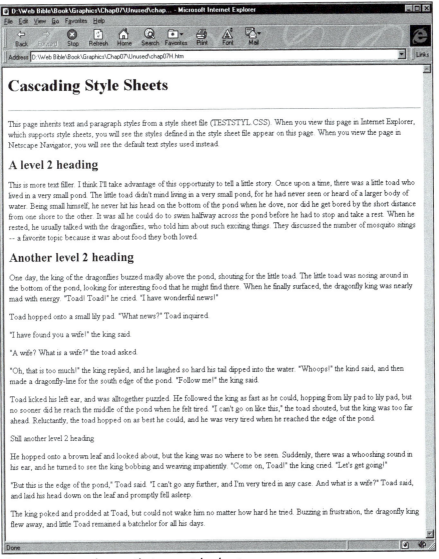

Figure 7-25: A web page that uses style sheets.

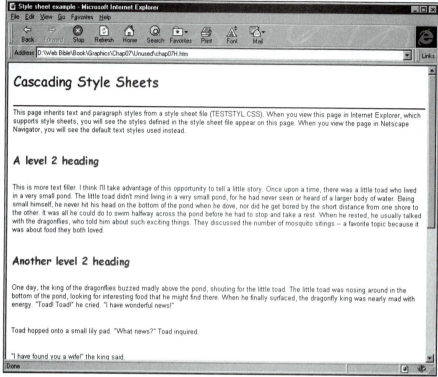

Figure 7-26: The same web page as in Figure 7-25, viewed in a browser that doesn't support style sheets.

The kinds of style information you can store in a style sheet file include: type size, font (typeface), weight, line height, colors, margins, and so on.

Font size

The *font-size* attribute sets the size of the text in points, inches, centimeters, or pixels. For example:

```
{font-size: 12pt}
```

Font name

The *font-family* attribute sets the font name used for text. You can specify one font:

```
{font-family: Arial}
```

or alternatives separated by commas:

```
{font-family: Arial, Helvetica}
```

Specifying a generic family name as the final alternative gives you a higher likelihood of getting a font similar to your design intentions:

```
{font-family: Arial, Helvetica, sans-serif}
```

You can use the generic family names (serif, sans-serif, cursive, fantasy, or monospace) to specify a font.

If you're referencing a typeface that consists of multiple words, use quotation marks:

```
{font-family: "Courier New"}
```

Weight

The *font-weight* attribute sets the thickness of the text:

```
{font-weight: bold}
```

There are several legal values for weight: extra-light, light, demi-light, medium, demi-bold, bold, and extra-bold. Not all fonts support all weights. For example, a user's computer may only have medium and bold typefaces installed for a given font.

Style

The *font-style* attribute sets italic text:

```
{font-style: italic}
```

Line height

The *line-height* attribute sets *leading,* the distance between the baselines of two lines of text. You can specify leading in points, inches, centimeters, or pixels. For example:

```
{line-height: 20pt}
```

You can also specify a percentage value of the default line height:

```
{line-height: 150%}
```

Colors

The *color* attribute sets the text to a named color or RGB value. You can use the 16 named colors or hexadecimal red-green-blue (RGB) color values. These are, respectively:

```
{color: teal}
```

or

```
{color: #33CC00}
```

The named colors are: black, silver, gray, white, maroon, red, purple, fuchsia, green, lime, olive, yellow, navy, blue, teal, and aqua.

Special text effects

The *text-decoration* attribute allows you to use underlining and strikethrough (called line-through in HTML-speak) for text. The supported values are underline, line-through, none, and italic. For example:

```
{text-decoration: underline}
```

Margins

The *margin-left, margin-right,* and *margin-top* attributes set the side margins and top margin. The margins apply to the specific HTML tag you associate them with. You can specify the margins in points, inches, centimeters, or pixels. For example, the following style definitions use pixels for margins:

```
BODY {margin-left: -10px;
      margin-right: -10px;
      margin-top: 20px}
  P {margin: 20px -10px-10px}
```

The BODY tag states each margin explictly. The P tag uses the default order for margins: top, right, and left. If you specify a single value, it will be applied to all three margins.

Alignment

The *text-align* attribute lets you left-justify, center, or right-justify HTML elements:

```
{text-align: left}
{text-align: center}
{text-align: right}
```

Indentation

In addition to using margins, you can also set additional indentations for sections of your page using the *text-indent* attribute. You can specify indentation in points, inches, centimeters, or pixels. For example:

```
H2 {text-indent: 0.5cm}
```

Background colors and images

The *background* attribute sets the background color or background image for a page. To set a color, specify a named color or use an RGB color value:

```
{background: red}
```

or

```
{background: #6633FF}
```

To place an image on the page background, specify the URL of the image in parentheses:

```
{background: URL(gifs/myimage.gif)}
```

You can control if and how the background repeats on the page. The values *repeat-x, repeat-y, repeat,* and *no-repeat* determine whether the background image is repeated horizontally, vertically, in both directions (default), or not at all:

```
{background: URL(gifs/myimage.gif) REPEAT-X}
```

The values *fixed* and *scroll* (default) determine whether the image is fixed on the page or scrolls with the page contents:

```
{background: URL(gifs/myimage.gif) FIXED}
```

You can specify the position of a background image with respect to a page element by specifying horizontal and vertical offsets. You can use the keywords *left, center, right* and *top, middle, bottom;* or percentage values; or distances in points, centimeters, inches, or pixels. For example, either of these definitions places the image at the lower left of the page:

```
{background: URL(myimage.gif) 0% 100%}
```

or

```
{background: URL(myimage.gif) left bottom}
```

Style blocks

Style blocks are intermediate in the cascade hierarchy. They appear in individual web pages, and override any style definitions in the imported style sheet for the page. These are blocks of HTML code that define (or redefine, if you are also using style sheets) style characteristics. Style blocks are declared with the STYLE tag, like this:

```
<STYLE TYPE="text/css">
  H1 {font: 18pt "Times"; color: "#FF00FF"}
</STYLE>
```

Use the TYPE parameter to define a cascading style sheet style within a web page. The definition overrides the definition in the style sheet, if one exists. In this example, the new font and color will apply to the entire web page that contains the style block.

Inline styles

Inline styles are the lowest level of the cascade hierarchy. They appear at one or more locations on a web page, and they change a single occurrence of a style. Instead of a STYLE tag, you use STYLE as a parameter of another tag. For example, to apply different font and color attributes to a single paragraph of Heading 1 style:

```
<H1 STYLE="font-weight: bold; color: blue">
```

You can span multiple paragraphs using the SPAN tag:

```
<SPAN STYLE="font-weight: bold; color: blue; margin-right:
      2in">
   <P>This paragraph will be bold, blue, and indented 2 inches
      from the right.</P>
   <P>This paragraph will also be bold, blue, and indented 2
      inches from the right.</P>
</SPAN>
<P>This paragraph will be in default weight, color, and
      location.</P>
```

In these examples, the styles will apply only to the paragraph(s) between the <SPAN> and </SPAN> tags; the rest of the page will inherit either the style blocks for that page, or the style sheet linked to the page.

Creating Gradient Text Effects with Photoshop

CD: A trial version of Photoshop is on the CD-ROM. To find out how to install it, view the web page at \demo\viewme.htm in your browser and click the \demo\adobe hyperlink.

Tutorial   **Level:** Fasten your seat belts!

Task: Add gradients to simulate a metallic surface

Before you start: Run Photoshop 4.0, either by double-clicking its icon, or using the Start | Adobe | Photoshop 4.0 menu item.

There are more graphic tricks to apply to fonts than any one book could ever describe. A hundred books might not be enough to describe just the tricks I've seen myself, let alone all the other tricks out there. This chapter will focus on the really cool font tricks, and you can build on those to create interesting effects of your own.

I've packed as many cool text effects into this tutorial as I could. The reason is simple: You can never know too many cool tricks. Pay close attention during the entire tutorial, as I will be slipping many innocent-looking tricks into the process, and you don't want to miss a single one.

Gradients

The metallic text effect makes your text (or any other object, for that matter) look like gleaming metal (see Figure 7-27). Photoshop 4.0 introduced a new tool, a Gradient Editor, that makes it very easy to create sophisticated metallic effects. Figure 7-28 shows several examples of a simple gradient that moves from black to white. Figure 7-29 shows more complex gradients that involve several color, value, and transparency changes.

Figure 7-27: A metallic text effect.

Linear gradients

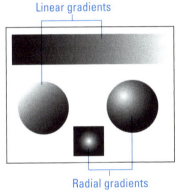

Radial gradients

Figure 7-28: Simple gradients.

Wavy gradient

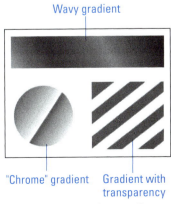

"Chrome" gradient   Gradient with transparency

Figure 7-29: Complex gradients.

Tip

Value refers to brightness or darkness without respect to color. Some colors have light values, such as yellow, while other colors have dark values, such as brown. Many colors, such as red and blue, can have either light or dark values. To see values clearly, temporarily convert an image to grayscale (Image | Mode | Grayscale menu selection).

1. Begin by creating a new file (File | New) that is 480 pixels wide and 180 pixels high in RGB color mode, with a white background (see Figure 7-30).

Figure 7-30: Creating a new file.

To keep the creation process well under control, begin by creating a new layer to which you will add the text.

2. Use the Layer | New menu selection to open the dialog shown in Figure 7-31.

Layer name

Figure 7-31: Adding a new layer.

3. Type in the layer name **Text Layer** and click OK to add the layer.

Figure 7-32 shows the Layers palette after the layer is added. If this palette is not displayed, you can use the Window | Show Layers menu selection to display it.

Figure 7-32: The Layers palette tells you everything you need to knowabout the layers in your image.

— New layer

Photoshop layers allow you to create objects that will remain separate from other objects in the image. For example, a common use of layers is to create an object on one layer, and its drop shadow on another layer. Objects in lower layers appear to be behind objects in higher layers.

4. To add text to the image, click on the Text tool (it's the big letter "T" at the middle right of the Photoshop toolbar) and click in the center of the image. This opens the Type Tool dialog box, shown in Figure 7-33.

Size   Font

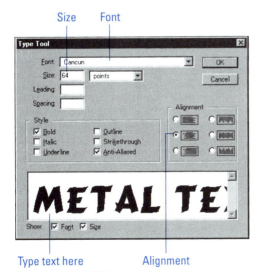

Type text here   Alignment

Figure 7-33: Adding text.

5. Duplicate the settings you see in Figure 7-33, as follows:

✦ Set the font to one that has fat letters. I used Cancun, but any font with wide, fat letters will work.

- ✦ Set the size to 64 points.

- ✦ Set the Style to Bold (see, I told you that you will encounter situations where bold is considered a style).

- ✦ Make sure that Anti-Aliased is checked

- ✦ Set the Alignment to horizontally centered.

- ✦ Type the all-uppercase text **METAL TEXT** into the white area at the bottom of the dialog box.

- ✦ To see the text in the selected font at the indicated size, make sure the Font and Size check boxes are checked.

6. When all is in order, click the OK button to add the text to the image.

Figure 7-34 shows the result. If you did not find the Cancun font on your computer, you will see letters that are shaped differently. As long as the letters are big and fat, you will be able to complete the tutorial. If the letters aren't fat enough, use Ctrl + Z (the keyboard shortcut for Undo) to remove the text and try a different font.

Figure 7-34: The text is now part of the image.

Tip
In Figure 7-34, the text is filled with black. The text will be filled with whatever the current foreground color is. For a standard gradient, this would be fine. However, you are going to create a gradient that uses transparency — the color of the text will show through some parts of the gradient. To fill the text with a color that will be suitable for the metallic gradient, click the Text layer in the Layers palette, and make sure that the Preserve Transparency check box is checked. Double-click the foreground color to open the Color picker, and set the RGB settings to Red=159, Green=134, Blue=33 (see Figure 7-35). Click OK. Use the Edit ∣ Fill menu selection to display the dialog box in Figure 7-36, and make sure the Contents are set to Foreground Color, that Opacity is 100%, and that Mode is Normal. Click OK to fill the text with this nice golden color. Edit ∣ Fill is much safer than using the Paint Bucket tool. Edit ∣ Fill always fills the entire selection. The Paint Bucket tool only fills adjoining pixels of identical color.

New color

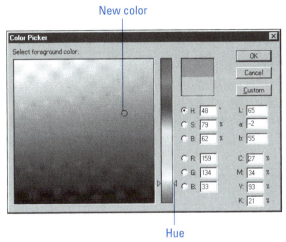

Hue

Figure 7-35: Setting foreground color.

Fill contents

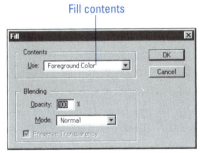

Figure 7-36: Filling the text with the foreground color.

Using the Gradient Editor

The Gradient tool has some very interesting options.

1. Click on the Gradient tool (see Figure 7-37). If the Gradient Tool Options palette (see Figure 7-38) is not currently displayed, double-click the Gradient tool to display the palette.

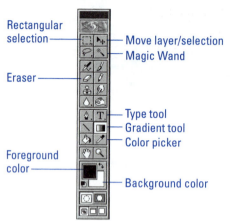

Rectangular selection

Move layer/selection

Magic Wand

Eraser

Type tool

Gradient tool

Color picker

Foreground color

Background color

Figure 7-37: Activating the Gradient tool.

Gradient type

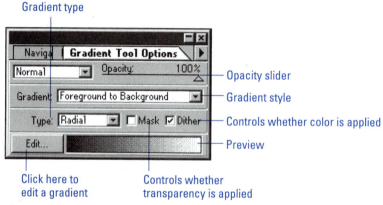

Opacity slider

Gradient style

Controls whether color is applied

Preview

Click here to edit a gradient

Controls whether transparency is applied

Figure 7-38: The Gradient Tool options.

2. Verify that the Opacity is set to 100% and that the current Gradient is Foreground to Background. The other settings do not matter at this point in the tutorial, but some of them will come into play later.

3. Click the Edit button at the lower left to display the Gradient Editor (see Figure 7-39).

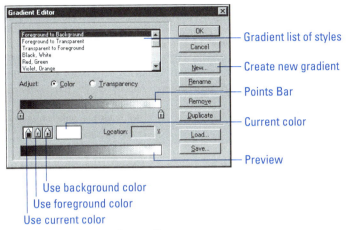

Gradient list of styles

Create new gradient

Points Bar

Current color

Preview

Use background color
Use foreground color
Use current color

Figure 7-39: The Gradient Editor.

There are a lot of buttons, lists, and odd-looking tools in this dialog box. Table 7-1 lists the primary tools in the Gradient Editor and describes their functions. The Gradient Editor's buttons are obvious in function and are not included in the table. For this tutorial, you'll only be using the New and OK buttons.

Table 7-1
The Gradient Editor Tools

Tool	Name	Description
Foreground to Background / Foreground to Transparent / Transparent to Foreground / Black, White / Red, Green / Violet, Orange	Gradient List	A list of the available gradients, by name.
○ Transparency	Transparency	When active, sets the Points Bar to transparency mode. All changes affect transparency at the current point.
⦿ Color	Color	When active, sets the Points Bar to color mode. All changes affect color at the current point.
(Points Bar graphic)	Points Bar	This is where you design the gradient. You can adjust both color and transparency at any point along the gradient.

(continued)

8. To add a new point, click just below the Points Bar where you want to add the point. For example, click just to the right of the leftmost point to add a new point at the location shown in Figure 7-43.

9. Then click the Opacity text box and set the Opacity at 25%.

Note the change that occurs on the Points Bar: The area above the new point is much lighter, and the overall gradient now starts at black, fades to 25% opacity, and then goes back to black at the right edge. The Preview Bar shows the actual transparency of the gradient. The gray-and-white checkered background is visible in the Preview Bar so you can get an idea of how the transparency will appear in the gradient.

Click in Points Bar to add new points

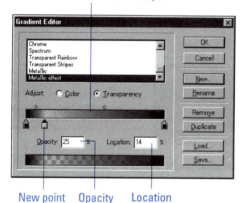

New point   Opacity   Location

Figure 7-43: Adding a new point.

Tip

The distance between any two points is a single gradient. When working in Transparency mode, the gradient between two points ranges from the Opacity value of one point to the Opacity value of the second point.

10. Add additional points until you have a total of 14 points, at approximately the locations shown in Figure 7-44.

The exact location of the points is not critical, as you will likely have to make adjustments to the points to get a good metallic effect later. The idea is to lay down a bunch of points, set some Opacity values, and then evaluate the results. You can adjust the location and opacity of individual points until the gradient effect is just right.

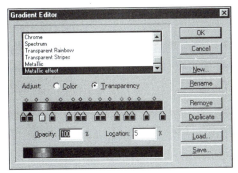

Figure 7-44: Adding 12 new points
(total points: 14).

Table 7-2 shows the locations and Opacity settings I used for the 14 points
you see in Figure 7-44. Point 1 is the point at the far left, and point 14 is the
point at the far right. Figure 7-45 shows the appearance of the Points Bar
with these settings applied. Note also the appearance of the Preview Bar,
which shows the transparency of the gradient.

11. Click each point and apply these settings if you want to duplicate exactly the
gradient that I designed.

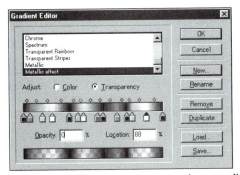

Figure 7-45: The transparency settings applied.

Table 7-2 Points and Their Opacity		
Point #	Opacity %	Location %
1	100	0
2	50	5
3	25	14
4	0	21
5	100	33
6	35	39
7	5	43
8	65	53
9	100	57
10	45	67
11	100	74
12	24	78
13	0	88
14	100	100

These settings will create a nice metallic effect, but adding even more points, and varying the settings of each, can create a more interesting and natural metallic effect. Figure 7-46 shows a more complex gradient, with 20 points. Figure 7-47 shows yet another variation on a metallic gradient, this time with 21 points. The gradient in Figure 7-46 has a high degree of contrast — the various Opacity settings range from 0 to 100. The gradient in Figure 7-47 has lower contrast — only the end points have a setting of 100; the other points range from 10 to 65.

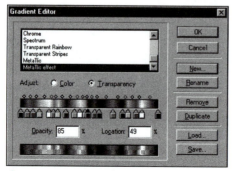

Figure 7-46: A completed gradient.

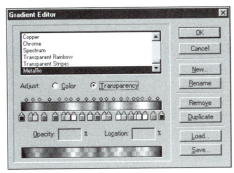

Figure 7-47: Another gradient.

As a general rule, the more points you add, the more natural the gradient will look. However, you can't really work with more than about 20 to 30 points in the small space available.

I suggest that you take a few moments to experiment with and expand upon the settings from Table 7-2 to create a gradient that appears metallic to you. Or, you can simply load the gradient you see in Figure 7-45 from the CD-ROM. It's located at \My Web Stuff\chap07\metalgrd.grd.

12. Click the Load button (in the Gradient Editor dialog box), locate the file (see Figure 7-48), and click the OK button to add the gradient to the list of gradients. The name of the gradient will be Ron's Metallic #1.

13. Locate the new gradient in the list of gradients, and click it to highlight it.

You can then continue with this exercise. However, note that the name of your gradient is Ron's Metallic #1 instead of Metallic Effect!

Figure 7-48: Loading a gradient from disk.

Tip

When you use the Save or Load buttons, you are saving or loading all of the gradients in a file. For example, if you were to click the Save button now and save your gradients, all of the gradients in the Gradient List would be saved to the file. To save just one gradient (or a subset of gradients), first save all of the current gradients to a temporary file. Then use the Remove button to remove all but the gradient(s) you want to save. Click the Save button, save to disk, remove the remaining gradient(s), and then reload all of your gradients from the temporary file. Gradients that you load are added to the existing gradients, thus the need to remove everything before you reload.

14. To gain control over the colors that the gradient uses, click the Color button so that the Points Bar displays the points associated with colors (see Figure 7-49).

    The default colors for a new gradient are black at the start (left) and black at the end (right).

15. Click to highlight the left color point, and then click the Foreground color (see Figure 7-50).

16. Click to highlight the right color point, and then click the Background color (see Figure 7-51). The gradient will now flow from whatever the current foreground color is to the background color.

Color radio button

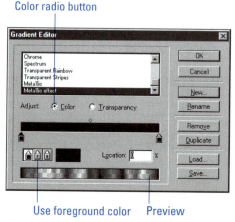

Use foreground color   Preview

Figure 7-49: Working with color instead of transparency.

In Figure 7-52, the foreground color is black, and the background color is white. Note how this affects the appearance of the gradient in the Preview Bar. The color at the left is black; the color at the right is white, and in between the transparency points affect how much black or white actually appears in the gradient.

17. Click OK in the Gradient Editor to save your gradient.

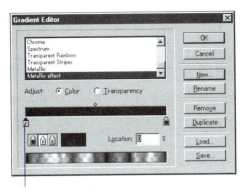

Foreground color

Figure 7-50: Setting foreground color.

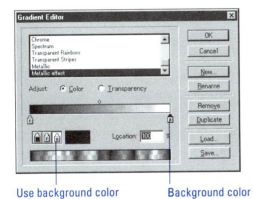

Use background color   Background color

Figure 7-51: Setting background color.

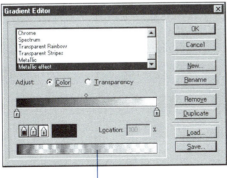

Preview changes to reflect new color

Figure 7-52: Viewing color and transparency simultaneously.

18. To use the gradient you designed, click the Gradient tool to activate it, and then select your gradient in the list of gradients in the Gradient Tool Options palette (see Figure 7-53).

Because your gradient uses both color and transparency, make sure that the Mask and Dither check boxes are checked. The Mask check box controls whether or not the transparency is applied, and the Dither check box controls whether or not the color is applied.

Figure 7-53: Selecting the current gradient.

19. To create a metallic gradient, set foreground and background colors appropriate to the metal you wish to imitate.

20. Double-click the foreground or background color on the toolbar to open the Color Picker dialog box.

21. Set the background color to RGB settings of Red=174, Green=138, Blue=12 (see Figure 7-55). For example, to get a bronze effect, set the foreground color to RGB settings of Red=217, Green=184, Blue=49 (see Figure 7-54).

New foreground color   New color   Old color

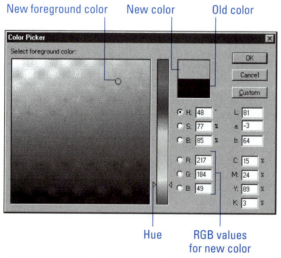

Hue   RGB values
for new color

Figure 7-54: Setting foreground color.

New background color

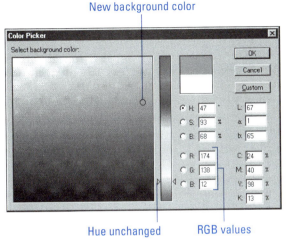

Hue unchanged   RGB values

Figure 7-55: Setting background color.

The colors visible in the Gradient Tool Options palette change to match the colors you just chose (see Figure 7-56).

Figure 7-56: The colors change in the Options palette.

Preview changes

Applying the gradient

To apply the gradient to the text, you must first select the text. The simplest way to do this is to use a little trick.

1. Click to activate the Selection tool.

2. Click and drag a rectangle around the text (see Figure 7-57). The text is on its own layer.

3. If you hold down the Ctrl key while pressing the Up arrow key, Photoshop does two things. It collapses the selection from a rectangle to just the area occupied by the text, and it moves the text upward one pixel. The collapse is good, because now the text is selected. The upward movement is not what we want, so . . . .

4. Hold down the Ctrl key while pressing the Down arrow key to move the text back.

Memorize this key sequence because it's the most convenient way I've found to quickly select all or part of the contents of a layer. Whenever I say to select something in what follows, use this trick.

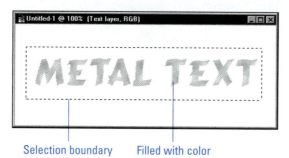

Selection boundary   Filled with color

Figure 7-57: Selecting an area around the text.

5. Click the Gradient tool to activate it.

6. Click just to the left of the text, near the bottom of the text, and then drag the mouse to a point near the top right of the text (see Figure 7-58).

7. Release the mouse button, and the text is filled with the gradient (see Figure 7-59).

Axis of gradient

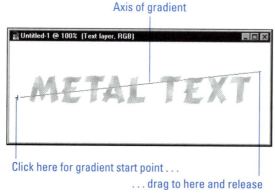

Click here for gradient start point . . .

. . . drag to here and release

Figure 7-58: Clicking and dragging to place a gradient.

This looks okay, but it's not very impressive. To get to impressive, you'll need to add a few details.

8. Begin by activating the Color Picker tool.

9. Click the very lightest pixels of the gradient to make that color the Foreground color.

10. Click the Background layer in the Layers palette to make it the active layer.

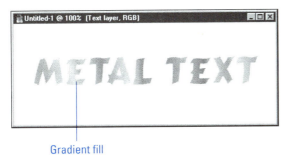

Gradient fill

Figure 7-59: The gradient applied to the text.

11. Use the Edit | Fill | Contents: Foreground menu selection to fill the background with the new Foreground color (see Figure 7-60).

    Note that this doesn't look great — but it's an intermediate step, so it doesn't matter.

12. Right-click the Text layer to display a pop-up menu.

13. Click the Duplicate Layer menu selection to display the dialog box shown in Figure 7-61.

Figure 7-60: Filling the background with color.

Figure 7-61: Duplicating a layer.

14. Give the new layer the name **Text drop shadow** and click OK. The new layer appears in the Layers palette (see Figure 7-62).

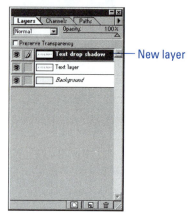

Figure 7-62: The new layer shows up in the Layers palette.

15. To make the new layer into a drop shadow, first click the layer and drag it to a position below the Text layer (see Figure 7-63). The new layer will now appear *below* the original layer.

16. Make sure that the Preserve Transparency check box is checked. When this is checked, only portions of the layer that already contain color can be changed.

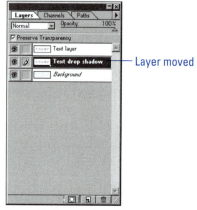

Figure 7-63: Moving a layer.

17. Now fill the layer with black (Edit | Fill | Contents: Black). You will not see any difference because the original Text layer is covering the new layer.

18. Click the Text layer's eye icon in the Layers palette (see Figure 7-64) to hide the Text layer (see Figure 7-65).

Preserve Transparency
┌ check box

Figure 7-64: Hiding a layer.

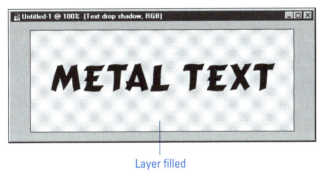

Layer filled

Figure 7-65: The Text layer is now hidden.

19. Make sure the Text drop shadow layer is selected in the Layers palette, and that the Preserve Transparency check box is *not* checked.

20. Use the Filter | Blur | Gaussian Blur menu selection to open the dialog box shown in Figure 7-66.

21. Set the radius of the blur to 3.0 pixels. You can see a preview of the blur in the small preview window at top left of the dialog box.

22. Click OK to apply the blur.

Blur preview

Figure 7-66: Applying a blur for a shadow.

Blur amount

Tip

If you had not unchecked the Preserve Transparency check box, you would not get a blur at all. In order to blur the contents of a layer, some transparent pixels must become nontransparent. Always turn off Transparency for a layer before you attempt a blur.

Figure 7-67 shows the blurred layer.

23. Click the space where the eye icon used to be on the Text layer to make it visible again (see Figure 7-68). You can just see the outer edges of the blurred layer beneath the Text layer.

Figure 7-67: The blurred layer.

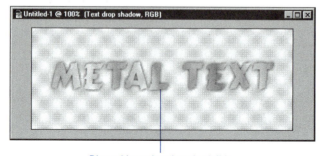

Blurred layer just barely visible

Figure 7-68: The blurred layer is under the Text layer.

24. Click the Text drop shadow layer on the Layers palette to make it the active layer.

25. Hold down the Ctrl key and press the Down and Right arrows repeatedly to move the shadow toward the bottom right (see Figure 7-69).

The further you move the drop shadow, the more pronounced the shadow effect will be. If you move the shadow too far, use Ctrl + Up and Left arrow keys to move it back.

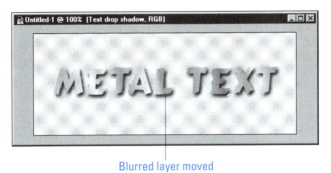

Blurred layer moved

Figure 7-69: The drop shadow moved into position.

Idea

Where to go from here:

✦ You can add highlights and dark areas to the text to create a rounded effect. Highlights are applied to the edges opposite the shadow, and dark areas mimic the shadowy areas. For example, you can select the text (just as you did earlier; refer to Figure 7-57), and then use the Linear Lasso tool to deselect part of each letter by hand. You can then lighten or darken the area that remains. For a softer edge, use the Select | Feather menu command to set a feather width that is about half the width of the selected areas (about three to four pixels in this example). Figure 7-70 shows a portion of the letter *M* being worked on in this way; Figure 7-71 shows several letters with partially selected areas. Figure 7-72 shows several letters with the highlights applied (Image | Adjust | Brightness and Contrast) and the areas selected for darkening. Figure 7-73 shows the completed effect, after darkening the selected portions of the letters.

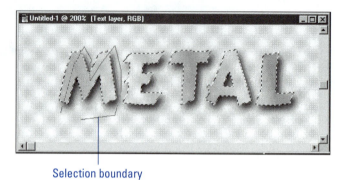

Selection boundary

Figure 7-70: Hand-selecting just a portion of a letter.

Remaining selection

Selection removed from this area

Figure 7-71: Several letters partially selected.

Highlight applied

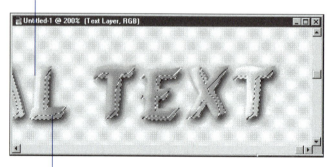

Remaining selection

Figure 7-72: Areas selected for darkening.

Figure 7-73: The completed 3-D effect.

✦ You can also add highlights using saved selections. Start by saving a selection (Select | Save Selection) and then offset the selection slightly (usually just a few pixels). Now reload the saved selection, but choose the Subtract from Selection radio button (see Figure 7-74). This leaves a thin selection that you can work with, lightening or darkening it as required. Figure 7-75 shows the selection to be highlighted, and Figure 7-76 shows the completed effect. Figure 7-73 shows a feathered edge on the highlights and darkening, while Figure 7-75 shows a hard edge. You can achieve feathered or hard edges with either of these techniques.

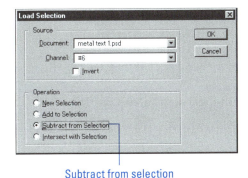

Figure 7-74: Subtracting from a selection.

Subtract from selection

Selected area

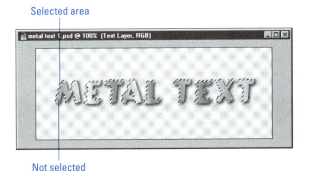

Not selected

Figure 7-75: Highlighting selected portions.

Beveled edge highlight

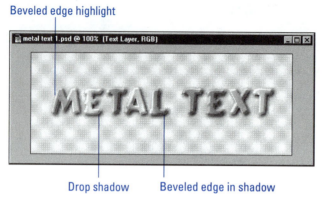

Drop shadow   Beveled edge in shadow

Figure 7-76: The completed effect.

✦ Select the text, and then use the Select | Modify | Contract menu selection to select only the central portion of each letter. You can do many things with this selection, using either a hard edge or a feathered selection:

- Fill the area with a color or gradient (see Figure 7-77)

- Lighten or darken the area

- Change the color of the area using the Image | Adjust | Hue/Saturation menu selection

- Apply a filter to the area, such as Filter | Artistic | Watercolor

Filled with color

Figure 7-77: The central portion of each letter is filled with a light green color.

Making Text Cutouts with Photoshop

CD: A trial version of Photoshop is on the CD-ROM. To find out how to install it, view the web page at \demo\viewme.htm in your browser and click the \demo\adobe hyperlink.

Tutorial   **Level:** Intermediate

Task: Add text cutouts to an image

Before you start: Run Photoshop 4.0, either by double-clicking its icon, or using the Start | Adobe | Photoshop 4.0 menu item.

A text cutout is text that appears to be cut out of a plate or block of color or texture, as in Figure 7-78. There are many variations on this effect. In this tutorial, you will create a cutout that includes metallic effects, engraved and raised effects, and a drop shadow.

Cutout

Figure 7-78: A text cutout.

1. Create a new file in Photoshop (File | New) with the following settings:
   - ✦Width: 420
   - ✦Height: 180
   - ✦Mode: RGB Color
   - ✦Contents: White

2. Select the gradient you used for the last tutorial. If the foreground and background colors are not set to the colors used in the last tutorial, set them now.

3. Click the Gradient tool to activate it, and drag out a gradient fill for the entire image as shown in Figure 7-79.

   Note that the start point is below the left corner of the image, and the end point is beyond the right edge of the image. The gradient looks like the image shown in Figure 7-80.

4. Select the rectangle as shown in Figure 7-80 using the rectangular Selection tool.

Axis of gradient   Gradient end

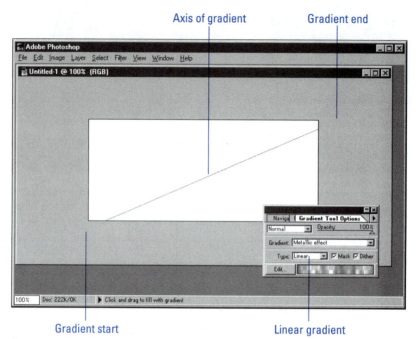

Gradient start   Linear gradient

Figure 7-79: Creating a gradient.

Selection boundary

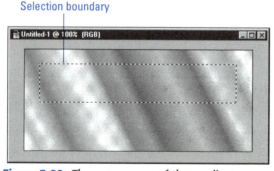

Figure 7-80: The appearance of the gradient.

Tip

In Photoshop versions prior to 4.0, gradients did not have transparency. If you made a mistake with a gradient (wrong angle, wrong color, or whatever), you could simply repeat the gradient with corrections and everything would be fine. This was true because the gradient fill covered everything beneath it. Many Photoshop 4.0 gradients include transparency. If you try again, you will still be able to see the previous gradient fill! Make sure you use the Undo command (Edit | Undo menu selection, or Ctrl+Z) to remove an incorrect gradient before trying again.

5. Use the Layer | New menu selection to create a new layer.

6. Give the layer the name **panel1** in the New Layer dialog (see Figure 7-81).

7. Fill the area within the selection in the new layer with the foreground color (Edit | Fill | Contents: Foreground Color; see Figure 7-82).

Layer name

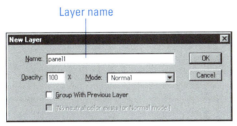

Figure 7-81: Creating a new layer.

Contents of new layer

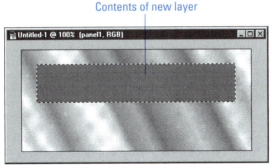

Figure 7-82: Filling the selection in the new layer.

8. Click the Text tool to activate it.

9. Click in the middle of the panel you created in the new layer to open the Type Tool dialog box (see Figure 7-83).

10. Click the Font drop-down list to choose a fat, heavy font; I used Cooper Black, but any heavy font will work if you don't have Cooper Black installed.

11. Set the size at 48 points, and the style as Bold.

12. Make sure Anti-Aliased is checked, and that Alignment is set to horizontally centered (refer to Figure 7-83).

13. Type in the text **Text Cutout** in the large box at the bottom of the dialog.

14. Click OK to add the text.

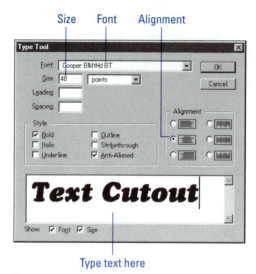

Figure 7-83: Adding text.

The actual color of the text does not matter; what you want to preserve is the selection that the text represents. However, you can fill the text with white to make it easy to see (Edit I Fill I Contents: White). To save the text selection, use the trick you learned in the previous tutorial:

15. Create a rectangular selection around the text (make sure the layer with the text is the selected layer in the Layers palette!), and hit the Up arrow and Down arrow keys one time each.

16. Then use the Select I Save Selection menu item to display the Save Selection dialog box (see Figure 7-84).

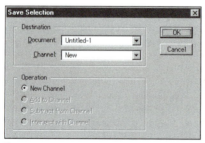

Figure 7-84: Saving a selection.

After you save the selection, you can delete the text layer because it is no longer needed; it was the selection we were after.

17. To delete a layer, right-click the layer in the Layers palette and choose the Delete Layer menu item on the pop-up menu (see Figure 7-85). You can also use the Layers | Delete Layer menu selection to remove a layer.

Figure 7-85: Deleting a layer.

18. Click the panel1 layer to activate it.

19. To create the cutout effect, load the selection you saved with the Select | Load Selection menu item.

20. Click the Eraser tool to activate it, and use it to erase the area within the selection (see Figure 7-86).

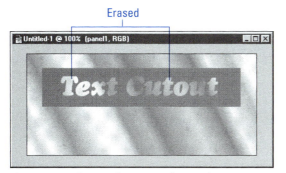

Figure 7-86: Create the cutout by erasing.

You can use this technique to create any kind of cutout, not just a text cutout. Any selection you create by any method can be used to create a cutout.

21. To create a drop shadow for the cutout layer, right-click the panel1 layer and click the Duplicate Layer menu selection. The Duplicate Layer dialog opens.

22. Type in a layer name of **panel1 shadow** and click OK. The duplicate layer appears above the original layer (see Figure 7-87).

23. In the Layers palette, click and drag the new layer to a position below the original layer and release the mouse button (see Figure 7-88).

24. Make sure the Preserve Transparency check box is checked.

Figure 7-87: The new layer is placed above the original layer.

Figure 7-88: The new layer is placed below the original layer, and Preserve Transparency is turned on.

25. Now fill the layer with black (Edit ǀ Fill ǀ Contents: Black).

26. Make sure the Preserve Transparency check box is not checked, and use the Effects ǀ Blur ǀ Gaussian Blur menu selection to open the Gaussian Blur dialog box (see Figure 7-89).

27. Set the Radius to 2.2 pixels, and click OK to apply the blur.

28. Hold down the Ctrl key and use the arrow keys to move the shadow layer down and to the right a few pixels (see Figure 7-90).

Blur   Blur amount

Figure 7-89: Applying a blur.

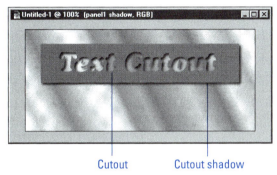

Cutout   Cutout shadow

Figure 7-90: Adjusting the drop shadow layer's position.

Tip

The background gradient visible in Figure 7-90 looks a bit too sharp to be effective. You can tone down the contrast in the gradient by applying a Gaussian Blur to it. Make sure the Background layer is the current layer, and then apply the blur using a radius of about 5.5 pixels. Figure 7-91 shows how the blur smoothes out the background gradient and makes it look more realistic. You can also lighten the background using Image I Adjust I Brightness and Contrast (Brightness: +16, Contrast: -31).

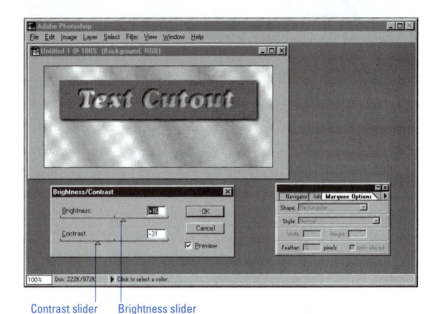

Contrast slider   Brightness slider

Figure 7-91: The background is less sharp after a blur and brightness/contrast adjustment.

Idea

Where to go from here:

✦ You can create other effects besides cutouts with a text selection. You can load the selection, select a layer (or the background), and then copy the selection to the Clipboard. Paste the selection back into the image (as a new layer, of course) and then lighten it. Repeat this again, but this time darken the new layer. If you line the layers up properly, you can get an engraved effect (see Figure 7-92) or raised effect (see Figure 7-93). Remember to position the layers appropriately above and below each other, and to use the Ctrl key plus the arrow keys to move the layer one pixel at a time.

Figure 7-92: An engraved effect.

Figure 7-93: A raised effect.

✦ The blur effect can be used on highlights as well as on shadows. Figure 7-94 shows both the highlight and shadow of a raised text block blurred.

Figure 7-94: Blurring creates an interesting look for raised text.

Adding Transparent Text with Photoshop

CD: A trial version of Photoshop is on the CD-ROM. To find out how to install it, view the web page at \demo\viewme.htm in your browser and click the \demo\adobe hyperlink.

Tutorial

Level: Intermediate to Advanced

Task: Add semi-transparent (see-through) text to an image

Before you start:

✦ Run Photoshop 4.0, either by double-clicking its icon, or using the Start | Adobe | Photoshop 4.0 menu item.

✦ Open the file \My Web Stuff\chap07\award.pcx in Photoshop.

✦ Set the foreground color to White.

It's easy to create transparent text in Photoshop. Every layer has properties you can set, and one of those properties is Opacity. But even something as simple as transparency can be spiced up and made challenging. In this tutorial, you'll learn not only how to make text transparent, but how to add highlights and shadows using saved selections.

1. Click at the lower left of the open image with the Text tool. Don't worry about the exact spot; you can move the layer later.

2. Choose a medium-weight font, such as Futura Heavy. This font is not as fat as the one used in the previous example, but it has enough thickness to work as transparent text. Text that is too thin might disappear if you made it transparent.

3. Set the point size very large (128 points), and make sure that Bold and Anti-Aliased are checked. The Alignment should be left aligned.

4. Make sure that you type the text **Award for Technical Flamboyance** on two lines, as shown in Figure 7-95.

5. Since the large point size will make it impossible to see what you are doing, if the Size check box is checked, uncheck it.

Font

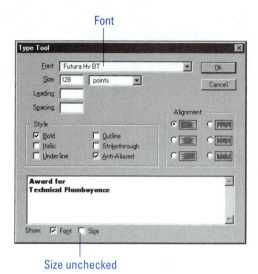

Size unchecked

Figure 7-95: Adding text.

Figure 7-96 shows what the text should look like on the image.

6. Hold down the Ctrl key and drag the text layer if it is not in the correct position.

7. If the text is too small or too large, delete the layer, adjust the font size, and try again.

Figure 7-96: The text is placed at the bottom of the image.

8. Right-click the Text layer in the layers palette, and click Layer Options to display the dialog box shown in Figure 7-97.

9. Set the Opacity to 60%, and click OK. Figure 7-98 shows the result.

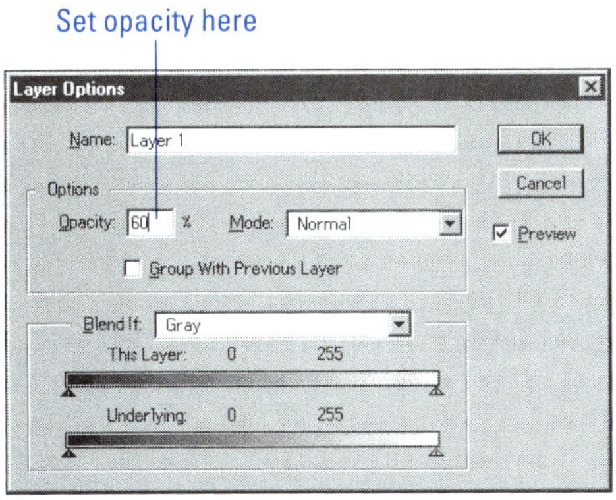

Figure 7-97: Setting layer opacity.

Figure 7-98: Transparent text.

If all you want to learn about is transparent text, you are done. Finished. Complete. But there is so much that you can do to enhance this text. For starters:

10. Add a new layer and add the same text to it, but in black.

11. Set the Opacity of this layer to 65%.

12. Move the new layer below the white text layer.

Tip

You could also create the new layer by duplicating the first layer, checking Preserve Transparency, and filling it with black.

13. Blur the black layer using the Effects | Blur | Gaussian Blur menu selection, using a radius of 3.5 pixels.

14. Move the black text layer down and to the right so it operates as a drop shadow. Ho hum; nothing new, but necessary to get the best eventual look for this text.

Now for the fun part.

15. Use the make-a-rectangular-selection-around-the-text trick to save the text selection (Select | Save Selection).

16. Activate the white text layer.

17. Hold down the Ctrl key, and use the arrow keys to move the selection up and to the left, three pixels in each direction.

18. Now load the selection you just saved, but click the Subtract from Selection radio button first.

The original selection is subtracted from the moved selection, leaving a thin selection area for each letter. This will become a highlight shortly. Figure 7-99 shows the thin selection.

The white text layer has an opacity setting of 60%, so filling the new selection with white won't do anything; the text already is white, but looks darker because of the transparency.

19. To deal with this, create a new layer (Layer | New).

20. Use the Edit | Fill | Contents: White menu selection to fill the selection with white in the new layer. Figure 7-100 shows the result.

Tip

If you prefer a wider highlight, and don't want to start over, you can use the Select | Modify | Expand menu selection to expand the highlight selection by one or two pixels and then refill it.

21. Repeat the move selection/subtract selection/fill selection process one more time, but fill with black instead of white, and move down and to the right.

Figure 7-101 shows the completed text. The central portion is transparent, but the top-left edge is highlighted, and the bottom-right edge is darkened. This creates a 3-D effect that stands out well in a crowd.

Selected area   Unselected

Figure 7-99: A thin selection for creating a highlight.

Highlight   Shadow

Figure 7-100: A white highlight on the text.

Figure 7-101: A stand-out example of transparent text.

Creating Fishtail Text Effects with Photoshop

CD: A trial version of Photoshop is on the CD-ROM. To find out how to install it, view the web page at `\demo\viewme.htm` in your browser and click the `\demo\adobe` hyperlink.

Tutorial

Level: Intermediate

Task: Add drop-shadowed, highlighted text

Before you start:

✦ Run Photoshop 4.0, either by double-clicking its icon, or using the Start | Adobe | Photoshop 4.0 menu item.

✦ Open the file `\My Web Stuff\chap07\fish.pcx` in Photoshop.

In this tutorial, you are building an image that is used again in Chapter 15 to create an image map. The text you add will be in the form of hotspots that can be used to jump to specific web pages.

1. Select the dark background with the Magic Wand tool using a Tolerance setting of 24.

Tip

Click below the fish's head to select the complete background at one time. If any areas remain unselected, hold down the Shift key while you click again near an unselected area. When the complete background is selected, fill the selected area with black. Then use Ctrl+D to deselect.

2. Use the rectangular Selection tool to select an area around the fish (see Figure 7-102).

3. Copy the selection to the Clipboard (Ctrl+C).

4. Use File | New to create a new file 200 pixels wider than the selection (about 900 pixels wide).

Click here to start

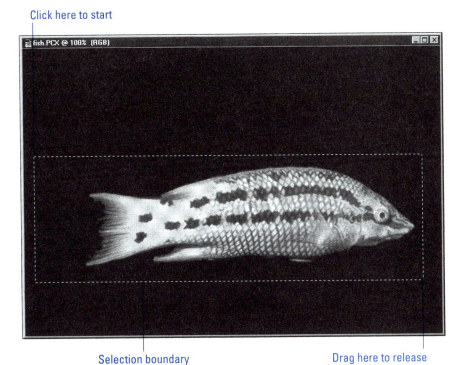

Selection boundary   Drag here to release

Figure 7-102: Selecting the fish.

5. Fill the new image with black (Edit | Fill | Contents: Black).

6. Paste the selection into the image (Ctrl+V).

7. Move the selection to the left edge of the image (hold down the Ctrl key and drag the new layer).

8. Use the Layer | Transform | Flip Horizontal menu selection to flip left to right.

9. Add a new layer (Layer | New | Layer).

10. Create a rectangular selection about one-third the height of the tail, and long enough for the required text (see Figure 7-103).

Figure 7-103: Creating a selection.

11. Set the foreground color to white and the background color to black.

12. Click to select the Gradient tool.

13. In the Gradient Options palette, set the gradient to Foreground to Background, and the Gradient type to Linear.

14. Click at the left edge of the selection and drag to the right edge, and release the mouse button. This fills the rectangle with a gradient from white to black (see Figure 7-104).

Figure 7-104: Filling with a gradient.

15. Select the rectangle.

16. Copy to the Clipboard (Ctrl+C).

17. Paste twice (Ctrl+V, Ctrl+V) to create two new layers, each with a rectangle at the center of the image.

18. If you can't see the new rectangles, hide the layer with the fish by clicking its eye icon in the Layers palette.

19. Move the rectangles so they stack neatly one above the other (see Figure 7-105).

20. Hide the fish layer while you do the preceding step if it is above the rectangles so you can see your work.

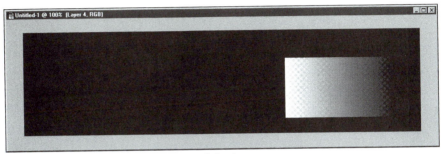

Figure 7-105: Adjusting the position of the layers.

21. Select the contents of the layer with the middle rectangle (see Figure 7-106).

22. Use the Layer | Transform | Flip Horizontal menu selection to flip it as shown in Figure 7-107.

Selected layer

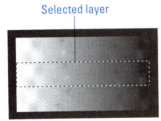

Figure 7-106: Selecting the middle rectangle.

Figure 7-107: The middle rectangle is flipped.

Tip

If the rectangles are too large, as shown in Figure 7-108, or too small, link all three layers (see Figure 7-109) and merge them into one layer (Ctrl+E). Select the contents of the layer. Use the Layer | Transform | Scale menu selection to scale the contents larger or smaller as needed to fit. Drag the selection handle at the top-middle or bottom-middle of the scale rectangle to increase or decrease the height of the rectangles. Because you merged the rectangles into one layer, all three will change by the same amount. This is a lot easier than starting over with a slightly smaller rectangle!

All on one layer

Figure 7-108: Problem: the rectangles are larger than the fish's tail!

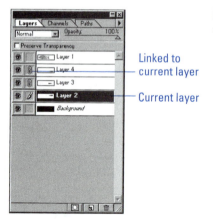

Linked to current layer

Current layer

Figure 7-109: Solution: link the layers and then resize them.

23. Choose a font you like (I used Ad Lib, 24-point).

24. Make the foreground color black, and add the text for the first hotspot (**DAILY SPECIALS**).

25. Add a second identical version of the text above the first version, but with white as the foreground color.

By default, each time you add text it is placed in its own layer with Preserve Transparency turned on.

26. Move the text layers so that the white version is two pixels left and two pixels above the black version.

Highlight the previous text's layer in the Layers palette before you place the text. The new layer will be added immediately above the selected layer.

27. Add one more version on top, and fill the text with a pink-to-white gradient opposite to the gradient in the underlying rectangle (see Figure 7-110).

To create a pink foreground color the easy way, use the Color Picker tool to select one of the shades of hot pink in the fish layer.

Highlight layer

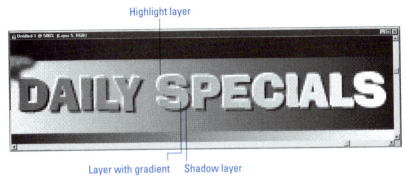

Layer with gradient   Shadow layer

Figure 7-110: Adding text.

To create a drop shadow from the black text layer, click that layer in the Layers palette. Make sure that the Preserve Transparency check box is unchecked. Use the Filter | Blur | Gaussian Blur menu selection to open the dialog box shown in Figure 7-111. Set the blur to 2.5 and click OK. The black text is now a drop shadow. Highlight the black text layer and hold down the Ctrl key while you drag it to the best position for a drop-shadow effect (see Figure 7-112).

Preview of blur

Figure 7-111: Blurring the black text layer.

Amount of blur

Blurred shadow

Figure 7-112: A drop-shadow effect.

28. Repeat these steps for two additional text strings:

    ORDER NOW!

    IN SEASON...

29. Remember to fill the text above each rectangle with a pink-to-white gradient *opposite* to the underlying rectangle's gradient (see Figure 7-113).

30. If you created a drop-shadow effect for the first text block, repeat it for the other two.

Figure 7-113: The completed image.

31. Take a moment to adjust the placement of all of the objects in all of the layers, and save your work.

If you want to preserve layers, save as a Photoshop file first (extension PSD), then save in a GIF or JPEG format. If you want to use PhotoImpact's SmartSavers to save the image in GIF or JPEG (I recommend JPEG), save the file from Photoshop in a noncompressed format such as PCX. Then open the image in PhotoImpact and use the JPEG SmartSaver to find the optimum level of compression interactively.

Hot Text and Cool Design

CD: A trial version of Photoshop is on the CD-ROM. To find out how to install it, view the web page at \demo\viewme.htm in your browser and click the \demo\adobe hyperlink.

Tutorial   **Level:** Advanced

Task: Create a neon text effect

Before you start: Run Photoshop 4.0, either by double-clicking its icon, or using the Start | Adobe | Photoshop 4.0 menu item.

This is a long chapter, but I'm not through parading cool text effects before your eyes. One neat effect that I haven't covered yet is neon text — text that appears to glow. The effect is easy to create using Photoshop's layers.

1. Run Photoshop 4.0 and create a new file with the following settings:

   ✦ Width: 280

   ✦ Height: 80

   ✦ Mode: RGB Color

   ✦ Contents: White

2. Fill the new image with black (Edit | File | Contents: Black). Figure 7-114 shows the result: a black rectangle.

3. Set the foreground color to white.

Figure 7-114: The new file.

4. Activate the Text tool, and click in the middle of the new image to open the Type Tool dialog box (see Figure 7-115).

5. Type in the text **HUMONGOUS** (yes, all upper case) and set the font to Arial Black, the Size to 36, and the Alignment to center.

6. Click OK to add the text to the image (see Figure 7-116).

7. If the text is not centered, hold down the Ctrl key and drag the text to the position shown in Figure 7-116.

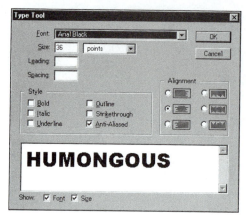

Figure 7-115: Adding text.

Figure 7-116: Text added to the image.

8. Use the Layers | Transform | Scale menu selection to stretch the text vertically, as shown in Figure 7-117. This makes the text *look* humongous.

This is going to be a company logo (used, by the way, in Chapter 15), and it should have the right feel to match the company name: Humongous Fish Company.

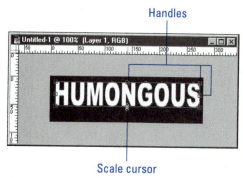

Figure 7-117: Scaling text by dragging.

To stretch the text only in the vertical direction, click the center-bottom handle and drag downward. The cursor changes to a small double-pointed arrowhead during the scale operation. When the text is the right size, click any tool in the toolbar to display the dialog box shown in Figure 7-118. Click Apply to apply the scaling.

Tip

Apply button

Figure 7-118: This dialog box appears after most of the Layer | Transform operations.

The text was automatically added as a layer when you created it.

9. To turn the text into a neon flight of fancy, begin by selecting the text. To select the text, use the old rectangular selection/Up- and Down-arrow trick.

10. Save the selection (Select | Save Selection).

Photoshop automatically puts newly pasted text and images into new layers if the image type is RGB Color.

Tip

11. Use the Select | Modify | Contract menu selection to display the dialog box shown in Figure 7-119.

12. Contract the selection by two pixels, and click OK. The selected area is now just the central portion of the letters (see Figure 7-120).

13. Save this selection as well.

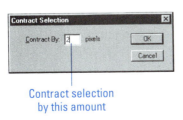

Figure 7-119: Contracting a selection by two pixels.

Contract selection by this amount

Contracted selection

Figure 7-120: Just the central portion of the text is selected.

Caution!

The font Arial Black is quite thick, and that's not ideal for neon text. A somewhat thinner font will give better-looking results, but the various operations are harder to see on thinner text. I used Arial Black so that you can see each step in the process clearly. At the end of the tutorial, you'll see an example that uses thinner text so you can compare. When using thinner text, you would contract by just one pixel.

14. Feather the current selection by two pixels (Select | Feather | Feather Radius: 2).

15. Save this as your third saved selection.

Tip

I'm being cautious by having you save each selection. You never know when you'll want to return to an intermediate step in the process to make an adjustment. When you save all of your selections, it's easier to return to an intermediate point and apply corrections. You are going to use the feathered version of the selection, but if it turns out that the feathering is too much or too little, you can go back to the second selection you saved and refeather it.

16. Load the first selection you saved. It will be channel number 4 (channels 1, 2, and 3 are the red, blue, and green channels for your image).

17. Load the selection using the Select | Load Selection menu item.

18. Now load the third selection you saved (the feathered one), but be sure to click the Subtract from Selection radio button (see Figure 7-121).

   The result is that you have a selection that consists of the outer edge of the letters, feathered toward the interior of the letters (see Figure 7-122).

Tip

You could also arrive near this point by selecting the letters and using the Select | Modify | Border menu item to create a narrow border. However, that border would extend beyond the confines of the letters, and you do not have the same degree of fine control that my method gives you.

19. Change the foreground color to a bright color, such as red or blue.

20. Make sure that the Preserve Transparency check box is checked, and fill the selection with that color. I used red, and Figure 7-123 shows the result.

Selection to use

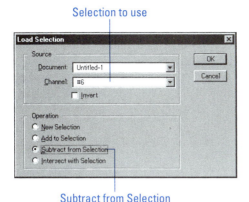

Figure 7-121: Subtracting from the current selection when loading a selection.

Subtract from Selection

Selected area   Unselected

Figure 7-122: The feathered, edge-of-the-letters selection.

Feathered fill

Figure 7-123: The almost-neon text.

This is okay, but you can create a soft outer glow that will really complete the neon text effect.

21. Create a new layer (Layers | New) and position it below the text layer (see Figure 7-124).

22. Click on the new layer in the Layers palette to make it the active layer.

23. Make sure that the Preserve Transparency check box is unchecked.

Figure 7-124: The new layer is below the text layer.

24. Load the first selection you saved (the full text, no feathering).

25. Use the Select | Modify | Expand menu item to enlarge the selection by one or two pixels.

Expanding by one pixel will create a slight halo effect; expanding by two pixels will create a dramatic halo effect. (If you were using thinner text, you would probably expand by just one pixel.) Figure 7-125 shows the result using a two-pixel expansion.

26. Fill the newly expanded selection with the same color you used earlier.

Figure 7-125: The expanded selection filled with color.

You could deselect the current selection using the Select | None menu item, but you can also deselect it by right-clicking the current layer to display a pop-up menu, and then clicking Select None (see Figure 7-126). Either way, you must deselect before you continue.

27. Use the Filter | Blur | Gaussian Blur menu selection to open the Gaussian Blur dialog box.

28. Use a Radius of 2.9 pixels to spread out the edge of the layer.

Figure 7-127 shows the result. The neon effect is now intense.

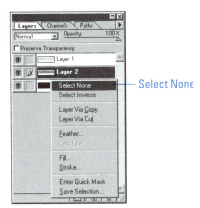

Figure 7-126: The right-click menu on the Layers palette is different when there is an active selection.

Select None

29. Add the rest of the company name in the same font (**Fish Company**), but use mixed case, 18-point text, and make sure the Bold style is checked.

30. Use the Layers | Transform | Scale menu selection to stretch the new text to the same width as the neon text (see Figure 7-128).

Figure 7-127: True neon text.

Figure 7-128: The company name stretched to match the width of the original text.

Figure 7-129 shows the promised alternative version that uses thinner text. The neon effect looks more like neon glass tubes because the text is uniformly thin throughout. In Figure 7-116, you can see that certain portions of certain letters glow more brightly because they are thicker.

Figure 7-129: A more subtle form of neon text.

Web Tour #7: Font Resources

To visit some web pages related to fonts, and to see even more examples of cool things you can do with fonts, double-click the file:

    \WebTour\Chapter07\index.htm

You'll see the web page for this chapter. Click the Web Tour icon and you will see a list of pages to visit. You'll also find some links to tools that help you work with fonts.

Graphics That Say "Wow!"

To prepare for this chapter's tutorials, copy the following folder from the CD-ROM to the \My Web Stuff folder on your hard drive:

    \tutorial\chap08

This will copy files for all of the tutorials in this chapter to your hard disk. See Chapter 1 for complete details on setting up for tutorials.

There are graphics, and then there are *graphics*. Knowing how to create *graphics* can make your web pages stand out from the sea of web pages that are out there on the Web.

There are some basic rules to learn about graphic design, and I spell them out in this chapter. I also include several tutorials designed to show you how great graphics are created. But the best way to learn about great graphics is to visit the web sites that use them, and learn by example. If you see a graphic that really grabs your attention, observe it. Meditate on it. Figure out how it does what it does.

Elements of Graphic Design

There are two levels of web graphic design: designing individual graphics, and designing web pages. A great web page will have both great graphics, and graphics that work great together.

At the individual level, graphics should have an organized, functional design and, of course, every graphic must do the job for which it is intended. For example, if you are designing a graphic that will be a button or a link to another web page, then the graphic has to look good and communicate its function, too.

At the page level, graphics have to work together. If your page design calls for a design theme, then all the graphics have to work within that theme. If the theme is a natural, woodsy look, then all the graphics should fit that design. If your theme is a hard, metallic, future-shock thing, then all the graphics should fit *that* design.

Designing an Image

There are some basic rules for designing graphics that have been around since about the time that mankind first put pigment to cave wall. Briefly, the standard rules are:

- ✦ Use the rule of thirds.
- ✦ Arrange on diagonals.
- ✦ Create a central focus.
- ✦ Background is background, foreground is foreground, and never the twain shall compete.
- ✦ Form follows function.

In addition, there is one rule that overrides all of the other rules, but only sometimes. That overriding rule is:

- ✦ Rules are made to be broken.

Use this last rule only when the other rules don't give you the result you want. This doesn't mean you should fall into the trap of "Ooh, this isn't working — I'll break the rules to fix it." The rules cover 98% of all graphic design cases. The time to break the rules is when you know that the rules aren't sufficient to solve whatever creative problem is facing you. Creativity is the key to graphic design, and it's easier to be creative than you think (see the sidebar, "What Is Creativity?")

To use the rules, you have to know what they really mean. The following sections present the rules in a form that should help them stick in your mind. I'll use very simple illustrations to make everything as clear as possible.

What Is Creativity?

Hey, don't ask me! Seriously, the debate about what constitutes creativity has been going on as long as there have been people on the planet. Creativity, many people say, has to do with breaking the rules and making something new and novel. This is too grand; the simple truth is that, 98% of the time, creativity is nothing more than using the rules in new ways.

Creativity, far from being something special and outrageous that only starving artists possess, is actually a very practical skill. There are many more examples of creativity in our daily lives than we realize. When you outmaneuver someone at work and get your idea accepted, that's creativity. When you finally get through to your teenager about some important life decision, that's creativity. Creativity isn't just about art, or being artsy. It's a daily part of our lives. If you've been telling yourself you're not creative enough to make neat-o keen-o graphics for web pages, guess again: You just need to channel the creativity you've already got into web graphics.

Why do I say this with such confidence? If you talk to artists, there is one common thread to all discussions about creativity. It turns out that creativity is the result of problem solving, not divine inspiration. As they say, creativity is 90% perspiration, 10% inspiration. If you want to be creative, learn your tools, study the problem at hand, and then let your creative self come up with a solution. That's creativity at its most wonderful, and its most mundane.

As often as not, when you are not feeling creative, it's because you either aren't fully comfortable with the tools you are using, or you haven't studied the problem at hand long enough for your creative juices to flow. The next time you have writer's block, the next time you just can't come up with a sketch for a graphic, simply reconsider the original problem, or refamiliarize yourself with your tools. Creativity is released by confidence, and confidence comes from knowing your tools and knowing the problem inside and out.

Rule of thirds

This rule is easy: Place important elements of the design on the one-third dividing lines of the image. Figure 8-1, a simple drawing of a man trying to decide whether he is seeing a mirage or a real lake in the desert, shows this rule being broken vertically: The horizon is at the vertical midpoint of the image. This divides the image into a top half and a bottom half. Horizontally, the rule of thirds is obeyed, more or less — the lake ends at the right third of the image, and the man is in the left third of the image. The sun is nearly in the middle, but not quite so far back as the one-third point. All in all, Figure 8-1 breaks more rules than it obeys.

Figure 8-1: An image that breaks the rule of thirds several times.

Figure 8-2 moves the horizon line down to the bottom third of the image. The sun is moved to the left, just a bit shy of the one-third point. The man is in almost the exact same position — having the man so far to the edge of the picture is a case of breaking the rule, but for a reason: It increases the sense of vastness and isolation he is facing.

Figure 8-2: Breaking the rule of thirds to create a stronger message.

Such lofty ambition for a lousy little line drawing! I suppose next you'll point out that placing the sun above this poor soul, but not vertically over him, shows that it is important to avoid lining up objects vertically and horizontally.

No, I cover that in the next section; one thing at a time! Note, dear reader, that I have also moved the lake to the bottom edge of the drawing. This makes for a more balanced drawing, and makes the lake look less cartoonish.

I have included Figure 8-3 to show how moving picture elements around can change the viewer's interpretation of the story that the picture tells. Remember — every picture tells a story (thank you, Rod Stewart) because every picture is worth a thousand words. By moving the sun away from the man, he is less oppressed by the heat, but more visually isolated. Granted, this is an absurdly simple drawing, but these changes still have a real effect. I leave it to you to decide which story you prefer.

Figure 8-3: Changing the position of an element changes the story behind the picture.

The horizon line can also move to the top third of the picture, as shown in Figure 8-4. This changes the feel of the picture — the sky no longer dominates; the desert dominates. I also enlarged the sun because I was getting carried away with creating trouble for the poor little stick man.

Figure 8-4: Setting the horizon at the top third.

 And so your true nature is revealed. I'll have no more of you calling me a curmudgeon from here on out; I come by my cynicism honestly!

And the sun rises in the west. Figure 8-4 is important for another reason: It makes strong use of diagonals, which is discussed more in the next section. The edge of the lake (perhaps it has grown to a sea, it is so large, but I wax poetic at the expense of clarity) is a strong diagonal, and the line between man and sun is a similar diagonal.

So far, I've been illustrating the rule of thirds exactly. Many classic painters used the rule of thirds as a guide, and then modified it to suit their subject. You can do the same. Figure 8-5 shows a painting by Botticelli that places figures at thirds, and then puts the focus of the painting near — but not exactly at — the center of the painting. This is an effective way to draw the viewer to the focus of the image, as discussed in a later section of this chapter.

In Figure 8-6, Botticelli shows in a simple sketch how to subtly and carefully use the rule of thirds to lay out an image. There are two strong figures that divide the picture into horizontal thirds, while the vertical third points are occupied by faces. Other painters in other periods likewise used the rule of thirds. Figure 8-7 shows an example by Monet. The moral of this little trip through the art museum is a simple one: Use the rule of thirds and your images will benefit.

Figure 8-5: Using thirds, and not using thirds, all at the same time.

Figure 8-6: Powerful use of thirds in a sketch.

Figure 8-13: A dark background establishes focus.

You can even use simple, crude pointing techniques to draw attention to a portion of an image. Figure 8-14 shows the monkey astride a red arrow, pointing at the dartboard. It's clear where the image's focus is; a diagonal helps to establish it. In this case, the eye starts at the strongest visual element (the monkey astride the arrow), and eventually follows this to the dartboard. There is a distinction between the most eye-arresting item in the visual field, and the focus to which the eye is eventually drawn.

Figure 8-14: Using crude tricks to establish focus.

You will find that the rule of thirds, diagonals, and center of focus are intensely interrelated aspects of an image. By gaining consciousness of the role that each plays in your graphics, you can create better-looking, more effective graphics. Hey, if it works for the great masters, it can work for you! Figure 8-15 shows a painting by Monet that uses strong diagonals to direct the eye to the center of focus. Figure 8-16 shows a more subtle use of diagonals to draw the viewer's eye to the upper right third of the painting. Both are superb examples of artfully engineered images — using the cheapest of cheap tricks. The art is not in the device you use to accomplish your goal, it is in the illusion of artlessness in the use of the device.

Figure 8-15: Strong diagonals create a center of focus.

Ugh! How artsy can you get and still get this by your editor? That's an appalling way to say what needs saying — that you can get away with anything, so long as the image does the job you want it to do. Never feel guilty about using these so-called cheap tricks. They are solid tools that deliver dependable results.

Figure 8-16: Subtle use of diagonals to draw the eye to the center of focus.

Background and foreground

Nearly every image must have a foreground and a background. The purpose of the background is to artfully support and draw attention to the foreground. If the background is distracting, it is committing the worst offense a background can commit. Busy backgrounds are the single greatest cause of disruption on today's web pages.

Figure 8-17 shows an example of a background that serves the purpose of the image. The graduated background helps draw attention to the dartboard, while still allowing the viewer to appreciate the humor of the monkey riding the red arrow. Figure 8-18 shows a background that distracts the viewer from the purpose of the drawing.

If that dartboard had been a hyperlink, Figure 8-17 would result in lots of visits to the linked page, while Figure 8-18 wouldn't result in anything but people running away from their computers, screaming about the horrors of distracting backgrounds.

There are many ways to make sure that a background functions as a background. You can lighten it, darken it, blur it, and so on. Anything that prevents competition between background and foreground is a good thing. For example, Figure 8-19 has a complex background, but a little blurring keeps it well in the background, allowing the foreground (text, in this case) to be read clearly. The effect is not as clear in black and white as it is in color, because in the original the background is red, and the foreground text is light blue. Adding a 3-D effect to the text draws it further into the foreground, and darkening the background further makes the text really stand out even in black and white (Figure 8-20).

Figure 8-17: A background that helps create a center of focus.

Figure 8-18: A distracting background.

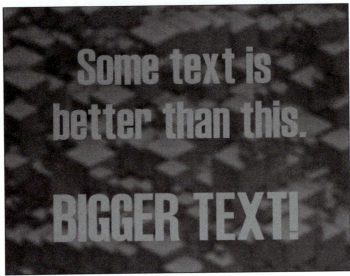

Figure 8-19: Background versus foreground.

Figure 8-20: Now the foreground stands out very clearly.

The entire trick to establishing the proper relationship between foreground and background is to do what you must to make the background less noticeable, and the foreground more noticeable. Techniques that work well for the background include:

- ✦ Using extremes of light and dark
- ✦ Blurring
- ✦ Soft colors
- ✦ Soft edges
- ✦ Low contrast (when there's not much difference between the lightest and darkest shades)
- ✦ Pleasant colors, such as green or blue
- ✦ Muted colors, such as grays and browns
- ✦ Large areas of color

Successful foreground objects in an image benefit from the opposite techniques:

- ✦ Middle shades of light and dark
- ✦ Shades opposite the background — dark for light backgrounds, light for dark backgrounds
- ✦ Hard colors
- ✦ Hard edges
- ✦ Hard contrast
- ✦ Irritating colors, such as neons or pink
- ✦ Edgy colors, such as reds and yellows
- ✦ Small areas of color

Some of the more sophisticated image editing programs, such as Photoshop and Painter, allow you to work with layers as you create your image. You can create the background in one layer, and the foreground in one or more layers on top of that. You can then adjust the appearance of both background and foreground to get the right balance between them.

Someone needs to say something about the modern trend toward backgrounds that confuse, overload, and dazzle the viewer. I'm talking about the sort of wild-eyed design you see in magazines like *Wired*. Is there really that much of a difference in the sensibility of the new generation, or is this just a fad that will fade as fast as the Peter Max illustrations of the 60s? It can't fade fast enough for me! If you like wild-eyed graphic design, and you can explain yourself clearly on the subject, please send mail to me in care of Mr. Author (ronw@mmadweb.com) because I am truly curious. The best answers will show up on the web site for this book.

Form follows function

Web graphics have a job to do. They must get a message across, identify a hyperlink, help the user to navigate to another web page, and so on. Web graphics are blue-collar images. The job comes first. Or, as Frank Lloyd Wright put it, form follows function.

Figure 8-21 shows an example of a web graphic that manages to do its job while still managing to be interesting. The graphic is from a Microsoft web page (the Site Builder Workshop, shown in Figure 8-22). The graphic, a hand holding out a key, also contains the text shown below it in Figure 8-22. Together, text and graphic convey the intended message: Become a member. The hand is open to an extraordinary degree so that it appears as inviting as possible. The key is a traditional key, to stir nostalgia and work on the subconscious. The soft edge of the graphic is part of the inviting, come-hither design philosophy behind the image. This simple graphic is actually very sophisticated, working at many levels to do its job.

Members Only

Figure 8-21: An illustration that straddles both sides of the form/function fence.

Text is a common element of web page graphics because often a graphic alone can't do the job. There are only so many universal icons out there. Most icons and buttons need a text label of some sort to make it clear what they do.

Figure 8-22 shows graphics that serve as buttons. By far the majority of graphics on the Web serve as some kind of button. The graphic either looks like a button or icon, or it is larger but still functions as a button. Whether a graphic looks like a button or not — and the trend is definitely away from literal buttons — the graphic will usually serve as a link to another web page.

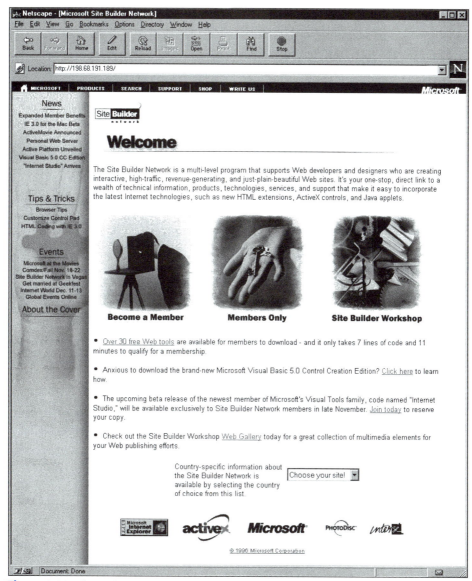

Figure 8-22: The web page containing the graphic from Figure 8-21.

Reprinted by permission from Microsoft Corporation.

However, there is still a place for a graphic that is just a graphic. One of the most common uses for such graphics is for company logos or the main illustration on a page. Figure 8-23 shows a nonlinked image from the home page of Number Nine Visual Technology. The page is a deliberately retro-looking affair (see Figure 8-24), and the cube fits the look of the overall page. However, there is no link to the cube; it's just there to anchor the page. The buttons floating around the cube are the hotspots. The cube, the buttons, and the text are all part of a single image with a transparent background.

Figure 8-23: A simple cube graphic.

Tip

Many main illustrations are actually image maps that can link to different web pages depending on what portion of the image is clicked. See Chapter 15 for information about creating and using image maps.

Putting Graphics Together

The purpose of good design at the level of the individual graphic is to create a well-designed web page. The whole idea of designing a web *page* seems to be a bit new, as any review of the pages out there on the Web will show. There are two reasons for this, and both reasons are beginning to go away.

The first reason: HTML, the language for constructing web pages, hasn't been sophisticated enough to support great page designs. While it has been possible to create a great web page with a great deal of effort, that's just too hard for the average person. HTML is evolving, however, and becoming a more powerful tool. Add to this the increasing sophistication of web page editors such as FrontPage and PageMill, and the days of average pages are nearly over.

The second reason: Most web pages have been amateur efforts. The number of pages created by paid staff is increasing, however.

Figure 8-24: The page that contains the image shown in Figure 8-23.

With more time available to create pages, and with better tools to work with, the level of web page design is advancing rapidly. In Chapter 1, I showed you the kinds of web pages you will find on the Net, and pointed out some of the basic elements you will find on most web pages. In this section, you'll see how to design three different kinds of web pages:

✦ Home page

✦ Detail page

✦ Feedback page

Each of these pages has a different function, and makes different demands on the page designer.

Tip

If the mass of web pages is moving from great individual graphics to great web pages, the cutting edge of web design is design of complete sites. This integrates the design of all web pages on a site. See Chapter 18 to learn how to design a complete site.

I always start the design of a page with pencil and paper. If other people are involved in the design, sit down with them and hack out the overall page design. Things to take into account are:

✦ The function of the page (to sell a product, convey an idea, entertain, and so on)

✦ Where the page fits into the overall site

✦ Common elements this page will share with other pages, such as navigation bars

✦ Links for the page

✦ Graphics needed for the page

✦ How to fit all of this onto the page for easy use by a visitor

All three of the following sample sites are actually fairly simple visually, but in two cases I had to use tricks to force the browser to arrange the page properly. All three pages are in the tutorial material you copied from the CD-ROM to your hard drive at the beginning of this chapter.

Home page

The first page is a home page for the Noodle Schmoodle company. The company makes noodles. They are famous for their slogan, shown below in the page requirements.

Page requirements

This page is the showcase page for the company's web site. It's important to have Wow! graphics and a clean design that reflect the company's down-home advertising.

Page function	Sell the company image ("We're the best darn noodle maker on the planet") and provide links to other company pages.
Page fit	Primary page for the site.
Common elements	Left-side navigation bar, large version of company logo.
Links	Links to main site pages: noodle manufacturing, how to identify a quality noodle, ordering noodles, noodle technical support. Also contains links for noodle chat and feedback.
Graphics	Logo, navigation bar, and one for each of the main links.

Page design

Figure 8-25 shows a paper sketch that lays out a page that meets the basic requirements. The next task is to create the individual graphics. That are true to the existing designs for Noodle Schmoodle ads, yet work properly on a web page.

Figure 8-25: The layout for the Noodle Schmoodle web page.

Figure 8-26 shows the completed page. The graphics were created with CorelDRAW, and you can learn how to create some of these graphics in the Victor Vector: CorelDRAW 7 tutorial in Chapter 12.

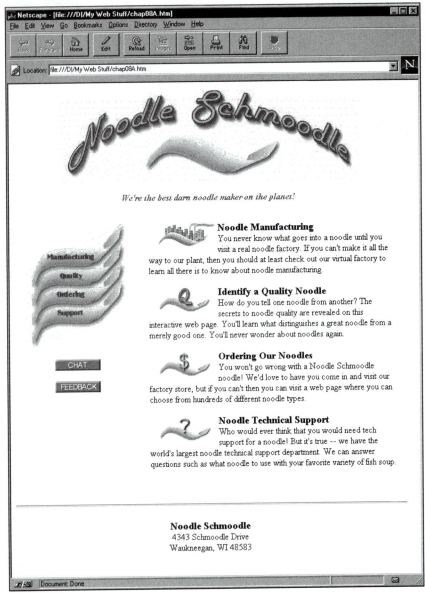

Figure 8-26: The complete Noodle Schmoodle page.

You can view this page as part of the tutorial files you copied at the beginning of the chapter. Double-click the files \My Web Stuff\Chap08\chap08A.htm and \My Web Stuff\Chap08\chap08B.htm to see two versions of the page.

Detail page

This page illustrates the details of a room in the Howard House bed and breakfast, a fine and expensive B&B on the shores of Lake Superior.

Page requirements

The house's classic features are to be reflected in the design of the page. The owner has requested that you use a diagonal layout similar to the brochure that the B&B has been using for seven years. You advise the owner that this is a more complex layout and will cost more, but the owner doesn't care; he wants what he wants. You sigh and sketch out a sample page.

Page function	Show the Howard House's Bergmann Room to be a classy room well worth its extravagant price.
Page fit	This is one of seven room pages on the site.
Common elements	The Howard House logo.
Links	Back to home page. The owner plans to have a map of all of the rooms made up at a later date, which you would implement as an image map (see Chapter 15).
Graphics	Logo, four photos of room details.

Page design

Figure 8-27 shows a paper sketch that lays out a page that meets the basic requirements. The owner has photographs of the room, and if they are good enough you can use them. If not, the next task is to get photographs that will look good at a small size on the web page.

Figure 8-27: A sketch of the detail page for the Howard House web page.

Figure 8-28 shows the completed page. The graphics are simple photographs of the room. I had thought to apply some enhancements with Auto F/X and Photoshop, but the images were too small to do this effectively. (See Chapter 3 for details on Auto F/X.)

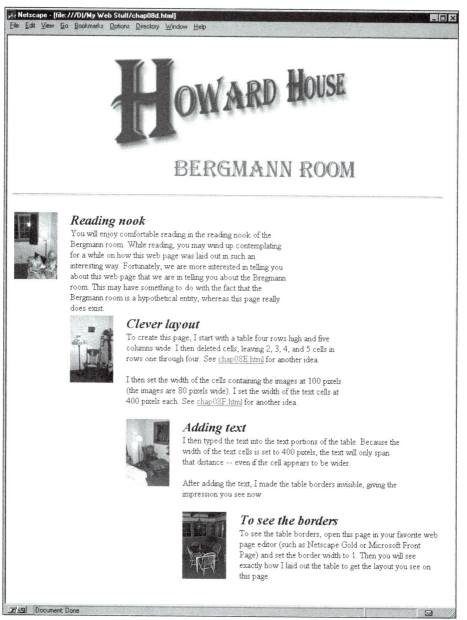

You can view this page as part of the tutorial files you copied at the beginning of the chapter. Double-click the file `\My Web Stuff\Chap08\chap08D.htm` or `\My Web Stuff\Chap08\chap08E.htm` to see one of two versions of the page. You'll find links to a third version as well, `\My Web Stuff\Chap08\chap08F.htm`.

Feedback page

This page for the Kute and Kudley Toy Bear Company provides an opportunity for visitors to provide feedback to the company.

Page requirements

Kute and Kudley needs a page so that visitors to the web site can provide feedback about three key issues: the company's toys, the company's web site, and reactions to the company catalog. The company has a webmaster who can write CGI (Common Gateway Interface) scripts to process form data, so that page is a form. Being a thoughtful webmaster, she wants a link for visitors who may prefer to send detailed e-mail messages.

Page function	Provides a form for user feedback on key issues.
Page fit	Only feedback page on the web site; covers three topics.
Common elements	Company logo, background image.
Links	Link to home page and buttons to send and reset form data.
Graphics	Logo, background, cute icon for feedback page top. Icon is larger version of button visitor clicked to get to feedback page.

Page design

Figure 8-29 shows a paper sketch that lays out a page that meets the basic requirements.

Figure 8-29: Sketch for the Kute and Kudley site.

Figure 8-30 shows the completed page. The images were created in Fractal Design Painter.

Figure 8-30: The completed Kute and Kudley site.

You can view this page as part of the tutorial files you copied at the beginning of the chapter. Double-click the file `\My Web Stuff\Chap08\chap08C.htm` to see a page similar to the one in Figure 8-30.

For more information about page and site design, visit Chapter 18.

Web Tour #8: Sophisticated Graphic Design on the Web

The graphics you've seen here are just the tip of the iceberg. You can further whet your appetite by visiting some of my favorite web sites to see not only some Wow! graphics, but also some Wow! pages.

To get started on the web tour, double-click the CD-ROM file:

`\WebTour\Chapter8\index.htm`

You'll see the web page for this chapter. Click the Web Tour icon to get started.

Music, let's start at the very beginning: the dough it takes to put those dear graphics on a web page. And the winner is…

A Film-to-Digital Bargain

If you already have a camera (and if you don't, pick up one of those $10 instant cardboard cameras — about which, more later), you have nearly everything you need to create digital images. You can take your film to just about any photo shop and say the magic words:

"Put these on a PhotoCD, please."

If you live in a large city, and happen to have gone to a photo shop that has its own PhotoCD setup (less than likely, but possible for the persistent), you can get your PhotoCD back in a day or even less — but expect to pay more for shorter turnaround times. If you live in a small city (or, like me, in a not-city), then you might have to wait a week or so while your film makes a cross-country journey to the nearest PhotoCD center and back.

However you manage it, expect to pay from $.25 to $1.00 for each image that you convert to PhotoCD. If you convert a whole roll of film at the same time it is developed, expect to pay less per image. If you hand over negatives and only want certain ones put on PhotoCD, expect to may more per image. Figure 9-1 shows a sample PhotoCD image. In my experience, the quality of the images is always extremely good — usually better than you could do yourself.

Figure 9-1: A sample PhotoCD image.

The advantages of PhotoCD are

+ More or less permanent storage for your photographs, which are available for digital use at a moment's notice

+ Stored in multiple formats, from wallet-sized to nearly-poster-sized

+ Convenient storage medium for photos — line up those jewel cases on your bookcase shelf

+ You can find the photo you want at a glance using the images on the cover of the CD-ROM jewel case

+ You can add additional rolls of film to that PhotoCD until it is filled

+ Image quality on PhotoCD is actually quite high, and almost always better than what you can get from an affordable scanner

The disadvantages of PhotoCD are

+ That week of waiting, in most cases

+ No prints unless you pay extra for them

+ It's hard to put a PhotoCD disc in your wallet

Does PhotoCD make sense for you? It does if you are patient about getting your pictures back, if you don't need pictures in your wallet (what are those wallet-sized PhotoCD images for, then?) and if you will need a limited number of images converted to PhotoCD.

If you pay $.35 per image, and need 100 images converted to PhotoCD, that's a cost of $35. A hand-held scanner costs $100 or more, so you just saved yourself some money. To find the nearest location for on-site creation of PhotoCDs, visit Kodak's web page at `http://www.kodak.com/digitalImaging/piwSites/piwSites.shtml` (see Figure 9-2). When I searched for the state of Washington, for example, I found two on-site PhotoCD providers. Both are located in the state's largest city, Seattle.

Some mail-order photo processing services also offer digital images on floppy, but this is not the same as PhotoCD! The image quality is less, but it may be more than suitable for web pages. Magazines such as *Peterson's* and *Popular Photography* have numerous ads near the back of the magazine for such processing.

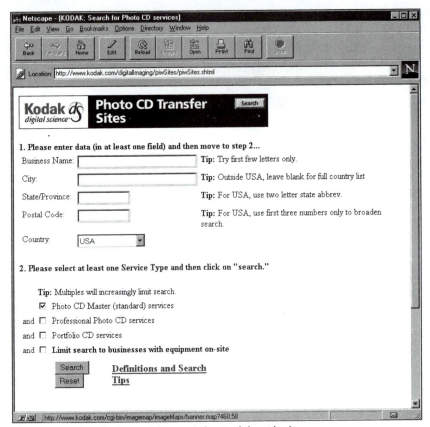

Figure 9-2: Virtual picture-taking on the Kodak web site.
Copyright©Eastman Kodak.

On the other hand, if you need more control over the process, if you need the images *now,* if you don't need the high quality of PhotoCD images, or if you have thousands of images, a scanner of some kind is probably a more useful choice for you. Not, of course, a . . .

Hand Scanner

Hand scanners are rapidly becoming the dinosaurs of the scanning world, and I'm not going to waste a lot of space on them. A hand scanner is a scanner that you hold in your hand. Okay, don't yell — I know that's obvious. It's also the whole problem with hand scanners. A little demonstration will show why.

Pick up a pencil. Grab a sheet of paper. Now draw a perfectly straight line.

It wasn't very straight, was it? Of course not. Hands are great for petting cats or picking fresh strawberries, but not for drawing straight lines. If you want straight lines, use a ruler and a pencil. If you want good scans, use a scanner that can shoot straight. That would be a . . .

Photo Scanner

Photo scanners are cute and they work. You stick a photograph in at one end, the scanner digests it, and a digital image shows up on your computer screen. Which leads to the primary point in favor of the new breed of photo scanners: They are easy to use.

The kind folks at Eastman Kodak Company sent me a Snapshot Photo Scanner 1 (see Figure 9-3). It took me less than ten minutes to

✦ Connect the cute little beast to the parallel port of my computer

✦ Connect my printer to the pass-through port on the scanner's cable

✦ Install the software

✦ Scan my first image

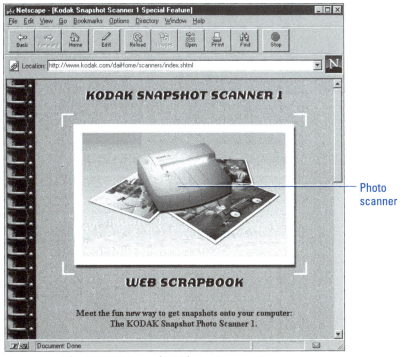

Figure 9-3: The KODAK Snapshot Photo Scanner 1.
Copyright©Eastman Kodak.

I've tested probably close to 1,000 different products over the last five years, and the Photo Scanner 1 is in the top ten, among the very easiest products I've ever installed (see the "Kodak Photo Scanner 1 Features" sidebar). The quality of the image scans is also very good. Figure 9-4 shows my son Justen all done up for Halloween.

Figure 9-4: A sample image scanned by the Kodak Photo Scanner 1.

This isn't the only Kodak product that I cover in this chapter; there are several others. All of them get great reviews — they install easily, they work well, and are generally user friendly. This suggests a trend, and I'm always glad to see a particular company whose products stand out for quality, reliability, and features. This bodes well for Kodak in the digital age. Heck, even their digital photography web site is cooler than cool. Check it out at `http://www.kodak.com/ digitalImaging/digitalImaging.shtml`.

For a look at how easily you can scan with the Photo Scanner 1 (and to see a completely humiliating picture of Mr. Author), see the section "Scanning with GOO," later in this chapter.

Kodak Photo Scanner 1 Features

Zoom Lens: 3:1 power zoom with a focal length of 37mm to 111mm.

Software: PHOTOENHANCER Special Fun Edition Software from PICTUREWORKS, KAI'S POWER GOO Software from METATOOLS, EASYPHOTO Software from STORM TECHNOLOGIES, TWAIN-compliant Software from Kodak

Resolution: Scans 800 x 1200 pixels from a 4" x 6" print, with up to 2.75 MB file size

Color: 24-bit, millions of colors

Scan Size: Up to 4" x 11.5" panoramic prints, including the new ADVANTIX Prints from Kodak

Scan and Display: Less than 30 seconds (based on a 4" x 6" print)

File Formats: BMP, TIFF, and JPEG

Optics: 8-bit A/D linear CCD with cold cathode mercury fluorescent lamp/square pixels

Interface: Parallel port cable (with pass-through port)

Photo scanners are inexpensive and work well, but if you need to scan larger images, get your hands on a . . .

Flatbed Scanner

If hand scanners are for the birds, and photo scanners are for small photographs, flatbed scanners are for anyone who is serious about scanning. You can scan lots of things: stamps, photos of all sizes, documents, cloth for textured backgrounds on web pages, and so on. I have used a Hewlett-Packard ScanJet III for years, and it has been completely reliable. It also makes great scans.

The ScanJet III is a flatbed scanner. It has a glass bed on which you lay the material you want to scan. For example, I took a stuffed animal that my dog, Picard (a Yorkshire Terrier) likes to chew on, and put it on the glass bed. Why a stuffed animal? I thought the fur might make a nice background texture for the collection of textures on the CD-ROM for this book.

I started up the DeskScan software that comes with the scanner (see Figure 9-5) using Photoshop's Import ∣ Twain_32 menu selection, and let the scanner do its job. It may not look like much, but later (in Chapter 17) you'll see how to transform this type of scan into a background texture in the form of a repeating tile.

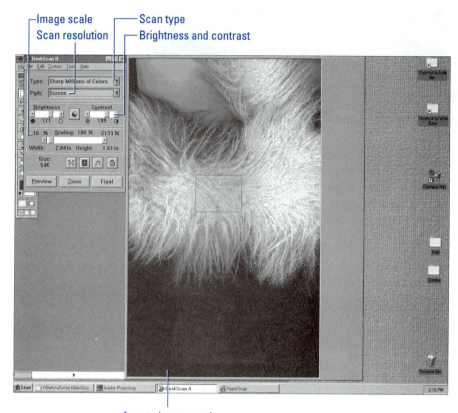

Figure 9-5: A typical example of scanning software.

The software automatically transferred the image to Photoshop (Figure 9-6), where I could make any necessary adjustments.

The result is shown in Figure 9-7. Okay; so I had a little fun in Photoshop.

That's really all there is to using a scanner. Oh, I suppose you can make major decisions like what size to make the image, or at what level of detail to do your scan, but that's easy, too. If you are serious about digitizing photographs, a flatbed scanner is an excellent choice. The HP ScanJets are time-tested units that are reliable and do a great job.

The main point to make about flatbed scanners is that they are easy to use. Probably the best news is that flatbed scanners, which only a year ago were going for more than $1,000, have dropped dramatically in price. You can get an excellent unit for less than $500. With little photo scanners (4 × 6-inch max) priced at $200, the flatbeds (8 × 14-inch max) are getting to be a very good deal.

Photoshop tools   Scanned image

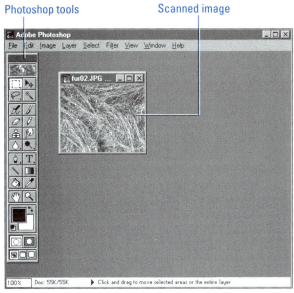

Figure 9-6: A scanned image in Photoshop.

Figure 9-7: A bit of fur, good for a textured background.

For flat-out, top-notch image quality, consider a . . .

Slide Scanner

You can also purchase scanners that will scan a slide or a negative and generate a digital image file. Nikon and Polaroid are the two primary manufacturers of such devices. Slide scanners are much more expensive than photo or flatbed scanners, and are useful only in extremely high-volume applications. If you are interested in more information about slide scanners, the Web Tour at the end of this chapter contains links to sites that provide details on these devices.

And now you can slide right into the Great Controversy of . . .

Digital Cameras Versus Cardboard Cameras

From everything I'd read before I sat down to write this section, I had a preconceived notion about digital cameras: cost too much, deliver too little. Most surveys compared the digital cameras to those little cardboard cameras ($10), and declared the cardboard cameras as the winner in image quality.

After all, you can get about 100 of those little cardboard cameras for the price of one digital camera ($1,000, give or take $500). Oops: I almost forgot. There's an extra $300 to $500 for additional memory so you can take more than 5–10 pictures with that digital camera.

Worse, if you want a digital camera that will do as well as an honest-to-goodness 35mm camera (around $300–700), then you'd better be prepared for a shock. Such a digital camera is going to set you back somewhere between $10,000 and $30,000. And it's probably going to have a hard drive, so get out the wrist exercisers.

Kodak DC50 Zoom Digital Camera Features

Zoom Lens: 3:1 power zoom with a focal length of 37mm to 111mm.

Flash: Three modes: automatic, on, or off. Up to a 14' range.

Sliding cover: Slide cover doubles as a power switch. Open it and the camera is ready to take pictures.

Viewfinder: Zooming optical viewfinder.

Timer LED: 10 or 20 second delay timer built in.

Multi-AF Photometric: The DC50 zoom camera automatically focuses from 0.7 m to infinity in normal mode, and from 0.5 m to infinity in Macro.

AE Photometric: In automatic mode, the light sensor measures the amount of flash you need.

Serial Port: Connects to your PC or Macintosh; cables included.

Viewfinder frame: The viewfinder has easy-to-see framing and target marks for the three different auto-focus settings:
Distance to infinity: Use the full frame and solid target mark to frame the shot.
Closer distances to 2.3 feet (70 cm): The frame marks are 85% of full frame.
Close-up: The frame marks are 60% of full frame.

PCMCIA Card slot: The DC50 zoom camera has optional removable memory, making your PCMCIA card your digital "roll of film." A 4MB card can hold from 28 to 88 images depending on the resolution quality you select for the pictures you're taking. There is also an internal 1MB memory that holds up to 22 "good," 11 "better," and 7 "best" quality pictures for up to 1 year.

Tripod socket: Mount your DC50 zoom camera on a standard tripod for steady, hands-free picture taking.

But we're talking about web pages; you can forget about a need for the high-end digital cameras. You can spend anywhere from $500 to $1,000 to get a usable digital camera for web page images. The reason: You're locked into using small graphics for the Web. What's the use of a gorgeous 10MB digital image file if what you need is a 30K highly compressed image file?

Never one to shoot down a product I hadn't even tried, I asked the folks at Eastman Kodak to send me one of their DC50 digital cameras. It's priced at the top end of the consumer market — around $900 street price as I write this. Unlike cheaper digital cameras, it has a zoom feature, a nice little LCD screen for status info, built-in flash, the ability to expand memory with PCMCIA memory cards, and more (see the sidebar, "Kodak DC50 Zoom Digital Camera Features"). And it takes great pictures (see Figure 9-8).

Figure 9-8: An image of my wife, Donna, taken with the Kodak digital camera.

When the camera arrived, I was underwhelmed. I had been expecting something glitzy and glorious, but the DC50 (see Figure 9-9) was a very workmanlike gray. It's smaller than a video camera, larger than a point-and-shoot camera, and fits comfortably in my hand. I turned it on, took a picture, walked over to the computer, downloaded the picture, used the PhotoImpact JPEG SmartSaver to minimize file size, and in minutes I had pictures of my daughter and my wife's dog for my web page (see Figure 9-10). I used PhotoImpact to get file sizes down to about 5K for JPEG file format for these pictures — the perfect size for a web page.

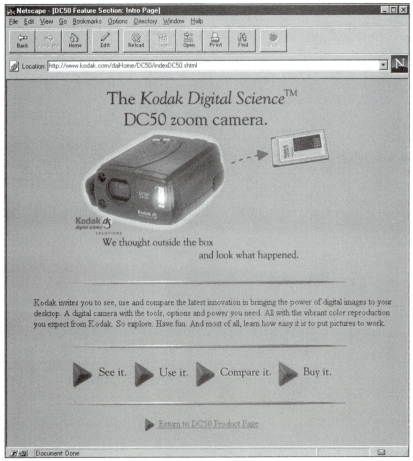

Figure 9-9: The KODAK DIGITAL SCIENCE DC50 Camera.
Copyright©Eastman Kodak.

Girl   Dog

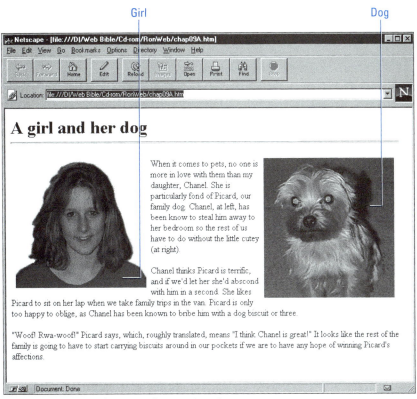

Figure 9-10: From dog to web page in minutes.

Hey, I thought: this is cool!

Now, I'm hooked. So what if I can get a better picture with a cardboard camera? Don't I need a scanner (can you say $200 to $1,000) to digitize it? Or I could wait a week to get the PhotoCD back (very inexpensive, however). But there is something to be said for instant gratification: from idea to web page in minutes. Don't you dare try to take my digital camera away!

Visit Kodak's web page at `http://www.kodak.com/daiHome/DC50/useIt.shtml` for an interactive session with the DC50 (see Figure 9-11). If the page is gone by the time you get there, you'll just have to take my gushing appreciation for the camera as your incentive to try it at a local camera store.

Click here to take a picture

Here's your chance to actually take some pictures with the KODAK DIGITAL SCIENCE(tm) DC50 zoom camera. As you will see, the 3x zoom feature allows you to frame just the shot you want without having to fiddle with changing lenses.

Just select the zoom level you want, then click on the "Take Picture" button and see the amazing clarity of color from Kodak coupled with the versatility of zoom.

1x ○ 2x ○ 3x ○

Take Picture.

Figure 9-11: Virtual picture-taking on the Kodak web site.

The DC50 isn't the only winner in this category. On the inexpensive side (around $400 street price as I write) is the Epson PhotoPC; it delivers the image quality of cameras costing $100–200 more. The Canon PowerShot 600 is also an excellent performer, and will satisfy your needs for web-level quality, and perhaps a bit beyond.

One of the diskettes that came with the unit Kodak sent to me for review was partially unreadable, so I needed to contact Kodak's technical support for assistance. I even made it a bit hard on the poor fellow who took my call. I started out by telling him that my software for the camera wasn't running properly. He asked all the right questions, figured out what the problem was, and took care of me in a very professional manner. We all know that poor service can ruin the out-of-box experience of new hardware, but Kodak took care of me and I always like that in a company. It makes for a sweet, long-lasting relationship that satisfies everyone.

See the tutorial near the end of this chapter to learn how to work with a digital camera.

If you already own a video camera, you can get very close to the convenience of a digital camera with a clever and relatively inexpensive device. It's called...

Snappy

It's a cool name, and it's a cool product: a palm-sized box that captures video images and stores them on your hard disk. I'm not the first to make this discovery, but if by some means you've managed to miss the myriad of positive reviews for the Snappy, allow me to introduce you to the neatest electronic toy since Pong. It doesn't look like much (see Figure 9-12), but a Snappy delivers a heck of a great-looking image.

Connect to parallel port   Video in and video thru

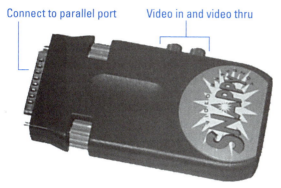

Figure 9-12: The Snappy.

For a list of many Snappy-related links (and tons of sample images), visit `http://www.pproducts.com/snlinx.html`. Or try the Snappy captures at the world-famous turtle cam, at `http://campusware.com/turtles`. You'll find all kinds of Snappy fanatics on the Web. The reason: It's easy to use, and delivers excellent video capture images.

To capture an image with Snappy, simply connect it to the parallel port of your computer, connect a video source to the Snappy, and start up the Snappy software. The Snappy does not have a pass-through feature for your printer. The most effective way to use the Snappy is with a data switch that provides one input (from your computer) and two outputs (one for Snappy, one for your printer). You can switch from printer to Snappy and back again easily this way. I was also able to connect the cable for the Kodak Photo Scanner 1 to the printer port, and then connect the Snappy to the pass-through connector for the Photo Scanner 1. I got excellent results with this setup, although it still left the printer out of the picture.

Leave the puns to me, sonny, or you'll get yourself into a heap of trouble.

Cool video images can find their way to your web site as easily as . . .

Capturing with Snappy

Tutorial

Download: Sorry, but there is simply no way to demo hardware! You can, however, visit the product information web site (`http://www.play.com`) where you can do everything but hold Snappy in your hands. To run this tutorial, you have to get your hands on a real Snappy.

Level: Easy as Pie

Task: Capture a video image to disk

Before you start: You must have the Snappy connected to your parallel port, and a video source (TV, VCR, camcorder, and so on) must be connected to the Snappy.

It's easy to use the Snappy, and I'm sure that is part of its charm. Figure 9-13 shows the Snappy software window. It's mostly splash and dash; a few buttons at the far left actually do something —a reasonable interface design when your product is very easy to use. The functions of the buttons are

Snap   Captures the current video frame into a window

Preview   Displays a small version of the incoming video signal, at about one frame per second

Adjust   Adjusts the captured picture (brightness, color, and so on)

Save   Saves the captured image to disk

Print   Prints the captured image

Setup   Sets up Snappy defaults

Help   Opens the help file (as if you'll need it!)

1. Double-click the Snappy software (Start | Snappy | Snappy) to run the program (see Figure 9-13).

2. Click the Snap button, and watch with delight as the row of buttons at the top of the screen flash red, yellow, and green. The captured image will fill your screen (with a black border if your screen size is larger than the capture size).

3. Click the image to continue. You'll return to the Snappy window, with the captured image sitting politely (and probably expectantly, for it will need some fine-tuning) in the background.

Cut the sarcasm, Sonny; it doesn't suit you. But the point is well made: Video images vary in color, brightness, and so on. You can get a much more useful image if you take the time to correct flaws.

Figure 9-13: The Snappy window.

4. Click the Adjust button to open the window shown in Figure 9-14. The captured image is shown as a small image in a little TV screen, and the adjustment controls are at the far right.

5. Move the little sliders left and right until the image looks good.

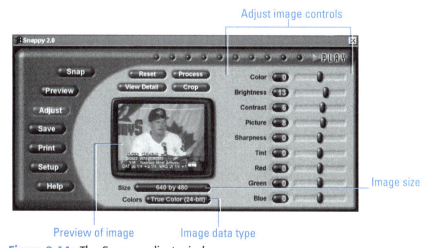

Figure 9-14: The Snappy adjust window.

The adjustments shown in Figure 9-14 are typical: Leave the color alone (the Snappy captures color accurately), increase the brightness and picture controls, and beef up the contrast a bit. You can select the image size and color depth by using settings located below the little TV screen. If you want to view the fine details of the image, click the View Detail button (located above the TV screen). Don't worry about getting the image perfect, as you can easily fine-tune the image at real size by using image-editing software.

6. To save the image to disk, click the Save button.

7. If you want to use the preview window, click on the Preview button to display it (see Figure 9-15).

Figure 9-15: The Snappy Preview window.

Setup options, shown in Figure 9-16, allow you to change the type of video source, adjust picture quality for moving or still scenes, save images in color or black and white, and so on. You can save settings so they will apply to all future sessions. That's all there is to image capturing with Snappy.

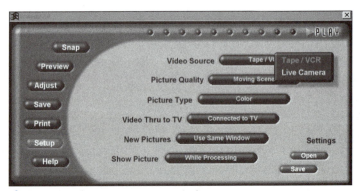

Figure 9-16: The Snappy Setup window.

Play, Inc., the folks who make Snappy, announced a new version of the Snappy software just as we were going to press. Figure 9-17 shows the appearance of the new software in Adjust mode. The changes are not as dramatic as they look; they are mostly cosmetic. I guess that proves the old adage: Don't mess with a winner.

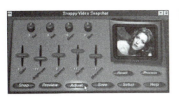

Figure 9-17: The Snappy Adjust window in version 2.0 of the software.

Snappy is great, but it only captures still images. It more or less lets you use your video camera as a digital still camera. It's better, actually, because you can store images on video tape cheaply and effectively — for much less than the cost of the flash memory used in many digital cameras. To top it off, the resolution of your Snappy images will be much better than the images you get with most of the digital cameras under $1,000. No wonder the Snappy, at less than $200, is such a big hit.

If you want to provide actual moving video footage on your web site, you are going to need a . . .

Motion-Video Capture Card

If graphics in general lead to large file sizes and slow downloads, video clips take things to another level. Video files can be huge. When you consider that a web graphic of 30K is considered large, and that video clips tend to take up 300K, 1MB, or more, you can understand why video clips are not common on the Web.

If you want to capture your own video, your primary concern will be which of the many video cards to purchase. The most recent generation of video capture cards finally makes use of the PCI bus for fast, efficient capturing. The older generation, which relied on the ISA bus, was much more troublesome to use. A rare exception to this was the Intel Smart Video Recorder Pro. Although an ISA card (and therefore inherently limited in speed and efficiency), the ISVR Pro (as it was affectionately known) was a real winner — heck I still use one in my Pentium. If you can get a good deal on an ISVR Pro, grab it.

If you want something from the new generation, Intel's entry is again one of the best. Like the ISVR Pro, it installs easily, works reliably, and captures excellent-looking video clips. Expect to pay a few hundred dollars for a quality capture card.

If you want to jump to the head of the class and create MPEG video clips, you are looking at much more expensive hardware. Even the cheapest units are several thousand dollars. The Sigma Designs ReelMagic Producer comes in at just under $2,500, for example.

For graphics purposes, a cordless pen has replaced the puck (see Figure 9-19). Although you can still digitize a drawing, you can also draw original art using the tablet.

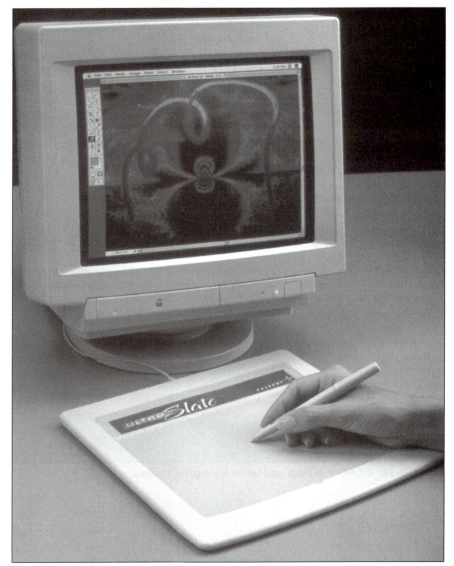

Figure 9-19: A typical pen and tablet combination, from CalComp.

The "pen" doesn't write anything on the tablet; the drawing appears on your computer screen in whatever image-editing software you use. Most tablets include a plastic layer; you can slip a drawing under the plastic and trace it with the pen.

The pen/tablet combination also serves as your mouse, so you get a whole new way to relate to your computer. Most tablets let you use both a mouse and a pen, though not both at the same time!

 Truth be told, these tablets are an excellent replacement for the mouse. The pen is so much less stressful to hold — my wrist doesn't give me problems when I use a pen and tablet. With the mouse, my hand aches after a few hours. The more you mouse around, the more you'll appreciate a pen-and-tablet. Gee — who'd have thought I had something nice to say? I'll make up for it, I promise you!

I use a prn-and-tablet for my graphics work. I've even been known to connect the graphics tablet to my laptop and take it along when I get out to draw for fun. As you'll see later in this chapter, combining a graphic tablet with software such as Fractal Design Painter can be a blast. My technical editor is a fan of Art Pad 2 by Watcom, similar in features and price to the Calcomp tablet.

If drawing your images seems a bit too much, create each artwork by . . .

Scanning with GOO

Tutorial

Download: I'd sure like to have provided a sample scanner with the book but space did not permit that. You can, however, visit the product information web site at `http://www.kodak.com`. If and when you get yourself one of these cute little scanners, you can step through the tutorial and have some fun. In the meantime, the tutorial will give you an idea of what it's like to work with the unit.

Level: Easy

Task: Scan a photo and make a mockery of it

Before you start:

✦ You must have the Photo Scanner 1 connected to your parallel port, and have a photo handy to feed it.

✦ You must also have Kai's Power GOO installed if you want to get into the mockery part. You can scan photos with other small-format scanners, but the software interface will be different from what's shown here.

Caution!

Warning: you are about to enter the Fun Zone. Please leave your sense of caution, but do bring along your willingness to be amazed. It's time for GOO.

One piece of software that is bundled with the Kodak Photo Scanner 1 is Kai's Power GOO. This is software that can best be compared to that staple of kindergarten known as finger painting.

The opening screen for GOO suggests that you are about to have a good time; it's got a definite sense of humor (see Figure 9-20). As if to remind you that whatever else you had in mind for your computer is meaningless, GOO fills your screen with black and centers it's own tools on that screen. You are now in the Fun Zone; there is no turning back.

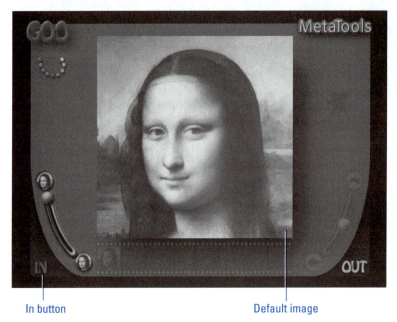

In button   Default image

Figure 9-20: The GOO opening screen.

1. To scan an image into GOO, click the IN hotspot at the lower left of the GOO screen (refer to Figure 9-21).

This displays your choices for obtaining images to work with (see Figure 9-21). Your choices include:

Get Image from Library	Load an image from the built-in library of fun faces.
Get Image from File	Open a graphic file; most popular formats are supported.
Get Goo from File	Get the Goo instructions (that's the finger-painting stuff you will see shortly) from an existing file.
Get Image from Digital Camera	Run the acquisition software for the Kodak DC20 digital camera (if you just happen to have one).

Get Image from Snapshot Scanner   Run the acquisition software for the Snapshot Scanner.

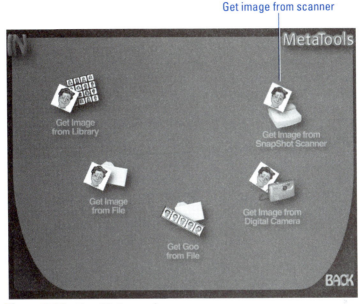

Figure 9-21: The GOO opening screen.

2. Click the top right button to run the software for the Kodak Photo Scanner 1. This displays the scanner software on top of the Goo screen (see Figure 9-22). You can choose Expert mode, or step-by-step mode. For this example, I will use the Expert mode.

3. After you click the Expert button, the window shown in Figure 9-22 appears.

Figure 9-22: Running the scanner software.

Expert Schmexpert! Who thought this stuff up? There isn't much difference between these two modes. So choose Expert and get flattered by whoever designed this software.

If you do not have a photo set up to feed into the scanner, you will see the preview window shown at the top left in Figure 9-23.

Preview area   Rotate button

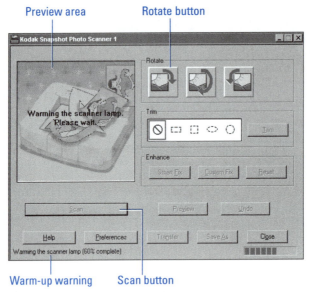

Warm-up warning   Scan button

Figure 9-23: The scanner window.

The preview window demonstrates that you should turn your photos face down to feed them into the scanner. To get clear colors, you must wait a few seconds while the scanner warms up its light. This is annoying, but lamp warm-up is a good idea. Even expensive scanners incorporate lamp warm-up. By allowing the lamp time to stabilize, you get more accurate color in your scan. When the lamp is warm, the message disappears from the preview screen, and the status line tells you to click the Scan button.

See what I mean? They call this Expert mode? Phooey! Even I could use this software.

During scanning, the image appears in the preview window. The scanner can handle up to a standard 4×6 photo, or any of the new Advantix formats (portrait, landscape, and panoramic). If the photo appears sideways in the preview window (as shown in Figure 9-24), you can click one of the rotate buttons to correct it.

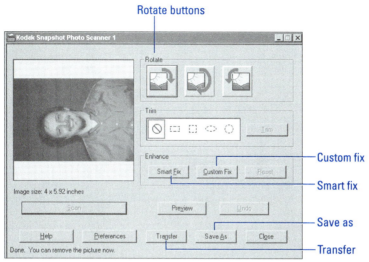

Figure 9-24: Scanning is complete.

You can adjust the brightness, contrast, saturation, and colors of the scanned photo manually or automatically.

4. To adjust manually, click the Custom Fix button, which displays two versions of your scan — before and after (see Figure 9-25).

5. Use the tabs at the upper right to select brightness/contrast, colors, or saturation; adjust the sliders until the image appears the way you want it.

   Most of the time, the Smart Fix button does a great job, and it's faster and easier than manual adjustments.

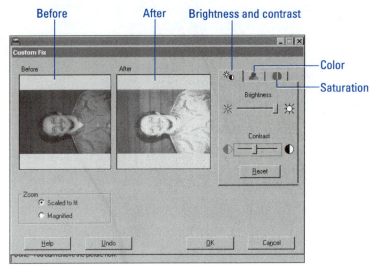

Figure 9-25: Adjusting the image manually.

You can either save the file to disk, or transfer it to the program that started up the scanning software (in this case, that would be GOO). Figure 9-26 shows the image rotated to the upright position.

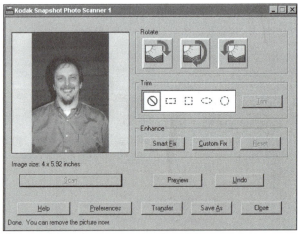

Figure 9-26: The image rotated upright.

6. Click the Transfer button to transfer the image to GOO (see Figure 9-27).

Beads

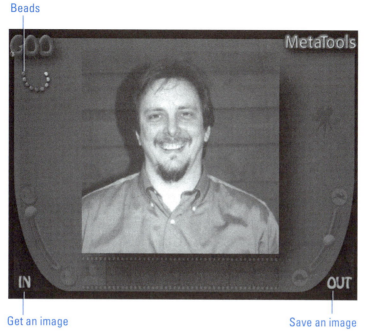

Get an image   Save an image

Figure 9-27: The image in GOO.

7. You can click and drag the image to see what GOO can do, but first click that chain of beads at the upper left, the GOO tools and controls(see Figure 9-28).

Figure 9-28: The GOO tools.

8. To activate a tool, just click it. (To deactivate a tool you click it again.) The tool changes to a highlight (see Figure 9-29) to indicate that it is active.

9. To hide the tools, click the chain of beads again.

Tip

The tool shown in Figure 9-29 is the Mirror Toggle. When this is on, any tool that you use is applied to the left and right halves of the image at the same time. This is ideal when you are working with a face-on image that is perfectly centered. If the image is off center (as in this example), do not use mirroring or you will create a mess! If you don't like your Goo, click the UnGoo tool (top right in Figure 9-28) to wipe it all away and start over.

Highlight

Figure 9-29: A GOO tool shown in unused mode (left) and highlighted (right).

Now for the fun!

10. If you followed my advice and scanned in an image of a person (in this case, it will be Mr. Author himself who will be made to look foolish), try clicking at one corner of the mouth and dragging a little outward.

11. Repeat this for the other corner of the mouth. Figure 9-30 shows the result for yours truly.

Figure 9-30: Mr. Author's smile begins to grow.

But let's face it: GOO is not about moderation. Go for it!

12. Drag those mouth corners way out!

13. Click on the eyebrows and drag up! Do it!

Figure 9-31 shows what GOO is all about: making people look silly. Isn't this fun? But wait — there's more!

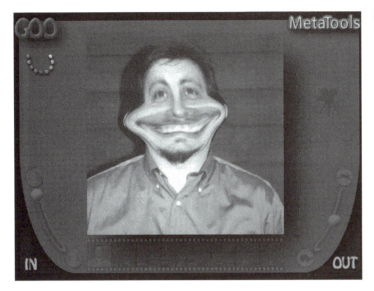

Figure 9-31: Now we're talking some serious GOO!

14. Drag out the cheek areas to widen the face, and then make those eyes as big as you can. Figure 9-32 shows the result.

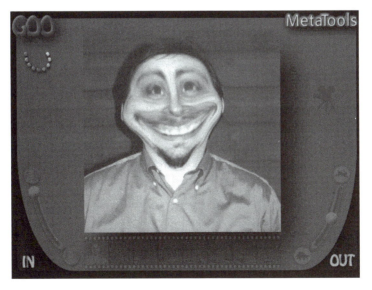

Figure 9-32: The author appears to have a fat head.

Cute, yes, but we're not done yet.

15. Drag out the neck area, and open up that chest.

Figure 9-33 shows me transformed into something just this side of Roger Rabbit. I haven't looked this good since I graduated from high school.

I suppose that you could create somewhat more subtle effects with GOO, but that's not my style.

 Harumph; Mr. Author couldn't do something subtle if he had to. Tell you what — you can certainly do better than Mr. Cretin. Why not e-mail Mr. Bigshot Author your best GOO examples so he can add them to a web page that I will insist he set aside just for this purpose? Send your best GOO examples as attachments to e-mail at goo@mmad.com.

Thanks, Unc; just what I needed — competition!

Ooh...sexy!

Figure 9-33: Give me a BIG smile!

16. To save your work, click the OUT hotspot at the lower right of the GOO screen. This displays your options for output:

Save Goovie Animation   Saves a special GOO animation file that you can only view in GOO.

Save Goovie with Image   Saves the animation and the GOO image in one file.

Save Image	Saves the image as a conventional graphic file that you can use in other applications (such as web pages, for one example).
Export AVI Animation	Saves the animation in a video for Windows format that you can play outside of GOO.
Print Image	Just what it says: prints the image to your printer.

If there is software that is cooler than GOO, I want to know what it is. In the meantime, I'm facing a serious GOO addiction. If you see this book in print, then you know I conquered my addiction and found enough time to continue writing.

If working with GOO is like fingerpainting, then the opposite would be . . .

Digital Photography

Download: Digital cameras are surprisingly easy to use. The quality level isn't there at the low end of the price scale, but the fun quotient is right up there. Visit the product web site at `http://www.kodak.com`.

Tutorial   **Level:** Easy

Task: Download a digital photo and save it to disk

Before you start:

   ◆ You must have the DC50 camera connected to a serial port, and have a photo or two sitting in the camera.

   ◆ Kodak's PhotoEnhancer software must also be installed.

The Kodak DC50 digital camera is very easy to use. As far as taking pictures is concerned, if you can think in terms of a camcorder, you have most of the skills you need to use a digital camera. The zoom controls are located at a handy point for your fingers, just like on most camcorders. The shutter button is near the zoom buttons, and works easily. The only thing missing is the click.

Before you go raving about this digital photography thing one more time, I have a complaint. That missing click — it's a mistake to leave out the click. And this is not just my curmudgeonly side looking for something to carp about. Digital cameras in general tend to have this annoying pause between the time you press the shutter button, and the time when the picture is actually taken. A little click would let you know when the shot is in the can. I hate standing there, with things blinking in my eye, wondering whether or not the durn picture got taken!

The camera fits easily into one hand. It has a handy strap that gives you a firm grip on the camera — just like a camcorder. The built-in flash works automatically. There is a small LCD on the back of the camera where you can change settings, switch to macro mode for close-ups (as close as 19 inches, but parallax will bite you every time, as with most cameras that do not use through-the-lens viewing).

Once you have taken all of your pictures, you can connect the camera to the serial port of your computer and run the PhotoEnhancer software (see Figure 9-34). Use the Camera ⏐ View Slides in Camera menu selection and the software will connect to the camera and download thumbnails of the images in the camera. You can choose to download all of them, or just a range of images.

The slides are displayed in a window. If, as shown in Figure 9-35, you happen to have used a vertical format, the images will be displayed sideways. This isn't a big deal for processing, as there is a tool built into the software for rotating images.

The number of images you see depends on the number of images you have taken with the camera. This in turn is controlled by how you have set up the camera. With the built-in memory (1MB), you can take 7 high-quality images, 11 medium-quality images, or 22 low-quality images. For most uses, the high-quality setting is more or less essential. All of the examples in this chapter use the high-quality setting unless otherwise indicated. All images are 756×504 pixels, but the lower-quality images are fuzzier than the higher-quality images. Figures 9-36, 9-37 and 9-38 show three images of my son Justen taken at the various levels of quality for comparison. The inset images are enlarged two times to show details more clearly.

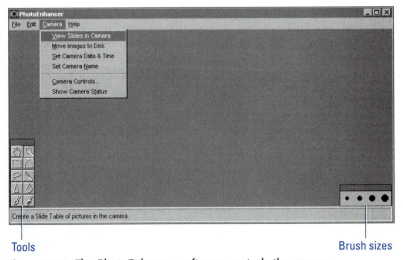

Tools   Brush sizes

Figure 9-34: The PhotoEnhancer software controls the camera.

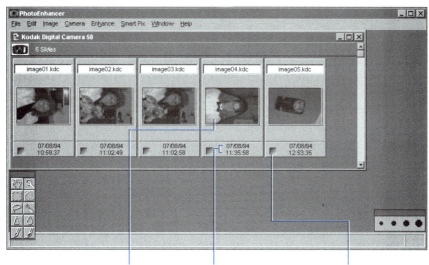

Figure 9-35: Viewing image thumbnails.

Figure 9-36: A high-quality image.

Figure 9-37: A medium-quality image.

Figure 9-38: A low-quality image.

If you want to take a larger number of high-quality pictures, use a PCMCIA memory card. The card is inserted into the bottom of the camera. You can copy images from the camera to a memory card. A 5MB memory card holds 35 high-quality images, 52 medium-quality images, and 90 low-quality images. A 40MB memory

Tip

card holds 280 high-quality images, 416 medium-quality images, and 720 low-quality images. That's a lot of images!

To see a complete image instead of a thumbnail, double-click the thumbnail. It takes a few seconds for the image to download from the camera, and then it appears in a window (see Figure 9-39). I used the Image | Rotate | 90 Degrees Left menu selection to orient the image correctly (Figure 9-40).

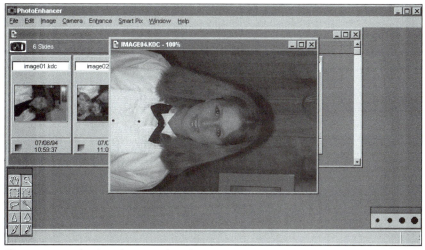

Figure 9-39: Viewing the complete image.

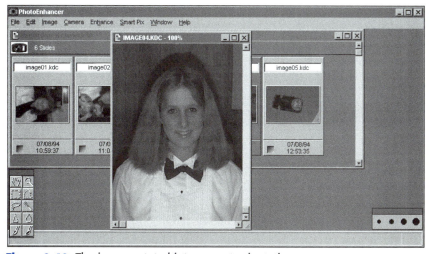

Figure 9-40: The image rotated into correct orientation.

I found that, in general, the images were a little on the dark side. The camera has a built-in exposure compensation setting that will lighten or darken all photos. If you do get a photo that is too dark or too light, you can adjust it using controls built into PhotoEnhancer. I applied the Smart Pix | Inside | Better filter to the image of my daughter Chanel (Figure 9-41) and the result was excellent (Figure 9-42). You can combine filters, or undo a filter that doesn't suit your needs, and this allows you to get a satisfactory result from just about any image.

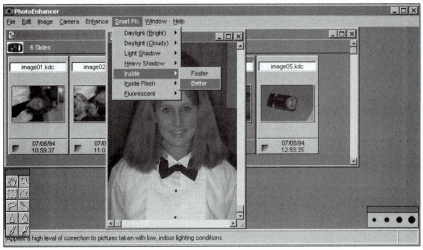

Figure 9-41: Applying a filter.

Figure 9-42: The image after filtering.

In this case, I saved my daughter's image to a file and loaded the file into Kai's Power GOO (see an earlier section of this chapter). The result is shown in Figure 9-43.

Figure 9-43: This is my daughter?!

So far I've talked about digital image acquisition. You can draw on your inner artist by . . .

Creating Images with a Graphic Tablet

Tutorial

Download: This tutorial involves some heavy hitters. The software part, Fractal Design Painter, is the easy part. It's the hardware — a graphic tablet — that you won't find in this book. Check out the software at http://www.fractal.com, and the hardware at http://www.calcomp.com.

Level: Intermediate and artsy

Task: Use a graphic tablet and Painter to create art

Before you start: You must have Fractal Design Painter installed, and a graphics tablet connected to your computer with its drivers installed.

In my original notes for this tutorial, I jotted down the phrase "free your inner artist." That's a pretty ambitious statement for a computer book, but it's absolutely true. The combination of sophisticated hardware and software can give the artist in you a chance to shine. By using the pen and tablet, you can work much more carefully than you can with a mouse. Trying to draw with a mouse is like trying to drive a car with your elbows on the gas and brakes, and your feet on the steering wheel.

Figure 9-44 shows the opening window for Fractal Design Painter. An image window is open at the upper left, and the various Painter panels are arranged at the right and bottom. These are only a few of the many, many tools and control panels that Painter offers. It's just not possible to show you everything this software can do; there's too much available.

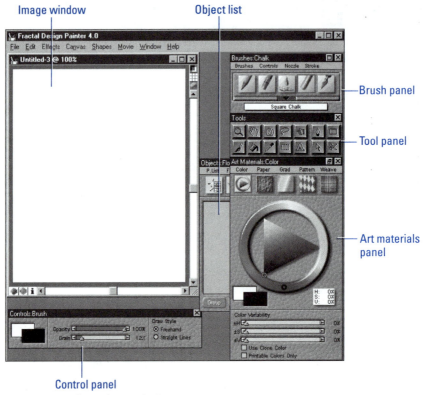

Figure 9-44: The Painter window.

For this exercise, I decided to draw a walrus. I had a nice sketch of a walrus handy (see Figure 9-45). I placed the sketch under the plastic cover of a Calcomp DrawingSlate II graphic tablet. My plan was to use the pencil sketch as a guide for a digital drawing using the tablet. You can use any image you like for this tutorial.

Figure 9-45: A sketch of a walrus.

The tablet I used for this tutorial measured 6" × 9". I've used larger tablets and smaller tablets, and this tablet size is ideal for web-sized images. A larger tablet takes up too much desk space, while a smaller tablet doesn't offer enough control while drawing.

Tip

I wanted more than just a sketch of a walrus; I wanted something that had color and background.

1. Begin the drawing by selecting the Gritty Charcoal tool, and then enlarging the brush. You must always click the Build button when changing brush settings. What is remarkable about selecting a brush, and setting its size? The other options available, that's what! Each of the visible settings — Gritty Charcoal brush, Cover method, and Grainy Soft Cover subcategory — is one out of many available. There are many other brush settings available — size variability, size stepping, squeeze factor, angle, and so on. This is why

Painter can be overwhelming at first — there are so many choices that you can't keep track of them all. Over time, as you use Painter's features, you begin to grasp more and more possibilities. Painter is a tool that rewards the large investment of time required to learn it.

2. With the larger Gritty Charcoal tool, and a light blue color selected, sketch in a rough sky (see Figure 9-46).

Figure 9-46: Sketching a sky.

3. Select a watercolor brush, and set it for Spatter brush, Wet method, and Grainy Wet Abrasive subcategory.

4. Chose a bright green color to suggest foliage. (Yes, they do have plants in the far north in the summertime!) I wiggled the pen to get the effect shown in Figure 9-47.

Figure 9-47: Adding a foreground. This wasn't quite what I wanted.

5. Open the Brush Looks panel and choose a Sponge look (see Figure 9-48).

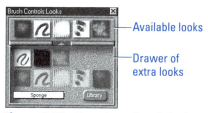

Figure 9-48: Choosing a brush look.

6. Apply three different shades of green with the sponge (see Figure 9-49).

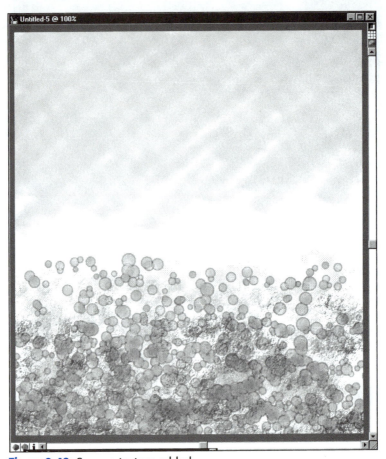

Figure 9-49: Sponge texture added.

7. Change the color to black; choose the Pen and Ink brush with default settings.

8. Trace the image. (As I traced somewhat haphazardly over the sketch that I had placed on the tablet, Painter put the "ink" on the "page." Figure 9-50 shows the result of this operation.)

Figure 9-50: The drawing of the walrus.

I had thought the drawing might look good with the sky and green stuff showing through the walrus drawing, but I was wrong. I needed to clear out the blue and green paint from the walrus outline.

9. Use the Edit | Magic Wand menu selection to open the dialog box shown in Figure 9-51. It looks strange and intimidating, but it's actually easy to use.

Figure 9-51: The Magic Wand dialog box.

10. While this dialog box is displayed, drag the cursor around in the part of the image that you want to select. All similar colors within that region get selected, as shown in Figure 9-52.

This is much easier than it sounds, and very intuitive once you get the hang of it. The area shown in red (the right-hand tooth) in Figure 9-52 is the area selected for this example.

Magic Wand selection

Figure 9-52: A portion of the image selected by waving the Magic Wand.

12. Once the portion of the image you want to fill is selected (in my case, the walrus's tusk), use the Effects | Fill menu selection to open the dialog box shown in Figure 9-53.

13. Set the current color to white, verify that the Fill With selection is set to Current Color, and click OK.

This fills the area with white; my walrus begins to emerge from the background (see Figure 9-54).

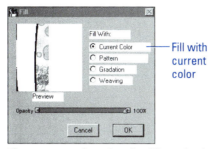

Fill with current color

Figure 9-53: Choosing the fill method.

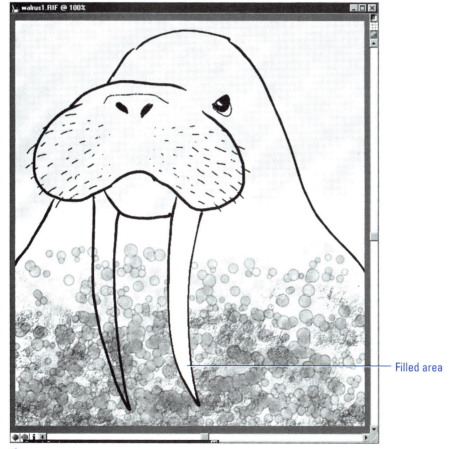

Filled area

Figure 9-54: The tusk is filled with white.

I continued to use the Magic Wand to select other areas of the drawing, and then filled each area with white. Figure 9-55 shows the result.

Filled area

Figure 9-55: The walrus now stands out neatly from the background.

14. Use the Magic Wand one more time to select the entire image (I selected the walrus, minus the tusks) and set the color (I used a suitable walrussy brown).

15. Use an enlarged charcoal brush to fill in the image (see Figure 9-56).

I used a smaller brush on my walrus and a darker brown to add some shadows in appropriate areas, such as the side of the head and under the tusks.

Figure 9-56: The nearly complete walrus.

For a final touch, I used the Magic Wand to select each of the tusks, and filled them with a gradient (see Figure 9-57).

Figure 9-57: The final result.

 Oh, aren't we the artist! I'll get you a beret for your birthday, Mr. Author. Actually, I think I like that marble texture for the walrus. It's not really a walrussy texture, but it's artsy. Now get back to work.

It would have been a nightmare to create such a complex drawing without the Calcomp graphic tablet. For serious artwork on the computer, you can't beat a good tablet and pen. This makes a nice conclusion for this chapter on hardware, because it shows an excellent example of how digital hardware can enhance, rather than substitute for, human creativity. If you need more information about all this hardware, take . . .

Web Tour #9: Web Sites for Cool Tools

The hardware described in this chapter — and many other items, too — are well represented on the Web. To visit web sites that describe this stuff, or offer examples of what you can create, or that I added just because I had a good reason to, double-click this file:

```
\WebTour\Chapter9\index.htm
```

You'll see the web page for this chapter. Click the Web Tour icon and you will see a list of sites that provide information about graphics hardware of various kinds.

Graphic Details

Publishing Strategies

To prepare for this chapter's tutorials, copy the following folder from the CD-ROM to the `\My Web Stuff` folder on your hard drive:

    \tutorial\chap10

This will copy files and folders for all of the tutorials in this chapter to your hard disk. See Chapter 1 for complete details on setting up for tutorials.

Most web pages start out on a hard drive on a desktop computer. Even if the computer has a modem, no one can see the web page unless someone copies the page to a *web server*. Web servers are otherwise perfectly ordinary computers that are physically connected to the Internet. This process of copying a web page (and any associated graphics or other files) to a web server is called web publishing.

Publishing Explained

There are things that the world has clearly needed at various times in history: a chicken in every pot, a good ten-cent cigar, an affordable cup of coffee. What the world really needs right now, if not sooner, is a standard method for publishing web pages. Every ISP (Internet Service Provider) establishes its own rules and procedures for publishing on the Web. As if that news wasn't bad enough, most web page editors have their own procedures for web publishing.

This double whammy means that I cannot simply jot down a list of steps that you can follow to publish your web pages.

Instead, I'm going to demonstrate several real-world publishing examples. Chances are that when you publish your web pages you'll find a situation that is at least similar to one of the examples in this chapter.

There are three basic methods for publishing your web pages:

♦ Using tools supplied by your ISP (or webmaster if an intranet is involved)

♦ Using tools built into a web page editor

♦ Using a general tool that you purchase specifically for web publishing

ISP-supplied publishing tools

If your ISP is a nationwide service, such as CompuServe or America Online, you can download tools for publishing your web pages. CompuServe supplies the Publishing Wizard, shown in Figure 10-1. It comes with a Home Page Wizard, which is a web page editor designed for creating personal web pages. The Publishing Wizard is required to upload web pages to CompuServe's Our World. You can visit Our World at `http://ourworld.compuserve.com`. The Home Page Wizard is not generally satisfactory for business web pages or web sites, but you can use other web page editors to create your web pages and then use the Publishing Wizard to upload the files to your Our World web site. CompuServe offers a selection of compatible editors on the Web at `http://ourworld.compuserve.com/ourworld/tools/authortools.html`.

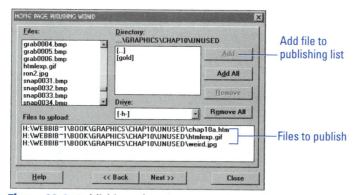

Figure 10-1: Publishing a home page on CompuServe.

CompuServe supplies only a small amount of space on its web server for your files. The Our World service is designed primarily for small, personal web pages. You would not have enough room for a large web site.

Caution!

The steps for uploading your files to CompuServe with the Publishing Wizard are:

1. Run the Publishing Wizard, and indicate whether you want to upload files, or delete existing files.

2. Provide personal information – name, address, interests.

3. Indicate which files you want to upload.

4. Specify which file is the default (home page) file.

5. Specify your CompuServe ID and password.

6. Publishing Wizard uploads your files to your web site.

The web site URL will have the form

where *yourname* is the name of the folder that contains your home page.

America Online (AOL) offers two methods for publishing your web pages: Personal Publisher and FTP. Personal Publisher is a point-and-click interface for creating very simple home pages. Figure 10-2 shows some of the steps you would use to create a web page with Personal Publisher. Figure 10-3 shows a page created with Personal Publisher. As you can see, it's extremely limited as a graphic design!

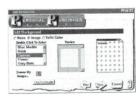

Figure 10-2: Creating a home page on AOL.

Figure 10-3: An AOL home page created with Personal Publisher.

Web sites uploaded with Personal Publisher have URLs with the form

```
http:// members.aol.com/<screen name>
```

Tip Yes, this means that everyone in your household (up to five different screen names) can have their own AOL web page. You will need to log in under the appropriate screen name, however, before you create each home page with Personal Publisher.

You can also create your web page using your own tools, and then upload it to AOL using FTP (File Transfer Protocol). This is the only way to upload a custom web page (or collection of pages and images, up to 2MB) to AOL's members area. Figure 10-4 shows where you start; use the keyword FTP to locate this tool. Click the GoTo FTP button at the lower right to display the list of FTP options, shown in Figure 10-5. Highlight the choice members.aol.com, and click the Connect button.

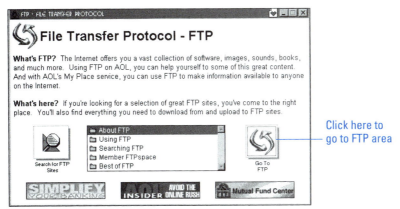

Click here to
go to FTP area

Figure 10-4: The FTP area of AOL.

AOL members' area

Figure 10-5: Choosing FTP options.

This displays the dialog box shown in Figure 10-6. You may not see any files listed, depending on whether you have previously created an AOL home page. I created a home page with Personal Publisher, and that is why there is an index.html file present. The images for that file are in the private directory. The exact list you see will depend on what files and directories are present.

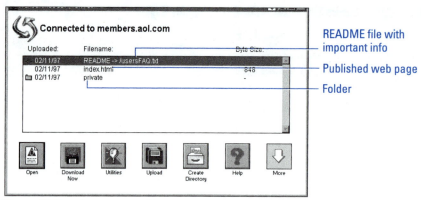

Figure 10-6: A home page directory on AOL.

You can get complete information about AOL's support for FTP by reading the file usersFAQ.txt (refer to Figure 10-6). Highlight this file and click the View button to read its contents.

The buttons at the bottom of the dialog box in Figure 10-6 control what you can do. From left to right:

Open	Open the file and view it.
Download Now	Download the file to your local hard disk.
Utilities	Access FTP utilities supplied by AOL.
Upload	Upload a file from your local hard disk.
Create Directory	Create a new directory.
Help	Get helpful information about FTP.
More	Display more files, if any.

To copy HTML pages and images for a web page to AOL, click the Upload button, identify the file(s) to upload, and click OK. The files will be copied into your user directory, and can be accessed at the appropriate URL. For example, if I create a directory called biz, containing a home page called index.htm, then the URL would be

```
http://members.aol.com/ronwodaski/biz/index.htm.
```

This gives you complete freedom to create and upload web pages and associated files, up to the limit of 2MB.

Web page editors that have publishing tools

Many web page editors come with built-in publishing tools. I'll show you several detailed examples of how to publish web pages using such tools. Examples of editors that come with tools include these:

✦ **Netscape Navigator Gold.** This is a basic web page editor, suitable for small web sites or single home pages. There are no web site management tools included, and web publishing is limited to publishing everything to one directory on the web server.

✦ **Microsoft FrontPage 97.** This is a powerful web page editor and site management tool. You can view your site graphically, and you can upload to a large number of directories on the server if necessary.

✦ **Net Object Fusion.** This editor is similar in scope to FrontPage 97. Templates are more tightly integrated into the software, but this can limit flexibility for the more adventurous web site designer.

You will see detailed examples of how to publish with these tools later in this chapter. Most web page editors do not come with publishing tools, and you will need to use a general-purpose tool such as FTP (File Transfer Protocol) to upload your files to the web server.

General-purpose publishing tools

There are a number of shareware and commercial products that use FTP to copy your files to a web server. The one that I like the best (and I'm not alone!) is called WS FTP Pro. You can download a shareware version of WS FTP Pro from `http://www.ipswitch.com`.

WS FTP Pro is the full-featured version of the program. A limited-edition version, WS FTP LE, is also available. The Pro version features drag-and-drop copy of files to and from the web server, and is an extremely flexible and reliable tool for copying pages to the web. However, the LE version is free for government employees, educators, and students. Visit `http://www.ipswitch.com` for more information about the LE version, and to see if you qualify for a free copy.

For my own purposes, I use WS FTP Pro for general web page publishing, with one exception: If I create a web site with FrontPage 97, I almost always use FrontPage 97 as my publishing tool; it's adept at managing large web sites with many pages. I have included detailed information about WS FTP Pro later in this chapter.

Servers and the Graphic Facts of Life

Although there is a great deal of variation in the specifics of web publishing, there are also some common factors that you should be aware of. The basic life cycle of a web site works like this:

1. Design the site.

2. Create the site on a local computer.

3. Publish the site to a web server.

4. Make revisions to the site on the local computer.

5. Publish revisions to the web server.

6. Repeat steps 4 and 5 until hell freezes over.

Before you publish your web pages, it is very important to make sure that the folder/directory structure you are using makes sense for the site. You can find details of how to organize a web site in Chapter 18. Essentially, the larger the site, the more important it is to organize your files — web pages, images, multimedia files, scripts, and so on — with some kind of structure.

The key point about structure is that you must use the same structure on the local computer as you will use on the web server. For example, if your images are all located in a folder called `img` on your local computer, then they must also reside in a folder/directory of the identical name on the web server.

Tip

Identical means exactly what it says. If the folder name is in lower case on the local computer, it must be in lower case on the web server, too. Not all servers are case-sensitive about folder and file names, however. If the server has naming restrictions, however — such as no spaces in folder or file names — then follow the same rules on the local computer. If I had a nickel for every time I solved a problem by removing spaces from filenames on a UNIX server, I could retire!

If all you need to retire is some nickels, I've got a pocket full of change I'm willing to contribute. As for failing to use legal filenames on the web server, it is one of the most common sources of trouble. Before you even start to create your web site, ask yourself some simple questions: What special characters, such as periods and underscores, are permitted on the server? How long can a filename be on the server? The more you know, the greater the chances that your web site will work properly after you publish it — or my name isn't Gustav Webb.

And I'll take it one step further than *that*. Your web pages may have hidden time bombs in them. There are plenty of Windows programs, in particular, that don't give a hoot about the need for case sensitivity in web filenames. For example, many image editors will apply an uppercase extension to your images. This often happens even if you type in a lowercase extension! For example, if you type in a filename as

```
myfile.gif
```

there is a good chance that the image editor will actually save the file as

```
myfile.GIF
```

Later, when you add the image to a web page, guess what gets stored in your web page? The HTML code will probably look like this:

```
<IMG SRC="myfile.GIF">
```

If your publishing tool preserves the case of filenames, you may not even notice that this has happened. However, many publishing tools allow you to enforce all-lowercase filenames, and that can cause problems if you are not aware of this tendency to create uppercase extensions.

The tools you use for editing images and web pages, and for publishing them afterwards, should be considered suspect in relation to file naming until proven reliable. Make some tests to determine how the various programs you use handle filenames. Check the documentation and/or help files carefully to determine whether there are controls for enforcing the case of filenames. Be sure to then run some tests to confirm proper operation of this feature.

Graphic strategies

Most users connect to the Internet using modems. Most of today's modems are operating at 28.8K or 33.6K bits per second. In reality, many users will actually connect at somewhat lower speeds because of line noise or other problems. In addition, the Internet itself adds a considerable amount of delay, further slowing down transmissions. At best, visitors to your page will receive data at around 3,500 bits per second, and usually at much slower speeds.

If there are graphics on your web pages, it is very important that the file sizes of those graphics be as small as is practical. (See Chapter 12 for important information about controlling the file size of your graphics.) The smaller your graphic files, the faster they will download, and the faster your web pages will display.

The best tools for visualizing the effect of smaller file sizes are the GIF and JPEG SmartSavers from Ulead. The best tools for optimizing file size are HVS Color and HVS JPEG from Digital Frontiers. See Chapters 12 and 14 for details.

ISP publishing requirements

Every ISP determines its own rules for uploading web pages, there is only one way to determine what those rules are. Any decent ISP has a web page somewhere on its web site that explains what you must do to upload your web pages.

If the ISP's web site has a search engine, you can usually find what you need by using PUBLISH as a keyword for the search. If there is no search engine, you may be able to find the information tucked away in the FAQ (Frequently Asked Questions) section of the web site.

If information is brief or lacking, I recommend that you attempt to connect to the web site using one of the FTP publishing tools, such as WS FTP LE or WS FTP Pro. As long as you can supply the path to the location of your web site, WS FTP Pro can usually figure out how to establish communication on its own. In most circumstances, if you know the path, your login name, and your password, the software will figure out the rest.

If you find yourself unable to locate publishing requirements on the ISP's web site, and you can't use WS FTP Pro to make the connection and do the publishing, you have a choice to make. You can either ask your ISP for the information, or find a new ISP that provides the info you need.

If you find yourself shopping around for an ISP, visit my web site at http://www.mmadweb.com/bible/isp.htm to find out which ISPs regularly receive good ratings from me, subscribers, and the press.

Help yourself

In addition to the physical requirements of publishing — that is, copying your web site's files from your local computer to a web server — there are some practical things you can do to enhance your web site's effectiveness:

✦ Check your links. Either manually test every link on your site, or use the tools built into your web page editor. FrontPage has a particularly good tool for testing the links in your site; it will report any broken links.

✦ Check your graphics. Make sure that every graphic on every page actually appears on the page when viewed in a browser.

✦ Check your layout. Load your pages into various browsers and confirm that the page displays properly. You will find problems in the pages as well as problems in the browsers, and sometimes it's hard to tell which is which. When in doubt, revise your page so it displays in the most important browsers: Netscape Navigator and Microsoft Internet Explorer. Don't forget to check using older versions of these browsers!

Tip

Your ISP may be able to tell you which browsers folks are using to visit your site. Such information, when available, appears in the daily, weekly, or monthly logs that your ISP provides. If your ISP doesn't provide such logs, ask for them — you should be getting them if you are paying for your web site! You can also write Perl scripts that detect the user's browser type.

✦ To let folks know about your web page, visit the web site at `http://www.submit-it.com/` and provide information about your web site for the various search engines.

One-Button Publishing with Navigator Gold

Tutorial

Download: Navigator Gold from the Netscape web pages at `http://www.netscape.com`. Look for the Download Now icon near the top of the web page.

Level: Deceptively Easy

Task: Publish a web page with Navigator Gold

Before you start:

✦ Install the trial version of Navigator Gold.

✦ Open the file `\tutorial\chap10\gold\chap10e.htm` in Navigator Gold.

✦ Click the Edit button to change to Edit mode.

Figure 10-7 shows what the open file looks like in Navigator Gold 3.0. The web page contains three images (one is hidden at the bottom of the page, but if you have the file open you can page down and have a peek at it).

Publish menu selection

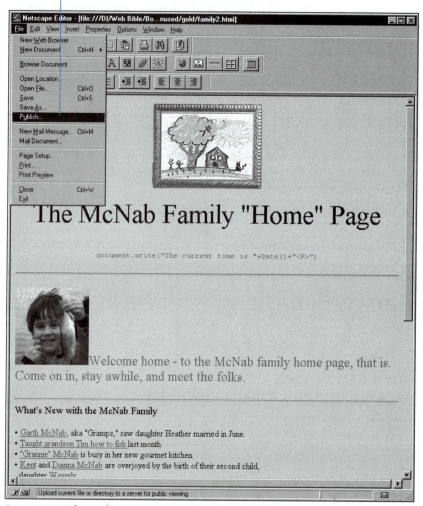

Figure 10-7: The web page you are about to publish.

1. To publish the page, click the File | Publish menu selection. This opens the dialog box shown in Figure 10-8.

There are two radio buttons at the top of the dialog box. "Images in the document" will publish the web page and the image files referenced in the page. "All files in document's folder" will publish every file in the same folder as the web page. In addition, there is a list of files.

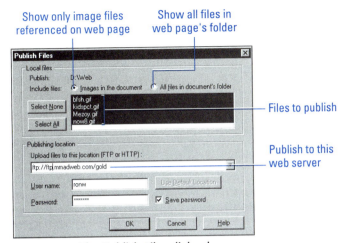

Figure 10-8: The Publish Files dialog box.

2. Click individual files to determine what gets published.

3. Specify the location to publish to in the box labeled Upload files to this location (FTP or HTTP).

What you put in this box depends on your ISP's requirements. My ISP requires that files get uploaded using the FTP protocol, and the location is based on my virtual domain name (http://www.mmadweb.com). The location I specified was:

```
ftp://ftp.mmadweb.com/gold
```

Note that the FTP domain name is just a variation of the HTTP (HyperText Transfer Protocol) domain name. The /gold directory is there because I wanted to keep these files separate from my home page files in the root directory.

Virtual domains are simply URLs that do not have their own physical web server. A server can host dozens, even hundreds, of virtual domain names. This is an economical way of obtaining a custom domain name of your very own. Some ISPs offer virtual domains, and some do not.

Uploading via FTP almost always requires a user name and password. These are normally the same user name and password you use to log in to your server to establish dial-up connections.

4. If you want to avoid entering your password every time, click to check the Save password check box in the Publish dialog box.

Caution!

If you do elect to save the password, anyone who has access to your computer will also have access to your web site. They will not need a password to publish files to your web site!

The exact location to publish to will vary from one ISP to another, and it also will vary depending on whether or not you have a virtual domain name. If your home page URL contains the domain name of your ISP, then you are not publishing to a virtual domain. For example, if your home page URL looks like this

```
http://www.somecompany.com/~myname
```

then you do not have a virtual domain. If your home page URL looks like this:

```
http://www.myname.com
```

then you do have a virtual domain, and you will probably publish using a location like the one in Figure 10-8.

Tip

Some virtual domains are not located on a separate web server, but share that server with other virtual domains. In such cases, you may not be able to use the virtual domain name with Navigator Gold. Instead, your ISP will provide you with the actual path to your files on the server. Figure 10-9 shows such a path for my virtual domain.

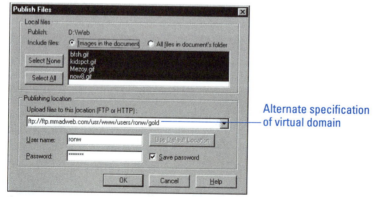

Alternate specification of virtual domain

Figure 10-9: An alternative location for a virtual domain.

5. When are you are sure that you have the correct publishing location, user name, and password entered, click OK to publish (also called uploading).

Caution!

If the location is not specified properly, you will see an error message. Error messages will also appear if the user name or password is incorrect. Your ISP may have FAQ files that will help you figure out exactly how to specify the location for publishing, or you can contact the ISP's phone or e-mail support for assistance. If your ISP supports FTP uploading of files, you should be able to use that information to construct the publishing location for Netscape Gold. You can find an example of such instructions on the web page at `http://support.pair.com/faq/ftp.html`.

During publishing, you will see the name of each file as it is uploaded, along with a running count of files uploaded so far and the total number of files to upload. After the upload is complete, you will see a dialog box telling you how many files were uploaded. The number should match the number you expected to upload.

6. To test the upload, run your browser and enter the URL for the page you uploaded. It will look something like this:

```
http://www.mmadweb.com/gold/chap10e.htm
```

If you cannot see the file at that location, you can use software such as WS FTP Pro for troubleshooting. See the section on WS FTP Pro later in this chapter for ideas.

Idea

Where to go from here:

✦ Create a simple web page with one or two graphics and try uploading it with Netscape Gold.

✦ The primary limitation of Netscape Gold is that it expects to upload all files into a single directory. You can overcome this by using a directory name as part of the publishing location. Then publish several times, publishing the files for a specific directory during each upload session.

Web-Site Publishing with FrontPage 97

Tutorial

Level: Deceptively Easy

Task: Publish a web page with FrontPage 97

Before you start:

✦ You must have a copy of FrontPage 97 loaded on your computer.

✦ A virtual domain, a complete web site reading for uploading and server extensions, must be installed by your ISP.

FrontPage 97 has very powerful publishing capabilities. Unlike Navigator Gold, FrontPage 97 has options that include Server Extensions that an ISP installs on the web server. If the Server Extensions are installed, you gain an enormous amount of control over publication of your web pages.

The downside is that is really isn't practical to create a FrontPage 97 publishing tutorial. To work a tutorial, you would need a virtual domain, a complete web site ready for uploading, and the Server Extensions installed by your ISP or webmaster. Instead of a traditional tutorial, I will provide a step-by-step description of the FrontPage 97 publishing process. The process isn't very complicated; setting up the process is where you'll find all the complications.

You do not have to have the Server Extensions installed on your web server in order to publish with FrontPage 97. FrontPage comes with a tool called the Personal Web Publisher that is also capable of handling simple publishing tasks. However, if you use the Personal Web Publisher instead of the Server Extensions, you will not be able to use any FrontPage features that rely on the Server Extensions, such as WebBots. WebBots add automatic features to web pages you create with FrontPage 97.

There are two ways you can interact with a web server using FrontPage 97. You can create your web pages locally and then publish them to the web server, or you can edit your files directly on the web server. If you are connecting with a modem, you will usually be better off creating your files locally and then publishing them. If you have a very fast connection to the server, such as ISDN or T1, you can experiment with editing files on the server.

FrontPage 97 consists of two major parts: the Explorer and the Editor. You use the Explorer to see and manage the various parts of your web site — pages, images, and the special components that FrontPage creates. You use the Editor to create or edit a web page.

When you see the word *web* used in a discussion of FrontPage, it means something specific to FrontPage. FrontPage refers to the collection of files you publish to the server as a web. This is distinct from the Web, web pages, and web sites. FrontPage opens webs, saves webs, and publishes webs. Everything associated with your web site is called a web in FrontPage. For example, instead of opening a file or a web site, you open a *web*.

This is, of course, just one more example of Microsoft hubris. It's not bad enough that the world is already confused about the difference between the Web and the Internet, now they have to waste time figuring out the differences among the Web (the World Wide Web), web (the adjective, as in web page or web site), and this amorphous thing-that-FrontPage-calls-a-web. It's enough to make a spider give up spinning.

You can also create sub-webs, for example to add additional features to a web. This allows you to break a large web into smaller chunks for easier management.

1. To open a web that is physically located on a web server, use the File | Open FrontPage Web menu selection in the FrontPage Explorer. This opens the dialog box shown in Figure 10-10.

2. Type the URL of the root directory of the web into the list box at the top of the dialog box, or select from the previously visited web servers by clicking on the little down arrow at the right of the list box.

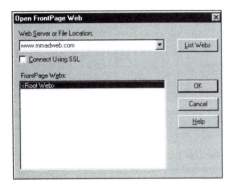

Figure 10-10: Opening an existing FrontPage Web.

3. To view the webs present on the server, click the List Webs button.

4. Click to highlight the web you want to open, and click OK.

In Figure 10-10, there is only one web: the root web. This is the first web that FrontPage creates on a server. You can create sub-webs if you desire. One example would be a sub-web that consists of a group of files and WebBots for a set of discussion pages. You could create the root web first, consisting of a home page and additional files. Then you could create the discussion pages as a sub-web. Breaking up a web site into sub-webs makes it easier to manage the site.

If the existing web is not already a FrontPage web, and if the Server Extensions are installed on the server, FrontPage will read the files on the server and create a FrontPage web automatically. Figure 10-11 shows how FrontPage reads the files on my web site (a virtual domain hosted by Pair Networks). The files are shown in the FrontPage Explorer.

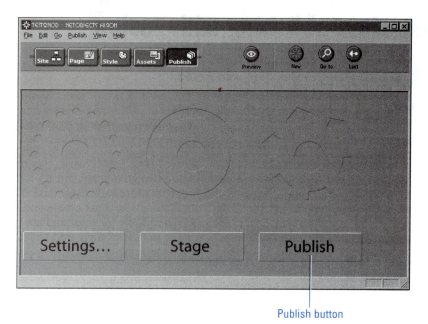

Figure 10-15: Publishing a web site with Fusion.

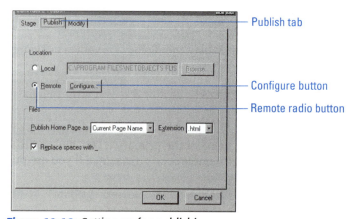

Figure 10-16: Setting up for publishing.

5. Click the Configure button to display YAD (Yet Another Dialog), shown in Figure 10-17.

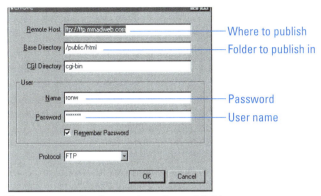

Figure 10-17: Setting options for publishing.

6. Enter the URL of the remote FTP host in the top text box, and the directory (if any) into which the files will be uploaded in the text box labeled Base Directory.

7. If there are any scripts involved in your web site, enter the directory into which the scripts will be uploaded in the CGI Directory text box.

8. Enter the appropriate user name and password for the FTP site, and check the Remember Password check box if you want Fusion to keep track of your password. There is only one protocol supported, FTP, so don't do anything with the Protocol list box.

9. Click OK and then click OK again to return to the dialog box in Figure 10-15.

10. Click the Stage button, and Fusion will gather information about the web site you have created.

11. Then click the Publish button. Fusion will use your modem to connect to the FTP server and upload the files for the web site.

Overall, I found that both Navigator Gold and FrontPage were more flexible in adapting to the difficulties of publishing to FTP servers. If you are unable to publish with Fusion (and in at least one case, that happened to me), check out the next tutorial and try it with an FTP tool like WS FTP Pro.

Publishing with WS FTP Pro

Level: Deceptively Easy

Task: Setting up WS FTP Pro

Tutorial

Before you start: You must have a copy of WS FTP Pro loaded on your computer.

Figure 10-18 shows the WS FTP Pro program in action. There are two panes visible. The left pane displays files on your local computer, and the right pane displays files on the remote web server.

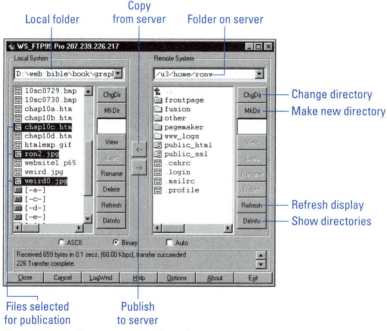

Figure 10-18: The WS FTP Pro interface.

There are three files selected in the left pane of Figure 10-18. You can select files using typical Windows 95 mouse/keystroke combinations. Shift + Click selects all files in a range, and Ctrl + Click selects noncontiguous files. To copy files to the server (also known as uploading or publishing), click the rightward-pointing arrow. To copy files from a server to the local hard disk, click the leftward-pointing arrow.

In addition to file copying, WS FTP Pro allows you to create subdirectories, remove subdirectories, view file contents, rename files, and delete files. You can perform these actions either locally or on the server. You can easily navigate directories on both local and remote machines by double-clicking the directory name. Figure 10-19 shows a different server directory, with the WS FTP Pro window expanded to show additional information about files (date, time, size, and so on.). You can also drag and drop files between windows instead of clicking the left and right arrows.

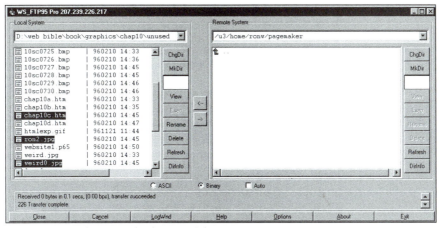

Figure 10-19: Changing the layout of the program.

WS FTP Pro reports the progress of copy operations in a dialog box. You can copy single files or groups of files at one time. The program will warn you if you try to copy over an older version of a file.

WS FTP Pro makes it extremely easy to maintain files for your web site. You can see all of the files in a traditional layout, and you can easily navigate to any directory or folder on your local computer or the web server. Even if you are using a web publishing tool that automates publishing procedures, such as FrontPage or Fusion, WS FTP Pro is still very handy. You can easily visualize your web site, and the many files that make it up, with WS FTP Pro. In addition, if you need to do any troubleshooting, you can use WS FTP Pro to upload single files, check file sizes to make sure an upload was completed, and a host of other tasks.

 WS FTP Pro is one piece of software that you should not be without. It works well, it's well designed, and it gives you complete control over your web site. Get it! If you are a home user or involved with government or education, you might even qualify for the free version, WS FTP LE.

For each web server you work with, you will have to set up WS FTP Pro using the Session Profile dialog box shown in Figure 10-20. The dialog box looks technical and daunting, but it's actually fairly simple to connect to a web server with WS FTP Pro. If you supply a few basic facts, WS FTP Pro will attempt to figure out how to connect to your web server. I have yet to find a web server that WS FTP Pro couldn't figure out.

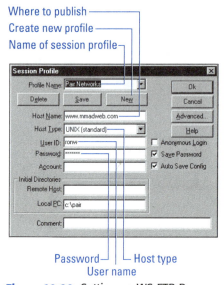

Figure 10-20: Setting up WS FTP Pro.

Follow these steps to set up WS FTP Pro:

1. WS FTP Pro comes with preinstalled session profiles for some major ISPs. Click the little arrow at the right of the Profile Name list to display the available profiles. If your ISP isn't in the list, click the New button to clear the dialog box's fields and enter your own ISP's session information.

2. Type a name for the server in the box at the top of the dialog box. Spaces are permitted; this is just a name, and isn't used to access the site. It is the name you will use to identify the site.

3. Type your host name in the Host Name box. This should be of the form `www.domain.com`.

4. Select the Host Type. If you are not sure of the type, select Auto detect. If the host is UNIX, try UNIX (standard).

5. Enter your user name in the user ID box.

6. Enter your password in the Password box. If you want WS FTP Pro to remember your password for future sessions, be sure to check the Save Password check box.

7. If you know the directory on the remote host that you want to connect to, enter it in the Initial Directories, Remote Host box. For your first connection, you may want to leave this blank. You can update it later when you know you have the connection working properly.

8. Enter the directory for your local machine in the Local PC box. This should be the directory that contains your web files.

9. Click OK to make the connection. If you are not already online, WS FTP Pro will display your connection dialog box. If you are online, WS FTP Pro will immediately attempt to connect to the server.

If the connection is made, you will see the two-window display shown in Figure 10-19. If not, check to make sure you are using the correct Host Name (contact your ISP if you are not sure about the Host Name). If WS FTP Pro has trouble auto-detecting your web server type, try setting the specific host type yourself and try to connect again.

Once you have set up the information for your web server, WS FTP Pro will connect automatically when you select the profile. By default, WS FTP Pro uses the last-used profile for a connection. This means that if you are publishing to only one server, you can connect very quickly with WS FTP Pro.

Web Tour #10: Real-Life Publishing

There are many ISPs that provide detailed information about publishing. I've tracked down some of the best and worst. To visit sites with information about publishing, double-click the file:

```
\WebTour\Chap10\index.htm
```

You'll see the Web Tour page for this chapter.

File Formats and Bit Depths

In This Chapter

Learning about graphic file formats

Exploring color depth

Using compression techniques

Converting graphics between formats

Dithering, and why it's bad for your images

Understanding palettes and their use

Using MIME file types for graphics

To prepare for this chapter's tutorials, copy the following folder from the CD-ROM to the \My Web Stuff folder on your hard drive:

    \tutorial\chap11

This will copy files for all of the tutorials in this chapter to your hard disk. See Chapter 1 for complete details on setting up for tutorials.

You don't have to know about file formats and other technical aspects of graphics files in order to work with them. However, if you do know your way around a file format, and especially if you understand bit depths and what they mean about image size, you can do a lot more with graphics on the Web.

There are just three file formats to learn about: GIF, JPEG, and PNG. And there are just two bit depths that matter: 8-bit images and 24-bit images. In fact, I can sum up this entire chapter in just four points:

+ Use the GIF file format for 8-bit images with broad areas of color, or images that require transparency.

+ Use the JPEG file format (file extension JPG) for photographic images and all true-color (24-bit) images.

+ Make your files as small as you can. For GIF images, use fewer than 256 colors. For JPEG images, use high compression factors.

+ The PNG format is new, and so far is receiving little support. It's supposed to replace both GIF and JPEG, but for now it's little more than a pipe dream. Ignore it.

If you understand those four points, then this chapter is redundant. If you don't understand those three sentences, you will by the time you finish this chapter. Either way, your knowledge of graphics should also include familiarity with palettes. See the section "Working with the Safety Palette," later in this chapter, for information about the way that palettes and GIF images work together.

I've read through this chapter, and I think a word or two of warning is needed before you wander any further. If you are already familiar with computer and graphics concepts, you can probably survive this chapter. If you don't have a grasp of key concepts, you ought to get a little background before you venture any further. Not that Mr. Author is derelict in his duties by throwing so much information at you. No, it would take a complete, separate book to cover these topics at an introductory level.

Graphic File Formats Explained

There are hundreds of different file formats used for storing graphics on computers. Some are rarely used, but even if you limit yourself to just the most commonly used image file formats, you will still have a long list. There is the bitmap format (extension: BMP), which is used by Windows and many Windows software programs. There is the venerable PCX format, still used by many image editors. Or the TIFF format (extension: TIF), often used by graphics professionals. Not to mention CMF, PCC, EPS, IFF, PSD, RAS, RLE, TGA, and a host of others.

The good news is that the Web only supports three image formats out of this alphabet soup of formats: GIF, JPEG, and PNG. Some browsers support other formats, but if you want images that just about any web browser can display properly, you should stick to these three formats. Two of the formats have a bit of history, while the third (PNG) is a recently developed format specific to the Web.

What's in a name? From GIF to JPEG, with a stop at PNG

GIF stands for Graphics Interchange Format, and was developed by CompuServe, a pre-Internet communications service. It uses compression to generate small image files. The compression scheme looks for redundant information in the image, and removes it. For example, if there are ten pixels of a certain color in a row, the GIF format will store that information in a shorthand way. Instead of storing all ten pixels, it will store the number 10 and the color — using just a few pixels instead of ten to store the information. This process is repeated throughout the image. When the file is read to redisplay the image, all of the pixels displayed are identical to the original image. There is no loss in quality from the compression.

Lossy and Lossless Compression

Image file compression is a mysterious art, and there is no getting around that fact. The technology used to compress images would probably humble the average mathematician, let alone the average person. However, there are two concepts that are very important to understand. I'm speaking of the difference between lossy and lossless compression.

Lossy compression is compression that actually throws away some of the image data. If the compression scheme is a good one, the loss will not be obvious. For example, the eye is less sensitive to color differences at the blue end of the color spectrum. Compression schemes that get rid of more blue than other colors can do so without degrading apparent image quality. What the eye can't see, it won't miss.

As to the manner in which lossy compression schemes toss out the data and achieve their compression, you are better off to assume it's magic. I've looked into it, and while I found the equations involved quite impressive, I understood less than 1 percent of what I saw. And I studied math a lot in college. This stuff is complicated in a major way, and is apparently not for mere mortals to grasp.

The point to remember is that with lossy compression some image data is truly lost, never to be recovered. You can usually adjust the compression level, and choose whether to lose only a little and maintain high image quality, or to lose a lot and wind up with lesser image quality.

Lossless compression takes advantage of redundancy in an image to achieve compression. This is at least an understandable concept. For example, if there are 20 red pixels in a row, the compression scheme can store the number 20 and the color red, instead of all those red pixels. This saves a surprising amount of space. There are also other lossless compression schemes, but the important point is that when the file is reopened and displayed on a web page, every pixel is there. Nothing is lost.

For the record, GIF files use lossless compression, and JPEG files use lossy compression.

By compressing the image this way, a GIF file is usually quite a bit smaller than an uncompressed file. For example, the image shown in Figure 11-1 uses 81,000 bytes when stored as a BMP file, and 9,000 bytes when stored as a GIF. That's a compression ratio of 9:1, and it represents a major savings in download time. A typical 28.8 modem connection, which can transfer at best around 3,000 bytes per second, would take almost 30 seconds to download the larger file, and three seconds to download the GIF.

Figure 11-1: An image that is very suitable for GIF compression.

The compression scheme used by GIF files allows a maximum of 256 different colors in the image. This is OK for some images, but not for others. GIF is a good choice for images that have many areas of a single color, such as cartoons like the one in Figure 11-1. You can use GIF for photographic images, but the size savings are not as substantial. Take Figure 11-2 for example. As a BMP file, it uses 1,036,856 bytes. As a GIF, it uses 272,847 bytes (a compression ratio of 4:1). That's still much too large for convenient downloading. For such images, a different compression scheme is available: JPEG. The same image, stored in the JPEG format, takes up only 105,885 bytes. That's still large (this is a large image at 640×480), but the JPEG image represents a compression ratio of 10:1.

Figure 11-2: An image that is very suitable for JPEG compression.

JPEG stands for Joint Photographic Experts Group, the folks who defined the JPEG compression standard. Unlike GIF files, JPEG files involve some loss of image data (see the sidebar "Lossy and Lossless Compression"). The formula that the JPEG format uses to compress an image is much more complex than the formula used in a GIF file. It involves factoring in such things as the colors to which the human eye is most and least sensitive, using mathematics to represent portions of the image, and so on. By carefully sacrificing color and image detail that is least noticeable to the human eye, a JPEG file becomes much smaller than the original. Visually, the image is so close to the original that it's hard to tell that it has been compressed. You can choose the amount of compression at the time you save an image to the JPEG format. There is an example of how to choose JPEG compression options explored in more detail in Chapter 14.

For example, the image shown in Figure 11-2 can be compressed to a higher degree. Figure 11-3 shows a high degree of compression, and the image quality is acceptable though noticeably degraded when viewed closely. Figure 11-4 shows what happens when you take JPEG too far — the image quality has degraded to the point where the image is useless. The file size for Figure 11-3 is 22,940 bytes (a compression ratio of 45:1), and the file size for Figure 11-4 is 13,456 bytes (a compression ratio of 77:1).

Figure 11-3: A highly compressed JPEG image.

Figure 11-4: An image that is compressed too much.

These high compression ratios would appear to make JPEG files the perfect answer for every image you put on the Web. That's not true. For example, when I saved the GIF file shown in Figure 11-1 as a JPEG file, the file size was 17,024 bytes — much larger than the 9,000 bytes for the GIF file. The following tip provides some rules you can live by:

Tip

If the image uses broad areas of color, GIF is the compression method to choose. If the image is photographic, or nearly so, then JPEG is the compression method to choose. If the image has characteristics of both types, then experiment to determine which type of compression to use. The primary exceptions involve situations where you need other features of these file formats that I have not touched on here. See Chapter 13 for a discussion of topics such as transparency and interlacing, which can affect your choice of image file format.

By now you are no doubt wondering about the third file format for graphics, PNG. The sad truth is that PNG is a latecomer to the scene, and most graphics are still being put on the Web in the GIF and JPEG formats. The idea behind PNG is that it includes the advantages of both GIF and JPEG, and will apply the best features of both according to the needs of the situation. Thus, the PNG format won't so much give you smaller file sizes (though it may give you a bit of that) as it will remove the need to choose between GIF and JPEG. There are still quite a few browsers in use that do not support the PNG format, and adoption of the new format has been slow. If and when the new format becomes popular, you will find that most image editing software includes the ability to save to the new format. You won't be left out in left field by change — at least not this time! For the time being, however, there isn't much reason to use PNG. So far, it's just a nice idea.

Color depth

You have probably heard phrases like "256 colors," "true color," 24-bit color," and "8-bit color" tossed around. These are not the random ravings of a madman; they are terms that have their roots in the very nature of digital (that is, computerized) data.

If the Web is like a Really Big Pig Farm, then digital data is very much like a mad tea party where everyone is either wearing a red toga, or wearing nothing at all. The madness is compounded by that word "digital." It means having to do with numbers (derived from the Latin, where a digit is a finger for counting those numbers on). Computers don't work with numbers; they work with bits. A bit, like the attendees at the mad tea party, has two possible states: 0 (not a stitch of clothing) and 1 (wearing a red toga).

 You could have used red togas and blue togas, and avoided the possibility of annoying those of your readers who are offended by the idea of imaginary partygoers who go about in the nude. But you didn't, and now I like you.

Thanks Webbsy; your enthusiasm is duly noted.

The bit is the fundamental unit of the "digital" world — and it has little to do with our counting system, which is based on ten (not surprisingly, that's the number of digits on both hands together). The bit-based counting system is based on two instead of ten. The relevant word here is *binary*, which means a system based on two. Instead of talking about digital computers, we should be talking about binary computers. Schoolchildren would have a much easier time with a binary number system. Instead of starting with 1-2-3-4-5-6-7-8-9-10, they would start with 1-10. This would speed up education dramatically, but I digress.

Counting with bits is tricky, but it can be done, and the results are instructive. Back to the world of our mad tea party: If we start with a party of one, there are two possibilities. That a partygoer can arrive in red, or sans toga entirely.

At a two-bit party, which is a party of two, either partygoer can arrive in either state. There are four possible combinations, as shown in Figure — oops; that wouldn't be nice, would it? It works just as well with ones and zeroes. If one is a red toga, and zero is no toga, the possibilities are

0	0
0	1
1	0
1	1

The number of possibilities grows rapidly every time you invite another person to the party. The number of combinations doubles with each new partygoer:

Number of persons at party	Number of possible costume combinations
3	8
4	16
5	32
6	64
7	128
8	256

Now it just so happens that the byte, the next higher unit for storing digital data, contains eight bits. Bytes are a conveniently sized collection of bits for computers to move around. Since a byte has 256 possible combinations of zero and one, it should come as no surprise that 256 colors is a common limit for images. The reason: Using one byte for each pixel in the image, each pixel can have one of the 256 possible values. That's a lot of parties, but these sound like *fun* parties.

 If you are still following this arcane discussion, the situation is actually far more complicated. Those values don't represent actual colors; they represent specific colors in a palette of 256 colors. Each pixel stores an index number that points to a position in the palette. That's why 256-color images are called indexed-color images.

The important point to remember is that an image that uses 256 colors is using one byte per pixel (eight bits) to store the image in a file. In other words, there is one complete eight-person party for every pixel in the image. Thus, a 256-color image is often called an 8-bit image. Eight-bits are used for every pixel in the image.

If the image is stored as a bitmap (BMP) file, there will be one byte per pixel, plus some overhead for that pesky palette. If the image is stored as a GIF file, compression will greatly reduce the file size because the GIF format doesn't store data pixel by pixel. It stores data about groups of pixels. It is as if the police show up at a party and send everyone home because there is already a party down the street with that same pattern of toga-wearing and toga-less partygoers. If you don't have a unique party (color), you're history as far as GIF is concerned.

And the JPEG format, which cheerfully throws away whole bytes of the image, provides even more compression and smaller file sizes for most images. It is as if the police show up at parties, declare them dull, and send everyone packing. If your party isn't unique *and* interesting, it's not part of the big picture.

That pun is so bad it makes even me cringe. Why don't we send you packing, and I'll write the book?

It'll never happen; you're an icon. Admit it: You've always been an icon, and you'll never be anything more than an icon. You're lucky I keep you on the payroll.

The advantage of 8-bit images is that they are smaller than images that use 16 bits (two bytes) or 24 bits (three bytes) per pixel. The compression used in GIF files reduces file size even more.

But the amazing fact buried in all this technospeak is that JPEG images aren't 8-bit images. They start out as 24-bit images, so-called true-color images. Consider the mathematical background for 16- and 24-bit images. One byte can hold 256 different values; that just happens to be two raised to the eighth power (2^8). Two bytes can hold 2^{16} values (that's 65,536 different colors in a 16-bit image), and three bytes can hold 2^{24} values (that's 16.7 million different colors in a 24-bit image). It just so happens that the average eye can distinguish about 16 million colors — hence the "true color" moniker for 24-bit images.

The amazing fact is, that despite starting out handicapped by a factor of three (a 24-bit image is three times the size of the equivalent, if less colorful, 8-bit image), JPEG compression achieves remarkable compression ratios. So not only is JPEG a useful tool for compressing photographic images for the Web, it does a better job of presenting graphics than GIF can. That's a second reason for choosing JPEG over GIF for photographic images: You're getting more bits per pixel, even when the file size is smaller.

Caution!

And now for the bad news. Many folks are using video displays that support only 8-bit color. That means that even if you put a great-looking 24-bit JPEG-compressed image on your web page, many folks will still only see it in 8-bit color. Worse, if there are several images on the page, they will all get displayed using the same 256 colors. That's not nice if you have a predominantly blue picture of your prize-winning 22-pound blueberry next to your mostly red picture of last week's fabulous sunset. A 256-color palette could handle a picture with lots of shades of blue, or a picture with lots of shades of red, but not one with lots of shades of blue and lots of shades of red. Too many shades makes for lots of dithering, and dithering leads to large file sizes. If there is a lot of dithering, it can also degrade image quality. See the section "Dithering for Fun and Profit: Not!" later in this chapter for detailed information about dithering and why it's bad for most images, and especially bad for web page images. (If you didn't already realize that the world of computers is crazy, now you know. Expect the best and prepare for the worst, and you'll get along just fine.)

Compression Clarified

Now that you know the essence of GIF, JPEG, 8-bit, and 24-bit, let's pause for a moment to consider how all of this fits together on the web page. Consider the raw facts:

✦ The GIF format is inherently an 8-bit format. It works best for images that have broad areas of single colors.

✦ The JPEG format is inherently a 24-bit format. Because it uses a lossy form of compression (that is, data is discarded forever when you save an image to JPEG format), JPEG files are not necessarily larger than GIF images. In fact, JPEG images are usually smaller than GIF images.

Transparency is the only feature of GIF files that might make you save an image in GIF format, even though it seems like a perfect image for JPEG. See Chapter 13 for information about image transparency.

The key point: The ultimate file size for an image does not depend on the bit depth of the image. If you save a 24-bit image using JPEG compression, then it will end up very small. If you save an 8-bit image using GIF, it will be small, but not necessarily (or even usually) smaller than a JPEG version of the image.

To get the smallest possible image sizes when compressing:

✦ For GIF files, use the fewest number of colors that still gives you a good-looking image. The two best methods for doing this are the PhotoImpact GIF SmartSaver and the HVS WebFocus for GIF files.

✦ For JPEG files, use the highest level of compression that still gives you a good-looking image. The two best methods for doing this are the PhotoImpact JPEG SmartSaver and the HVS WebFocus for JPEG files.

If you are unsure about whether to use GIF or JPEG compression for an image, try both of them to see which results in the smallest file size. Image compression is more art than science, and trial and error are sometimes the best tools to use.

Using HiJaak Pro, All-Purpose Converter

Download: A trial version was not available at press time. Check the Quarterdeck web site at `http://arachnid.qdeck.com/qdeck/demosoft` to see if this changes.

Tutorial   **Level:** Easy as Pie

Task: Convert files with HiJaak Pro

Before you start: Have HiJaak Pro installed and running on your machine. (You might want to download the demo version if it's available by the time you read this.)

So far, I've been yakking on and on about the GIF and JPEG file formats. Those are the file formats you will use for images that appear in web pages. However, you may need to convert to GIF and JPEG from many other file formats. I've said this before: There are a frightening number of odd image formats out there. The chances are good that, sooner or later, you will wind up having an image handed to you that is in some obscure file format. What do you do?

One option is to get your hands on a software package that understands even the obscure file formats. Yes, I know that today's image editors support a large number of image formats. The simple truth is that even the best of today's image editors handles about a dozen file formats. When it comes to obscure image formats, you need a specialized tool that knows hundreds of file formats.

One such program is HiJaak Pro. Figure 11-5 shows the easiest way to use HiJaak. When you install HiJaak, it installs a number of its utilities.

1. Right-click a file in a folder. The utilities become available. You can adjust these options with the Preference setting in HiJaak Pro.

2. Click the HiJaak Convert option to display the dialog box shown in Figure 11-6. This is a very important option.

For a book on graphics, it's sure been a long time since the last figure. Give me a break next time!

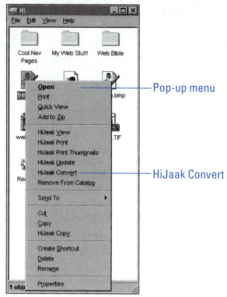

Figure 11-5: Accessing HiJaak Pro
with a right-click menu.

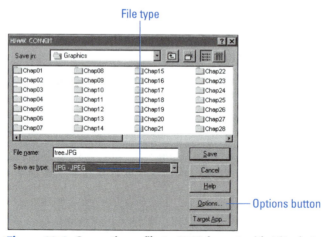

Figure 11-6: Converting a file to JPEG format with HiJaak Convert.

This dialog box allows you to specify the type of file to convert to. In this example, the file \My Web Stuff\Chap11\tree.bmp (that's the file I right-clicked to display the dialog box in Figure 11-5) is being converted to the JPEG format.

You can convert more than one file at a time. Simply use Shift + Click or Ctrl + Click to select the files you want to convert before you invoke the right-click menu; then pick HiJaak Convert. Be sure to specify *.jpg as the filename, or you will get a sequentially numbered series of files instead of files with the same base names and a new extension.

3. Click the Options button (see Figure 11-6) to display the dialog box shown in Figure 11-7.

The options shown are the raster processing options for converting to the JPEG format; you will see different options when converting to other formats. The most useful options are quality setting (top right) and smoothing (a check box at center right). The other settings allow you to adjust image size, colors, and so on. Unfortunately, HiJaak does not display the image as you adjust the quality (compression) setting, so it isn't as useful as PhotoImpact's JPEG SmartSaver.

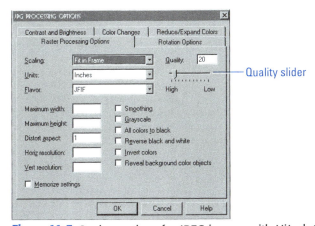

Figure 11-7: Setting options for JPEG images with HiJaak Convert.

If you were converting to the GIF format, you would see the raster processing options shown in Figure 11-8. Note that you can apply transparency, but only to the colors black and white; you cannot select the color you want to be transparent. Again, this is less useful than PhotoImpact. There is also a check box to specify interlacing at the bottom right.

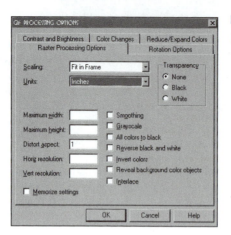

Figure 11-8: Setting raster processing options.

4. If you are saving to the GIF format, you can also click the Reduce/Expand Colors tab to change the number of colors used in the image (see Figure 11-9). HiJaak does not offer the 216-color Netscape safe palette, however.

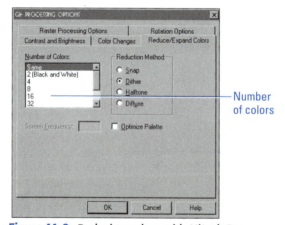

Figure 11-9: Reducing colors with HiJaak Pro.

The main advantage of HiJaak is that it will convert lots of files at one time. This is convenient if you need to manage a large number of files. If you need to optimize individual graphics for web pages, you are better off using products such as HVS Color or PhotoImpact.

Dithering for Fun and Profit: Not!

In nearly every image editor I've worked with, converting from a true-color (aka 24-bit color) image to an 8-bit image involves dithering. Dithering involves mixing pixels of different colors to create the illusion of some other color.

If you want the best possible image and you have a limited number of colors to work with, dithering sometimes makes sense. If you need to compress an image for downloading over the Web, dithering is bad news.

Figure 11-10 shows how dithering is accomplished. The small figure at the bottom right is actual size; the background figure is the same image, pixel for pixel, but blown up eight times. The enlarged figure shows how pixels of completely different colors can blend to form new colors. This is the basis of dithering.

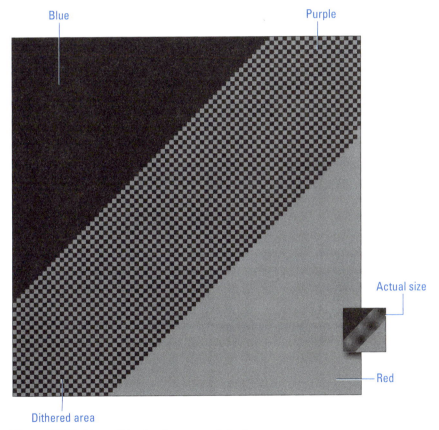

Figure 11-10: How dithering is accomplished.

Unfortunately, when it comes to web pages, dithered images aren't fun, and there's no profit in it at all. Dithering results in larger files when using the GIF format. You are almost always better off to simply save the file in the JPEG format and choose a suitable compression level.

Why is dithering such a poor choice? Examine what happens when you apply dithering to an image. Figure 11-11 shows a small portion of a typical true-color image, enlarged to show the pixels that make up the image. Note that the transition between colors is smooth because there are so many colors to use for the transition.

Figure 11-11: A true-color image, with a close-up showing individual pixels.

Figure 11-12 shows a small portion of the same image after it has been converted to 216 colors and saved as a GIF file. Because there are fewer colors to work with, the converter (Photoshop) mixed pixels of the basic 216 colors to approximate the colors used in the original image. There are fewer colors, but the colors are intimately mixed. GIF compression works best on broad areas of color. Dithered images will not compress well because there are no broad areas of color, just lots of little areas.

Figure 11-12: A 216-color image, with a close-up showing individual pixels.

If you reduce the colors further, the dithering gets further out of hand, as shown in Figure 11-13. Generally speaking, this is why it is best to use JPEG compression, rather than GIF compression, for photographic images.

Figure 11-13: A 32-color image, with a close-up showing individual pixels.

If you simply must convert a true-color image to an 8-bit image (or better yet a 216-color image using a safe palette; see the next section, "Working with the Safety

Palette"), use one of the HVS tools. They use better methods than dithering to get good-looking results. The methods are too complicated to explain (and proprietary as well!) but they work. In the broadest possible terms, the HVS tools use cleverly constructed bands of color rather than dithered, intermixed colors. This means that GIF compression is more effective for images whose colors are reduced with the HVS tools.

Working with the Safety Palette

Most of the people who view your web pages will do so with a computer that uses only 256 colors at a time. If you want your web pages to look their best, you will have to pay attention to this fact.

These 256 colors are called a palette. All palettes do not have 256 colors. Some images have 2, 4, 16, 32, 64, or other numbers of colors in them. The palette is like a painter's palette: The colors in the palette are all the colors available for representing a given image. Blending the colors — dithering — will simulate additional colors. This comes at the cost of a larger file size if the image is compressed, as explained earlier in this chapter.

Each time an image is displayed, the computer looks at the image's file, determines the palette of colors that the image uses, and then renders the image using those colors. Any images that are displayed at the same time will be redisplayed using the same palette. The result is that in order to make the current image look good, the other images often wind up looking terrible.

Web browsers get around this problem by using a single palette to display all images on the web page. It is called the *safety palette* because, if you use this palette, your colors will display safely on the page as pure colors, without dithering. Dithering can make an image look out of focus or sloppy, and is something well worth avoiding whenever possible.

It's not good enough to simply use the same palette of colors for each image. You cannot improve your web pages by using any set of 256 colors. Because web images can be displayed on many different platforms, a means had to be found to come up with a palette that would safely display on almost any computer. That is the function of the safety palette. You must use the safety palette to consistently get rich, solid colors. This is most important for GIF images, which often use solid colors. JPEG images are usually photographic in nature, and you will usually have to accept dithering for your JPEG images. You can convert your JPEG images to the safety palette, but you may still get dithering because when the JPEG file is reconstructed from its compressed form, there is no guarantee that the colors you get back will be the same as the colors that went in!

It's worth a few paragraphs to discover how the safety palette was created. First, consider how colors are represented on a computer. There are three colors which, when blended in the proper proportions, can be used to represent any color the eye can see (see the section, "Color depth," earlier in this chapter). These colors are red, blue, and green. White is made up of full portions of all three colors, black is made up of zero portions of all three colors, yellow is made up of equal parts red and green, and so on.

For each of the three colors, there are 256 possible values. Remember this number, which is two raised to the eighth power. This just happens to be eight bits (one byte). Thus, with three bytes, your computer can represent any color in the rainbow.

Strictly speaking, this is not true, and I am nothing if I am not a strict speaker. The human eye is a marvelous instrument, and can see colors beyond what monitors, printed paper, televisions, and other media can present. However, the statement is close enough to true to be widely regarded as true, and that will be adequate for Mr. Author's purposes. However, you and I will know that the truth stretches a bit further than the color gamut of your average computer monitor.

True enough, but beside the point. Come to think of it, Webbsy, you've spent most of your life standing beside various points of interest, haven't you?

It might surprise you to know that (virtually) every color the eye can see can be represented by 256 values of just three colors. However, this is actually a lot of colors. How many? A total of 256 cubed (256^3), or more than 16 million colors.

It is a shame to have to reduce this vast number of colors to a mere 256 in total, but it must be done if you want your graphics to display cleanly on all monitors.

Or you could be an elitist, and insist that visitors to your web pages invest in true-color video cards. A solution, and one I support. Let them view dithered colors if they wish, but why should you sacrifice your images for the rude masses of humanity? Encourage them instead to upgrade and move into the future.

Elitist poppycock, Webbsy. One's web pages should invite visitors, not challenge them to spend money! Sometimes I regret I invited you to participate.

The proper way to represent 16 million+ colors with a palette of only 256 colors is to divide the color scale into 256 equal divisions, and use those colors for the palette. The math works out like this:

```
256³  =  16,777,216
16,777,216 ÷ 256 = 65,536
```

That means that, if we take every 65,536th color, we get a 256-color palette whose colors are equally spaced across the entire color spectrum. However, this creates problems. What about shades of gray? The sad truth is that we cannot use all 256 colors for our palette, because we need to stack the palette with some predetermined choices.

If web pages were only viewed with Windows machines, the number of colors to use would be 236. Windows reserves 20 colors for its own use, leaving 236 for our safety palette. But other machines handle palettes in their own ways, and the sad fact is that the safety palette, in order to actually be safe, must use no more than 216 colors. This just happens to be 6^3 (six cubed), which has some nice benefits that will become clear in a moment.

Every color you view on your monitor is composed of one or more shades of red, green, and blue. The shorthand reference for this is RGB. RGB is just one color model. You can also create colors using cyan, magenta, yellow, and black (the CMYK color model). There are different color models for different uses of color. RGB is commonly used on computer displays; CMYK is commonly used for color printing.

To create the safety palette, start with the fundamental fact of 24-bit (three-byte) color: There are 256 possible values for red, 256 for green, and 256 for blue. If you divide each of these numbers of colors by six, there are 51 units between colors. It works out like this:

Red	Green	Blue
0	0	0
51	0	0
51	51	0
51	51	51
102	0	0
102	51	0
102	51	51
102	102	0
102	102	51
102	102	102
153	0	0
...		
255	255	51
255	255	102
255	255	153
255	255	255

Figure 11-14 shows an example of some colors obtained using this method. Figure 11-15 shows the red, green, and blue values for these colors. There are 36 colors in this example, making up just one-sixth of the safety palette. Figure 11-16 shows the complete safety palette, including the 40 spaces reserved for use by the operating system. See the color section at the back of the book for a color representation of the safety palette.

Figure 11-14: A range of colors that make up a portion of the safety palette.

R=0 G=0 B=0	R=0 G=0 B=51	R=0 G=0 B=102	R=0 G=0 B=153	R=0 G=0 B=204	R=0 G=0 B=255
R=51 G=0 B=0	R=51 G=0 B=51	R=51 G=0 B=102	R=51 G=0 B=153	R=51 G=0 B=204	R=51 G=0 B=255
R=102 G=0 B=0	R=102 G=0 B=51	R=102 G=0 B=102	R=102 G=0 B=153	R=102 G=0 B=204	R=102 G=0 B=255
R=153 G=0 B=0	R=153 G=0 B=51	R=153 G=0 B=102	R=153 G=0 B=153	R=153 G=0 B=204	R=153 G=0 B=255
R=204 G=0 B=0	R=204 G=0 B=51	R=204 G=0 B=102	R=204 G=0 B=153	R=204 G=0 B=204	R=204 G=0 B=255
R=255 G=0 B=0	R=255 G=0 B=51	R=255 G=0 B=102	R=255 G=0 B=153	R=255 G=0 B=204	R=255 G=0 B=255

Figure 11-15: The color values displayed.

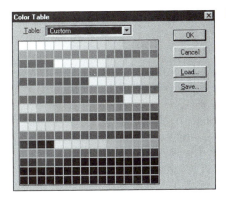

Figure 11-16: The complete range of colors that make up the safety palette.

I mentioned earlier that you can get dithering with JPEG images, even if the original image uses only colors in the safety palette. Figure 11-17 shows that this is true. I took the image from Figure 11-14 and saved it as a GIF image and, using different colors from the safety palette, as a JPEG image. I then created a web page that uses both images. Note that the GIF image (at the top of the page) uses pure, undithered safe colors, while the JPEG image's colors, which were taken from the safety palette before compression, are nonetheless dithered when displayed on the web page.

To view this page and see the dithering for yourself, double-click the file `\My Web Stuff\Chap11\chap11A.htm` included on the CD-ROM.

There are two ways to use the safety palette. Some image editors, such as Photoshop, have built in the safety palette, and you can choose it when converting a true-color image to 8-bit color, or you can apply the safety palette to an existing 8-bit image that uses a different palette.

To apply the safety palette when reducing colors from true color to 8-bit color in Photoshop, follow these steps:

1. Use the Image | Mode | Indexed Color menu selection to open the Palette dialog box.

2. Select Web as the Palette type. Set dither to None whenever possible. Use a diffusion dither only if the None setting generates unpleasant results.

3. Click OK to reduce the color count to 216 using the safety palette.

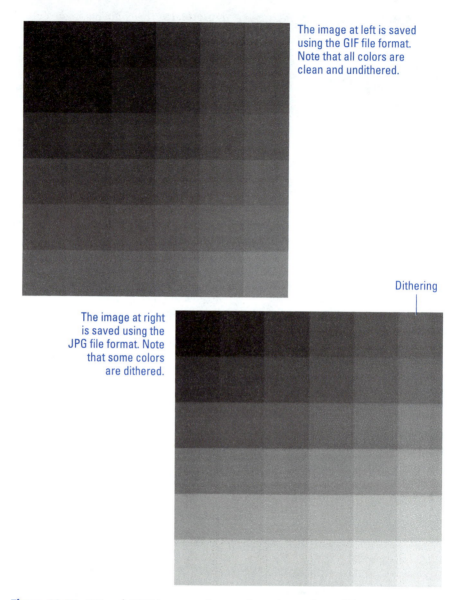

The image at left is saved using the GIF file format. Note that all colors are clean and undithered.

Dithering

The image at right is saved using the JPG file format. Note that some colors are dithered.

Figure 11-17: GIF and JPEG images relate to the safety palette differently.

Other image editors may have a similar process available; check their documentation. If not, you may be able to apply the safety palette as a custom palette. To apply the safety palette to an existing 8-bit image in Photoshop:

1. Open the image with the incorrect palette, and click the Image I Mode I RGB color menu selection. This converts the image to true color.

2. Apply the preceding set of steps.

I have supplied a collection of palettes for various image editors on the CD-ROM. Each of the palettes is the 216-color safety palette. A safety palette in the proper format for each editor is located in a folder named for the editor. For example, the safety palette for Photoshop is located in the file \palettes\photoshp\ safety.act.

Setting MIME File Types

MIME (Multipurpose Internet Mail Extensions) is a system for identifying file types and transferring them across the Internet. Different types of files have designated MIME types that are stored and used by your browser — often without you even knowing that MIME types are involved.

The MIME types for various graphics file types are shown in Table 11-1. The MIME type is added to the file (usually at the start of the file) for transmission via e-mail, or across the Web as part of a web page. Your browser or e-mail reader will read the MIME type, discard it, and then display the file appropriately if possible, or present a dialog box if it doesn't know what to do with the MIME file type.

Table 11-1 MIME File Types	
MIME type	**Extension(s)**
image/ief	ief
image/x-png	png
image/x-photo-cd	pcd
image/x-MS-bmp	bmp
image/x-rgb	rgb
image/x-portable-pixmap	ppm
image/x-portable-graymap	pgm
image/x-portable-bitmap	pbm
image/x-portable-anymap	pnm
image/x-xwindowdump	xwd
image/x-xpixmap	xpm

(continued)

Table 11-1 (continued)	
MIME type	**Extension(s)**
image/x-xbitmap	xbm
image/x-cmu-raster	ras
image/tiff	tiff, tif
image/jpeg	jpeg, jpg, jpe
image/gif	gif

The last two entries in Table 11-1 are the two most commonly used image types on the Web, and the most widely supported by browsers.

Various web browsers support these file types in different ways. To access the MIME types with the Netscape Navigator browser, use the Options | General Preferences menu selection to display the dialog box shown in Figure 11-18. If the Helpers tab is not active, click it to activate it. Note the column labeled Action. There is an action for each MIME type. In some cases, as for JPEG and GIF files, the browser itself will handle the display of the image. For others, such as TIFF and RAS, the browser will display a dialog box (see Figure 11-19) asking you what you want to do with the image.

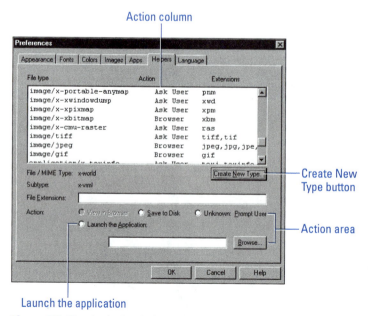

Figure 11-18: Displaying helpers in Navigator.

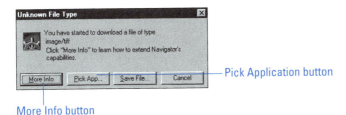

Figure 11-19: Dialog box for unsupported image types in Navigator.

You can create new MIME types with the Create New Type button (see Figure 11-18), and change the action for a MIME type using the radio button near the bottom of the dialog box. Note the radio button called Launch the Application. You can browse to find an application that can display image types that aren't supported by your browser. For example, you could invoke your favorite image editor to display a TIF image.

You can also choose how to handle unsupported MIME types in creative ways when the dialog box in Figure 11-19 presents itself. If you click the More Info button, Navigator will display a new browser window with a list of software products that plug right into Navigator (see Figure 11-20). Oddly enough, they are called plug-ins.

You can read about each of the products that Netscape lists, and then click the appropriate link to download one of them. In most cases, you will download a trial version of the software, and you will have to buy the software to continue using it. After you download the software and install it, that software will automatically be used to display the MIME type(s) it supports.

If you click the Pick App button, you can choose an existing application to view the file (see Figure 11-21). Click the Browse button to look for an application that can display the file type involved, such as Photoshop for a TIF file (see Figure 11-22).

This puts the full pathname for the chosen application into the dialog box (see Figure 11-23). Click OK to display the image. From now on, any time you click images of this MIME type, they will be displayed automatically in whatever application you designated.

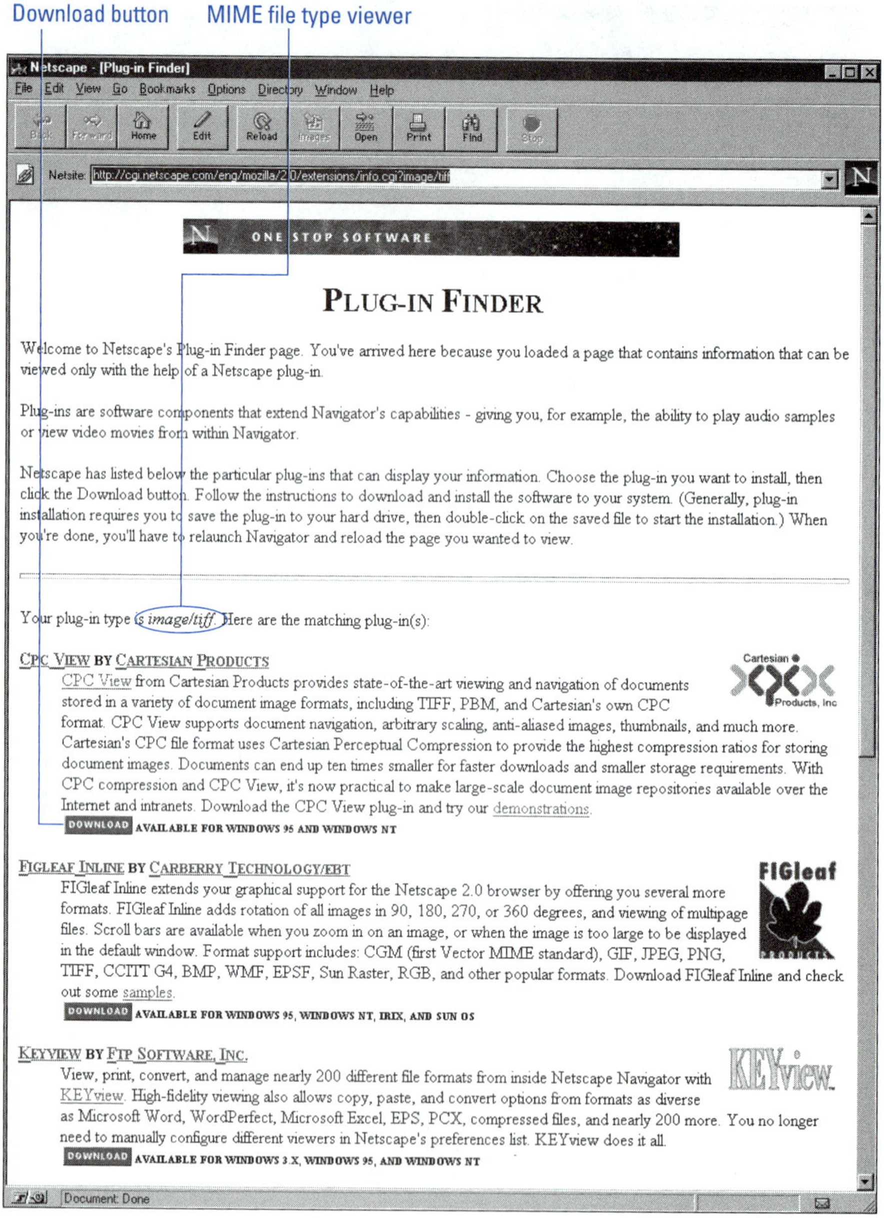

Download button   MIME file type viewer

Figure 11-20: Choosing a plug-in to display a MIME file type.

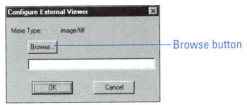

Figure 11-21: Configuring an external image viewer.

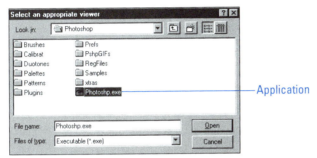

Figure 11-22: Choosing the external viewer.

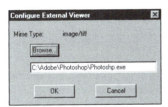

Figure 11-23: The external viewer added to the dialog box.

The General Preferences dialog box Helpers tab (see Figure 11-24) shows that the external viewer is now the method of choice for displaying the TIF image type. You can change the setting in the General Preferences dialog box back to its original setting (see Figure 11-25) at any time if you change your mind about how to display TIF or any other MIME file types.

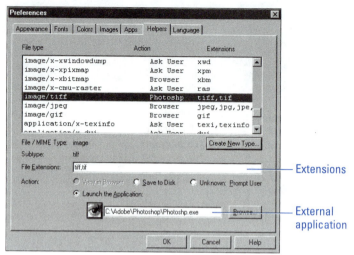

Figure 11-24: The Action for TIF files is changed.

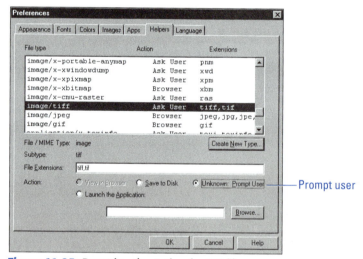

Figure 11-25: Resetting the Action for TIF files.

If you are using Microsoft Internet Explorer as your browser, there are two ways to choose how to display MIME file types for images. By far the easiest way is simply to double-click a file of the given type, and when Windows asks you to supply a program to display the image, locate the appropriate program's file. This is very similar to what you can do with Netscape, but you can do it even if you are not browsing the Web at the time.

You can also use the View | Options menu selection in Internet Explorer to display the dialog box shown in Figure 11-26. If the Programs tab is not active, click it to make it active. Click the File Types button to access the File Types dialog box. This lists all of the file type associations for Windows 95.

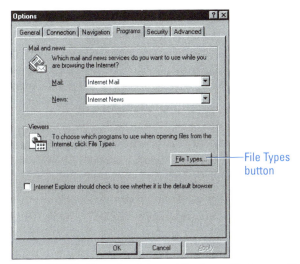

Figure 11-26: Changing Internet Explorer file type settings.

If the file type you want to view is not shown, click the New Type button and enter the appropriate information (see Figure 11-27). This is, however, the hard way. It's much, much easier to let Windows 95 do the work for you. Close all these dialog boxes, double-click a file that uses the extension of the file type, and let Windows 95 fill in all the blanks for you.

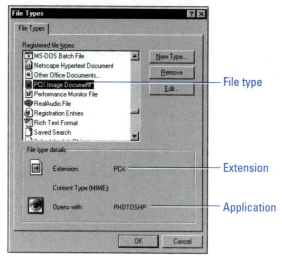

Figure 11-27: Adding a new file type.

Web Tour #11: Interesting Image Tools

The Web is full of cool tools for working with images. Come along for a tour of the stuff that's out there waiting for you to try. Visit some of my favorites by double-clicking the file:

```
\WebTour\Chap11\index.htm
```

You'll see the Web Tour page for this chapter.

Small Is Beautiful

To prepare for this chapter's tutorials, copy the following folders from the CD-ROM to the \My Web Stuff folder on your hard drive:

    \tutorial\chap12

    \palettes

This will copy files for all of the tutorials in this chapter to your hard disk. See Chapter 1 for complete details on setting up for tutorials.

I f you just arrived here from Chapter 11, congratulations. You have earned a degree in computer graphics theory. Now it's time to consider the practical application of smallness to the world of web page graphics.

Fortunately, you don't have to know very much theory in order to make use of the tools available. As long as you are clear about the need to keep graphics file sizes small, you can use the tools to achieve small file sizes with relatively little pain.

 This chapter includes several tutorials for reducing the number of colors. I hope you will keep in mind that no matter how much Mr. Author prattles on about color reduction, the right way to shrink file sizes is interactively. The best tools are therefore PhotoImpact and HVS Color. I will assume, out of the kindness of my heart, that Mr. Author feels a need to cover the subject completely, but let's face it — seeing the effect of compression while you set compression levels is the only way to fly. And fly your web pages will if the graphics in them use small file sizes.

For once, I agree with you, Uncle. PhotoImpact and the tools from Digital Frontiers are far ahead of the pack for color reduction and file size control. But, for the sake of comparison, let's see how some other tools work their magic at color reduction.

Bandwidth and Image Size

As long as people use modems to connect to the Internet, it is going to be important to keep graphics file sizes as small as possible. Even with fast modems (28.8, 33.6, or even 56 Kbps), graphics files still take a long time to download. Even if you have the cleanest possible connection, actual data transfer rates of 3,000 to 6,000 bytes per second are the very best you can hope for — and you won't often get that. Given that a large graphics file is something on the order of 50,000 to 100,000 bytes, that's 8 to 34 seconds to download, depending on your modem's speed. That's a very long time to wait for one image.

If you assume that most modems are in the range of 28.8 to 33.6 Kbps, and that the average Internet transfer rate is about 2,500 bytes per second (and those are both very generous assumptions), then a 10,000-byte graphic is going to take 4 seconds to download. If you use five such graphics on a page, that's 20 seconds of download time. You can ignore the time to download the text on the average page because that part takes just fractions of a second.

However, these are peak transfer rates. What about those precious seconds lost while your browser reconnects to get the next portion of the page? The reality is that even a well-designed web page, with small graphics file sizes, can take 30 seconds to a minute to fully display for the visitor. A page that does not use small graphics files can take much, much longer.

There are two ways to cut file size:

✦ Reduce the number of colors

✦ Use compression

Reducing the number of colors

Color reduction applies to 8-bit images. The fewer the colors in the image, the smaller the image file will be. There is one exception to this: Images that use dithering can actually increase in file size when the number of colors is reduced. As a general rule, color reduction has the greatest impact on file size when you avoid dithering. The sad part of this is that for photographic images, dithering is almost essential to get a decent-looking image after color reduction. Figure 12-1 shows an image whose colors were reduced without dithering, and Figure 12-2 shows the image when dithering was used.

Severe color banding

Figure 12-1: This image had its colors reduced without benefit of dithering.

Dithering

Figure 12-2: This image's colors were reduced with dithering.

This is where Digital Frontiers HVS Color comes in. It uses mostly non-dithered techniques to achieve color reduction; the images save at much smaller file sizes.

Using compression

Compression is covered extensively in Chapter 11, so I won't repeat myself a great deal here. I will remind you about the two kinds of compression — lossless (employed with GIF files), and lossy (employed with JPEG files). Lossless compression exploits redundancy in the image colors; lossy compression sacrifices some image quality to achieve compression.

Lossless compression looks for repeating colors or repeated patterns in the image, and stores colors and patterns in a kind of dictionary. It compresses the image by storing references to the dictionary, or to the number of repeated pixels, instead of the pixels themselves. Lossless compression works best with images that have large areas of a single color, such as cartoons. Since lossless compression doesn't destroy any part of the image, you can use it with complete safety.

Lossy compression uses fancy mathematical maneuvers to achieve very high levels of compression. Colors to which the human eye is least sensitive are pulled out, and areas of color are reduced to mathematical formulae. This mishmash of image data and formulae is stored in the file. When the image is reconstructed, it will have lost some quality. You can adjust how much quality is sacrificed when you apply the compression. If you use lossy compression, keep an uncompressed version of the image handy for editing. Lossy compression permanently removes portions of the image; having the original on hand is useful if you need to make changes. Changing compressed images and saving it again degrades image quality. It's like making photocopies of photocopies — after a while, the image is junk. Thus the title for this chapter: Small Is Beautiful. I'm going to assume that you are now a convert, and cut to the how-to.

Graphic Reductions with Paint Shop Pro

Download: A shareware version of Paint Shop Pro from Jasc's web site at `http://www.jasc.com`.

CD: Paint Shop Pro is also on the CD-ROM.

Tutorial

Level: Easy

Task: Reduce colors and apply the safety palette

Before you start:

> ✦ Download and install the shareware version of Paint Shop Pro.
>
> ✦ Open the file `\My Web Stuff\Chap12\fly.jpg` in Paint Shop Pro (that's the File | Open menu selection).

Figure 12-3 shows two images open in Paint Shop Pro. An image of a fly (yes, that's the same fly you saw earlier in the chapter) and an image of a helicopter. Both images are included on the Paint Shop Pro CD-ROM as royalty-free images for your use. There are about 100 such images on the disc.

To reduce colors in an image with Paint Shop Pro, you can use the Colors | Decrease Color Depth | X Colors (8 bit) menu selection (see Figure 12-4). Note that you also have the option of selecting from predetermined color depths as well.

This opens the dialog box shown in Figure 12-5. Here you can set the number of colors. In Figure 12-5, I've entered 216, the number of colors in the safety palette. Unfortunately, you cannot control which colors are used in the palette, and you will not get the safety palette. Instead, you'll get the best 216 colors that fit the image you are working with. The fly image is mostly reds and maroons, so the palette will consist predominantly of those colors. This is not the kind of color reduction that is appropriate for web images.

Settings for current tool   Toolbars

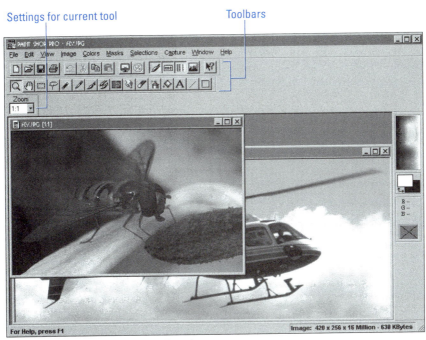

Figure 12-3: Two images in Paint Shop Pro.

Set number of colors

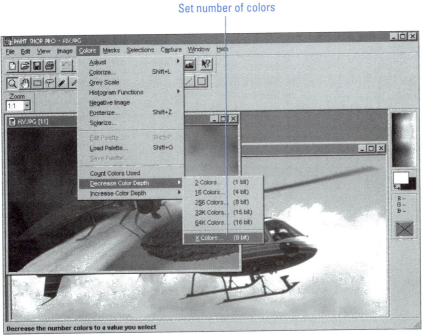

Figure 12-4: Decreasing the number of colors.

Number of colors

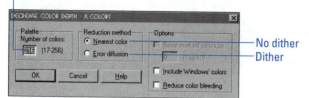

Figure 12-5: Decreasing color depth.

Another approach is to use the Colors | Load Palette menu selection to load a safety palette from disk. I have included a safety palette for Paint Shop Pro on the CD-ROM in the file \My Web Stuff\palettes\paintshp\safety.pal.

To begin the tutorial:

1. Open the file \tutorial\chap12\fly.jpg from the CD-ROM in Paint Shop Pro using the File | Open menu selection. Because this file is a JPEG file, you know that it uses true color (24-bit color, with 16.7 million possible colors).

2. To load this palette and simultaneously convert the image to 216 colors, use the Color | Load Palette menu selection to open the dialog box shown in Figure 12-6.

3. Locate the file \My Web Stuff\palettes\paintshp\safety.pal, and click it to highlight it as shown in Figure 12-6.

4. Verify that the radio button Error diffusion dithering is highlighted, as shown in Figure 12-6.

5. Click Open to open the palette file and apply it to the image.

Figure 12-7 shows the original fly image, and Figure 12-8 shows the reduced-color version. You can find the originals on the CD-ROM in the files:

\tutorial\chap12\fly.jpg

\tutorial\chap12\fly256.gif

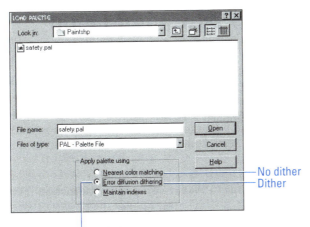

Error diffusion radio button

Figure 12-6: Loading a palette.

Figure 12-7: The original true-color image.

Figure 12-8: The image with colors reduced to 216 using the safety palette.

While it is possible to use Paint Shop Pro to reduce colors for web pages, it is not the most convenient tool for the process.

Palettes and Indexed Color

The Photoshop dialog box used to set the palette is titled *Indexed Color*. There is a little history behind this phrase, and a little bit of technical jargon. The colors in a palette are numbered. If the palette has 256 colors, each color has a number associated with it. The actual color isn't stored in the image; the palette is stored in the image, and each pixel has the number of the palette color attached to it. Thus, if a light red color is color #211, and the very first pixel uses that color, the number 211 is stored at the pixel location, not the red/green/blue settings.

The red/green/blue settings are stored in the palette at palette location 211. This is called the index. Thus the term indexed color to refer to images that use palettes.

For example, if you convert a true-color image to 216 colors, you can say that you changed the image to indexed color. This proliferation of terms for color depths (8-bit color, 256-color images, 216-color images, safety palette, indexed color image, and so on) isn't my fault, so don't kill the messenger!

How much difference does dithering make? The original JPEG file size for the fly image was 31,792 bytes. The GIF file was significantly larger (49,326 bytes), and the image quality was much reduced. The images look nearly identical because the web page is 256-color — a JPEG file's superior color depth is meaningless in this situation. However, the JPEG file is still smaller, and that counts for something! To see this web page for yourself, double-click the file `\My Web Stuff\Chap12\Chap12A.htm`.

The lesson learned here is that photographic images almost always do better as JPEG images. There are two distinct advantages to JPEG for photos:

✦ The file size is almost always smaller than an equivalent GIF file.

✦ The image appearance will be as good as a GIF file on a 256-color display, and superior to GIF files on true-color and high-color displays.

However, if you require transparency (see Chapter 13 for details), you will need to save your image in the GIF format since the JPEG format does not support transparency.

Idea

Where to go from here:

✦ Experiment by converting to indexed color with Dither set to none. The image quality will be poor because there aren't enough colors in the safety palette to match the colors in the image. Try it and see.

✦ Carefully use the lasso tool to select just the fly, and then apply a solid color to the background. When you use the File | Export | GIF 89a menu selection to save the file, you can set the background color as transparent.

Graphic Reductions with HVS Color and HVS JPEG

Tutorial

CD: Trial versions of the HVS tools are on the CD-ROM. They are seven-day trials, so don't install them until you are ready to work with them. Visit the Digital Frontiers web site at http://www.digfrontiers.com.

Level: Easy

Task: Install HVS tools and use them for color reduction

Before you start:

✦ Photoshop 4.0 must be installed on your hard drive.

✦ Install HVS Color and HVS JPEG (instructions included here).

HVS Color and HVS JPEG are two very powerful tools for balancing the tradeoffs between image file size and image quality. These plug-ins use sophisticated algorithms to analyze many aspects of the colors used in the images before determining exactly how to reduce the number of colors.

Caution!

The demo versions of these plug-ins expire in seven days. That means that you have seven days to play with them before they become useless. I suggest that you install the HVS plug-ins only when you are ready to work with them.

To install HVS Color:

1. Open the plug-in folder for Photoshop. This is usually found at \Adobe\Photoshop\plugins on your hard drive.

2. Open the folder \demo\HVSColor on the CD-ROM.

3. Drag the following files from the CD-ROM folder to the \plugins folder:

   HVSColor.8BF
   HVSColor.hlp

4. Drag the following files from the CD-ROM folder to the Photoshop folder (\Adobe\Photoshop):

   RSDLL.DLL
   RSAGNT32.DLL
   RSAGENT.HLP

To install HVS JPEG:

1. Open the plug-in folder for Photoshop. This is usually found at \Adobe\Photoshop\Plugins on your hard drive.

2. Open the folder \demo\HVSColor on the CD-ROM.

3. Drag the following files from the CD-ROM folder to the \plugins folder:

```
HVSJPEG.8BF
HVSColor.hlp
```

You will also find the files from Step 4 of the Installation HVS Color procedure in the HVSJPEG folder, but you do not need to copy them again. They are identical to the files you copied already.

Using HVS Color

I have included a sample image in the tutorial files for this chapter, which you can use to demonstrate the capabilities of the HVS plug-ins.

1. Open the file \My Web Stuff\Chap12\exampl1.pcx in Photoshop 4.0.

I selected this image because it presents significant challenges to any color-reduction utility. It contains fine detail, gradient values, and sharp edges. Figure 12-12 shows the file open in Photoshop, with the Filter menu pulled down to show where you will find the HVS plug-ins.

Figure 12-12: Accessing theHVS plug-ins.

2. To explore the features and possibilities of HVS Color, click the menu choice Filter | HVS Color | HVS Color. The actual filters you see may vary, depending on which Photoshop plug-ins are installed on your computer.

This tutorial features version 1.5 of HVS Color. Version 2.0 of the product should be available by the time you read this. Visit the Digital Frontiers web site at `http://www.digfrontiers.com` and download the latest and greatest version of this powerful tool.

Tip

If you do not see the HVS Color or HVS JPEG menu choices, it is likely that the files for these plug-ins did not get copied to the proper folders. Check to see that all files are in the proper folders, and try again.

Tip

Figure 12-13 shows the appearance of the Basic version of the HVS Color dialog box.

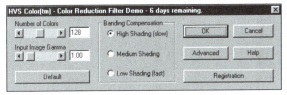

Figure 12-13: The HVS Color dialog box.

3. Set the number of colors to 128, and the Banding Compensation to High Shading (slow), and click OK. This reduces the number of colors from 16.7 million to 216.

4. If you see a dialog box warning you that the image is still in RGB mode, click OK to continue.

Figure 12-14 shows the image after color reduction. Note that although the number of colors used is small, the image looks sharp and colorful.

I also tested HVS Color with smaller numbers of colors, converting each time from the full-color original. Black-and-white images are insufficient to see what happens when you use fewer and fewer colors. You can look at full-color versions of these images in the tutorial folder. The files are

Ex216.pcx (216 colors)
Ex96.pcx (96 colors)
Ex48.pcx (48 colors)

Figure 12-14: A version of the image that uses 216 colors.

These files demonstrate the effects of extreme color reduction. The images stay sharp, but the color contrast is reduced. In plain English, colors tend to become washed out. I suggest that you try different numbers of colors to see what works best for your needs. The fewer the number of colors, the smaller the file size — and the paler your images.

The settings available in the Basic dialog box include

Number of Colors	Determines the number of colors present in the images palette.
Input Image Gamma	Gamma correction is a calculation that compensates for the way brightness appears on your monitor. Many monitors have a nonlinear brightness curve. This means that the difference in brightness values (from 0 to 255) is not uniform at all points between 0 and 255. The difference between 10 and 20, for example, may not equal the difference between 130 and 140. If you know the gamma setting for your monitor (programs such as PhotoImpact can help you determine this), enter that value here. If you do not know, experiment with different values to see which value gives you the best result. Typical input image gamma values are from 1.8 to 2.4.

(continued)

Banding Compensation	This setting determines the size of the blocks that HVS uses to process the image. When set to High Shading, color shading is emphasized more than color transitions at the edges of color areas. When set to Low Shading, edges between colors are treated as most important. Low shading works with strong colors with sharp divisions, and High shading works best with natural, photographic images. Use Medium Shading for images that have aspects of both types.
Default button	Returns all settings to their default values.
OK button	When clicked, converts the colors in the original image using the settings in the dialog box.

If you click the Registration button at lower right of the Basic dialog box (refer to Figure 12-13), you can get a fully working version of this tool for use after the seven-day trial period. If you click the Advanced button, you see the intimidating-but-powerful dialog box shown in Figure 12-15.

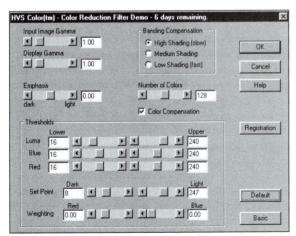

Figure 12-15: The Advanced version of the HVS Color dialog box.

The advanced settings allow you to tune the results of HVS Color reduction to a very fine degree. The additional settings available to you include these:

Display Gamma   This value applies to the gamma correction required for the monitor on which the image will be displayed. For web images, this doesn't matter; you can't predict what monitor folks will be using! For images viewed locally, you can use this setting to apply gamma correction.

Emphasis   Allows you to emphasize either dark or light colors in the color reduction. If you shift the emphasis toward dark, more palette colors are reserved for dark colors. If you shift the emphasis toward light, there will be more light colors in the palette.

Luma Threshold   Determines the degree of compression used on the darkest and lightest colors in the image. All colors with a brightness value lower than the lower threshold or higher than the higher threshold will be set to that value. For example, if you set the lower threshold to 30, all color values below 30 (remember that zero is black) will be rendered at a value of 30. This has the effect of removing pure blacks from the image, and thus reduces overall image contrast.

Red Threshold   Determines lower and upper limits for the red component of each pixel's color. This does not correspond to the blue value in RGB (Red/Green/Blue), but to the red component of the YCrCb color model. Y is for Luma (brightness), Cr is for Color red, and Cb is for Color blue.

Blue Threshold   Determines lower and upper limits for the blue component of each pixel's color. This does not correspond to the blue value in RGB (Red/Green/Blue), but to the blue component of the YCrCb color model.

Red Weighting   This value provides a degree of "spread" to the lower Luma threshold value. A higher setting reduces the number of red values mapped to a single threshold value. To obtain equal dark thresholds for red, green, and blue, set Red Weighting to 1.5 and Blue Weighting to 2.4. For images with lots of flesh tones, set Blue Weighting to zero and Red Weighting to 1.5. For outdoor scenes dominated by blues and greens, set Blue Weighting to 2.4 and Red Weighting to zero.

Blue Weighting   This value provides a degree of "spread" to the lower Luma threshold value. A higher setting reduces the number of blue values mapped to a single threshold value. See also Red Weighting.

(continued)

Dark Set Point	Determines the value for colors that are darker than the lower Luma Threshold. By setting this number lower than the lower Luma Threshold, you can retain contrast in the output image.
Light Set Point	Determines the value for colors that are brighter than the upper Luma Threshold. By setting this number higher than the upper Luma Threshold, you can retain contrast in the output image.
Color Compensation	If this is checked, the converter will make an extra pass in which the RBG values in the palette are compared to the average colors in the original image. Leave this checked unless it causes noticeable color problems in the output.

The features in the Advanced version of the dialog box take some time and effort to understand and use effectively. However, you gain a very high degree of control over the appearance of the output image. If you are serious about color reduction, the Advanced dialog box gives you tools you will find almost nowhere else.

Close all files when you are done testing HVS Color, and before you start the HVS JPEG tutorial.

Using HVS JPEG

HVS JPEG allows you to interactively choose not the just the quality level but many other JPEG-related settings. This can result in significantly smaller files — and in significantly better-looking images, too.

This tutorial features version 1.5 of HVS JPEG. Version 2.0 of the product should be available by the time you read this. Visit the Digital Frontiers web site at http://www.digfrontiers.com and download the latest version of this powerful tool.

1. Open the file \My Web Stuff\Chap12\Exampl1.pcx in Photoshop 4.0. This is the same file you used for the HVS Color tutorial.

2. Use the Filter | HVS JPEG | Save selection on the JPEG menu to access the HVS JPEG plug-in. This displays the Save As dialog box.

3. Enter a filename of **test.JPG**, and specify the \My Web Stuff folder. Click Save.

This opens the HVS JPEG dialog box, which has many settings. You can simply accept the default settings, adjust the Q (Quality) Setting, and click Export to create the JPEG file. Or you can use the settings to get a little extra compression. You've faced scary dialog boxes before. Test your mastery — put this one on-screen by yourself, and examine some controls:

Prefilter Detail	Determines the amount of detail that is filtered out of the image prior to applying JPEG compression. If your image has a lot of detailed textures, you will probably want a setting at or near the Sharp setting. If the image has broad areas with only minor color changes, use Soft.
Prefilter Strength	Determines the amount of prefiltering applied to the image. A Low setting results in very little prefiltering, and a High setting results in the maximum amount of prefiltering.
Q-Table	The JPEG compression standard uses a Q-Table to determine how to process various aspects of an image. You can either choose one of the default Q-Tables (General, Portraits, or Textured Images buttons), or have HVS generate a custom table (Generate Optimized Q-Table button). If you ask HVS to generate a custom Q-Table, it will ask you for a target compression level. This is the same as the Q setting at the far right in the dialog box. This is required because the custom Q-Table will vary for different levels of compression.
Progressive Display	Controls whether or not the JPEG image displays in multiple passes.
Show Compressed	Determines whether the preview pane at the upper right shows a compressed version of the image.
Q Setting	Sets the quality level for JPEG compression.
Statistics	Shows the estimated output file size, the estimated compression ratio, and the estimated time to download the image with a 28.8 modem.
Export button	Saves the JPEG file to your hard disk.
Done button	Closes the dialog box. Nothing is saved if you click here before you click the Export button.

By far the most powerful feature of this dialog box is the capability to generate a customized Q-Table for each image. You can experiment with the custom Q-Table feature by first adjusting the Q Setting for best results, and then generating a custom Q-Table. In most cases, you will find that you can use a lower Q Setting (and generate a smaller output file) after generating a custom Q-Table.

Figure 12-16 shows enlarged portions of three different images. The image at far left is the original. The image in the middle uses a very high level of compression, and the image at far right uses a moderate level of compression. These images show the differences in the fine detail caused by JPEG compression techniques.

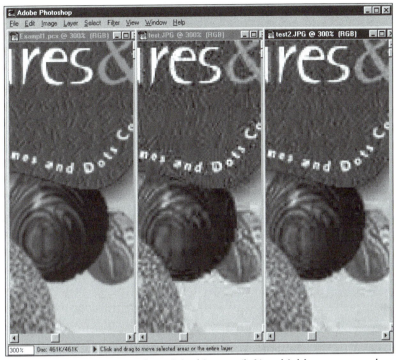

Figure 12-16: Comparing the original image (left), a highly compressed image (center), and a moderately compressed image (right).

You can compare the original with the JPEG compression files by looking at these files in \My Web Stuff\Chap12:

```
Exampl1.pcx
Test1.jpg
test2.jpg
```

Where to go from here:

Idea

The controls for HVS Color and HVS JPEG are complicated; there's no doubt about that! I suggest that you experiment with the sample image for this tutorial, as well as other images, using various settings and see how those settings effect the output. At first, change only one setting at a time so you can see the effect of that setting. Then work on combinations, such as changing the Luma Threshold while also changing the Dark Set Point. It takes time to learn how these controls affect your images, but the payoff in smaller file sizes is worth the effort.

Victor Vector: CorelDRAW 7

I think it's time to introduce a new method for creating images. If you think that all web images tend to look alike, consider using some tools that grew out of the need to create scaleable images for the world of print publishing. Most of the images you find on web pages are created as bitmaps — pixels of color that make up an image. Bitmaps don't scale well, as you'll see shortly. There is another way to create web page images, called *vector drawing*. Vector drawing involves some new ideas that differentiate it from bitmap-based drawing. Vector images are specifically designed to be scaleable — you can print a vector drawing small or large, and it looks great. You don't need (and often can't use) scaleability on a web page, but some of the tools used in print publishing offer unique tools for creating such graphics.

Tip

Although vector-based drawing tools such as CorelDRAW use different methods for many operations, they do share some characteristics of bitmap drawing tools such as Photoshop. Even if you use a vector-based program to create graphics, you will still need to save it to a bitmap format for use on the Web. There is limited support for vector image formats on the Web; if you want anyone and everyone to appreciate your graphics, stick to the GIF and JPEG image formats. Figure 12-17 shows a web page from Chapter 8. All of the graphics on the page were created as vector graphics in CorelDRAW, then saved in JPEG format.

To get started with the world of vector art, you need to know that there are two kinds of graphics files in common use on computers: raster files, and vector files. Raster files are bitmaps, and file formats such as TIFF, BMP, TGA, PCX, GIF, and JPEG are all raster formats. In simplest terms, a raster image file is composed of pixels. Raster files tend to be large because every pixel must be recorded in the file. Compressed formats like GIF and JPEG reduce the size of the image file to a greater or lesser degree either by storing redundant pixel data in a compact form, or by simply eliminating some of the pixels altogether (Chapter 11 covers the GIF and JPEG file formats in depth).

If you try to enlarge a rasterized image, the pixels that make up the image become all too visible. Figure 12-18 shows an image at actual size, and Figure 12-19 shows the image enlarged several times. The pixels are visible in the enlarged image. If this were a rasterized image, no pixelation would occur. As it happens, only raster image formats are widely supported on the Web. This means you can use vector drawing programs to create graphics, but in the end you will probably have to convert to one of the web-supported raster formats, GIF and JPEG. To minimize pixel problems, convert to GIF or JPEG only when you complete work on the vector image.

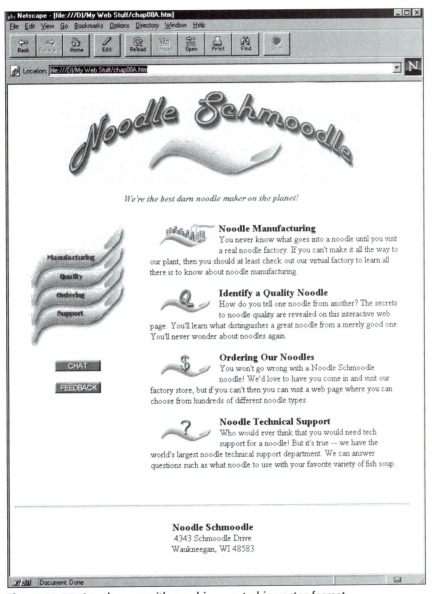

Figure 12-17: A web page with graphics created in vector format.

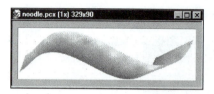

Figure 12-18: A rasterized image of a noodle.

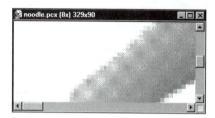

Figure 12-19: Enlarged eight times, the pixelated nature of a rasterized image shows clearly.

Vector images explained

Vector images, unlike rasterized images, do not store pixels. They store a mathematical description of the image. For example, if there is a curved line in the image, the path of the curve is stored, not the curve itself. When you open a vector file, the image editor reconstructs the drawing from the mathematical descriptions contained in the file.

For the most part, image editing programs are divided into those that are primarily designed to work with vector graphics, and those that are primarily for rasterized graphics. Photoshop is for raster images, CorelDRAW for vector images. The division is not absolute: Photoshop has some limited abilities for creating vector drawings, and CorelDRAW supports rasterized images.

Vector images are used primarily for print publishing. Unlike rasterized images, which show pixelation when enlarged, vector images have sharp, clear edges at every size. Instead of enlarging the image by adding pixels, software enlarges vector images by recalculating the mathematical formulas for the new size.

Why all this discussion about vector and raster? Because for the first time in this book you are about to step through a tutorial using an image editor designed for vector graphics: CorelDRAW 7. Figure 12-20 shows CorelDRAW when you begin a session. Tools and palettes are arranged around the window edge, and a blank sheet of paper sits in the middle of the window. This sheet of paper betrays CorelDRAW's origins as a vector graphics program designed for print use.

Sheet of paper

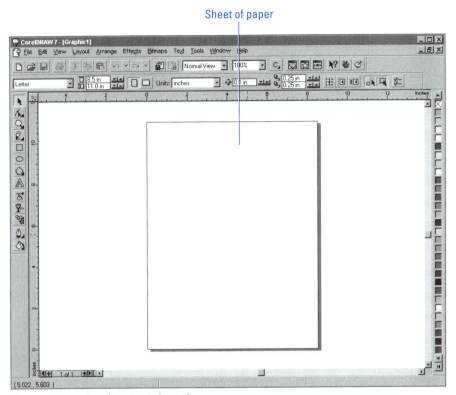

Figure 12-20: CorelDRAW 7 in action.

Creating a Vector Graphic

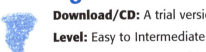

Download/CD: A trial version of CorelDRAW 7 was not available at press time.

Level: Easy to Intermediate

Task: Create vector graphics and save in JPEG format

Tutorial

Before you start: Install and run version 7 of CorelDRAW.

To create a logo for Noodle Schmoodle, the company introduced in Chapter 8:

1. Select the text tool from the CorelDRAW toolbar at the left side of the window (see Figure 12-21).

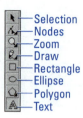

Figure 12-21: Choose the text tool.

- Selection
- Nodes
- Zoom
- Draw
- Rectangle
- Ellipse
- Polygon
- Text

2. Position the text cursor on the drawing surface (that's supposed to represent a sheet of paper) near the top left and click. The exact position doesn't matter, as you will be saving the image to a file, not printing to a sheet of paper. You'll see a vertical bar, which marks the insertion point for adding text.

3. Type the company name, **Noodle Schmoodle** (see Figure 12-22).

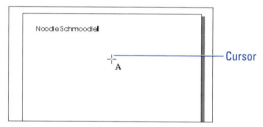

Noodle Schmoodle

——— Cursor

A

Figure 12-22: Adding text.

4. Click the selection tool to make the text the currently selected object (see Figure 12-23).

5. If the text is not the selected object — that is, if the text does not have those big old black squares around it — click the text to select it.

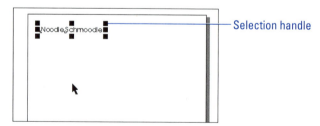

Noodle Schmoodle

——— Selection handle

Figure 12-23: Text as an object.

As the text stands now, it's horrible and useless as a logo. We need to jazz it up.

6. Use the Text | Format Text menu selection to open the dialog box shown in Figure 12-24.

7. Click the Font tab to activate it.

The text used is the default font and size. In my case, that was Avant Garde and 24.0 points. You may see something different.

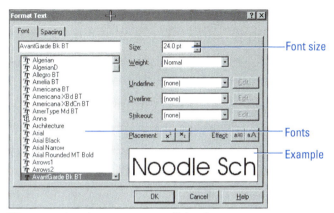

Figure 12-24: The Format Text dialog box.

8. Change the size of the font to 64.0 points, and choose the Harlow font. If you do not have the Harlow font installed, pick any interesting font that appeals to you. A font with oversize capitals, as shown in Figure 12-25, is ideal.

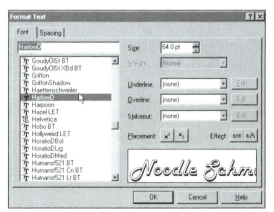

Figure 12-25: Choosing a new font and size.

Tip

For best results, click the Spacing tab in the Format Text dialog box, and set the Word spacing to 150.0. This puts a little more space between words, and gives a more balanced appearance to the logo. Click the Center radio button as well, to center the text.

9. Click OK when you are done making changes to the Format Text dialog box.

The text will now be larger (64 points instead of 24), and offset to the left. The offset occurred because the text is centered on the original insertion point.

10. Click and drag the text to the center of the page (see Figure 12-26).

Dragging an object

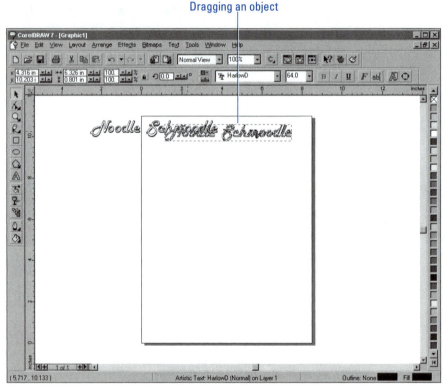

Figure 12-26: Recentering the text.

11. To change the color of the text, click any of the colors at the right of the CorelDRAW window (see Figure 12-27, which shows an enlargement for your viewing pleasure).

12. You can create a custom color by clicking the Color flyout (see Figure 12-28) and choosing the fill option. This displays a color dialog box similar to the one used in Photoshop (see Figure 12-29).

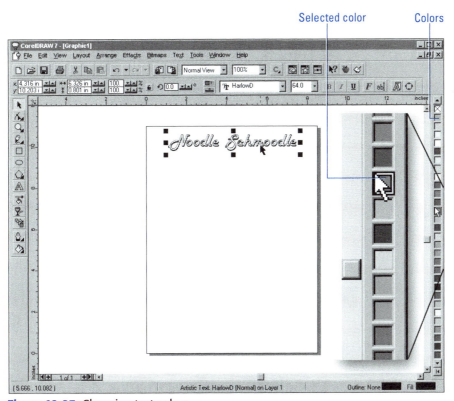

Figure 12-27: Changing text colors.

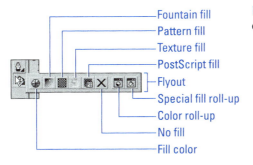

Figure 12-28: Customizing text colors with a fill.

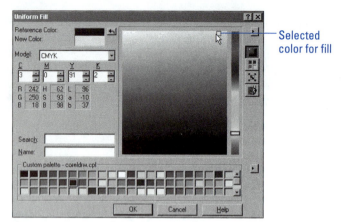

Figure 12-29: Creating a custom color.

Tip   Although vector and raster programs deal with drastically different kinds of files, you may have noticed already that there are only minor differences between how you work with those images using the tools in the software. An image is an image, and the file format used to store it is becoming less and less important. However, as you progress through this tutorial, you will begin to see that vector files have distinct advantages. This is especially true when working with text.

Modifying vector drawings

To make this text work as a logo, it needs to be stretched out a bit to elongate the letters. The next task is to wrap the text to an ellipse, and it will look better elongated.

1. Click the text to select it (Figure 12-30), and click and drag the right-center selection handle to the right (see Figure 12-31).

2. Continue to drag off the right edge of the paper. When you release the mouse button, the text will be wider (see Figure 12-32).

Figure 12-30: Select a handle and drag.

└─ Cursor

Figure 12-31: The cursor changes as you drag.

Figure 12-32: The elongated text.

The action you just performed is one that shows off the value of vector-based drawing. Although you increased the width of the text, you did not create new pixels. The elongated text is still created using a mathematical formula, and is completely smooth. If the text had been composed of pixels, stretching it would have blurred the edges and created a less sharp result. Figure 12-33 shows what the text looks like when stretched as pixels in PhotoImpact. The bottom image shows the effects of stretching.

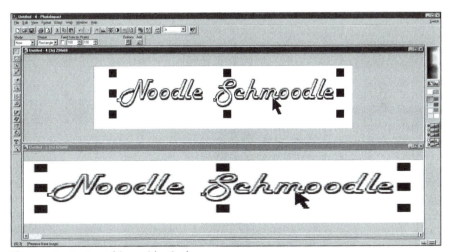

Figure 12-33: Stretching with pixels.

Fitting text to a curve

The next task is to curve the text. This is accomplished in CorelDRAW by first creating a curve, and then fitting the text to the curve.

1. To create an ellipse, click the ellipse tool and then drag to form an ellipse that is slightly larger than the width of the text. Figure 12-34 shows the approximate dimensions and shape of the desired ellipse.

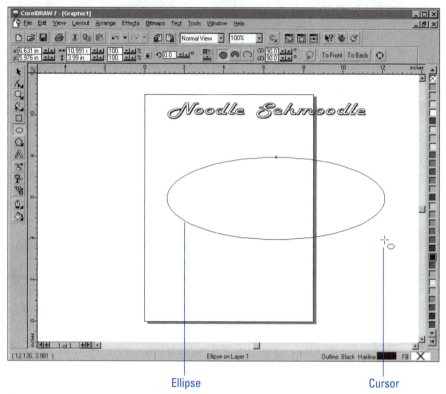

Figure 12-34: Creating an ellipse.

For example, click below the left end of the text object, and then drag down and to the right. You do not need to match the size and proportion exactly.

2. Before you can fit the text to the ellipse, click to select the ellipse, and then Shift + Click to add the text object to the selection. Selection handles will appear surrounding both objects (see Figure 12-35).

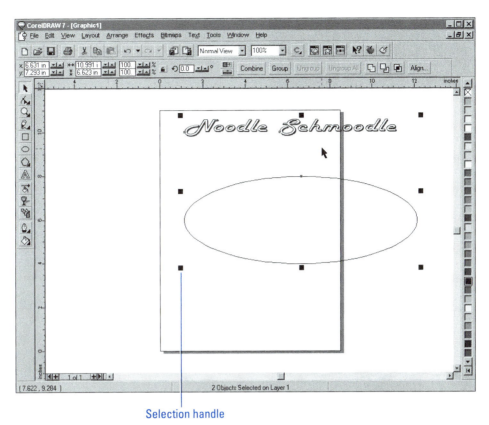

Selection handle

Figure 12-35: Selecting more than one object.

3. Now use the Text | Fit Text to Path menu selection to open the Fit Text to Path roll-up (see Figure 12-36). (Look at the nearby Tip if you're wondering what a roll-up is.)

——Apply button

Figure 12-36: The Fit Text to Path roll-up.

The Fit Text to Path roll-up displays several choices for fitting text in the drop-down list at the top of the roll-up, as shown in Figure 12-36.

Tip

Roll-ups are semipermanent dialogs unique to CorelDRAW. They "roll up" so that only the title bar displays when you click the middle button at upper right of the roll-up.

4. Choose the option that keeps the text vertical, as shown, and click the Apply button to fit the text to the path. The text jumps to the top of the ellipse.

5. Move the combined ellipse and text to center it at the top of the page. Figure 12-37 shows the result. Don't worry if the text overlaps the edge of the page.

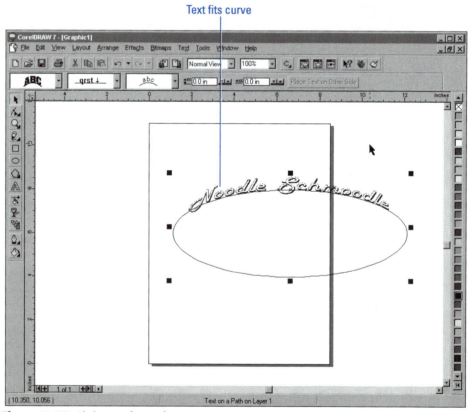

Figure 12-37: Fitting to the path.

Fitting text to a path is another vector-specific feature of CorelDRAW. It is available in most vector-based image editors, such as Freehand and Adobe Illustrator.

6. The ellipse doesn't belong as part of the logo. To get rid of it, make sure the text and ellipse are selected (click either one to select both), and use the Arrange | Separate menu selection to break them into separate objects. The text will retain the shape of the ellipse.

7. You can now select just the ellipse, and remove it with the Edit | Cut menu selection. This leaves just the text (see Figure 12-38).

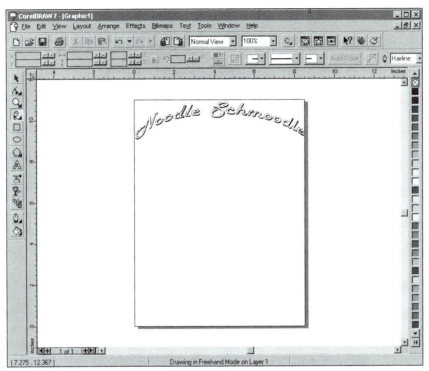

Figure 12-38: The text remains after the ellipse is removed.

Saving a vector drawing as a raster image

If you save your work in CorelDRAW, it is saved as a vector drawing in Corel's proprietary format. That format is unsuitable for a web page. You could select File | Export to save the image to Corel's CMX format (see Figure 12-39), or you could convert the graphic to the standard GIF or JPEG file formats.

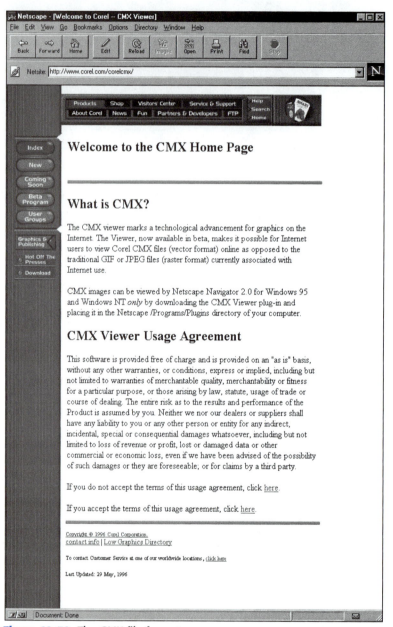

Figure 12-39: The CMX file format.

If you export to the CMX format, anyone viewing your web page will need to download Corel's CMX Viewer from `http://www.corel.com/corelcmx/` and install it as a Netscape plug-in. Unless you are willing to require this of your visitors, saving as GIF or JPEG is a better option. In fact, in a test, the CMX file was about twice the size of the JPEG file, so there was no size advantage. JPEG is often a good option for an image, as it results in very small file sizes.

To save the logo as a JPEG image file:

1. Use the File | Export menu selection. This opens the Export dialog box (see Figure 12-40).

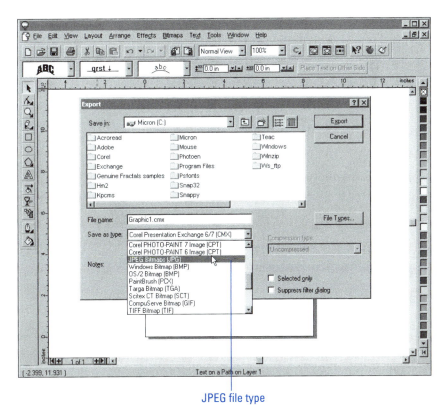

JPEG file type

Figure 12-40: Exporting to a file.

2. Choose JPEG Bitmaps as the file type. Give the image a filename (**graphic1.jpg** will work just fine) and click the Export button to display the dialog box shown in Figure 12-41.

3. Use the default values with one exception: Click the Super-sampling radio button at the bottom right. This will give you the highest possible image quality.

4. Click OK to continue.

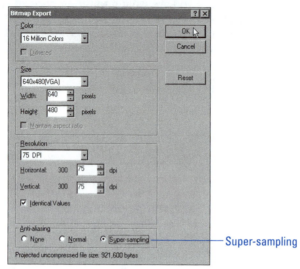

Figure 12-41: Export options.

This displays the compression settings for JPEG files (see Figure 12-42). I chose the highest possible quality setting to preserve the appearance of the logo. For use on the Web, I would eventually use a higher compression setting to get a smaller file size.

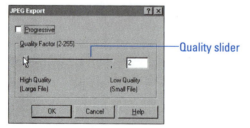

Figure 12-42: Set JPEG compression for the highest possible image quality.

It's always a good idea to use as little compression as possible until you are certain that are you completely done editing an image. If you do make changes, you want to make them to a very high-quality version of the image. I usually work at minimal compression levels until I'm ready to copy the image to the web server. At that time, I use a tool like HVS Color or PhotoImpact's JPEG SmartSaver to determine how much compression to use.

Idea

Where to go from here:

✦ CorelDRAW includes many other features that are unique to vector-based drawing software. You can experiment with them to see how they work. These include spline-based drawing using Bezier curves and freehand drawing that is converted to Bezier curves.

✦ The logo could use a noodle under the text. To create a noodle, draw a line with the freehand tool, extrude it; resize it if necessary, and give it noodle-like colors (see Figure 12-43).

Figure 12-43: The completed noodle.

The completed logo is shown in Figure 12-44. I loaded the logo into Fractal Design Painter and added drop shadows to both the text and the noodle.

Figure 12-44: The completed logo.

When Zero Is the Perfect Image Size

Wouldn't it be great if you could create image files that were so small that they consisted of zero bytes? That sounds too good to be true, and it is. You can have image files with zero bytes, but they still take time to download.

Yes, you read that correctly, but it is a misleading statement. I'm talking about generating images on the fly. Instead of downloading a preexisting graphic image from the web server, your web page downloads an image created by a program on the server. The image has zero bytes on the server because there is no image file on the server. But when the server creates the image on the fly, there are bytes that must be sent across the Internet, and that takes download time.

At the risk of saying something over Mr. Author's head, you do get something for nothing, but you still pay for it with download time.

The trick is to run a program on the web server that generates a stream of bytes that is exactly the same as the stream of bytes that makes up an image file. Before I go too far out on a limb, let's take a look at the steps in displaying the typical web page graphic.

1. Your browser requests a page from a web server.

2. The web server starts sending the text on the page.

3. If a graphics file is included, your browser requests the graphics file.

4. When the web server finds the graphics file, it starts sending it. The graphics file is preceded by some bytes that say, in essence "here comes a graphics file."

5. Your web browser receives the bytes for the graphics file, and displays them on the page as a graphic.

Your web browser doesn't care where the bytes that make up the image come from. They could be in a file on the web server, they could be under a napkin in the cafeteria. As long as the bytes get to your browser, the browser is happy to display them. The key is that the bytes have to be organized in the same format as a real graphics file.

This means that if there is software running on the web server that can create graphics files on the fly, and send the bytes (along with those bytes that say "here comes a graphics file"), then it's possible to display images that don't "really" exist.

Got that? Now for the bad news: It's not an easy thing to do. If you want to create images on the fly, you need to learn how to write computer programs. If you already know something about programming, you can probably handle the programming required to create graphics on the fly. The trick is to use existing libraries that handle the hard-core stuff for you. This allows you to write fairly simple programs that will generate the graphics for you. Unfortunately, before you can write those simple programs you need to do quite a bit of technical work to install the various pieces that make up the tools, and then learn how to use them.

If that doesn't scare you away from the idea of generating images on the fly, I can point you to online information about installing such a library, writing Perl scripts to generate graphics, and writing the HTML code to generate graphics on the fly on web pages. A good starting point is the web page at
`http://www.genome.wi.mit.edu/ftp/pub/software/WWW/GD.html`.

The next question is a natural one: For what, exactly, does one use these on-the-fly graphics? I dug up only a few sites making use of them. Figure 12-46 shows a page called Web-a-Sketch that allows you to draw interactively on a web page. It's slow, but for a cheap thrill, visit `http://www.digitalstuff.com/web-a-sketch/`.

Figure 12-45: Web-a-Sketch uses generated GIF images.

More mundane uses might include live data graphs ("Care for a pie chart with your data, sir? The *Year-to-Date Cherry Shipments* is excellent."), graphic web-page counters, simple maps, interactive graphics, keypads, calculators, and so on. The Web Tour for this chapter points you to some sites that use on-the-fly GIF images.

Web Tour #12: Real-Life Examples

Small images exist all over the Web, and there are even some web sites that make almost exclusive use of small graphics files. To see examples of small graphics used well, and even some on-the-fly generated graphics, double-click the file:

```
\WebTour\Chap12\index.htm
```

You'll see the Web Tour page for this chapter.

Interlacing and Transparency

To prepare for this chapter's tutorials, copy the following folder from the CD-ROM to the `\My Web Stuff` folder on your hard drive:

`\tutorial\chap13`

This will copy files for all of the tutorials in this chapter to your hard disk. See Chapter 1 for complete details on setting up for tutorials.

You've seen transparency and interlacing a million times if you've been on the Web for more than a week. These two image features are pervasive. They are found on small pages and large, complex web sites and simple home pages. There is a good reason for such ubiquity: Transparency and interlacing are very, very useful.

Interlacing Isn't Just for Sneakers

If you peruse the computer ads in the magazines and the Sunday paper, you have probably noticed that most monitors sold today have a feature called *non-interlaced.* An interlaced monitor isn't good for you, but interlaced web page images are. Your television is interlaced, but movies are not.

The interlacing on a television or an older computer monitor has to do with the way that these devices operate. There is an electron gun at the back of the tube inside the TV or monitor. The gun "paints" images on the screen by scanning back and forth in horizontal lines. On an interlaced computer monitor or a TV screen, the gun skips a line when it paints. On the first pass, it paints all of the odd lines. On the second pass, it paints all of the even lines.

As if Mr. Author really knows whether odd or even lines get painted first. The point is the skipping; it's the very essence of interlacing.

The skipping technique means that it takes two passes to paint one screen image. The good news is that motion video looks better on an interlaced monitor, and that's why TVs continue to use interlacing. The bad news is that stationary images flicker on an interlaced monitor, and that's why computer monitors are advertised as *non-interlaced*. Today's computer monitors don't do the skipping thing: They paint every line from top to bottom. This results in a steadier display with very little flickering. Interlacing is making a comeback on web pages. This time, the interlacing doesn't have anything to do with the electron guns in your monitor. It has to do with how a GIF image gets displayed on a web page.

The interlaced technique — skipping lines — gradually displays a web image. Images are made up of rows of pixels; each row corresponds to a line. Your browser displays images one line at a time, displaying a non-interlaced image from the top down; the visitor has to wait to see what the image looks like. Your browser displays an interlaced image by skipping lines, blending together the lines it does display. At first, the image is fuzzy and indistinct (as in Figure 13-1). As additional portions display during the download, the image gets clearer.

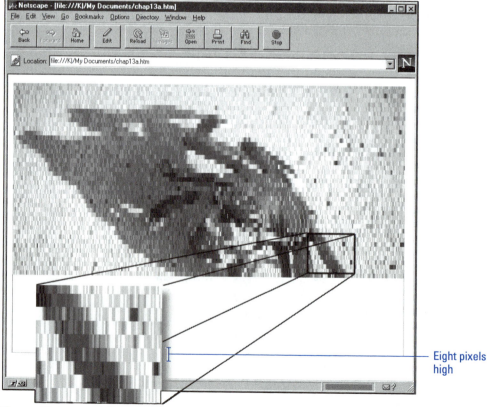

Eight pixels high

Figure 13-1: A partially displayed interlaced image.

CD

In the case of interlaced web page images, the skipping doesn't involve every other line. The skipping pattern for GIF images is more complicated than that. In the first stage of its display, an interlaced image is very low quality because, in fact, most of the image is missing. To view the file yourself, double-click the file on the CD-ROM: \tutorial\chap13\chap13a.htm. If you do not have the CD-ROM installed, you can view the file \My Web Stuff\chap13\chap13a.htm. The file will load more slowly from CD-ROM, and the effect will be more visible.

In Figure 13-1, every eighth line of pixels is displayed. If this were all that were happening, the image would actually look as shown in Figure 13-2, with most of the lines missing. Your browser plays a little trick and temporarily expands the visible lines so each line is eight pixels high (see the close-up detail in Figure 13-1).

Figure 13-2: Every eighth line of an image.

On the next pass, the lines midway between the already displayed lines get displayed. This shows a bit more image detail. As before, the missing pixels are filled in by stretching the visible pixels vertically. Figure 13-3 shows an image after the second pass and just before the end of the third pass. The detail shown at the right of the image shows how the image looks after the second pass. The pixels are still stretched vertically but not as much as before — each pixel is stretched four pixels high. The detail shown at the left of Figure 13-3 shows a portion of the image with three passes. The pixels are only slightly stretched vertically; they are two pixels high.

To get a sense of the actual image pixels present in Figure 13-3, look at Figure 13-4. It shows the image during the middle of the second pass, but with no stretching. Most web browsers provide the stretching feature because unstretched pixels are hard to discern.

Figure 13-3: A partially displayed GIF image.

This process continues until the complete image is displayed in detail (as in Figure 13-5). The advantage of interlacing is that the complete image gets displayed at low resolution quickly, giving the visitor a quick idea of what the image is about.

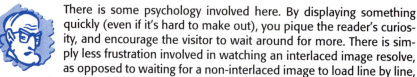 There is some psychology involved here. By displaying something quickly (even if it's hard to make out), you pique the reader's curiosity, and encourage the visitor to wait around for more. There is simply less frustration involved in watching an interlaced image resolve, as opposed to waiting for a non-interlaced image to load line by line, from top to bottom, slowly. An interlaced image provides some instant gratification, while a non-interlaced image provides little but frustration.

Figure 13-4: A partially displayed interlaced image, in the middle of the second pass.

Figure 13-5: The completely displayed image.

The larger an image, the more important it is to interlace that image. There are several tutorials later in the chapter that show how easy it is to create interlaced images. Interlacing, however, only applies to GIF images. If you have a JPEG image, you can take advantage of a recent development called progressive JPEG. It is explained in the next section.

Tip

GIF images are literally interlaced. The rows are stored in the GIF file out of order so that they display in an interlaced fashion. Since JPEG images aren't actually composed of rows of pixels (remember, there is all that fancy compression going on), the term interlacing just doesn't apply, but progressive *sounds* great.

Get Progressive with JPEG

Until fairly recently, interlacing was strictly for GIF files. Anyone using JPEG files for their images had to take the bad with the good. The good: JPEG image files are very highly compressed, and therefore small and quick to download. The bad: JPEG files display from the top down, frustrating visitors to the page.

The advent of progressive JPEG changes all of that. Progressive JPEG allows you to save JPEG images so that they will display gradually, just like an interlaced GIF image. Figure 13-6 shows an example of an early stage in the display of a progressive JPEG image. Note that the first scan is still line by line, but it is at a lower overall resolution. The pixel stretching is not nearly as obvious. To see this for yourself, double-click the file `\My Web Stuff\chap13\chap13d.htm` to view it in your browser.

Figure 13-6: An early step in scan one.

Figure 13-7 shows the end of the first full scan. You can specify the number of scans when you save the file as progressive JPEG. Figure 13-8 shows the dialog box for saving as JPEG in Photoshop. There is a drop-down list that allows you to choose 3, 4, or 5 scans.

Edges soft

Figure 13-7: The end of the first full scan.

Progressive
radio button   Quality level

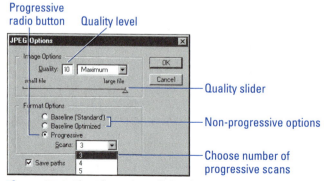

Quality slider

Non-progressive options

Choose number of
progressive scans

Figure 13-8: The Photoshop dialog box allows you to choose
the number of scans.

Figure 13-9 shows the image after the final scan. You may not be able to see it here in black and white, but the image quality is better than in the first full scan. You can compare the images directly on the CD-ROM. Load the files from the CD by double-clicking the file \tutorial\chap13\chap13b.htm. I suggest loading the file from the CD because it will make the progressive nature of the display easier to see. The CD-ROM is slower than your hard disk, and the image will take a bit longer to display.

Edges sharp

Figure 13-9: The completed progressive image display.

See the tutorials later in this chapter for information about saving images in the progressive JPEG format.

I've noticed that progressive JPEG images actually tend to be slightly smaller in size than standard JPEG images, so now you have a second reason for using the progressive JPEG file format.

Transparency Tricks

Transparency is the art of making the background of an image disappear, leaving an irregular outline around some object or image. Figure 13-10 shows this better than words can. The file is `\My Web Stuff\Chap13\chap13i.htm`. You've probably seen similar images around the Internet on a variety of web pages. If you've been wondering how it's done, it's incredibly easy. You'll learn how in the first tutorial in this chapter.

Figure 13-10: The upper image has a transparent background.

Although adding transparency to an image is easy, you can improve the overall look of your transparent images by knowing a few simple tricks. All of the tricks have to do with preserving a hard edge on the image, so that there is a clean break between the image and its background.

8-bit versus 24-bit

Most image editing software allows you to create either 8-bit or 24-bit images. Often, it is desirable to create 24-bit images to maintain the highest possible image quality while you work on the image. However, if you plan to create transparency in an image, 24 bits may hurt rather than help.

Figure 13-11 shows a red button in Photoshop. I created the red button by

✦ Creating a new file (80 × 80 pixels)

✦ Dragging out a circular selection

✦ Turning on anti-aliasing

✦ Filling the selection with red

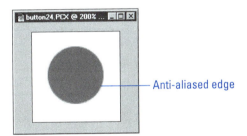

Figure 13-11: A 24-bit red button with anti-aliasing on.

The edge of the button is soft because it blends neatly into the background. The anti-aliasing accounts for the smooth blending, as explained in the sidebar "Auntie Alias Strikes Again." Figure 13-12 shows the same kind of circular button created in an 8-bit image, but with anti-aliasing turned off.

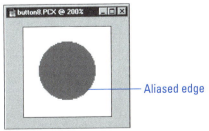

Figure 13-12: A red button with anti-aliasing turned off.

Auntie Alias Strikes Again

The term anti-aliasing can be confusing. I want to take a moment to help you get a clear understanding of the term. You won't find anti-aliasing in your dictionary (at least I couldn't find it in my rather large unabridged dictionary). And if the word "alias" means a false name, it's hard to see how "anti-alias" can refer to a few faded pixels.

Figure 13-13 shows what you get when you turn anti-aliasing *on*. The image editor adds pixels that are intermediate in color between the two original colors to smooth

the appearance of the edge between those two colors. The pixels in Figure 13-13 are greatly enlarged. This is a very small section of the round button in Figure 13-11.

Figure 13-14 shows what you get when you turn anti-aliasing *off*. There are no intermediate pixels to soften the edge between the two colors. This is called a hard edge, and it is highly desirable when you are creating images with transparent backgrounds. You'll see the advantages of turning anti-aliasing off in the Photoshop tutorial later in this chapter.

Figure 13-13: An image with anti-aliasing on.

Figure 13-14: An image with anti-aliasing off.

Figure 13-15 shows a web page that uses the two red buttons shown in Figures 13-11 and 13-12. On a white background, the two images look equally good. In fact, the image with the anti-aliasing turned on looks a bit better because it blends more smoothly into the background. This is true because the images were originally created with a white background. You can see this for yourself in the file \My Web Stuff\Chap13\chap13E.htm.

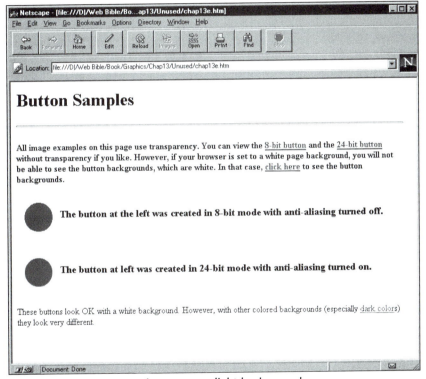

Figure 13-15: Transparent images on a light background.

Figure 13-16 shows a web page that uses a dark background. Now, the light pixels created with anti-aliasing on stand out and create an unnatural white fringe around one of the buttons. You can see this for yourself in the file \My Web Stuff\Chap13\chap13F.htm.

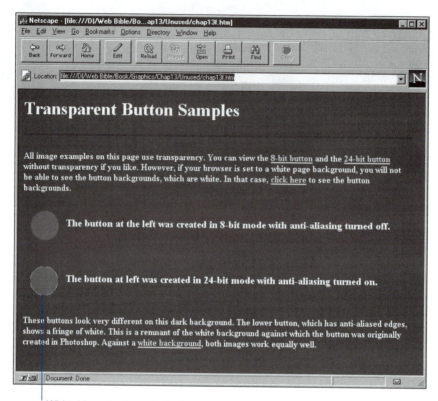

White fringe due to anti-aliasing

Figure 13-16: Only the non-anti-aliased image looks good on a dark background.

Tip

If the button images had been created against a dark background, their behavior would be opposite. They would both look good on a dark background, while only the non-anti-aliased image would look good on a light background. This is why it is a good idea to create your buttons and doodads without using anti-aliasing — you can create them with any kind of background, and use them against any kind of background. This avoids the necessity of recreating transparent images for various background colors.

Beware of shadows and aliasing

Just as anti-aliasing can create problems with transparency, any part of an image that fades into the image's background color can cause trouble. A drop shadow is a good example. Figure 13-17 shows a web page with two buttons on it. One of the buttons has a drop shadow, and one does not. Both buttons were created with white backgrounds, and the background was then made transparent. The button with the drop shadow appears to have a white shadow instead of a dark one. This happens because the background color is darker than most of the shadow. You can see this for yourself in the file `\My Web Stuff\Chap13\chap13H.htm`.

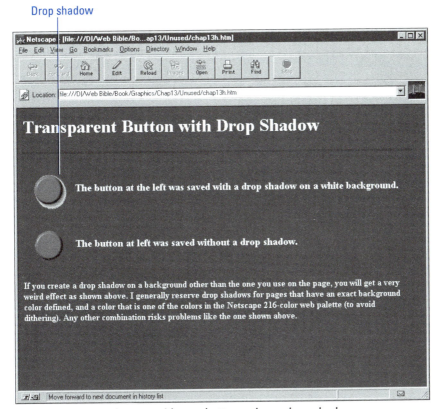

Figure 13-17: A web page with one button using a drop shadow.

This points out a fundamental limitation of transparency on web pages: The edge between the image and the background is always a hard edge. You cannot fade something like a shadow into the background. Keep this one fact in mind:

Always give your objects hard edges by turning anti-aliasing off.

If you do, you will seldom have trouble with transparency.

Figure 13-18 shows the drop-shadow problem up close and personal. As the shadow fades from dark gray to the background (white in this case), it takes on more and more of the background color.

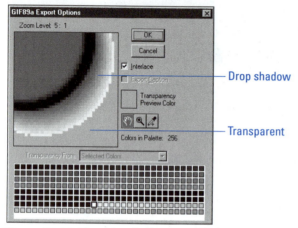

— Drop shadow

— Transparent

Figure 13-18: The drop shadow actually has a fringe that matches the background against which it was created.

Tip

There are times when you can exploit anti-aliasing when using transparency. Probably the most dramatic example is the use of anti-aliasing to create a smooth fade from the page's background color to another color. Figure 13-19 shows an example. The dark-blue background color at the image's edge fades to a much lighter color. Note that you do not need to match the page's background color exactly. The color around the outside edge of the image only needs to be similar because transparency helps cover any slight mismatch of color. You can see this effect for yourself in the file `\My Web Stuff\Chap13\chap13j.htm`.

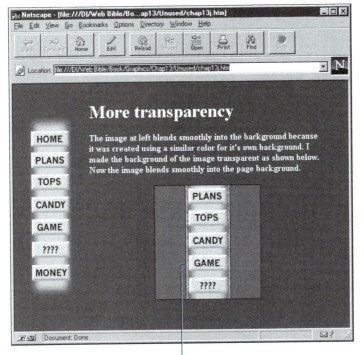

Transparent pixels at edge

Figure 13-19: Using transparency in a different way.

Interlacing and Transparency with HyperSnap

CD: You'll find HyperSnap on the CD-ROM. To install, double-click the file
`\demo\hypersnp\hysnap.exe`.

Level: Easy as Pie

Tutorial

Task: Add transparency and interlacing to a GIF image

Before you start: Install and register the shareware version of HyperSnap. Note that this tutorial will not work with the unregistered version of HyperSnap, as that version will not save GIF images.

If your image editor does not support transparency or interlacing, you can still work with your familiar editor to create/edit images, and use HyperSnap to add these features. HyperSnap is a shareware screen-capture utility, but it includes some nice Web-aware features. If you use it be sure to pay the current shareware fee.

1. Double-click the HyperSnap icon to open HyperSnap.

   Figure 13-20 shows what you'll see: a very unassuming and simple interface. Most of HyperSnap's features are oriented toward screen capture. I recommend it highly, by the way, for this primary function. I can attest to its usefulness and reliability, as I used it to capture all of the screen images in this book.

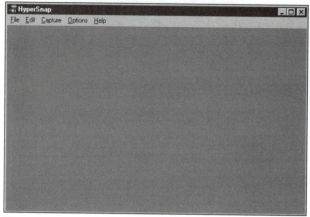

Figure 13-20: HyperSnap's interface looks blank, but isn't.

2. To use HyperSnap for its web features, use the File | Open menu selection to open the Open dialog box. (How's that for redundancy? See Figure 13-21.)

3. Locate the file \My Web Stuff\Chap13\myDuck.gif, click to highlight it, and click the OK button to open it (see Figure 13-22).

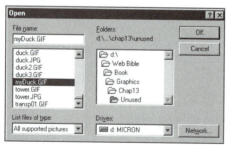

Figure 13-21: Opening a file with HyperSnap.

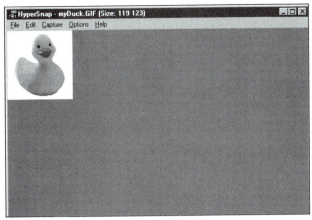

Figure 13-22: An image loaded into HyperSnap.

4. Click the File |Save As menu selection to open the Save As dialog box (see Figure 13-23). This dialog box is where you can access Web-related features.

5. Locate the original file \My Web Stuff\Chap13\myDuck.gif and click it to put the correct filename in the File name box.

6. Click the Options button to open YAD (Yet Another Dialog; see Figure 13-24). This dialog box is for GIF images, and there is a corresponding dialog box for JPEG images that lets you set compression levels.

Filename

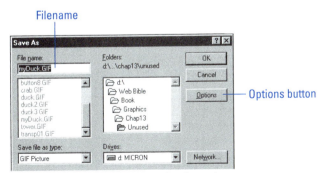

Options button

Figure 13-23: The Save As dialog box gives you access to web-related features.

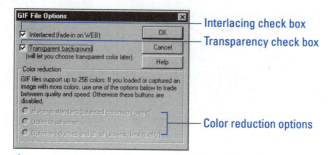

Interlacing check box
Transparency check box
Color reduction options

Figure 13-24: Web features for GIF files dialog box.

7. Click the two check boxes to turn them on. The top check box causes the file to be interlaced, and the second check box is for transparency. The options at the bottom of the dialog box are for images that have more than 256 colors; they are grayed out and unavailable because the duck image uses 8-bit color.

8. Click the OK button. The GIF File Options dialog box closes. Click OK again.

And now for the tricky part: Look at the title bar for the HyperSnap window (see Figure 13-25, and compare it to Figure 13-22). Instead of the image filename, the title bar is blinking a message at you:

```
Click on transparent color, or abort with right button
```

Note changed caption in title bar

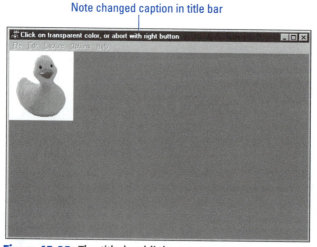

Figure 13-25: The title bar blinks a message at you.

Making Great Web Graphics

The following section sparks your creativity and adds to your learning experience by showing many web graphics and processes in color. Enjoy!

Look for this icon in this color section; it tells you where to find more information on a topic.

For additional ideas, more full-color graphics, and software, check out the accompanying CD-ROM. You can access the fun stuff on the CD-ROM by double-clicking on the file `viewme.htm` in the root directory.

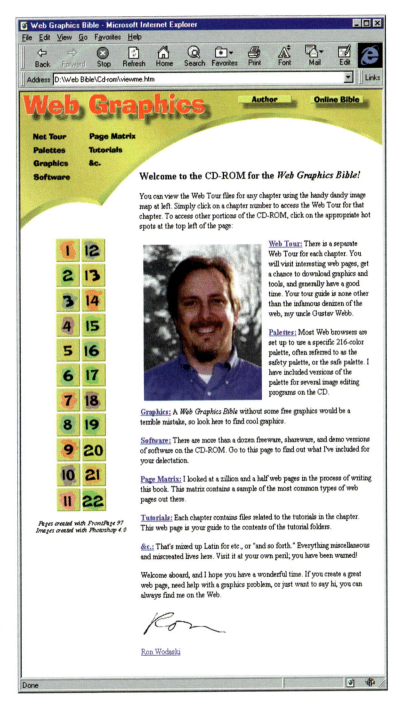

Anti-Aliasing Creates an Edge Effect

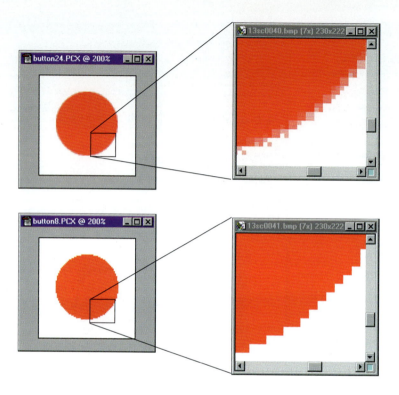

When you create a button (or any web image) that will have a transparent background, decide early whether you want to use anti-aliasing. Anti-aliasing adds transition pixels at the edge of an image (the top set of images shows this), but this causes a halo effect if the page background is a different color than the image background. In most cases, leave out the anti-aliasing so you can get a clean edge, as shown in the lower pair of images. Yes, you wind up with a more ragged-looking edge, but it's much better than a glowing halo.

Square or rectangular images do not need special attention regarding anti-aliasing. And don't ever hesitate to use anti-aliasing everywhere except the edge, because it will always make your image look more natural.

See Chapter 13

JPEG Compression Works Well for Photos

Probably the most important thing to know about web graphics is that they should be small files. Small files download more quickly. The faster a page displays, the more likely your visitor is to stick around and read it. The best road to small image files is image compression.

See Chapter 14

The image below left is the uncompressed version. It's a real monster in web terms, almost 180,000 bytes (about 175K). Here's a reality check: The total size for all web images on a basic page should usually be under 50K.

The image on the right is the compressed version. JPEG compression is better for photographs than GIF compression (see next color page for GIF info). JPEG compression can deal with lots and lots of differently colored pixels, while GIF is very poor at that. The dialog box below shows the PhotoImpact JPEG SmartSaver in use to determine the optimal amount of compression. You can change the amount of compression with the slider at the bottom of the dialog box and immediately view the effect in the right-hand image. Even with heavy compression (the quality setting of 24), the image still looks good, and it now takes up just 6,500 bytes. This is a major savings.

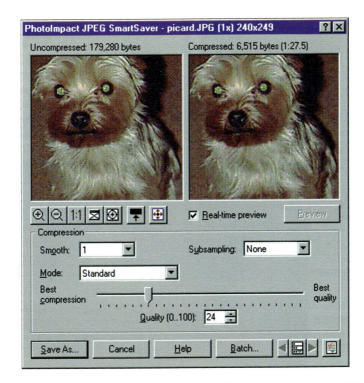

Create Seamless Tiles in Photoshop 4.0

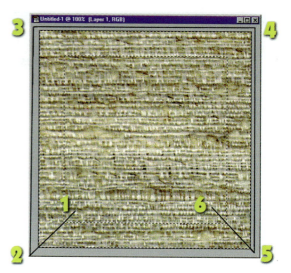

Start with a scanned or painted image. Above is a scan of a piece of linen. To turn it into a seamless background

- Create a fat border selection and then remove all but a picture-frame-shaped piece at the bottom. Hint: Hold down the Alt key and use the Linear Lasso tool to click at the locations shown in the sequence at right.

- Copy the selection and paste it into a new layer (see below left). Flip the layer vertically, and move it to the top of the image.

- Create a layer mask by clicking the Make Mask icon in the layers palette (see below center).

- Use the eraser tool with the airbrush variant to blend the edge of the layer.

- Repeat for the left edge of the image. See below right, which shows the two layers flipped and blended. The original image is hidden to show the blending more clearly.

On these two pages, you'll find the secret to creating seamless tiled backgrounds. Enjoy!

You could just make the original layer visible, save the result to a JPG file, and have a nice enough background image. To enhance the image further, you can

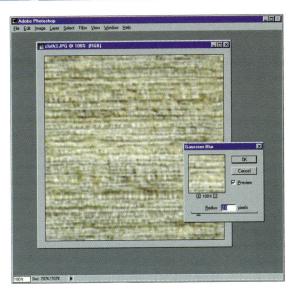

■ Use the Layer⇨Transform⇨Skew menu to bend the selection so that it lines up exactly with the original image. The figure above illustrates the skewing in action.

■ Use the Filter⇨Blur⇨Gaussian Blur menu to apply a subtle blur to the image (see figure above right). This allows the background to recede into the background of the web page, rather than fight for attention with the text and images on the page.

The web page below shows a seamless background at work.

See Chapter 17

It's usually a good idea to incorporate GIF images that use transparency when working with textured backgrounds like the one shown here.

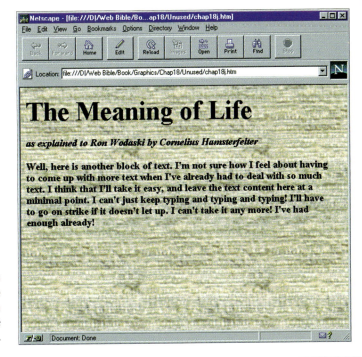

Enhance Buttons and Doodads with Tools and Imagination

Use your imagination to create web graphics.

There are many, many ways you can use layers in Photoshop 4.0 to create sophisticated, realistic 3-D objects. The four at right are a few samples of what you can accomplish. The metallic effects are applied with a custom gradient you'll find on the CD-ROM in the tutorial files for Chapter 7. See Chapter 16 for information about the little rivets.

This is some text for example.

Images you capture for yourself or that you purchase in clip art collections may not have uniform backgrounds. The first hat image at left is a typical example. Take some time to select the background and fill it with white (bottom image) before you use the image on a web page.

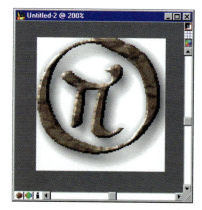

See Chapter 16

Fractal Design Painter makes it especially easy to create cool 3-D and shadow effects, as you see above.

9. Click the white background, which displays the dialog box shown in Figure 13-26. This tells you that all white pixels in the image will become transparent when viewed on a web page.

10. Click the Accept button if you agree, the Change button if you don't, or the Cancel button to abort.

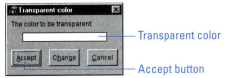

Figure 13-26: Verifying transparent color.

In this example, you set both interlacing and transparency. You can set one option or the other; you do not have to set both at one time.

Interlacing and Transparency with PhotoDeluxe

Tutorial

Download: A trial version of PhotoDeluxe is not available. Visit the Adobe web site at `http://www.adobe.com` for more information about PhotoDeluxe.

Level: Easy

Task: Add transparency and interlacing to an image

Before you start:

✦ Download and install PhotoDeluxe.

✦ Open the file `\My Web Stuff\Chap13\beary.pcx` (use File | Open, or a variety of other methods available).

PhotoDeluxe is designed to be easy to use. It has the world's friendliest image editor interface, as you can see in Figure 13-27. How friendly? Figure 13-27 shows the "On Your Own" mode, which fills about a quarter of your screen. The assisted mode is even friendlier.

If you already know how to use an image editor, let me be plain about this: PhotoDeluxe is not for you. If you want to have your hand held (tightly, I might add) while you learn about image editing, then PhotoDeluxe is for you.

Big buttons

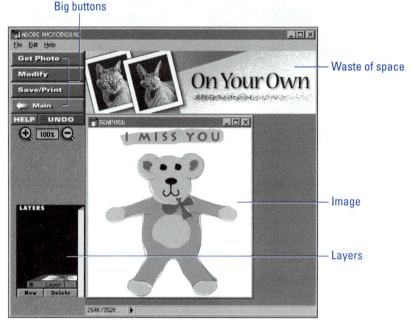

Waste of space

Image

Layers

Figure 13-27: Working in PhotoDeluxe.

To save the beary.pcx file with interlacing and/or transparency:

1. Use the File | Export | GIF98a Export menu selection to open the dialog box shown in Figure 13-28. (To simply save an image in GIF format, you would click OK.)

   To set interlacing or transparency, you need YAD (Yet Another Dialog; PhotoDeluxe is YAD City).

2. Click the Advanced button to display the dialog box shown in Figure 13-29.

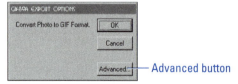

Advanced button

Figure 13-28: The Export Options dialog box.

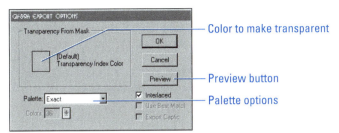

Figure 13-29: The advanced version of the Export Options dialog box.

Tip

By default, GIF images are interlaced. If that's all you want to do, and you haven't changed the Interlaced setting previously, you don't need to access the Advanced options; just click the OK button when you get to the dialog box in Figure 13-28.

3. The default transparency color is a medium gray. To change this to white (the actual background color of this image), click the color square to open YAD (see Figure 13-30).

4. Click the color square to display YAD (see Figure 13-31), and click the white square to pick it as the transparent color.

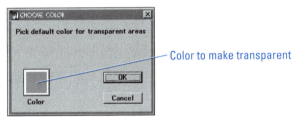

Figure 13-30: The Choose Color dialog box.

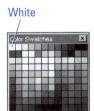

Figure 13-31: A dialog box for choosing a transparent color.

Clicking a color in a dialog box is a terrible way to pick your background color. The only correct way to select a transparency color is to click an actual color in the image. Fortunately, there is a way to do this. Unfortunately, it's totally non-obvious. You have to click the Preview button (refer all the way back to Figure 13-29) to display YAD (see Figure 13-32; how many $&^#$^ dialogs do we have to deal with here?) where you can actually click a color to indicate it should be the transparent color.

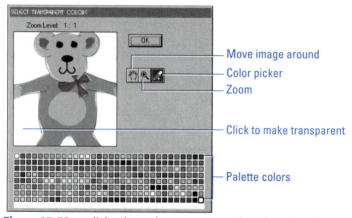

Figure 13-32: A dialog box where you can select the color for transparency.

5. However you choose your transparency color, click the OK button in the dialog box shown in Figure 13-29. This opens the dialog box shown in Figure 13-33, where you can locate the folder to save the file to, and enter a filename.

6. Save to the \My Web Stuff folder using the filename **beary.gif**.

7. Click the Save button to display YAD (see Figure 13-34), and click OK to return to PhotoDeluxe.

Figure 13-33: Entering the filename to save to.

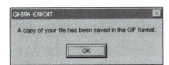

Figure 13-34: The final dialog box.

PhotoDeluxe certainly wins the award for most dialog boxes per given activity. If you have experience, you can see why it would be frustrating to deal with all these dialog boxes. If you are new to image editing, you might find all of this very helpful. However, PhotoDeluxe is at its best when you are doing nontechnical things. Unfortunately, saving as a GIF image appears to be on the technical side. For actually working with an image, PhotoDeluxe shines for the new user.

Interlacing and Transparency with Photoshop

CD: A trial version of Photoshop is on the CD-ROM. To find out how to install it, view the web page at \demo\viewme.htm in your browser and click the \demo\adobe hyperlink.

Tutorial   **Level:** Easy

Task: Add transparency and interlacing to an image

Before you start:

✦ You must have Photoshop 4.0 installed on your computer to work with this tutorial.

✦ Open the file \My Web Stuff\Chap13\duck.pcx (File | Open) in Photoshop 4.0.

Figure 13-35 shows the file open in Photoshop. The image background is shaded. Before you can make the background transparent, you must select the background and fill it with a solid color.

The best tool for selecting similar colors is the Magic Wand tool (see Figure 13-36). Click the Magic Wand to make it the active tool. Double-click it to display the tool's options (see Figure 13-37).

Figure 13-35: A file open in Photoshop.

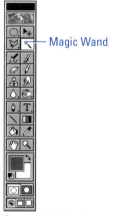

— Magic Wand

Figure 13-36: The Photoshop tools.

— Option tab

— Anti-aliased check box

—Tolerance

Figure 13-37: Magic Wand options.

The Tolerance setting is similar to the Similar setting in PhotoImpact (according to the Dept. of Redundancy Department; see Chapter 13). This setting defines the reach of the Magic Wand. If the Tolerance setting is high, many similar pixels will be selected when you click a pixel. If the Tolerance setting is low, only extremely similar pixels get selected. For example, if the Tolerance setting is 1, only identical pixels get selected. For this exercise, use a Tolerance setting of 32 (see Figure 13-37).

To avoid any nasty anti-aliasing at the edge of the duck, make sure that the Anti-aliased check box is unchecked as shown in Figure 13-37.

To add interlacing and transparency to the image:

1. Begin by clicking near the top of the image, which will select a range of similar colors. The exact area selected will vary depending on where you click. Figure 13-38 shows a rough approximation of what you will see.

Click here to add to selection

Figure 13-38: A selection created with the Magic Wand.

2. To select more of the background, hold down the Shift key and click near the "crawling ants" at the bottom edge of the selection you just created (refer to Figure 13-38).

   Make sure to click within the existing selection so that the addition is contiguous. Figure 13-39 shows what you should see. The exact shape of your selection area will probably be slightly different.

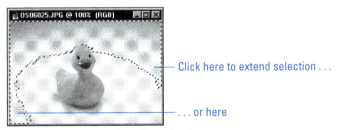
Click here to extend selection . . .

. . . or here

Figure 13-39: Expanding the selection.

3. Continue in this manner until you have selected nearly the entire background. The shadow below the duck cannot be selected using this technique because the colors are so similar to the duck's colors.

4. When you have selected as much as you see selected in Figure 13-40, click to select the lasso tool (see Figure 13-41).

5. If the linear lasso tool is not already the active tool, click and hold on the lasso tool and choose the linear lasso tool from the flyout.

Figure 13-40: Most of the background is selected.

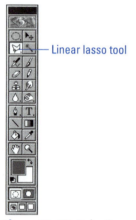

— Linear lasso tool

Figure 13-41: Selecting the linear lasso tool.

6. Press Ctrl and the Plus key on the numeric keypad as many times as needed to zoom in to a 400% view of the base of the duck. This shows the unselected pixels clearly (see Figure 13-42).

7. Use the linear lasso tool to select the area below the duck: Hold down the Shift key and click near the upper left of the unselected background area, then click several more times to carefully outline the area along the base of the duck, and then click a few points below the area to surround it (see Figure 13-43).

8. Make the last click a double-click to close the selection.

9. When you are done, use the Ctrl and the Minus key on the numeric keypad several times to return to a 100% view. Figure 13-44 shows the background completely selected.

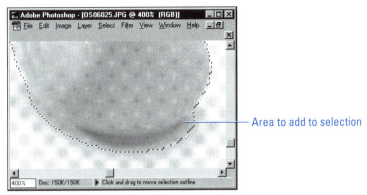

Area to add to selection

Figure 13-42: The unselected background area.

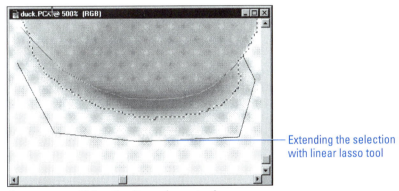

Extending the selection
with linear lasso tool

Figure 13-43: Using the linear lasso tool.

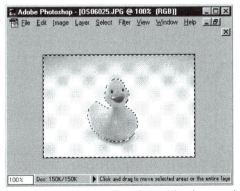

Figure 13-44: The fully selected background.

10. Fill the background with white (choose the Edit | Fill menu selection, and pick White in the Use drop-down box).

11. Use the Select | Inverse menu selection to select the duck instead of the background (see Figure 13-45).

Figure 13-45: Inverted selection.

The duck contains some white and some light pixels. When you make the white background transparent, some of the white pixels in the duck will become transparent, too. In addition, even though you turned off anti-aliasing, there are still some very light pixels at the edge of the duck. Darkening all of the pixels in the duck will eliminate the problem.

12. Use the Image | Adjust | Brightness and Contrast menu selection to open the dialog box shown in Figure 13-46.

Figure 13-46: Adjusting brightness and contrast.

13. Use the sliders in the dialog box to make the duck slightly darker (I used a setting of -18) and to slightly increase contrast (+8). If the Preview check box is checked, you will see the results of your changes as you make them.

14. Click OK when you are satisfied.

15. Change the Mode of the file to 8-bit color with the Image | Mode | Indexed Color menu selection.

16. Choose Web as your palette type, and set the Options to Dither. Dithering is essential because the duck uses many more shades of yellow than are available in the 216-color Web palette.

The background in this image is very large. You will probably want to save the image with a smaller background for general use. To do this, use the rectangular selection tool to select a rectangle that is slightly larger than the duck, copy it to the Clipboard, create a new file, and paste the duck into the new file. By default, Photoshop will create the new file to be the same size as the contents of the Clipboard. Change to 8-bit mode (Image | Mode | Indexed Color) and continue with the tutorial.

Tip

17. To save as a GIF file, use the File | Export | GIF89a menu selection. This displays the dialog box shown in Figure13-47.

18. Click the white background to make it transparent, and make sure that the Interlace check box is checked. Figure 13-48 shows the result.

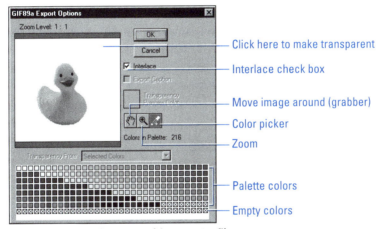

Figure 13-47: Saving a graphic as a GIF file.

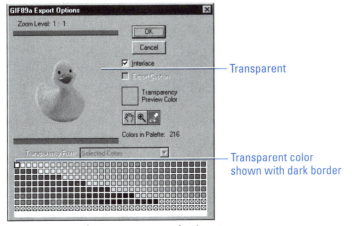

Figure 13-48: The transparent color is set.

You can use the zoom tool to enlarge the view of the duck and verify that there are no nasty anti-aliased pixels around the edge (see Figure 13-49). If you had turned anti-aliasing on, you would see something like Figure 13-50. With no anti-aliased pixels, the duck image is suitable for use on any color background.

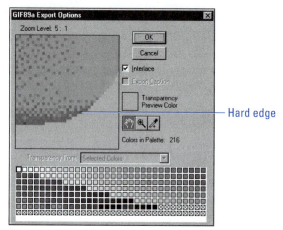

— Hard edge

Figure 13-49: No anti-aliased pixels here to create problems.

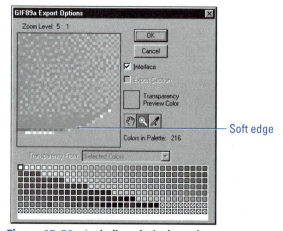

— Soft edge

Figure 13-50: Anti-aliased pixels at the edge of the duck.

Idea

Where to go from here:

✦ A more subtle way to darken just the lightest pixels in the duck is to use the Image | Adjust | Variations menu selection, and to set the variations to adjust only the highlight pixels. Try it and see. Figure 13-51 shows the Variations dialog box. You can use it to adjust colors as well as brightness.

✦ Experiment with creating transparent images while anti-aliasing is turned on. If you *know* you can use the same background color for the image and the page, you can achieve smoother, nicer-looking edges on your images.

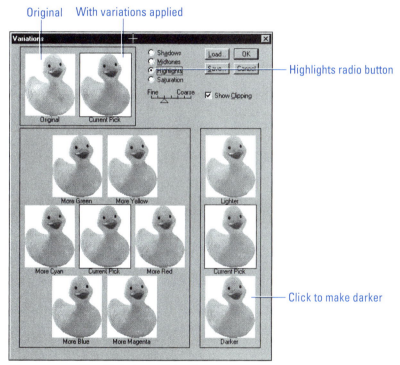

Figure 13-51: The Variations dialog box.

Interlacing and Transparency with Fractal Design Painter

Tutorial

CD: To install the trial version of Painter from the CD, double-click the file `\demo\fractal\painter4\setup.exe`.

Level: Easy

Task: Add transparency and interlacing to an image

Before you start: Install the trial version of Painter.

To add transparency and interlacing in Fractal Design Painter:

1. Begin by creating a new file (File | New, 80 pixels wide, 80 pixels high; see Figure 13-52).

2. Click on the Selection tool (see Figure 13-53) and choose the Elliptical variant in the Controls: Selection dialog box (see Figure 13-54).

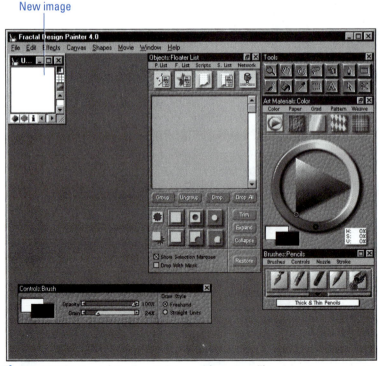

Figure 13-52: Fractal Design Painter with a new file open.

Figure 13-53: Choosing a tool.

Figure 13-54: Choosing the type of selection.

3. Click and drag out a circle in the new file (see Figure 13-55). If you want to add a drop shadow at a later time, leave a little extra room at the bottom and right edges.

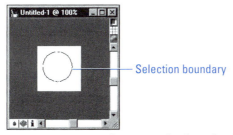

Figure 13-55: Dragging out a circular selection.

4. Use the Edit │ Float menu selection to turn the circular selection into an object.

You will see a black and yellow band around the object, but not the object itself (see Figure 13-56). This is the outer boundary of the object, which is larger than the object itself. The object itself has the same color as the background, and therefore has no visible edges.

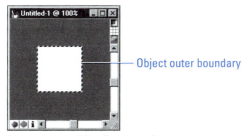

Figure 13-56: The floating object.

To create a button, you must fill the object with color.

5. Click in the Art Materials palette (click the Color icon if the palette doesn't look like Figure 13-57) and choose a red color in the outer ring, and a rich red color at the right apex of the triangle (see Figure 13-57).

6. Use the Effects | Fill menu selection to open the Fill dialog box (see Figure 13-58).

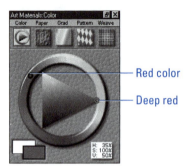

Figure 13-57: Selecting a color.

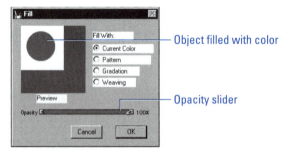

Figure 13-58: Filling an object with color.

7. Make sure that the Current Color radio button is selected, and click OK. The button is now filled with red.

8. Use the Effects | Surface Control | Apply Surface Texture menu selection to open the Apply Surface Texture dialog box (see Figure 13-59). The default texture is paper grain.

9. Click the Paper Grain button to display an alternate list of methods, as shown in Figure 13-59.

10. Choose Mask.

   The preview window at the upper left of the dialog box changes to show the effect of the Mask method. The button now has a very thin shadow on the lower right side.

11. Move the Softness slider toward the right until the value shows as 6.5, as shown in Figure 13-60.

This broadens the 3-D effect as shown in the preview window.

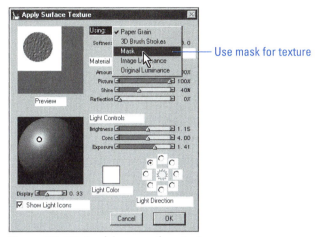

Figure 13-59: Applying a surface texture.

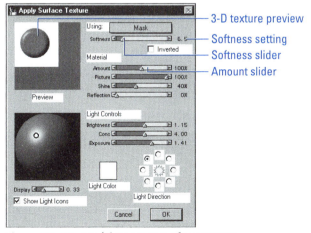

Figure 13-60: Applying a 3-D surface texture.

12. Click the OK button.

Figure 13-61 shows the appearance of the button.

Figure 13-61: The revised button.

13. To save the button with a transparent background, use the File | Save As menu selection to open the dialog box shown in Figure 13-62.

Figure 13-62: Saving an image as a GIF file.

14. Click the Save as type drop-down arrow, and choose GIF Files (*.GIF).

15. Enter a filename of **redbtn2.GIF**, and locate the folder \My Web Stuff as the destination for saving the file.

16. Click the Save button.

   This displays a dialog box that warns you that "The floaters in this image are merged with the canvas layer when saving to this format — save as RIFF to save the floaters as independent objects."

17. Since you want to save as GIF, you can click OK and ignore the message. This displays the dialog box shown in Figure 13-63, where you can set the options for the GIF file format.

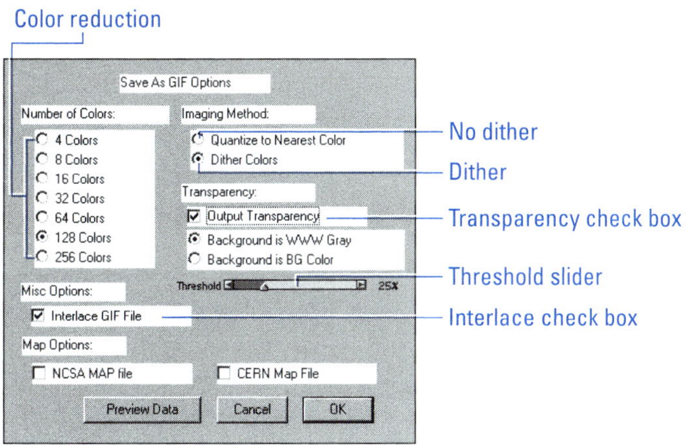

Color reduction

Figure 13-63: Setting GIF options.

The options in this dialog box are

Number of Colors
Choose the number of colors to be used in the image. I chose 128 colors for this button, but different numbers of colors will be suitable for different images. Painter does not give you the option of using a Web palette. If you want to use a Web palette, save the image in a 24-bit format, such as PCX, and use another tool to reduce colors, such as PhotoImpact.

Misc Options
Check the Interlace GIF File check box to interlace the image.

Map Options
Map Options are not used here. They are used when saving an image to be used as an image map. See Chapter 15 for information about image maps.

Imaging Method
Quantize will avoid dithering, and Dither colors will do just what it says. For mostly monochrome images like this one, dithering is needed.

Transparency
Check the Output Transparency check box to have Painter save the image with transparency. The rule is simple: Objects will be visible, and the background will be transparent. The two radio buttons determine whether to use medium gray as the background, or the existing background color. The threshold slide controls the degree of anti-aliasing. Larger numbers result in more pixels being included; smaller numbers have the effect of limiting anti-aliasing. There is always some degree of anti-aliasing present, however, so Painter is not ideal for creating backgrounds.

18. Once you have the options set as shown in Figure 13-63, click the Preview Data button to check the results.

19. Click OK on the preview to close it.

20. If you need to make changes, move the Threshold slider and preview until you get it right.

21. Click OK in the GIF Options dialog box to save the file.

You can see this for yourself in the file \My Web Stuff\Chap13\chap13L.htm.

Idea

Where to go from here:

✦ If you have too many objects present in the image, Painter may not evaluate the transparency correctly. The symptoms: missing objects in the GIF file. If this happens, try grouping the objects and then collapsing them into a single object. Buttons for both actions are on the Floaters palette.

✦ Try a drop shadow on an object to see how it affects transparency.

✦ Create see-through objects by drawing on the background, selecting the irregular shape with the Magic Wand, and then choose Edit | Float to place it into an object. Drop shadows on objects with cutouts are often visually very effective, but transparency is out of the question for such objects. Figure 13-64 shows an object created with cutouts.

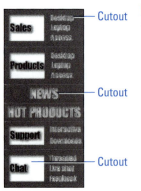
— Cutout

— Cutout

— Cutout

Figure 13-64: A floating navigation bar that uses cutouts and a drop shadow.

Web Tour #13: More Image Tools

Interlacing and transparency are two of the most common image attributes you will encounter on web pages. Most web pages, in fact, use one or both of them. To visit some web pages that make use of transparency and/or interlacing, double-click the file:

    \WebTour\Chap13\index.htm

You'll see the Web Tour page for this chapter.

SmartSavers 4 U

To prepare for this chapter's tutorials, copy the following folder from the CD-ROM to the \My Web Stuff folder on your hard drive:

    \tutorial\chap14

This will copy files for all of the tutorials in this chapter to your hard disk. See Chapter 1 for complete details on setting up for tutorials.

SmartSaver Tools

Of all the tools I've worked with for saving GIF and JPEG images, Ulead's SmartSaver tools built into PhotoImpact (and available as plug-ins for Photoshop) are simply the best. With these tools you can make more tests and you have more options at your fingertips. Nothing else comes close. (The color-reduction tools from Digital Frontiers are also useful, but have a different function and are explored in detail in Chapter 12). Simply put, if you want web pages with small, efficient graphics, the SmartSavers are just what their name says they are: a smart way to save your image files.

There are two major tutorials in this chapter — one for GIF images, one for JPEG images. Both tutorials operate on the same base image, shown in Figure 14-1; just as I got it from a clip art collection from Planet Art. I was writing this chapter around Christmastime so forgive me if you're reading this chapter in July! Read both tutorials carefully, then come back to the image and open its file as they show you; we have to fix the image up a bit.

Although these tutorials show the SmartSavers being used in PhotoImpact, Ulead also offers the SmartSavers as Photoshop plug-ins. This means that you can use the SmartSavers in any image editing program that supports Photoshop plug-ins. The processes outlined in these tutorials are standard for all types of web images.

Figure 14-1: The base image for both tutorials.

The background presents a few problems — there is a black border, and the overall background is too dark. Use the PhotoImpact Magic Wand tool to select the entire background (see Figure 14-2); fill it with white (see Figure 14-3), set the Add option, and use a Similarity setting of 48.

Rectangular selection tool
Magic Wand tool   Selection boundary

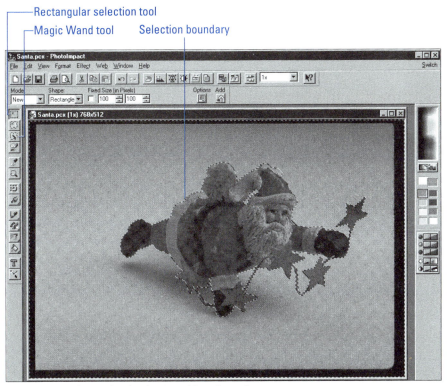

Figure 14-2: The entire background is selected.

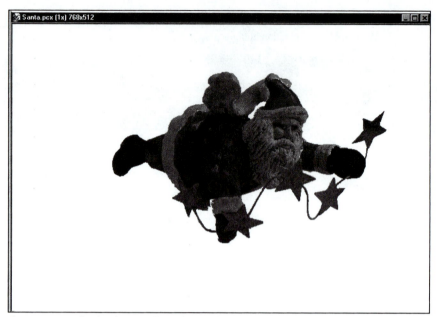

Figure 14-3: The background is filled with white.

Tip

The Magic Wand selects adjoining pixels that are similar in color and value to the pixel you click. When creating a selection with the Magic Wand, it's important to set the Similarity box to an appropriate number. Small numbers mean that only pixels that are very similar to the clicked pixel will be selected. Large numbers mean that many adjoining pixels are likely to be selected. Usually, you will have to experiment to figure out what number to use. With PhotoImpact, you can set the Line option (see Figure 14-4) and drag a line through the area you want to select. This is very useful with a graduated background like the background in the Santa image.

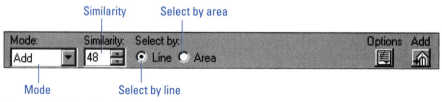

Figure 14-4: The Magic Wand options.

If you over-select — that is, if you accidentally select some part of the Santa figure — you can switch to Subtract selection mode temporarily by holding down the S key while you click. Another alternative: Press Ctrl + Z to undo the last selection, reduce the Similarity number, and select again.

Once you have selected just the background, fill it with white (Edit | Fill). The white boundary is too large, so select just the area around the Santa (see Figure 14-5) and paste it into a new image (see Figure 14-6) using the Edit | Paste | As New Image menu selection. The white background makes it very clear that the Santa image is too dark. Adjust the image using the Format | Brightness and Contrast menu selection, and the image is ready for use. Save the image (File | Save As) as a true-color (24-bit color) image with the filename santa1.pcx.

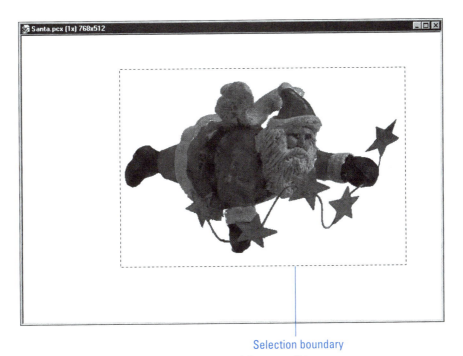

Selection boundary

Figure 14-5: Selecting a smaller portion of the overall image.

Figure 14-6: The new image.

Tip

The Paste As New Image menu selection is extremely convenient, and is just one more example of why PhotoImpact is such a neat and productive tool. I find myself using PhotoImpact for many of my image editing needs because it includes such cool tools. In just this short exercise, the Line setting for the Magic Wand and the Paste As New Image menu selection alone saved me a lot of time and effort. Working with images can be tedious; tools that make the process move quickly and efficiently are highly desirable.

Using the JPEG SmartSaver

Tutorial

CD: To install the trial version of the PhotoImpact SmartSavers, double-click the file `\demo\ulead\smrtsave\uss12t.exe`. If you want to try the Photoshop plug-in trial versions, double-click `\demo\ulead\webext\we4ps14t.exe`.

Level: Intermediate

Task: Learn to use the JPEG SmartSaver

Before you start:

✦ Install the JPEG SmartSaver trial version from the CD-ROM .

Open the file `\My Web Stuff\Chap14\santa1.pcx` in PhotoImpact (or in Photoshop if you are using the Photoshop plug-in versions of the SmartSavers).

✦ If you want to make any changes to the image (lighten it, sharpen it, blur it, and so on), make the changes before you continue.

To use the JPEG SmartSaver:

1. Use the Web | JPEG SmartSaver menu selection to open the dialog box shown in Figure 14-7.

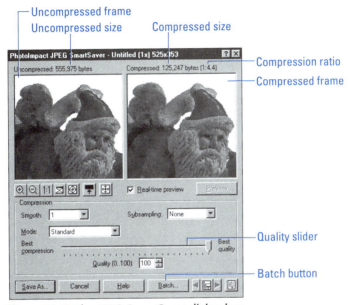

Figure 14-7: The JPEG SmartSaver dialog box.

2. Access all of the features desired of the JPEG SmartSaver from this dialog box.

JPEG options

The image at top left of the dialog box is the source image frame, exactly as you left it in PhotoImpact. If you made any changes, they will appear here. The image frame at top right is the compressed version of the image. The file size of the uncompressed and compressed images is shown above the images. In this example, with the settings shown below the images, the uncompressed image is 555,975 bytes, and the compressed image is 125,247 bytes. The compressed image is less than one-fourth the size of the original (the compression ratio is 1:4.4), but carefully adjusting the JPEG settings can give you much higher compression.

The row of buttons below the uncompressed image allows you to change the way you view the image. Table 14-1 shows what each of the buttons is for.

Table 14-1
JPEG SmartSaver Buttons

Button	Name	Description
⊕	Zoom in	Shows a closer view of the images in the frames. See Figure 14-8.
⊖	Zoom out	Shows more of the images in the frames.
1:1	Actual size	Displays the images in the frames at actual size. This is the default when you start the JPEG SmartSaver.
⊠	Resize to frame	Resizes the images in the compressed and uncompressed image frames so they fit the frames.
⊡	Center images	Centers the images in the frames.
⬆	Toggle	Toggles between displaying both frames, and only the compressed frame. When the compressed frame only is displayed, it is the full width of the dialog box (see Figure 14-9).
⊞	Full screen	Shows a full-screen view of the compressed image at actual (1:1) size. Useful for getting a feel for the exact appearance of the image. See Figure 14-10 for an example.

Figure 14-8: Zooming in to see details.

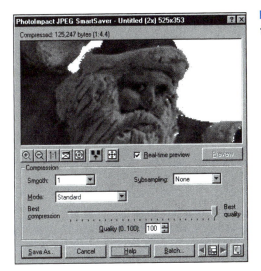

Figure 14-9: Showing only the compressed frame.

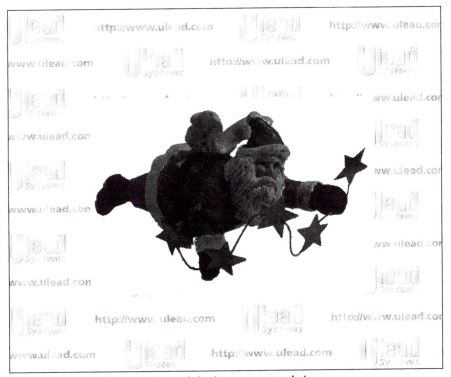

Figure 14-10: A full-screen view of the image at actual size.

The portion of the JPEG SmartSaver you will use most often is the quality slider (see Figure 14-11). At the extreme left of the slider, image quality is least, and compression is greatest. At the extreme right, image quality is at its best, and compression is least. By adjusting this slider, and checking the appearance of the image in the compressed frame, you can gauge the best setting for compression. Some of the other settings in the dialog box can be used to tweak the appearance of the compressed image.

Figure 14-11: The quality/compression slider.

For example, in Figure 14-12, the quality slider is set fairly far to the left. The face of the Santa is noticeably degraded. However, the compression ratio is very high. The compressed image is only 11,505 bytes, a compression ratio of more than 1:48!

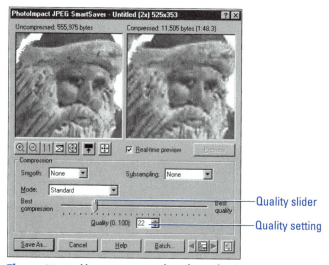

Figure 14-12: Heavy compression degrades image quality.

If you really, really need a high compression setting, you can improve the appearance of the image by using a higher Smooth factor. Figure 14-13 shows the appearance of the compressed image with the highest Smooth setting, 10. The image looks a bit fuzzier, but not quite as horrible as in Figure 14-12. Remember that you are looking at the image zoomed in; it will not be as fuzzy at actual size (see Figure 14-14).

Figure 14-13: Using a higher Smooth setting.

Tip

To create a progressive JPEG file, click the drop-down arrow on the box labeled Mode, and choose Progressive. A progressive JPEG image displays gradually, similar to an interlaced GIF image. See Chapters 13 and 14 for information about interlaced GIFs and progressive JPEGs.

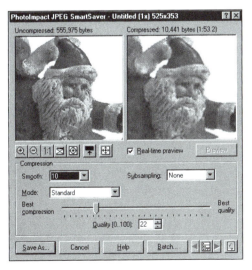

Figure 14-14: Images at actual size.

By experimenting with the various settings (Smoothing, Subsampling, Mode, and the quality slider) I was able to come up with an image that looked good to me, while still providing extremely high compression (a 57.8:1 compression ratio). It is shown in Figure 14-15.

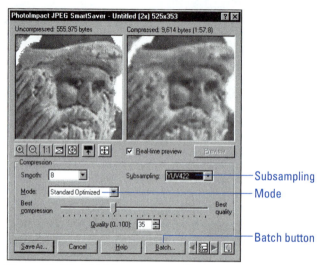

Figure 14-15: A highly compressed image.

 The Subsampling settings force the compression algorithm to go beyond the pixel level to improve the appearance of the image. The Mode setting offers different modes that may or may not improve the appearance of a particular image. The best way to tell is by trial and error.

Batch mode

In addition to testing various settings by trial and error, you can use the JPEG SmartSaver's Batch mode to test many different variations quickly. In Batch mode, the SmartSaver generates a number of samples that you can check visually while comparing file sizes and image quality. You can then pick the best of the batch, and save using those parameters.

1. To use the Batch mode, click the Batch button at the bottom of the JPEG SmartSaver dialog box (see Figure 14-15). This opens the dialog box shown in Figure 14-16.

   There are four settings in the Batch dialog box: Lowest quality, Highest quality, Number of tests, and Increment.

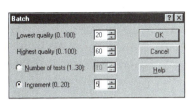

Figure 14-16: The Batch dialog box.

2. To create a batch, enter a number for the lowest quality you think you can tolerate (low quality = high compression and small file sizes), and the highest quality you expect to use (which yields large file sizes).

You can then choose one of two methods to create the batch:

- You can enter the number of tests to generate, in which case the Batch will consist of that number of text cases, evenly spaced across the range of quality settings you specified.

- Or you can enter the increment, in which case the number of test cases will be the difference between the quality levels, divided by the increment.

But that explanation is the long way around. An example will show what I mean. Look again at Figure 14-16. The lowest quality setting is 20, and the highest is 60. I have set the increment at 5. This means that the test cases will have quality settings of 20, 25, 30, 35, 50, 45, 50, 55, and 60. Figure 14-17 shows the test cases ready to be viewed.

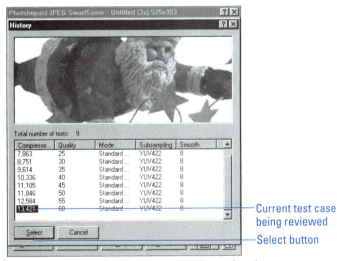

Figure 14-17: Viewing the test cases in the batch.

3. To view each test case, click it and the compressed image at the top changes to reflect the settings for that test case.

4. When you find the right combination of compression and image quality, click the Select button (see Figure 14-17) to return to the original JPEG SmartSaver dialog box.

5. You can continue to tweak the settings, or click the Save As button to save the file.

6. If you want to view other test cases from the batch, use the batch arrow buttons at the bottom right of the dialog box, and then click the Save As button to save the image as a JPEG file.

If you are serious about getting the best-looking images, this JPEG SmartSaver is one heck of a great tool. You just can't beat the thoroughness of its approach to the problem of finding the right combination of settings for optimal JPEG compression. I am in awe of whoever designed this thing: It's brilliant. Get it.

Figure 14-17 displayed the test case with the highest quality. The compressed file size is 13,421 bytes, and the image quality is very good. In Figure 14-18, the test case for a quality setting of 40 is displayed. The image quality is still good, and the file size is down to 10,336 bytes.

Figure 14-18: This is how the image appears at a quality setting of 40.

Using the GIF SmartSaver

Tutorial

CD: To install the trial version of the PhotoImpact SmartSavers, double-click the file `\demo\ulead\smrtsave\uss12t.exe`. If you want to try the Photoshop plug-in trial versions, double-click `\demo\ulead\webext\we4ps14t.exe`.

Level: Intermediate

Task: Learn to use the GIF SmartSaver

Before you start:

✦ Install the GIF SmartSaver trial version from the CD-ROM.

✦ Open the file `\My Web Stuff\Chap14\santa2.pcx` in PhotoImpact (or in Photoshop if you are using the Photoshop plug-in version of SmartSavers).

The Santa image isn't well-suited for saving as a GIF image, so I modified it to make it more suitable. I used the PhotoImpact Level dialog box (Format | Level menu selection; see Figure 14-19) to change the number of colors used in the various channels (Master, Red, Green, and Blue).

I did this until I got a brighter-looking Santa that uses just a small set of colors. This creates an image with broad areas of single colors — ideal for GIF compression (see Figure 14-20). If you are using the trial version of the SmartSavers, you can use your favorite image editor to make a similar change if it supports this feature.

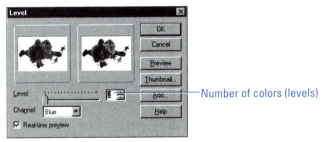

Figure 14-19: Reducing levels (colors) one channel at a time.

Figure 14-20: The image uses fewer colors.

Then I adjusted the brightness and contrast (see Figure 14-21) to arrive at a final image that is brighter and more useful (see Figure 14-22).

See the color section of the book to see just how impressively colorful this version of Santa really is.

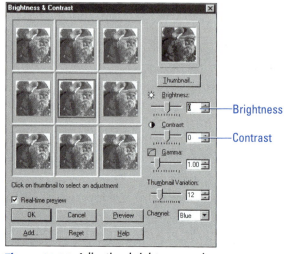

Figure 14-21: Adjusting brightness and contrast.

Figure 14-22: The final image ready for GIF SmartSaver.

Now, to use the GIF SmartSaver:

1. With the file `santa2.pcx` open, use the Web | GIF SmartSaver menu
   selection to open the dialog box shown in Figure 14-23.

   This dialog box is very similar to the dialog box for the JPEG SmartSaver.
   There are two frames at the top — uncompressed at the left, compressed at
   the right. The uncompressed image size is the same as the previous example:
   555,975 bytes. The compressed size is 29,207 bytes. Despite color reduction,
   the compression from JPEG is greater than the compression from GIF.

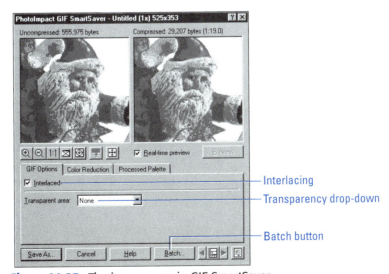

Figure 14-23: The image open in GIF SmartSaver.

By default, the image will be interlaced. The first step in the process is to make the white background transparent (see Chapter 13 for details on transparency and interlacing).

2. Click the Transparent area drop-down list, and click the Pick colors selection (see Figure 14-24). This tells the GIF SmartSaver that you intend to pick the color to use for transparency.

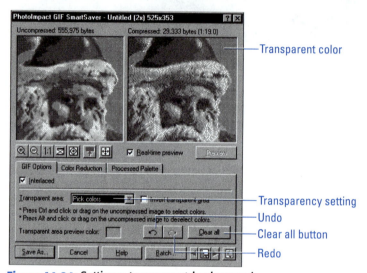

Figure 14-24: Setting a transparent background.

The text below the Transparent area drop-down list explains how to set the transparent area. Your options are:

• Press the Ctrl key and click a pixel in the uncompressed image to select a transparent color.

• Press the Ctrl key and click additional pixels to expand the range of colors that are transparent.

• Press the Ctrl key and click and drag on a range of colors in the uncompressed image to select colors for transparency.

You can also press the Alt key, and then click or drag in any of the three ways listed above to remove a color from the transparency setting.

3. Pick a color; as you do, all the pixels of that color in the image will turn to a medium gray. Only one color in a GIF file can be transparent. The medium gray color replaces whatever colors you select for transparency.

Tip

The transparent color should be a color that is not otherwise used in the image. Otherwise, you will create transparency in places where you do not want it. You can click the transparent color at the bottom center of the dialog box to change it. You can also use the Undo and Redo buttons at bottom right if you change your mind about a particular color selection. To start over from scratch, click the Clear all button.

In this example, the entire background is white, so you only need to click once on the uncompressed image to choose the transparent color. The background will change to a medium gray, as shown in Figure 14-24.

4. Click the Color Reduction tab (see Figure 14-25).

   This displays settings you can use to reduce the number of colors used in the image. Note that, by default, color reduction is accomplished by dithering. This accounts for the dithered appearance of the compressed image at the top right.

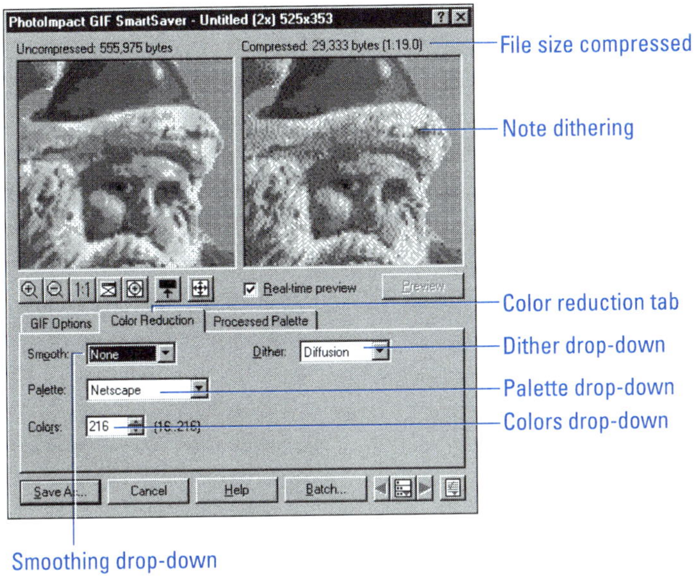

Figure 14-25: The Color Reduction tab.

5. Click the Dither drop-down list and select None.

   The right-hand image changes to reflect the lack of dithering (see Figure 14-26), and as a bonus the file size for the compressed image goes down to 16,733 bytes. This is as clear a demonstration as you can get for how dithering increases GIF file size.

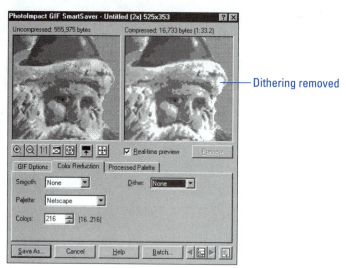

Figure 14-26: Dithering set to None reduces file size.

You can add smoothing to GIF images with the Smooth drop-down list, but smoothing doesn't improve the appearance of this particular image (see Figure 14-27).

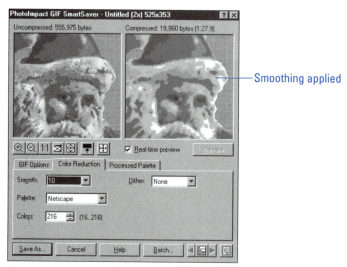

Figure 14-27: Smoothing applied to the image.

So far, the Palette list has been left at the default setting of Netscape. You can also choose other palettes, as shown in Figure 14-28. These include an Internet Explorer palette, an optimized palette, or a palette file from another image. PhotoImpact allows you to save palettes to a file using the Format | Color Table | Save menu selection.

An optimized palette uses colors that best represent the range of colors used in the image. If you choose Netscape, Internet Explorer, or a file palette, the image will be forced to use just the colors from that palette. If you specify an optimized palette, the colors in the palette will result in a more natural appearance for the compressed image. However, if two images on a web page use different palettes, then the browser will be forced to find a common palette for the images — and that takes control over image appearance away from you.

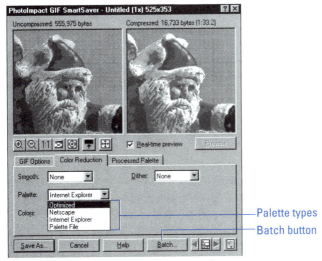

Figure 14-28: Selecting an alternate palette.

6. Whichever palette you use, reduce the number of colors that are used by changing the number in the Colors drop-down list. The fewer colors you use, the smaller the compressed image will be.

As with the JPEG SmartSaver, you can create a batch of test cases to see the effect of various settings on image quality and file size. Figure 14-29 shows the Batch dialog box for GIF files. For this example, I set the fewest colors at 16, the most colors at 216, and asked for 15 test cases.

7. Click OK, and the test cases appear in the dialog box shown in Figure 14-30.

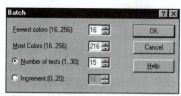

Figure 14-29: Creating a batch of test cases.

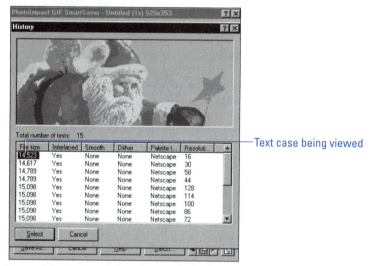

Figure 14-30: Examining the batch for image quality and file size.

Because this image already uses only a few colors, the savings from color reduction are minimal. A 16-color image would be 14,523 bytes, while an image with 128 colors would be 15,098 bytes. Not shown is the file size for 216 colors, which would be 16,733 bytes.

8. To see the colors used in the palette, click the Processed Palette tab. This displays the colors in a table, as shown in Figure 14-31.

9. Click the Save button to save the palette to a file, if desired.

10. To see the red, green, and blue color values for any color in the palette, click to highlight the color entry in the palette. In Figure 14-31, the highlighted color has the values Red=153, Green=0, Blue=51.

The best file size for this image as a GIF file was 14,523 bytes (see Figure 14-32).

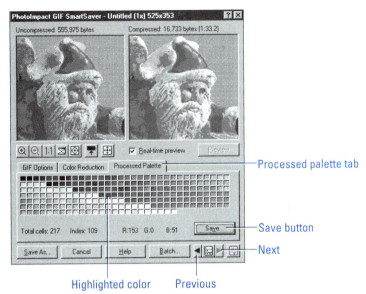

Figure 14-31: Checking colors in a palette.

Figure 14-32: Viewing my best GIF file size as a test case.

Using the JPEG SmartSaver, and adjusting for compression without too much image degradation, I could get a file size of 10,685 bytes (see Figure 14-33). This is almost a third smaller than the best GIF file size. However, the GIF file allows transparency, and the JPEG file does not. If you need a transparent image, you would have to choose GIF even though the file size is larger.

The GIF image is grainier at close range, but sharper at actual size. The JPEG image blends more smoothly in the inset, but looks washed out at actual size. This is a good example of a simple fact: The proof of your compression is always in the final image appearance.

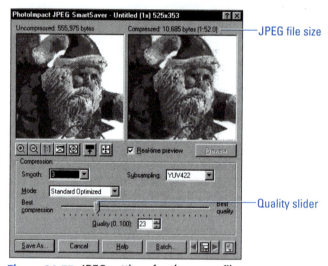

Figure 14-33: JPEG settings for the same file.

Nothing would please me more than to lay out clear rules for when to use GIF and when to use JPEG. As you can see from these examples, the line between the formats crosses many boundaries — compression, transparency, graininess, and so on. If your web pages must look their best, you should take some time with these two SmartSavers to test out all aspects of your images to determine what settings to use for GIF and JPEG, and which of the two best suits your purposes.

Web Tour #14: Ulead's Web Site

This chapter was completely dedicated to Ulead's PhotoImpact and its SmartSavers, so the Web Tour for this chapter is likewise focused. To visit Ulead's web site, double-click the file:

```
\WebTour\Chap14\index.htm
```

You'll see the Web Tour page for this chapter. You can also visit Ulead's site directly at http://www.ulead.com.

Image Maps: Jump for Joy

To prepare for this chapter's tutorials, copy the following folder from the CD-ROM to the \My Web Stuff folder on your hard drive:

    \tutorial\chap15

This will copy files for all of the tutorials in this chapter to your hard disk. See Chapter 1 for complete details on setting up for tutorials.

You caught your first look at image maps in Chapter 5. You used FrontPage 97 not only to add graphics, but also to add multiple hyperlinks to a graphic. There are many other ways to create image maps, but the mechanics of implementing image maps is only part of the story. Creating image maps that look good and function as intended is also important.

Images can be plain or fancy, but whatever the level of graphic design involved, the behind-the-scenes operation of all image maps falls into two broad categories: server-side image maps, and client-side image maps. Server-side image maps reside on the web server, and almost any browser can work with a server-side image map. Client-side image maps reside on the visitor's machine. Only the very newest versions of browsers support client-side image maps.

There are some important benefits of using client-side image maps. If you are willing to accept that some visitors may not be able to use your client-side image maps, you can enjoy those benefits. See the section "Server Versus Client Image Maps," later in this chapter.

In this chapter, you'll learn how image maps work and what kinds of image map options are available to you. You'll find out some keys to designing good image maps, and you'll also learn how to use a variety of tools to create image maps.

Image Maps Mean Multiple Links

An image map has two parts: the image and the map. The image is the visible part. The image, such as the one shown in Figure 15-1, has different areas that the visitor can identify visually. The invisible part is a map that specifies the exact coordinates of the different areas on the image. These areas are referred to as *hotspots*. Hotspots can be rectangular, elliptical, or polygonal. Figure 15-2 shows examples of these shapes. On an image map, each shape has a URL (a web page, an image, or some other valid URL) associated with it.

Figure 15-1: A simple image map created in Fractal Design Painter.

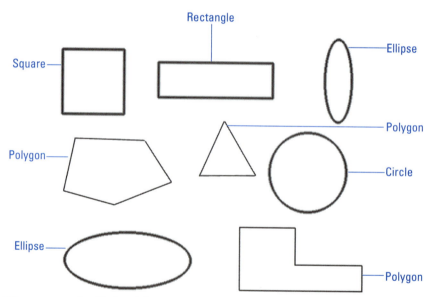

Figure 15-2: The kinds of shapes you might use on an image map.

When you click the image, either the browser or the web server looks up the shape associated with that location on the image (by referring to the shape definitions in the map file) and jumps to the URL for the area you click.

Examples of image maps

To see how image maps work, I'm going to show you several images and the maps associated with them. The map for the image in Figure 15-1 is shown in Figure 15-3.

The map shows 11 hotspots (areas 1 through 11); each would have its own associated URL .

Area 1		Area 2
Area 1		Area 3
Area 6	Area 9	Area 4
Area 7	Area 10	Area 4
Area 8	Area 11	Area 5

Figure 15-3: The map implied by Figure 15-1.

Figure 15-4 shows two separate image maps. The large image at the top contains four "buttons." These are not separate buttons; they are part of a single image, shown in Figure 15-5.

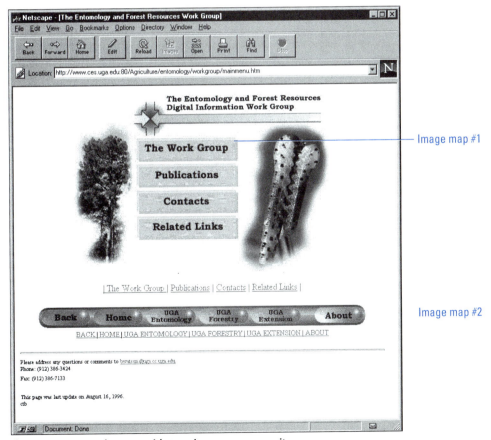

Figure 15-4: A web page with two image maps on it.
Courtesy of the Entomology and Forest Resources Digital Information Work Group, now at
http://www.bugwood.caes.uga.edu/.

Figure 15-5: The image that makes up the top image map in Figure 15-4. Courtesy of the Entomology and Forest Resources Digital Information Work Group, now at http://www.bugwood.caes.uga.edu/.

Stacked Graphics and Image Maps

You may be wondering how to decide whether to use stacked graphics or an image map on any given web page. The answer is, there is no easy answer. Here are the main issues to consider when choosing between stacked graphics and image maps:

✦ If you want to be sure that the most visitors will see the image(s) arranged correctly on the page, use stacked graphics.

✦ Some web page editors introduce small spaces between vertically stacked graphics, requiring you to edit the HTML code by hand to get the display you want. For example, if you use Netscape Gold to create web pages, it adds a carriage return between vertically stacked graphics, and you will have to manually edit out the extra spaces in the HTML file. Use an editor such as Notepad to do this. If your web page editor adds vertical space between graphics, and you don't want to change editors, then image maps are a simpler choice.

✦ Client-side maps and stacked graphics behave similarly, in that the visitor will see the destination URL in the status line of the browser when he passes the mouse cursor over an image. Server-side maps display only map coordinates. Because they display URL information, client-side maps and stacked graphics have a small but useful advantage over server-side image maps. Be sure to see the section on server-side and client-side maps later in this chapter if you are not already familiar with these terms.

✦ When you use an image map, there is only one image to be concerned with. With proper compression (that means JPEG), a single image will usually download more quickly than a bunch of smaller images.

The bottom line is that you will probably always be able to use image maps, and image maps (especially client-side image maps) are easier to maintain in many ways. However, when you are dealing with a simple horizontal row of buttons, stacked graphics can be very easy and are often a good choice in that particular situation. It's also important to consider the practical differences between server-side and client-side image maps, as explained later in the chapter.

The second image map in Figure 15-4 is the navigation bar at the bottom of the page. There are six hotspots in the navigation bar.

Another option is *image stacking* — combining separate images with no space between the images, either vertically or horizontally. (To learn more about when to use image stacking versus image maps, see the sidebar, "Stacked Graphics and Image Maps.")

What Mr. Equivocator is trying to say is that there isn't a heck of a lot of difference, in practice, between image maps and stacked graphics. If you prefer one method over another, that preference alone is sufficient justification. You don't need fancy reasons! Use whichever method you like. Of course, image maps look more sophisticated; if you want to impress your visitors, a fancy image map gets 'em every time.

Figure 15-6 shows an image map at `www.geocities.com/TheTropics/`. This one is 95% graphic, with a few hotspots of text at the right edge. It is fairly common for hotspots to consist of text. Likewise, Figure 15-7 has a nice graphic, and some hotspots defined by text.

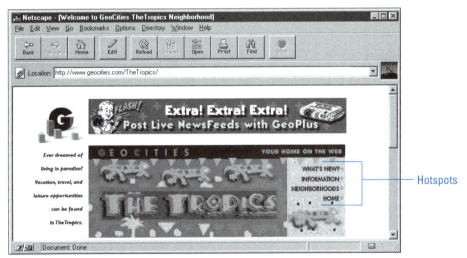

Figure 15-6: An image map containing only a small area with hotspots.

Figure 15-7: Another image map with text hotspots.

Figure 15-8 shows a very attractive approach to creating an image map. The hotspots are strictly text, but they fade into the graphic of a stringed instrument in an interesting and effective way. The page itself is also attractively designed.

Designing an image map

There are many ways to design an image map. The examples you've just seen show a variety of designs, and there are plenty of others out there on the Web. The easiest way to learn how to turn your list of URLs into an image map is to look at some practical examples.

Example 1: The Humongous Fish Company

The Humongous Fish Company specializes in shipping freshly caught fish to its customers. Only large fish are involved, such as tuna and swordfish. The company's web page has three hotspots to add to an image map:

   ✦ Daily Specials

   ✦ Order Now

   ✦ What's in Season

Figure 15-8: An attractive image map.

The company logo will appear separate from the image map. Naturally, the president of the company, Bob Humongous, wants an image of a fish to be the dominant design element in the image map. During a three-martini business lunch, you learn that he likes the idea of a fish in profile, with the three hotspots near the tail of the fish. You make a quick sketch on a napkin (see Figure 15-9), and then work for hours at your computer to come up with the image shown on the web page in Figure 15-10. You can find the file in
`\My Web Stuff\chap15\chap15A.htm`.

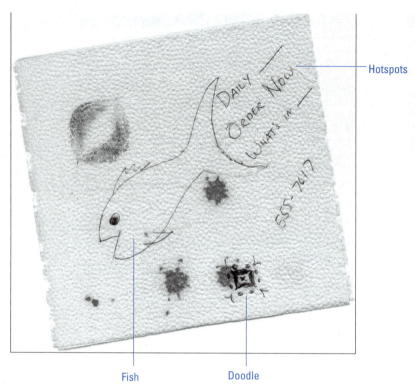

Hotspots

Fish   Doodle

Figure 15-9: A rough outline for an image map, including lipstick
and Tabasco Sauce™ stains.

The fish image was created using clip art and Photoshop. To create this image
yourself, see the detailed tutorial in Chapter 7, "Working with Text." To learn how
to add multiple hyperlinks to this image, see the tutorial, "Creating an Image Map
with LiveImage" later in this chapter.

Example 2: Dada Consulting

Dada Consulting is a company with a clearly defined mission: to bring the
serendipity of the Dadaist movement to the business world. As part of their
relentless campaign, they wish to create a web page listing the services they
provide to large, wealthy companies looking for ways to spend money to improve
themselves. There are four hotspot items on their list, all drawing from famous
Dadaist works of art:

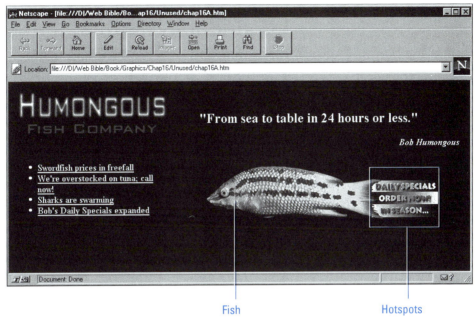

Fish   Hotspots

Figure 15-10: The Humongous web page.

◆ Dude Descending from a Job (downsizing re-euphemized)

◆ Molten Watches (time is money!)

◆ Da Champ and the Bicycle Seat (don't overspend on office equipment)

◆ Andy Loosian's Dog (as in work like a …)

The company has no logo, of course, and wants something as surreal as possible for the image map. During lunch with the president of the company, Stevedore Dahlia, you learn that he takes a fancy to animal images, and you, thinking to pull a surreal fast one, propose a collage of everyday objects. After a hearty laugh, Stevedore suggests that you add some crawling ants to the mix, and you agree, although you aren't quite sure how the hotspots will fit into the overall design. You make a quick sketch on a napkin (see Figure 15-11), and then spend about 15 minutes on the phone with a consultant who drops off a sample image (see Figure 15-12).

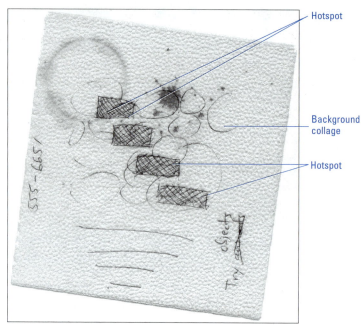

Figure 15-11: The original layout for the Dada image map.

Figure 15-12: The first version of the image map.

The folks at Dada Consulting were happy with the result: chaos and confusion, with the background competing with the foreground for attention. However, upon seeing the version of the image in Figure 15-13, which completely hides the hours and hours of work put into the objects in the background (but still retains a few of the ants), they were ecstatic. "This totally captures the essence of what we're trying to do," said Dahlia. Bemused but with payment in hand, you can't help but agree. The file is shown in \My Web Stuff\chap15\chap15B.htm.

Figure 15-13: The Dada web page.

The image was created using clip art and Fractal Design Painter. To create this kind of image yourself, follow these steps:

1. Identify the images in one or more clip art collections that appeal to you, or that focus on a subject relevant to the web page.

2. Copy the images to a working directory on your hard disk. Change the file attributes from read-only so that you can edit the files. Hint: Select the files and right-click; select the Properties menu item. In the Properties dialog box, uncheck the Read Only box.

3. Load the file into Photoshop, and use the Magic Wand and/or lasso tools to select the background. Fill the background with white.

4. Reduce the size of the image to thumbnail size.

5. Select the white background with the Magic Wand, apply the Select | Inverse menu selection to select only the image instead of the background. Save the image to hard disk.

6. Repeat Step 5 until you have processed all images. Close Photoshop.

7. Open Painter, and create a new file large enough for your design.

8. Open the thumbnail images in Painter, one at a time. For each image, use the Magic Wand to select the background, then apply the Edit | Mask | Invert Mask menu selection so that the object is selected.

9. Copy the image to the Clipboard and paste the image into the newly created Painter file. Hint: If the object has internal white space, remember to use the rectangular selection tool to select the entire object before you use the Magic Wand. That allows you to include all white background areas with the Magic Wand, rather than only contiguous white areas.

10. Add drop shadows to any images that require them. Apply any other changes — filters, natural media painting, Surface Textures, and so on — before moving to the next thumbnail file. Repeat this step until all of the small files you created in Photoshop are added to the Painter file.

11. Rearrange the images in the Painter file until you are satisfied with the composition.

12. Create a rectangular selection of the required size for one of the four buttons on the image.

13. Use the Edit | Float menu selection to make the button into an object.

14. Use the Canvas | Canvas Size menu selection to add 10 pixels to all four sides of the button (see Figure 15-14). This doesn't add pixels to an object. It adds an area for effects such as Surface Texture and Feathering.

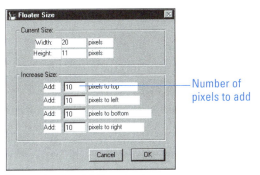

Number of
pixels to add

Figure 15-14: Adding size to a canvas.

15. While the button object is selected, set Opacity on the Control palette to an appropriate value, such as 50% (see Figure 15-15). You want some of the background to show through, but not enough to interfere with the legibility of the text.

16. Set Feather to 5 pixels (or any other value that appeals to you, but no more than the 10 pixels you added to the canvas size) to create a soft edge effect (see Figure 15-15).

Opacity slider

Feather slider

Figure 15-15: Setting Opacity and Feathering for an object.

17. Repeat steps 12 to 16 for the other buttons.

18. Select the Image Hose and a Nozzle, and paint the background. The background is still empty of images or paint, since everything you've done so far created a new object.

19. Apply a slight blur (Effect ┃ Focus ┃ Blur menu selection) to the background to blur your paint job.

20. Select all of the objects except the buttons, and drop them to the background with the Edit ┃ Drop menu selection.

21. Add text to buttons; use a font that reads clearly — the background is horribly noisy, and the plainer the text the better.

22. Apply Surface Texture and a drop shadow to text if desired; both help to make the text more readable.

23. Make any final adjustments, and save your work.

To learn how to add multiple hyperlinks to this image, see the tutorial, "Creating an Image Map with MapEdit," later in this chapter.

Example 3: Frontier Makers, Inc.

Frontier Makers offers something that few businesses can offer: a chance for glory. They meet with the top executives of a company and design a foolish but grand expedition to some bizarre and little-known backwater country. The company executives bond under the searing pressure of imminent hazard, and the company later goes bankrupt because the executives now realize how truly boring their jobs actually are. Still, the idea has a lot of prestige, and the bankruptcies inevitably happen months, or even years later, when executive ennui becomes too much.

The Frontier Makers web page is to have a list of the ten most dangerous expeditions mounted during the last year:

- ✦ Komodo, featuring large, fast dragons
- ✦ Malawi, featuring a pack of starving lions
- ✦ Botswana, featuring a staged coup
- ✦ Antarctica, featuring the Budweiser penguins
- ✦ Sahara Desert, featuring perpetual sand between your toes
- ✦ Alaska, featuring wrestling with Kodiak bears
- ✦ Hawaiian Islands, featuring wrestling with Pele in the wee hours of the morning
- ✦ Himalayas, featuring night climbing on K2
- ✦ Namib Desert, featuring Welwitchia (*Welwitchia Mirabilis*) wrestling
- ✦ Newark, N.J., featuring a walk through the city at night

During lunch with the Frontier Makers company president, Chris Columbine, you learn two things: where the company name comes from ("There are no more frontiers," Chris says to you, adding, "so we make our own"), and that the company wants a separate graphic-and-text for each hotspot. You assure Chris that all of the best image maps use this technique, quote an outrageous price for all the original graphics, and hand the project over to your assistant who spends two weeks deciphering your napkin drawings (see Figure 15-16) to arrive at the image map shown in Figure 15-17.

The file is shown in `\My Web Stuff\chap15\chap15C.htm`.

I created this image from clip art in Photoshop. For the various animal images, I created thumbnails of suitable images in the same manner as described for the Dada Consulting page. I carefully selected the background of each image, and then filled it with white. I used the Image | Image Size menu selection, and set the width of the images to about 140 pixels. I copied each image to the Clipboard and pasted it into the final image in a new layer.

For each scenic image in the Frontier Makers image map, I created an oval selection (ellipse variant of the rectangle selection tool) and used the Select | Inverse menu item to select the area around the image. I feathered the selection by 32 pixels and filled it with white. I then reduced the image to about 140 pixels, copied it to the Clipboard, and pasted it into a new layer in the final image. I repeated this process for each image.

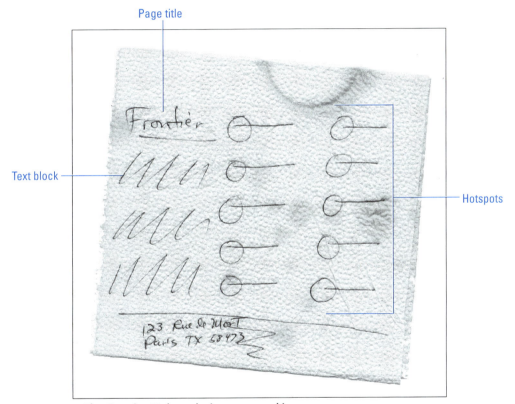

Figure 15-16: The Frontier Makers design on a napkin.

I rearranged the various images (easy to do since each was in a separate layer) and then added the text. Any exotic font is suitable for Frontier Makers. To see how to add hotspots to the image, see the tutorial, "Creating Image Maps with Web Page Editors," later in this chapter.

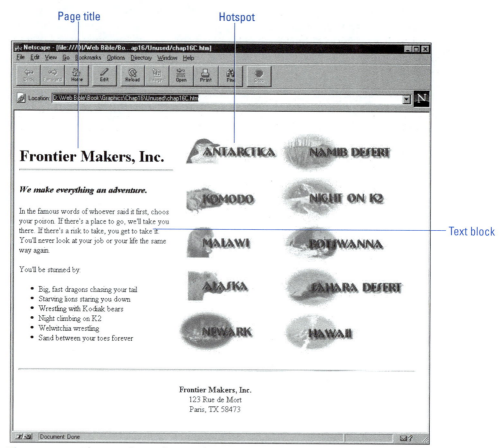

Figure 15-17: The Frontier Makers web page.

Server Versus Client Image Maps

Before moving on to creating image maps, I want to pause for a moment to consider the implications of server-side and client-side image maps in considerable detail. There is a strong trend away from server-side image maps, but trends are like "one-size-fits-all" clothing: They *don't* fit everyone. Server-side maps may not be cool right now, but sometimes they are still the best solution.

Originally, server-side image maps were the only choice. The only way to create an image map was to place both the map and the image on the web server. Not all web servers supported image maps, and those that did support image maps did it in different ways. This created a lot of confusion, and the result was that only the brave and daring bothered with image maps at all.

Server-side image maps

To some extent, the problems associated with server-side image maps have been reduced, but they aren't completely gone. It's worth some consideration to choose one type of image map and work consistently with that type.

Server-side image maps have an important benefit: The vast majority of browsers in use today support them. The downside is that the first few server-side image maps you create are very likely to be a learning experience. You'll need to allow time to learn how your specific ISP (Internet Service Provider) handles server-side maps.That is, if your ISP supports them; some still don't.

Client-side image maps also have an important positive side: They are easy to create and test. There is no time spent learning how your ISP handles them; the ISP isn't involved at all. The downside: Older browsers do not support them.

If you decide to go with server-side image maps, your primary concern will be learning the details of your ISP's implementation. I use Pair Networks, and they use a very straightforward server-side implementation. I create the image map locally, copy it to the server, and then I can access the map using the appropriate syntax in my web pages. I've included an example of a server-side image map a little later in the chapter.

With some ISPs, you'll find that the map files must be placed in specific directories, and sometimes you have to ask the ISP to copy the file to the directory for you. If you run into these kinds of problems, perhaps you should consider switching to client-side maps.

 I'm sure you wish that this section contained detailed instructions on how to conquer the world of server-side image maps. Well, the fact is that there are so $^*#&$ many ways to do it that Mr. Author and I can't do that. If you've got a good ISP, there is a FAQ sheet somewhere on the server that lays out how to create server-side image maps in step-by-step detail. If you don't have a good ISP, find one — a good ISP is worth the effort.

One thing I can tell you is that there are two kinds of server-side image maps: the NCSA (National Center for Supercomputing Applications) and CERN (*Conseil Européenne pour la Recherche Nucléaire,* a.k.a. the European Laboratory for Particle Physics) conventions. The differences are in the internal layout of the map file. Most software that can create an image map allows you to create either kind of image map. Be sure to check with your ISP or its FAQ page to find out which of these two conventions it supports.

Client-side image maps

If you decide to go with client-side maps, your primary concern will be whether to provide alternate hyperlinks for the hotspot links. This allows visitors to your page to jump to the required locations even if they can't use the image map itself. In Figure 15-10 you can see a subtle way of doing this: The text on the page contains links to the same URLs as the image map.

Creating an Image Map with LiveImage

Tutorial

Download: To install the free version of LiveImage, go to
`www.mediatec.com`.

Level: Easy

Task: Add hotspots to an image

Before you start: Install and run LiveImage software.

Note: As this book went to press, the product known as MapTHIS! was sold, upgraded, and renamed LiveImage. This accounts for references to MapTHIS! in the figures.

The Humongous Fish Company web page, shown earlier in Figure 15-16, contains an image — not an image map. To turn the image into an image map, you must indicate which regions on the image are hotspots, and identify the URL each hotspot is linked to. In this tutorial, you will use MapTHIS! to turn the image into an image map. I like creating image maps with MapTHIS! because it is so easy to use. Open the image, draw the hotspots, add the URLs, and save the map. MapTHIS! is not an image editor, and will not make changes to your images other than identifying hotspots.

Running MapTHIS! displays the program window shown in Figure 15-18.

1. Use the File | New menu selection, which displays the dialog box shown in Figure 15-19.

2. Click the Okay button to go in search of the image file. This displays the Open an Existing Image dialog box (see Figure 15-20).

3. Locate the file `\My Web Stuff\Chap15\fish2.gif`. Highlight the filename and click the Open button to load the file into MapTHIS!.

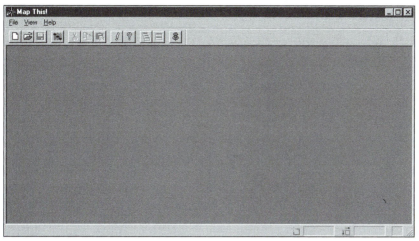

Figure 15-18: The LiveImage program window.

Figure 15-19: An image map starts with an image.

Okay button

Figure 15-20: Locating an image for your map.

Image filename

The image opens in the LiveImage window as shown in Figure 15-21. This image has a transparent background. The entire area shown in gray is transparent when the image is displayed on a web page. Since the Humongous web page has a black background, this works nicely.

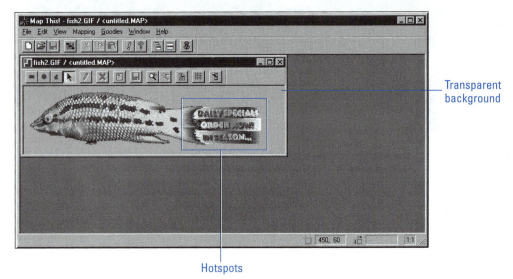

Figure 15-21: The image opened in LiveImage

LiveImage tools

There is a row of tools at the top of the image window. From left to right, these tools perform the functions listed in Table 15-1. You can also hold the mouse over any tool to display a tool tag that identifies the tool's function. A more detailed description of each tool appears in the status bar at the bottom of the program window.

	Table 15-1	
	LiveImage Tools	
Tool	**Name**	**Description**
▬	Rectangle	Creates a square or rectangular hotspot
✦	Ellipse	Creates an elliptical or circular hotspot

Tool	Name	Description
	Polygon	Creates a polygonal hotspot
	Selection	Selects a hotspot so you can edit it
	Edit Hot Spot	Edits the settings for the currently selected hotspot
	Delete Hot Spot	Deletes the currently selected hotspot
	Toggle List	Shows/Hides hotspot list
	Save	Saves the image map to disk
	Zoom In	Enlarges your view of the image
	Zoom Out	Reduces your view of the image
	Edit Map	Edits map information (title, author, and so on)
	Toggle Grid	Displays/hides grid
	Test	Tests the map interactively

If the image size is too small, you can click the Zoom In tool to enlarge your view of the image (see Figure 15-22).

Adding hotspots

The next step is to add hotspots to the text floating away from the fish's tail. These will be rectangular hotspots.

1. Click the Rectangle tool to activate it. The cursor changes to a small rectangle with an arrow. Zoom in on the image with the Zoom In tool (see Figure 15-22).

Zoom tool

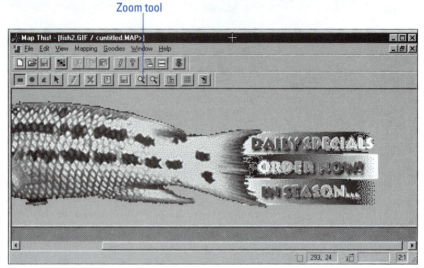

Figure 15-22: Enlarging the view with the Zoom In tool.

2. Click at the top-left corner of the upper hotspot (see Figure 15-23) and drag to the lower-right corner (see Figure 15-24).

3. Release the mouse button, and you have yourself a nice little hotspot (see Figure 15-25).

Cursor for rectanglar hotspot

Figure 15-23: The upper-left corner of the hotspot.

Hotspot boundary

Figure 15-24: The lower-right corner of the hotspot.

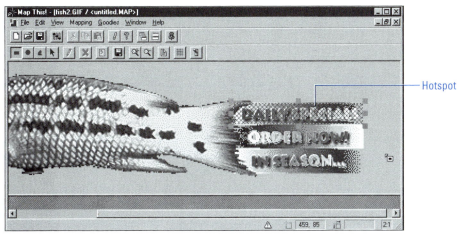

Figure 15-25: The completed hotspot.

Note that the hotspot has selection handles on it. You can adjust the size of the hotspot with these handles.

4. If you need to adjust the size or borders of the hotspot, first click the Selection tool, then click on the hotspot to select it, and *then* make any necessary adjustments by dragging one of the handles.

5. Repeat Step 4 two more times, once for each line of text at the right of the tail. Figure 15-26 shows the three hotspots.

6. If the hotspots are not exactly right, select each one in turn and adjust its size and/or position. Figure 15-27 shows a hotspot being moved, and Figure 15-28 shows a hotspot being resized.

If you need to change the position of the hotspot, select it and click anywhere within the hotspot; drag it to its new destination. Figure 15-27 shows how the cursor changes during a resize, and Figure 15-28 shows how the cursor appears while you're dragging a hot spot.

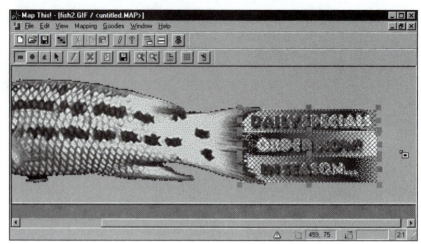

Figure 15-26: Three hotspots.

Figure 15-27: Moving a hotspot.

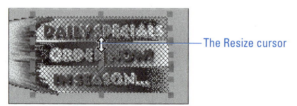

Figure 15-28: Resizing a hotspot.

Adding URLs to hotspots

Follow these steps to add a URL to a hotspot:

1. Click the selection tool to activate it.

2. To indicate the URL that the visitor will jump to when a hotspot is clicked, highlight the top hotspot and double-click it. This displays the Area Settings dialog box shown in Figure 15-29.

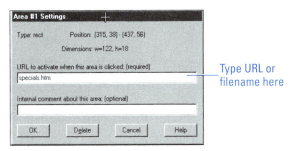

Type URL or
filename here

Figure 15-29: Entering the URL for a hotspot.

3. Type the URL into the top text box.

4. If you want to add a comment, you may do so in the lower text box. For the top hotspot, enter the hypothetical URL of a web page on the hypothetical Humongous web site: **specials.htm**.

5. Click the OK button.

6. Continue by adding two more URLs for the two remaining hotspots: **order.htm** and **season.htm**.

7. You can also view and edit hotspot URLs by clicking the Toggle List button (refer to Table 15-1). This displays the list of hotspots, shown in Figure 15-30.

8. Using the list, you can click the Pencil tool at the right of the list to edit the URL for the currently selected hotspot.

In Figure 15-30, none of the hotspots has URLs, so they are all shown in red with alert triangles to the left of each hotspot. When you add a URL to a hotspot, its position in the list changes color and appearance as shown in Figure 15-31.

List

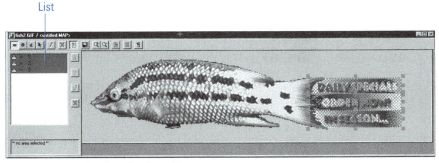

Figure 15-30: Viewing the list of hotspots.

Figure 15-31: The first hotspot now has a URL.

Nonrectangular hotspots

You can create elliptical or polygonal hotspots in the same manner as rectangular hotspots: Click the appropriate tool, drag out the size and shape of the hotspot, and add the URL.

The Ellipse tool works just like the Rectangle tool; click and drag to indicate a shape.

The Polygon tool is a bit different. To make the fish itself a hotspot:

1. Click the Polygon tool. The cursor changes to a small polygon with an arrow; the tip of the arrow (upper left of the cursor) indicates where a click operates.

2. To indicate the shape of the polygon, click at the points (technically, vertices) of the polygon.

   For the fish, these are various points around the outline of the fish. The exact points aren't critical. Figure 15-32 shows the sequence of points I clicked to outline the fish.

3. Double-click to close the polygon. Figure 15-33 shows the hotspot.

To complete the polygon, click one last time as close as you can to the start point of the polygon. LiveImage will sense that you are close to the start point, and close the polygon automatically.

4. Highlight the new hotspot, and double-click it. Enter the filename **fish.htm** as the URL (see Figure 15-34).

5. Before you save your work, use the Mapping | Edit Map Info menu selection to display the Settings for this Mapfile dialog box (see Figure 15-35).

6. Enter the title **fishmap**, your own name as Author, and a default URL of **home.htm**. The default URL is the page to jump to if the visitor clicks outside the hotspots, and it is required. If you like, add a description as well.

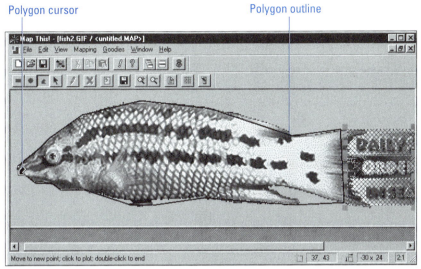

Figure 15-32: Creating a polygonal hotspot.

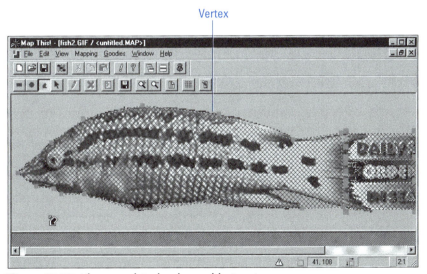

Figure 15-33: The completed polygonal hotspot.

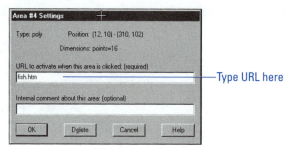

Figure 15-34: Adding a URL for the new hotspot.

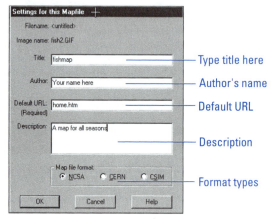

Figure 15-35: Setting map file information.

At the bottom of the dialog box there are three radio buttons, one for each type of image map that MapTHIS! can create. The three kinds of map file are

◆ **NCSA** — Create a server-side map file using the NCSA convention.

◆ **CERN** — Create a server-side map file using the CERN convention.

◆ **CSIM** — Create a client-side image map.

7. Click the NCSA radio button, and then click OK to save the changes.

8. To save the map file, use the File | Save menu selection to open the dialog box shown in Figure 15-36.

9. Make sure you save the file to the \My Web Stuff\Chap15 folder. To save the file using the NCSA convention, verify that the NCSA radio button is active at the bottom of the dialog box, and enter the filename **fishncsa.map**.

10. Click Save to save the file.

Figure 15-36: Saving the map file.

Tip

Those radio buttons at the bottom of the Save dialog box in Figure 15-41 are very handy. You can change the server-side convention, or save a client-side file, all with the click of a radio button. If you save with the NCSA or CERN convention, make sure that you use the extensions .map or .imp for the file. If you save as client-side, use the .htm or .html extensions. Note that while the client-side image map was called CSIM in the Map Info dialog box, here it is referred to as HTML. CSIM and HTML behave identically, and a future version of the software will probably fix this minor bug.

File conventions

I suggest that you save the file using all three available options (NCSA, CERN, HTML) to see what you get. Listing 15-1 shows the contents of an NCSA file; Listing 15-2 shows the contents of a CERN file, and Listing 15-3 shows the contents of an HTML/CSIM file.

Listing 15-1: NCSA version of the map file

```
#$MTIMFH
#$-:Image Map file created by Map THIS!
#$-:Map THIS! free image map editor by Todd C. Wilson
#$-:Please do not edit lines starting with "#$"
#$VERSION:1.30
#$TITLE:fishmap
#$DESCRIPTION:A map for all seasons
#$AUTHOR:Your name here
#$DATE:Mon Jan 20 07:51:42 1997
#$PATH:D:\My Web Stuff\Chap15\
#$GIF:fish2.GIF
#$FORMAT:ncsa
#$EOH
```

(continued)

Listing 15-1 (continued)

```
default home.htm
rect specials.htm 315,36 437,59
rect order.htm 315,59 438,79
rect season.htm 315,80 438,103
poly fish.htm 12,70 29,82 45,84 52,89 73,89 116,102 137,102
          186,96 272,102 310,101 308,35 264,41 196,18 126,10 72,22
          43,43 12,70
```

The lines in Listing 15-1 that begin with a pound sign and dollar sign (#$) are comments added by LiveImage. They are ignored by the server-side software accessing the file. The four hotspots are defined at the bottom of the listing — three rectangles and a polygon. Compare these hotspot definitions to the hotspot definitions in Listing 15-2. The default URL for clicks outside the defined hotspots appears just above the hotspot definitions.

The lines in Listing 15-2 that begin with

```
rect (4096,4096) (4096,4096) mt:#$
```

are comment lines. The CERN convention doesn't support pure comments, so LiveImage adds false hotspot definitions and follows those with comments. Ugly, but it works. The hotspot definitions themselves are at the bottom of the listing. Compare them to the slightly different definitions used in Listing 15-1 for the NCSA convention. The default URL for clicks outside the defined hotspots appears just above the hotspot definitions.

Listing 15-2: CERN version of the map file

```
rect (4096,4096) (4096,4096) mt:#$MTIMFH
rect (4096,4096) (4096,4096) mt:#$-
        :Image%20Map%20file%20created%20by%20Map%20THIS!
rect (4096,4096) (4096,4096) mt:#$-
        :Map%20THIS!%20free%20image%20map%20editor%20by%20Todd%20
        C.%20Wilson
rect (4096,4096) (4096,4096) mt:#$-
        :Please%20do%20not%20edit%20lines%20starting%20with%20"#$
        "
rect (4096,4096) (4096,4096) mt:#$VERSION:1.30
rect (4096,4096) (4096,4096) mt:#$TITLE:fishmap
rect (4096,4096) (4096,4096)
        mt:#$DESCRIPTION:A%20map%20for%20all%20seasons
rect (4096,4096) (4096,4096) mt:#$AUTHOR:Your%20name%20here
        mt:#$AUTHOR:Your%20name%20here
rect (4096,4096) (4096,4096)
        mt:#$DATE:Mon%20Jan%2020%2007:51:55%201997
```

```
rect (4096,4096) (4096,4096)
     mt:#$PATH:D:\My%20Web%20Stuff\Chap15\
rect (4096,4096) (4096,4096) mt:#$GIF:fish2.GIF
rect (4096,4096) (4096,4096) mt:#$FORMAT:cern
rect (4096,4096) (4096,4096) mt:#$EOH
default home.htm
rectangle (315,36) (437,59) specials.htm
rectangle (315,59) (438,79) order.htm
rectangle (315,80) (438,103) season.htm
polygon (12,70) (29,82) (45,84) (52,89) (73,89) (116,102)
        (137,102) (186,96) (272,102) (310,101) (308,35) (264,41)
        (196,18) (126,10) (72,22) (43,43) (12,70) fish.htm
```

If you save a file as HTML/CSIM, you get the bare bones of an HTML file as shown in Listing 15-3. Since you probably are using some kind of web page or HTML editor to create your web pages, you will need to open the HTML file LiveImage creates, copy the image map definitions to the Clipboard, and then paste them into your web page. The map definition is everything except the <BODY> and </BODY> tags. You do not have to keep the comments when you paste the map definition into the actual web page. Keep the comments in the LiveImage file, however, so that LiveImage knows what the map file is about.

Listing 15-3: HTML/CSIM version of the map file

```
<BODY>
<MAP NAME="fishmap">
<!- #$-:Image Map file created by Map THIS! ->
<!- #$-:Map THIS! free image map editor by Todd C. Wilson ->
<!- #$-:Please do not edit lines starting with "#$" ->
<!- #$VERSION:1.30 ->
<!- #$DESCRIPTION:A map for all seasons ->
<!- #$AUTHOR:Your name here ->
<!- #$DATE:Mon Jan 20 07:52:11 1997 ->
<!- #$PATH:D:\My Web Stuff\Chap15\ ->
<!- #$GIF:fish2.GIF ->
<AREA SHAPE=RECT COORDS="315,36,437,59" HREF="specials.htm">
<AREA SHAPE=RECT COORDS="315,59,438,79" HREF="order.htm">
<AREA SHAPE=RECT COORDS="315,80,438,103" HREF="season.htm">
<AREA SHAPE=POLY
        COORDS="12,70,29,82,45,84,52,89,73,89,116,102,137,102,186
        ,96,272,102,310,101,308,35,264,41,196,18,126,10,72,22,43,
        43,12,70" HREF="fish.htm">
<AREA SHAPE=default HREF="home.htm">
</MAP></BODY>
```

Case study: Server-side map file

To use either of the server-side map files, you must:

◆ Change the web page so the browser will know that the image has an associated map file.

◆ Upload the map file to the web server.

◆ Perform any additional ISP-specific actions required.

You can change the web page in an editor such as Notepad, or with your web page editing software. To change the web page in Notepad or a similar editor:

1. Open the web page file and find the image reference. For example, the Humongous web page has the following HTML code for the image:

```
<IMG SRC="fish2.GIF" HEIGHT=121 WIDTH=480>
```

2. To change this image reference so it works as an image map, using the NCSA map file, you need to add a hyperlink to the map file, and the ISMAP parameter to the IMG tag.

   The location of the map file is up to your ISP. One example of a map file's location is shown here:

```
<A HREF="../maps/fishncsa.map"><IMG SRC="fish2.GIF" ISMAP
       HEIGHT=121 WIDTH=480></A>
```

3. After you add the hyperlink and ISMAP parameter, save the file.

4. You must upload the map file to the server before you can test your image map. How you upload to the server varies from one ISP to the next.

You can also change the image reference using some web page editors. The exact method will vary from one editor to another, but the basic process involves creating a hyperlink to the image map file, and adding that ISMAP parameter to the IMG tag. Some editors will allow you to simply check a box to add the ISMAP parameter, while others may require you to add it manually.

For example, to make an image into a server-side image map with FrontPage 97:

1. Right-click the image to display the Image Properties dialog box (see Figure 15-37).

2. Enter the URL of the image map file into the Location text box in the Default Hyperlink area of the dialog box.

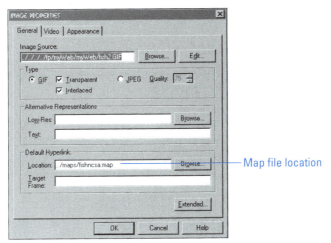

Figure 15-37: Image properties in FrontPage 97.

The hyperlink alone isn't enough to make the image map work.

3. Click the Extended button to display YAD (Yet Another Dialog), shown in Figure 15-38.

The Extended Attributes dialog box allows you to add parameters (FrontPage 97 insists on calling them attributes) and their values (if any) to an HTML tag. In this case, the tag is the IMG tag, and the parameter you should add is ISMAP.

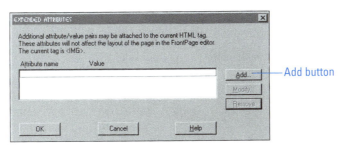

Figure 15-38: Adding parameters to an HTML tag.

4. Click the Add button to open YAD, shown in Figure 15-39.

5. Enter **ISMAP** as the name, and leave the Value text box blank. This parameter has no value associated with it.

6. Click OK.

Parameter goes here

Figure 15-39: Adding a parameter.

The appearance of the Extended Attributes dialog box changes to show the new attribute/parameter (see Figure 15-40).

7. Click OK. Now, when you save the web page, the hyperlink and additional parameter are added to the HTML code.

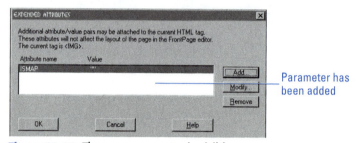

Parameter has been added

Figure 15-40: The new parameter is visible.

Here is the HTML code as written to the file by FrontPage 97:

```
<a href="../maps/fishncsa.map"><img src="fish2.gif" border="0"
     width="480" height="121" ismap></a>
```

Note that it looks very much like the code shown near the beginning of this section:

```
<A HREF="../maps/fishncsa.map"><IMG SRC="fish2.GIF" ISMAP
     HEIGHT=121 WIDTH=480></A>
```

The only notable difference (besides the fact that FrontPage 97 uses lowercase) is the addition of the BORDER parameter, setting the image border to zero. FrontPage97 omits borders around hyperlinked images by default, which is the norm for today's web pages. This is a nice touch, as most editors default to including the border, and you have to take steps to remove the border yourself.

You must upload the map file to the server before you can test your image map.

How you upload to the server varies from one ISP to the next. FrontPage 97 includes publishing tools that are supported by some ISPs, and some of the other web page editors also include publishing tools. As always, check with your ISP to find out exactly which tools are supported, and any special instructions you need.

If you had used the CERN map file instead of the NCSA map file, the steps involved would have been exactly the same. Only the internal contents of the map file would be different.

Case study: Client-side map file

Big-time editors like FrontPage 97 and Fusion, among others, have built-in support for client-side image maps. To use the client-side image map file created with LiveImage in other editors (such as Navigator Gold) requires some manual work.

1. Open the client-side map file \My Web Stuff\Chap15\fishmap.htm in Notepad (see Figure 15-41).

2. Copy everything except the BODY tags to the Clipboard (see Figure 15-42).

```
<BODY>
<MAP NAME="fishmap">
<!-- #$-:Image Map file created by Map THIS! -->
<!-- #$-:Map THIS! free image map editor by Todd C. Wilson -->
<!-- #$-:Please do not edit lines starting with "#$" -->
<!-- #$VERSION:1.30 -->
<!-- #$DESCRIPTION:A map for all seasons -->
<!-- #$AUTHOR:Your name here -->
<!-- #$DATE:Mon Jan 20 07:52:11 1997 -->
<!-- #$PATH:D:\My Web Stuff\Chap16\ -->
<!-- #$GIF:fish2.GIF -->
<AREA SHAPE=RECT COORDS="315,36,437,59" HREF="specials.htm">
<AREA SHAPE=RECT COORDS="315,59,438,79" HREF="order.htm">
<AREA SHAPE=RECT COORDS="315,80,438,103" HREF="season.htm">
<AREA SHAPE=POLY
COORDS="12,70,29,82,45,84,52,89,73,89,116,102,137,102,186,96,272,102,
310,101,308,35,264,41,196,18,126,10,72,22,43,43,12,70"
HREF="fish.htm">
<AREA SHAPE=default HREF="home.htm">
</MAP></BODY>
```

Figure 15-41: The client-side image map file.

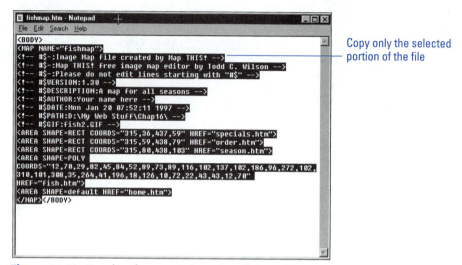

Figure 15-42: Copying the map info to the Clipboard.

3. Now open the file \My Web Stuff\Chap15\chap15A.htm in Notepad.

4. Position the cursor in the open line just after the <BODY> tag (see Figure 15-43).

5. Paste the contents of the Clipboard at this location (see Figure 15-44).

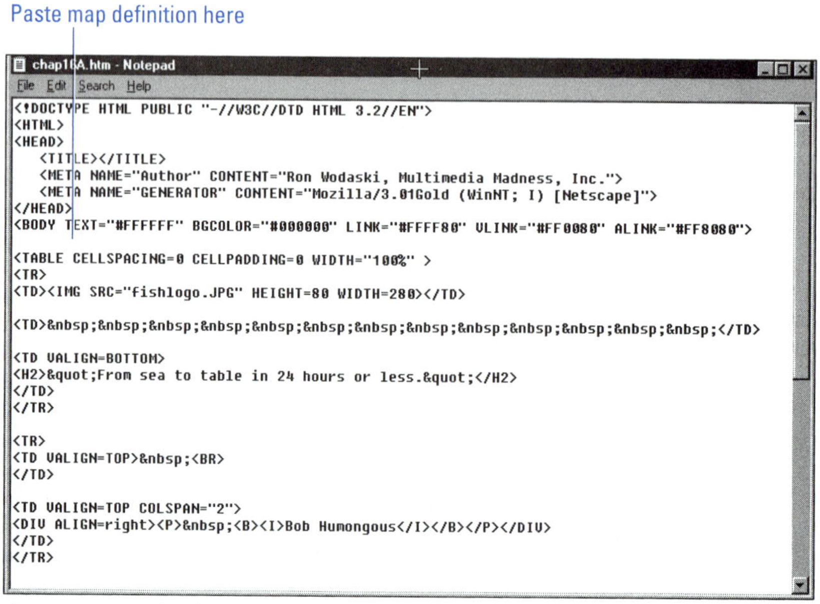

Figure 15-43: The location for pasting the map info.

Beginning of map definition   End of map definition

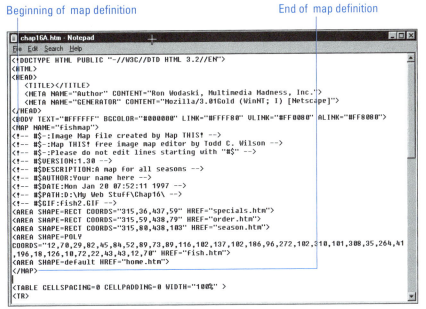

Figure 15-44: The map info pasted into the file.

You do not need the comments created by MapTHIS!; they are stored in the original map file. You can delete them if you wish. The comment lines all start with `<!-- #$` and end with `-->`.

6. Go to the bottom of the file and locate the line shown as selected in Figure 15-45. You are going to modify this line to work with the map definition you just pasted into the web page.

   The existing contents of the line are:

   ```
   <TD><IMG SRC="fish2.GIF" HEIGHT=121 WIDTH=480></TD>
   ```

7. Change this to:

   ```
   <TD><IMG SRC="fish2.GIF" USEMAP="#fishmap" BORDER=0
        HEIGHT=121 WIDTH=480></TD>
   ```

8. Before you continue, save the file with a new name: **\My Web Stuff\Chap15\myFish.htm.**

The changes you made added two parameters. The first, USEMAP, tells the browser which map definition to use. There is only one map definition, but you still have to specify it. The second, BORDER, sets the image border to zero. Most browsers will add a border around an image that uses the USEMAP parameter. Figure 15-46 shows the border — and it does nothing to enhance the appearance of the page.

You can see these changes in the file `\My Web Stuff\Chap15\ Chap15A2.htm`.

```
<TR>
<TD VALIGN=TOP> <BR>
</TD>

<TD VALIGN=TOP COLSPAN="2">
<DIV ALIGN=right><P> <B><I>Bob Humongous</I></B></P></DIV>
</TD>
</TR>

<TR>
<TD>
<UL>
<LI><B><A HREF="temp.htm">Swordfish prices in freefall</A></B></LI>

<LI><B><A HREF="temp.htm">We're overstocked on tuna; call now!</A></B></LI>

<LI><B><A HREF="temp.htm">Sharks are swarming</A></B></LI>

<LI><B><A HREF="temp.htm">Bob's Daily Specials expanded</A></B></LI>
</UL>
</TD>

<TD>     </TD>

<TD><IMG SRC="fish2.GIF" HEIGHT=121 WIDTH=480></TD>
</TR>
</TABLE>
```

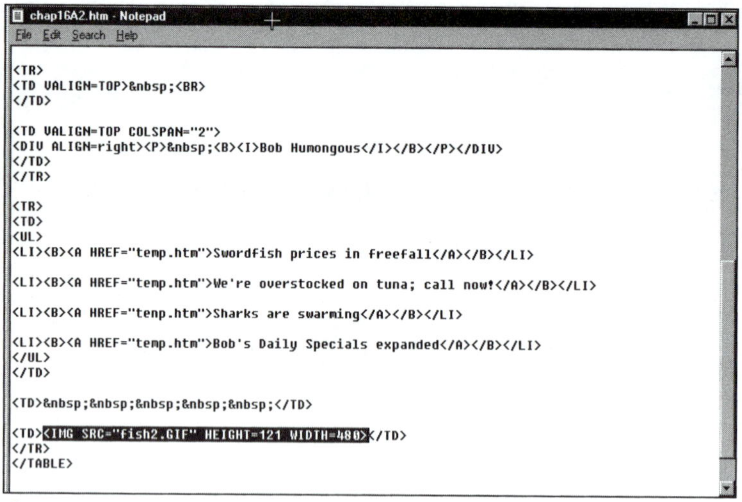

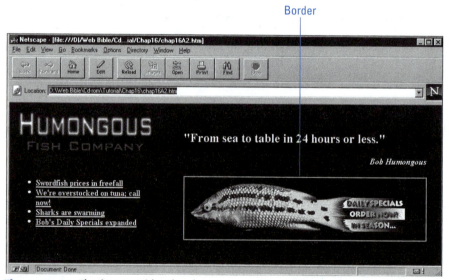

Figure 15-45: The line of HTML code you are going to modify.

Figure 15-46: The image with a border.

You can open the web page in your browser to test it, and then upload to the web server when everything works correctly. Browsers such as Navigator Gold and Internet Explorer, which support client-side image maps, will operate the image map properly. Older browsers may not. If a browser doesn't support your image map, the image will fail completely: It will not have working hotspots. To cover this situation, you can add a line of text hyperlinks below the image map for users whose browsers do not support client-side image maps. Figure 15-47 shows how this looks. The file is \My Web Stuff\Chap15\Chap15A3.htm.

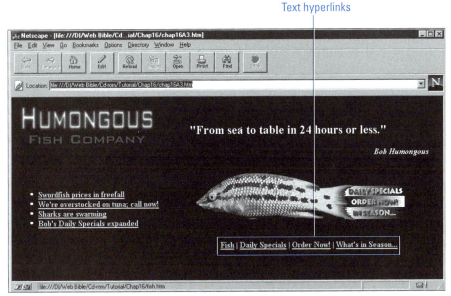

Figure 15-47: The page with text hyperlinks added below the image map.

Server-side meets client-side

You can have images that support both sides of the fence simultaneously. This is accomplished by adding the HTML codes for both server-side and client-side mapping to the same web page.

For this example, first set up the page for server-side mapping by uploading the map file, and changing the HTML code for the image tag as shown earlier:

```
<A HREF="../maps/fishncsa.map"><IMG SRC="fish2.GIF" ISMAP
     HEIGHT=121 WIDTH=480></A>
```

Then open the page in Notepad and add the client-side map definition to the top of the file (just after the <BODY> tag), and add the client-side HTML codes:

```
<A HREF="../maps/fishncsa.map"><IMG SRC="fish2.GIF" ISMAP
     USEMAP="#fishmap" HEIGHT=121 WIDTH=480></A>
```

Browsers that support client-side mapping will use this client-side definition. Browsers that do not will use the server-side map.

Creating an Image Map with MapEdit

Download: For a trial version of MapEdit, go to `www.boutell.com/mapedit/`.

Level: Easy

Tutorial

Task: Add hotspots to an image

Before you start: Install and run MapEdit software.

Working with MapEdit isn't a whole lot different from working with LiveImage. Other than the lack of an exclamation point in the name, MapEdit operates in a very similar fashion: Define the hotspot size and shape, add a URL, and output a server-side map file or a client-side image map definition.

However, MapEdit has a very different overall feel. For example, it starts up differently from most Windows programs. It begins with a dialog box, shown in Figure 15-48. This is unconventional, but it reveals a neat feature of MapEdit. If you put an HTML filename in the top text box (don't type it in; use the Browse button!), you see the dialog box that lists all of the images on that web page. Where LiveImage makes you copy the map definition by hand, MapEdit will do it for you.

Browse button for locating an existing map file or web page

Browse button for locating an image file

Figure 15-48: The starting dialog box for MapEdit.

Overall, I rate LiveImage as the program with the better interface, and MapEdit as the program with more clever features. In my estimation, the LiveImage interface is worth more points than the MapEdit features. I would like to use MapEdit for its features, but when MapEdit falls down, it falls down hard.

Creating a client-side map

To convert the Dada Consulting image into a client-side image map:

1. Double-click the MapEdit icon. You'll see the dialog box in Figure 15-48.

2. Click the Browse button and locate the file `\My Web Stuff\Chap15\Chap15B.htm` in the Open dialog box.

3. Highlight the file and click the Open button.

This displays a list of the images in the file (see Figure 15-49). There is only one image in this file: dada6.jpg.

4. Click the image to highlight its name, and then click OK. This returns you to the starting dialog box, but with the HTML and image filenames filled in (see Figure 15-50).

Figure 15-49: A list of the images in the file.

Figure 15-50: The Open/Create Map dialog box.

If you want to create an image map for a specific image (that is, if you want to create a server-side image map), click the Browse button for the Image Filename instead of the Map or HTML File Browse button.

5. Click OK to finally get to the MapEdit program window (see Figure 15-51).

Toolbar

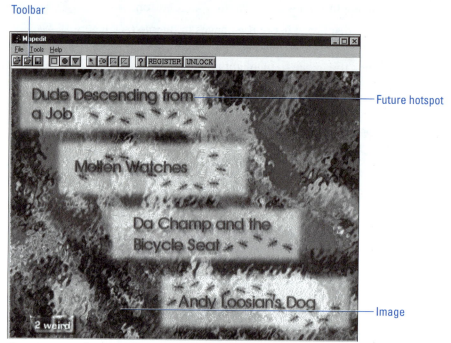

Future hotspot

Image

Figure 15-51: The MapEdit program window.

MapEdit tools

There is a row of tools at the top of the image window. From left to right, these tools perform the functions listed in Table 15-2. Holding the mouse over any tool may not display a tool tag. If this is the first time you are using MapEdit, clicking a tool will display a little window with a brief description of the tool's function. When you no longer want to see the hints, click the No More Hints button, and you will not be bothered with them again.

Tool	Name	Description
	Open	Opens a file
	Close	Closes this file
	Save	Saves to disk
	Rectangle	Creates a square or rectangular hotspot
	Ellipse	Creates an elliptical or circular hotspot
	Polygon	Creates a polygonal hotspot
	Test/Edit	Tests and edits a hotspot
	Move	Moves a hotspot around
	Add Points	Adds points to a polygon
	Remove Points	Removes points from a polygon

Table 15-2
MapEdit Tools

This image requires five rectangular hotspots. There are four large buttons on the image, and a small button at lower left. The button at lower left provides a link to the hypothetical graphic design firm that handled the design: 2 Weird, Inc.

1. Click the Rectangle tool and then click at the upper left of the top button ("Dude Descending from a Job").

2. Click again at the lower-right corner to complete the rectangle. You will see a thin line that defines the hotspot, and the dialog box shown in Figure 15-52 displays.

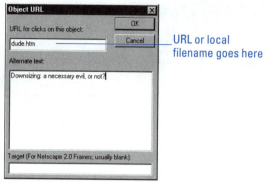

Figure 15-52: Defining a hotspot's
URL and alternate text.

You can enter three kinds of information in the dialog box. For this example, enter the URL and alternate text shown in Figure 15-52 (and in Table 15-3).

3. At the top, enter the URL for the web page displayed when the hotspot is clicked.

4. In the central box, enter alternate text.

Some browsers, such as Internet Explorer, display the alternate text when the cursor lingers on a hotspot for more than a second. The bottom box is for entering a target. This is used with pages that have frames, and the target is usually the name of a specific frame on the page.

5. Click OK to save the URL and alternate text. A thin line appears, defining the hotspot (see Figure 15-53).

6. Add four more hotspots, using the URLs and alternate text from Table 15-3.

Table 15-3 Dada Consulting Hotspots		
Button text	**URL**	**Alternate text**
Dude...	dude.htm	Downsizing: a necessary evil, or not?
Molten Watches	time.htm	Time management
Da Champ...	equip.htm	Office equipment: control expenditures
Andy Loosians...	work.htm	Working too hard?
2 Weird	http://www.2weird.com	Page and image created by 2 Weird, Inc.

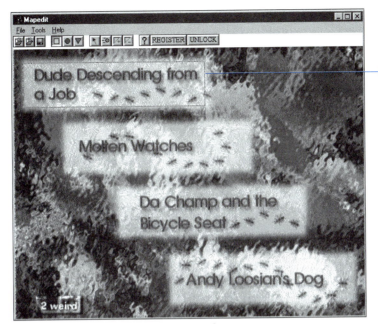

Figure 15-53: The first hotspot defined.

The ability to add the alternate text so easily is a nice feature of MapEdit. However, it created a hot philosophical debate at Dada Consulting. Both sides in the debate felt that it gave visitors some clues about the nature of the web pages behind the buttons. One side thought this was a good thing, since the page was obscure. The other side felt that this interfered with the purity of the Dada/surreal aspects of the site. Fortunately, the more sensible view prevailed, and the alternate text stayed. The reason? Even those opposed realized that, because only certain browsers support alternate text, the page would still possess a bizarre nature.

Somebody want to call the white coats? Mr. Author has done gone over whatever fine edge of sanity he had left.

Figure 15-54 shows the image with all five hotspots added. Unlike LiveImage, MapEdit makes it hard to see the hotspots.

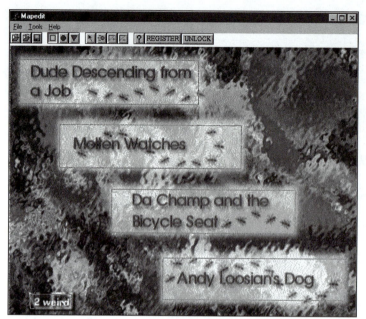

Figure 15-54: All hotspots created.

Caution!

Hard-to-see hotspots are the least of the problem with MapEdit. If you try to resize or move a hotspot, you will find it very difficult to locate the handles. You can only move a hotspot by clicking a nearly-invisible cross at the center of the hotspot, and the selection handles are, as far as I could tell, invisible. These problems are by far the most serious shortcoming of MapEdit. This is a shame, because so many other aspects of the program are so cleverly designed.

7. To check the contents of any hotspot, or to edit the contents, click the Test/Edit tool and then click a hotspot. The hotspot appears in reverse color, and the Object URL dialog box appears (see Figure 15-55).

Tip

To specify a default URL for all areas of the image outside of the hotspots, activate the Test/Edit tool and click anywhere outside the hotspots. This displays the dialog box shown in Figure 15-56. Type in the default URL, and click OK.

Reverse color

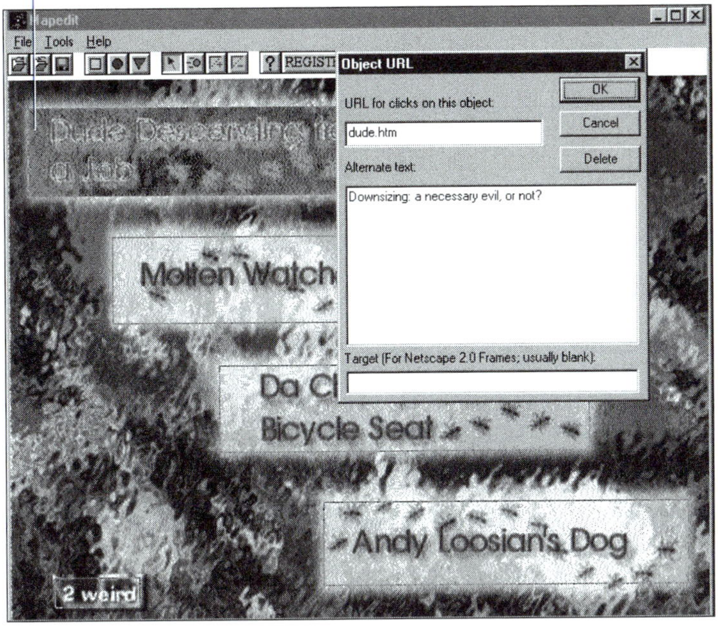

Figure 15-55: Editing a hotspot's URL.

Default URL or
local filename

Figure 15-56: Specifying the default URL.

8. To save the hotspots as a client-side image map, use the File | Save As menu selection.

9. Click the Client Side Map (HTML) radio button, and change the filename to **\My Web Stuff\Chap15\Chap15B3.htm**.

10. Click OK to save the file.

11. To save as an NCSA or CERN server-side image map file, click the appropriate button and enter an appropriate name such as (**\My Web Stuff\Chap15\dadancsa.map** or **\My Web Stuff\Chap15\dadacern.map**).

If you save as a server-side map, be sure to edit the image reference in the web page file to add the hyperlink to the map file, and the ISMAP parameter.

Figure 15-57 shows the Dada Consulting web page in action. Note that the cursor changes to a pointing hand over the hotspots on the image map. The file is `\My Web Stuff\chap15\chap15B2.htm`.

Figure 15-57: The page in action.

If you save in NCSA format, MapEdit uses the alternate text as comments in the file, as shown in Listing 15-4. Compare this to Listing 15-1 (the NCSA output from LiveImage).

Listing 15-4: MapEdit NCSA output

```
#Downsizing: a necessary evil, or not?
rect dude.htm 17,24 349,103
#Time management
rect time.htm 94,140 428,217
#Office equipment: control expenditures.
rect equip.htm 191,255 528,332
#Working too hard?
rect work.htm 286,377 620,451
#Page and image created by 2 Weird, Inc.
rect http://www.2weird.com 40,443 117,469
default dada.htm
```

Creating Image Maps with Web Page Editors

In addition to using tools like LiveImage and MapEdit, many of the web page editors available today allow you to interactively add hotspots to an image on a web page. You can see one example using FrontPage 97 in Chapter 5. Net Objects Fusion also allows you to add hotspots to web page images.

Caution!

When you add hotspots interactively on a web page, you are almost always creating a client-side image map. While client-side maps are certainly the wave of the future, if you need a server-side map, look to tools like the map editors described in the preceding sections: LiveImage and MapEdit.

Fusion isn't a page editor; it's a site editor. That means that you use it for managing a complete web site (creating templates, publishing, rearranging the site, and so on); page editing is just one feature of Fusion. You shouldn't expect to load a single page into Fusion to edit it. Why not? Because Fusion uses a large set of sophisticated templates for creating its web pages. As you lay out a page, you use elements from the template for the page headers, body, and footers.

If you really and truly want to edit a page in Fusion, use the File | Import Page menu selection to add the page to an existing web site.

Figure 15-58 shows Fusion in action. Note the areas at the top and bottom of the page; these are the header and footer, respectively. I made the header and footer as small as I could to focus attention on the image map.

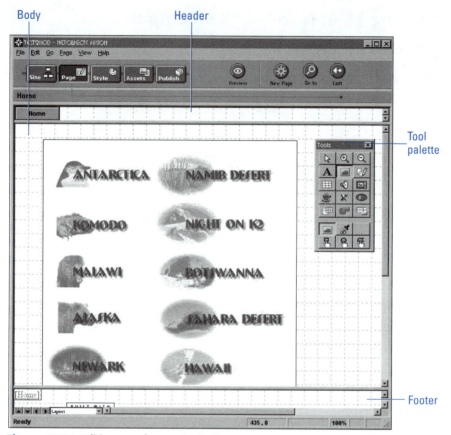

Body   Header   Tool palette   Footer

Figure 15-58: Editing a web page in Fusion.

Figure 15-59 shows the Fusion toolbar. The Picture button is depressed, making it the active tool. To add a picture, follow these steps:

1. Click the page to establish the upper left corner of the image. An Open dialog box appears.

2. Locate the file `\My Web Stuff\Chap15\frontier.gif`.

3. Click OK to load it, and it appears on the page.

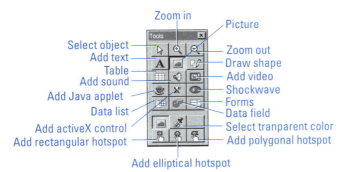

Figure 15-59: The Fusion toolbar.

4. To add hotspots to the image, click the appropriate button at the bottom of the toolbar.

5. Click and drag the image to indicate the extent of the hotspot. The dialog box shown in Figure 15-60 appears.

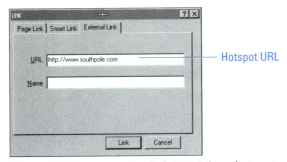

Figure 15-60: Entering the link (URL) for a hotspot.

6. Type the URL for the link in the space provided.

7. Click the Link button to establish the link. This closes the Link dialog box, and a box appears in the location of the hotspot (see Figure 15-61).

8. You can resize or move the link by clicking and dragging.

9. To edit the hotspot's properties, click the link to highlight it, and click the Hot Spot tab in the Properties dialog box (see Figure 15-62). (You can display any item's properties by pressing Alt+Enter.)

There is only one property: the URL of the link. The remaining hotspots would be added in the same manner.

Image handle   Hotspot handle

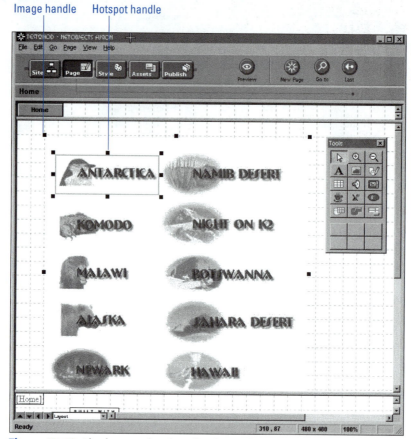

Figure 15-61: The hotspot has handles for resizing.

10. Click the Preview button at the top of the Fusion window to view the page in your default browser.

11. To test the Frontier Makers page for yourself (the basic version, not one created in Fusion), double-click the file `\My Web Stuff\Chap15\chap15C.htm`.

Image maps are a compact and effective way to add links to a web page. The trend is toward client-side image maps, but you will find many server-side image maps around the Web. Image maps offer an opportunity for a grand graphic on a web page. Several of the examples in this chapter are quite large. This runs counter to my philosophy of small is beautiful, but the fact is that the Web is littered with large image maps. If an image map looks good enough, your visitors will indulge you.

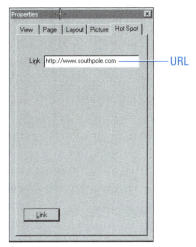

Figure 15-62: The hotspot's one and only property.

Web Tour #15: Image Maps of the World Wide Web

There are many web sites out there using interesting image maps. To visit sites with image maps, double-click the file:

```
\WebTour\Chap15\index.htm
```

You'll see the Web Tour pages for this chapter.

Graphic
by Design

P A R T

The Best of Buttons and Doodads

To prepare for this chapter's tutorials, copy the following folder from the CD-ROM to the \My Web Stuff folder on your hard drive:

    \tutorial\chap16

This will copy files and folders for all of the tutorials in this chapter to your hard disk. See Chapter 1 for complete details on setting up for tutorials.

The two best tools for creating the miscellaneous graphics you need on a web page are, without question, Adobe Photoshop and Fractal Design Painter. The latest version of Photoshop, version 4.0, includes features that make the web page designer's job a lot easier. In particular, you can use layers and Photoshop's Batch mode to accomplish new tricks with buttons, icons, page headers, and all the other graphics that have become important parts of a web page.

I'd better put in my two cents before Mr. Author goes overboard with his glowing recommendations. Someone has to say it: It's all too easy to reach graphic overkill on a web page. Mr. Author will be showing you some nice 3-D graphics and metallic effects, but ask yourself: At what point do the graphics overwhelm the page and create chaos? Think about it; there will be a test at the end of the semester.

Old Mr. Fuddy Duddy roars back and lands another bite on the hindquarters. Of course it's possible to overdo your graphics. Remember, there are two levels of design:

individual graphics, and the complete web page. No matter how much you fall in love with a particular graphic, if it doesn't fit into the web page, it doesn't fit into the web page.

Creating Basic Buttons with Photoshop

CD: A trial version of Photoshop is on the CD-ROM. To find out how to install it, view the web page at `\demo\viewme.htm` in your browser and click the `\demo\adobe` hyperlink.

Tutorial   **Level:** Easy

Task: Create a 3-D button

Before you start:

  ✦ Run Photoshop 4.0.

The two most common graphic elements on web pages are buttons and bullets. Most buttons can work as bullets if you shrink them down, and many bullets work well as buttons if you make them larger. I'm going to treat buttons and bullets as one category for now. In the last section of this chapter, I'll make some important distinctions between these mostly similar graphic elements.

1. To create a simple button, create a new file that is 40 pixels by 40 pixels (File | New menu item).

2. Activate the oval selection tool by clicking and holding the selection tool in the toolbar and then selecting the oval variant (see Figure 16-1).

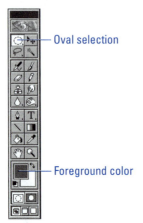

Figure 16-1: Activating the oval selection tool.

There are two ways to build this button: with or without transparency (see Chapter 13, "Interlacing and Transparency," for the details of GIF transparency). To create the button with a transparent background, you must create the base layer of the button with anti-aliasing turned off.

3. Double-click the oval selection tool to display the tool's options (see Figure 16-2).

4. Make sure that the Anti-aliased check box is unchecked.

 — Anti-aliased check box

Figure 16-2: Turning off anti-aliasing.

5. Click and drag out a circle that is slightly smaller than the full size of the canvas (see Figure 16-3). To make sure you get a circle, hold down the Shift key while you click and drag.

 — Selection

Figure 16-3: Creating a round selection.

6. Set the foreground color by clicking its icon in the toolbar. This opens the dialog box shown in Figure 16-4.

7. Set the current color to forest green using the RGB settings shown in Figure 16-4 (Red=0, Green=102, and Blue=51).

 — Color — RGB values

Figure 16-4: Setting the foreground color.

8. Add a new layer to the image using the Layer | New Layer menu selection. The layer appears as Layer 1 in the layers palette (see Figure 16-5).

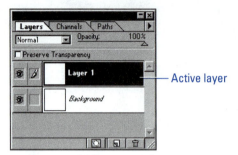

Figure 16-5: Adding a new layer.

Tip

This button is too small to work efficiently at 100% size. Use the "Ctrl +" (Control and Plus key) combination six times to enlarge the button to 700%.

9. Use the Edit | Fill menu selection to open the Fill dialog box (see Figure 16-6).

10. Set the Contents to Foreground Color, and verify that the Opacity is 100% and the Mode is Normal. The Preserve Transparency check box should be unchecked.

11. Click OK to fill the circular selection.

Figure 16-7 shows the filled selection. Note the jagged edge of the selection. This is the penalty for using a non-anti-aliased selection: Anti-aliasing smoothes the edges between object and background.

I apologize for Mr. Author's crazy use of the language: double negatives appear to be back in style. Let's get this straight: if you get rid of the jaggies, that's anti-aliasing. So shouldn't jagged edges be called aliased? No, that would be too easy. Jagged edges are non-anti-aliased. Spare me the double-speak!

Oh honorable Mr. Uncle, you speak with great wisdom. Except everyone else on the planet is calling it non-anti-aliased, and I'm just going with the flow.

Figure 16-6: Filling the selection with the current foreground color.

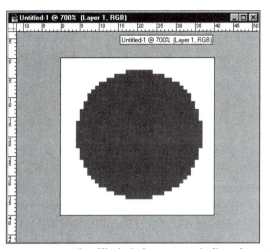

Figure 16-7: The filled circle, non-anti-aliased version.

Tip

You may also want to have an anti-aliased version of the button available for situations where the page background closely matches the image background. You can use Photoshop's layers to create an alternate version of the button base and have the best of both worlds. Turn anti-aliasing back on, create a new layer and a new (but identical!) circular selection, and fill it with the foreground color. Turn one circle off and the other on to switch between aliased and anti-aliased versions of the button. Figure 16-8 shows the appearance of the anti-aliased circle. It looks much smoother than the circle in Figure 16-7.

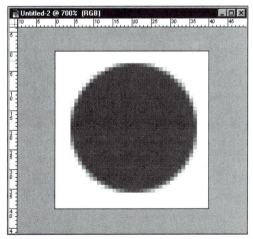

Figure 16-8: The filled circle when an anti-aliased selection is used.

The next step is to use a slightly smaller circular selection to create a 3-D detail on the button base. You could use the Select | Modify | Contract menu selection to reduce the size of the selection by two pixels. However, the current selection is non-anti-aliased. It's bad enough that this creates a jagged outer edge.

12. Click the Anti-aliased check box on the selection tool's option palette to turn it back on.

   This allows you to use anti-aliasing for all of the interior work on the button. The button will have a jagged outer edge to satisfy the needs of transparency, but the inner portions of the button will be as smooth as possible.

13. Create a new layer (Layer | New Layer).

14. Make sure that the rulers are turned on (View | Show Rulers; verify that rulers are set to pixels, not inches, via File | Preferences | Units & Rulers).

15. Create a second selection by clicking and dragging.

16. Click at a point two pixels to the right of the left edge of the existing circle, and two pixels below the top edge of the existing circle.

   Figure 16-9 shows the starting and ending points I used, and the resulting circular selection that is two pixels smaller in radius than the original selection.

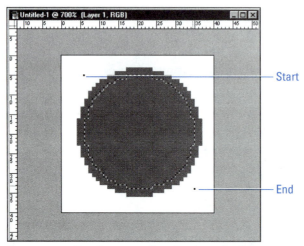

Figure 16-9: Creating a smaller circular selection.

17. Make sure the new layer is the active layer (click it in the Layers palette to highlight it).

18. Click the Gradient tool (see Figure 16-10) to activate it.

19. Click the background color to open the Color Picker dialog box (see Figure 16-11).

20. Set the new color as Red=124, Green=219, and Blue=173.

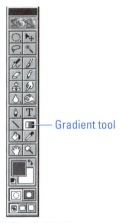

Gradient tool

Figure 16-10:
The Gradient tool.

Color

RGB values

Figure 16-11: Setting a new background color.

21. Double-click the gradient tool to view the tool's options (see Figure 16-12).

22. Select the Foreground to Background gradient, and set the type to Linear.

Figure 16-12: Selecting gradient options.

23. Click at the upper left of the current selection, drag to the lower right, and release the mouse button.

Figure 16-13 shows the starting and ending points for the gradient. Figure 16-14 shows the appearance of the gradient fill. Because the dark area is at the top left, the area you filled appears to be recessed.

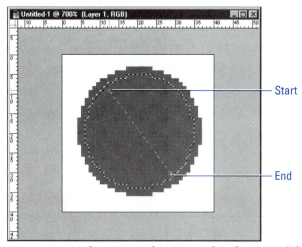

Figure 16-13: Where to set the start and end points of the gradient.

If the top left of an area is bright, the eye interprets it (most of the time) as a raised edge. If the top left is dark, the eye interprets is as sunken. The opposite is true of the bottom right of an object: brightness indicates sunken, darkness indicates raised. Try it and see! There's some terribly interesting visual psychology going on here, but I leave it to the scholars to tell us what that might be.

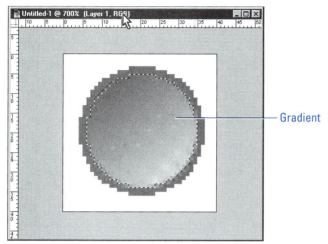

Figure 16-14: The gradient fill completed.

This looks good, but the outer ring of the underlying button is all one flat color, and that spoils the 3-D effect. There are two approaches to fixing this:

✦ Apply an opposite gradient to the circle in Layer 1.

✦ Select just the outer ring of Layer 1, and apply the opposite gradient to that.

The first choice is easy — just repeat the steps you used on this layer on Layer 1. To select just the outer portions of Layer 1 (that is, the portion of Layer 1 visible outside the edges of Layer 2):

1. Save the current selection (Select | Save Selection).

2. Make Layer 1 the active layer.

3. Load the Layer 1 Transparency as a selection (Select | Load Selection) to make it the current selection.

4. Subtract the selection you saved in Step 1 from the current selection (Select | Load Selection | Subtract from Selection).

This leaves just the outer ring selected (see Figure 16-15). Using the start and end points shown in Figure 16-16, apply a gradient to the current selection. Figure 16-17 shows the result: a completed button. To view the button at actual size, use the "Ctrl -" (Control and minus) key combination six times to switch to 100% view.

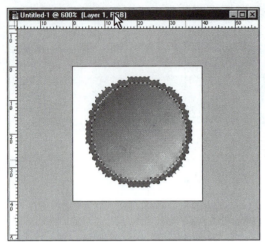

Figure 16-15: The resulting selection.

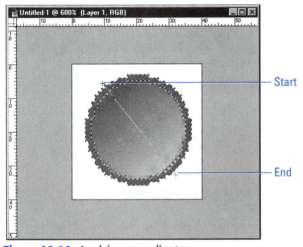

Figure 16-16: Applying a gradient.

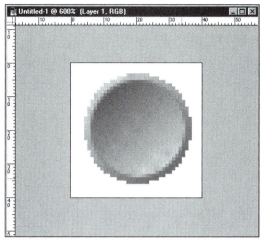

Figure 16-17: The gradient applied.

Idea

Where to go from here:

✦ You can use gradients to create all kinds of 3-D effects. Instead of a circular selection for the middle of the button, try a square or polygon shape instead.

✦ Look at the button with Layer 2 made invisible. The edge gradient you applied to Layer 1 created an interesting button shape all by itself.

✦ There are many, many effects possible using selections and gradient fills. Experiment by adding additional layers to create additional bumps or indentations. The direction of the gradient determines whether the area you fill appears to be raised or inset.

Creating Button Effects with Photoshop

CD: A trial version of Photoshop is on the CD-ROM. To find out how to install it, view the web page at \demo\viewme.htm in your browser and click the \demo\adobe hyperlink.

Tutorial

Level: Easy to Intermediate

Task: Create a 3-D button

Before you start:

✦ Run Photoshop 4.0.

✦ Create a new file 40 pixels by 40 pixels (File | New).

The previous tutorial shows some of the possibilities available to you using bright and dark areas to create the illusion of three dimensions on a button. In this tutorial, we'll dig a little deeper into the bag of tricks.

1. Fill the image with the same forest green color you used in the last tutorial (Red=0, Green=102, and Blue=51).

2. Press Ctrl+A to select the entire image.

3. Use the Select I Modify I Border menu selection to open the Border dialog box (see Figure 16-18).

4. Enter a value of **4**, and click OK. This selects just the outer four pixels all around the image (see Figure 16-19).

Figure 16-18: Setting the Border amount.

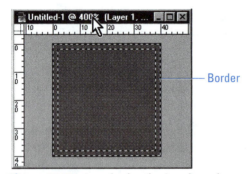

Border

Figure 16-19: Just the border is selected.

5. Save this selection (Select I Save Selection) as a new selection.

6. Activate the linear lasso tool (click and hold the lasso tool, and click the Linear variant from the flyout).

7. Use the linear lasso to remove half of the border.

8. Click at the numbered points in Figure 16-20 in sequence while holding down the Alt key.

9. Continuing to hold the Alt key, double-click the last point to close the selection. This will subtract from the current selection because you are holding down the Alt key.

This technique leaves a diagonal edge at the top right and lower left. Figure 16-21 shows the shape of the selection that is to remain.

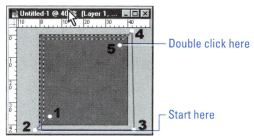

Figure 16-20: How to subtract from the selection.

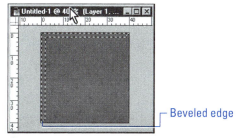

Figure 16-21: This selection will be the highlight area of the button.

10. Feather the selection by two pixels (Select | Feather). For the round button, the 3-D edges between layers were hard. Feathering will create a soft, rounded 3-D edge.

11. Use the Image | Adjust | Brightness and Contrast menu selection to open the dialog box shown in Figure 16-22.

12. Set the brightness of the selection to +75.

13. Click OK.

Repeat this process to create a shaded 3-D effect on the opposite sides of the button:

14. Load the border selection (Select | Load Selection | #4).

15. Use the linear lasso tool to remove the top and left portions of the border, leaving the right and bottom portions (see Figure 16-23).

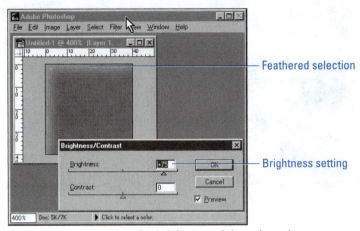

Figure 16-22: Increasing the brightness of the selected area.

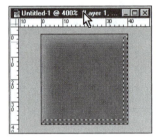

Figure 16-23: The correct selection.

16. Feather the selection by two pixels.

17. Darken the selection (Image | Adjust | Brightness and Contrast, -57; see Figure 16-24). This completes the basic button.

You can combine the ideas from the first tutorial with this button. Create a new layer, create a circular selection, and fill it with a gradient. The gradient should start at the upper left with a darker green than the green of the button, and end at the lower right with a lighter green (see Figure 16-25).

Tip

Use the Color Picker tool to set both the foreground and background color to the green of the button, and then edit them to set a darker foreground and a lighter background.

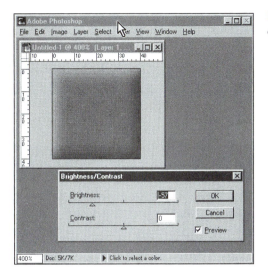

Figure 16-24: Darkening the edge of the button.

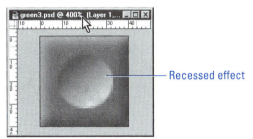

Figure 16-25: An incised area.

You can reverse the direction of the gradient to create a raised effect (see Figure 16-26).

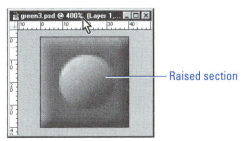

Figure 16-26: A raised area.

You can use Photoshop's guides to create a rounded bar across the top of the button. Set the guides as shown in Figure 16-27.

Tip

To create a guide, click in the ruler and drag out into the drawing. Release the mouse button when the guide is at the proper location. If you want to move a guide, click the Move tool (the tool at the top right of the tool panel) and drag the guide to the correct location.

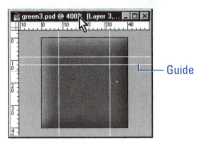
— Guide

Figure 16-27: Setting guides.

18. Enlarge your view of the image with the "Ctrl+" key combination to about 1600% (see Figure 16-28).

19. Make sure that the left vertical guide at 8 pixels is visible.

Note that because I applied the guide before I zoomed into the image, the top horizontal guide is slightly off — it is between 8 and 9 pixels on the left ruler. Observe how Photoshop handles this during the next few steps.

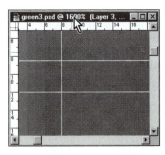

Figure 16-28: Zooming in to view the guides in detail.

20. Create a tiny circular selection using the guides. Hold down the Shift key while doing this to make sure you get a circle.

Figure 16-29 shows the size of the circle: the distance between the horizontal guides. When you release the mouse, the selection appears as shown in Figure 16-30. It looks strange, but Photoshop will use anti-aliasing to make this tiny selection look reasonably circular.

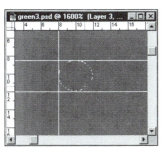

Figure 16-29: Dragging out a small circular selection.

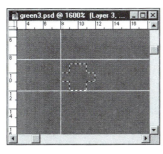

Figure 16-30: The actual appearance of the selection after you release the mouse button.

21. Click with the mouse and drag the selection border two pixels to the left (use those rulers at the top!) so that it straddles the vertical guide. Be sure that the move tool is not the current tool, or dragging will drag the contents of the selection, not the border!

22. Hold down the Shift key and drag to create a second small circular selection that straddles the right vertical guide (see Figure 16-31).

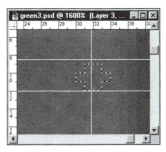

Figure 16-31: The second small circular selection.

23. Zoom back out to 700% using the "Ctrl-" key combination repeatedly.

24. Change to the rectangular variant of the selection tool.

25. Hold down the Shift key and drag out a rectangle, starting at the upper left of the box formed by the guides, and dragging to the lower right of that box.

When you release the mouse button, you should have a selection that looks like the one shown in Figure 16-32. It is built up from the two small circular selections and the rectangular selection you just created.

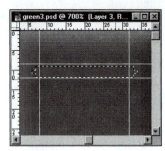

Figure 16-32: The completed multi-selection.

To use this selection to create a raised bar on the green button:

26. Create a new layer, and fill the selection with a darker green than the green of the button (click the foreground color, change it to a darker green, and use the Edit | Fill menu item to fill the selection with the foreground color).

27. Create another new layer, and fill it with the green of the button face (use the Color Picker to pick up the button's color).

28. Create a third new layer, and fill it with a lighter green color. The order of the three new layers should now be: lightest green on top, regular green in the middle, and dark green on the bottom.

29. Move the light green layer between the normal and dark green layers (click and drag the layer in the Layers palette to a position between those other two layers).

30. Make the light green layer the active layer in the Layers palette. Hold down the Ctrl key, and hit the Up arrow once, and the Left arrow once. This moves the layer up and to the left so that the light green layer shows behind the normal green layer.

31. Make the dark green layer the active layer. Hold down the Ctrl key, and hit the Down arrow and the Right arrow once each.

    Figure 16-33 shows the result: a 3-D effect for the horizontal bar.

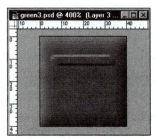

Figure 16-33: A 3-D bar added to the button.

Where to go from here:

✦ Reverse the offset of the light green and dark green bars to create a recessed effect (see Figure 16-34).

✦ Use a different color for the normal green bar. Figure 16-35 shows the effect of a red bar that uses a gradient from light red at the top to dark red at the bottom. Open the file `\My Web Stuff\chap16A.htm` to see this in color.

✦ Figure 16-36 shows how a radial gradient looks in place of the linear gradient used in Figure 16-35.

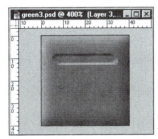

Figure 16-34: A recessed bar.

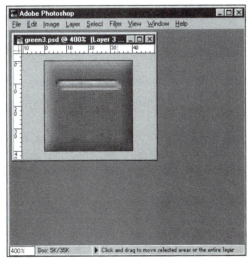

Figure 16-35: A red recessed bar.

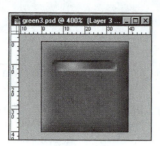

Figure 16-36: A red recessed bar with a radial gradient.

Creating Icons with Fractal Design Painter

Tutorial

CD: To install the trial version of Painter from the CD, double-click the file `\demo\fractal\painter4\setup.exe`.

Level: Easy to Intermediate

Task: Create a 3-D icon

Before you start:

✦ Run Painter 4.0

Buttons are dandy, but sometimes you want an image on the page that doesn't really look like a button. You can create dazzling iconic masterpieces with Fractal Design Painter.

1. Create a new file measuring 120 pixels by 120 pixels in Painter and zoom to 200% (Press Ctrl+ as shown in Figure 16-37).

   This is larger than the button image you just created, but that doesn't mean all icons are larger than all buttons.

2. Select the pen tool and the Calligraphy variant (see Figure 16-38).

3. Draw a circle that is just slightly smaller than the size of the canvas, as shown in Figure 16-39.

4. Add a decorative or other element to the inside of the circle. I chose the Greek letter Pi (see Figure 16-40). You could draw a face inside the circle, a cob of corn, or anything else that you want to add to it.

Image enlarged to 200% (Ctrl +)

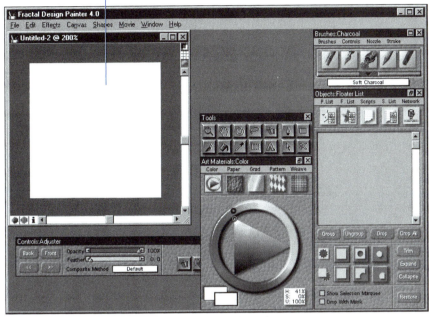

Figure 16-37: Starting a new file for an icon in Painter.

Pen tool

Calligraphy variant

Figure 16-38: The pen tool options.

Figure 16-39: Drawing a circle.

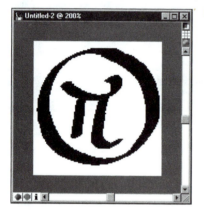

Figure 16-40: Enhancing the circle.

The next step is to turn the painted image into an object.

5. Click the selection tool (see Figure 16-41), and select the entire drawing by clicking and dragging from the top left to the bottom right.

6. Use the Edit | Magic Wand menu item to display the Magic Wand dialog box (see Figure 16-42).

— Selection tool

Figure 16-41: The 6election tool.

Tip

When you use the Magic Wand with a selection, the wand will select similar colors within the selection. Without a selection, the Magic Wand only selects colors that are contiguous. Since the Pi symbol is not connected to the outer circle, a selection allows the Magic Wand to select both the circle and the Pi symbol.

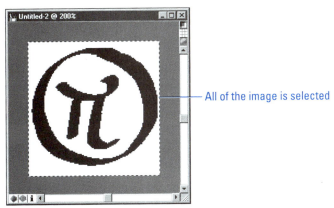

All of the image is selected

Figure 16-42: The Magic Wand dialog box.

7. Click anywhere on the circle or Pi symbol to select all black pixels.

8. Click OK. A flashing red border appears around the black pixels.

9. Use the Edit | Float menu selection to turn the black pixels into a floating object. A yellow and black border appears outside the object, as shown in Figure 16-43.

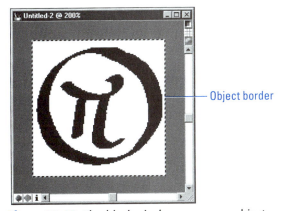

Object border

Figure 16-43: The black pixels are now an object.

Because the black pixels are now a floating object, you can use various Painter tools on the object. For example, you can use the Effects | Object | Create Drop Shadow menu item to add a drop shadow to the object. I used the settings shown in Figure 16-44. The drop shadow is shown in Figure 16-45.

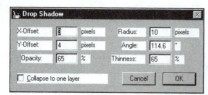

Figure 16-44: Adding a drop shadow.

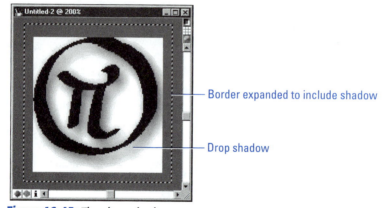

Border expanded to include shadow

Drop shadow

Figure 16-45: The drop shadow.

You can apply other Painter effects, too. Figure 16-46 shows a texture applied to the object (Effects ┃ Fill ┃ Pattern), and Figure 16-47 shows a 3-D effect (Effects ┃ Surface Control ┃ Apply Surface Texture ┃ Mask).

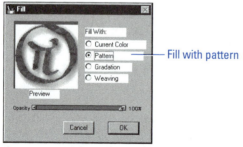

Fill with pattern

Figure 16-46: Applying a pattern to the object.

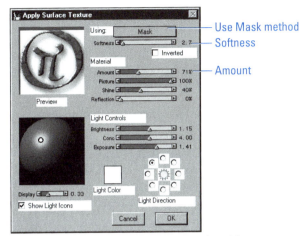

Figure 16-47: Adding a 3-D effect to the object.

Figure 16-48 shows the final result.

Figure 16-48: The completed icon/doodad.

Where to go from here:

✦ Painter contains a multitude of interesting tools and effects. Try applying them to the object to see what happens. For example, you can fill the object with a color or pattern, and then apply the various effects to it. You can find these effects on the Effects menu, of course.

✦ Create a matched set of icons and other page elements. Figure 16-49 shows a page header I created using the same pattern I used on the icon. See the tutorial section that follows for details.

Figure 16-49: A matching page header.

Creating a Page Header with Photoshop

CD: A trial version of Photoshop is on the CD-ROM. To find out how to install it, view the web page at `\demo\viewme.htm` in your browser and click the `\demo\adobe hyperlink`.

Tutorial

Level: Advanced

Task: Create a 3-D page header

Before you start:

✦ Run Photoshop 4.0.

1. Create a new file measuring 420 pixels wide and 80 pixels high (File | New).

2. Verify that the Contents are set to white, and the Mode is RGB Color.

3. View the image at 200% and add four guide lines: two vertical (15 pixels in from the side edges) and two horizontal (10 pixels in from the top and bottom edges).

Figure 16-50 shows the proper position for the guides. These guides, along with the additional guides you are about to add, form a grid on which to create a precise, complex selection.

Guide

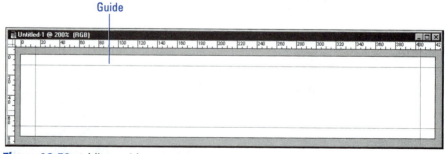

Figure 16-50: Adding guides, step one.

4. Add additional horizontal and vertical guides at the following points:

✦ Vertical guide at 60 pixels

✦ Vertical guide at 130 pixels

✦ Vertical guide at 290 pixels

✦ Vertical guide at 360 pixels

✦ Horizontal guide at 20 pixels

✦ Horizontal guide at 25 pixels

✦ Horizontal guide at 55 pixels

✦ Horizontal guide at 60 pixels (see Figure 16-51)

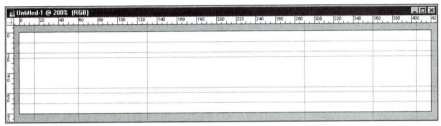

Figure 16-51: Adding guides, step two.

5. Use the guides to drag out a rectangular selection as shown in Figure 16-52.

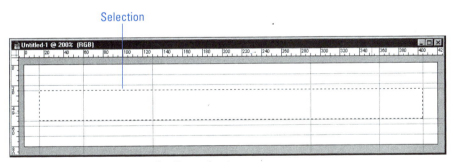

Figure 16-52: Dragging out the first selection.

6. Hold down the Shift key and drag out a second selection, as shown in Figure 16-53.

7. Hold down the Shift key and drag out a third selection as shown in Figure 16-54. Then hide the guides so you can see what you are doing! I had to hide the guides for Figure 16-54 because it was not possible to even see the selection.

8. Save the selection (Select | Save Selection) as a new selection just in case you need it later.

Added selection

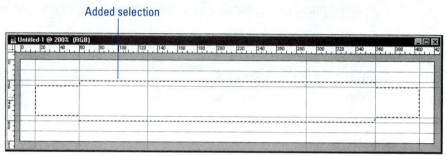

Figure 16-53: Adding a second selection.

Selection

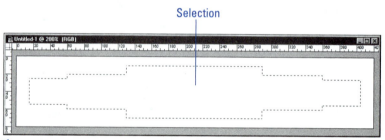

Figure 16-54: The completed, three-part selection.

9. Add a new layer (Layer | New Layer). Invert the selection (Select | Inverse; see Figure 16-55).

Selection

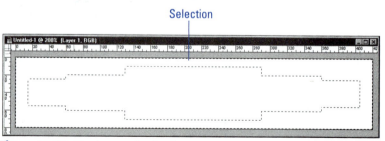

Figure 16-55: The inverted selection.

10. Click the Foreground color and set the color to a gold tone (Red=255, Green=212, and Blue=79; see Figure 16-56).

11. Fill the selection with the new color (Edit | Fill | Foreground Color; see Figure 16-57).

Figure 16-56: Setting a new foreground color.

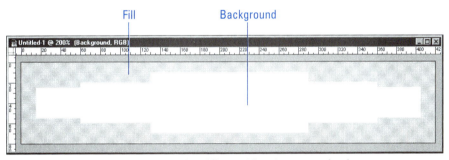

Figure 16-57: The layer contents after filling with a foreground color.

12. Open the file \My Web Stuff\Chap16\wood01.psd (see Figure 16-58).

13. Select the entire image with the Select | All menu item.

14. Use the Edit | Define Pattern menu item to define the selection as the pattern to use for fills.

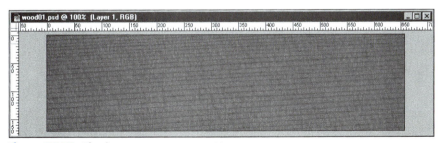

Figure 16-58: The image to use as a pattern.

15. Make the background the active layer (click Background in the Layers palette).

16. Use the Edit | Fill | Pattern menu selection to fill the background with the wood pattern. Figure 16-59 shows the result.

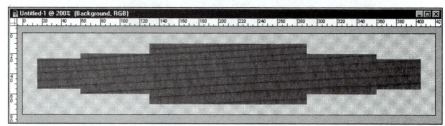

Figure 16-59: The background filled with the pattern.

17. Make Layer 1 the active layer.

18. Right-click Layer 1 in the Layers palette and choose Duplicate layer. A new layer named Layer 1 Copy appears in the Layers palette.

19. Click the new layer and drag it below the original Layer 1 (see Figure 16-60).

20. Click Preserve Transparency to turn it on.

21. Click the eye icon for Layer 1 to make it invisible (see Figure 16-60).

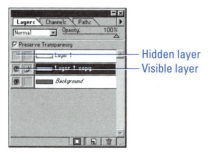

Figure 16-60: The state of the Layers palette after completing the actions through Step 21.

22. Fill Layer 1 Copy with black (Edit | Fill | Black; see Figure 16-61).

23. Turn off Preserve Transparency.

24. Apply a Gaussian blur of 4.1 pixels (Filter | Blur | Gaussian Blur). Figure 16-62 shows the result.

25. Make Layer 1 visible again (click where the eye icon was), then click the Layer 1 Copy in the Layers palette to activate it.

26. Hold down the Ctrl key and drag Layer 1 Copy down and to the right to create a drop shadow for Layer 1 (see Figure 16-63 for guidance).

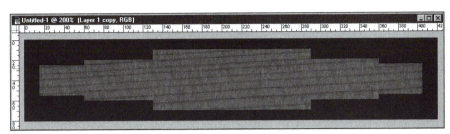

Figure 16-61: Layer 1 Copy filled with black.

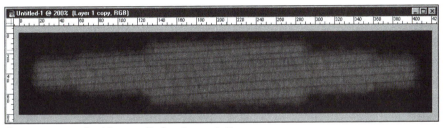

Figure 16-62: The blur applied to Layer 1 Copy.

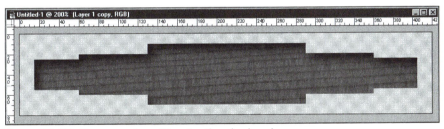

Figure 16-63: The correct position for the shadow layer.

27. Make sure Layer 1 is the active layer.

28. Load the Layer 1 transparency (Select | Load Selection | Layer Transparency).

29. Use the Select | Modify | Contract menu item to reduce the size of the selection by one pixel (see Figure 16-64).

30. Save the selection (Select | Save Selection).

31. Load the Layer 1 transparency again.

32. Load the selection you just saved, but be sure to click the Subtract from Selection radio button before you click OK. Only the inner edge of the layer remains selected.

Figure 16-64: Creating a border selection.

33. Create a new layer (Layer 2).

34. Set the Foreground color to Red=228, Green=181, Blue=35. This is a very light gold color.

35. Fill the one-pixel-wide selection with this color. This creates a nice highlight on the edge of the gold layer (see Figure 16-65, although it shows up better in color).

Highlighted edge

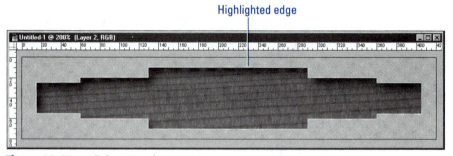

Figure 16-65: A slight 3-D edge on Layer 1.

36. Set the Foreground and Background colors to Red=126, Green=99, Blue=18. This is a dark gold color.

37. Click to activate the gradient tool.

38. Choose the Metallic effect gradient, such as you created in Chapter 7 (see Figure 16-66 and the next Tip).

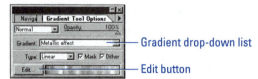

Gradient drop-down list

Edit button

Figure 16-66: The Gradient options.

If you have not created this gradient yet, you can load it from the chapter files you copied at the start of the chapter. Click the Edit button in the Gradient options dialog box (see Figure 16-66). This displays the Gradient Editor. Click the Load button, and locate the file `\My Web Stuff\Chap16\metalgrd.grd` (see Figure 16-67). Click to highlight it, and click the Open button. Click the OK button in the Gradient Editor. The gradient is now available in the Gradient drop-down list (see Figure 16-66).

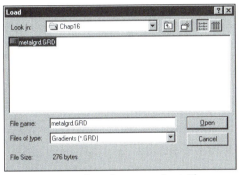

Figure 16-67: Choosing a gradient file.

39. Verify that the Opacity is set to 100%, the Type is linear, and that the Gradient is Metallic effect.

40. Click in the Layers palette to make Layer 2 the active layer.

41. Verify that Preserve Transparency is checked.

42. Click and drag from the upper right to the lower left to apply the gradient.

Figure 16-68 shows what the gradient should look like. This provides a sophisticated page header that will look great on a web page. Be sure to process the image with either HVS JPEG (see Chapter 12, "Small is Beautiful,") or the Ulead JPEG SmartSaver (see Chapter 14, "SmartSavers 4 U") to compress the file effectively.

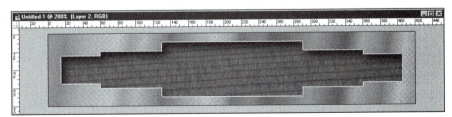

Figure 16-68: The gradient provides a metallic sheen to the gold layer.

If you make a mistake applying a gradient that uses transparency, you must use Ctrl+Z to undo the gradient. If you try to reapply the gradient without undoing the first one, the transparency allows the previous gradient to show through. A non-transparent gradient, on the other hand, completely covers the previous gradient.

Idea

Where to go from here:

✦ Add a few rivets to the corners of the metal plate. Add a new layer and make a small circular selection while the layer is active (see Figure 16-69). Set the foreground color to a light gold, and the background color to a very dark gold. Use a gradient fill, with the gradient type set to Foreground to Background. Click in the upper left third of the selection, and drag to the lower right edge. Figure 16-70 shows the rivet. Copy the layer three times. Activate each layer in turn, and then hold down the Ctrl key and drag the layer's rivet into a corner. Figure 16-71 shows the completed metal plate.

✦ Add a text title to the wood. You can layer light text above the wood, add a drop shadow to the text, or create incised or raised lettering. Figure 16-72 shows an example of text added using lighter and darker versions of the background texture. Figure 16-73 shows an example of incised text.

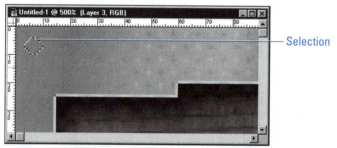

Figure 16-69: Creating a small circular selection at the upper left of the metal plate.

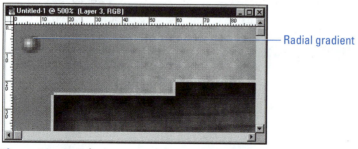

Figure 16-70: A rivet.

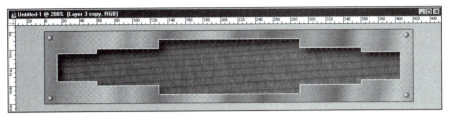

Figure 16-71: The page header with four rivets.

Figure 16-72: An example of text added to the page header.

Figure 16-73: Incised text.

Creating a Page Header with Painter

CD: To install the trial version of Painter from the CD, double-click the file `\demo\fractal\painter4\setup.exe`.

Level: Easy to Intermediate

Tutorial

Task: Create a web page header

Before you start:

✦ Run Painter 4.0

✦ Create a new image that is 420 pixels wide and 80 pixels high.

When you have created your new image, you are ready to follow these steps:

1. Select a rectangular portion of the image that is smaller than the image and offset toward the upper left, as shown in Figure 16-74.

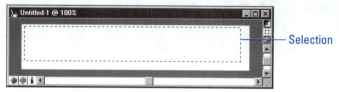

Figure 16-74: Selecting a region in the image.

2. Fill the selection with black (Effects ⎮ Fill ⎮ Current Color).

3. Click in the Control panel to change the selection type to ellipse.

4. Select a small ellipse at the left edge of the black area, and fill it with white (see Figure 16-75).

5. Change back to the rectangular selection tool, and select a vertical rectangle at the right edge of the black area (see Figure 16-75) and fill it with white (see Figure 16-76).

6. Use the Magic Wand (Edit ⎮ Magic Wand) to select all of the black area.

7. Turn the selection into an object with the Edit ⎮ Float menu item.

Figure 16-75: Adding a white ellipse.

Figure 16-76: The completed object.

8. Create a second copy of the object: Use Ctrl+C to copy to the Clipboard, and Ctrl+V to paste the copy. The copy is now on top of the original.

9. Make sure that the copy is the currently selected object (click it, so that it has a black and yellow outline as shown in Figure 16-76).

10. Select the paper pattern in the Art Materials: Pattern panel (see Figure 16-77).

11. If the Pattern panel is not the current view in the Art Materials panel, click the Pattern icon.

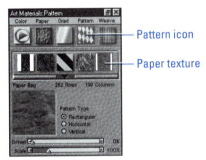

Figure 16-77: Choosing a pattern.

12. Use the Edit ∣ Fill ∣ Pattern menu selection to fill the object with the current pattern. Figure 16-78 shows the result.

Figure 16-78: The filled object.

You can add some color and spice to the image by adding a third copy of the object, and filling it with a bright color. Drag the new copy in the Floaters panel so that it lies between the black copy and the pattern-filled copy. Offset each copy so that the bright copy is at the upper left, the black original is at the lower right, and the pattern-filled copy is neatly in the middle (see Figure 16-79). You can experiment with different colors and brightness levels for the bright copy. I liked a nice hot orange best.

Figure 16-79: A three-layered sandwich.

If the hard-edge black layer doesn't suit your tastes (it is perfect for situations that require a transparent background), you can apply a drop shadow instead.

13. Use the Effects | Object | Create Drop Shadow menu selection, and use the settings shown in Figure 16-80).

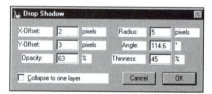

Figure 16-80: Settings for adding a drop shadow.

14. Be sure to turn off the visibility of the black layer if you use a drop shadow; click the eye icon in the Floaters panel. Figure 16-81 shows the appearance of the drop shadow.

Figure 16-81: A drop shadow in place.

Idea

Where to go from here:

✦ Add an object, logo, or freehand design to the open oval. If you add it in Painter, you can also add a drop shadow to it.

✦ Add the page title in white or light-colored text.

✦ Check out the many textures Painter offers, and apply those to the page header.

✦ Create a collection of page images consisting of a page header, icons, buttons, bullets, and divider lines using the same texture and overall design.

Batch Image Manipulation with BatchMaster

Tutorial

Download: You can download a trial version of BatchMaster from the Jasc web site at http://www.jasc.com.

Level: Intermediate

Task: Operate on more than one file at a time

Before you start:

✦ Download and install the trial version of BatchMaster.

Consider the following not-so-hypothetical situation. You go to a lot of trouble to create a collection of graphics. You are happy with them. Then something comes along — an irritated client, an indigo mood, a full moon — and you decide you want to change something. Perhaps it is the color of the collection, perhaps it is the texture. Whatever it is, it sure would be nice to have a simple way to apply the change to all of the images in the collection.

One potential solution: BatchMaster, from Jasc. BatchMaster allows you to apply one or more effects to a collection of images. Figure 16-82 shows the BatchMaster window. The available tools are in a list at the upper left. The image at the lower left is for sampling the results of the batch change. The white area at the upper right shows the currently selected tools. The gray area at the lower right displays the settings for the currently highlighted tool.

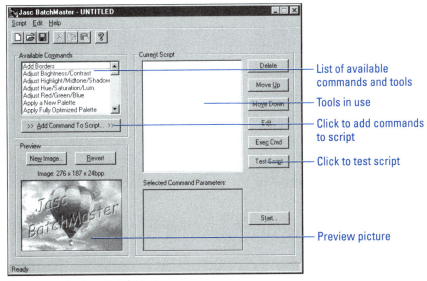

Figure 16-82: Jasc BatchMaster.

I have included five sample files that you can use to test BatchMaster. They are located in the folder `\My Web Stuff\Chap16\images1`. You can load one of the sample images in place of the default image shown at the lower left of Figure 16-82. Click the New Image button, and locate the file `\My Web Stuff\Chap16\images1\btn01.bmp`. Click Open to open this file as the sample image. It is a silly sample image, as you can see in Figure 16-83.

For this example, you will change the color of the image and apply a new palette to the image.

1. Begin by clicking Adjust Hue/Saturation/Lum in the list of available commands to highlight it.

2. Click the Add Commands to Script button. This opens the dialog box shown in Figure 16-83. The sample image appears in the preview window at the right.

3. Set the % Hue to -75, the % Saturation to 100, and the % Luminance to 60.

4. Click OK. Adjust Hue/Saturation/Lum is added to the Current Script list at the upper right.

— Preview

Figure 16-83: Setting values.

5. Click Apply a New Palette in the list of available commands.

6. Click the Add Commands to Script button. This opens the Apply a New Palette dialog box (see Figure 16-84).

7. Locate the file `\My Web Stuff\Chap16\Paintshop\safety.pal`.

8. Click the radio button Nearest color matching. This prevents dithering.

9. Click Open.

The two commands are now in the Current Script list (see Figure 16-85).

10. To view the settings for any item in the Current Script list, click the item to highlight it. The settings appear in the window at the bottom right.

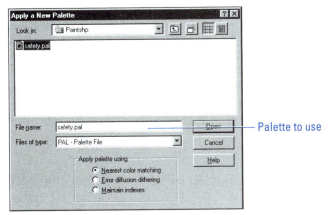

Figure 16-84: Choosing the palette.

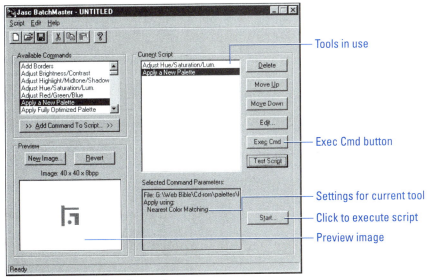

Figure 16-85: Viewing the settings.

Tip

To save the script for later use, use the Script I Save As menu item and supply a filename.

11. To apply the script to a group of files, click the Exec Cmd button at the middle right of the BatchMaster window. This opens the Batch Process Input Files dialog box, shown in Figure 16-86. Locate the folder \My Web Stuff \Chap16\images1.

12. Hold down the Ctrl key and select each file one at a time; or click the first file, hold down the Shift key, and click on the last file. Note that the filenames appear in the File name text box, with each filename in double quotes.

13. Click Next when you have selected the input files for the batch.

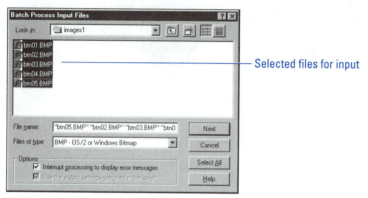

Figure 16-86: Selecting input files for the batch.

This displays the Batch Process Output Options dialog box, shown in Figure 16-87.

14. Locate the folder `\My Web Stuff\Chap16\images2` in the Save in drop-down list. The files output by the batch operation will be saved in this folder.

15. Verify that the Save as type is BMP — OS/2 or Windows Bitmap — and click the Finish button.

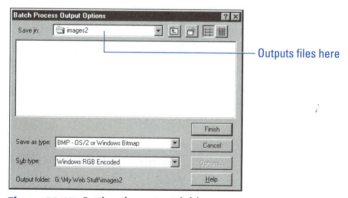

Figure 16-87: Setting the output folder.

During batch processing, BatchMaster will display details of the batch operation in the Batch Processing Status window (see Figure 16-88).

16. When the batch process is complete, click OK.

17. Open the files in `\My Web Stuff\Chap16\images2` in your favorite image editor to verify that the images are 8-bit color and that the original green images are now orange-red.

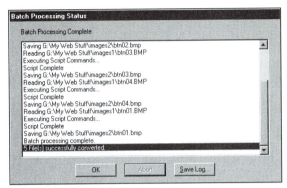

Figure 16-88: Batch status.

BatchMaster is easy to use, and it offers a large number of commands you can apply to images. However, if you really have a complex set of operations to perform, you'll want to take a look at the next section. It provides details on the batch capabilities built into Photoshop 4.0.

Where to go from here:

✦ The Jasc web site has some useful web-related tools located in the `ftp://ftp.jasc.com/WEBTOOLS` directory (the exact tools may vary over time):

- `htmlasst.zip:`   HTML Assistant for Windows freeware HTML editor
- `htmlwrit.zip:`   HTML Writer for Windows HTML editor
- `hotdog24:`   Hot Dog shareware HTML editor
- `mpths130.exe:`   Map This freeware Image Map utility (Win 95 only)
- `163_text.zip:`   163 seamless textures for Web page backgrounds
- `bullets.zip:`   Bullet images for Web page bullet points
- `line_bar.zip:`   Lines and bars for Web page dividers
- `netpal.zip:`   Netscape color palette saved as a JASC palette
- `rgb2hex2.zip:`   RGB to Hex converter (Windows 95)

Batch Image Manipulation with Photoshop

CD: A trial version of Photoshop is on the CD-ROM. To find out how to install it, view the web page at `\demo\viewme.htm` in your browser and click the `\demo\adobe` hyperlink.

Tutorial   **Level:** Intermediate to Advanced

Task: Operate on more than one file at a time

Before you start:

✦ Run Photoshop 4.0.

For years, visual artists have been having the same dream: a version of Photoshop that allows you to apply repeated operations to multiple files. In version 4.0, this dream is finally realized. Photoshop allows you to record operations and store them in the Actions palette. In addition, you can apply any action to multiple files using a batch operation.

Figure 16-89 shows a collection of five buttons I created for this exercise. They look the same as the buttons in the BatchMaster section (just previous to this section), but there is a critical difference: These are true Photoshop files, complete with layers, saved selections, and any other Photoshop feature you care to use.

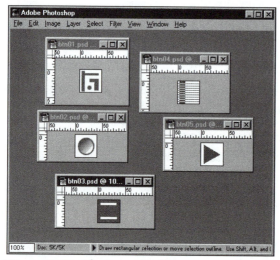

Figure 16-89: A button collection.

The buttons are all green, and they are all 24-bit images. In this tutorial, you will record an action script that will make the images orange and convert them to 8-bit color using a Web-safe palette.

1. In order to record a set of actions to apply to all of the images, open one of the image files for this chapter: \My Web Stuff\Chap16\images1\ btn01.psd.

2. Use the Color Picker tool to set the foreground color to the green used in the button.

Tip

By setting the foreground color to the color used in the image, you will be able to preview the change in hue later in the tutorial.

3. Click the menu arrow at the top right of the Actions palette (see Figure 16-90). (If the Actions palette is not displayed, use the Window | Show Actions menu item to display it.)

4. Click the New Action menu item.

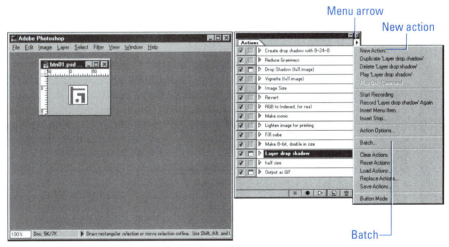

Figure 16-90: Menu for accessing Action choices.

This displays the New Action dialog box.

5. Give the new action a name: **Green to Orange + 8-bit** and click Record.

The new action appears at the bottom of the list of actions (see Figure 16-91). The actions you see will vary from the ones displayed in Figure 16-91 depending on how you have used the Actions palette. You may see more or fewer actions listed.

Stop recording

New action

Figure 16-91: The list of actions. Your list may vary from what is shown.

Once you click the Record button, just about anything you do in Photoshop is recorded as part of the action. There are some activities that will not be recorded; consult the Photoshop documentation for complete details. For example, if you click and drag a selection, the movement is not recorded.

6. To change the hue of the open image from green to orange, use the Image | Adjust | Hue/Saturation menu item. This opens the Hue/Saturation dialog box (see Figure 16-92).

7. Move the Hue slider to the left until a value of -99 appears in the window above the slider (see Figure 16-93).

8. Adjust the Saturation setting to +85, and the Lightness setting to +48. The preview box at the bottom center of the dialog box shows the change in the current foreground color.

9. Click OK.

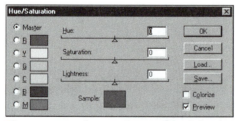

Figure 16-92: The Hue/Saturation dialog box.

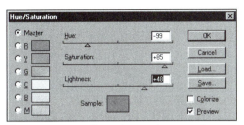

Figure 16-93: Adjust the settings as shown.

Photoshop has been dutifully recording your activity. Look at the Actions palette (see Figure 16-94). The Hue/Saturation settings have been added to the action you are recording. If you do not see the details shown in Figure 16-94, click the triangle at the left of the entry for Hue/Saturation to expand the list.

Figure 16-94: The recording in progress.

The next step is to convert the image to 8-bit color using the Web palette.

10. Use the Image | Mode | Indexed Color menu selection to open the Indexed Color dialog box (see Figure 16-95).

11. Set the Palette to Web and the Color Depth will automatically be set to Other.

12. Make sure that the Dither option is set to none — the green is a solid color, and by eliminating dithering you force Photoshop to match the orange color to the nearest Web-safe color.

13. Click OK.

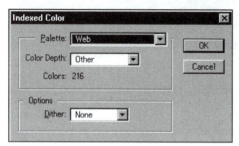

Figure 16-95: Applying a Web-safe palette.

You now have two options. If you stop here, you can use the Batch feature to save the files as PSD files in a new folder. If you want to save the files as GIF files, you will need to continue to add a third step to the recording.

14. Use the File ❘ Export ❘ GIF89a menu selection to open the GIF Export Options dialog box, shown in Figure 16-96.

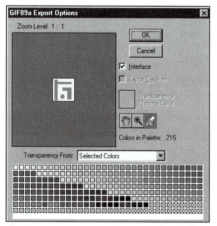

Figure 16-96: Saving as a GIF file.

Normally, you would choose a transparent color for the GIF image. However, the actual save operation will occur during the batch operation.

15. Simply click OK to display the Export GIF89 dialog box, shown in Figure 16-97.

16. Locate the folder in which you want to save the output images: `\My Web Stuff\Chap16\images2`.

17. Enter a filename such as **junk.gif**, and click Save.

Figure 16-97: Saving the file to disk.

This completes the steps you need to record.

18. Click the Stop Recording button on the Actions palette (see Figure16-98).

19. Close the file you opened, choosing not to save any changes you made.

20. Delete the file you created, `junk.gif`.

21. To run the action on a batch of files, highlight the name of the action you just recorded (on the Actions palette).

22. Click the menu arrow at the top right of the Actions palette.

23. Click the Batch item, which opens the dialog box shown in Figure 16-99.

24. Verify that the Source is folder, and that the Action is Green to Orange + 8-bit.

25. Click on the upper Choose button, and locate the folder `\My Web Stuff\ chap16\images1`. This is the input folder (the source for the files the action will act on).

26. Click OK. This folder name appears in the Batch dialog box (see Figure 16-100).

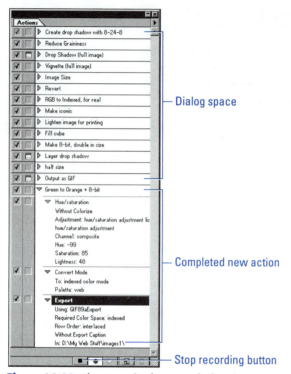

Figure 16-98 callouts:
— Dialog space
— Completed new action
— Stop recording button

Figure 16-98: The steps in the recorded action.

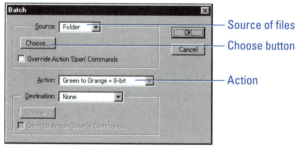

Figure 16-99 callouts:
— Source of files
— Choose button
— Action

Figure 16-99: The Batch dialog box.

Figure 16-100: The Batch dialog box with input folder set.

27. Click OK to process the batch. You will have a set of five GIF files as output.

If you want to interact with the dialogs for the Export GIF dialogs, click in the dialog box space to the left of the Export item in the action (refer to Figure 16-98). A tiny dialog box appears in the space. When you run the action, you will see the dialogs for that action displayed.

Tip

Where to go from here:

Idea

✦ You can also use the batch operation to save your files in the same format as the input files. Omit recording the save operation, and set the Destination in the Batch dialog box to Folder. Use the lower Choose button to select the output folder (see Figure 16-101).

✦ Photoshop contains a wealth of operations that go far beyond the capabilities of BatchMaster. Try recording more complex operations, or visit my web site at `http://www.mmadweb.com/bible` to find interesting and useful recorded actions.

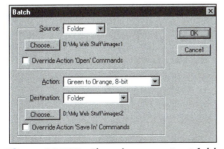

Figure 16-101: Choosing an output folder.

Button and Doodad Collections

If you can design one button, you can design a collection of buttons using varia-tions on that design. Figure 16-102 shows a variety of buttons, doodads, and what-nots that all use the same color or design. You can find most of these images as part of the Labyrinth collection on the CD-ROM at \graphics\styles\ labyrinth.

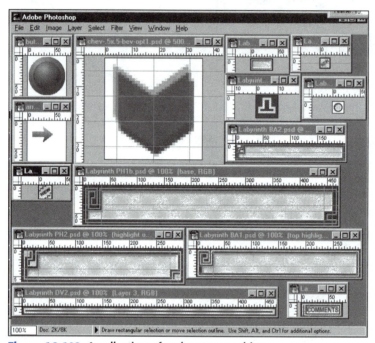

Figure 16-102: A collection of web page graphics.

When you are creating a collection in Photoshop, you can take advantage of Photoshop features to store your items efficiently. For example, consider the button \My Web Stuff\Chap16\button.psd. It has a rounded top and a ledge. There are five layers in addition to the background. In fact, none of the button is drawn on the background; it's all in the layers. By turning various layers on and off, you can change the appearance of the button.

Tip

To output GIF or JPEG files from these multilayered graphics, simply choose the layers you want to be visible, and use the File | Save a Copy menu selection to save the file using any format you choose.

This technique is particularly useful when you have a number of text strings to apply to a button. A different text string appears on each layer. For each button you want to create, you create a separate text string. You can then save button images in GIF or JPEG format one at a time, with the correct text string visible for each button.

Web Tour #16: Sources for Doodad Graphics

You can visit some of my favorite buttons and doodads on the Web. There are many web sites out there that offer interesting images. Some of these sites offer free images, and some of them offer ideas you can build on to create your own graphics. To visit sites with cool images, double-click the file:

    \WebTour\Chap16\index.htm

You'll see the Web Tour page for this chapter.

Backgrounds

To prepare for this chapter's tutorials, copy the following folder from the CD-ROM to the \My Web Stuff folder on your hard drive:

   \tutorial\chap17

This will copy files for all of the tutorials in this chapter to your hard disk. See Chapter 1 for complete details on setting up for tutorials.

There are three kinds of backgrounds possible on a web page: no background, color background, and image background. Unless you specify a color or an image for a background, the page will have a default background. That will be either a neutral gray, or a color selected as a browser option by the visitor to your page.

Color backgrounds are easy to create and most web page editors support them. You simply point to a color you like in a dialog box, and that becomes the color background for that page. Many pages use color backgrounds, such as http://www.hwg.org.

Image backgrounds are somewhat trickier. There are many variations, some of them quite subtle. The web site at www.broflo.com.au/ shows a typical background image in action. You can download background images from a variety of web sites, but that's too easy. In this chapter, you'll learn to create your own from scratch. Background images are often small. The browser repeats a background image. This is called *tiling* because the images repeat much like tiles on a wall. Most of the time, background images are created in such a way that they tile seamlessly, so that you cannot tell where one tile ends and the next begins. You'll learn how to create seamless tiles later in this chapter.

What Makes a Good Background Image?

Backgrounds can make or break a web page. A good background makes a page almost three-dimensional, while a bad background makes a page useless. Too many web pages overemphasize the background image. The very word "background" itself tells you what a good background image should do: It should stay in the background.

Figure 17-1 shows an example of a background image that does what it's supposed to do. The text is clearly readable. The background adds a touch of texture to the page without getting in the way of the work the page has to accomplish. Figure 17-2 shows the background image used on this page.

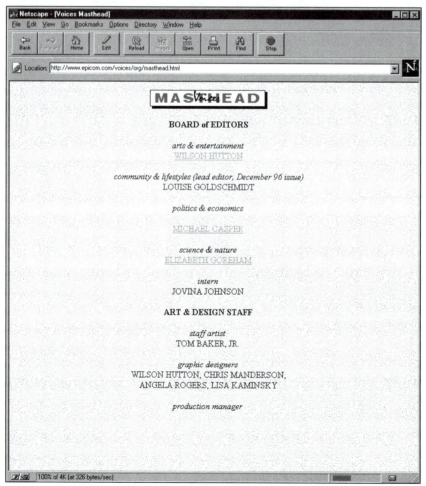

Figure 17-1: A subtle background image that manages to stay in the background.
Wilson Hutton, designer. Copyright © VOCP, Inc.

Figure 17-2: The background image for Figure 17-1.

The web page at `www.koala.net/` has a somewhat intrusive background. The text at the bottom of the page is a challenge to read, and the background image interferes with the layout of the graphics on the page; it competes for attention. If this were my page, I would probably apply a blur to the background to take the edge off it.

The site at `www.lib.virginia.edu/cataloging/vnp/mast/masterhead.html` shows another page where the background is a little too strong to work well on the page. The background intrudes sharply into the foreground, and makes the page hard to read. The background again interferes with the graphic images on the page.

Later in this chapter, you'll learn some tricks for taming an unruly background image. Not all interactions between foreground and background are necessarily harmful. Figure 17-3 shows an example of a page that repeats blocks of color from the background in the foreground images to get an interesting effect (the file is `\My Web Stuff\Chap17\chap17s.htm`). The background image for this page is shown in Figure 17-4.

Figure 17-3: Repeating background colors in foreground images.

Figure 17-4: Background image for Figure 17-13.

Background Types

The backgrounds you've seen so far are all literally tiles — square or rectangular images that repeat in vertical and horizontal directions across the page. Although all background images repeat like this, there are some tricks you can use to create the *appearance* of very different backgrounds. The types I am about to list refer to the appearance of the actual background on the page. All background images tile automatically, but with a little trickery you can disguise that fact. For example, you can create the illusion of a border along the left edge of a web page by using a very wide background image. You'll learn the specific details for creating this and other backgrounds in this chapter.

I divide background images into six general types. There is some overlap between the categories, but they are still useful for discussing background images. The categories are:

✦ **Left edge** — The background is mostly white, with a border of some kind along the left edge of the page. Figure 17-5 shows an example (the file is \My Web Stuff\Chap17\chap17a.htm); the background image is shown in Figure 17-6. The left-edge background is fairly common, but it requires some special handling to get it working right on the page. The most common method for keeping text off of the left edge is a table with a blank column of cells on the left. See the section, "Adding Backgrounds," later in this chapter for more information. If the left border is light-colored, as shown in Figure 17-7 (the file is \My Web Stuff\Chap17\chap17c.htm), the text can easily cover a portion of the background image without confusion.

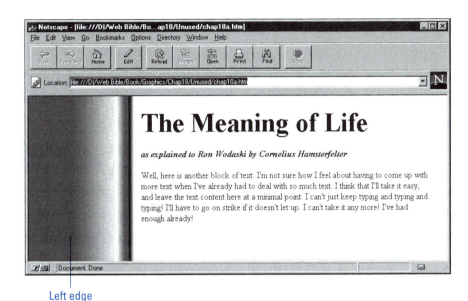

Left edge

Figure 17-5: A page with a left-edge background image.

Figure 17-6: The background image for Figure 17-15.

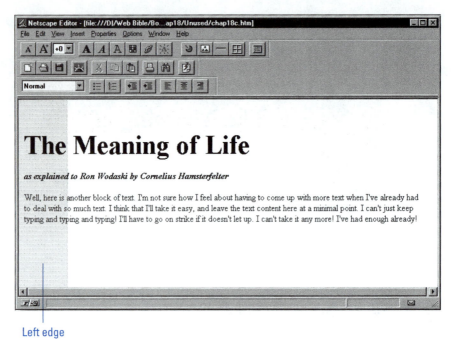

Left edge

Figure 17-7: A lighter background image with text over it.

✦ **Top edge** — The background is mostly white, with a border of some kind at the top of the page. This isn't all that common, but the basic technique is similar to the technique for a left border. This type of background is seen less frequently than it once was; I couldn't find one even with hours of looking, so I created a simple sample page for Figure 17-8 (the file is \My Web Stuff\Chap17\chap17b.htm). Yes, that's the same image used in Figure 17-5, but rotated 90 degrees. Note how the image seems much more dominating when used at the top of the page instead of at the side of the page. The background image used in Figure 17-8 is shown in Figure 17-9. Depending on the exact nature of the background, you may or may not need to use spacing to keep text off of the top portion of the background.

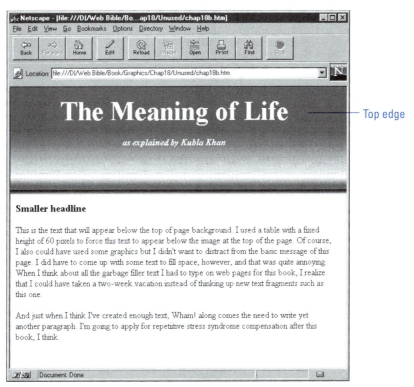

Top edge

Figure 17-8: A page with a top-edge background image.

Figure 17-9: The background image for Figure 17-8.

◆ **Image background** — This refers to backgrounds that consist almost entirely of a photograph, logo, or other image that repeats across the background. Unlike textured backgrounds, which are usually subtle, image backgrounds tend to jump out and bite you on the nose. Image backgrounds can be intrusive, but blurring, lightening, and contrast reduction can all help to reduce the problem. See the page at `resort-travel.com/`.

◆ **Subtle background** — You can generate interesting background effects with an image that doesn't vary much in color or brightness. Figure 17-10 shows an example of a thin, horizontal image as the background (giving the effect of a soft left-edge background), and Figure 17-11 shows an image background that is subtle enough to be effective. To work well, this type of background image shouldn't vary much in color or brightness so it can appear behind any text or graphic. There should be no need to arrange the page in any special way to accommodate the background.

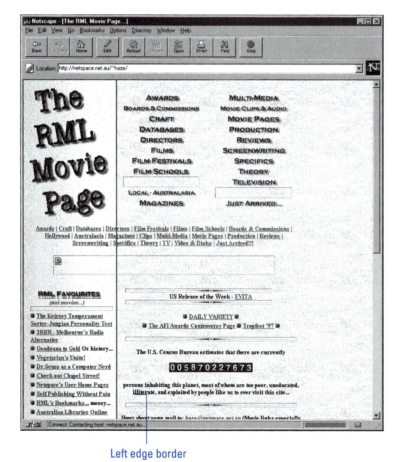

Left edge border

Figure 17-10: A subtle left-edge background.

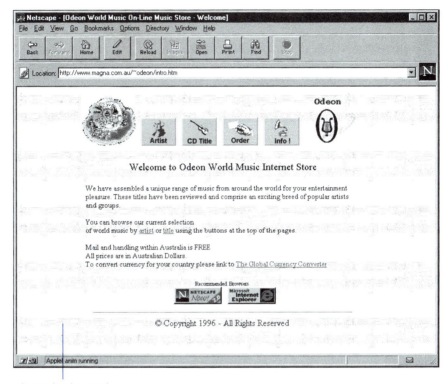

Image background

Figure 17-11: A subtle background.

✦ **Over-the-top** — This is my term for a background that is so outrageous it becomes the dominant factor on the page. It is rare when a page of this type can be called tasteful. As often as not, such pages are created to deliberately flaunt their garish appearance. Another word that describes this kind of background is dramatic.

✦ **Reversal** — I use this term to describe any and all dark backgrounds. By dark I mean any background image that requires you to use white or light text for clarity.

These types are not meant to be a definitive classification of backgrounds, but they are useful for discussing many of the backgrounds that you will see and learn how to create in this chapter. I feel certain that, now that I've laid down these categories, someone will come along with one that I did not think of.

Adding Backgrounds

Different web page editors use different methods for adding background images to a page. However, in each case, as long as you know where the information is stored, it's very easy to add or change the background image for a page.

Navigator Gold backgrounds

Figure 17-12 shows the Navigator Gold dialog box for adding a background image to a page. This dialog box is reached through the Properties | Document menu selection. It provides access to many other document properties besides the background image. To add a background image to a page, click the Browse for File button to open the Open dialog box. Locate the image file and click the Open button. When you return to the Document Properties dialog box, the Use Image check box will be checked, and the filename of the image file will appear as shown in Figure 17-12.

Click here to set
solid color background

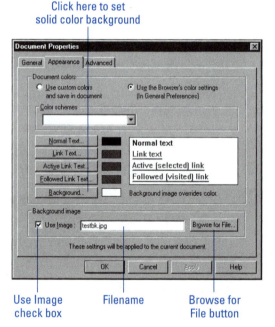

Figure 17-12: Setting the document background image in Navigator Gold.

Use Image
check box

Filename

Browse for
File button

FrontPage 97 backgrounds

If you are using FrontPage 97 to create your web pages, use the Format |
Background menu selection to open the dialog box shown in Figure 17-13. By
default, the Background tab at the top of the dialog box is active. This is the Page
Properties dialog box (such a difference from Document Properties!). By default,
the background and colors are inherited from the page shown at the bottom of the
dialog box. Some FrontPage wizards and templates use this type of page to specify
defaults, and some do not. You can also create your own default pages, and enter
them manually. To specify different settings for the current page (that is, the page
whose properties you are viewing in the dialog box), click the Specify Background
and Colors radio button at the top of the dialog box. The appearance of the dialog
box changes, as shown in Figure 17-14.

Click the check box for Background Image, and then click the Browse button. This
opens YAD (which as you probably know by this point in the book, stands for Yet
Another Dialog) shown in Figure 17-15. If the image for the background is already
part of the images set aside for the web site, locate the image and click OK. If the
image is not part of the web site yet, click the Other Location tab to display YAD
shown in Figure 17-16.

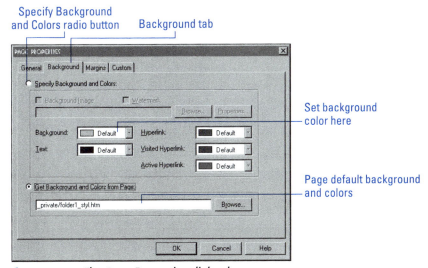

Figure 17-13: The Page Properties dialog box.

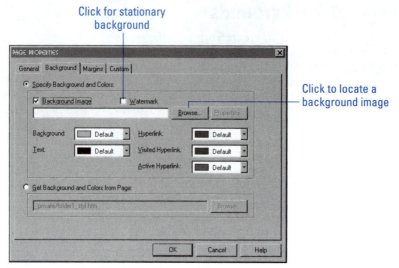

Figure 17-14: Setting the background image.

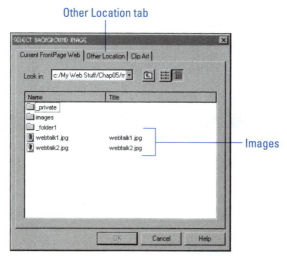

Figure 17-15: Selecting an image from the current web as the background image.

Click here to locate
an image file   Browse button

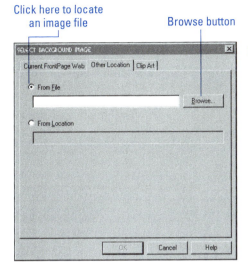

Figure 17-16: Selecting a non-web image for the background.

Click the From File radio button (if it is not already active), click the Browse button, and locate the file. Click OK to return to the original dialog box. If the image were somewhere on the Web, you would use the From Location radio button, and type the URL for the image into the text box. However, unless the image is somewhere on a web server that you control, it is almost always bad form to load images from someone else's web server to use on your pages — it places an unreasonable burden on the owner of that other web server, because that server will be accessed every time your web page gets displayed.

 Amen! Don't you ever show such bad manners. Load all of your images locally. While we're on the subject of FrontPage 97, I have to vent a little steam. It's a great web page editor, so don't get me wrong. But who in the world thought up all those dialog boxes? You can get yourself lost trying to accomplish something in FrontPage! I suggest leaving a trail of breadcrumbs anytime you venture into new territory.

When you return to the Page Properties dialog box, the filename for the background image will appear. Click OK, and you can relax. You've added one background to one page, as shown in Figure 17-17.

 If you want to add the same background to all pages, take advantage of FrontPage's ability to work from templates. That file listed at the bottom of the Page Properties dialog box is the file from which this page (and probably a lot of other pages) takes its properties, including background image. Change the background image for that page, and it will change on all pages that use that page as a template.

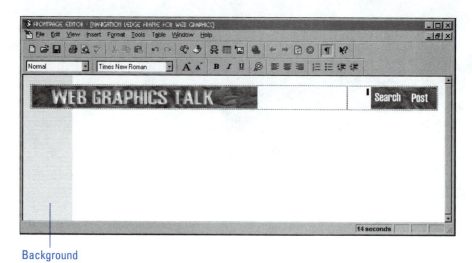

Background

Figure 17-17: The web page has a background.

Fusion backgrounds

Figure 17-18 shows Net Object's Fusion, another web page editor. Like FrontPage 97, Fusion includes many features for managing a web site, as well as page-design tools. The dialog box shown in Figure 17-18 is called the Properties dialog box. Do you sense a certain consistency from program to program? Yes, that's right: In web editor after web editor, you can change the page background by finding the Properties dialog box for that page. In Fusion, the Properties dialog box is visible by default. Click the Layout tab if it is not already active, and then click the Picture radio button. This opens a Locate dialog box. There is no need to click the Browse button; Fusion anticipates your moves. Locate the file for the background, and click Open. This returns you to the Properties dialog box, with the image filename neatly appearing next to the Picture radio button. Figure 17-19 shows the web page with the background added.

Click here to create a
solid color background   Properties dialog

Click here to add a background image

Figure 17-18: The Fusion Properties dialog box and a web page.

Whatever tools you use for editing web pages, you can usually set the background
image by displaying the page (or document) properties dialog box. In some cases,
(as with FrontPage 97), you can specify a standard background image for all pages.

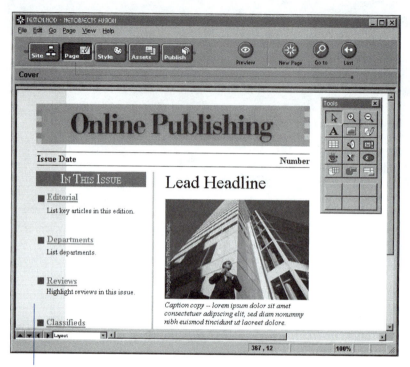

Background

Figure 17-19: The web page now has a background.

Whipping Up Quick Patterns with Painter

CD: To install the trial version of Painter from the CD, double-click the file `\demo\fractal\painter4\setup.exe`.

Level: Easy

Tutorial

Task: Create a repeating background tile for a web page

Before you start: Download and install the demo version of Painter.

The page background shown in Figure 17-20 can be created easily in Fractal Design Painter. The concept behind a page background is a simple one: The edges of the pattern must match exactly so that when the pattern is automatically repeated by the browser, there are no visible seams. This tutorial covers the basic process of creating a background tile. The tile you create in this tutorial was used for the web page originally described in Chapter 8, "Graphics That Say Wow!."

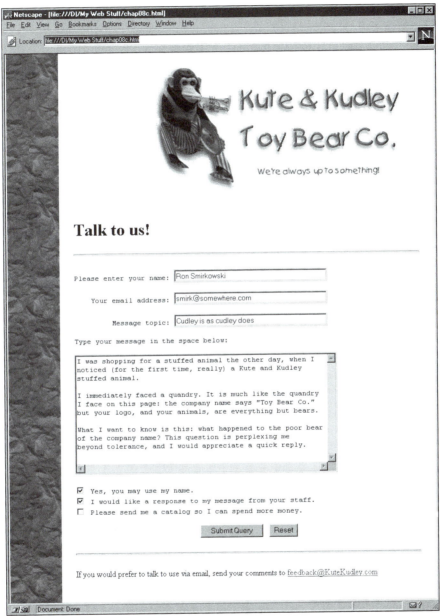

Figure 17-20: A web page that uses a background image.

Figure 17-21 shows Fractal Design Painter open for creating a background. I scanned the page layout using my Hewlett-Packard ScanJet IIC, saved it as a file, and opened it in Painter to use as a reference guide for creating various elements of the page. To create the background:

1. Choose a pattern (I chose Paper Bag) and then click the Pattern | Check Out Pattern menu selection of the Art Materials panel.

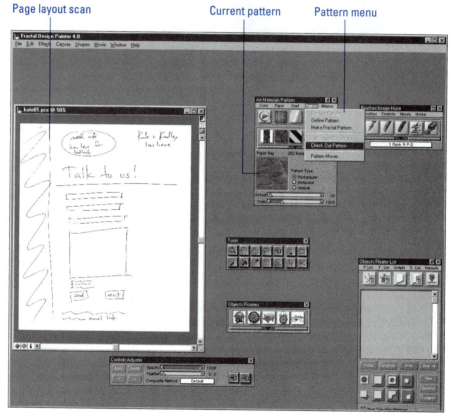

Figure 17-21: Fractal Design Painter ready to create a background.

This opens a copy of the current pattern as an image file (see Figure 17-22).

2. Click the selection tool (see Figure 17-23) and then click and drag a selection of the approximate width desired for the repeating pattern at the left edge of the page design (see Figure 17-24).

Figure 17-22: The Paper Bag pattern as an image.

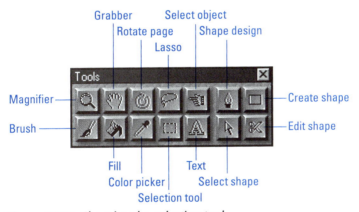

Figure 17-23: Choosing the selection tool.

Figure 17-24: A portion of the image is selected.

3. Copy the selected portion of the image to the Clipboard using the Edit |
Copy menu selection. The Control panel (see Figure 17-25) shows the size of
my selection. It is 262 pixels high.

4. Use the File | New menu selection to create a new file. I set the width at 1024
pixels (wider than the usual web browser window) and 262 pixels high.

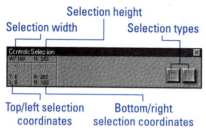

Figure 17-25: The Control panel shows
selection width and height.

5. Paste the selection into the new image, and carefully move it to the exact left
edge of the image (see Figure 17-26). (Because the image I selected was
already a repeating pattern, the top and bottom edges match and create a
seamless background.)

Figure 17-26: The new image with the selection pasted in and moved.

6. To test that the image really is seamless, save the image as a JPEG file (I
saved it as kutebrd2.jpg) and use it as a background for a web page. Figure
17-27 shows the appearance of the background.

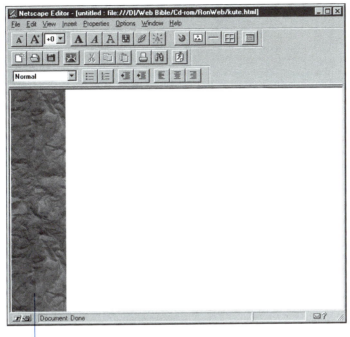

Background

Figure 17-27: The background on a blank web page.

Idea

Where to go from here:

✦ To give the background a 3-D look, use the Effects | Apply Surface Texture menu selection to open the Surface Texture dialog box. Choose Mask as your method, and set softness at about 3 or 4. Adjust the Amount slider to get a good 3-D edge.

✦ A drop shadow will increase the 3-D look. Use the Effects | Object | Create Drop Shadow menu selection to add the drop shadow. Experiment with different settings to get the right look.

✦ Painter also has a feature for creating original seamless backgrounds. Try creating your own seamless patterns using the Pattern | Define Pattern menu selection on the Art Materials panel. Create an image before you try to use this technique. When you draw, your strokes continue to the opposite edge so the tile is seamless. Experiment with different natural brushes.

Seamy, or Seamless?

The background you created in the previous tutorial is seamless, because it is built from a pattern that is already seamless in Painter. You can take almost any image and convert it into a seamless pattern for a background in any image editor. You can also use a special feature of Painter to create your own seamless background from scratch.

Even if you use seamless background images, you will have to be careful about whether the pattern appears to repeat. A very dark or light area, a sharp line, or some other feature of the pattern may easily give the appearance of a seam even if none is present. Figure 17-28 shows a web page that uses a seamless background, but still appears to have a seam. The image is quite dark (see Figure 17-29), so the seams may not show clearly here on the page. You can check out the web page yourself at http://www.magna.com.au/~odeon/.

Figure 17-28: A not-quite-seamless background.

Figure 17-29: The background image for Figure 17-28.

Even without considering the still-slightly-visible seams, the stars in the image are obviously repeating. I know I have pushed for small images, but in this case the background image is too small to work effectively. Figure 17-30 shows a page with a background that uses a somewhat larger star image that isn't as obviously repeating. I also took the liberty of making the background of the image of the hands darker and transparent so some background image stars show through. Otherwise, the image tended to have an obvious border around it.

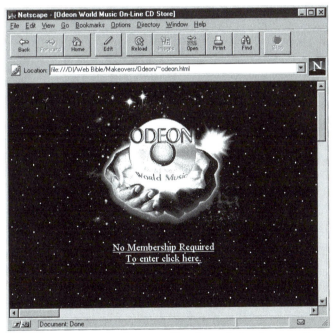

Figure 17-30: A revised page with a less obviously repeating background.

A careful look at this page shows that the background image is repeating, but it is much less obvious. The background image is still quite small (120 pixels by 120 pixels; see Figure 17-31). If it is really, really important to have a diverse background of stars, a still larger image is necessary.

Figure 17-31: The background image for Figure 17-30.

Using Watermarks

All of the background images so far tend to be small images (or at least very thin images). There is another type of background image that is supported only by Microsoft Internet Explorer: watermarks. The name is taken from paper publishing. Watermarks are added to some paper to indicate who made the paper. They are called watermarks because they are faint marks made on the paper as part of the water removal process. (If you aren't familiar with paper making, paper starts as a slurry of wood products, water, and chemicals that is spread or squeezed into sheets and then dried.)

The only difference between a watermark and a normal background is that a watermark does not move as the page is scrolled. You add a watermark in exactly the same way as you add any background image, the method of course depending on the web page editor you are using. There will either be a check box of some sort to indicate that the background image should act as a watermark (see Figure 17-32, which shows the appropriate dialog box from FrontPage 97), or you will need to modify the HTML source code to make the background image behave like a watermark.

Filename   Watermark check box

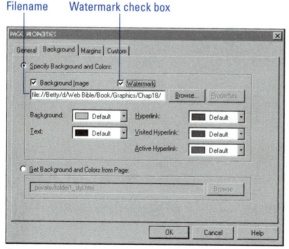

Figure 17-32: The Page Properties dialog box from FrontPage 97.

The following HTML code for the BODY tag adds a background image to a web page:

```
<BODY BACKGROUND="image.gif">
```

To make the image behave like a watermark, you must add a BGPROPERTIES tag to it, like this:

```
<BODY BACKGROUND="image.gif" BGPROPERTIES=FIXED>
```

You can make these changes using any text editor that doesn't add special codes to files, such as Notepad. When you alter HTML codes like this, be very careful to make only the changes you actually need to make. Even small changes in the BODY tag can lead to major changes in the appearance of the page.

If you have Microsoft's Internet Explorer browser available, double-click the file `\My Web Stuff\chap17\chap17d.htm` to see an example of a web page with a watermark. Images used as watermarks can be quite large, and it is usually a good idea to keep the majority of the image as simple as possible — a single color would be ideal. Figure 17-33 shows the type of image that works well as a watermark; the web page is shown in Figure 17-34.

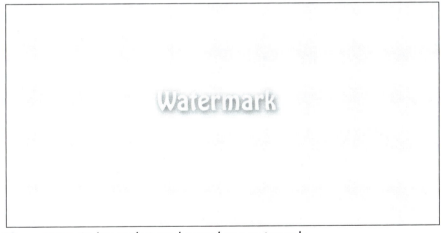

Figure 17-33: An image that can be used as a watermark.

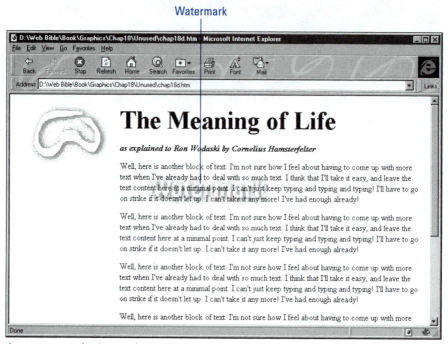

Figure 17-34: The image from Figure 17-33 used as a watermark.

The central-image-on-a-blank-background is not the only kind of watermark that you can use. Most subtle images work well as watermarks — after all, despite the cute terminology, the real point of a watermark is that it doesn't move. Most background images look great as watermarks. However, if you decide to use watermarks, remember that, unless and until Netscape and other browsers support it, only Internet Explorer users will see it as a stationary background. (The BGPROPERTIES parameter does no harm for most browsers; they will display the watermark as a regular, scrolling background.)

Figure 17-35 shows that even when the text scrolls, the background image does not.

The way HTML is set up, when a browser encounters a tag or a parameter it does not understand, it just ignores the tag or parameter. This prevents messy errors, and allows older browsers to display pages that use more recent HTML features — like watermarks.

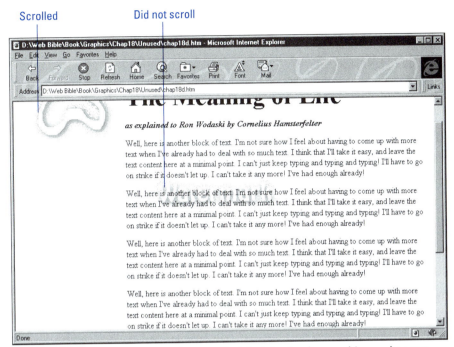

Figure 17-35: The page content has scrolled, but the background image has not.

A smaller image can work as a watermark, as shown in Figure 17-36 (the file is \My Web Stuff\Chap17\chap17d.htm). Smaller images, however, tend to look crowded and the watermark effect (stationary background) can get lost. Some textured backgrounds look good as a watermark because the text and images appear to scroll over the stationary background, enhancing the illusion of a real material background.

There is something special about the background image used for Figure 17-36. The very first reader who can tell me what it is wins a free T-shirt. How's that for cheap sensationalism?

Image on page (not watermark)   Repeating watermark

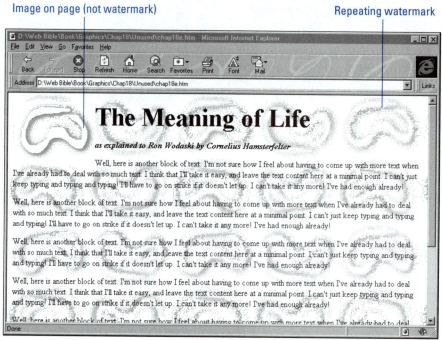

Figure 17-36: A smaller image used as a watermark.

Creating Seamless Tiles with Fractal Design Painter

CD: To install the trial version of Painter from the CD, double-click the file `\demo\fractal\painter4\setup.exe`.

Level: Easy

Tutorial

Task: Create a repeating background tile for a web page

Before you start: Download and install the demo version of Painter.

So far, you have been studying the appearance of backgrounds on the web page. The actual act of creation has been lurking in the background like the smell of apple pie during dinner. Your appetite need not wait any longer; it's time to chow down on some hard-core techniques.

The easiest way to create a background is with Fractal Design Painter. In just a few easy steps, you can have a wild or tame background that fits your needs.

1. Begin by creating a new file with the appropriate dimensions for a background image. For starters, try a Width and Height of about 160.

2. Use the File | New menu selection to create the file. Figure 17-37 shows the newly created file, along with some of Painter's various palettes.

New image   Art Materials palette

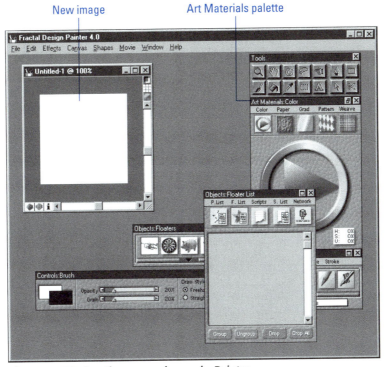

Figure 17-37: Creating a new image in Painter.

3. Click the Pattern menu on the Art Materials palette to display the menu shown in Figure 17-38.

4. Click Define Pattern. This converts what was once a typical image into a very special and very convenient pattern/image.

Define Pattern selection

Figure 17-38: The Pattern menu.

Whenever you draw in the pattern/image, lines that touch a border automatically extend to the opposite edge. To test this, draw a line from the left to the right, but at a slight angle and do not stop when you get to the right edge. The line magically reappears at the left edge. Press Ctrl+Z to remove the test line.

Once you define an image as a pattern, almost anything you draw or apply to the page will automatically extend to the opposite edge. You can paint with natural media, apply the Image Hose to the canvas, and so on. However, if you paste an object, or create a floater, the floater will not automatically extend across edges. The edge phenomenon applies only when you are actually drawing in some manner.

Tip

If you simply must paste something into your pattern/image, paste it twice, once at one edge, and once at the other edge. Make certain that the dividing line you use at each edge is correct down to the exact pixel or you won't get a truly seamless tile.

6. Click the Image Hose tool (see Figure 17-39) to select it as the active brush.

7. In the Brush Controls: Nozzle palette (see Figure 17-40), choose Nasturtiums as the active hose. If this hose is not visible, click the drawer handle to open the drawer where you can find additional hoses. You do not need to make any changes to the default settings in this dialog box.

Tip

If the Brush Controls palette is not visible, use the Nozzle menu in the Brushes palette to select Nozzle. Now you can select the Nasturtiums nozzle.

Figure 17-39: Selecting a brush.

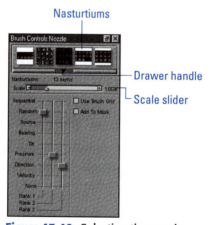

Figure 17-40: Selecting the nozzle.

8. Modify the opacity of the Image Hose using the Controls: Brush palette, shown in Figure 17-41.

Since it is desirable to have a background that does not conflict with the foreground, choose an opacity level that seems suitable for a given web page. Usually, a setting somewhere between 10 and 50% will be effective in fading the image sufficiently for it to behave like a background. If you want light text against a dark background, you might get good results even with a 100% setting.

Opacity slider

Figure 17-41: Setting opacity.

After setting opacity, start to draw in the image with the Image Hose. The hose sprays images like paint, as shown in Figure 17-42.

9. Spray a single line of nasturtiums along the right edge, and watch as they fold neatly to the left edge automatically.

10. Continue to spray nasturtiums until you cover the image, as shown in Figure 17-43.

Figure 17-42: Painting with nasturtiums.

Figure 17-43: The image is covered with nasturtiums.

The nasturtiums in Figure 17-43 were applied with an opacity of 50%. Using a setting of 10% the nasturtiums are much lighter, as shown in Figure 17-44. Figure 17-45 shows the appearance of the lighter image as a background for a web page; the file is \My Web Stuff\Chap17\chap17n.htm. Figure 17-46 shows the darker version of the image with a bit of blurring (Effect | Focus | Soften menu selection) applied. The file is \My Web Stuff\Chap17\chap17m.htm. Also take a look at the file \My Web Stuff\Chap17\chap17L.htm to see a version that uses neither softening nor lightening.

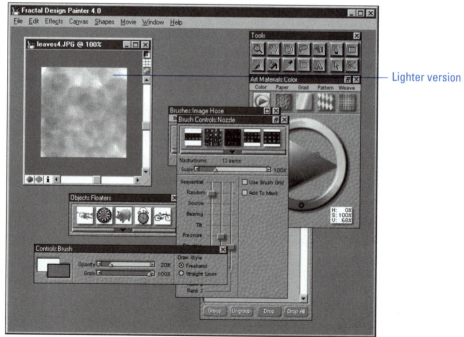

Figure 17-44: A lighter version of the nasturtium background.

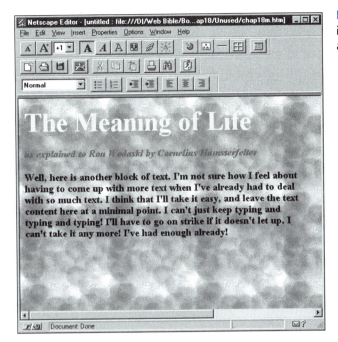

Figure 17-45: The nasturtium image as a background on a web page.

Figure 17-46: The darker version of the image as a web page background.

Idea

Where to go from here:

✦ The Image Hose is cool, but Painter offers a lot more power. Try creating a simple background image using the drawing tools available in Painter.

✦ After you create an image, you can use various Painter tools to add interest to the image, or to make it more suitable as a background. Lightening, darkening, and softening all enhance an image for use as a background.

✦ Sculpt images in 3-D using the Effects | Apply Surface Texture menu selection, then soften the 3-D effect.

Creating Seamless Backgrounds with Photoshop

Tutorial

CD: A trial version of Photoshop is on the CD-ROM. To find out how to install it, view the web page at \demo\viewme.htm in your browser and click the \demo\adobe hyperlink.

Level: Advanced

Task: Create a repeating background tile for a web page

Before you start:

✦ Run Photoshop version 4.0.

✦ Open the file \My Web Stuff\Chap17\cloth2.pcx in Photoshop (File | Open menu selection; see Figure 17-47).

If you do not have Photoshop installed, you may be able to adapt the steps in this tutorial to your favorite image editor. The key element of the process is the ability to divide an image into layers. If your image editor supports layers, it is most likely that some variation of this tutorial will work.

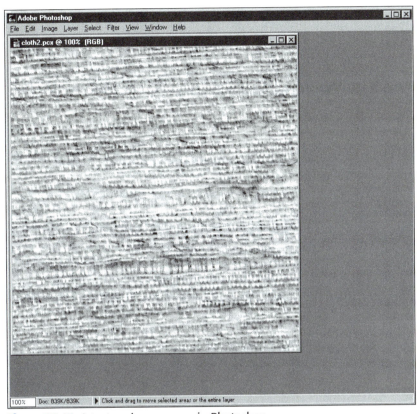

Figure 17-47: A texture image open in Photoshop.

Figure 17-47 contains a highly textured image with lots of subtle variation and detail. This is the easiest kind of image to turn into a seamless background tile. Images with larger detail, such as a close-up of a pile of rocks, are more challenging but not impossible.

To create the image, I draped a pair of linen shorts across my Hewlett-Packard flatbed scanner and scanned the image at a high resolution to show lots of detail. I used a very small portion of the total image. The bed of the scanner is roughly 8.5 inches by 14 inches, and the image shown in Figure 17-47 is less than one inch on a side. See Chapter 9 for an example of image scanning.

If you look carefully at Figure 17-47, you'll notice that the horizontal lines aren't exactly horizontal. To correct this, follow these steps:

1. Use the Image ⏐ Rotate Canvas ⏐ Arbitrary menu selection to open the dialog box shown in Figure 17-48.

2. Set the Angle of rotation at 2 degrees, and the direction at °CW (clockwise).

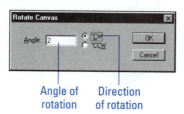

Figure 17-48: Setting the angle of rotation.

Angle of rotation   Direction of rotation

This makes the image nearly horizontal, as shown in Figure 17-49. The exact color of the added portions of the image will vary according to the current background color.

3. To select just the useful portion of the image, click the rectangular selection tool in the Photoshop toolbar (see Figure 17-50).

4. Click at the upper left and drag to the lower right, then release. You should have a roughly square selection, as shown in Figure 17-51.

2°

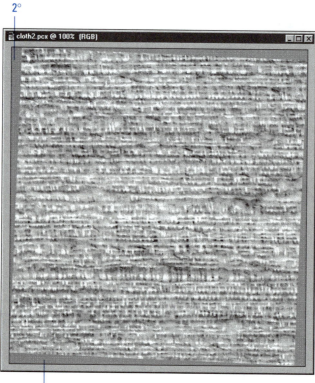

Figure 17-49:
The rotated image.

Background color fills "empty" space

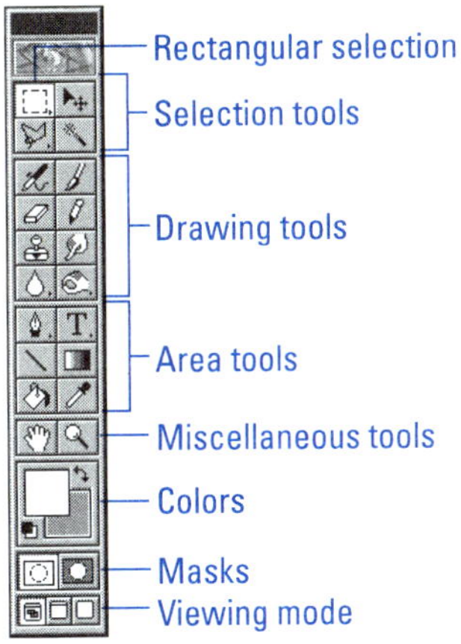

Figure 17-50: The Photoshop toolbar.

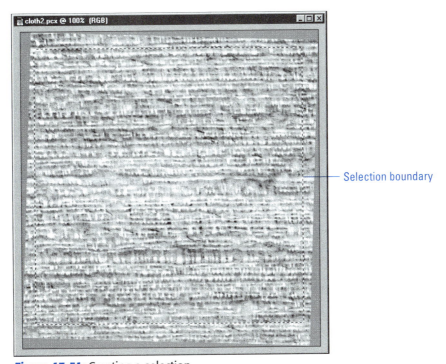

— Rectangular selection

— Selection tools

— Drawing tools

— Area tools

— Miscellaneous tools

— Colors

— Masks
— Viewing mode

cloth2.pcx @ 100% (RGB)

— Selection boundary

Figure 17-51: Creating a selection.

5. Copy the selection to the Clipboard (the Edit ∣ Copy menu selection or use the Ctrl+C key combination).

6. Use the File ∣ New menu selection to open the New dialog box shown in Figure 17-52. The height and width you see will probably be different, but they will match the height and width of the image you just copied to the Clipboard.

7. Click OK to create the new file.

8. Now use the Ctrl+V key combination to paste the Clipboard contents into the image. Figure 17-53 shows the result.

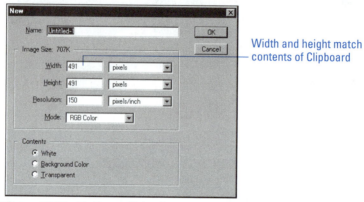

Width and height match contents of Clipboard

Figure 17-52: The New dialog box.

Figure 17-53: The new image.

9. Save the newly created image before you continue.

10. Use the File | Save As menu selection, and type in the filename **myCloth.psd**.

11. Make sure the image type is Photoshop so that you will retain layer information.

12. Save to the \My Web Stuff directory.

Theory of seamless backgrounds

The essence of a seamless background tile is that the opposite edges match exactly. Figure 17-54 shows this in a simple example. The image on the left in the figure will not create a seamless background, but the image on the right will. The lines in the image on the right match exactly at the top/bottom and left/right edges.

Figure 17-54: The image on the left will not be seamless, but the image on the right will be.

Figure 17-55 shows a web page that uses the image on the left in Figure 17-54 for a background (the file is \My Web Stuff\Chap17\chap17o.htm). Figure 17-56 shows a web page that uses the image on the right in Figure 17-54 for a background (the file is \My Web Stuff\Chap17\chap17p.htm).

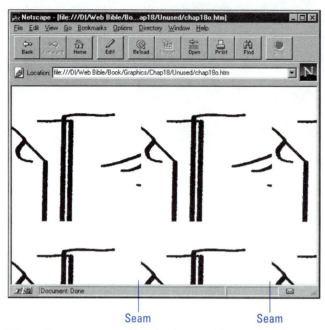

Figure 17-55: A page with a background image that does not tile seamlessly.

Figure 17-56: A page with a seamless tiled background.

In the same way, the image shown in Figure 17-53 will not be seamless. Figure 17-57 shows what this image looks like on a web page (the file is \My Web Stuff\ Chap17\chap17R.htm). The point where the tiles come together makes a subtle but noticeable line. This is why images with lots of subtle variations make such good background images — you do not have to get the edges perfectly seamless. They tend to disappear amid the confusion and chaos inherent in the texture.

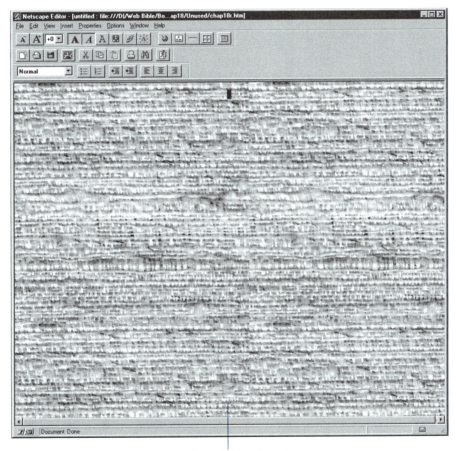

Edge between tiles (seam)

Figure 17-57: The texture from Figure 17-53 as a background image on a web page.

To get the edges of the image to match at the top/bottom and left/right, you will copy the bottom edge to the top, and the right edge to the left edge. Then apply softening and blending to merge the copied portions with the underlying image.

Adjusting the selection

Begin by selecting the entire image in Photoshop.

1. Press Ctrl+A, or use the Select | All menu selection. A selection border appears around the edge of the image.

2. While holding down the Alt key, use the rectangle selection tool to remove the central portion of the selection.

   This leaves a selection around the outside edge of the image. It should be about 10 to 20% of the width of the image, as shown in Figure 17-58.

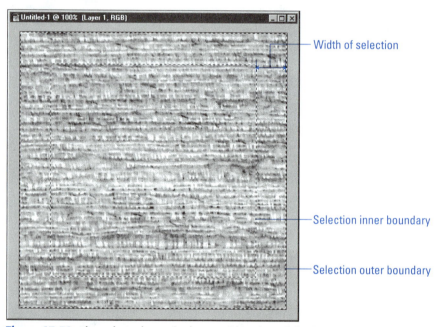

Figure 17-58: The selected area is the outside edge of the image.

3. Click and hold the lasso tool to select the linear lasso (see Figure 17-59). The linear lasso selects an irregular area.

4. Click a series of points to establish an outline.

5. Double-click the last point to complete the outline, and everything within the outline is selected.

   You can also use the linear lasso tool to add to or remove from an existing selection. Holding down the Shift key while clicking with any selection tool adds to a selection. Holding down the Alt key while clicking removes from a selection. Your next step is to remove most of the selection, leaving just the bottom portion of the area still selected. The bottom portion will have the shape of the bottom piece of wood in a typical picture frame. Peak ahead to Figure 17-61 to see what the shape of the selection will be.

Linear lasso

Figure 17-59: The linear lasso tool.

6. To remove all but this bottom portion of the selection, hold down the Alt key while clicking with the lasso tool at the six points shown in Figure 17-60.

7. Be sure to double-click the last point to complete the outline. The area within the outline is removed from the selection, leaving the selection shown in Figure 17-61.

8. Copy this selection to the Clipboard using the Ctrl+C key combination.

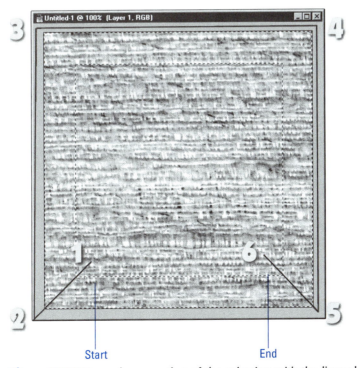

Start   End

Figure 17-60: Removing a portion of the selection with the linear lasso tool.

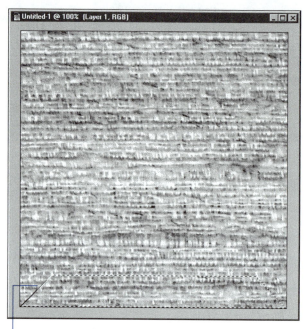

Selection boundary

Figure 17-61: The remaining selection.

Creating layers automatically

1. Use Ctrl+D to deselect all. There is now no selection at all.

2. Press Ctrl+V to paste a copy of the bottom portion of the image as a new layer.

You will not see much visible difference because the pasted area is so similar. Look at the Layers palette, shown in Figure 17-62. The palette shows a thumbnail of the contents of each layer, as well as several indicators that give you information about each layer. From left to right, these are

✦ Visibility toggle (determines if a layer is visible)

✦ Mode toggle (determines if you are painting on a layer or layer mask)

✦ Thumbnail (a small picture of the layer's contents)

✦ Layer name

If the Layers palette is not visible, use the Window | Show Layers menu selection to display it.

Tip

The paste operation didn't just add a selection; it added a completely new layer called Layer 2.

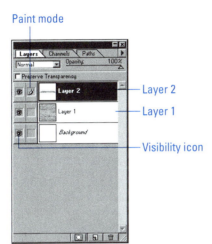

Figure 17-62: The Layers palette.

You can operate on just the Layer 2 contents by clicking it to highlight it. You can work on any other layer by clicking to highlight that layer. You can also control which layers are visible by clicking the eye icon for each layer. Figure 17-63 shows Layer 1 turned off. Later, you will click the eye again to turn Layer 1 back on. When the layer is off, it is invisible, as shown in Figure 17-64.

Figure 17-63: Turning off a layer.

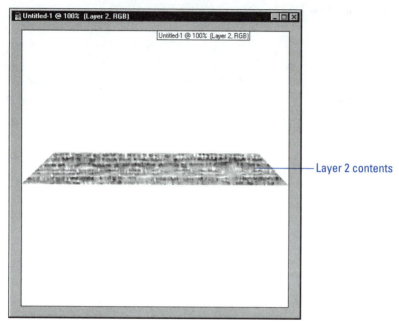

Figure 17-64: Layer 1 is off and is therefore invisible.

Flipping the new layer

To fit the Layer 2 contents correctly in the overall image, flip it vertically.

1. Use the Layer | Transform | Flip Vertical menu selection to do this. The layer's contents flip as shown in Figure 17-65.

2. Hold down the Ctrl key and click and drag the layer's contents to the exact top edge of the image (see Figure 17-66).

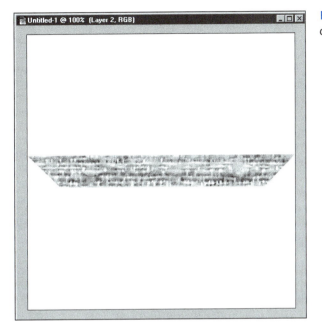

Figure 17-65: The layer's contents have flipped.

Match carefully!

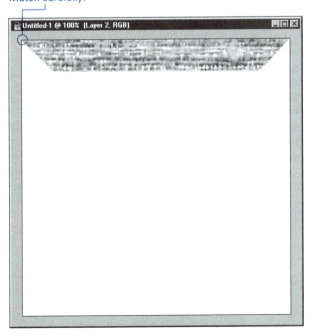

Figure 17-66: The layer's contents at the top of the image.

Creating a layer mask

At this point, the top and bottom now match, although the bottom is temporarily invisible. To complete the operation, it is only necessary to blend the new layer into the original layer. The simplest way to do this is to select the Dodge/Burn tool (also called the Toning tool; see Figure 17-67), and then create a mask for Layer 2. The mask controls which pixels in the layer are visible, and to what degree.

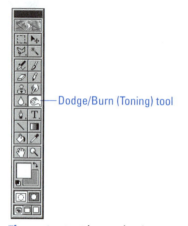

—Dodge/Burn (Toning) tool

Figure 17-67: The Dodge/Burn tool.

1. To create a mask for Layer 2, click Layer 2 in the Layers palette if it is not already highlighted.

2. Now click the Make Mask icon at the bottom center of the Layers palette (see Figure 17-68).

   A small thumbnail appears at the right of the layer thumbnail, as shown in Figure 17-68. A small chain icon between the thumbnails indicates that the layer and its mask are linked. Any changes you make to the mask while it is linked to the layer's contents will change the transparency of the layer.

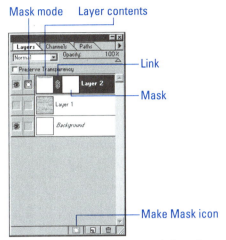

Figure 17-68: Creating a mask for a layer.

Altering the layer mask

Before you begin altering the Layer 2 mask, set the Toning tools options.

1. If the Options palette is not visible, double-click the Toning tool to display it. Figure 17-69 shows the options.

2. Select Highlights from the drop-down list, Exposure for 50%, and the Tool as Burn. If you are not using a tablet and stylus (see Chapter 9, "Graphic Hardware," for more information on tablets), the Size and Exposure check boxes will be gray.

3. Set the brush size as shown in Figure 17-70. If the Brush Size palette is not visible, use the Window ⏐ Show Brush menu selection to display it.

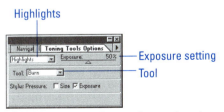

Figure 17-69: Setting Toning tool options.

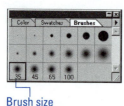

Figure 17-70: Setting brush size.

Brush size

4. Use the Burn tool to lighten the edges of the image in Layer 2, as shown in Figure 17-71.

   You may need to go over the edges several times to get the proper degree of lightening. You are not changing the image itself; you are changing the transparency of the image.

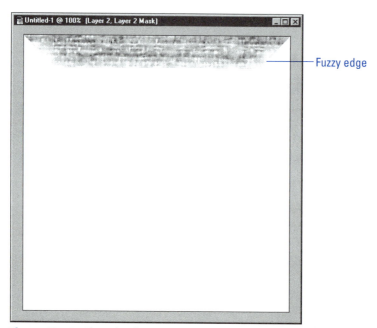

Fuzzy edge

Figure 17-71: Changing image transparency interactively.

Tip

You do not have to use the Burn option of the Toning tool to create transparency. You can also paint onto the mask with the Airbrush tool or other tools if you wish. (The Burn and Dodge tools come from photography, and refer to adding or subtracting light when printing from a negative.)

5. To check your work, click the eye icon for Layer 1 in the Layers palette to make the contents of Layer 1 visible again (see Figure 17-72). When you can no longer easily distinguish the boundary between layers, you are done.

6. Save your work (File | Save menu selection).

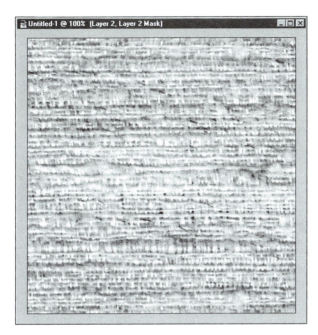

Figure 17-72: The layers blend neatly.

Adding a new layer

To complete the pattern, repeat these steps on the left and right edges of the image:

1. Select the entire image, then remove the central portion. Leave 10 to 20% of the image width as a border around the image.

2. Use the Alt key and the linear lasso tool to remove all but the left edge of the selection.

3. Copy the remaining selection to the Clipboard, and use Ctrl+D to remove the selection. Paste with Ctrl+V.

4. The horizontal rows may not match exactly (see Figure 17-73). You can use the Layer | Transform | Skew menu selection to bend the contents of Layer 3 so they line up exactly with Layer 1.

5. Once you start the skew, handles appear around the contents of Layer 3. Click and drag the left-center handle (see Figure 17-74) and move it up or down a small amount.

When you get the position just right, the lines seem to blend into one another. Keep at it until you get the best compromise.

6. To lock in the changes, click any other tool and the Apply Transformation dialog box appears. Or you can double-click the selection to immediately accept the changes.

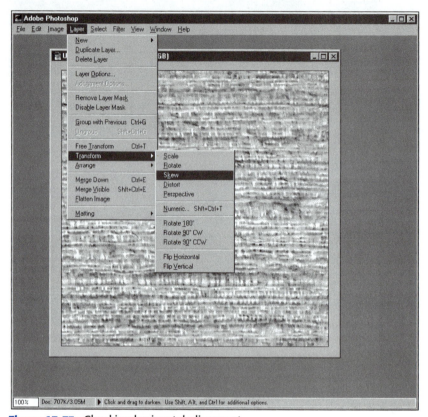

Figure 17-73: Checking horizontal alignment.

7. Click the Apply button if the Skew transformation is acceptable to you.

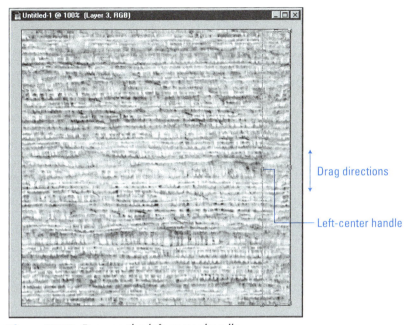

Figure 17-74: Drag on the left-center handle.

Figure 17-75 shows a more extreme example of applying a skew to a selection. This is another image that I converted into a background. In this case, the degree of skew required was much larger, and shows the effect of skewing more clearly. The nice thing about using skew is that the edge pixels are not affected by the change. This gives you a powerful tool for merging between the background image and the edge of the new layer.

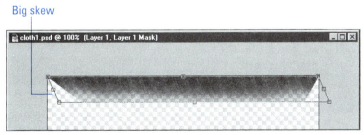

Figure 17-75: A more extreme example of skew.

8. Hide Layer 1 (see Figure17-76).

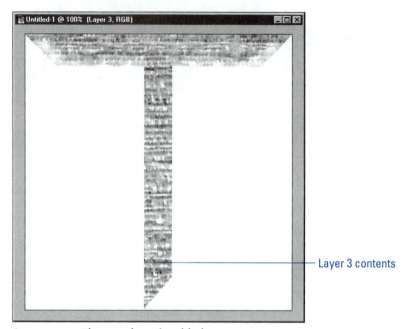

Figure 17-76: The new layer is added.

9. Select Layer 3 by clicking it in the Layers palette.

10. Flip the layer image horizontally (Layer | Transform | Flip Horizontal) and move it to the right edge.

11. Create a mask (click the Make Mask button) and soften the edge of Layer 3 (see Figure 17-77).

12. Click the eye icon for Layer 1 to make it visible, and check your work. When you can no longer see the boundary between Layers 1 and 3, your work is complete.

13. Save the image to disk. To use the image as a background, save it as a JPEG file. Use the File | Save as Copy menu selection. Use the filename **myCloth.JPG**.

Figure 17-78 shows an example of a web page that uses a modified version of the background. Why modified? The background image was based on a scan, and the scan shows a lot of sharp detail. By lightening or darkening the image, it is easier to put either dark or light text in front of the image. The text is more readable. By blurring the background image, the sharp text shows up more clearly against the background. The physical size of the image is also fairly large, and can be cut by a factor of two or three for typical web page use. To reduce image size in Photoshop, use the Image | Resize menu selection.

Soft edge

Figure 17-77: Softening the edge of Layer 3.

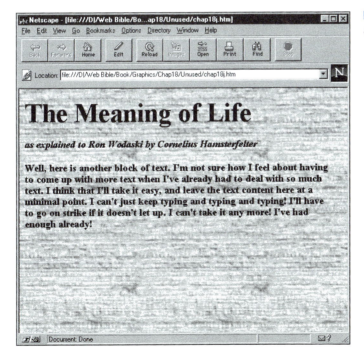

Figure 17-78: The image as a web page background.

Brightness and contrast are controlled with the Image | Adjust | Brightness and Contrast menu selection. For best results when blurring, use the Filter | Blur | Gaussian Blur menu selection. The blur dialog box allows you to change the degree of blur interactively.

Where to go from here:

✦ You can use this process to create background images out of almost any texture. Textures with small details, as shown in this tutorial, are the easiest to work with. If you work with less-detailed textures, you can use the Smudge tool to shove pixels around and join the various layers together. You may need to use the Layer | Flatten Image menu selection first, to put all the layers on a single layer. Otherwise, you won't be able to move pixels from layer to layer.

✦ Try working with the Airbrush tool instead of the Toning tool to soften the edges of layers.

✦ Create seamless tiles with a wide variety of images, just to see what results you can get. You can sometimes get especially interesting effects when working from scanned photographs that include a combination of objects and textures.

The Logic of Backgrounds

Throughout this chapter, I have described many different types of backgrounds. Now it's time to classify the images that are used to create backgrounds. While there are an infinite number of possibilities, most background images fall into easily identifiable groups.

Thin horizontal images

The thin horizontal type of image is often just a few pixels high, and repeats from the top to the bottom of the page. Figure 17-6 shows a typical thin horizontal image. When viewed on the page, this type of background image always creates a left-edge type of background. The width of the line must be greater than the typical width of a browser window to avoid duplication of the background. For most situations, a width of about 1,024 pixels is adequate.

Thin vertical images

Thin vertical images are often just a few pixels wide, and repeat from left to right across the page. Figure 17-9 shows a typical thin vertical image. When viewed on the page, this type of background image always creates a top-edge type of background. The height of the image must be larger than the likely page height of the user's browser. A height of 1,024 is a safe figure, but if you want to be *really* safe, use 1,200 pixels high. The larger height will work for folks who are using a $1,600 \times 1,200$ screen size.

Blocks

Blocks are small square or rectangular images that repeat in normal tile fashion on the page. The most common form is a seamless tile, but if you have the right image, seams can look good. This is the largest category of background images you will find on the Web. Sizes range from very small (such as 10×10 pixels) to very large (400×400 pixels and up).

With all of these background images, there are some interesting possibilities for interactions between the foreground and background. By definition, foreground images overlay background images. You can cover selected portions of the background to create interesting effects. Figure 17-2 shows one possibility.

Web Tour #17: Sources for Background Graphics

There are many web sites out there that offer interesting images you can use as backgrounds. Many of them offer free images. To visit sites with background images, double-click this file:

```
\WebTour\Chap17\index.htm
```

You'll see the Web Tour page for this chapter.

Site and Page Design

To prepare to follow along with this chapter, copy the following
folder from the CD-ROM to the \My Web Stuff folder on your
hard drive:

    \tutorial\chap18

This will copy files for this chapter to your hard disk. See Chapter 1
for complete details on setting up for tutorials.

In Chapter 8, you saw three web pages go from a pencil
sketch to a web page. But there is much more to web
design than sketching on napkins and throwing a page
together. Most web sites consist of many pages. In this
chapter, you will learn how to put the various pieces together
into a coherent whole. Navigation bars, hot graphics, image
maps, and other page elements can be combined into a
design that works across an entire web site.

You'll start by learning how to create a site design, and then
move on to creating pages that utilize the basic design.

Creating a Site Design

If there is one topic that is the easiest to identify and at the
same time the hardest to explain properly, it is site design.
Good site design is critical. The whole point of a web site is
to deliver information. If a visitor can't find that information
on your site, or can't navigate around your site to explore,
then your web site isn't getting the job done.

It's easy to identify a web site with poor design. After about a
minute at the site, you begin to experience a queasy feeling
in your stomach. Little irritations start to mount. You can't
find the stuff you are looking for. You try to explore, but you

keep coming back to the same pages. Eventually, you leave, and perhaps you never come back.

It's much harder to address these problems and come up with practical solutions. (You can find some ideas in Chapter 19, where I do some web page makeovers.) Organizing a web site is at least as much art as science; there isn't a fixed set of rules you can follow and Presto! you get a wonderful web site. The reality is that site design involves more trial and error than directness, more plodding progress than speedy resolution.

But do not despair! There are some guidelines you can live by and learn from. All is not lost. There are good web sites out there, and yours can be one of them.

The most basic principles of site design involve more than graphics. Graphics are just one element in the well-designed site, and graphics should always serve the greater good. A splashy graphic that confuses your visitors is more trouble than it is worth.

Principles of site design

To guide you in organizing your web site into a coherent whole, I have formulated some principles that sum up the basics of good site design. Let's take a break from all the pretty graphics and get down to some hard-core information. The next eight points can make or break your site design. I don't want to get all alarmist on you, but ignore them at your peril!

✦ *Examine every element of your site from one perspective, and one perspective only: that of the visitor to the site.* What is good for the visitor is good for the site. That which hinders the visitor, obscures necessary information, or introduces ambiguity is bad for the site.

✦ *The larger the site, the greater the need for clear, concise organization of information.* Organization applies at two levels: to the site as a whole, and for the individual page. For very large sites, there is a third level between these two: the collection of pages, or the subsite.

✦ *The page that loads quickly is better than the slow page.* This rule doesn't apply to every site, but it does apply to the vast majority of web sites. If you can't get your pages in front of the visitor quickly, the visitor leaves. It's as simple as that.

✦ *Don't provide distracting links on pages where the distraction isn't warranted.* It's fine to have a links page that is 98% links; it's not so fine to plow through text with every other word a hyperlink. Provide useful links, and pare out the useless ones.

✦ *Make sure you've got the right images.* That old saying a picture is worth a thousand words isn't exactly correct. The correct saying is the *right* picture is worth a thousand words. The wrong picture is just a waste of someone's download time. On the other hand, a little decoration can be a good thing if it's done tastefully. Don't eliminate every unnecessary graphic, or your pages will look sterile and uninviting. This is a perfect example of why it's hard to lay down exact rules for site design — finding the perfect balance between graphics and text is an art, not a science.

✦ *Know the purpose of every graphic so you can decide if the time it takes to download the graphic is justified.* Does the graphic have meaning on the page? If it is just decoration, is it a good and satisfying decoration? Does the graphic have a specific function — such as a link or a MAILTO? Knowing what the graphic is doing on the page will often result in recreating the graphic because you'll realize it's not doing its job effectively. This takes time, but your web pages will be better for the effort.

✦ *Check the organization of your site.* Find someone to cruise your web site before you publish it, and find out where the rough spots are. When all is said and done, how long does it take for a new visitor to understand how your web site is organized? You can't figure this out yourself, because you already *know* how it's organized.

✦ *Prototype your web site before you release it on an unsuspecting world.* To be good, the typical large web site needs to go through several cycles of revision. You can no more think of all aspects of using a web site than you can write a large computer program perfectly on your first try. This analogy is more apt than we like to think. Both are works in progress. Understanding this simple truth can save an awful lot of finger pointing when the web site is published. *Assume* your web site is full of holes, and you are much more likely to find them. Oh — don't forget to allow time for fixing the problems you find!

A web site is a living thing. A large web site is more like an ant colony. The larger the web site, the harder it is to control. A good site design will allow the site to grow and evolve without major headaches. You can't anticipate everything; there will be some headaches. All you can hope to do is minimize them.

There is nothing worse than a total redesign of a large web site. As hard as it is to work through three or four prototypes, it's nothing compared to shifting your entire web site to a new design.

If you want a short version of the above lecture to stick next to your monitor, here it is. Or cut it out and paste it on the inside of your glasses. Or just photocopy Figure 18-1 and tape it to your mirror.

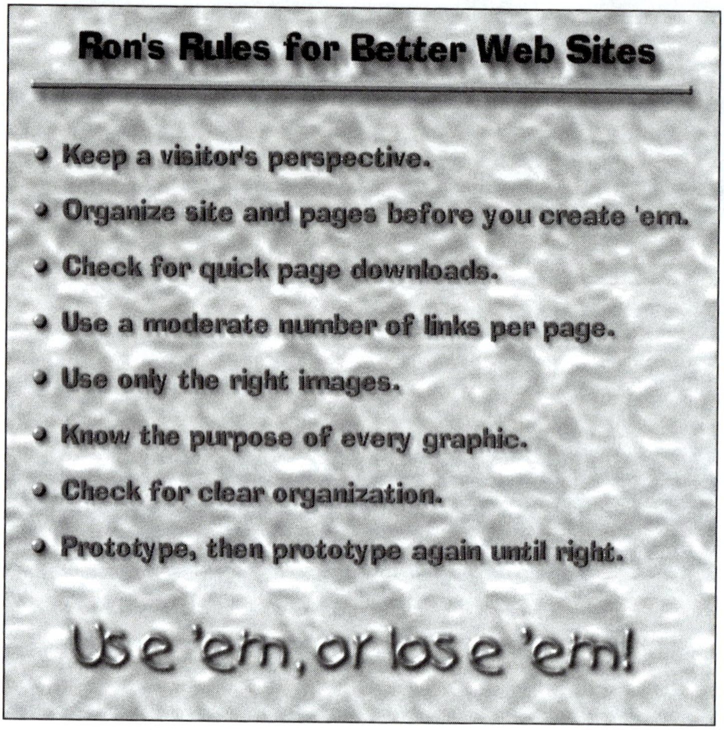

Ron's Rules for Better Web Sites

- Keep a visitor's perspective.
- Organize site and pages before you create 'em.
- Check for quick page downloads.
- Use a moderate number of links per page.
- Use only the right images.
- Know the purpose of every graphic.
- Check for clear organization.
- Prototype, then prototype again until right.

Use 'em, or lose 'em!

Figure 18-1: The rules for creating great web sites.

Design alternatives

There are alternatives to creating your own web site from scratch. There was a time when the only templates you were likely to find on the web were for single pages. At some point, these templates evolved to include multiple pages, but that wasn't the same thing as a template for an entire site design.

With the introduction of site-management products like FrontPage, Fusion, and others, however, the need for site templates grew exponentially. FrontPage 97, in particular, sets a new standard for the level of site design possible using templates. This is because FrontPage 97 allows third parties to create templates that dovetail right into FrontPage. This means that templates for everything from chat groups to web-based catalogs and shopping baskets are available right out of the box.

Even if you plan to explore site templates, I recommend reading all the way through this chapter on site design. There isn't a template anywhere that will meet all of your needs. Some degree of customization is nearly always required, and often rather more than less. The guidelines above, and the discussion that follows, can help you modify a template so that it does meet your needs.

Implementing a Design

I've broken site design and implementation into ten steps. Still, it's hard to separate design from implementation. Often, as you implement, you realize new things about the site and must change the design. Site design is best described as an iterative process. You create a prototype, you examine it for flaws, and then you change it and try again. My ten-step site planning process involves just two iterations (overall structure versions 1 and 2), but you may need more iterations depending on the complexity and sheer obtuseness of your site.

The ten steps are

1. Come up with a site concept.
2. Lay out the overall site structure.
3. Establish navigation requirements.
4. Identify major page types.
5. Design the navigation bar.
6. Create a generic page design.
7. Establish themes.
8. Refine the overall site structure.
9. Create a home page design.
10. Create major page designs.

There is an eleventh step that makes me shudder just to think about it. However, it's been proven over and over again, in study after study: To generate return traffic, your web site has to present new data. Otherwise there's no reason to come back. Allowing for the growth and change to meet this requirement is probably the toughest part of designing and maintaining a good web site. The eleventh step is

11. Revise existing content and add new content.

 If I had my way, every web site would have to pass muster with my own hand-picked corps of web site testers. If the site doesn't fly, they'll shoot it down and the designer can get back to the drawing board. The best way to generate web traffic isn't marketing your web site; it's creating a good web site in the first place. If you build it, they will come — but will they come back?

The following sections explore each of the ten steps in enough detail to either convert you to my system, drive you nuts with the implications of site design, or make you give up on web design entirely.

To give the discussion a focal point, imagine a nice little hypothetical company. The company is called MegaMany Computers, Inc. The company manufactures and sells giant computers that can out-compute anything else on the market. The company wants to create a web site that will give visitors access to all parts of the company, and that will take advantage of the Web to offer additional services, such as visitor feedback and interactive support.

Start with the site concept

The site must provide information about all divisions and operations of the company:

✦ Direct sales

- Desktop computers

- Laptop computers

- Accessories

- Third-party products

- Special offers, overstocks, refurbished computers, and so on

✦ Service for current owners

- Standard service contact info

- E-mail links to service, by product/division

✦ Product info, by product line

- Desktop computers

- Laptop computers

- Accessories

✦ Company contact information

The site will also make use of the Web to provide services that are not otherwise offered by the company:

✦ Interactive support

- Do-it-yourself support

- Feedback

- Threaded discussions

- Chat

✦ Links to related sites

✦ Updated driver downloads

✦ Upload area for customer bug reports

Because MegaMany Computers, Inc. is a forward-thinking company, it has decided to follow the short form of my rules for better web sites. Here's how they plan to implement the rules:

✦ **Keep a visitor's perspective**. The company is so large that it would not be possible to review every page with customers. Instead, the policy for page creation requires that pages get created in the field, with the emphasis on content. A new page (or even raw content) is sent to the newly formed MegaMany Web Division, where pages are completed by experienced web designers. Random pages are periodically tested with focus groups consisting of customers who are interviewed by the web designers to see how well the web pages work.

✦ **Organize the site and pages before creation.** The company followed a sound route by first putting up a simple web page announcing the future web site, and then setting aside a month to come up with the first site design.

✦ **Check for quick page downloads.** All pages are tested for time to download over standard 28.8 modem connections at various sites. The results are averaged, and stored in a database. Once a month, page download times are reviewed to catch any "bad" (too-large) pages.

✦ **Use a moderate number of links per page.** This is the hardest to enforce, since everyone seems to want a lot of links so their pages look nice and Webby. The MegaMany president has announced a 10% across-the-board cut in the number of links per page, which has the web staff up in arms. This is turning into a real problem, with the managers insisting on the cuts, and the staff screaming that a more sensible approach is needed.

✦ **Use only the right images.** The budget for graphics is minimal, so there is a lot of reuse of existing graphics. Unfortunately, there is inadequate training of the web staff for working with graphics, and there are plenty of too-large graphics and many improperly converted graphics. The too-large graphics will be caught as part of the check for quick page downloads (see earlier point), but the ugly graphics are going to be harder to fix. No one wants *his* graphics called ugly!

✦ **Know the purpose of every graphic.** Because of the effort required to convert existing graphics, there is a tendency to use graphics only when they are truly needed. The bottom line is that scant attention is being paid to this area. MegaMany isn't alone in that regard.

✦ **Check for clear organization.** MegaMany's strength shows here. Thanks to the month for planning, it looks like the overall site design will be a strong point. No web site has it all, and organization is probably more important than some of the other problem areas. The webmaster for the whole site, who is aware of the problem areas but powerless to make the necessary changes, plans to address the problem areas after the site is up and running. She realizes that this probably means higher overall costs for the web site, but it's politically expedient.

✦ **Prototype, then prototype again.** The month-long planning stage works very well for prototyping. The webmaster has broken the month down into two segments. The first segment is just shy of three weeks, and consists of a series of department meetings to identify the content that various departments can place on the Web. The second segment involves mostly the web staff, who will develop two alternate site organization plans, and then begin implementing the better of the two plans as soon thereafter as practical.

The next section describes the final site organizational plan to be developed by the webmaster.

Create an overall site structure

At the end of the month, the webmaster presented the two versions of the plan to the company's management committee. Being a smart webmaster, she knew which was the better plan and made sure that the committee understood which plan they should approve. Here's the plan she presented:

Company page

- ✦ Sales
  - Desktop computers
  - Laptop computers
  - Accessories
  - Threaded discussions
  - Live chat
- ✦ Product info
  - Desktop computers
  - Laptop computers
  - Accessories
  - Third-party sales
- ✦ MegaMany News
- ✦ Hot Products
- ✦ Support
  - Do-it-yourself interactive support
  - Driver downloads
  - E-mail to service department
  - Feedback

- ✦ Special offers
  - Special offers
  - Threaded discussions
  - Live chat
  - Links to related sites
- ✦ Contact info
  - Non-web contacts
  - Web contacts, with e-mail links (MAILTO)

Figure 18-2 shows a graphic representation of the plan. Later, when the site is up and running, a version of this graphic could be used as a site map, with hotspots to all the features of the site.

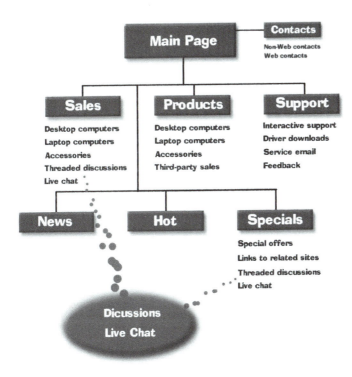

Figure 18-2: The MegaMany Computers site plan.

The site plan is similar to the original site concept, but key portions of the concept have been moved around, either so they fit better on a web site, or to satisfy the requirements of company politics. It's a good idea to realize that there will always be non-web-related reasons for particular aspects of any site design.

Important changes from concept to site design (and their reasons) include these:

✦ Third-party sales were moved out of the company sales area. This decision was one of the big wars of the planning phase. The sales team wanted to keep the third-party products close to the MegaMany products because they felt there was a sales synergy. The management types noted that the profit margin on third-party sales was so low as to be nearly meaningless. The management types won, and the third-party sales page was moved to the product info area of the site.

✦ As a result of the move of third-party products from Sales to Product info, a number of the third-party vendors stepped in and agreed to provide links to their own web sites, where MegaMany customers could purchase the third-party products. In some cases, the third-party vendors sell products that compete with MegaMany's products. Providing links to sites with competing products was one of the main reasons that the management types hated to sell the third-party products from the MegaMany Sales web pages.

 You may be squirming in your seat right now, asking what the heck all this has to do with site design. Welcome to the real world, where the prejudices and expectations of nontechnical folks can have major effects on site design.

✦ The MegaMany News and Hot Products sections were added to the main page. Some folks thought this was overloading the main page, while others felt that it was important to bring these things to the visitor's attention. Initially, the news section was offered as a lower-cost way to bring visitors back — the news would be changed daily or weekly. This was done to discourage spending money on the discussion and chat pages, but in the end *all* of them were approved. The result was a main page that is overcrowded, creating some serious problems for the web staff.

✦ The web staff was extremely successful in overcoming initial management resistance to threaded discussions and a chat section. At first, management staff felt that the cost to develop and maintain these features was prohibitive. Web staff eventually showed that such features are actually a low-cost way to constantly provide new and stimulating material on the site. In the end, the managers agreed not only to a chat section, but to *live* chat. The web staff is planning to add real-time audio and video services using the same arguments they advanced to get discussions and chat approved.

✦ Service was incorporated into Support. The top priority for support is the introduction of a system for interactive self-help. There is great hope that such a system will reduce the huge burden of support calls. A significant staff increase will be required to design, develop, install, and maintain the self-help support system, but the company expects to cut three telephone support persons for every self-help staff person hired. This will still be a major effort, and the group will also have programming and maintenance responsibilities for the threaded discussions and live chat features of the web site.

✦ Feedback and driver downloads were made part of the Support portion of the site. The logic for this was overwhelming enough to overcome initial management resistance. The only penalty paid by the web staff was that there was no permission for customers to upload to the web servers. Telephone and on-site support were viewed as lower-cost alternatives.

✦ Contact information was moved to the company's main page in the form of a link to a contact page. The contact page will include both standard and web contact info.

✦ The Special offers page has moved out of Sales and onto the company's main page. The cost per unit sale for overstocked items, refurbished computers, and other special offers was too high, and offering these over the web is an opportunity to cut those costs. To that end, the special offers will be featured at the top level of the site to see if it will stimulate sales. In addition, to help draw visitors to special offers, links to the threaded discussions and live chat are included here; note their "impressive" graphics.

Like most site plans, this one was the result of a mixture of web-related and politically motivated forces. The webmaster realizes it is a plan that the company and its workers can all live with, although there are some definite shortcomings from a webmaster's point of view. There is substantial initial development required beyond just graphics and content, thanks to the triple-threat of threaded discussions, live chat, and the self-help support system.

Specify navigation requirements

The webmaster managed to convince the company to add a navigation panel to every page. Initially, this will be done with a stack of graphic buttons at the left of the page, and eventually the webmaster hopes to use frames to isolate navigation so that the navigation panel is always visible and available.

There will be a single navigation bar, with four buttons:

✦ Sales

✦ Product info

✦ Discussion and Chat

✦ Do-it-yourself support system

The assumption is that these buttons will jump to the highest-level appropriate page, and the visitor can jump to specific pages within the section using links on that page. For example, if the visitor wants to get product information about desktop computers, the visitor clicks the Product button, jumps to the Product page, then clicks on Desktops, and then on a specific model.

Identify major page types

The page types come right out of the site plan:

✦ Main company page, a one-of-a-kind page

✦ Section pages: Sales, Products, Support, Special Offers, Contacts

✦ Within sections, subsection pages (desktops, laptops, do-it-yourself support, and so on)

✦ Special subsection pages for the high-profile "treats": Threaded Discussions and Live Chat

✦ Forms for placing orders (and probably a Java-based shopping basket system)

✦ Detailed pages at the bottom of the design hierarchy. Whenever possible, such pages will fit into the overall page design, but special-purpose pages, such as Feedback and Driver downloads, will have a unique look.

The main purpose behind identifying page types is to know what kinds of features are going to be needed on typical pages. This allows the page designers to identify common elements between pages.

Create a navigation bar

Given the simple nature of the navigation bar, and that blue and white are the company colors, the web design team developed the 3-D control shown in Figure 18-3. No sooner was the design tried out than it was discovered that users were unsatisfied with the large number of clicks required to get to a destination.

Figure 18-3: The initial navigation bar.

A new navigation bar was eventually designed, and is shown in Figure 18-4. The new navigation bar has more options, and allows visitors to go straight to their destination. It also has a more graphically refined look, and is probably a better solution for the MegaMany Computer company. After design review, the version in Figure 18-5 was adopted as the final navigation bar. However, the navigation bar is getting dangerously overloaded, and a second overhaul is probably not far off.

Figure 18-4: The revised navigation bar.

Figure 18-5: The revised revised navigation bar.

How, you may ask, did I create the navigation bar in Figure 18-4? I started in Fractal Design Painter, where I created blue boxes of appropriate height for buttons with none, two, or three secondary entries. I added the white boxes to the multi-entry buttons by selecting the background, floating, and filling it with white. I then added the text. Finally, I dropped all objects, and then used the Magic Wand to select just the blue stuff, which I floated. I then added a drop shadow offset by a small amount for the 3-D effect.

Create a generic page design

To kick off the process of generating a basic page design, the webmaster designed a prototype for the company's main page. Figure 18-6 shows her original sketch created on a napkin at a local diner.

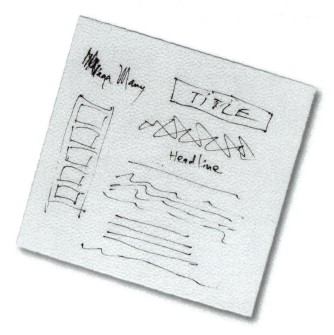

Figure 18-6: The original sketch for the MegaMany main page.

The basic elements of this page were retained in the design for the generic web page for the site. The next few figures show the building blocks that were available to create the page. Figure 18-7 shows the company logo. Figure 18-8 shows the template for the page title, which borrows on the design of the navigation bar (see Figure 18-4).

Figure 18-7: The company logo.

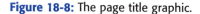

Figure 18-8: The page title graphic.

In actual use, the page title graphic gets a text title in the company font (Ad Lib), and a subgraphic if appropriate to the page. Figure 18-9 shows an example. Many pages probably will not have subgraphics, as they take time to create.

Figure 18-9: The page title graphic with title and subgraphic added.

Figure 18-10 shows the first version of the generic page. It includes the elements just described, and adds sample text content as a guide. You can view this file yourself by double-clicking the file \My Web Stuff\Chap18\chap18a.htm. The page layout is largely controlled using a table with invisible borders. The table's borders, when revealed as in Figure 18-11, show how the page layout is arranged. The file \My Web Stuff\Chap18\chap18b.htm shows the page with table borders visible.

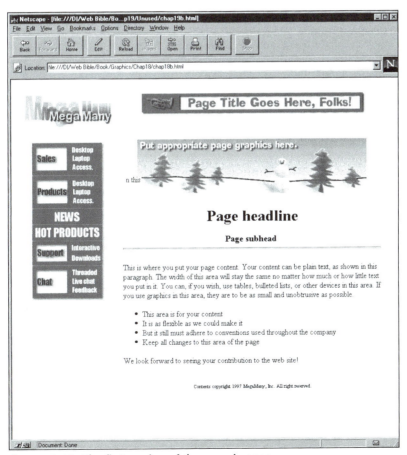

Figure 18-10: The first version of the generic page.

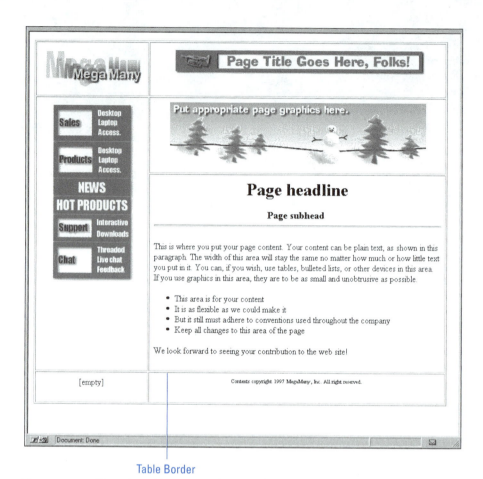

Table Border

Figure 18-11: How the table sets up the page layout.

After review, the team in charge of page design suggested that the navigation bar be moved further down the page — exactly even with the start of the page's content, and below the page graphic.

Figure 18-12 shows the revised page design (see the file \My Web Stuff\Chap18\chap18c.htm), and Figure 18-13 shows how a table is used to control placement of page elements (see the file \My Web Stuff\Chap18\chap18d.htm).

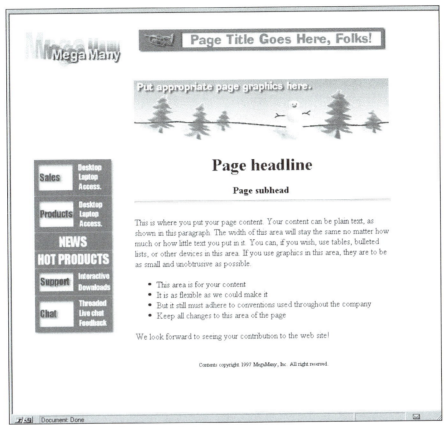

Figure 18-12: The revised page design.

Most of the web pages on the site will be built using the page in Figure 18-12 as a template. The page titles will vary, as will the page graphic and the page content, but the company logo, the form for the page title, and the navigation bar will be constant on the majority of pages.

Pages with a special purpose, or pages that require special features, will vary from this basic design. As much as possible, however, the site will keep the company logo at the top left, and the navigation bar on the left.

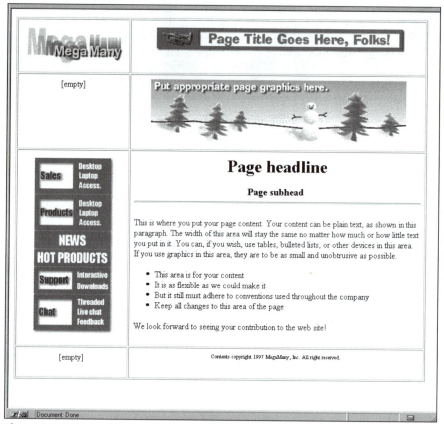

Figure 18-13: The table borders made visible to show page structure.

Review pages and determine themes

At this point in the process, it is time to take stock of the page designs and site design created so far. Some pages will have been built using the generic design, and they will look great. Some pages will bend the generic design to the breaking point, and some pages will be unique. Someone, usually a small design team of no more than two to four people, must then review these various pages to see what works and what doesn't.

Out of this review will come a fairly workable set of themes. Some of the themes are already clear — the company logo at the top left, the navigation bar on the left. Other themes might be more subtle. For example, the designer used a trumpet as the subgraphic on the generic page title. Musical instruments, or music itself, might become a web site theme.

Another possible theme could evolve from the drawing style of the snowman image. This example has a largely hand-drawn effect (although it was created in Fractal Design Painter with lots of non-freehand help!). This could become a standard "look" for page graphics. Other possible looks include

- ✦ Transparent icons with drop shadows
- ✦ Black-and-white line drawings
- ✦ Pencil drawings on crumpled Kraft paper, with drop shadows behind the scraps of paper

The possibilities are endless. By deciding on various themes, the pages take on a character and a life of their own. For many companies, it is important that the themes remain consistent with the character of the company.

Revisit the overall site design

Knowing when it's time to revisit the overall site design isn't critical; do it as often as you can. When you get a gut feeling that tells you something is wrong, don't forget to review the site design to see if it is limiting your implementation of individual pages.

On the other hand, the cost of making changes late in the cycle can be high. For example, if there are dozens of pages whose content takes it for granted that there will be a live chat page, removing live chat to save money may wind up actually costing time and money. Balancing the cost of revisions against the cost of not making those revisions is a decision that I can't make for anyone. But it is critical to know what works and what doesn't, so that when the opportunity presents itself for changes, you can take advantage of it.

In the case of MegaMany's web site, there has been ongoing discussion about whether the News page and the Contacts page will really be useful. In the case of the News page, there are those who feel that it will clutter up the main page and the navigation bar — not to mention the cost of creating and laying out the weekly news "broadcasts." And then there are those who feel that the company will benefit from updated news pages because they will draw repeating traffic. With no clear winner on either side of this debate, the News page is staying by default.

The Contacts page has proven to be a problem as originally conceived. The plan was to put the entire company phone directory on the Web. The phone system uses a computerized database of names and extensions, and the programming staff assured management that a program could be written to export the names and extensions to a series of indexed web pages. As it turns out, the cost to develop these programs will be ten times larger than the original estimate. As a result, the Contacts page will be retained, but it will be limited to department-level contacts, and it will be created monthly by hand.

Create the main page

You saw the webmaster's original design for the main page in Figure 18-6. At some point in the original development cycle, the actual page must be created so that the various departments and managers can hack at it and reduce it to the least common denominator of Design Hell.

 And if you don't think that this sort of thing goes on, I'm here to tell you that it goes on more often than you think! Just look at large corporate web pages. IBM's web page, while beautiful in many respects, is so crowded that it probably scares half of its visitors away.

As the design review process for the main page proceeds, the webmaster is probably wishing that the site map (back in Figure 18-2) could be used as the main page. Once the main page is nearly complete, it can be placed on the web server as a tease for visitors. Remember to stub out links — all links should point either to a blank version of the page that will eventually be there, or to a common blank page (with an appropriate name such as `temp.htm` or `blank.htm`).

Complete major page-type designs

The generic design mentioned earlier will work fine for many pages. But there will be special-purpose pages that cannot use that design, or that can only use part of that design. Now, as the planning process nears its end, is the time to nail down specifics of design for these pages.

At MegaMany, the webmaster has set a hard and early date for completion of page design for the live chat and threaded discussion pages. The primary reason for being so tough is that there is programming work required to implement these pages, and the programmers need to know what the pages are supposed to look like before they can write many of the programs. Even though page design will be complete, the graphics for the pages don't necessarily need to be completed. Simple temporary graphics will be used by the programmers until the final graphics are ready. Since the size of the graphics is known, and since size is the only issue relevant to the programming team, this leaves some freedom of scheduling for the graphic design team.

Other special-purpose pages, such as News and Contacts, have more flexible schedules but design still must be completed just prior to the end of the planning phase. At the end of the planning phase, pages will be assigned priority levels. High-priority pages will be completed first, and lower-priority pages later. This allows the site to go online without waiting for everything to be complete.

As the site goes online, it's very important to stub out missing pages. The same techniques mentioned earlier work best — either link stubs to a blank page with some text or graphic to indicate that it is a work in progress, or link to a standard temporary page.

Revise existing content and add new content

It's very easy to republish a web page. On the one hand, this allows you to put up a page fast and revise it or add to it later. On the other hand, you can wind up with too many half-done web pages that become a burden to any organization. It's a good idea to limit the number of in-progress web pages to a small fraction of the total number of web pages. Yes, this means that you are going to have to say no at times to requests for changes to web pages.

Where to Go from Here: Search Tools, Site Maps, and More

I've covered a lot of ground in a very short space, and I've focused on two aspects of web site development: graphics, and outside factors than can influence design and development. There are many features you can add to a web site beyond those I've covered in this example.

If the site is even moderately large, a search engine is a useful addition. Users can search your site for keywords, ideas, or concepts. Many of the major search engines, such as Excite at `http://www.excite.com`, provide smaller versions of their engines for use on a web site.

I made slight mention of a site map (see Figure 18-2), but site maps are becoming essential for medium to large web sites. The visitor sees only one page at a time, and having a convenient way to quickly get to the right spot is important. Avoid unnecessarily complex text-based site maps. Graphical site maps are easier to understand, even if they do not provide access to every single web page.

Software to visualize and manage your web site is also important. Products such as Fusion and FrontPage 97 allow you to see your web site at a glance, and are invaluable for maintaining a large web site. Such tools also assist with publishing your web pages. Anything that will automate publishing and maintenance is a good idea.

Web Tour #18: The Top Ten Interesting Web Sites

Web sites come and web sites go, but the best-organized ones tend to stick around. I've collected some of my favorites for you to visit. To see them, double-click the file

```
\WebTour\Chap18\index.htm
```

You'll see the Web Tour page for this chapter.

Web Page Make-Ups and Makeovers

> To prepare for this chapter's tutorials, copy the following folder from the CD-ROM to the `\My Web Stuff` folder on your hard drive:
>
> `\tutorial\chap19`
>
> This will copy files for all of the tutorials in this chapter to your hard disk. The contents of this chapter are split between the book and the CD-ROM; you are copying files for both the book and CD portions when you copy as instructed here. See Chapter 1 for complete details on setting up for tutorials.

Of all the web pages out there in this crazy Internet World of ours, there are more than a few that need some help. Uncle Webb would probably say that *every* web page needs some help, but some need more than others.

If you look at the history of human endeavor, one thing is obvious: The first version of everything is a mess. This is why writers re-write, and why artists sketch a subject until they are ready to paint it. This is why computer programmers test, test, and test before a piece of software leaves the factory door.

 I don't think you have it quite right. This is why computer programmers *should* test, test, and test. Has anyone noticed that computer software is worse than ever? Now they expect us to download bug fixes over the Web, allowing companies to ship software before it's finished. Hey, Mr. CEO, this is wonderful for your cash flow, but it sure beats the rest of us over the head. And while I'm up on my soapbox, yes indeed, there isn't a web page out there that couldn't be improved. If you see a web page that is simply awful, tell me about it. Send e-mail to unc@mmadweb.com.

Web pages are no different. The process of perfecting a web page is exactly that: a process. Whether you start with a sketch on a napkin, or create a draft web page with your favorite web page editor, the best way to create a great web page is to go through several iterations. It's easy to throw a web page together; anyone can do it. Creating a web page that really works, and that looks great doing it, is another matter. In a sense, every web page is the result of a makeover.

Tip   The best way to view a web page is online. To give you the best overview of how a web page makeover works, this brief chapter gives you a quick overview of one such makeover; it is intended to be used in conjunction with the Web Tour material on the CD.

Major Makeover

Sometimes you inherit a web page that needs to be revised, either because of new content or the design is no longer suitable. Figure 19-1 shows a web page in need of a makeover. This page has several problems that need to be solved:

- ✦ The background image is much too dominant.
- ✦ The background image doesn't tile very effectively; it collides with itself!
- ✦ Most of the text can't be read clearly.
- ✦ The logo at the top left has anti-aliasing problems (a white glow around it).
- ✦ The form elements at the bottom of the page are a confusing jumble.
- ✦ Overall, the page is hard to figure out: too much stuff.

The first problem I addressed was the background; it had to change if this page was to be readable. I tried lightening the background, blurring it, reducing contrast — but none of these efforts was quite enough. The background image was simply too aggressive. In desperation (I was determined to use the same background, if only to prove that it could be done!), I tried to create a pure black and white version of the image, using the Image | Adjust | Threshold menu selection (see Figure 19-2). Note that I had replaced the water in the foreground with a cloned version of the values in the middle of the image. The result wasn't yet useful, but after I applied a -92 contrast setting and a radius 3.1 Gaussian blur, there was finally some hope that I could use the image (see Figure 19-3).

Unfortunately, there was still too much contrast in the image. I had to start over. I used Image | Adjust | Posterize this time, using a value of 5, and converted to Grayscale (Image | Mode | Grayscale). I then used the Select | Color Range menu selection. In the dialog box that opened I set fuzziness to a value of 29 so that the edges of the selection would not be harsh and visible. I saved the initial selection, and then used Select | Color Range several more times until I had selected all of the high-contrast elements in the image (consisting mostly of the tower and the islands). Figure 19-4 shows the image after lightening. I later added a few touch-ups with the brush tool to show the suspension bridge elements more clearly.

Figure 19-1: A web page in need of a makeover.

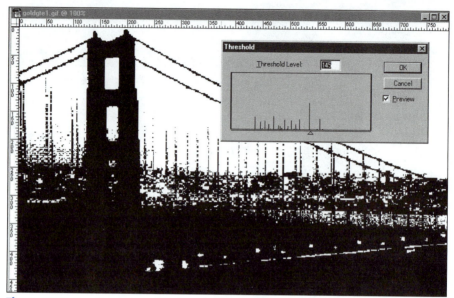

Figure 19-2: Creating a pure black and white version of the image.

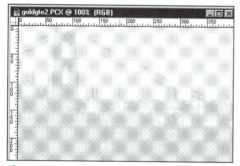

Figure 19-3: A light, fuzzy version of the image.

Unfortunately, there was still too much contrast in the image. I had to start over. I used Image ⏐ Adjust ⏐ Posterize this time, using a value of 5, and converted to Grayscale (Image ⏐ Mode ⏐ Grayscale). I then used the Select ⏐ Color Range menu selection. In the dialog box that opened I set fuzziness to a value of 29 so that the edges of the selection would not be harsh and visible. I saved the initial selection, and then used Select ⏐ Color Range several more times until I had selected all of the high-contrast elements in the image (consisting mostly of the tower and the islands). Figure 19-4 shows the image after lightening. I later added a few touchups with the brush tool to show the suspension bridge elements more clearly.

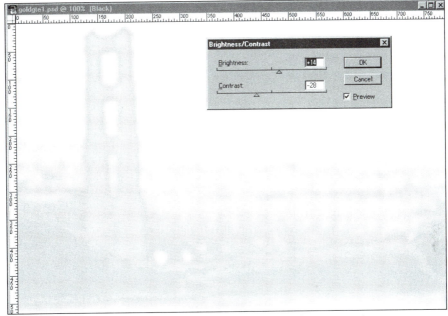

Figure 19-4: The entire image now has a similar value (low contrast).

The next issue I tackled was the logo and the central image of a building. I used new fonts for the logo, and added drop shadows. I placed a semi-transparent rectangle behind the logo, and added the logo to the building image at the upper left. Figure 19-5 shows my first attempt.

I added the logo at the upper left because it had been located at the upper left of the page in the original. However, it just didn't work in that location; the center of the overall image was uncertain – the eye tends to wander around. I moved the logo and backup rectangle to the bottom of the image (see Figure 19-6) where it works much better. The eye is now attracted to the logo instead of somewhere on the building.

Using normal text in the page layout doesn't cut it: the text is too wimpy to be effective. I created new headings and hotspot text in Photoshop, and placed those on the page (see Figure 19-7).

Figure 19-5: The revised logo and image.

Figure 19-6: The final version.

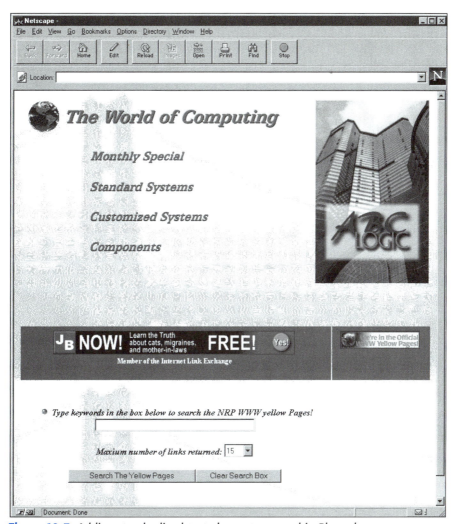

Figure 19-7: Adding standardized text elements created in Photoshop.

The page is better, but it's still not right. I added a table to the page to try to control the placement of individual elements. I added a background color to one cell of the table to try to bring the form elements at the bottom of the page into some kind of order. But this was barely adequate. The best solution would be to hire a programmer to develop a Java applet that would display the various required graphic elements and text in a more arranged (and somewhat more compact) manner. Figure 19-8 shows how such a Java applet might look. Figure 19-8 was also my final redesign of the page. The elements are now in reasonable balance. I'm not convinced the page is perfect, but it's much better than it was, and it still uses most of the original design elements. Each element has been modified in some way to bring everything into close harmony.

Figure 19-8: Using a Java applet to really organize the page.

It's easy to criticize, Mr. Author. How about showing us this wonderful web page process you talked about earlier — using some of your own pages? Have you got the guts?

Looks like you've sunk to a new low, Unc. Of course I have the guts! But let's step over to the CD-ROM, where I can parade my efforts in full color. Check out the Web Tour for this chapter, where I'll demonstrate how even a weak beginning can lead to a web page that works well.

Web Tour #19: Web Page Makeovers

I have included a two-part Web Tour for this chapter, thanks in part to Uncle Webb's cranky suggestion.

Web Tour, Part 1: Want to see how I create a web page, through several iterations? Double-click the file:

```
\WebTour\Chap19\makeover\extra.htm
```

You'll find a web page with detailed, step-by-step coverage of a web page I created for a small business.

Web Tour, Part 2: Want to try your hand at improving web pages? I've scoured the Web to find pages that need help. To visit pages that you can practice on, double-click the file:

```
\WebTour\Chap19\index.htm
```

You'll see the Web Tour page for this chapter.

Tables + Graphics = Hot Pages

CHAPTER

20

To prepare for this chapter, copy the following folder from the CD-ROM to the \My Web Stuff folder on your hard drive:

```
\tutorial\chap20
```

This will copy files and subfolders for all of the tutorials in this chapter to your hard disk. See Chapter 1 for complete details on setting up for tutorials.

I f there is one thing about web pages that has both everything and nothing to do with graphics, it is tables. On the one hand, tables are the most powerful layout tool available when you are creating a web page. On the other hand, what could be more innocuous than a simple table?

The reason for this apparent disparity is that HTML, the language used to specify web pages, is actually very primitive. There are many things you can do in a word processor that you cannot do on a web page — add footnotes, annotations, or tabs; make precise paragraph indents; or flow text around images, to name a few things.

You can approximate some of these missing features using tables. The regimented nature of tables (I'm talking about rows and columns here) lends itself to bringing order to the otherwise chaotic web page.

That chaos comes from the simplicity of HTML. HTML was originally conceived of as an extremely simpleminded way to describe the contents of a page. On this fragile foundation, we have communally built a huge office building. This chapter is about ways you can cope with the mess that results from adding features to a once-simple design. They call it feature creep, and today's browsers are ready to break under the strain.

Hold your horses, Uncle. The *real* problem stems from the very nature of the web page. Try changing the window size of your typical web browser — the web page is realigned to fit the new window width. This is called flexibility. It's a far more important factor than the original simplicity of HTML. HTML has grown with the times, but great page layout and flexibility don't fit easily together. Tables can take away some, even most, of that flexibility and put it into the hands of the page designer. *That's* what this chapter is about.

Using Transparent Images and Tables

When I introduced the subject of image transparency in Chapter 13, "Interlacing and Transparency," the primary use of transparency was to make the background of an image disappear. In this section, you will learn that you can gain a lot of control over page design by using images that disappear completely. You can't simply position a graphic at a specific place on a web page. You have to use tricks to accomplish this feat.

 This situation of not being able to place a graphic at a specific place on the web page will probably change when the next generation of browsers is introduced. It will take some time, probably well into 1998, before any important graphics changes percolate through to the majority of web browsers.

You heard me right: By making an image completely invisible, you can get some real use out of it. The invisible image occupies space on the page. You can use it to push other elements of the page — other images, or some text — into the exact position you require.

These invisible images are often referred to as *spacers*. To create a spacer, simply create an image that is wide enough or high enough to do the job. For example, if you have a background image that occupies the left page margin, you can use a spacer and a table to keep all of the text away from the left margin. Create a new image that is one pixel high, and a bit wider than the background image's left margin. For example, if the background image will occupy 60 pixels at the left edge of the page, a spacer 70 or 80 pixels wide will do the job. The exact size depends on the situation and your preferences. Figure 20-1 shows a typical spacer image in Photoshop. It's just one pixel high, and 80 pixels wide. I created the image as a 24-bit image (an RGB image, in Photoshop lingo) so I could control the palette used for the image. Convert the image to 8-bit color using the Web safety palette (see Figure 20-2 to see how to do it in Photoshop with the Image | Mode | Indexed Color menu selection). (See Chapter 11, "File Formats and Bit Depths," for detailed information about 8-bit palettes.)

Figure 20-1: An image that works well as a spacer.

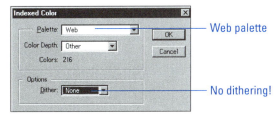

Figure 20-2: Setting the Web safety palette.

Caution!

Do not use dithering when converting to the safety palette. This will protect you from problems that arise if the background of the spacer image isn't already one of the safety palette colors. If the background color isn't a safe color, you could wind up with two or more colors in a dithered pattern. You want only one color because you can make only one color transparent.

To save the image as a GIF file in Photoshop, use the File | Export | GIF89a menu selection to display the dialog box shown in Figure 20-3. Click anywhere in the image to select its one and only color as the transparent color. Click OK, and then supply a filename in the Export GIF89a dialog box.

To use the spacer on a web page, create a two-column, one-row table. Put all of the page's content in the rightmost cell, and add the spacer image to the leftmost cell. The spacer image pushes the contents of the rightmost cell away from the page edge, as shown in Figure 20-4.

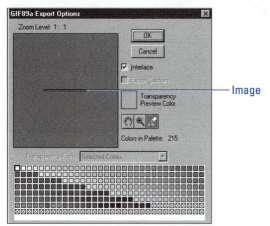

Figure 20-3: Use this dialog box to make the image transparent.

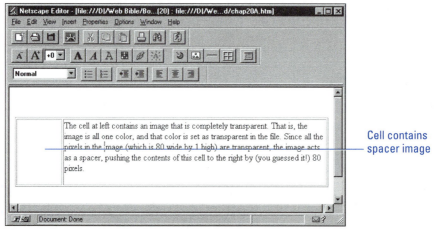

Figure 20-4: Using the spacer image and a table to move page contents away from the page border.

Strictly speaking, you could set the width of the leftmost cell to force the page content away from the left edge. In fact, if you look at how tables are supposed to work, this is by far the easiest way to accomplish the task. The reality is that different browsers interpret the cell width differently, and you can never be sure that your page will display correctly under all conditions in all browsers. A spacer image, on the other hand, provides almost exactly the same spacing every time, and is therefore a better choice for the serious page artist.

Figure 20-5 shows a web page with the background graphic added, and the table border set to zero. The table and the spacer image invisibly force the page content to stay away from the page border image.

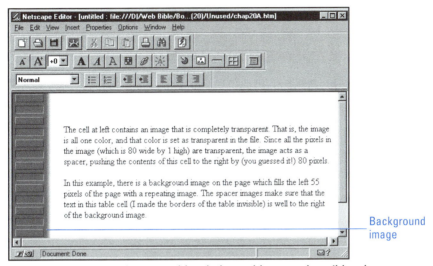

Figure 20-5: A spacer image and borderless table tame the wild web page.

Figure 20-6 is almost identical to Figure 20-5, but I clicked the spacer image to highlight it so you can see that it really and truly is doing its job.

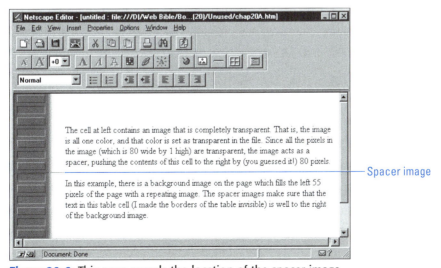

Figure 20-6: This page reveals the location of the spacer image.

Figure 20-7 shows how I created the page background in Photoshop. I set a guide at 80 pixels while creating the background image so that none of the non-white pixels would come close to the width of the spacer image. I created the background using a gradient between purple and white, and added the 3-D effects using overlapping rectangles and color variations. You can look at my handiwork on the web page \My Web Stuff\chap20\chap20A.htm.

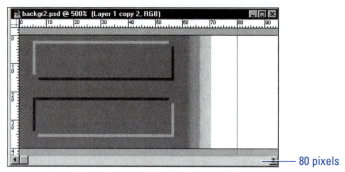

— 80 pixels

Figure 20-7: How I created the background image.

You can also use spacer images to move a single line of text away from its natural left margin. Figure 20-8 shows a much smaller spacer image, and Figure 20-9 shows the spacer image at work on a web page to create a precise indent for three paragraphs. The spacer image is made visible next to the third indented line so you can see its size and location.

— Image

Figure 20-8: A smaller spacer image.

Tip

You can use a spacer image to move text away from the right margin, too. A table cell will work to keep an entire page of content away from the right margin, and you can use spacer images to keep right-aligned text away from the right margin.

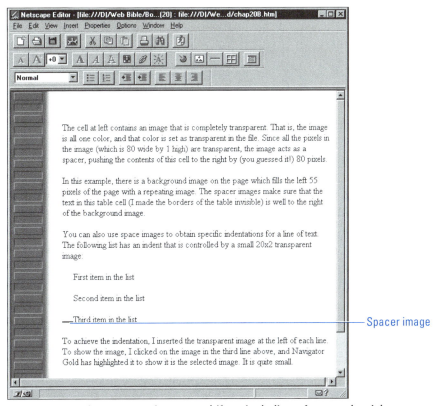

Figure 20-9: Using a spacer image to shift a single line of text to the right.

Setting Column and Row Spanning

Figure 20-10 shows a newly created table (the editor is Netscape Navigator Gold). Every row in the table has the same number of cells. You can also create tables that have different numbers of cells per row, and/or tables with different numbers of cells in each column. The usual procedure in most web page editors is to delete specific cells, and to extend the size of remaining cells using column and row spanning.

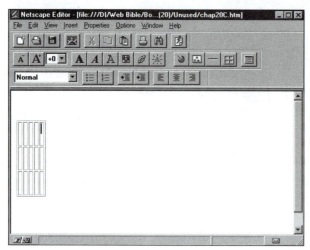

Figure 20-10: An empty table on a web page.

Column span refers to the number of columns that a cell crosses. The row with the largest number of cells in it (including cells from other columns that span across the largest column) determines the number of cells spanned.

Row span refers to the number of rows that a cell crosses. The column with the largest number of cells in it (including cells from other rows that span across the largest row) determines the number of cells spanned.

That's all theory, however; building a table that uses column and row spanning will make this much clearer. The following example uses Netscape's Navigator Gold as the web page editor, but any editor that supports tables will work just as well. If you want to follow along, create a table with three rows and five columns in the editor of your choice.

The first step in the process is to create a layout of the final appearance of the table. Figure 20-11 shows my sketch for how the table should look. Each row has five cells across. By deleting the appropriate number of cells in each row, and then setting column and row spanning for the remaining cells, the table will look like Figure 20-11.

The final design calls for just two cells in row one, so delete three cells. In Navigator Gold, the easiest way to delete a cell is to right-click the cell, and choose the Delete I Cell menu selection (see Figure 20-12). As you delete cells, your web page editor will adjust the appearance of the table. Most editors show the missing cells as filled-in cells at the right edge of the row (see Figure 20-13).

Figure 20-11: A design for a table.

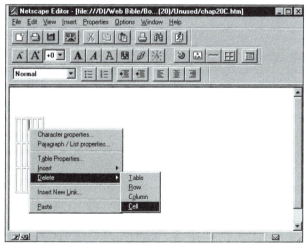

Figure 20-12: Deleting a cell in a table.

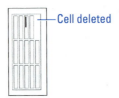

Figure 20-13: One cell
in the top row has
been deleted.

Delete two more cells from the top row. Click the rightmost remaining cell in the top row (see Figure 20-14) and right-click the Properties menu selection to display the Table Properties dialog box (see Figure 20-15). Click the Cell tab if it is not already active. Set the column span for this cell to 4 and click OK.

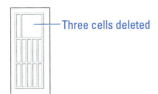

Figure 20-14: Three cells
have been removed from
the top row.

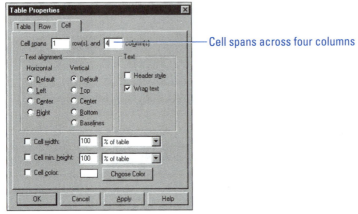

Figure 20-15: Setting column span
for a cell in Navigator Gold.

The table design calls for five cells in the middle row. However, one of those cells is actually the leftmost cell in the top row, which will span all three rows. Delete one cell in the middle row (but don't change any cell's properties), and delete three cells in the bottom row. Right-click the leftmost cell in the bottom row and display the Table Properties dialog box. Set the column span to 3 and click OK.

The table looks a little funky at this point (see Figure 20-16); two rows are "missing" a cell. To correct the appearance of the table, set the row span for the left cell in the top row to 3 (see Figure 20-17). Figure 20-18 shows the appearance of the table.

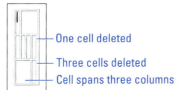

— One cell deleted

— Three cells deleted

— Cell spans three columns

Figure 20-16: The table after cells are deleted and column spanning is set, but before row span has been set.

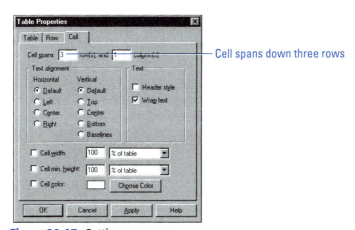

— Cell spans down three rows

Figure 20-17: Setting row span.

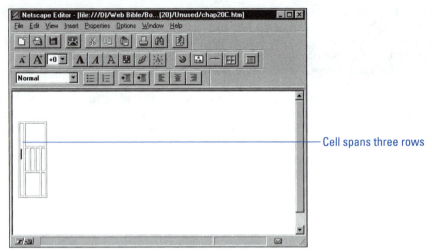

Figure 20-18: The table layout completed.

Of course, this is just an empty table. To see how you can use this kind of table to control page layout (including both text and graphics), follow the steps below. This example uses Navigator Gold; your editor may require slightly different steps.

1. Right-click the leftmost cell (the one that spans three rows) and use the Table Properties menu selection to display the cell's properties.

2. Set Text Alignment | Vertical to Top, then click OK.

3. Position the cursor in the same cell, and insert the image file `\My Web Stuff\chap20\logo1.jpg`.

4. Press Enter to create a new line. Insert the image file `\My Web Stuff\chap20\btns1.jpg`.

   Figure 20-19 shows how the web page should look. Note that the images created for this cell are very narrow. This is necessary to fit the overall page design. Wider images would stretch the width of the page too far. If you are using a different web page editor, the exact appearance of the page may be a little different.

5. Position the cursor in the rightmost cell in the top row.

6. Insert the image file `\My Web Stuff\chap20\banner1.jpg`.

   Note that this image is very wide, but not very tall. The image defines the width of the overall table. Optionally, you could set the width of the cell to match the width of the image to gain tighter control.

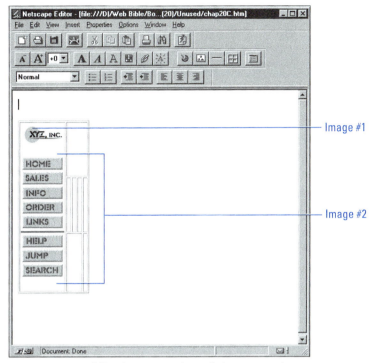

Figure 20-19: Adding images to the cell that spans three rows.

7. Set the width of the three middle cells in the middle row to 100 pixels each.

8. Position the cursor in the rightmost cell in the middle row. Insert the image file `\My Web Stuff\chap20\text1.jpg`.

9. Position the cursor in the rightmost cell in the bottom row. Insert the image file `\My Web Stuff\chap20\text2.jpg`.

10. Add text to the three middle cells in the middle row as shown in Figure 20-20.

11. Apply font+1, bold, and italic formatting to the headline portion of the text, and font-1 to the rest of the text.

12. Set paragraph alignment to Center.

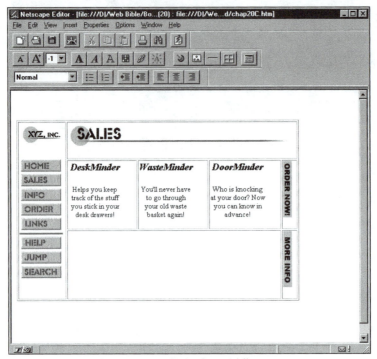

Figure 20-20: Adding text to cells in the middle row.

There is still one cell in the table that has no contents. I added a form to the cell, as shown in Figure 20-21. This view of the page is in Navigator Gold's Edit mode, showing the form as it would look on the Web. As you can see, the form elements are spread out in different directions. In a word, the form looks terrible.

There are two ways to fix the form. The old-fashioned method is to apply the PREFORMATTED style to the entire block of text, and to use spaces to make everything line up. This will work, but it also changes the text to a Courier font. This is an inelegant solution. A better solution is to create a table within a table.

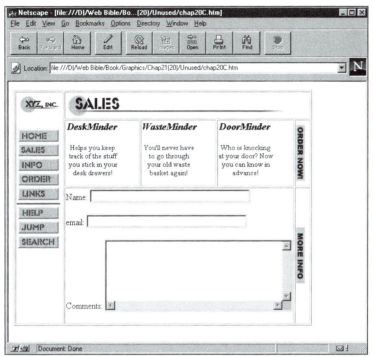

Figure 20-21: Putting a form in the middle cell of the bottom row completes the page.

Using Nested Tables and Complex Tables

By moving each of the form elements into separate table cells, you can line them up easily. Figure 20-22 shows the form in Navigator Gold (this time, back in Edit mode). The little yellow tags indicate the form elements. I created a two-column, three-row table. I put the text elements (Name, email, and Comments) in the left column and the form elements in the right column.

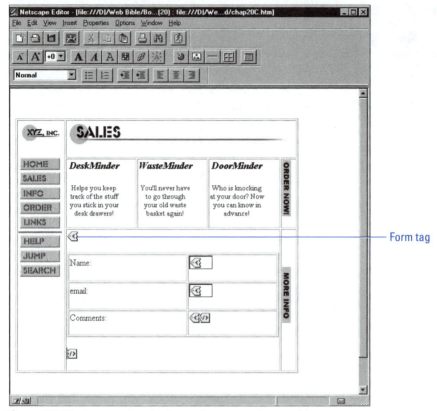

Figure 20-22: Rearranging the form elements using a table.

When viewed in Browse mode (see Figure 20-23), the form elements line up perfectly.

As you can see in Figure 20-23, everything on the web page lines up, not just the form elements. Unfortunately, with all those table borders, the page *still* looks terrible. The next step is to make the table borders invisible.

In Navigator Gold, you can set table properties by right-clicking the table to display the Table Properties menu selection. Set the borders of both tables to zero. Figure 20-24 shows the result. Note that I made a change to one of the graphic images. I added more orange to the MORE INFO graphic so that it lines up better with the form elements. The alignment between the graphic and form elements isn't perfect, but I'll address that shortly.

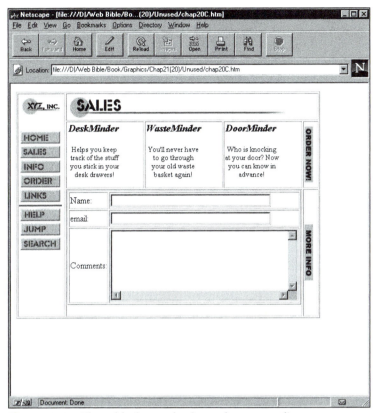

Figure 20-23: The table forces the form elements to line up.

The main point is that by setting table borders to zero, you can use tables (or tables within tables (or tables within tables within tables)) to gain a tremendous amount of control over page layout. For an extreme example of this technique, try building a web page with Adobe's PageMaker 6.5. PageMaker is a desktop publishing program that now also creates web pages. I created a simple web page in PageMaker (see Figure 20-25). I purposely mingled text and graphics in ways that I knew would be hard to translate to a web page.

I then output the page as a web page, using the HTML publishing tools built into PageMaker 6.5 (see Figure 20-26). PageMaker gives you clear options for converting PageMaker styles into web-legal styles (see Figure 20-27). The dialog box shown in Figure 20-27 also allows you to control output of graphics; PageMaker will convert all images to GIF, JPEG, or decide on its own which format to convert to.

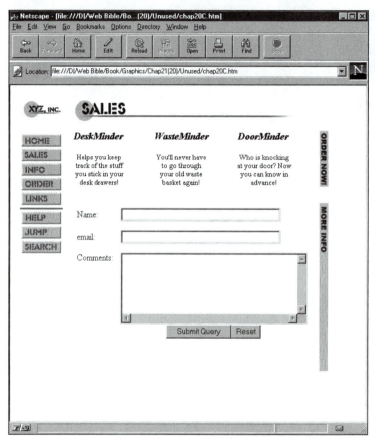

Figure 20-24: Removing the borders reveals the page in all its glory.

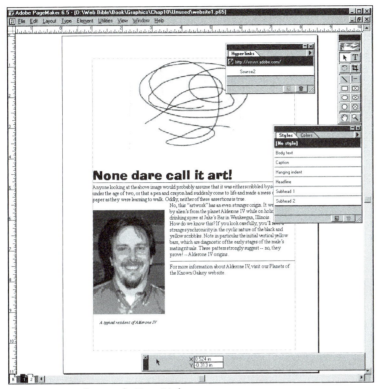

Figure 20-25: A page in PageMaker.

Output text, images,
and layout

Output text only

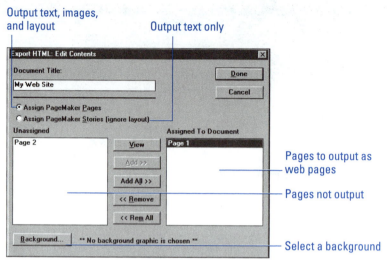

Figure 20-26: Determining which pages to output as web pages.

Pages to output as
web pages

Pages not output

Select a background

Tip

In PageMaker, to keep image file sizes small, be sure to check the Downsample to 72 dpi check box. This converts the high-resolution images typically used for desktop publishing into smaller images appropriate for a web page.

Use table for layout

Page width in pixels

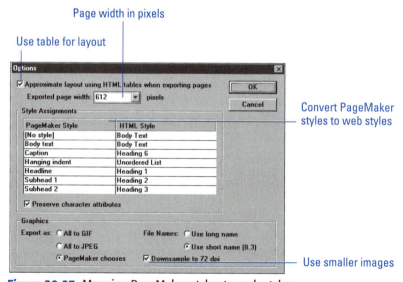

Convert PageMaker
styles to web styles

Use smaller images

Figure 20-27: Mapping PageMaker styles to web styles.

Figure 20-28 shows the web page that PageMaker generated. It is reasonably similar to the original shown in Figure 20-25. Figure 20-29 shows the same page with table borders turned on — PageMaker performs its tricks with some *very* fancy cell work in a table.

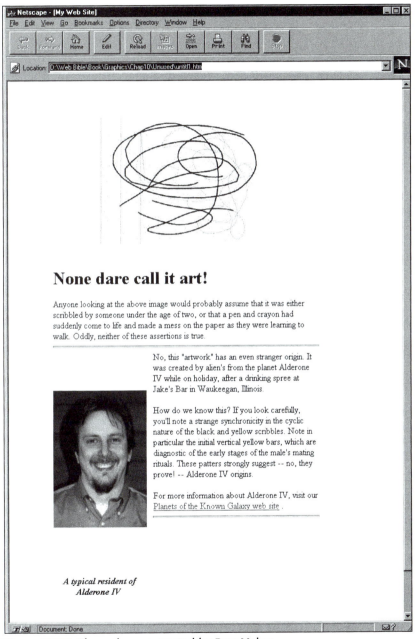

Figure 20-28: The web page created by PageMaker.

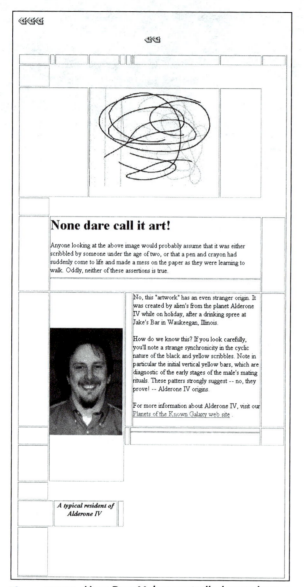

Figure 20-29: How PageMaker controlled page layout.

For serious page design (or, for that matter, seriously frivolous page design), you can't beat the control and leverage that tables give you. If you create enough table cells, you can create great pages.

Creating Colorful Tables

Earlier, I pointed out that the alignment of a graphic and the form elements (see Figure 20-24) wasn't quite right. The graphic extended below the form elements, giving the bottom of the page a ragged and unprofessional appearance.

One solution is to add color to the table cell that contains the table that contains the form elements. In Navigator Gold, cell color is just one more table property that you can set, and most other page editors also allow you to set the color of table cells. Figure 20-30 shows the page with color added to the cell. Now the MORE INFO image and the cell match up perfectly.

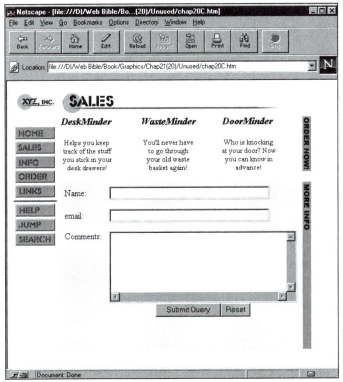

Figure 20-30: Adding color to the form cell restores balance to the page.

Some browsers, most notably Microsoft Internet Explorer, also support background images for individual table cells. You could apply a texture to the cell instead of just a single color if you knew that the majority of your users would be viewing the page with Internet Explorer. Look for other browsers to support this feature soon.

You can also use multiple colors in a table, or different colors in nested tables, to create areas of color on the web page. This can be an effective design tool, but it is also easy to overdo it. Follow the same rules for background colors for tables and table cells as for page backgrounds: Make sure you can still read the text, and that the colors are compatible with the graphics used on the page. To see the actual color in the final version of this web page, look at the file \My Web Stuff\chap20\chap20c.htm.

Under the Table: Table Secrets

In addition to the table tricks I've already shown you in this chapter, there are more table options provided in HTML, the language of web pages. The next generation of web page editors will no doubt support these HTML features directly. If you are interested in using the most advanced table features right away, you can learn how to use HTML to create unique table designs. You can add and edit HTML in your web pages either by using a web page editor that supports direct HTML editing, or by opening your web pages in a generic text editor such as Notepad.

In this section, you'll learn the newest and most useful table HTML tags and how to use them to control the appearance and layout of tables on a web page.

In this section, the following shorthand notations are used:

<URL>	This refers to any valid URL, including local filenames/ pathnames, HTTP and FTP, and so on. For example, http://www.mmadweb.com/index.htm.
"#RRGGBB"	This refers to a hex representation of a color using red, green, and blue numeric values. For example, red is specified as #FF0000, and #777777 is a neutral gray.
Number	This refers to any valid number, with enclosing double quotes optional. For example, WIDTH=50 shows usage without quotes, and WIDTH="50" shows usage with quotes. Generally, you don't need quotes for a number, but when in doubt, use quotes.

TABLE parameters

Table parameters are used with the <TABLE>, <TH>, <TR>, and <TD> tags. These parameters are described and illustrated in the following sections.

ALIGN

Options: LEFT, RIGHT

Description: Used to set text alignment. LEFT is the default alignment for the `<TABLE>`, `<TR>`, and `<TD>` tags. The default for the `<TH>` tag is center aligned (see Figure 20-31).

HTML example (`\My Web Stuff\Chap20\chap20D.htm`):

```
<TABLE ALIGN=RIGHT BORDER=1>
<TR><TH>Column Header #1</TH>
<TH>Column Header #2</TH></TR>
<TR><TD ALIGN=RIGHT>Cell one</TD>
<TD ALIGN=RIGHT>Cell two</TD></TR>
</TABLE>
```

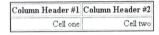

Figure 20-31: The Table ALIGN parameter.

BACKGROUND

Options: "<URL>"

Description: Applies a background image to a table or cell (see Figure 20-32)

HTML example (`\My Web Stuff\Chap20\chap20E.htm`):

```
<TABLE ALIGN=RIGHT BORDER=1 BACKGROUND=bg1.jpg>
<TR><TD><B>Cell one</B></TD>
<TD><B>Cell two</B></TD></TR>
<TR><TD ALIGN=RIGHT><B>Cell three</B></TD>
<TD ALIGN=RIGHT BACKGROUND=bg2.jpg>
<FONT COLOR="#FFFFFF"><B>Cell four</B></FONT></TD></TR>
</TABLE>
```

Figure 20-32: The Table BACKGROUND parameter.

BGCOLOR

Options: "#RRGGBB" or the name of a color

Description: Sets the background color of a table or cell (Figure 20-33)

HTML example (\My Web Stuff\Chap20\chap20F.htm):

```
<TABLE ALIGN=RIGHT BORDER=1 BGCOLOR="#0080FF">
<TR><TD BGCOLOR="#FFFF80"><B>Cell one</B></TD>
<TD><B>Cell two</B></TD></TR>
<TR><TD ALIGN=RIGHT><B>Cell three</B></TD>
<TD ALIGN=RIGHT BGCOLOR="#804040">
<B><FONT COLOR="#FFFFFF">Cell four</FONT></B></TD></TR>
</TABLE>
```

Figure 20-33: The Table BGCOLOR parameter.

BORDERCOLOR

Options: "#RRGGBB" or the name of a color

Description: Sets the color of a table border. Otherwise, the default border color is derived from the background color. Only applies when the table BORDER is 1 or larger (Figure 20-34).

HTML example (\My Web Stuff\Chap20\chap20G.htm):

```
<TABLE BORDER=4 BORDERCOLOR="#115540">
<TR><TD>Cell one</TD>
<TD>Cell two</TD></TR>
<TR><TD >Cell three</TD>
<TD>Cell four</TD></TR>
</TABLE>
```

Figure 20-34: The Table BORDERCOLOR parameter.

BORDERCOLORLIGHT / BORDERCOLORDARK

Options: "#RRGGBB" or the name of a color

Description: The table border consists of two colors: a light highlight, and a dark shadow. You can use the BORDERCOLORLIGHT and BORDERCOLORDARK parameters to set these colors independently. Otherwise, light and dark variations of the BORDERCOLOR are used to determine the border colors (Figure 20-35).

HTML example (\My Web Stuff\Chap20\chap20H.htm):

```
<TABLE BORDER=4 BORDERCOLORDARK="#115540"
       BORDERCOLORLIGHT="#61b5a0">
<TR><TD>Cell one</TD>
<TD>Cell two</TD></TR>
<TR><TD >Cell three</TD>
<TD>Cell four</TD></TR>
</TABLE>
```

Figure 20-35: The Table BORDERCOLORLIGHT and BORDERCOLORDARK parameters.

VALIGN

Options: TOP, BOTTOM

Description: Specifies top or bottom text alignment within a table or cell. Default alignment is the center of the cell (Figure 20-36).

HTML example (\My Web Stuff\Chap20\chap20I.htm):

```
<TABLE BORDER=1>
<TR><TD>Cell one<BR>is right here.</TD>
<TD VALIGN=BOTTOM>Cell two</TD></TR>
<TR><TD >Cell three<BR>is this one.</TD>
<TD VALIGN=TOP>Cell four</TD></TR>
</TABLE>
```

Figure 20-36: The Table VALIGN parameter.

CAPTION parameters

The <CAPTION> tag is used in a table to define a caption for the table. The parameters of the <CAPTION> tag are described and illustrated in this section.

ALIGN

Options: LEFT, RIGHT, CENTER

Description: Sets the horizontal text alignment of a caption (Figure 20-37)

HTML example (\My Web Stuff\Chap20\chap20J.htm):

```
<TABLE BORDER=1>
<CAPTION ALIGN=CENTER>This is the table caption.
<TR><TD>Cell one is right where it should be.</TD>
<TD>Cell two is to the right of cell one.</TD></TR>
<TR><TD >Cell three is here; it has few pretensions.</TD>
<TD>Cell four showed up under protest.</TD></TR>
</TABLE>
```

This is the table caption.	
Cell one is right where it should be.	Cell two is to the right of cell one.
Cell three is here; it has few pretensions.	Cell four showed up under protest.

Figure 20-37: The Caption ALIGN parameter.

VALIGN

Options: TOP, BOTTOM

Description: Specifies whether the table caption appears above or below a table (Figure 20-38)

HTML example (\My Web Stuff\Chap20\chap20K.htm):

```
<TABLE BORDER=1>
<CAPTION ALIGN=LEFT VALIGN=BOTTOM>This is the table caption.
<TR><TD>Cell one is right where it should be.</TD>
<TD>Cell two is to the right of cell one.</TD></TR>
<TR><TD >Cell three is here; it has few pretensions.</TD>
<TD>Cell four showed up under protest.</TD></TR>
</TABLE>
```

Cell one is right where it should be.	Cell two is to the right of cell one.
Cell three is here; it has few pretensions.	Cell four showed up under protest.
This is the table caption.	

Figure 20-38: The Caption VALIGN parameter.

HTML 3.2 TABLE parameters

These are parameters that are only suitable for use with browsers that support the HTML 3.2 standard.

THEAD, TBODY, TFOOT

Options: None

Description: THEAD defines groups of rows in a table. Other row-oriented groups are TBODY and TFOOT. You can set the properties of a group, and the properties apply to all rows in the group. See also COLGROUP, which defines groups of columns in a table (Figure 20-39).

HTML example (\My Web Stuff\Chap20\chap20L.htm):

```
<TABLE BORDER=1>
<THEAD>This is the header section of the table.
<TR><TD>Cell one, header section.</TD>
<TD> Cell two, header section.</TD></TR>
<TR><TD> Cell three, header section.</TD>
<TD> Cell four, header section.</TD></TR>
</THEAD>
<TBODY>This is the body section of the table.
<TR><TD>Cell one, body section.</TD>
<TD> Cell two, body section.</TD></TR>
<TR><TD> Cell three, body section.</TD>
<TD> Cell four, body section.</TD></TR>
</TBODY>
<TFOOT>This is the foot section of the table.
<TR><TD>Cell one, foot section.</TD>
<TD> Cell two, foot section.</TD></TR>
<TR><TD> Cell three, foot section.</TD>
<TD> Cell four, foot section.</TD></TR>
</TFOOT>
</TABLE>
```

This is the header section of the table.	
Cell one, header section.	Cell two, header section.
Cell three, header section.	Cell four, header section.
This is the body section of the table.	
Cell one, body section.	Cell two, body section.
Cell three, body section.	Cell four, body section.
This is the foot section of the table.	
Cell one, foot section.	Cell two, foot section.
Cell three, foot section.	Cell four, foot section.

Figure 20-39: The THEAD, TBODY, and TFOOT parameters.

COLGROUP

Options: None

Description: Defines a group of columns within a table. THEAD, TBODY, and TFOOT define groups of rows. Each COLGROUP tag defines the properties of one or more columns (Figure 20-40).

HTML example (\My Web Stuff\Chap20\chap20M.htm):

```
<TABLE BORDER>
<COLGROUP ALIGN=CENTER>
<COLGROUP ALIGN=RIGHT>
<COLGROUP ALIGN=RIGHT>
<THEAD>
     <TR><TH>Really Neat Stuff</TH><TH>Old and Ancient
       Stuff</TH><TH>Totally Useless Stuff</TH>
   </THEAD>
   <TBODY>
     <TR><TD>Pool table</TD><TD>Model A Ford</TD><TD>Broken
       record</TD>
     <TR><TD>Ferrari</TD><TD>Pyramids</TD><TD>Used tape</TD>
     <TR><TD>Ice</TD><TD>My diapers</TD><TD>Adolescent
       jokes</TD>
   </TBODY>
</TABLE>
```

Really Neat Stuff	Old and Ancient Stuff	Totally Useless Stuff
Pool table	Model A Ford	Broken record
Ferrari	Pyramids	Used tape
Ice	My diapers	Adolescent jokes

Figure 20-40: The COLGROUP parameter.

COL

Options: None

Description: Used to specify the properties of a column group (see "COL/COLGROUP Parameters" below for details)

FRAME

Options: None

Description: Controls display of the outer border of a table (See "FRAME Parameters" for details)

RULES

Options: None

Description: Controls display of the inner rules of a table (See "RULE Parameters" for details)

COL/COLGROUP parameters

These are parameters that are only suitable for use with the <COL> and <COLGROUP> tags. They determine the size and arrangement of columns.

COL SPAN

Options: Number

Description: Determines arrangement of column spanning (Figure 20-41)

HTML example (\My Web Stuff\Chap20\chap20N.htm):

```
<TABLE BORDER>
<COLGROUP>
   <COL ALIGN=CENTER SPAN=1>
<COLGROUP>
   <COL ALIGN=LEFT SPAN=2>
   <THEAD>
     <TR><TH>Really Neat Stuff</TH><TH>Old and Ancient
       Stuff</TH><TH>Totally Useless Stuff</TH>
   </THEAD>
   <TBODY>
     <TR><TD>Pool table</TD><TD>Model A Ford</TD><TD>Broken
       record</TD>
     <TR><TD>Ferrari</TD><TD>Pyramids</TD><TD>Used tape</TD>
     <TR><TD>Ice</TD><TD>My diapers</TD><TD>Adolescent
       jokes</TD>
   </TBODY>
</TABLE>
```

Really Neat Stuff	Old and Ancient Stuff	Totally Useless Stuff
Pool table	Model A Ford	Broken record
Ferrari	Pyramids	Used tape
Ice	My diapers	Adolescent jokes

Figure 20-41: The COLSPAN parameter.

COL ALIGN

Options: CENTER, JUSTIFY, RIGHT, LEFT

Description and examples: See COL SPAN

COLGROUP ALIGN

Options: CENTER, JUSTIFY, RIGHT, LEFT

Description and examples: See COLGROUP

COLGROUP VALIGN

Options: BASELINE, BOTTOM, MIDDLE, TOP

Description: Specifies the vertical alignment of a group of columns (Figure 20-42)

HTML example (\My Web Stuff\Chap20\chap200.htm):

```
<TABLE BORDER WIDTH=250>
<COLGROUP VALIGN=BOTTOM>
<COLGROUP VALIGN=MIDDLE>
<COLGROUP VALIGN=TOP>
<THEAD>
     <TR><TH>Really Neat Stuff</TH><TH>Old and Ancient
       Stuff</TH><TH>Totally Useless Stuff</TH>
   </THEAD>
   <TBODY>
     <TR><TD>Pool table</TD><TD>Model A Ford</TD><TD>Broken
       record</TD>
     <TR><TD>Ferrari</TD><TD>Pyramids</TD><TD>Used tape</TD>
     <TR><TD>Ice</TD><TD>My diapers</TD><TD>Adolescent
       jokes</TD>
   </TBODY>
</TABLE>
```

Really Neat Stuff	Old and Ancient Stuff	Totally Useless Stuff
Pool table	Model A Ford	Broken vinyl 10" record
Ferrari	Pyramids	Used tape recordings
Ice	My 200-year-old diapers	Jokes

Figure 20-42: The COLGROUP VALIGN parameter.

FRAME parameters

FRAME parameters determine how the outside borders of a table display.

VOID

Options: None

Description: Removes a table's outside borders. It has no effect on the inside borders (Figure 20-43).

HTML example (`\My Web Stuff\Chap20\chap20P.htm`):

```
<TABLE BORDER=1 FRAME=VOID>
<TR><TD>X</TD><TD>X</TD><TD>O</TD></TR>
<TR><TD>O</TD><TD>X</TD><TD>X</TD></TR>
<TR><TD>O</TD><TD>O</TD><TD>X</TD></TR>
</TABLE>
```

 Figure 20-43: The VOID parameter.

ABOVE

Options: None

Description: Displays only the top outside border for a table. It has no effect on the inside borders (Figure 20-44).

HTML example (`\My Web Stuff\Chap20\chap20Q.htm`):

```
<TABLE BORDER=1 FRAME=ABOVE>
<TR><TD>X</TD><TD>X</TD><TD>O</TD></TR>
<TR><TD>O</TD><TD>X</TD><TD>X</TD></TR>
<TR><TD>O</TD><TD>O</TD><TD>X</TD></TR>
</TABLE>
```

 Figure 20-44: The ABOVE parameter.

BELOW

Options: None

Description: Displays only the bottom outside border for a table. It has no effect on the inside borders (Figure 20-45).

HTML example (\My Web Stuff\Chap20\chap20R.htm):

```
<TABLE BORDER=1 FRAME=BELOW>
<TR><TD>X</TD><TD>X</TD><TD>O</TD></TR>
<TR><TD>O</TD><TD>X</TD><TD>X</TD></TR>
<TR><TD>O</TD><TD>O</TD><TD>X</TD></TR>
</TABLE>
```

Figure 20-45: The BELOW parameter.

HSIDES

Options: None

Description: Displays only the top and bottom outside borders for a table. It has no effect on the inside borders (Figure 20-46).

HTML example (\My Web Stuff\Chap20\chap20S.htm):

```
<TABLE BORDER=1 FRAME=HSIDES>
<TR><TD>X</TD><TD>X</TD><TD>O</TD></TR>
<TR><TD>O</TD><TD>X</TD><TD>X</TD></TR>
<TR><TD>O</TD><TD>O</TD><TD>X</TD></TR>
</TABLE>
```

Figure 20-46: The HSIDES parameter.

LHS

Options: None

Description: Displays only the left outside border for a table. It has no effect on the inside borders (Figure 20-47).

HTML example (\My Web Stuff\Chap20\chap20T.htm):

```
<TABLE BORDER=1 FRAME=LHS>
<TR><TD>X</TD><TD>X</TD><TD>O</TD></TR>
<TR><TD>O</TD><TD>X</TD><TD>X</TD></TR>
<TR><TD>O</TD><TD>O</TD><TD>X</TD></TR>
</TABLE>
```

Figure 20-47: The LHS parameter.

RHS

Options: None

Description: Displays only the right outside border for a table. It has no effect on the inside borders (Figure 20-48).

HTML example (\My Web Stuff\Chap20\chap20U.htm):

```
<TABLE BORDER=1 FRAME=RHS>
<TR><TD>X</TD><TD>X</TD><TD>O</TD></TR>
<TR><TD>O</TD><TD>X</TD><TD>X</TD></TR>
<TR><TD>O</TD><TD>O</TD><TD>X</TD></TR>
</TABLE>
```

Figure 20-48: The RHS parameter.

VSIDES

Options: None

Description: Displays only the left and right outside borders for a table. It has no effect on the inside borders (Figure 20-49).

HTML example (\My Web Stuff\Chap20\chap20V.htm):

```
<TABLE BORDER=1 FRAME=VSIDES>
<TR><TD>X</TD><TD>X</TD><TD>O</TD></TR>
<TR><TD>O</TD><TD>X</TD><TD>X</TD></TR>
<TR><TD>O</TD><TD>O</TD><TD>X</TD></TR>
</TABLE>
```

Figure 20-49: The VSIDES parameter.

BOX

Options: None

Description: Displays the complete outside border of a table (Figure 20-50)

HTML example (`\My Web Stuff\Chap20\chap20W.htm`):

```
<TABLE BORDER=1 FRAME=BOX>
<TR><TD>X</TD><TD>X</TD><TD>O</TD></TR>
<TR><TD>O</TD><TD>X</TD><TD>X</TD></TR>
<TR><TD>O</TD><TD>O</TD><TD>X</TD></TR>
</TABLE>
```

Figure 20-50: The BOX parameter.

RULE parameters

RULE parameters determine how the inside borders of a table display.

NONE

Options: None

Description: None of the inside borders display (Figure 20-51).

HTML example (`\My Web Stuff\Chap20\chap20X.htm`):

```
<TABLE BORDER FRAME=BOX RULES=NONE>
<TR><TD>X</TD><TD>X</TD><TD>O</TD></TR>
<TR><TD>O</TD><TD>X</TD><TD>X</TD></TR>
<TR><TD>O</TD><TD>O</TD><TD>X</TD></TR>
</TABLE>
```

Figure 20-51: The NONE parameter.

GROUPS

Options: None

Description: Displays inside borders between the THEAD, TBODY, and TFOOT sections of a table (Figure 20-52)

HTML example (\My Web Stuff\Chap20\chap20Y.htm):

```
<TABLE border FRAME=BOX RULES=GROUPS>
<COLGROUP ALIGN=RIGHT SPAN=2>
<COLGROUP ALIGN=CENTER>
<THEAD>
<TR><TD>Cell one, header section.</TD>
<TD>Cell two, header section.</TD><TD>Cell three, header
      section</TD></TR>
<TR><TD>Cell four, header section.</TD>
<TD> Cell five, header section.</TD><TD>Cell six, header
      section.</TD></TR>
</THEAD>
<TBODY>
<TR><TD>Cell one, body section.</TD>
<TD>Cell two, body section.</TD><TD>Cell three, body
      section</TD></TR>
<TR><TD>Cell four, body section.</TD>
<TD> Cell five, body section.</TD><TD>Cell six, body
      section.</TD></TR>
</TBODY>
<TFOOT>
<TR><TD>Cell one, foot section.</TD>
<TD>Cell two, foot section.</TD><TD>Cell three, foot
      section</TD></TR>
<TR><TD>Cell four, foot section.</TD>
<TD>Cell five, foot section.</TD><TD>Cell six, foot
      section.</TD></TR>
</TFOOT>
</TABLE>
```

Cell one, header section.	Cell two, header section.	Cell three, header section
Cell four, header section.	Cell five, header section.	Cell six, header section.
Cell one, body section.	Cell two, body section.	Cell three, body section
Cell four, body section.	Cell five, body section.	Cell six, body section.
Cell one, foot section.	Cell two, foot section.	Cell three, foot section
Cell four, foot section.	Cell five, foot section.	Cell six, foot section.

Figure 20-52: The GROUPS parameter.

ROWS

Options: None

Description: Displays borders between rows in the table, but not between columns (Figure 20-53)

HTML example (`\My Web Stuff\Chap20\chap20Z.htm`):

```
<TABLE border FRAME=BOX RULES=ROWS>
<COLGROUP ALIGN=RIGHT SPAN=2>
<COLGROUP ALIGN=CENTER>
<THEAD>
<TR><TD>Cell one, header section.</TD>
<TD>Cell two, header section.</TD><TD>Cell three, header
      section</TD></TR>
<TR><TD>Cell four, header section.</TD>
<TD> Cell five, header section.</TD><TD>Cell six, header
      section.</TD></TR>
</THEAD>
<TBODY>
<TR><TD>Cell one, body section.</TD>
<TD>Cell two, body section.</TD><TD>Cell three, body
      section</TD></TR>
<TR><TD>Cell four, body section.</TD>
<TD> Cell five, body section.</TD><TD>Cell six, body
      section.</TD></TR>
</TBODY>
<TFOOT>
<TR><TD>Cell one, foot section.</TD>
<TD>Cell two, foot section.</TD><TD>Cell three, foot
      section</TD></TR>
<TR><TD>Cell four, foot section.</TD></TR>
</TFOOT>
</TABLE>
```

Cell one, header section.	Cell two, header section.	Cell three, header section
Cell four, header section.	Cell five, header section.	Cell six, header section.
Cell one, body section.	Cell two, body section.	Cell three, body section
Cell four, body section.	Cell five, body section.	Cell six, body section.
Cell one, foot section.	Cell two, foot section.	Cell three, foot section
Cell four, foot section.		

Figure 20-53: The ROWS parameter.

COLS

Options: None

Description: Displays borders between columns in the table, but not between rows (Figure 20-54)

HTML example (`\My Web Stuff\Chap20\chap20AA.htm`):

```
<TABLE border FRAME=BOX RULES=COLS>
<COLGROUP ALIGN=RIGHT SPAN=2>
<COLGROUP ALIGN=CENTER>
<THEAD>
<TR><TD>Cell one, header section.</TD>
<TD>Cell two, header section.</TD><TD>Cell three, header
      section</TD></TR>
<TR><TD>Cell four, header section.</TD>
<TD> Cell five, header section.</TD><TD>Cell six, header
      section.</TD></TR>
</THEAD>
<TBODY>
<TR><TD>Cell one, body section.</TD>
<TD>Cell two, body section.</TD><TD>Cell three, body
      section</TD></TR>
<TR><TD>Cell four, body section.</TD>
<TD> Cell five, body section.</TD><TD>Cell six, body
      section.</TD></TR>
</TBODY>
<TFOOT>
<TR><TD>Cell one, foot section.</TD>
<TD>Cell two, foot section.</TD><TD>Cell three, foot
      section</TD></TR>
<TR><TD>Cell four, foot section.</TD></TR>
</TFOOT>
</TABLE>
```

Cell one, header section.	Cell two, header section.	Cell three, header section
Cell four, header section.	Cell five, header section.	Cell six, header section.
Cell one, body section.	Cell two, body section.	Cell three, body section
Cell four, body section.	Cell five, body section.	Cell six, body section.
Cell one, foot section.	Cell two, foot section.	Cell three, foot section
	Cell four, foot section.	

Figure 20-54: The COLS parameter.

ALL

Options: None

Description: Displays all internal borders (Figure 20-55)

HTML example (`\My Web Stuff\Chap20\chap20AB.htm`):

```
<TABLE border FRAME=BOX RULES=ALL>
<COLGROUP ALIGN=RIGHT SPAN=2>
<COLGROUP ALIGN=CENTER>
<THEAD>
<TR><TD>Cell one, header section.</TD>
<TD>Cell two, header section.</TD><TD>Cell three, header
        section</TD></TR>
<TR><TD>Cell four, header section.</TD>
<TD> Cell five, header section.</TD><TD>Cell six, header
        section.</TD></TR>
</THEAD>
<TBODY>
<TR><TD>Cell one, body section.</TD>
<TD>Cell two, body section.</TD><TD>Cell three, body
        section</TD></TR>
<TR><TD>Cell four, body section.</TD>
<TD> Cell five, body section.</TD><TD>Cell six, body
        section.</TD></TR>
</TBODY>
<TFOOT>
<TR><TD>Cell one, foot section.</TD>
<TD>Cell two, foot section.</TD><TD>Cell three, foot
        section</TD></TR>
<TR><TD>Cell four, foot section.</TD></TR>
</TFOOT>
</TABLE>
```

Cell one, header section.	Cell two, header section.	Cell three, header section
Cell four, header section.	Cell five, header section.	Cell six, header section.
Cell one, body section.	Cell two, body section.	Cell three, body section
Cell four, body section.	Cell five, body section.	Cell six, body section.
Cell one, foot section.	Cell two, foot section.	Cell three, foot section
Cell four, foot section.		

Figure 20-55: The ALL parameter.

Web Tour #20: The Best of Web Tables

Tables are everywhere on the Web. As I pointed out in the section, "Invisible Tables," you may not realize how many pages are using tables until you look for the evidence. To visit sites that make clever use of tables, double-click this file:

```
\WebTour\Chap20\index.htm
```

You'll see the Web Tour page for this chapter.

Framing Your Graphics

To prepare for this chapter's tutorials, copy the following folder from the CD-ROM to the \My Web Stuff folder on your hard drive:

    \tutorial\chap21

This will copy files and folders for all of the tutorials in this chapter to your hard disk. See Chapter 1 for complete details on setting up for tutorials.

Frames are a recent addition to web page layout tools. Frames divide the browser window into two or more sections, each containing a different web page. For example, if you visit a web page and see three frames (see Figure 21-1), you are looking at three separate web pages. This is very different from tables. Tables divide a web page into sections, but the images and/or text in a table cell are fixed. Because each frame contains its own web page, you can dynamically alter the contents of frames on the fly. Frames are much more powerful tools than tables, but they are also significantly more complicated.

Typically, the web page in a given frame has a certain function, and the page layout takes this into account. For example, a tall, thin frame at the left of the browser window is often used to show the contents of a web site. You can quickly jump to any part of the site by clicking in this frame.

Frame descriptions are stored in a web page using HTML tags; these tags are explained in detail in the next section. However, you can also use web page editors like FrontPage to create and manage your frames. Each approach to working with frames has its advantages and disadvantages. However, I'll start with the HTML approach to creating frames. It's tedious and guaranteed to be challenging, but understanding how frames work at the nuts and bolts level gives you greater understanding of what you are doing when you create frames the easy way, with a web page editor. If you have no interest in the mechanics of frames, you can skip ahead to the section, "Creating a Web Page with Frames," which explains how to create frames with FrontPage 97.

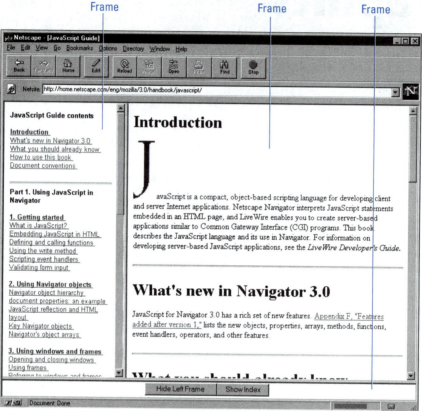

Figure 21-1: A web page that uses frames.

Frames Explained

Figure 21-2 shows a basic arrangement of frames. It is similar to Figure 21-1, but with the small horizontal frame at the top. Listing 21-1 shows the HTML code that creates this arrangement of frames.

Frame

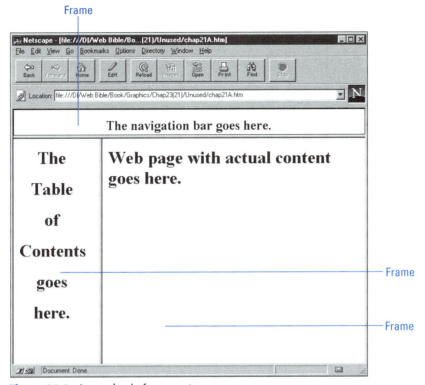

Figure 21-2: A very basic frame setup.

Listing 21-1: HTML code for three frames.

```
<frameset rows="11%,89%">
  <frame src="nav.htm" name="navbar" scrolling="no">
  <frameset cols="25%,75%">
    <frame src="toc.htm" name="toc">
    <frame src="index.htm" name="webpage">
  </frameset>
  <noframes>
  <body>
<p>This web page uses frames, but your browser doesn't support
      them.</p>
<p>Please visit our <A HREF="nfindex.htm">non-frame version</A>
      of this page, or press your browser's back button to
      return from whence you came.</p>
  </body>
  </noframes>
</frameset>
```

The HTML in Listing 21-1 has a very definite structure. If I remove everything but the structure, you can see the structure more clearly:

```
<frameset> Start of first set of frames.
<frameset>    Start of nested set of frames.
</frameset>   End of nested set of frames.
<noframes>    Begin section that will display if
         browser does not support frames.
<body> Begin BODY section for non-frame browser.
    Everything between body tags displays only
    in a non-frame browser.
</body> End of BODY section.
</noframes> End of section for browsers that do not
         support frames.
</frameset> End of first set of frames.
```

I can translate the HTML in Listing 21-1 into plain English for you. If you were a browser, this is what the HTML would tell you:

HTML: `<frameset rows="11%,89%">`

Translation: "Hey, Mr. Browser — create two frames for me, one above the other. The frame on top should take up 11% of the browser, and the frame on the bottom 89%."

HTML: `<frame src="nav.htm" name="navbar"`
                    `scrolling="no">`

Translation: "Now, in that top frame, load the contents of the web page `nav.htm`. I'll be referring to the top frame using the name `navbar`. By the way, don't allow the user to scroll the contents of this frame. That's it for the top frame."

HTML: `<frameset cols="25%,75%">`

Translation: "Hey, Mr. Browser! I want to create another set of frames inside the bottom frame. Divide the bottom frame into two frames for me, side by side. The frame on the left occupies 25% of the available space, and the frame on the right 75%."

HTML: `<frame src="toc.htm" name="toc">`

Translation: "In the left frame, display the contents of the web page `toc.htm`. I'll be referring to this frame using the name `toc`. That's it for the left frame."

HTML: `<frame src="index.htm" name="webpage">`

Translation:	"In the right frame, display the contents of the web page `index.htm`. I'll be referring to this frame using the name `webpage`. That's it for the right frame."
HTML:	`</frameset>`
Translation:	"That's it for the second set of frames."
HTML:	From `<noframes>` to `</noframes>`
Translation:	"Um, if you haven't heard a thing I've said so far, that means you don't know anything about frames. So here's what I'm going to do. Take all this stuff between these two tags and display it on the web page. Forget entirely about anything having to do with frames. Heh, heh — that frame stuff is just our little secret. Don't put any of it on the page! Just this stuff between the tags. OK?"
HTML:	`</frameset>`
Translation:	"That's it for frame stuff."

There are some key points that are clear from this translation:

✦ Frames are arranged into framesets.

✦ Framesets can be nested.

✦ Individual frames have names.

✦ Each frame displays a web page.

✦ You can tell a non-frame browser what to display instead of the frames. This can be a warning that the page uses frames ("Hey, Mr. Visitor! You can't see anything here because this page uses frames!"), or an alternate non-frame version of the page. You might want to include a link to a download site for a browser that supports frames.

Of these key points, one stands out as the most important: Each frame displays a web page. If you are not used to working with frames, you equate "web page" with "what I see in the browser window." In fact, frames allow you to display more than one web page at a time in the browser window.

Figure 21-3 shows a web page from the Microsoft Site Builder Network. This page looks like any other web page, but it's actually a collection of three web pages. The page uses frames, but the frames have their MARGINWIDTH set to zero and there are no borders between frames. Listing 21-2 shows the HTML used to display the page in Figure 21-3.

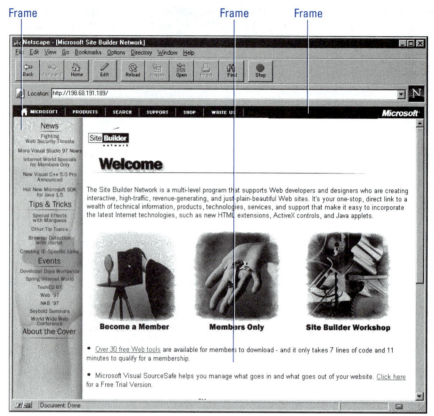

Figure 21-3: A web page that uses borderless frames.

Reprinted by permission from Microsoft Corporation.

Listing 21-2: Microsoft Site Builder Network frame page.

```
<frameset rows="24,*" border=0 framespacing=0 frameborder=no>
    <frame src="nav.htm" scrolling=no marginheight=0
    marginwidth=0 noresize>
    <frameset cols="144,*" border=0 framespacing=0
    frameborder=no>
        <frame src="side_barx.htm" scrolling=no marginwidth=0
        marginheight=0 noresize>
        <frame src="content.htm" marginheight=0 marginwidth=4
        name="content">
    </frameset>
</frameset>
```

The first line of HTML uses a different method for specifying the relative sizes of the two frames in the frameset. The division is top to bottom, with the top frame 24 pixels high, and the bottom frame taking up whatever space remains. This is indicated by

```
Rows="24,*"
```

The asterisk is used whenever you want to let the browser allocate all remaining space to a frame.

The nice thing about frames is that once you have a working frame setup, you can put whatever pages you wish into it. Figure 21-4 shows a web page that uses exactly the same frames as those used in Figure 21-3, but different web pages are displayed in each frame. This was done by using a different URL with the SRC parameter of the FRAME tag:

```
<frame src="nav2.htm" scrolling=no marginheight=0 marginwidth=0
       noresize>
```

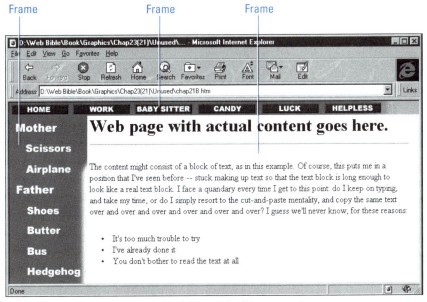

Figure 21-4: You can reuse a frameset with different web pages.

The lack of borders is essential to the appearance of the pages in Figures 21-3 and 21-4. Figure 21-5 shows the web page of Figure 21-4 with borders — it just doesn't look right.

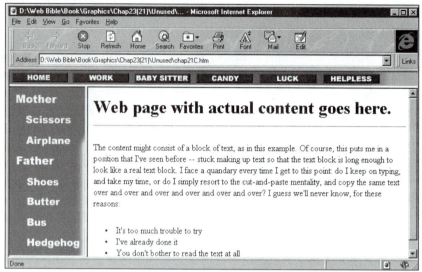

Figure 21-5: The web page from Figure 21-4 with frame borders visible.

You can create multiple nested framesets as well. Figure 21-6 shows another web page from Microsoft, the ActiveX HTML Reference. There are four frames on the page. They are created using the HTML shown in Listing 21-3.

Listing 21-3: Microsoft Internet Workshop frame page.

```
<frameset frameborder="3" framespacing="3" rows="49,*">
    <frame marginwidth="0" marginheight="0" src="nav.htm"
    name="topic-nav" noresize scrolling="no">
    <frameset frameborder="3" framespacing="3" cols="160,*">
        <frameset frameborder="3" framespacing="3"
        rows="80,*">
        <frame marginwidth="0" marginheight="2" src="head.htm"
        name="article-head" scrolling="no">
        <frame marginwidth="4" marginheight="0"
        src="contents2.htm" name="article-nav"
        scrolling="yes">
    </frameset>
    <frame marginwidth="9" marginheight="0" src="htmlref.htm"
    name="text" scrolling="yes">
</frameset>
```

Figure 21-6: Another web page that uses frames.

Reprinted by permission from Microsoft Corporation.

I found that frames did not display identically between different browsers. For example, Figure 21-7 shows the same web page shown in Figure 21-4, but in Navigator instead of Internet Explorer. Note the white space between frames, even though margins and borders are set to zero. It's always a good idea to check your web page layouts in several different browsers!

Figure 21-7: All browsers are not created equal; always check your pages!

Controlling Frames

You can use various HTML tags and parameters to control the appearance of frames, or to control which web page displays in what frame.

In this section, the following shorthand notations are used:

<URL>	Refers to any valid URL, including local filenames/pathnames, HTTP and FTP, and so on. Example: `http://www.mmadweb.com/index.htm`.
Number	Refers to any valid number, with enclosing double quotes optional. For example, `WIDTH=50` shows usage without quotes, and `WIDTH="50"` shows usage with quotes. Generally, you don't need quotes for a number, but when in doubt, use quotes.
Percentage	Refers to any valid number (100 or less!) followed by a percent sign: `50%`, `22%`, and so on.
Relative (*)	Refers to the one or more items in a sequence of numbers and/or percentages. It indicates that remaining space should be divided among the items according to the number next to the asterisk. For example: `25%`, `1*`, `2*` results in 25% of the space for the first item, one-third of the remaining space for the second item, and two-thirds of the remaining space for the third item.

Parameters for the FRAME tag

The parameters for the FRAME tag determine the appearance of the frame borders, and the distance between the frame and the contents of the web page it contains.

FRAMEBORDER

Options: YES, NO

Description: Determines whether or not a frame displays its borders (Figure 21-8)

HTML example (\My Web Stuff\Chap21\chap21D.htm):

```
<frameset rows="28,*">
<frame src="nav2.htm" FRAMEBORDER="NO" SCROLLING=NO>
<frameset cols="144,*">
<frame src="toc2.htm" FRAMEBORDER="NO" SCROLLING=NO>
<frame src="index2.htm" FRAMEBORDER="NO" name="content">
</frameset>
</frameset>
```

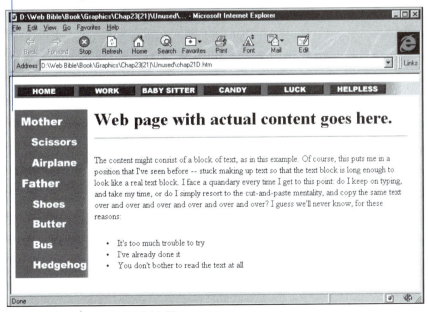

Figure 21-8: The FRAMEBORDER parameter.

MARGINHEIGHT

Options: Number

Description: Determines the number of pixels between the top edge of the frame and the frame's contents (Figure 21-9)

HTML example (\My Web Stuff\Chap21\chap21D.htm):

```
<frameset rows="28,*">
<frame src="nav2.htm" FRAMEBORDER="NO" MARGINHEIGHT=0
      MARGINWIDTH=0 SCROLLING=NO>
<frameset cols="144,*">
<frame src="toc2.htm" FRAMEBORDER="NO" SCROLLING=NO>
<frame src="index2.htm" FRAMEBORDER="NO" name="content">
</frameset>
</frameset>
```

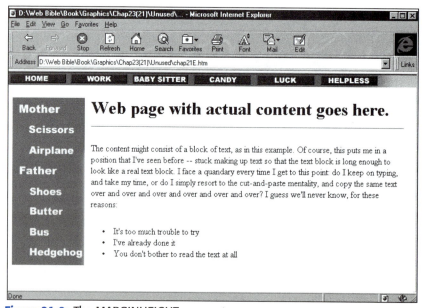

Figure 21-9: The MARGINHEIGHT parameter.

MARGINWIDTH

Options: None

Description: Determines the number of pixels between the left and right edges of the frame and the frame's contents

Example: See MARGINHEIGHT.

NAME

Options: None

Description: The NAME is used to refer to the frame. For example, you can use the name to set a TARGET frame for a web page; the web page will display in that frame (Figure 21-10).

HTML example (\My Web Stuff\Chap21\chap21F.htm):

Contents of the page that defines the frames:

```
<frameset rows="28,*">
<frame src="nav2.htm" FRAMEBORDER="NO" MARGINHEIGHT=0
     MARGINWIDTH=0 SCROLLING=NO>
<frameset cols="144,*">
<frame src="toc2.htm" FRAMEBORDER="NO" SCROLLING=NO name="toc">
<frame src="index3.htm" FRAMEBORDER="NO" name="content">
</frameset>
</frameset>
```

Contents of the page index.htm, located in the frame named "content":

```
<P><A TARGET="toc" HREF="toc3.htm">Click me</A> to display a
     new web page in the table of contents frame.</P>
```

Clicking the hyperlink above displays a new version of the table of contents page (toc3.htm instead of toc2.htm) in the frame with the name toc. This is the bottom left-frame in the visual example.

NORESIZE

Options: None

Description: Prevents the visitor from resizing the frame (Figure 21-11)

HTML example (\My Web Stuff\Chap21\chap21G.htm):

```
<frameset rows="28,*">
<frame src="nav2.htm" MARGINHEIGHT=0 MARGINWIDTH=0 SCROLLING=NO
     NORESIZE>
<frame src="index2.htm" name="content">
</frameset>
```

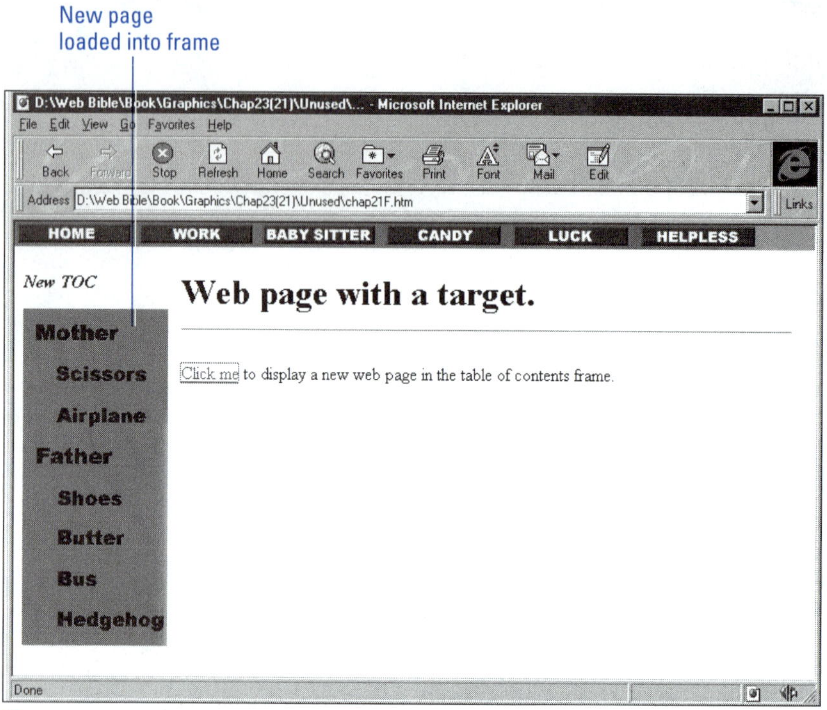

New page
loaded into frame

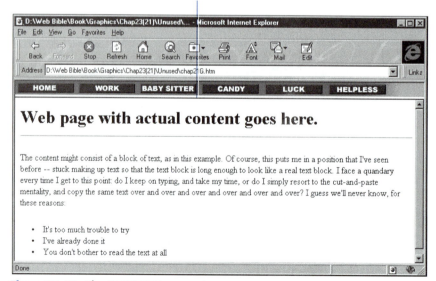

Figure 21-10: The NAME parameter.

Frame border cannot be moved

Figure 21-11: The NORESIZE parameter.

SCROLLING

Options: YES, NO

Description: Determines whether scroll bars are displayed for the frame. Scrolling is usually set to NO for frames that display the same web page at all times, particularly when navigation bars are involved. When scrolling is set to NO, you may want to also use NORESIZE for the frame (Figure 21-12).

HTML example (\My Web Stuff\Chap21\chap21H.htm):

```
<frameset rows="28,*">
<frame src="nav2.htm" FRAMEBORDER="NO" MARGINHEIGHT=0
      MARGINWIDTH=0 SCROLLING=NO NORESIZE>
<frame src="index2.htm" SCROLLING=YES FRAMEBORDER="NO"
      name="content">
</frameset>
```

Figure 21-12: The SCROLLING parameter.

SRC

Options: "<URL>"

Description: Specifies the URL of the web page that is displayed in the frame (Figure 21-13)

HTML example (\My Web Stuff\Chap21\chap21I.htm):

```
<frameset rows="24,24,*" FRAMESPACING=0>
<frame src="nav2.htm" MARGINHEIGHT=0 MARGINWIDTH=0
      FRAMEBORDER="NO" SCROLLING=NO>
```

```
<frame src="nav3.htm" MARGINHEIGHT=0 MARGINWIDTH=0
        FRAMEBORDER="NO" SCROLLING=NO>
<frame src="index2.htm" SCROLLING=YES FRAMEBORDER="NO"
        name="content">
</frameset>
```

Figure 21-13: The SRC parameter.

Parameters for the FRAMESET tag

The parameters of the FRAMESET tag determine the characteristics of all of the frames in a frameset.

COLS

Options: Percentage, number, relative (*)

Description: Determines the number of columns allocated to each frame in the frameset (Figure 21-14)

HTML example (\My Web Stuff\Chap21\chap21J.htm):

```
<frameset cols="42,1*,2*,3*" FRAMESPACING=0>
<frame src="nav4.htm" MARGINHEIGHT=0 MARGINWIDTH=0
        SCROLLING=NO>
<frame src="cols1.htm" name="content1">
<frame src="cols2.htm" name="content2">
<frame src="cols3.htm" name="content3">
</frameset>
```

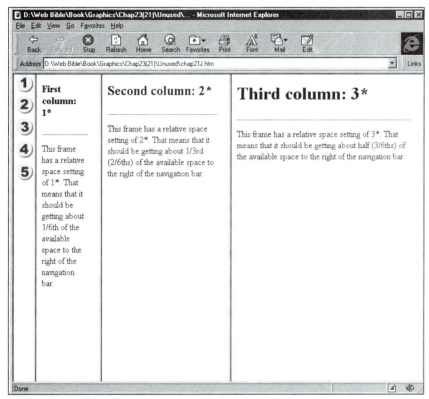

Figure 21-14: The COLS parameter.

ROWS

Options: Percentage, number, relative (*)

Description: Determines the number of rows allocated to each frame in the frameset (Figure 21-15)

HTML example (\My Web Stuff\Chap21\chap21K.htm):

```
<frameset rows="24,1*,2*,3*" FRAMESPACING=0>
<frame src="nav2.htm" MARGINHEIGHT=0 MARGINWIDTH=0
    SCROLLING=NO>
<frame src="rows1.htm" name="content1">
<frame src="rows2.htm" name="content2">
<frame src="rows3.htm" name="content3">
</frameset>
```

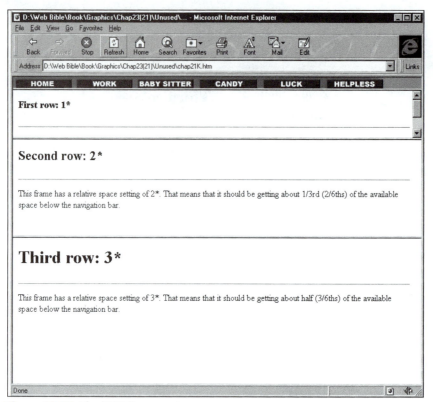

Figure 21-15: The ROWS parameter.

BORDER/FRAMEBORDER

Options: YES, NO

Description: Determines whether or not borders display between frames in the frameset. Even if borders are turned off, if SCROLLING is on, scrollbars will display for all frames that contain text that extends beyond the visible limits of a frame (Figure 21-16).

HTML example (\My Web Stuff\Chap21\chap21L.htm):

```
<frameset cols="42,1*,2*,3*" FRAMEBORDER=NO>
<frame src="nav4.htm" MARGINHEIGHT=0 MARGINWIDTH=0
     SCROLLING=NO>
<frame src="cols1.htm" name="content1">
<frame src="cols2.htm" name="content2">
<frame src="cols3.htm" name="content3">
</frameset>
```

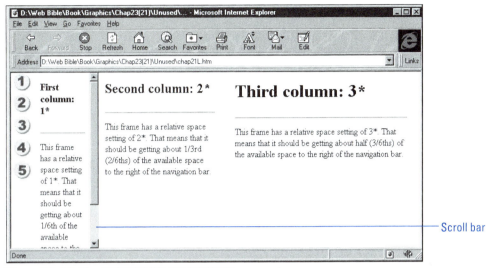

Figure 21-16: The BORDER/FRAMEBORDER parameter.

FRAMESPACING

Options: Number

Description: Determines the width of frame borders (Figure 21-17)

HTML example (\My Web Stuff\Chap21\chap21D.htm):

```
<frameset cols="42,1*,2*,3*" FRAMESPACING=30>
<frame src="nav4.htm" MARGINHEIGHT=0 MARGINWIDTH=10
      SCROLLING=NO>
<frame src="cols1.htm" name="content1">
<frame src="cols2.htm" name="content2">
<frame src="cols3.htm" name="content3">
</frameset>
```

TARGET as a parameter

You can use the TARGET parameter with the A, AREA, BASE, and FORM tags to determine in which window or frame a web page displays. Table 21-1 lists the valid targets you can use. Typical HTML code for a target is shown in the HTML example for the NAME parameter of the FRAME tag discussed earlier in this chapter:

```
<P><A TARGET="toc" HREF="toc3.htm">Click me</A> to display a
      new web page in the table of contents frame.</P>
```

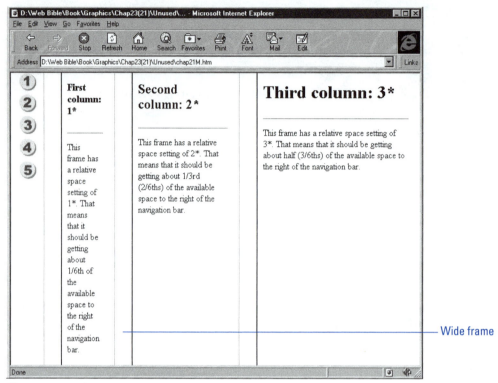

Figure 21-17: The FRAMESPACING parameter.

	Table 21-1 Valid TARGETs	

Target specified	Description
window or **frame**	Displays the web page in the named window or frame.
_blank	Displays the web page in a new, blank window.
_parent	Displays the web page in the parent window of the window containing the web page with the link.
_self	Displays the web page in the same window or frame as the window or frame containing the web page with the link.
_top	Displays the web page in the full body of the current window. If the web page containing the link is displayed in a frame, the window containing that frame is the window used to display the linked page.

Additional examples of how to use the TARGET tag can be found in the next section.

Using the TARGET tag

The TARGET tag is very important for working with frames. Displaying the correct page in the correct frame is the name of the frame game. Before you can use the TARGET tag, you must make sure that all frames that will be displaying web pages have a name. All names must be alphanumeric, contain nothing but letters and numbers, and must always start with a letter.

Hyperlink targets

You use the A tag to indicate hyperlinks with HTML. For example, in the following sentence, the text "aviation museum" is hyperlinked to the web page `avmuseum.html`.

```
Visit the <A HREF="avmuseum.html">aviation museum</A> web page
        for more information.
```

To specify a frame as a target for the new web page, use the TARGET parameter to specify a named frame — in this case, the frame `mainpage` is assumed to exist:

```
Visit the <A HREF="avmuseum.html" TARGET="mainpage">aviation
        museum</A> web page for more information.
```

Client-side image map targets

You can include TARGETs in the definition of a client-side image map. (See Chapter 15, " Image Maps: Jump for Joy," for details about image maps.) A typical hotspot on a client-side image map looks like this:

```
<AREA HREF="avmuseum.html" SHAPE=RECT COORDS="50,50, 100,100">
```

To specify a target to display the web page, use the TARGET parameter:

```
<AREA TARGET="mainpage" HREF="avmuseum.html" SHAPE=RECT
        COORDS="50,50, 100,100">
```

Default target for a page

You can use the BASE tag to specify a default frame that all links on the page should use. You can override the BASE target by specifying a different TARGET in an individual link. For example, to display all links in the current frame:

```
<BASE HREF="http://www.avmuseum.org/index.htm"
        TARGET="mainpage">
```

All links on the page will display in the `mainpage` frame.

Target for form results

When you click the SUBMIT button of a form, the results of the submission are displayed. You can control where the results display by adding the TARGET parameter to the FORM tag:

```
<FORM TARGET="mainpage" ACTION="/cgi-bin/myscript.cgi>
```

Creating a Web Page with Frames

Download: A trial version of FrontPage 97 is not available. Check the web site at http://www.microsoft.com to see if this changes.

Level: Easier than you think

Tutorial

Task: Create a web page with frames

Before you begin:

✦ Install and run FrontPage 97.

The first thing you see when you run FrontPage 97 is the Getting Started dialog box, shown in Figure 21-18. FrontPage speaks in terms of webs. A web is simply a collection of web pages and all the files that go along with them — images, scripts, WebBots, and so on. To create a web that uses frames:

1. Click the From a Wizard or Template radio button in the Getting Started dialog box, and click OK.

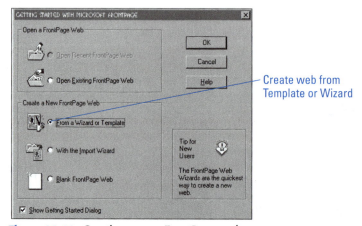

Create web from Template or Wizard

Figure 21-18: Creating a new FrontPage web.

Tip

If you don't want to see the Getting Started dialog box, uncheck the check box at the bottom of the dialog box. If you do this, you can create new webs using the File | New | FrontPage Web menu selection.

This displays the New FrontPage Web dialog box (see Figure 21-19). There are nine options.

2. Click to highlight Discussion Web Wizard, and click OK.

This wizard walks you through the creation of a set of web pages for an online discussion group that supports threaded messages, a table of contents, and full-text searching.

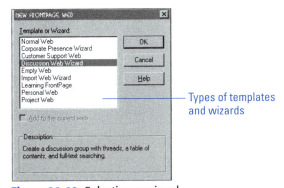

Types of templates and wizards

Figure 21-19: Selecting a wizard.

You are prompted to specify the location and name of the new web. I suggest saving the new web in the folder c:\fp\myWeb (where c: is the letter of your drive), but if you want to save the new web in a different location, it will not affect the tutorial significantly. Simply note the location, and use it wherever the location is referenced in the tutorial.

3. Specify the name **myWeb** for the new web. Whatever folder you specify, if it does not exist, FrontPage will ask if you want to create it.

4. Click Yes to create the folder. FrontPage will then ask you if you want to convert the folder to a FrontPage web.

5. Click Yes.

That completes the preliminary work; you will now see the first panel in the Discussion Web Wizard (see Figure 21-20). This is a typical FrontPage Wizard panel, with a cute graphic at the left, explanatory text and fill-ins on the right, and a set of buttons at the bottom: Cancel, Back, Next, and Finish.

6. Click Next to get started.

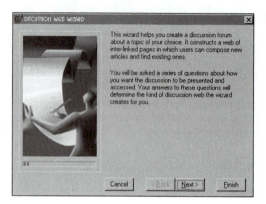

Figure 21-20: The first panel presented by the Discussion Web Wizard.

This displays the panel shown in Figure 21-21. You can select the features you want on your discussion web. These include:

✦ Submission form (this is required; you can't uncheck it), which you use to submit messages to the discussion.

✦ Table of contents, which displays the messages in the discussion.

✦ Search form, which is used to search for messages that contain a text string you enter.

✦ Threaded replies, which causes the messages to be joined into threads. This means that messages and their replies will be grouped for quick reference.

✦ Confirmation page, which is a page displayed when a message is added to a thread.

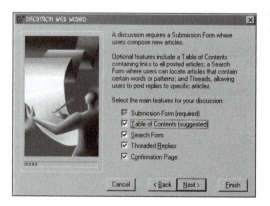

Figure 21-21: Choosing which pages to include in the new web.

7. Select all of the features, and click the Next button.

This displays a panel asking for two pieces of information: first, the title of the discussion.

8. Enter **Web Graphics**.

   The second item is the name for the folder that will contain the discussion's web pages.

   Accept the default of _folder1.

10. Click Next.

    A panel displays asking you to choose the input fields for the submission form. These will be the default fields; you can add more fields later in the FrontPage Editor.

11. Select the first choice: Subject, Comments, and click Next.

    The next four panels ask you whether the discussion should be in a protected web, how to sort the Table of Contents, whether the Table of Contents should be the home page for this web, and what information to display on the Search form. In the next four steps you answer these questions.

12. Select No, anyone can post articles, and click Next.

13. Select Oldest to newest, and click Next.

14. Select Yes, and click Next.

15. Select Subject, Size, Date, Score and click Next.

    Now a panel displays that allows you set up the colors and background for your web page (see Figure 21-22).

16. Click the Colors | Custom radio button, and click the Solid box.

17. Pick white as the page background color.

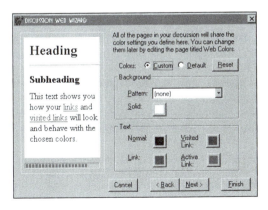

Figure 21-22: Setting page colors in the Discussion Web Wizard.

18. Click Next

    The suggested frame layout for the Discussion Web appears (see Figure 21-23). You have four options for frame support:

✦ No frames, in which case the page layout will use standard non-frame HTML tags.

✦ Dual interface, in which case both a frame and a non-frame version of the web will be created. Browsers that support frames will automatically see the frame version. Other browsers will automatically see the non-frame version.

✦ Contents above current article, in which case the frames are arranged so that the site contents appear above the currently displayed message.

✦ Contents beside current article, in which case the frame layout appears as shown in Figure 21-23.

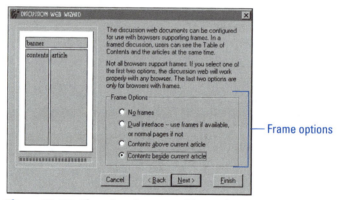

Figure 21-23: Choosing the type of frame layout to use.

19. Choose the fourth option, Contents beside current article, and click Next. This displays the final panel.

20. Click Finish to complete the Wizard.

FrontPage will work for a few moments, and then display the new web in FrontPage Explorer (see Figure 21-24). The various portions of the web are shown in the left pane, and the interconnections of the pieces appear in the right pane of Explorer. If you cannot see all of the components in the left pane of Explorer, click the little plus signs to expand the list.

To view any of the pages in the web in the FrontPage Editor, double-click the item in the left pane. Figure 21-25 shows the Navigation Ledge Frame for Web Graphics in the Editor. The page consists of a two-column, one-row table, with a text title in the left cell and two text hyperlinks in the right cell.

You can edit the page to suit your requirements. For example, Figure 21-26 shows the title and links replaced with graphics.

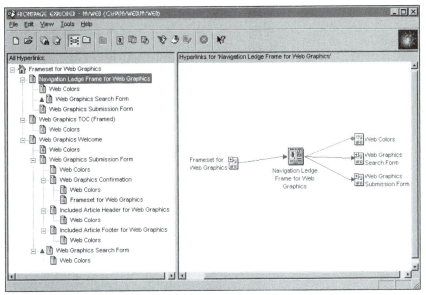

Figure 21-24: The completed web in FrontPage Explorer.

Left table cell   Right table cell

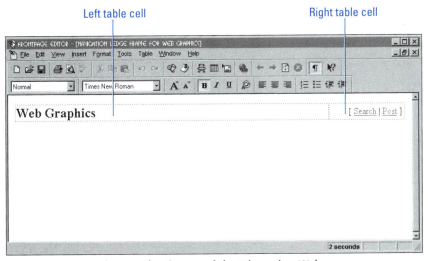

Figure 21-25: A web page that is part of the Discussion Web.

I created the title graphic (left cell in Figure 21-26) in Fractal Design Painter as a text cutout. The dash of red is simply an object located between the top textured object and the background.

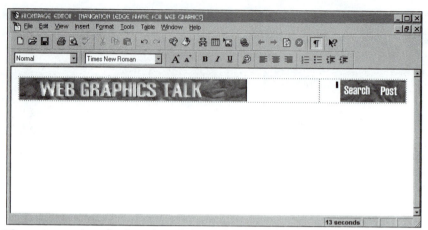

Figure 21-26: An edited version of the web page shown in Figure 21-25.

Figure 21-27 shows the Discussion Web in action. The Navigation Ledge Frame is the top frame. The left frame shows the web's contents — there is none because no messages have been added yet. The right frame shows the welcome message for the web. It includes two text links: one for posting new articles, and one for performing a search. As with all of the web pages in all of the frames, you can edit the web page in the Editor and make whatever changes you require.

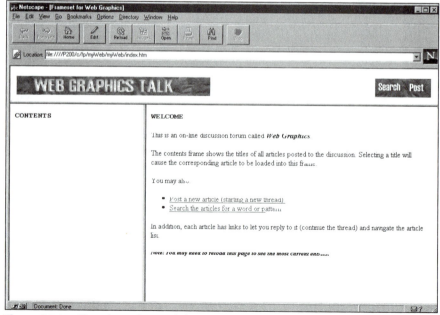

Figure 21-27: The Discussion Web home page.

Figure 21-28 shows the Search page. It includes a place to enter the search string, and a button to initiate the search.

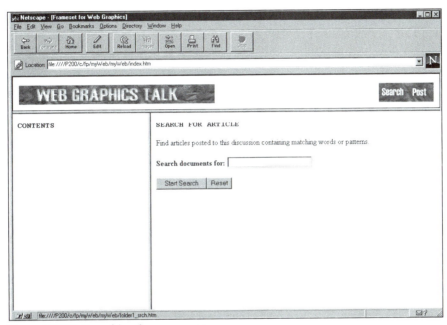

Figure 21-28: Searching for messages.

Figure 21-29 shows the web page for adding new messages to the discussion. It includes the three fields you selected using the Discussion Web Wizard, as well as a button to post the article, and a button to clear (reset) the form and try again.

This is not the only FrontPage Wizard that includes options for frames. However, you don't have to add a complete new web to use frames. You can add a frameset at any time in the FrontPage Editor.

Figure 21-29: Posting a new message.

Creating Custom Frames in FrontPage 97

FrontPage Editor includes a Wizard for creating custom framesets.

1. Create a new page using the File | New menu selection in the FrontPage Editor.

2. Highlight Frames Wizard, and click OK.

    The first panel of the Frames Wizard displays (see Figure 21-30). You have two choices: You can create a frameset from a template, or you can create a custom frameset.

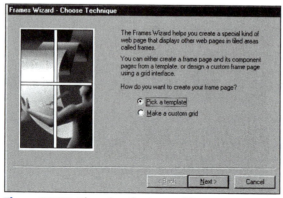

Figure 21-30: Choosing the type of frameset to create.

If you choose to create a frameset from a template, you will see the panel shown in Figure 21-31.

3. Simply click the available options to preview the frame layout on the left side of the panel. After you choose a frameset template, you can specify an alternate non-frame page and the name for the frameset.

If you choose to create a custom frameset, you'll see the panel shown in Figure 21-32. It allows you to create new frames, set the number of rows and columns, merge cells, split cells, and so on. Figure 21-33 shows a complex frameset I created in less than a minute using this panel. It's very easy to create exactly the frameset you want. However, make sure you decide on the total number of rows and columns before you try to split and merge cells. Otherwise, you'll find you have to start all over again.

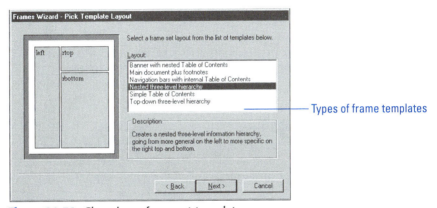

Figure 21-31: Choosing a frameset template.

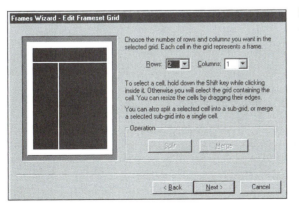

Figure 21-32: Creating a custom frameset.

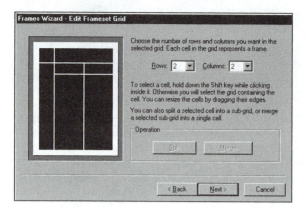

Figure 21-33: You can easily create fairly complex framesets.

Figure 21-34 shows the next step: naming your frames and setting their properties.

4. Click each frame in turn to supply its name, default URL, MARGINWIDTH and MARGINHEIGHT, scrolling, and whether the frame should resize.

Current frame   Name for frame

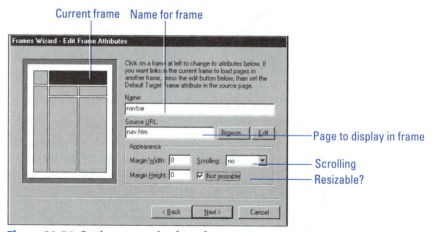

Page to display in frame

Scrolling
Resizable?

Figure 21-34: Setting properties for a frame.

Tip

As with other frameset templates, you can specify an alternate web page to display in browsers that do not support frames.

You complete the process by giving the frameset a name. Figure 21-35 shows two framesets I created in less than five minutes, one from a template (Frameset 1) and one custom frameset (Frameset 2).

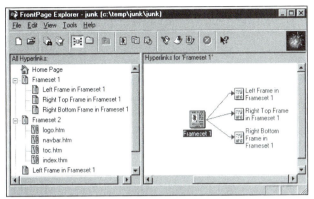

Figure 21-35: Two framesets created in FrontPage 97.

Using Graphics with Frames

The relationship between frames and graphics is similar to the relationship between tables and graphics: You get more control over page layout with frames. However, by putting a different web page in each frame, you also gain a tremendous amount of flexibility. By careful management of MARGINWIDTH, MARGINHEIGHT, and other parameters for the FRAME and FRAMESET tags, you can create versatile and interesting web sites.

However, working with frames requires either a lot of hand-coding of HTML, or the use of a fairly sophisticated web page editor. I have to give the nod to FrontPage when it comes to working with frames. Frames are often an option when creating web sites with Wizards, and you can use the Frames Wizard to add individual framesets to your web site.

The design rules for adding graphics to pages that are used in frames aren't really any different from the design rules for graphics on individual web pages. The key difference is that you will display more than one page at a time, and you should pay close attention to the way that graphics in different pages interact.

Web Tour #21: The Best of Web Frames

Frames are not as common as tables, but there are quite a few frame-based web sites on the Web. There are also sites that use invisible frames; many of these exist on Microsoft's web site. To visit sites that make clever use of frames, double-click the file:

```
\WebTour\Chap21\index.htm
```

You'll see the Web Tour page for this chapter.

Dynamic Graphics: Animation

> To prepare for this chapter's tutorials, copy the following folder from the CD-ROM to the \My Web Stuff folder on your hard drive:
>
> \tutorial\chap22
>
> This will copy files for all of the tutorials in this chapter to your hard disk. See Chapter 1 for complete details on setting up for tutorials.

Depending on your point of view, web page animation is either the best thing ever to happen to web pages, or the worst. When I see a web page that dances every which way, without planning or design, I shudder and move on, convinced that animation is a dangerous development. When I see animation used to entertain or help make a web page more effective, I smile and get involved with the page.

There's a lot to be said for subtlety in animation. It's too easy to get carried away with the possibilities and create a monster. In this chapter, you learn to create the different kinds of animation possible on a web page. If you are interested in web pages that make maximal use of animation, you will need to study up on the heavy stuff like Shockwave animation and video production.

Principles of Animation

Animation is just a series of graphic images showing successive steps. Figure 22-1 shows a simple animation sequence. A wave moves from left to right across a blue line, peaks, and splits off a drop of liquid that falls back onto the blue line. Each image is called a frame of the animation. An animation can have just a few simple frames, or many frames.

You can see this animation in action in the files for this chapter. Double-click the file `\My Web Stuff\chap22\chap22A.htm` to see the animation in action.

There are many ways to present an animation, and many ways to create the animation in the first place. You can add an animation to a web page using GIF files, or by converting the animation to a video clip and adding the clip to the web page. The simplest method by far is to use GIF animation, and that is the focus of this chapter.

A number of software packages can assist you in creating animations. There are two basic animation techniques: interpolation and keyframing.

Interpolation

To create an interpolated animation, you create a starting frame and an ending frame, and then use software to create the intervening frames. For example, you could create a starting frame with a ball at the lower left corner, and an ending frame with the ball at the upper right corner. Many animation software packages can then create intervening frames showing the ball moving from the start position to the end position. You'll see an example of interpolation later in this chapter.

Keyframing

To create keyframe animation, you must draw every frame in the animation individually. Most animation software allows you to draw on top of a shaded version of the prior frame. This allows you to draw the new frame accurately. The technique of viewing one or more prior frames while drawing the current frame is called *onionskin*. It is named after the type of tracing paper used by animators who work with paper and pencil. Onionskin paper is so thin that you can see through it. By tracing out a new frame on onionskin, a traditional animator was able to accurately draw each succeeding frame of an animation sequence. You'll see an example of keyframing using onionskin in the next section.

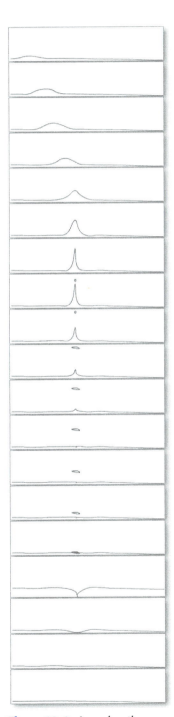

Figure 22-1: An animation sequence.

Animating a Bird

Tutorial

CD: To install the trial version of Painter from the CD, double-click the file `\demo\fractal\painter4\setup.exe`. Note that the trial version does not support movies; you'll need the full version of Painter to work this tutorial.

Level: Easy

Task: Create a flying bird animation

Before you start:

✦ Install Fractal Design Painter.

The best way to learn to create an animation is to do it. This example shows how to create an animation in Fractal Design Painter. The basic steps will be similar in other animation software. Painter is not specifically designed for animation, so there are only a few tools to assist you in creating the animation. Later in this chapter you'll learn how to create an animation using FutureSplash Animator, a software package whose only purpose is to create animations.

When you create a new file in Painter, there are two radio buttons at the bottom of the New Picture dialog box (see Figure 22-2).

1. Use the File | New menu selection to open the dialog box. By default, the Image radio button is active.

2. Click the Movie with radio button and enter **8** for the number of frames.

3. Click OK. This opens the dialog box shown in Figure 22-3.

   Painter wants a name for the animation (which Painter insists on calling a movie).

4. Type in the name **anim01**, and locate the `\My Web Stuff` folder using the Save in drop-down list at the top of the dialog box.

5. Click the Save button to save the eight empty frames. This displays the dialog box shown in Figure 22-4.

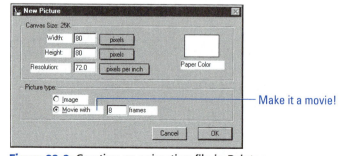

Figure 22-2: Creating an animation file in Painter.

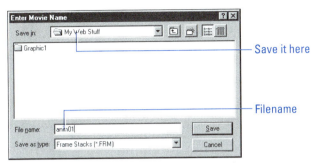

Figure 22-3: Saving the empty animation file.

6. Set the layers of onionskin at two, and the storage type as 24-bit color.

7. Click OK.

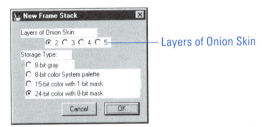

Figure 22-4: Setting properties for the animation file.

This opens the animation file in Painter (see Figure 22-5). In addition to the image window itself, there is a control window that allows you to pick which frame displays in the image window.

8. For convenience while drawing, I suggest that you enlarge the view of the image window with "Ctrl+" (using the + key on the numeric keypad) (see Figure 22-6).

9. Enlarge the size of the image window by clicking and dragging as needed.

The pen tool is ideal for drawing this animation of a bird in flight.

10. Click the pen tool to activate it (see Figure 22-7). If the pen tool is not active, click the drawer handle (just below the tools) and click the pen.

11. If the active variant isn't already Fine Point, click the white drop-down list, located just below the image tools, to select that variant.

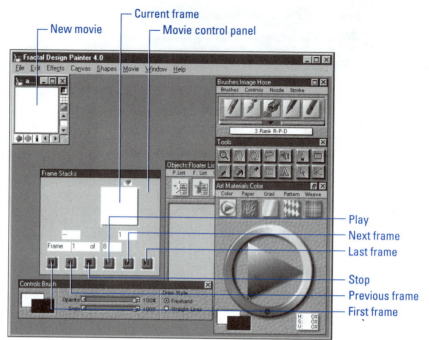

Figure 22-5: A new animation file open in Painter.

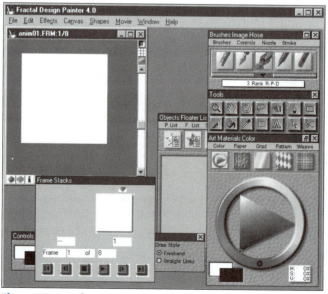

Figure 22-6: Enlarge your view of the animation for more control.

Pen

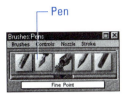

Figure 22-7: Selecting the pen tool.

12. Confirm that the active frame is frame 1 (look in the animation control window), and then draw a simple bird, as shown in Figure 22-8.

   Don't worry about details; just draw this simple outline. If you have a pen and tablet it will be easier to draw, but you can draw simple outlines with the mouse, too.

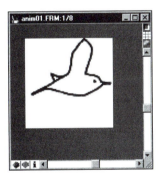

Figure 22-8: How to draw a bird.

13. When you are done drawing this frame, click the Next button in the control window to move to frame 2.

   Figure 22-9 shows the control panel, with frame 1 at the left, and frame 2 at the right. The little red doohickey at the top of frame 2 indicates that it is the active frame (that is, the frame displayed in the image window).

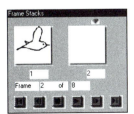

Figure 22-9: The control window shows a miniature version of the contents of frame 1.

Figure 22-10 shows the appearance of the image window when frame 2 is active. If you see a blank frame instead, click the onionskin button (at the top right edge of the image window) to turn on the onionskin. This is a gray version of the image in frame 1.

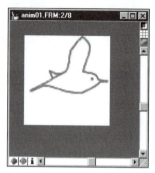

Figure 22-10: The image window shows an onionskin version of the image in frame 1.

14. Draw the second bird image by tracing over the onionskin image.

Figure 22-11 shows the appearance of frame 2 with onionskin on, and Figure 22-12 shows the appearance of frame 2 with onionskin off. It's always a good idea to turn off onionskin before moving on to the next frame, so you can check your work for completeness.

Figure 22-11: Drawing the second frame.

15. Use the Next button in the control window to move to the next frame.

16. Figures 22-13 through 22-16 show frames 3 through 6; draw the bird images for these frames.

Each figure shows both onionskin and non-onionskin versions of each frame.

Figure 22-12: The second frame without onionskin.

Figure 22-13: The third frame with (left) and without (right) onionskin.

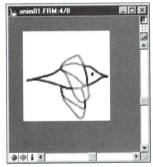 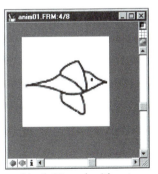

Figure 22-14: The fourth frame with (left) and without (right) onionskin.

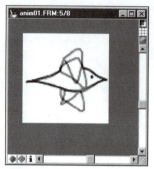 

Figure 22-15: The fifth frame with (left) and without (right) onionskin.

Figure 22-16: The sixth frame with (left) and without (right) onionskin.

There are only six frames in the animation.

17. To delete the extra frames, use the Movie | Delete Frames menu selection to display the dialog box shown in Figure 22-17.

18. Delete frames 7 through 8.

19. Click OK to delete the extra frames.

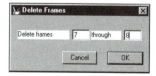

Figure 22-17: Deleting frames.

You don't need to worry about adding frames to an animation; they are added automatically. If you are at the last frame, simply click the button to go to the next frame and Painter creates the new frame for you.

As you move from frame to frame, Painter is automatically saving your changes to the file `anim01.frm`.

20. To use the animation on a web page, use the File | Save As menu selection to display the dialog box shown in Figure 22-18.

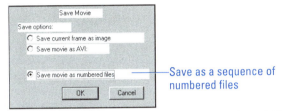

Figure 22-18: Saving the animation as numbered files.

By default, you can save the movie as a video clip (sometimes called an AVI file). The preferred file type for most animations is GIF because more browsers can display GIF animations.

21. Click the radio button for Save movie as numbered files and click OK.

This opens the Save Image As dialog box, shown in Figure 22-19.

22. Enter the filename **bird0001**, and set the Save as type to Bitmap Files (*.BMP).

23. Locate the `\My Web Stuff` folder in the Save in list at the top of the dialog box and click the Save button.

Painter will save six files, numbered in sequence from `bird0001.bmp` to `bird0006.bmp`. Figure 22-20 shows the six files open in Photoshop.

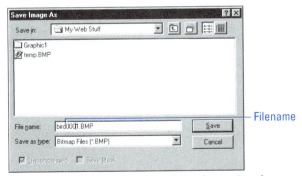

Figure 22-19: Saving numbered files by setting the number of the first file.

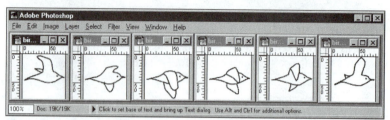

Figure 22-20: The six frames of the animation.

To turn the numbered files into a GIF animation, you'll need to use a GIF animator. The next section shows how this is done.

Idea

Where to go from here:

✦ Paint the bird using Painter's natural media tools. For example, you could use a small version of the Soft Charcoal tool (see Figure 22-21 and Figure 22-22) to create a bluebird (see Figure 22-23 and Figure 22-24). Be sure to paint all of the frames, and save the frames as a numbered sequence of BMP files.

Figure 22-21: Selecting the Soft Charcoal tool.

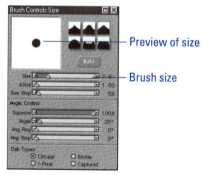

Figure 22-22: Changing the tool size so it is small enough to paint the bird.

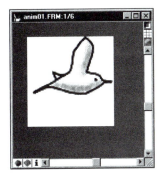

Figure 22-23: Painting dark blue on the bird.

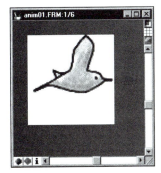

Figure 22-24: Painting a lighter blue on the bird.

Figure 22-25 shows the original and blue versions of the animation frames.

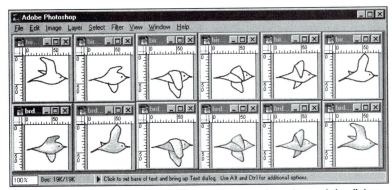

Figure 22-25: Comparing the outline and painted versions of the flying bird animation.

Using a GIF Animator

Tutorial

CD: To install the trial version of PhotoImpact GIF Animator, double-click the file `\demo\ulead\GIFAnim\ga12t.exe`.

Level: Easy

Task: Assemble a flying bird animation

Before you start:

✦ Install the trial version of the PhotoImpact GIF Animator.

Painter is one of the software packages you can use to create numbered animation files. There are several software packages whose main purpose is to take numbered animation files (or video clips or other forms of animation) and output them as animated GIF files. The best of the lot is Ulead's PhotoImpact GIF Animator.

To turn the numbered files of the flying bird animation into a GIF animation, follow these steps:

1. Open the PhotoImpact GIF Animator (see Figure 22-26).

2. To load a numbered image file, click the Add Image button. You can also use the Layer | Add Image menu selection. Either way, the Add Image dialog box (see Figure 22-27) opens.

3. Press and hold Ctrl and click to select the files you want to load. The files to select are `brdB0001.BMP`, `brdB0002.BMP`, `brdB0003.BMP`, `brdB0004.BMP`, `brdB0005.BMP`, and `brdB0006.BMP`.

4. Click the Open button.

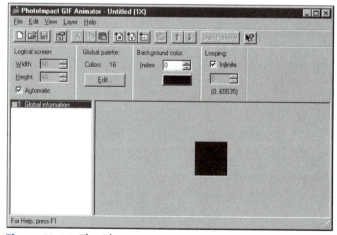

Figure 22-26: The PhotoImpact GIF Animator, version 2.0, in action.

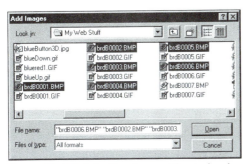

Figure 22-27: Selecting image files to load.

The dialog box shown in Figure 22-28 appears. It shows the first numbered image file (`birdB0001.bmp`). You can set the options for loading the image into GIF Animator as shown in Figure 22-28. I elected to set Dithering to None, but this did degrade image quality a bit. Note the right-hand image, which shows color conversion to the Netscape Safe Palette. It is coarser than the original image. You can use the appearance of the right-hand image to set the various options for the best results.

5. Click the Insert button.

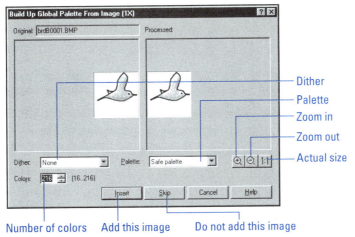

Figure 22-28: Setting load options for the first image.

The load options for the second through sixth images are slightly different (see Figure 22-29). There are two check boxes: The top one will apply the settings to additional images, and the lower one, if checked, will automatically apply the settings and load all images without further interruption.

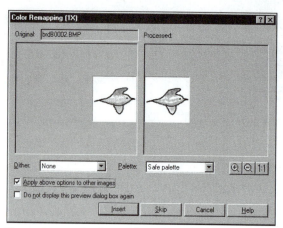

Figure 22-29: Setting options for subsequent images.

6. For this example, check both boxes and then click Insert.

This displays the GIF Animator window, with the six images listed in the file list at the left (see Figure 22-30).

7. To view an image, click to highlight it in the list.

Note that the default delay (the length of time the image will be displayed) is set to 50 hundredths (or ½) of a second. This is a relatively long time in animation terms.

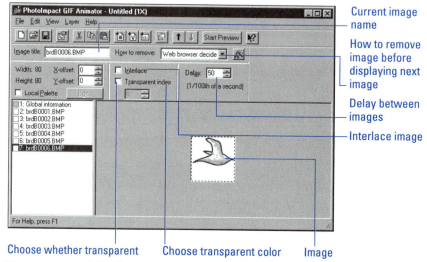

Figure 22-30: All six files are open in GIF Animator.

To change the delay time for all frames, you can either highlight each frame and manually change the value for delay to 12 (12 hundredths of a second), or change the delay on one frame and then click the Global Attribute tool to display the dialog box shown in Figure 22-31.

8. Check Delay, and click the Apply to all images radio button, then click OK. The new delay value will be applied to all images.

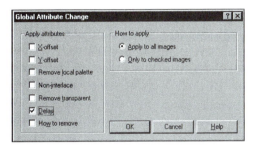

Figure 22-31: Applying attributes globally. Note that you can limit changes to only those images that are checked in the image list.

9. Save the GIF animation using the File | Save As menu selection. Use the filename **bird1.gif**.

Figure 22-32 shows the animation on a web page. You can view the animation on the web page `\My Web Stuff\chap22\chap22B.htm` in your browser.

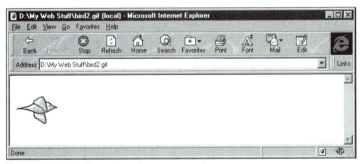

Figure 22-32: The animation on a web page.

Other GIF animators are similar to PhotoImpact GIF Animator, but they lack the depth of features of GIF Animator, or are more clumsy to use. Microsoft's GIF Animator (why do all of these programs have the same name?), shown in Figure 22-33, offers fewer options and has a particularly clumsy interface.

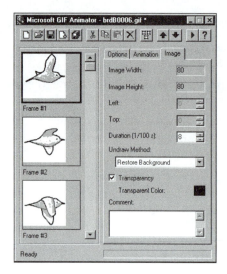

Figure 22-33: Microsoft's GIF Animator is awkward to use.

Idea

Where to go from here:

✦ The PhotoImpact GIF Animator provides transition effects that you can use to move from one image to another. You can use this to create slide shows within a GIF animation. Use the Layer | Add Transition menu selection to access this feature.

✦ You can use PhotoImpact GIF Animator to save GIF animations as numbered files. Use the Export Images button in the toolbar (see Figure 22-34) to identify which frames in the animation should be saved in this fashion.

✦ The How to remove list of options controls how each image changes to the next image. The default is to let the web browser decide, but for some animations you may need to use other options. For example, if you have problems with pixels from previous frames hanging around, use the To Background Color option instead of the default option.

✦ You can use transparency to remove the background color from an animation. You can set a different background color for each frame, if necessary. Click the color box next to the Transparency check box to set the transparent color for the currently selected frame.

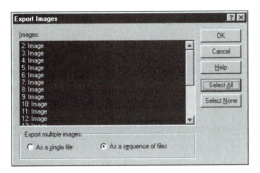

Figure 22-34: Exporting frames from a GIF animation. This is handy for GIF animations you download and want to edit.

Animating Objects

Tutorial

CD: To install the trial version of PhotoImpact GIF Animator, double-click the file `\demo\ulead\GIFAnim\ga12t.exe`.

Level: Easy as pie

Task: Animate a fixed image

Before you start:

✦ Install the trial version of PhotoImpact GIF Animator.

In addition to frame-based animations, you can use the settings of the PhotoImpact GIF Animator to animate a single image. In this example, you'll learn how to move an image of a ball from side to side.

I created a ball image in Photoshop for this tutorial. I started with a 16×16 pixel new image (File | New). I then selected a circle 15×15 pixels and filled it with a radial gradient fill from white to red. This selection is deliberately one pixel smaller than the image size to allow a border around the ball. Figure 22-35 shows the ball image.

Before saving the image as a GIF file, I converted it from RGB Color to Indexed Color (Image | Adjust | Indexed Color) and chose the Web palette with a diffusion dither. I used the Export | GIF89a menu selection to save to disk. I did not select a transparent color because you can use GIF Animator to set transparency.

Figure 22-35: Using a radial gradient to create a simple ball (shown enlarged).

To animate the ball using PhotoImpact GIF Animator, use the following steps:

1. Load the single image \My Web Stuff\Chap22\ball.gif into GIF Animator (see Figure 22-36) five times. The easiest way to add an image multiple times is to click the Add an Image button to insert each copy.

2. Click the second image in the list of images to activate it. Set the X-offset for the second image to 5 pixels (see Figure 22-37). Note how the five pixels are added to the left of the ball image in the preview pane.

3. Set the X-offset for the remaining images in increments of five: 10, 15, and 20 pixels. Figure 22-38 shows the offset for the last image.

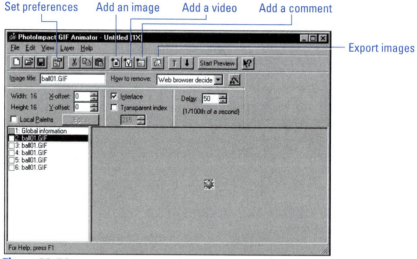

Figure 22-36: Loading the same image multiple times.

4. Set the delay for each image to 12 hundredths of a second, and save the file as **ball.gif**.

5. Open the file \My Web Stuff\chap22\chap22C.htm to see the animation in action.

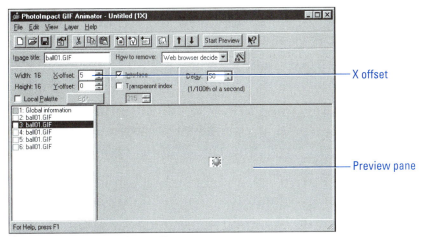

Figure 22-37: Setting the X-offset.

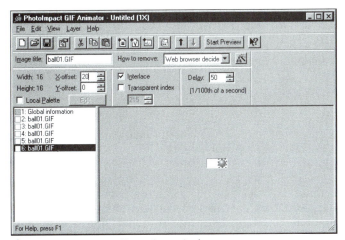

Figure 22-38: An X-offset of 20 pixels.

Where to go from here:

✦ You can use negative numbers in the X-offset box to move an image to the left.

✦ The Y-offset box allows you to move an image up and down.

✦ By carefully setting the numbers in the X-offset and Y-offset boxes, you can move images in circles, at an angle, and so on. Experiment to learn how these two values interact. Try both positive and negative numbers in various combinations.

✦ Use different delay values for different images to cause the movement to speed up and/or slow down.

✦ Use GIF Optimization (the File | GIF Optimization menu selection) to reduce file size by eliminating duplicate pixels from successive animation frames. Figure 22-39 shows the results of an optimization pass — the file size was reduced by one-third. You won't always see such spectacular results, but you will almost always see worthwhile savings.

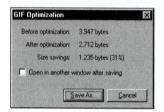

Figure 22-39: Reducing file size with GIF Optimization.

Creating an Interpolated Animation

Download: To install the 30-day trial version of Macromedia Flash download it from www.macromedia.com/futurewave and follow the instructions.

Task: Create an interpolated animation

Tutorial

Before you begin:

✦ Install and run the trial version of Macromedia Flash.

✦ If a blank document does not appear automatically, use the File | New menu selection to create a blank document.

This tutorial is based on an animation tool that goes well beyond the animation features of programs like Painter or GIF animators. It's called Macromedia Flash, and it includes tools that are designed specifically for creating dazzling animations. Figure 22-40 shows the program at startup. Note that FutureSplash Animator appears in the title bar. The product's name was changed to Macromedia Flash as we went to press.

The program window has six major areas that are worth a close look before trying to accomplish anything. You will interact with most of these areas during the next two tutorials.

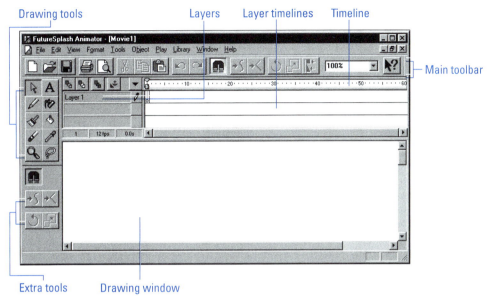

Figure 22-40: The Macromedia Flash Animator window.

Main toolbar	These tools are used in a variety of situations. They include file save/open buttons, undo/redo buttons, and so on.
Drawing tools	These tools are used to draw in the drawing window.
Extra tools	The tools visible here vary, depending on which drawing tool is currently active.
Layers	This area contains a list of layers, as well as buttons for controlling the onionskin feature.
Timeline	This provides frame-by-frame breakdown of the animation(s) present on each layer.
Drawing window	Displays the contents of the current frame.

The default size for an animation document is 7.5 × 10 inches. That's way too large for a web page graphic! First you'll change the document size.

1. Use the Format ǀ Document menu selection to open the dialog box shown in Figure 22-41.

2. Set the document width to 4, and the height to 1.

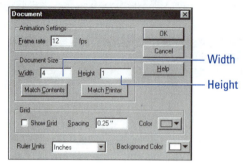

Figure 22-41: Changing the document size.

 You can use this dialog box to change other aspects of the animation document, such as background color, the spacing of the snap-to grid, and the animation frame rate (that is, how many frames display each second).

Figure 22-42 shows the new document size. The exact relationship between document size and the Macromedia Flash window will vary, depending on your screen size and resolution.

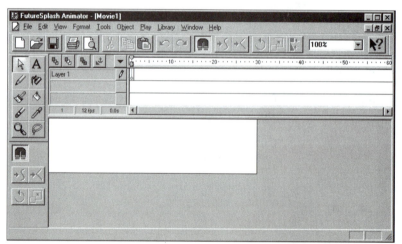

Figure 22-42: This document size is more appropriate for a web page. In other words, it's small.

To create an interpolated animation, you must specify the contents of the first and last frames. In this example, you will create a very wide ellipse in the first frame, change it to a very narrow but tall ellipse in the last frame, and then create the interpolation frames between them.

3. Begin by clicking the pencil tool. Note that the extra tools area changes when the Pencil tool is active (see Figure 22-43).

4. Click on the topmost extra tool to display the available variations (see Figure 22-44).

5. Click the oval tool. This replaces the former tool at this location (see Figure 22-45).

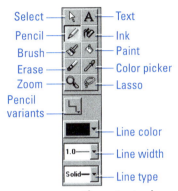

Select — Text
Pencil — Ink
Brush — Paint
Erase — Color picker
Zoom — Lasso
Pencil variants —

Line color
1.0 — Line width
Solid — Line type

Figure 22-43: The extra tools associated with the pencil tool.

Straighten
Smooth
Ink
Oval
Rectangle
Line

Figure 22-44: Picking a variant of the pencil tool.

Figure 22-45: The oval variant of the pencil tool is active.

6. Click and drag in the drawing window to create a wide, thin oval as shown in Figure 22-46.

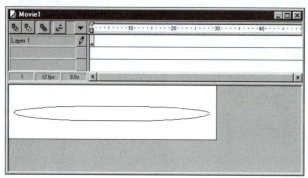

Figure 22-46: Creating an oval.

Uppercase Timeline refers to the bar that contains numbers at the top of the Timeline section. Lowercase timeline refers to the white rows at the right of each layer. Right now, there is only one layer, called Layer 1.

The Timeline shows that only one frame exists at this point.

7. To create a bunch of new frames, click the timeline for Layer 1 (refer to Figure 22-47) under the numeral 20 in the Timeline.

A small 3-D rectangle appears, as well as an Insertion cursor (both shown in Figure 22-47). This location is position 20 on the Timeline.

Figure 22-47: Getting ready to insert a new frame.

8. Right-click the 3-D rectangle to display a pop-up menu (see Figure 22-48).

9. Click the Insert Frame menu selection.

Not only does Macromedia Flash insert a frame at position 20, it also inserts frames between the first frame at position 1 and the new frame. Figure 22-49 shows the added frames.

If you are referring to a position on the layer's timeline where a frame does not exist, that is called position <number>, where the number matches the number on the Timeline. If you are referring to a position on the layer's timeline where a frame does exist, that is called frame <number>.

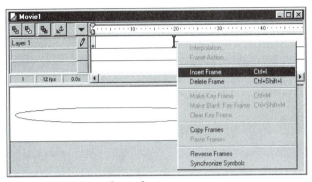

Figure 22-48: Inserting a frame.

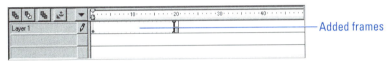

Figure 22-49: The animation now contains a total of 20 frames.

Note that frame 1 contains a small, solid blue dot. This indicates that frame 1 is a keyframe, and that the frame contains something (in this case, an oval). Frame 1 is always a keyframe. A keyframe that does not yet contain something is shown as a hollow blue circle.

Tip

Don't confuse this use of the term keyframe with keyframe animations, which are covered in the next section. A keyframe here is simply a frame that contains some kind of change from the preceding frame(s). An interpolated animation always contains two keyframes: the start and end frames of the interpolation.

To use the oval in an interpolated animation, you must first turn it into a symbol.

10. Click the oval to select it. *This is very important;* if the oval is not selected, Macromedia Flash will create a new symbol object, instead of converting the oval into a symbol. The outline of the oval will thicken to indicate that it is selected.

11. Use the Object | Create Symbol menu selection to open the dialog box shown in Figure 22-50.

12. Type the name **oval1** and click OK.

Figure 22-50: Naming a symbol.

The appearance of the oval changes to indicate that it is now a symbol (see Figure 22-51).

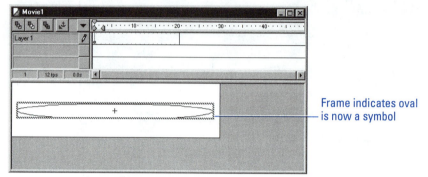

Frame indicates oval is now a symbol

Figure 22-51: The oval is now a symbol, and is putting on airs.

13. Right-click the 3-D rectangle in frame 20.

14. This time, click the Make Key Frame menu selection. A small blue dot appears in the frame marker (refer to Figure 22-52).

15. To make frame 20 the active frame, click the Timeline at the number 20. The current frame indicator moves to frame 20.

16. Right-click the oval and choose Scale in the pop-up menu.

17. Drag either the left or right selection handle close to the middle of the frame, and drag the top or bottom selection handle toward the edge of the frame.

    Your goal is to change the shape of the oval to look like the example in Figure 22-52.

18. Click frame 1 in the Layer 1 timeline.

19. Right-click the 3-D rectangle, and click the Interpolation menu item. This displays the Interpolation dialog box, shown in Figure 22-53.

If you click the Interpolation menu item and nothing happens, you probably didn't left-click on frame 1 before right-clicking it. Left-click in frame 1 on the Layer 1 timeline, then right-click.

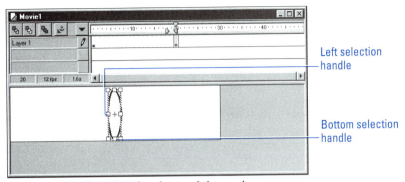

Figure 22-52: Changing the shape of the oval.

Figure 22-53: The Interpolation dialog box.

20. Click the drop-down list that currently says None, and choose Motion.

The dialog box changes, as shown in Figure 22-54. You can choose to perform interpolation on rotation, scaling (that's what I did to the oval), and whether or not to rotate an object with a path (if a path is involved; no path is involved here).

Figure 22-54: Working with the Interpolation dialog box.

The slider at the bottom of the dialog box controls the speed of the interpolation at the beginning and end. If you move the slider toward Ease in, the interpolation will start slowly and then speed up. If you move the slider toward Ease out, the interpolation will start quickly and then slow down.

21. Click OK to create the interpolation. A red arrow appears in the Layer 1 timeline to indicate that the interpolation exists (refer to Figure 22-55).

22. To verify proper operation of the interpolation, click the Timeline at frame 10. This is halfway between the two keyframes. The size of the oval should be halfway between the start and end sizes (see Figure 22-55).

Red arrow indicates interpolation   Current frame indicator

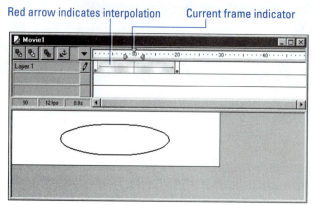

Figure 22-55: An intermediate frame of the interpolated animation.

Caution!

If you do not convert the oval into a symbol, the interpolation will not work properly. In that case, the oval will stay the same size for 19 frames, and then suddenly jump to the other size in frame 20. If this occurs, start over, and remember to convert the oval into a symbol.

23. To test the animation, press Enter. You will see the oval shrink before your eyes.

24. To save your work for later editing, use the File | Save As menu selection. This displays a Save As dialog box. Set the Save as Type to the Flash native format, .SPA. This saves all aspects of the animation, including proprietary Flash information. Save the file in the \My Web Stuff\chap22 folder.

25. To save in the Shockwave Flash format (.SPL), which allows the animation to appear on a web page, use the File | Export Movie menu selection and accept the default Save as Type setting (FutureSplash Player).

26. Type in a filename such as **oval1** and click Save.

    Only browsers using the Shockwave Flash plug-in will display the animation. Visitors can download the player from http://www.macromedia.com/futurewave/.

27. To save as an animated GIF, use the File | Export Movie menu selection and choose the Save As Type Animated GIF.

    Figure 22-56 shows the GIF animation in a browser. Open the file \My Web Stuff\chap22D.htm to see the animation in action.

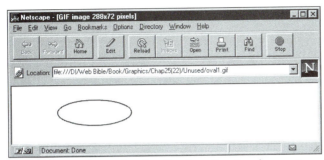

Figure 22-56: The oval animation in action in a browser.

Idea

Where to go from here:

✦ You can perform interpolated animation on any object that you can turn into a symbol. Try different starting and ending shapes and sizes.

✦ You can create an interpolated animation for text without converting it into a symbol.

✦ You can create an interpolated animation along a path. After you create the interpolation on a layer, right-click the layer and choose Add Motion Guide. A new layer appears below the original layer. Use the Pencil tool to create the motion path. In the original layer, move the anchor point for the symbol object so that it aligns *exactly* with an end point of the path. This is easy to do if snap-to-grid is active (it is active by default, unless you turn it off). The object must be exactly on an end point in both the start and end frames of the original interpolation for this to work. Press Enter to test the animation along a path.

Creating a Keyframe Animation

Tutorial

Download: To install the 30-day trial version of Macromedia Flash, download it from `www.macromedia.com\futurewave` and follow the instructions.

Level: Tedious, but charming

Task: Create a keyframe animation of a wavy line

Before you begin:

✦ Install and run the trial version of Macromedia Flash.

To create a keyframe animation, you draw a new animation for each frame. In most cases, the image from the last frame is only slightly modified. By default, Flash displays the contents of the last frame in the current frame. You can simply modify the image in front of you to create the new frame.

One particular feature of Flash makes this even easier. When you draw with the pencil or brush tool, the line you create isn't cast in stone. You can bend it, twist it, and otherwise reshape it. This is particularly valuable for keyframe animation, as you'll see during this tutorial.

Tip

The previous tutorial introduces a number of key features of Flash. Check out the opening section of that tutorial for important information you will need in this tutorial.

When you run Flash, it opens a blank document. If this does not happen, create a new blank document with the File | New menu item. Then change the size of the document:

1. Use the Format | Document menu selection to set the document size: width of 4, height of .5 (see Figure 22-57).

2. Click OK, and the document size is set (see Figure 22-58).

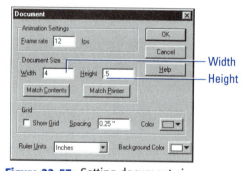

Figure 22-57: Setting document size.

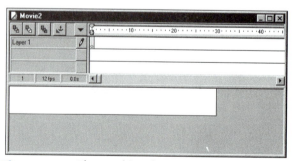

Figure 22-58: The resulting document is wide and short.

3. Click the pencil tool (see Figure 22-59) to activate it.

4. Use the extra tools below the drawing tools to set up the type of line the pencil will draw.

5. Click the variant icon, and choose the Smooth variant (the curvy line).

6. Click the color icon, and select a medium blue color.

7. Click the line width icon, and set line width to 2.0.

8. Verify that the line type is set to solid.

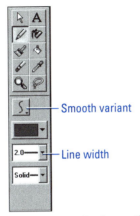

Figure 22-59: Setting options for the pencil tool.

9. Draw a line across the bottom of the animation document, as shown in Figure 22-60.

   Try to keep the line as straight as you can, but don't worry about being perfect. You'll use the line-editing abilities of Flash to create a perfectly straight line.

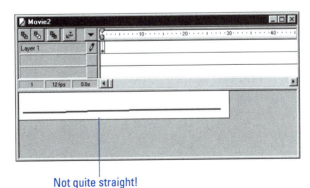

Figure 22-60: Drawing a line.

10. Click the pointer tool (refer to Figure 22-59) to activate it.

Use the tool to push the line around. If there is a part of the line that dips down, locate the center of the dip.

11. Click the line at that point while "pushing" upward with the pointer tool. Notice how a short segment of the line curves in the direction of the push.

12. When you release the mouse button, the line segment stays at the new position.

13. Repeat steps 11 and 12 until the line is perfectly straight.

All of your work so far has taken place in frame 1.

14. Create a new frame by clicking in the Layer 1 timeline at position 2.

15. Right-click the little 3-D rectangle to display a pop-up menu, and click Insert Frame. You can also use the keys Ctrl+I to insert a new frame at the current position.

16. To make the new frame a keyframe (all of the frames in this tutorial are going to be keyframes), either use the right-click menu to click Make Keyframe, or use the keys Ctrl+M.

Figure 22-61 shows that Layer 1 now has two keyframes (that is, two frames, and both with blue dots).

17. Make sure that the pointer on the Timeline is set to frame 2 before you start editing.

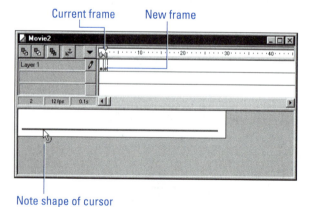

Figure 22-61: Where to push against the line.

18. Position the cursor at the location shown in Figure 22-62.

19. Click and move the cursor upward just a little bit, until the line looks like the one shown in Figure 22-62.

20. Release the mouse button and the line now has a wave in it.

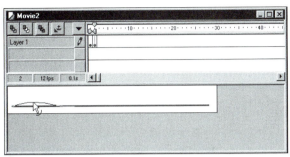

Figure 22-62: Pushing a segment of the line upward.

21. Create a new keyframe (insert frame, then make it a keyframe).

22. Click in the Timeline to make frame 3 the current frame.

23. Click the Show Onionskin button, just above the name of the Layer 1 layer. Note that faint versions of the previous frames are visible underneath the current frame.

24. Click and drag to make the line in frame 3 perfectly straight (see Figure 22-63). You can now see the outline of frame 2.

25. Click a bit to the right of the center of the wave in frame 2, and drag upward to create a wave in frame 3, as shown in Figure 22-64.

   The wave in frame 3 must be to the right of the wave in frame 2. Note that Figure 22-64 shows onionskin versions of all three frames. You can control the number of onionskins visible by moving the two sliders at the bottom edge of the Timeline. The slider at the top of the Timeline determines the current frame for editing purposes.

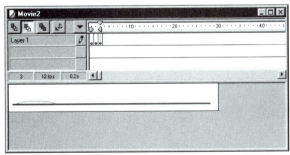

Figure 22-63: Straightening the line.

Limit of onionskins in prior frame   Limit of onionskin frames

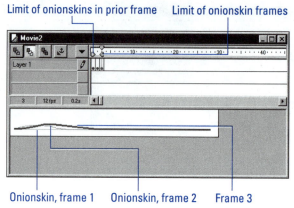

Onionskin, frame 1   Onionskin, frame 2   Frame 3

Figure 22-64: A wave in frame 3.

Tip

This is the essence of keyframe animation in Flash. You add, edit, or remove some-thing from the previous frame to create the proper degree of motion in the current frame. You can learn how much to add, edit, or remove by experimenting with var-ious changes and seeing how they look when animated. You can test an animation at any point by pressing the Enter key.

26. To complete the animation, repeat the steps for frame 3 until the wave moves completely to the right end of the line:

✦ Insert a new frame.

✦ Make it a keyframe.

✦ Straighten the line in the new frame.

✦ Create a wave to the right of the previous frame's wave.

Figure 22-65 shows the waves I created for each frame. I next created a little wiggle at the end of the line, and the very last frame adds a wiggle at the beginning of the line. You can create the wiggles by dragging the exact end of the line upward. When the animation loops (that is, plays over and over), the wiggles cause the end to flow neatly into the beginning. Open the file \My Web Stuff\chap22E.htm to see the animation in action.

27. To save the animation as an animated GIF, use the File | Export Movie menu selection. See the previous tutorial for detailed steps.

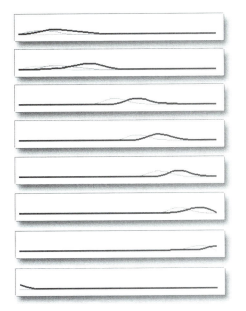

Figure 22-65: Creating a series of waves from left to right.

Idea

Where to go from here:

✦ Flash is so powerful, there are probably a million different directions you could take. For some real excitement, try adding one of the symbols included with Flash. Some of them are animations — yes, you can have animations within animations. For example, how about a spinning leaf that moves across the animation?

✦ You can save your animations as video clips, and then edit them as video clips in Adobe Premiere, where you can create all kinds of special effects and transitions. Figure 22-66 shows one of the two dialogs you'll encounter when you save the animation as a video clip. The Width and Height settings will vary depending on the size of your animation. I suggest that you use the other settings in the dialog box for your video clips until you are ready to experiment.

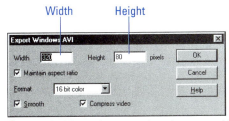

Figure 22-66: Saving an animation as a video clip.

A Peek at Adobe Premiere

Speaking of Premiere, Figure 22-67 shows what this powerful program looks like. The two most important parts of the program are the Construction window and the Transition window.

You can load a single animation or video clip into the Construction window (see Figure 22-68) and apply filters to it. Premiere supports a very large number of filters. Many of them are similar to the effect filters you find in image editing software, such as blurring, color changes, and so on. Other effects are more oriented toward video clips — you can change the settings for some effects over time. Figure 22-69 shows a portion of the effects available. To add an effect to a clip, click the effect in the left pane, click the Add button, and then set any required parameters. To set different parameters for the start and end of the clip, use the Start and End buttons.

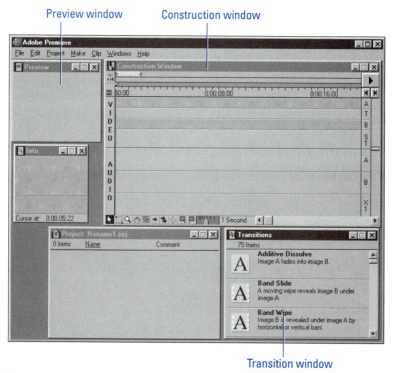

Figure 22-67: Working with Adobe Premiere.

Frame from clip

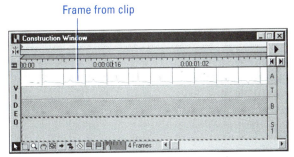

Figure 22-68: Editing a video clip in Premiere.

Remove filter   Add filter

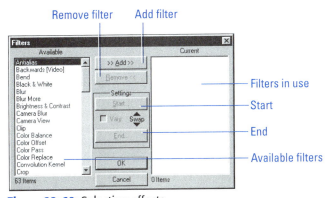

Filters in use

Start

End

Available filters

Figure 22-69: Selecting effects.

Figure 22-70 shows how the Bend filter affects a video clip. The blue line in the clip is actually straight, but the Bend filter distorts it horizontally and vertically. Note the extensive set of controls for fine-tuning the effect. You can view the original video clip by double-clicking the file \My Web Stuff \drop1.avi. The version created in Premiere is file \My Web Stuff \drop2.avi.

Filter preview

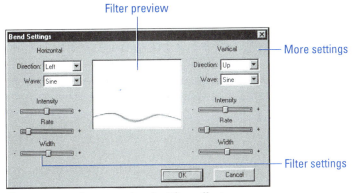

More settings

Filter settings

Figure 22-70: An example of a filter effect.

You can have a combination of effects at work: In the video clip shown in `\My Web Stuff \drop5.avi`, the blue line is doubled into a blue and yellow line, a lens flare filter shines at the center of the clip, and the background is broken into small tiles.

You can also place two or more video clips or animations into the Premiere Construction window (see Figure 22-71). You can then drag transition effects from the Transition window to the transition track between the video tracks. These transitions provide clever and artistic ways to switch from one video clip to another.

Figure 22-71: Working with multiple video clips.

You can even load the same video clip into two video tracks, apply different filters to each clip, and use transitions to switch from one effect to another. Figure 22-72 shows a transition that rips through one clip to reveal another clip. You can preview the transition while you work on it.

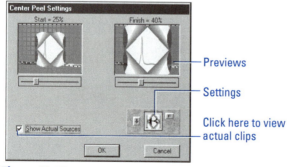

Figure 22-72: Setting up a transition between two video clips.

You can view the video clip by double-clicking the file \My Web Stuff \drop7.avi. For that matter, I created a number of video clips; check out all of the drop files in that folder. My personal favorite is drop10.avi.

This is just the barest introduction to working with video clips and animations in Premiere. Much more is possible. Explore!

 I bet you didn't think I could keep my trap shut for a whole chapter. Well, I could have, but I have two cents worth of actual thought to apply to this whole topic of animation. It's easy to create a web page that will make the average visitor seasick if you overdo the animation. Please be considerate of your visitors' well-being, and keep your animations useful, informative, or at least fun.

Web Tour #22: The Best of Dynamic Graphics

I've scoured the Web to find interesting examples of animations and video clips. I have also included some fun animations on the CD-ROM for you to explore. To visit sites that make clever use of animation, double-click the file

    \WebTour\Chap22\index.htm

You'll see the Web Tour page for this chapter.

Contents of the CD-ROM

The CD-ROM that comes with this book is filled with as many cool goodies as I could find. I've also tried to make it as easy to use as possible.

Installing the CD-ROM and Running Programs

When you insert the CD-ROM into a Windows 95 or Windows NT 4 CD-ROM drive, you will see a screen similar to the one shown in Figure A-1 (The demos listed are different due to last-minute changes to the CD-ROM.). This program runs automatically unless you have turned off the CD-ROM Autorun feature. If you want to run the program manually, double-click on the file `autorun.exe` in the root directory of the CD-ROM.

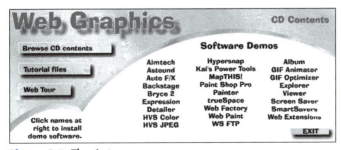

Figure A-1: The Autorun program.

There are three buttons at the left of the Autorun program. You can click these buttons to display web pages from the CD-ROM in your default browser. These buttons are

Browse CD contents

Opens a web page on the CD-ROM in your browser. This page, which will look similar to Figure A-2, allows you to browse through the various contents of the CD-ROM.

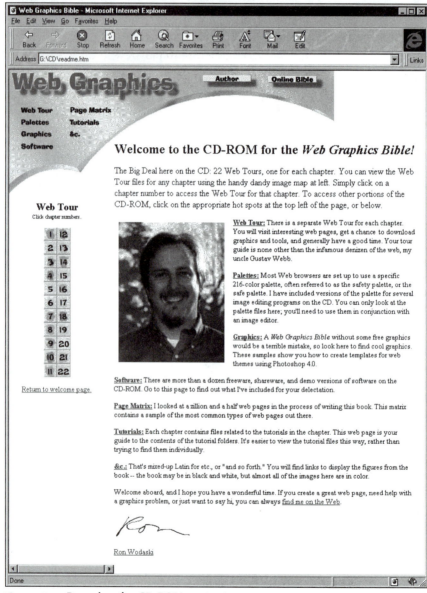

Figure A-2: Browsing the CD-ROM contents.

| Tutorial files | Opens a web page that provides quick, easy access to the various files used in the tutorials in the book. |
| Web Tour | Opens a web page that provides instant access to all 22 Web Tours (one for each chapter). |

The central portion of the Autorun program displays the software included on the CD-ROM. These are mostly timed-trial demos (except for the Adobe Acrobat Reader, which is a full version) that allow you to play with the software for 7 to 30 days to see how it works. Three products (HyperSnap, WS_FTP, and Paint Shop Pro) are shareware. These are fully functional; try the program for a limited period and register it with the developer for a small fee if you decide to continue using it. To install a particular piece of software, click on the program's name.

 Be careful with those timed-trial programs! Don't just install all of them and then try them out. There are too many programs here, and most are complex and interesting. You want time to play with them. Install a trial version only when you are ready to spend serious time with it.

The following demos and shareware are on the CD-ROM. (Adobe Acrobat Reader is a full version, as noted earlier.)

Adobe: Acrobat Reader lets you view any Portable Document Format (PDF) file. Install the Acrobat Reader before any of the other software on the CD-ROM. **Photoshop** is a first-class, professional image editing program. **Premiere** is one of the best video editors available. **PageMaker,** while initially designed as a layout program for the printed page, has evolved into a powerful tool for creating highly customized web pages.

Astound WebMotion: Tool for developing interactive web pages.

Auto F/X: These are Photoshop plug-ins. **Photo/Graphic Edges** applies stylized edge effects. **Photo/Graphic Patterns** applies cool patterns to your images. **Typo/Graphic Edges** adds edge effects to type and clip art. **Ultimate Texture Collection** creates cool textures.

Caligari trueSpace3: Tool for creating and animating 3-D models and photorealistic images. You can also use it to generate VRML objects and worlds for your web pages.

Corel WebMaster Suite: Collection of tools for creating and maintaining compelling Intranet and Internet sites.

Digital Frontiers: These are Photoshop plug-ins. **HVS Color** gives greater control over color reduction for GIF images. **HVS JPEG** provides greater control over JPEG compression of true-color images. Both include sophisticated algorithms that enable you to create the smallest possible graphic files for fast downloads, without sacrificing image quality.

Fractal Design: Includes **Painter,** a powerful image creation tool with natural media; **Detailer,** a 3-D painting program; and **Expression,** a natural-media vector drawing program.

Hyperionics HyperSnap: Screen capture and GIF transparency tool.

Ipswitch WS_FTP: The best FTP tool for uploading web pages.

Jasc Paint Shop Pro: Popular shareware image editor.

Macromedia Flash: The leading tool for creating animation for web pages.

MetaTools: Kai's Power Tools is a hot plug-in for creating stunning image effects in Photoshop. **Bryce 2** is sophisticated program for creating 3-D scenes.

Thunder & Lightning Web Factory: Web page editing tool with integrated image editing.

Ulead: A whole pile of tools. **PhotoImpact GIF Animator** creates sophisticated animated GIF files from videos or still images. **PhotoImpact GIF/JPEG SmartSavers** optimize image size and quality for your web pages. **PhotoImpact GIF Optimizer** enhances compressibility of GIF images. **PhotoImpact Screen Capture** captures all or part of your screen to an image file. **PhotoImpact Album** manages collections of images efficiently. **PhotoImpact Explorer** displays image files interactively. **PhotoImpact Viewer** displays images quickly. **Web Extensions for Photoshop** adds SmartSaver technology to Photoshop.

Use the web page shown in Figure A-2 to view the CD-ROM contents more specifically. You display this page by clicking the Browse CD contents button, as mentioned, or by double-clicking `readme.htm` in the root directory of the CD-ROM.

There are numerous hotspots on this web page that you can use to view the contents of the CD-ROM. For example, click the image map hotspots at top left, just under the page title, to gain access to key areas of the CD-ROM described next. You can also click the text hyperlinks of the same names on the web page.

Web Tours

The 22 numbers in the left frame of the web page shown in Figure A-2 provide instant access to the Web Tours for each chapter. Figure A-3 shows the Web Tour for Chapter 16, for example. The format for each of the Web Tours is different; I arranged the material to suit the content of each chapter.

To take each tour, read the material and click the links. That's all there is to it.

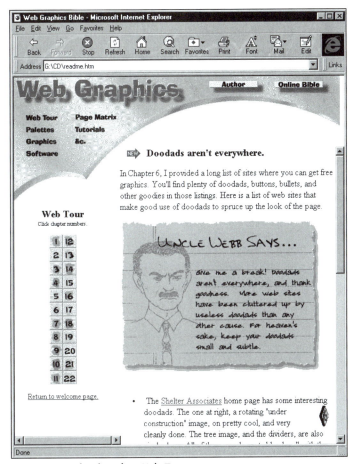

Figure A-3: Viewing the Web Tour pages.

Demo Software

You can examine the files for the various programs on the CD-ROM. Figure A-4 shows the page that lists the software programs available for installation. The actual screen may look slightly different due to changes as this book went to press.

There's a lot of material on this page. Each company in the list of companies at the left of the page has two hyperlinked images next to it. Clicking the *B* will take you to the bookmark on the page for that company. Clicking the *S* will take you to the company's web site.

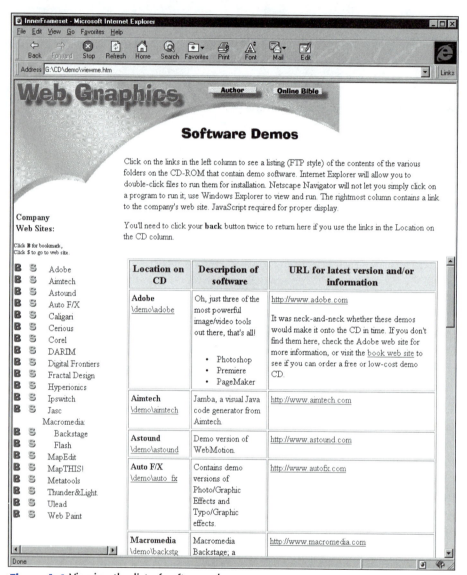

Figure A-4: Viewing the list of software demos.

There are three columns in the table of demos. The left column contains links that display the files included on the CD-ROM. In most cases, there is a setup file you can double-click to install the demo. In other cases, you will see instructions that tell you how to install the demo (usually this involves copying files from the CD-ROM to your hard disk; follow these instructions carefully).

How you interact with these lists of files depends on the browser you are using. If Netscape Navigator is your browser, you will only be able to look at the file lists. If you try to double-click a file to install the demo, you will see a dialog box offering to download the file to your hard disk. This is a security feature of Navigator; it refuses to run software on your computer.

If Internet Explorer is your browser, you can install programs by double-clicking the appropriate file.

In most cases, life will be easier if you install the demo programs using the Autorun program. If you like to live dangerously, you can find the demo folders in the \demos folder on the CD-ROM.

Graphics Samples

I have included two families of graphics on the CD-ROM that show how you can use the layer features of Photoshop to create web page graphics that adhere to a design theme. You can view the individual graphics that make up each theme, and you can view web pages that illustrate how the graphics work together.

You will need Photoshop 4.0 to view the versions of these images that use layers. The images are located in the folders \graphics\styles\labyrinth and \graphics\styles\Blueston.

Tutorial Support

Most of the chapters in this book feature tutorials. You can find the tutorial support files, as well as some extra files that illustrate topics in each chapter, in the \tutorial folder on the CD-ROM. I have also included a web page that lists the support files and extra files for each chapter. The page is located at \tutorial\viewme.htm. You can quickly access the files for any chapter using the hyperlinks at the top of the page (one for each chapter, of course).

Note that the pages that display are images, not the actual pages. You can use the URL visible in the image to locate the original page if you want to use it as a template.

Palettes

Various image editors use different file formats to store indexed color palettes. I have included 216-color, Web-safe palettes in formats for several popular image editors. You can find the palettes in the \palette folder on the CD-ROM.

Other Buttons

There are two other buttons on the `readme.htm` web page worth noting: Author and Online Bible. The Author button will take you to my personal web page; drop in and say hello. The Online Bible button will take you to the web page for the book. You will find goodies, last-minute features, links to book-related web sites, additional demo downloads, and other material related to the book on that web page.

Index

SYMBOLS & NUMBERS

A

C

(continued)

E

F

(continued)

M

X

Y

Z

NOTES

NOTES

NOTES

NOTES

NOTES

NOTES

NOTES

NOTES

NOTES

NOTES

NOTES

NOTES

IDG BOOKS WORLDWIDE, INC.
END-USER LICENSE AGREEMENT

Read This. You should carefully read these terms and conditions before opening the software packet(s) included with this book ("Book"). This is a license agreement ("Agreement") between you and IDG Books Worldwide, Inc. ("IDGB"). By opening the accompanying software packet(s), you acknowledge that you have read and accept the following terms and conditions. If you do not agree and do not want to be bound by such terms and conditions, promptly return the Book and the unopened software packet(s) to the place you obtained them for a full refund.

1. **License Grant.** IDGB grants to you (either an individual or entity) a nonexclusive license to use one copy of the enclosed software program(s) (collectively, the "Software") solely for your own personal or business purposes on a single computer (whether a standard computer or a workstation component of a multiuser network). The Software is in use on a computer when it is loaded into temporary memory (i.e., RAM) or installed into permanent memory (e.g., hard disk, CD-ROM, or other storage device). IDGB reserves all rights not expressly granted herein.

2. **Ownership.** IDGB is the owner of all right, title, and interest, including copyright, in and to the compilation of the Software recorded on the CD-ROM. Copyright to the individual programs on the CD-ROM is owned by the author or other authorized copyright owner of each program. Ownership of the Software and all proprietary rights relating thereto remain with IDGB and its licensors.

3. **Restrictions on Use and Transfer.**

   (a) You may only (i) make one copy of the Software for backup or archival purposes, or (ii) transfer the Software to a single hard disk, provided that you keep the original for backup or archival purposes. You may not (i) rent or lease the Software, (ii) copy or reproduce the Software through a LAN or other network system or through any computer subscriber system or bulletin-board system, or (iii) modify, adapt, or create derivative works based on the Software.

   (b) You may not reverse engineer, decompile, or disassemble the Software. You may transfer the Software and user documentation on a permanent basis, provided that the transferee agrees to accept the terms and conditions of this Agreement and you retain no copies. If the Software is an update or has been updated, any transfer must include the most recent update and all prior versions.

4. **Restrictions on Use of Individual Programs.** You must follow the individual requirements and restrictions detailed for each individual program in the Appendix of this Book. These limitations are contained in the individual license agreements recorded on the CD-ROM. These restrictions may include a requirement that after using the program for the period of time specified in its text, the user must pay a registration fee or discontinue use. By opening the Software packet(s), you will be agreeing to abide by the licenses and restrictions for these individual programs. None of the material on this disc or listed in this Book may ever be distributed, in original or modified form, for commercial purposes.

5. Limited Warranty.

(a) IDGB warrants that the Software and disk(s)/CD-ROM are free from defects in materials and workmanship under normal use for a period of sixty (60) days from the date of purchase of this Book. If IDGB receives notification within the warranty period of defects in materials or workmanship, IDGB will replace the defective disk(s)/CD-ROM.

(b) IDGB AND THE AUTHORS OF THE BOOK DISCLAIM ALL OTHER WARRANTIES, EXPRESS OR IMPLIED, INCLUDING WITHOUT LIMITATION IMPLIED WARRANTIES OF MERCHANTABILITY AND FITNESS FOR A PARTICULAR PURPOSE, WITH RESPECT TO THE SOFTWARE, THE PROGRAMS, THE SOURCE CODE CONTAINED THEREIN, AND/OR THE TECHNIQUES DESCRIBED IN THIS BOOK. IDGB DOES NOT WARRANT THAT THE FUNCTIONS CONTAINED IN THE SOFTWARE WILL MEET YOUR REQUIREMENTS OR THAT THE OPERATION OF THE SOFTWARE WILL BE ERROR FREE.

(c) This limited warranty gives you specific legal rights, and you may have other rights which vary from jurisdiction to jurisdiction.

6. Remedies.

(a) IDGB's entire liability and your exclusive remedy for defects in materials and workmanship shall be limited to replacement of the Software, which may be returned to IDGB with a copy of your receipt at the following address: Disk Fulfillment Department, Attn: *Web Graphics Bible*, IDG Books Worldwide, Inc., 7260 Shadeland Station, Ste. 100, Indianapolis, IN 46256, or call 1-800-762-2974. Please allow 3–4 weeks for delivery. This Limited Warranty is void if failure of the Software has resulted from accident, abuse, or misapplication. Any replacement Software will be warranted for the remainder of the original warranty period or thirty (30) days, whichever is longer.

(b) In no event shall IDGB or the author be liable for any damages whatsoever (including without limitation damages for loss of business profits, business interruption, loss of business information, or any other pecuniary loss) arising from the use of or inability to use the Book or the Software, even if IDGB has been advised of the possibility of such damages.

(c) Because some jurisdictions do not allow the exclusion or limitation of liability for consequential or incidental damages, the above limitation or exclusion may not apply to you.

7. U.S. Government Restricted Rights.
Use, duplication, or disclosure of the Software by the U.S. Government is subject to restrictions stated in paragraph (c) (1) (ii) of the Rights in Technical Data and Computer Software clause of DFARS 252.227-7013, and in subparagraphs (a) through (d) of the Commercial Computer—Restricted Rights clause at FAR 52.227-19, and in similar clauses in the NASA FAR supplement, when applicable.

8. General.
This Agreement constitutes the entire understanding of the parties and revokes and supersedes all prior agreements, oral or written, between them and may not be modified or amended except in a writing signed by both parties hereto which specifically refers to this Agreement. This Agreement shall take precedence over any other documents that may be in conflict herewith. If any one or more provisions contained in this Agreement are held by any court or tribunal to be invalid, illegal, or otherwise unenforceable, each and every other provision shall remain in full force and effect.

Installing the CD-ROM

Follow these simple steps to access the material on the accompanying CD-ROM.

1. Insert the CD-ROM in your CD-ROM drive.

2. In a few moments, the Windows 95 AutoRun feature automatically displays a list of options, including the software available for installation.

3. Click a program's name.

4. Follow the instructions that appear on your screen to install the software.

Please see the appendix for more information.

IDG BOOKS WORLDWIDE REGISTRATION CARD

Visit our Web site at http://www.idgbooks.com

ISBN Number: 0-7645-3055-0

Title of this book: Web Graphics Bible

My overall rating of this book: ❑ Very good [1] ❑ Good [2] ❑ Satisfactory [3] ❑ Fair [4] ❑ Poor [5]

How I first heard about this book:

❑ Found in bookstore; name: [6] _____

❑ Advertisement: [8]

❑ Word of mouth; heard about book from friend, co-worker, etc.: [10]

❑ Book review: [7]

❑ Catalog: [9]

❑ Other: [11]

What I liked most about this book:

_____

What I would change, add, delete, etc., in future editions of this book:

_____

Other comments:

_____

Number of computer books I purchase in a year: ❑ 1 [12] ❑ 2-5 [13] ❑ 6-10 [14] ❑ More than 10 [15]

I would characterize my computer skills as: ❑ Beginner [16] ❑ Intermediate [17] ❑ Advanced [18] ❑ Professional [19]

I use ❑ DOS [20] ❑ Windows [21] ❑ OS/2 [22] ❑ Unix [23] ❑ Macintosh [24] ❑ Other: [25] _____
(please specify)

I would be interested in new books on the following subjects:

(please check all that apply, and use the spaces provided to identify specific software)

❑ Word processing: [26]

❑ Data bases: [28]

❑ File Utilities: [30]

❑ Networking: [32]

❑ Other: [34]

❑ Spreadsheets: [27]

❑ Desktop publishing: [29]

❑ Money management: [31]

❑ Programming languages: [33]

I use a PC at (please check all that apply): ❑ home [35] ❑ work [36] ❑ school [37] ❑ other: [38] _____

The disks I prefer to use are ❑ 5.25 [39] ❑ 3.5 [40] ❑ other: [41] _____

I have a CD ROM: ❑ yes [42] ❑ no [43]

I plan to buy or upgrade computer hardware this year: ❑ yes [44] ❑ no [45]

I plan to buy or upgrade computer software this year: ❑ yes [46] ❑ no [47]

Name: _____ Business title: [48] _____ Type of Business: [49] _____

Address (❑ home [50] ❑ work [51] /Company name: _____)

Street/Suite# _____

City [52] /State [53] /Zip code [54]: _____ Country [55] _____

❑ **I liked this book!** You may quote me by name in future IDG Books Worldwide promotional materials.

My daytime phone number is _____

IDG BOOKS WORLDWIDE™

THE WORLD OF COMPUTER KNOWLEDGE®

❏ YES!

Please keep me informed about IDG Books Worldwide's World of Computer Knowledge. Send me your latest catalog.